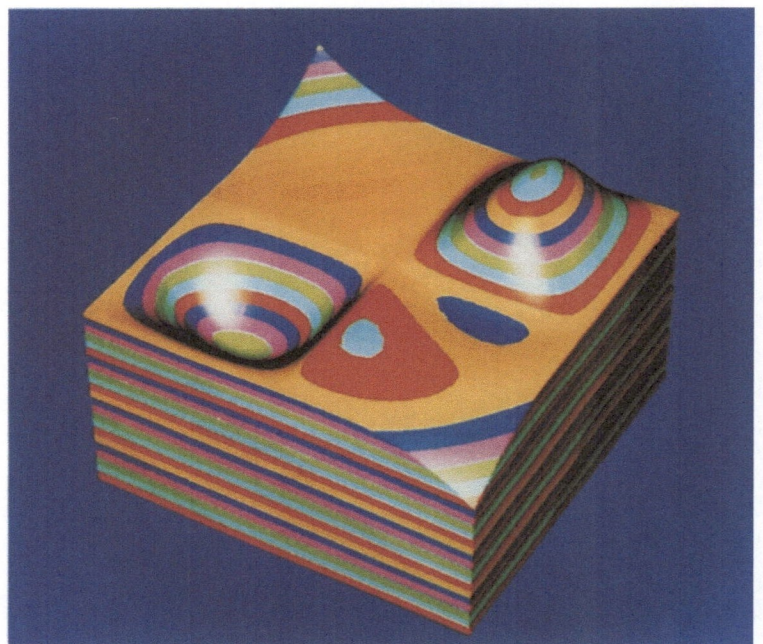

Gregory Patches                    © Software Research Center of Ricoh Co., Ltd.

# Advanced Computer Graphics

Proceedings of
Computer Graphics Tokyo '86

Edited by Tosiyasu L. Kunii

With 264 Figures
97 of them in Color

Springer-Verlag
Tokyo Berlin Heidelberg New York

Dr. Tosiyasu L. Kunii
Professor and Director
Kunii Laboratory of Computer Science
Department of Information Science
Faculty of Science
The University of Tokyo

Cover Design: Maple tree images generated by A-System.
© Kunii Laboratory of Computer Science, The University of Tokyo and Software
Research Center, Ricoh Co,. Ltd.


ISBN-13:978-4-431-68038-3          e-ISBN-13:978-4-431-68036-9
DOI: 10.1007/978-4-431-68036-9

# Preface

Computer Graphics Tokyo, now in its fourth year, has established a world-wide reputation as an international technical conference, presenting work of high quality in the field of computer graphics. Each conference has been attended by a couple of thousand participants from all over the world and tens of thousands have visited the exhibition. After strict peer review, 34 papers were accepted this year, of which about 40% were from the USA, 30% from Japan, 20% from Europe, and 10% from Canada. A good balance of papers on advanced research results, industrial/marketing surveys, and computer art technology has made Computer Graphics Tokyo an indispensable forum for researchers, engineers, and administrators working in this field. Computer graphics is a rapidly developing and expanding area and it is not easy to keep abreast of all the progress that has been made. This volume contains the proceedings of Computer Graphics Tokyo '86 and provides the reader with a comprehensive survey of the state of the art in computer graphics.

Computational geometry (Chapter 1) is one of the fastest growing areas in computer graphics. This is well recognized as the basis of shape modeling. After shapes are modeled, they are displayed for visual observation. Chapter 2 on rendering presents various novel methods and technological innovations for visualizing shapes. To make display systems more accessible to users, rich visual interfaces and languages are being designed, as shown in Chapter 3. Visual data bases for sharing graphics- and image-data are handled in Chapter 4. Computer animation, dealt with in Chapter 5, will be of great interest to anyone fascinated by moving pictures. Chapter 6 charts the recent progress in graphics hardware/software systems. Chapters 7 and 8 are concerned with CAD/CAM — Chapter 7 on mechanical and general purpose CAD/CAM and Chapter 8 on VLSI CAD/CAM. Finally, marketing and business/technical trends are surveyed in Chapter 9.

The conference is organized by the Computer Graphics Society (CGS) and sponsored by Japan Management Association (JMA) in cooperation with the Association for Computing Machinery (ACM), IEEE Computer Society, and European Association for Computer Graphics (Eurographics).

I would like to express by most cordial thanks to Springer-Verlag, which as an established scientific/technical publisher has ensured ever since the first conference that the proceedings have reached a wide readership throughout the world. Selected papers have also been published in the journals *IEEE Computer Graphics and Applications* and *The Visual Computer: An International Journal of Computer Graphics.*

Tosiyasu L. Kunii

# Table of Contents

# List of Contributors

The page numbers given below refer to the page on which contribution begins.

Chapter 1

# Computational Geometry

# Localized Surface Interpolation Method for Irregular Meshes

Hiroaki Chiyokura

Software Research Center, Ricoh Co., Ltd., Koishikawa, Bunkyo-ku, Tokyo, 112 Japan

## ABSTRACT

A surface interpolation method for irregular meshes of curves is proposed. When a face in the mesh is interpolated, a surface patch on the face is individually generated from localized boundary information. The tangent planes of generated patches are continuous. This method employs an extended Bezier patch as a surface equation. The patch can be defined, specifying independently normal derivatives along the boundary curves. The total procedure of generating patches is simple and quick.

Keywords: CAD/CAM, Free-form surfaces, Solid modeling, Irregular mesh, Gregory patches

## 1. INTRODUCTION

The importance of representing free-form surfaces in a computer has been widely recognized in CAD/CAM field. The representation can support a wide variety of activities in CAD/CAM such as numerically controlled machining and graphical displays. This paper proposes a method for representing the shape of an engineering object with free-form surfaces.

In designing free-form surfaces with a computer, a designer first produces a curve mesh model, using tools available in the design system. He represents the characteristics of the desired free-form surfaces in terms of curves. Then, the system generates surfaces interpolating to the mesh model. The advantage of this method is that a user can easily handle free-form surfaces, modifying the curve shapes in the curve mesh model. In this approach the mesh becomes irregular, if a user freely adds to or deletes curves in the model. For example, the mesh model contains triangular side faces and nodes connected to three curves. Therefore, we propose a new method for generating free-form surfaces over irregular curve meshes.

## 2. INTERPOLATION OF IRREGULAR CURVE MESHES

In our previous interpolation method[1,2] for irregular meshes of curves, shown in Figure 1, free-form surfaces over the mesh are generated from localized boundary information. The tangent plane of the surfaces are continuous. Figure 2 illustrates that when a face Fl is interpolated, a free-form surface is generated from boundaries of edges El, E2, E3 and E4. This localized interpolation method has the following advantages:

(1) The procedure for generating surfaces is simple because only local information is referenced.

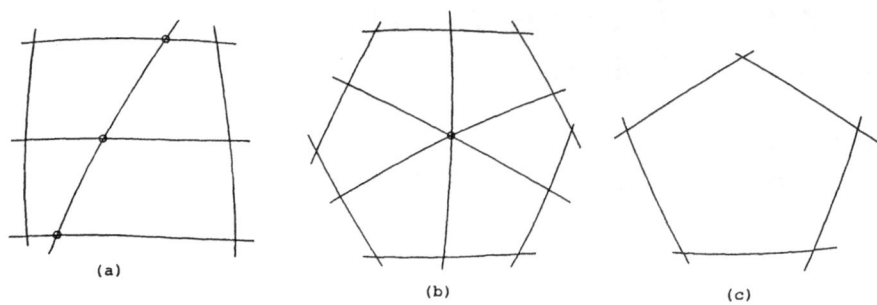

Figure 1 Irregular mesh of curves

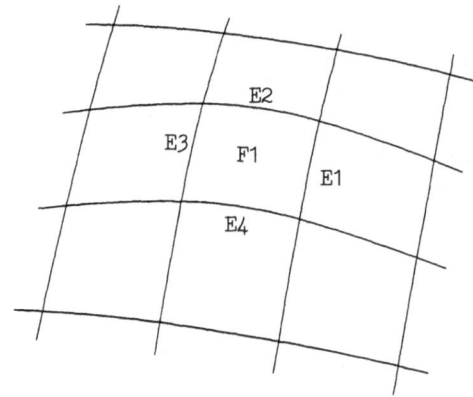

Figure 2 Interpolated face and its boundary


(2) The internal representation of the designing system need not include surface equations because surfaces can be quickly generated. Therefore, the
internal representation requires a small memory space.

The previous method, referencing extremely localized information alone, contains
the following two problems:

(1) Globally unsmooth surfaces are occasionally generated.
(2) It is very difficult to generate surfaces which are tangent plane continuous over the curve meshes shown in Figure 3. This figure shows that a vertex
V1 is connected to three edges E1, E2 and E3, and the curves of two edges E1
and E2 are tangent continuous. The node V1 shown in this figure is called a
"T-node".

T-nodes often appear in meshs of curves representing the characteristics of
free-form surfaces. Figure 4 shows T-nodes Vi(i=1..4) in the model. T-nodes V1
and V2 appear when an edge E1 is added in a face F1, as shown in Figure 5.

This paper presents a new localized surface interpolation method to solve
these problems. When a face F1 shown in Figure 6 is interpolated by our method,
the surface is generated from the boundary edges Ei(i=1..5) and edges
Ej(j=6..14) attached to these boundary edges. This new method has been
developed in our solid modeling system DESIGNBASE[3].

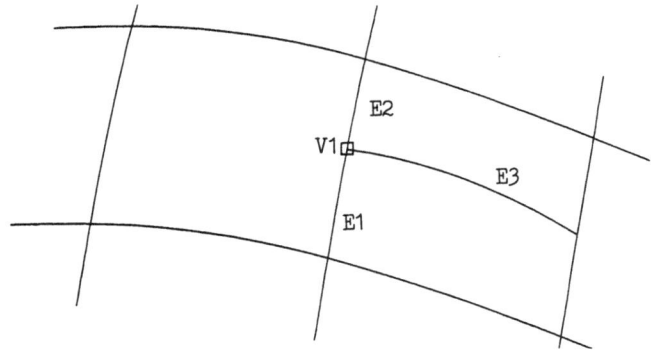

Figure 3 Irregular mesh of curves

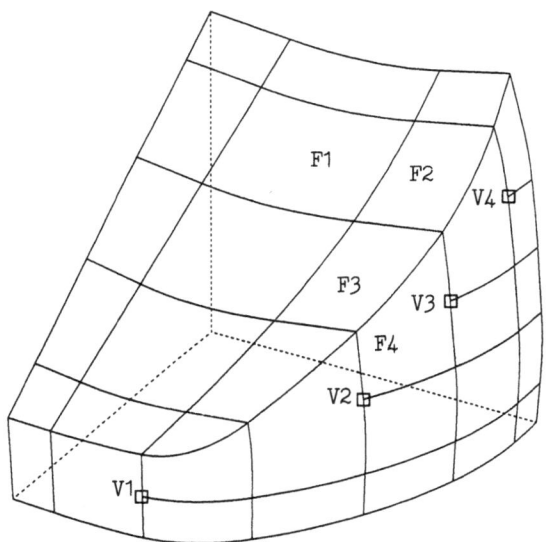

Figure 4 Curve mesh with T-nodes

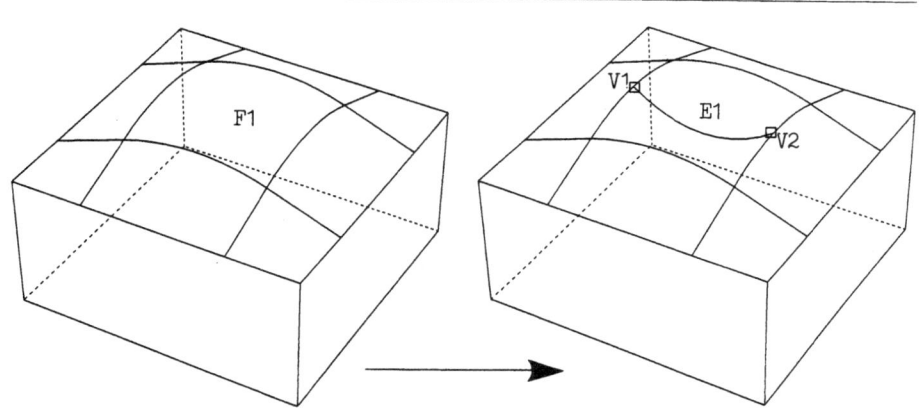

Figure 5 Curve mesh with T-nodes

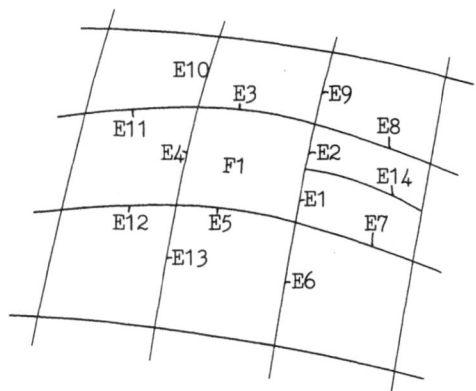

Figure 6 Interpolated face and its surrounding edges

## 3. INPUT METHODS OF FREE-FORM SURFACES

### 3.1 Conventional Input Method

Broadly speaking, conventional input methods of free-form surfaces can be grouped into two kinds. One is the "cross-sectional design" (CS-design)[4] and the other is the "characteristic polyhedron design" (CP-design). In the CS-design, a user first defines cross-sections of the desired shapes. Then, lets the system generate the surface, interpolating the given cross-sections. Advantages of the CS-method are that a user can precisely define the shape and that he can make subtle shape modifications by retouching cross-sections directly. However, it is not easy to make gross shape changes.

In the CP-design, a user defines free-form surfaces through the characteristic polyhedron. The typical CP-design method uses B-spline surfaces[5]. To define B-spline surfaces, a user inputs a polyhedron in which all faces are rectangular and vertices are attached to four edges. In the CP-method, it is easy to modify the shape roughly by manipulating the polyhedron. However, to give the precise definition is not easy. Some attempts[6,7,8] have been made in recent years to extend the B-spline method. These approaches do not, however, allow subtle definitions and modifications as permitted in the CS-design approach.

In DESIGNBASE, a user first inputs a characteristic polyhedron. The polyhedron does not define surfaces but mesh models of curves. Then, the system interpolates the mesh models. For rough modifications, the characteristic polyhedron is altered. For subtle modifications, the curves in the mesh model are changed. Thus, in our method, a user can enjoy advantages of both the CS-design and CP-design.

### 3.2 Input Method in DESIGNBASE

In our system, the input of solids with free-form surfaces is done, using the following steps:

[STEP 1] Design of Skeleton Model
Using local operations and set operations, a user make a "skeleton model" roughly representing the desired shape. All edges of the solid are straight lines, but faces need not be flat. Figure 7 shows the skeleton model of a telephone.

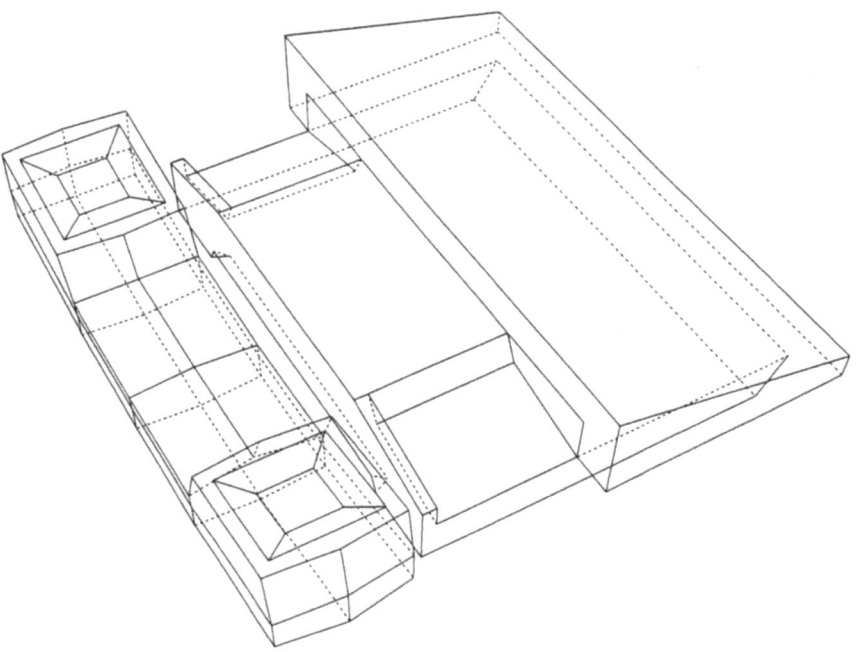

Figure 7 Skeleton model of a telephone

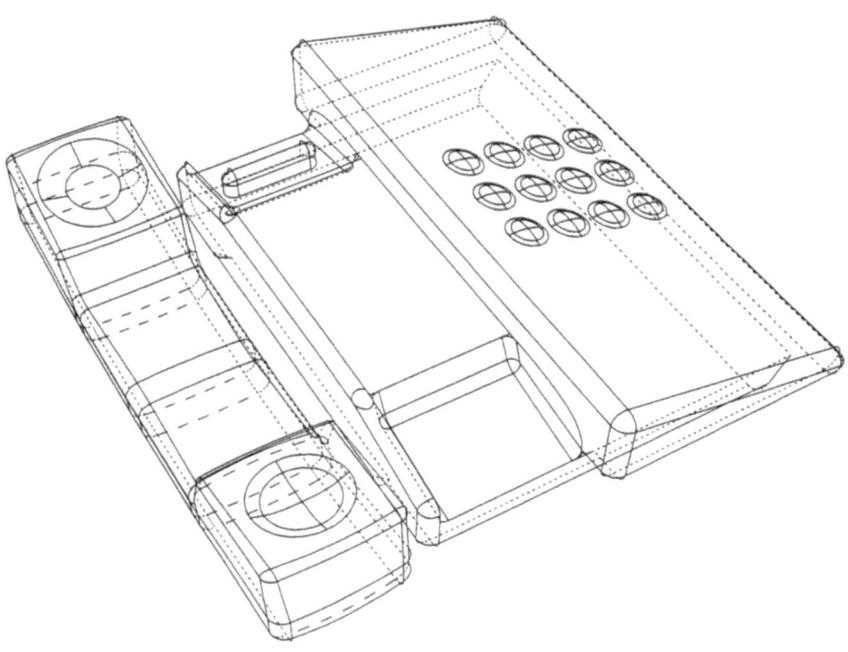

Figure 8 Curve  mesh of a telephone

[STEP 2] Design of Curve Mesh Model
Using the rounding operation[1], the curve mesh model is generated from the skeleton model. Before the rounding operation, a user assigns a rounding value to each edge of the model by selecting from the three values 0, 1 and 2:

0: The edge is rounded. When free-form surfaces are generated, this is used.
1: The edge remains unchanged, e.g. as sharp as before. Depending on the values of neighboring edges, the specified edge turns into a curved one.
2: The edge is rounded in accord with a radius specified. This edge turns into a fillet surface.

In a fine tuning, a user has either to add an edge to the model or modify the curved edge. Figure 8 shows the curve mesh model of a telephone which is generated from the skeleton model.

[STEP 3] Generation of Free-form Surfaces
Free-form surfaces are generated on faces of curve mesh models. This paper describes in depth an algorithm for generating surfaces. As a demonstration of a free-form surface in our system, cross-section pictures and color shaded pictures are generated on a CRT screen.


## 4. GREGORY PATCH

Gregory [9] have extended a coons patch so that the normal derivatives across the patch boundaries can be independently specified. This extension has been called "compatibility correction" [10]. Chiyokura and Kimura [1] applied the same extension to a bicubic Bezier patch. In our interpolation method, the extended Bezier patch is employed as mathematical equations, and called a "Gregory patch". As a preparatory step for describing the interpolation method itself, we explain the properties of the Gregory patches and the connection between two such patches.

### 4.1 Gregory Patch's Properties

As shown in Figure 9, a Gregory patch is defined by a set of twenty control points $P_{i,j,k}(i=0..3, j=0..3, k=0..1)$. Its equations of the patch are as follows:

$$S(u,w) = \sum_{i=0}^{3} \sum_{j=0}^{3} B_i(u)B_j(w)Q_{i,j}(u,w) \qquad 0 \le u, w \le 1$$

$$B_i(u) = \binom{3}{i}u^i(1-u)^{3-i}$$

$$Q_{i,j}(u,w) = P_{i,j,0} = P_{i,j,1} \quad (\text{except for } Q_{1,1}, Q_{2,1}, Q_{1,2} \text{ and } Q_{2,2})$$

$$Q_{1,1}(u,w) = \frac{uP_{1,1,0} + wP_{1,1,1}}{u + w}$$

$$Q_{2,1}(u,w) = \frac{(1-u)P_{2,1,0} + wP_{2,1,1}}{1-u + w}$$

$$Q1,2(u,w) = \frac{uP1,2,0 + (1-w)P1,2,1}{u + 1-w}$$

$$Q2,2(u,w) = \frac{(1-u)P2,2,0 + (1-w)P2,2,1}{1-u + 1-w}$$

The Gregory patch has the following three major properties:
(1) The Gregory patch has the convex hull property similar to that of the Bezier patch. Namely, any point on a patch is always contained in a convex hull defined by 20 control points. This property is advantageous for a rough interference checking.
(2) The Gregory patch in one case degenerates to a bicubic Bezier patch. When all the eight inside control points satisfy the equation $Pi,j,0 = Pi,j,1$ (i=1..2, j=1..2), the Gregory patch is a Bezier patch.
(3) Four normal derivatives across the patch boundaries can be independently specified as cubics.
The normal derivatives of the patch S(u,w) are hereafter expressed as follows:

$$\partial S(u,w)/\partial w\Big|_{w=0} = Sw(u,0).$$

Then, these normal derivatives can be defined by control points as follows:

$$Sw(u,0) = 3\sum_{i=0}^{3} Bi(u)(Pi,1,0 - Pi,0,0)$$

$$Sw(u,1) = 3\sum_{i=0}^{3} Bi(u)(Pi,3,0 - Pi,2,0)$$

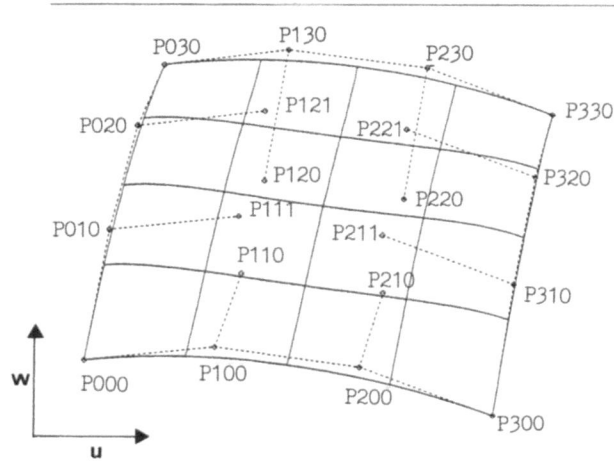

Figure 9 Control points of a Gregory patch

$$Su(0,w) = 3\sum_{i=0}^{3} Bi(w)(P1,i,0 - P0,i,1)$$

$$Su(1,w) = 3\sum_{i=0}^{3} Bi(w)(P3,i,0 - P2,i,1)$$

The last property makes it possible to generate our localized interpolation method.

## 4.2 Patch Connection

This section describes the connection of two Gregory patches under the condition of tangent plane continuity. Figure 10 shows two Gregory patches $S(u,w)$ and $S'(u,w)$, to be connected. In this figure, vectors $ai(i=0..3)$, $bi(i=0..3)$ and $ci(i=0..2)$ are

    ai = P3,i,1 - P2,i,0
    bi = P'1,i,1 - P'0,i,0
    ci = P'0,i+1,0 - P'0,i,0

where $Pi,j,k$ and $P'i,j,k$ are control points of patches $S(u,w)$ and $S'(u,w)$, respectively. For two patches to be tangent plane continuous with regard to the boundary, three vectors a0, b0 and c0 attached to a vertex V0 must be on the same plane. Vectors a3, b3 and c2 must also be on the same plane. This is expressed as follows:

    b0 = k0a0 + h0c0
    b3 = k1a3 + h1c2

where k0, k1, h0 and h1 are scalar values. The conditions for two patches to be tangent plane continuous are that $Su(1,w)$ is quadratic, and that the relations of the vectors between control points satisfy the following relations[1]:

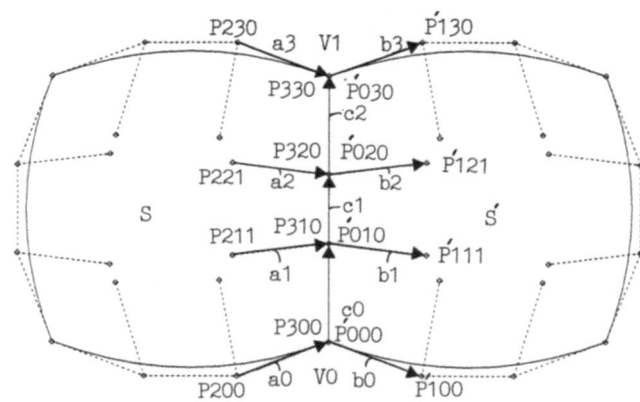

Figure 10 Connection of Gregory patches

$$b1 = (k1-k0)a0/3 + k0a1 + 2h0c1/3 + h1c0/3$$
$$b2 = k1a2 - (k1-k0)a3/3 + h0c2/3 + 2h1c0/3 .  (1)$$

Since Su(1,w) is a quadratic equation, its quadratic Bezier function must be defined by three vectors a0, q and a3. Next, vectors a1 and a2 are to be determined, using the following equations:

$$a1 = (a0 + 2q)/3$$
$$a2 = (2q + a3)/3  (2)$$

## 5. GREGORY PATCHES GENERATING PROCESS

Figure 11 shows a face F to be interpolated by a Gregory patch. The patchs generation process is described below.

(1) Definition of the Cross-Boundary Tangent

We define the "cross-boundary tangents" $gi(ti)$ $(0 \leq ti \leq 1)$ $(i=1..4)$ along edges $Ei(i=1..5)$ of a face F. Along an edge E1 shown in Figure 11, two tangents g1(t1) and g'1(t1) are defined for the interpolation of two faces F and F' respectively. When tangent planes of the patches on two faces F and F' are continuous, the two tangents along the edge E1 become g1(t1) = -g'1(t1). In this figure, edge E3 and E4 are attached to a T-node vertex V1. Since edges E3 and E4 can be represented as one cubic Bezier curve, one cross-boundary tangent g3(t3) is defined along edges E3 and E4. The tangent is quadratic so that it can be transformed into a normal derivative of a patch by equations (1) and (2).

(2) Determination of Control Points

The cross-boundary tangent can be expressed in the quadratic Bezier function, which is defined by three vectors a0, a1 and a2. Once three vectors are given, control points defining normal derivatives of a patch are determined using equations (1) and (2). The control points thus derived define one Gregory patch itself, when the number of the cross-boundary tangent is four, completing the whole process.

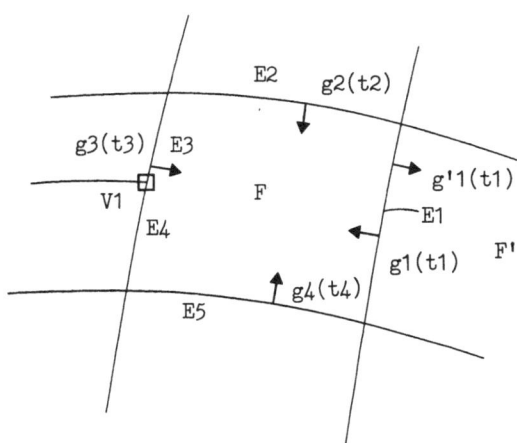

Figure 11  Boundary  curves  and  cross-boundary
           tangents

(3) Subdivision of a Face

When a face is non-rectangular, it must be subdivided into some rectangle faces to generate a Gregory patch on each face, as shown in Figure 12. In our system, all faces are interpolated by the rectangular Gregory patch alone. Non-rectangular patches[11,12] have been already proposed. If triangular or pentagonal patches are also used as an internal representation of the system, each patch will require its own program for its manipulation. For instance, a separate program for calculating each of cross sections between patches and a flat plane. This enlarges the program size of the system. So, only the rectangular Gregory patch is employed in our system.

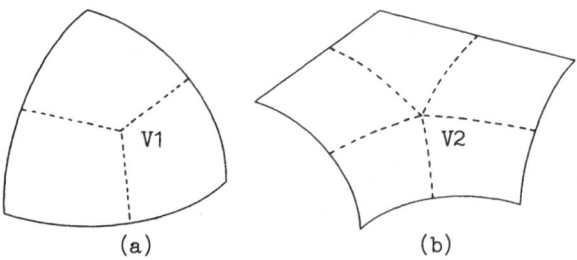

Figure 12 Subdivision of non-rectangular faces

## 6. A DEFINITION OF A CROSS-BOUNDARY TANGENT

The major difference between our new interpolation method and the previous one lies in the definition of the cross-boundary tangent on the boundary edge. This section describes the method for defining the tangent in detail. Definition methods for such tangents on an edge differ, depending on whether the edges are connected to T-nodes or not. Each case is given below.

### 6.1 The Case That an Edges Is Not Connected to T-nodes

Figure 13 describes how we define a cross-boundary tangent on an edge E0 where two faces F1 and F2 meet. In this figure, the edge E0 runs between two vertices V1 and V2. Points Z1 and Z2 are control points of the edge E0 of a Bezier curve. Edges E1 and E2 are attached to the edge E0 and the face F1. Similarly, edges E3 and E4 are attached to the edge E0 and the face F2. Let points P1, P2, p3 and P4 near vertices V1 and V2 be control points of the Bezier curves expressing edges E1, E2, E3 and E4, respectively. The definition process of the tangent consists of three steps:

(1) Calculation of Normal Vectors

Our system automatically generates interpolating surfaces to a curve mesh made by a user. The boundary curves in general denote the tangent plane continuity of surfaces to be generated on two faces which meet at an edge. For example, the surfaces on two faces F1 and F2 shown in Figure 4 become continuous. On the other hand, the surfaces on faces F3 and F4 are independently generated. To check the continuity of two faces F1 and F2 shown in Figure 13, a comparison must be made between the value of normal vector $n_{1,1}$ of the plane defined by three points V1, P1 and Z1 and that of $n_{1,2}$ of the plane defined by points V1, P4 and Z1. If the vector values turn out the same, faces F1 and F2 should be made continuous around vertex V1. Otherwise, not. The same is to be repeated on vectors $n_{2,1}$ and $n_{2,2}$ to determine the necessity of continuity around V2.

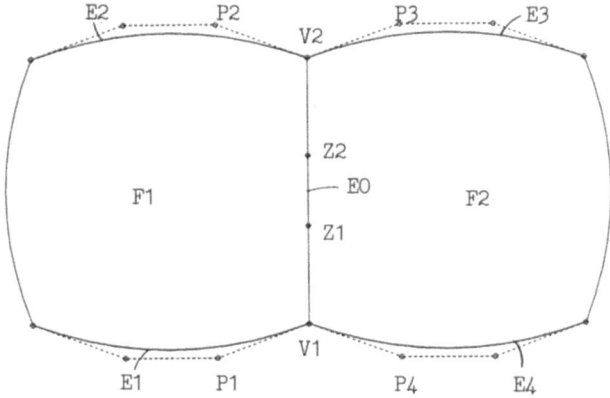

Figure 13 Boundary curves

(2) Determination of Vectors a0 and a2

The cross-boundary tangent on an edge El is a quadratic Bezier function to be
defined by three vectors a0, a1 and a2. This section describes how to determine
the tangent vectors a0 and a2 at vertices V0 and V2. Although the directions of
the tangent vectors have geometric meaning here, their magnitudes have none.
Let the vectors a0 and a2 be unit vectors. To generate a smooth surface only
on a face F1, it is desired to let a0 and a2 be vectors parallel to vectors P1V1
and P2V2, respectively. To connect faces F1 and F2, let the average of vectors
P1V1 and V2P4 the unit vector a0. Define vector a2 similarly. The vectors a0 and
a2 are expressed as follows:

if $n1,1 = n1,2$
then $a0 = (P1 - P4) / |P1 - P4|$

else $a0 = (P1 - V1) / |P1 - V1|$  (3)

if $n2,1 = n2,2$
then $a2 = (P2 - P3) / |P2 - P3|$

else $a2 = (P2 - V2) / |P2 - V2|$

(3) Determination of Vector a2

To generate a smooth surface, the cross-boundary tangent must be smooth. For
simplicity, let the tangent be linear. The vector a1 can be expressed as

$a1 = (a0 + a2) / 2$  (4)

6.2 The Case that an Edge Is Connected to T-nodes

Figure 14 shows a face F1 to be interpolated. It is attached to a T-node
vertex V3 and vertices V1 and V2. The vertex V3 is connected to three edges E1,
E2 and E3. Edges E1 and E2 were originally represented in a cubic Bezier curve,
until a vertex V3 is made, dividing the original edge. Let control points on
edges E1, E2 and E3 of Bezier curve be Z1, Z2 and P5. We describe how to define
the tangent on edges E1 and E2 as follows:

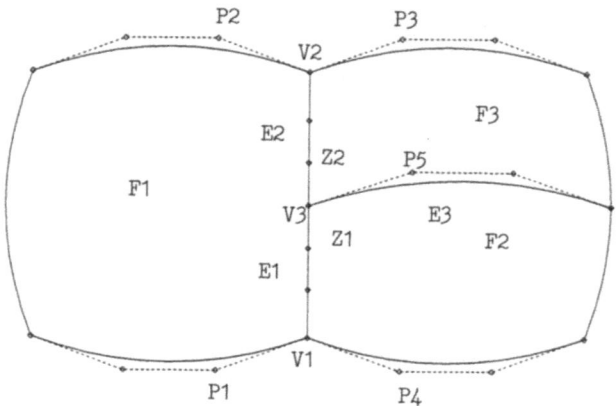

Figure 14 Boundary curves attached to a T-node

(1) Calculation of Normal Vectors

The normal vectors $n1,1$ and $n1,2$ at the vertex V1, and vectors $n2,1$ and $n2,2$ at vertex V2 are computed by the method described in Section 6.1(1).

(2) Determination of Vectors a0 and a2

The tangents a0 and a2 are determined by equations (3).

(3) Determination of Vector a1

If $n1,1 \neq n1,2$ and $n2,1 \neq n2,2$, then a vector a1 is determined using a equation (4). Otherwise, the unit tangent vector b3 at the vertex V3 is first calculated by

$$b3 = (V3 - P5) / |V3 - P5| .$$

When edges E1 and E2 can be represented as one cubic Bezier curve, the parameter value t3 at the position of the vertex V3 is given by

$$t3 = |V3 - Z1| / |Z2 - Z1| .$$

The vector a1 in the quadratic Bezier function

$$P(t) = \sum_{i=0}^{2} Bi(t)ai$$

interpolating three points V1(t=0), V3(t=t3) and V2(t= 1) is given as follows:

$$a1 = (b3 - B0(t3)a0 + B2(t3)a2) / B1(t3) .$$

This vector defines the cross-boundary tangent.

7. EXAMPLES

Figure 15 shows an example of an irregular mesh model. A face F1 in the model is attached to two T-node vertices V1 and V2. Figure 16 shows cross-sections of free-form surfaces generated in the model. Further, Figures 17 and 18 show cross-sections of free-form surfaces in the model depicted in Figures 4 and 5, respectively. Figures 19 and 20 show shading pictures of the telephone model depicted in Figure 8.

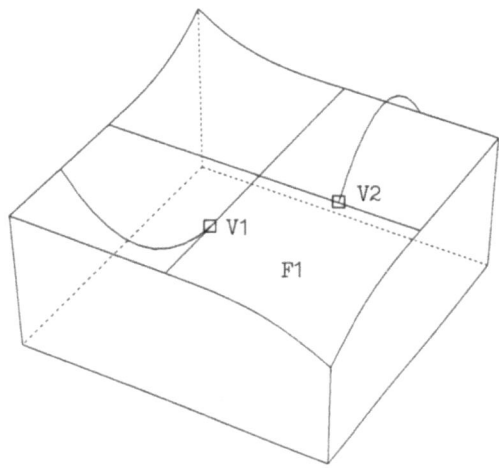

Figure 15 Curve  mesh with T-nodes

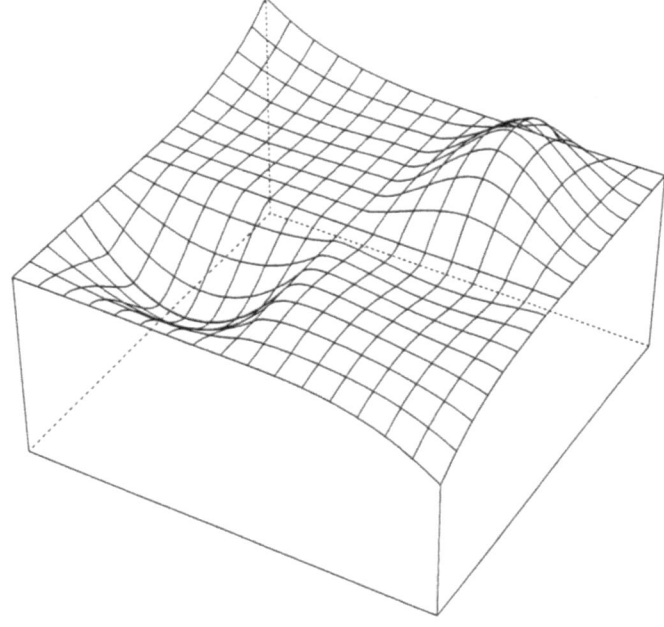

Figure 16 Cross-sections of surfaces

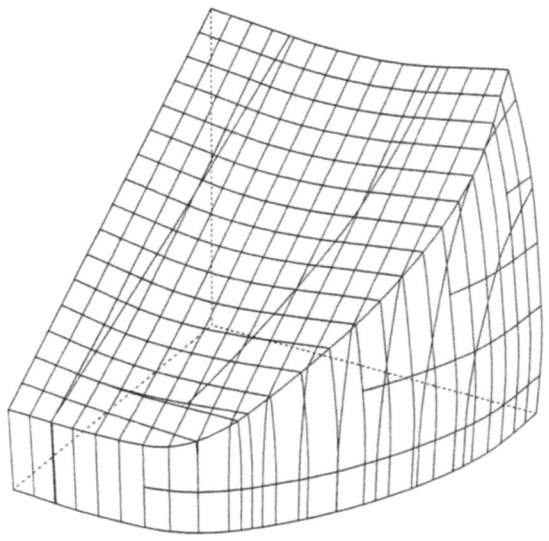

Figure 17 Cross-sections of surfaces

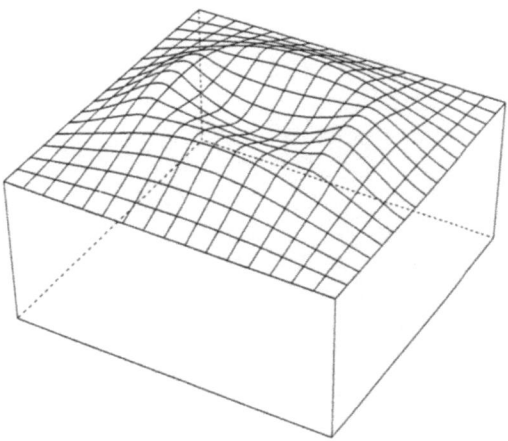

Figure 18 Cross-sections of surfaces

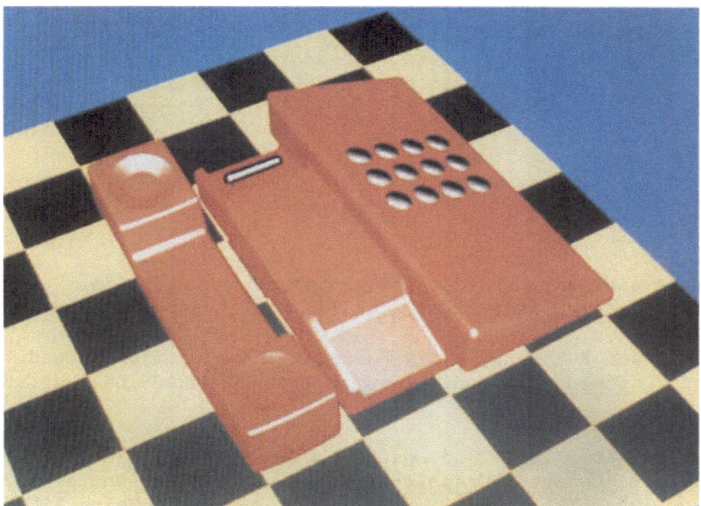

Figure 19 Shaded picture

Figure 20 Shaded picture

## 8. CONCLUSION

This paper proposed an interpolation method for irregular meshes of curves including T-nodes. In this method a free-form surface interpolating to one face is individually generated from localized boundary information. Because of this, our procedure is simple and quick.

The Gregory patch is used as a surface equation. This patch, defined by 20 control points in all, also has the convex hull property. Further, the patch can interpolate to four normal derivatives which are independently specified on the boundary curves.

## ACKNOWLEDGEMENT

Authors would like to thank Masaaki Kagawa, of Ricoh Co., for his making programs of shaded pictures; Associate Professor Fumihiko Kimura, of the University of Tokyo for his valuable suggestions; Dr. Hideko S. Kunii, General Manager of Ricoh's Software Research Center, for her valuable comments and discussion.

## REFERENCE

[1] H.Chiyokura and F.Kimura, "Design of Solids with Free-form Surfaces," Computer Graphics (Proc. SIGGRAPH'83), Vol.17, No.3, July 1983, pp.289-298.

[2] H.Chiyokura and F.Kimura, A New Surface "Interpolation Method for Irregular Curve Models," Computer Graphic Forum (J. of EUROGRAPHICS), Vol.3, No.3, 1984, pp.209-218.

[3] H.Toriya, T.Sato, K.Ueda and H.Chiyokura, "Invertible Set Operation for Solid Modeling," Computer Graphics - Visual Technology and Art (Proc. Computer Graphics Tokyo '85), T.L. Kunii (ed.), Springer-Verlag, Tokyo, 1985, pp.3-20.

[4] I.D.Faux and M.J.Pratt, Computational Geometry for Design and Manufacture, Ellis Horwood, London, 1979.

[5] R.F.Riesenfeld, Applications of B-spline Approximation to Geometric Problems of Computer Aided Design, Ph.D. thesis, Syracuse University, May 1973.

[6] D.Doo, "A Subdivision Algorithm for Smoothing Down Irregular Shaped Polyhedrons," Proc. Conf. Interactive Technique in CAD, IEEE Computer Society, 1978, pp.157-165.

[7] E.Catmull, and J.Clark, "Recursively Generated B-spline Surfaces on Arbitrary Topological Meshes," Computer Aided Design, Vol.10, No.6, November 1978, pp.350-355.

[8] B.A. Barsky and J.C.Beatty, "Local Control and Bias and Tension in Beta-spline," Computer Graphics (Proc. SIGGRAPH'83), Vol.17, No.3, July 1983, pp.193-218.

[9] J.A.Gregory, "Smooth Interpolation Without Twist Constraints," Computer Aided Geometric Design, R.E. Barnhill and R.F. Riesenfeld (Eds.), Academic Press, New York, 1974, pp.71-87.

[10] R.E.Barnhill, J.H.Brown and I.M.Klucewicz, "A New Twist in Computer Aided Geometric Design," Computer Graphics and Image Processing, Vol.8, 1978, pp.78-91.

[11] M.A.Sabin, "Non-Rectangular Surface Patches Suitable for Inclusion in a B-spline Surface," EUROGRAPHICS'83, P. ten Hagen (Ed.), North-Holland, Amsterdam, 1983, pp.57-69.

[12] M.Hosaka and F.Kimura, "Non-four Sided Patch Expression with Control Points," Computer Aided Geometric Design, Vol.1, No.1, 1984.

**Hiroaki Chiyokura** directs the 3D CAD project at the
Software Research Center of Ricoh Co., Ltd.  His
research intersts are solid modeling, computer
graphics, and their applications to computer-aided
design and manufacturing.  He received his BS
and MS degrees in mathematics from Keio University
in 1979 and 1981, respectively.  He earned his
Dr. Eng. in precision machinery engineering from the
University of Tokyo in 1984.  He is a member of
ACM SIGGRAPH.

The authors' address is Software Research Center,
Ricoh Co., Ltd., 1-1-17, Koishikawa, Bunkyo-ku,
Tokyo, 112 Japan.

# Environment for Fast Elaboration of Constructive Solid Geometry

Akira Fujimoto, Christopher G. Perrott and Kansei Iwata

Graphica Computer Corporation, Nagayama, Tama, Tokyo, 192-02 Japan

ABSTRACT:

This paper describes a set of software entities, both algorithms and data structures, which together comprise a system for the efficient elaboration of complex shapes defined by arbitrary volumetric Boolean constructs.

The three key elements in this system are:
    Spatially Enumerated Auxiliary Data Structure (SEADS),
    Boolean Compiler (B-COM)
    Accelerated Ray Tracer (ART).

SEADS is a structure which allows high speed access to the data associated with each cuboid voxel of the object space. B-COM is reponsible for resolving most of the CSG definitions while compiling them into SEADS. ART, partially the result of previous development, has been extended to handle the residual Boolean information in SEADS for various purposes (including mass properties calculation, rendering etc.).

The major significance of the system, as demonstrated by many experimental results, is its speed. ART provides practically constant processing time, virtually independent of both the number of objects and the complexity of the CSG description. B-COM processing time is to a certain extent influenced by the number of objects and the complexity, but in almost all practical cases it represents only a small fraction of the total processing time.

INTRODUCTION

Current solid modeling systems support very powerful, high-level operations but users generally find them rather slow. For this reason much recent research effort on solid modeling has concentrated on improving the computational speed (Atherton 1983; Sears 1984). The possibilities for increasing the efficiency of any solid modeler are closely related to the representation it uses. This subject has been elaborated in depth by Requicha and Voelcker (1983) and by Atherton (1983). The superior precision and compactness of the Constructive Solid Geometry representation, discussed on many occasions in the literature, contribute to the growing popularity of CSG representation (Wyvill 1985). (CSG represents objects by applying Boolean operations such as "union" and "intersection" to primitive solid building blocks). Unfortunately direct elaboration of CSG representation has been infamous for its long processing time. In order to improve CSG rendering speed, some researchers have chosen to sacrifice some of the precision and compactness, and have proposed simplified solutions (Atherton 1983; Sears 1984).

Two general approaches are commonly used to generate shaded surface images from CSG models (Atherton 1983; Requicha and Voelcker 1983)

    1.   direct      ray-firing or casting

    2.   indirect   resolving CSG a priori by transforming it to another representation such as boundary representation and then applying a hidden surface removal procedure.

CSG representation, however, is best suited to ray tracing. This is the only practical method which supports refraction and reflection and it provides the highest degree of realism currently available. It is commonly believed that ray tracing (even if limited to ray-casting) is extremely inefficient (Whitted 1980). It is sometimes argued that it cannot take advantage of coherence properties (Atherton 1983).

Our recent developments showed that ray tracing speed could be dramatically improved by means of an auxiliary data structure which not only possessed a high degree of coherence in itself but also did in fact take advantage of the coherence present in the original model (Fujimoto et al. 1985). The coherence represented in this structure could then be exploited by a fast traversing tool in the form of a 3D line generator used directly for ray tracing. Experimental results showed that a spatially enumerated uniform 3D grid provided far better performance than, for example, the octree approach (Fujimoto et al. 1985) for any spatial resolution. The superiority of this structure in comparison to the hybrid octree decomposition approach was confirmed by experiment. In particular, rendering time by the use of ray tracing was found to be virtually independent of the number of objects in the scene. In fact, for highly complex scenes involving thousands of objects, accelerated ray tracing was actually found to be faster than popular scan line methods. (Fujimoto et al. 1985)

The above developments were the starting point for our current research on the rendering of complex CSG constructs by the use of ray tracing. The essential advantage of the Spatially Enumerated Auxiliary Data Structure (SEADS) over octree is the fact that its final structure is independent of object shape; parameters such as the number of voxels in each direction can be fixed before actual enumeration takes place. This property of SEADS, as will be shown below, provides an excellent environment for efficient preprocessing of all kinds of volumetric operations prior to actual rendering. This feature, for example, is essential in implementing the plane generator, which is one of the basic tools of the Boolean Compiler (B-COM).

ENVIRONMENT COMPONENTS

As suggested by Requicha and Voelcker (1983), a modeling system can be regarded as

    1.   a specific collection of representations, some exact, some approximate, some auxiliary

together with

2. a collection of procedures for managing the representations and doing representation conversion and other geometrical calculations.

Below we present a suite of such representations and procedures which constitute the working environment for our CSG system.

-Line Generator (3DDDA): a fast traversing tool used to identify all voxels which are pierced by an arbitrarily placed ray.

-Spatially Enumerated Auxiliary Data Structure (SEADS): a structure characterized by a high level of coherence independent of the model.

-Boolean Compiler (B-COM): a set of efficient procedures for resolving a significant proportion of the volumetric Boolean operations in the preprocessing phase, while compiling the model into SEADS.

-Surface Generator (3DSG): procedures used by B-COM to perform efficient enumeration of the voxels intersected by the surface of an object. (The notion of 3DDDA has been extended from line to surface.)

We shall now discuss these tools in more detail:

SEADS & 3DDDA

SEADS (a representation) and 3DDDA (a procedure and algorithm) were developed by the authors and reported in our previous work (Fujimoto et al. 1985). (The acronym "SEADS" was not used in the earlier paper, but it is introduced in the present paper for the sake of clarity.) Only the essentials of the previous work will be repeated here. Prior to rendering of a model by the ray tracing technique its boundary is compiled into a spatially indexed data structure, SEADS, which conceptually corresponds to the decomposition of the scene into a 3D matrix of subspaces (voxels). The voxels are disjoint hexahedrons, in fact cuboids. (See Fig.1. for a 2D example.) After enumeration of all the voxels intersected by any object boundary, each voxel in decomposed space will be either HETEROgeneous (voxel containing any object boundary) or HOMOgeneous (voxel completely inside or outside all real objects).

3DDDA is responsible for generating only those voxels in SEADS which are pierced by the processed ray. 3DDDA ignores all HOMO voxels and continues generation until either a HETERO voxel is found or the end of the domain is encountered. When a HETERO voxel is found, objects in the voxel are checked for intersection with the ray. If an intersection is found then the shader is invoked and the pixel corresponding to that particular ray can be displayed (ray casting) or reflected and refracted rays can be spawned and processed (ray tracing). If all intersection tests fail, 3DDDA continues processing as if the voxel had been HOMO.

The above scheme of SEADS and 3DDDA is adopted in the present work without any major changes. In this paper we show how it can be extended to support efficient image rendering of complex shapes defined by CSG. (The approach can also easily be extended to support mass properties calculations (Roth 1982).)

B-COM and 3DSG

The essential tool developed for handling CSG constructs is the Boolean Compiler (B-COM). B-COM is a powerful preprocessor which uses efficient algorithms to preprocess a significant part of any typical, even very complex, CSG description. Information on Boolean operations which it cannot resolve at the voxel level (residual Booleans) is stored in SEADS in a form which is easily processed by the ray tracing renderer (and the mass properties evaluators). Although the primary purpose of the Boolean Compiler is maximum resolution of CSG volumetric Boolean operations prior to the rendering phase, it is also responsible for resolution of visibility (hidden surface removal).

The basic notion of B-COM is as follows:

For any Boolean construct it is possible to enumerate all relevant voxels simply by visiting all HETERO voxels (all voxels which happen to contain any part of the boundary of a cluster - by cluster we understand any Boolean definition) and evaluating the construct for the voxel as a whole.

Such evaluation will yield three and only three possible situations:

1.  FALSE          : voxel is ignored
2.  TRUE           : voxel is ignored
3.  UNRESOLVED     : voxel has to be enumerated.

Before discussing Boolean compilation algorithms, however, we have to address the problem of efficient identification of HETERO voxels. We wish to avoid the use of a computationally intensive approach, such as using clipping algorithms (Glassner 1984), or invoking a penalty function for several points in a voxel in order to check for each voxel in the primitive's domain whether it has HETERO or HOMO status toward the object (Hashimoto et al.). (A domain in this case is defined as the smallest parallelepiped in which the particular primitive can be embedded.) In the above mentioned methods the status of every voxel in the primitive's domain has to be checked; the ideal enumeration algorithm will directly identify all HETERO voxels without referring to irrelevant HOMO voxels.

Such algorithms, identifying only HETERO voxels, have been developed by extending the notion of 3DDDA in order to create a set of surface generators (3DSG).

Different surface generators have been developed for each primitive. For example, in the case of the plane surface generator, the notion of the Driving Axis (Fujimoto et al. 1985) was extended to the notion of Driving Plane which in turn forms the basis for incremental generation of all voxels which intersect the particular surface. The key feature of each surface generator is that it addresses only HETERO voxels without ever visiting any others.

Now we shall outline the main algorithm used by B-COM:

```
FOR each Boolean construct
   FOR each primitive
      FOR all HETERO voxels (generated by 3DSG)
         evaluate the Boolean construct for this voxel
         IF Boolean construct is unresolved
            store 'residual Boolean' information in SEADS
```

The above algorithm will enumerate only those voxels which contribute to the final shape of the construct. The unresolved information corresponds to residual Boolean constructs which in the worst case (fortunately never encountered in practice) reproduce the original Boolean definition and in the best case (most frequently encountered) refer only to a single primitive which happens to intersect the voxel.

We shall explain this using a simple example of an AND (intersection) construct (Fig.1.). After compiling the original definition A-B-C (=A*negB*negC) into SEADS, 22 HETEROgeneous voxels will be enumerated. Most of them (19 voxels) will contain completely resolved information which corresponds to a single primitive forming the logically true boundary of an object. Only three HETERO voxels contain residual Boolean constructs, and the residual Booleans are much simpler than the original Boolean definition. The uppermost voxel will be elaborated with A*negB, the middle voxel (in which primitives B and C intersect) will be enumerated with negB*negC and the lowest voxel with A*negC.

Now, using this very simple example let us discuss the merit of the proposed B-COM.

Let us first consider the processing required if ray tracing were used to evaluate the geometry of the object without any compilation. First each traced ray would have to be checked for intersection and if an intersection were found then the whole Boolean construct would still have to be evaluated in order to determine whether this intersection is logically true.

Now if we enumerate all HETERO voxels without Boolean compilation then in this particular case we will identify 77, all with the complete, unabbreviated Boolean definition. This situation corresponds to our previously developed Accelerated Ray Tracing. A ray is evaluated against a given Boolean only if it enters a HETERO voxel. Although the complete Boolean must be processed for each HETERO voxel, this nevertheless represents a considerable improvement, as shown in (Fujimoto et al. 1985).

B-COM, however, dramatically reduces the complexity of the Boolean construct for each voxel. In this particular case 22 voxels with complete Boolean definition were replaced by only 3 voxels with residual Booleans. In the three-dimensional case the number of voxels with residual Booleans will generally be greater, but only in the same proportion as the total number of HETERO voxels. For fairly complex operations involving a great number of objects B-COM can be expected to reduce by several orders of magnitude the amount of Boolean processing which must be performed by subsequent phases, such as the ray tracing renderer.

It is possible to increase the efficiency of the above B-COM algorithm in some cases where long strings of AND (intersection) operations are involved in the definition of a single object. In Fig.2, for example, "Boolean Cheese" is actually defined as a single object corresponding to a cluster of more than a thousand primitives most of which participate in an AND operation.

Although all the primitives are logically related, the dominant majority do not actually influence each other. A significant number of the holes do not contribute to the visible boundary of the object (do not intersect the bounding sphere, bounding planes or cutting planes).

Unless further Boolean operations on the model are envisioned or the model is transparent, their enumeration in SEADS is meaningless. Also, the majority of the holes which are actually visible have no common intersections. Adopting the Boolean enumeration algorithm where for each encoded primitive, each generated HETERO voxel must be processed for Boolean operations involving thousands of primitives would in this case require excessive compilation time. Fortunately during the enumeration phase it is possible to skip all those primitives which do not intersect the one which is actually being enumerated.

EXPERIMENTAL RESULTS

The representations and procedures described above have been implemented in Fortran 77 and tested using a DEC VAX 11/785 under VMS operation system. Many experiments have been performed, using various numbers of primitives and CSG constructs with various levels of complexity. Lack of space prevents us from showing all the results and instead we present details of just one of the most complex models we have used in our experiments. The images shown in Fig.3 were all generated and displayed using a resolution of 512x512 pixels. Boolean Cheese was mentioned in the previous section. A similar representation is often desired by chemists investigating molecular structures. It enables them to view their models in complementary fashion in order to grasp the topology of a molecule. In order to display such (and other) structures in any desired manner we have implemented the notion of a 'knife'. A knife is a CSG cluster related to all objects in the scene by an AND operation. A knife can be as simple as a single cutting plane; then everything which is on its FALSE side will be removed. On the other hand, it may be as complex as any general cluster. In general the existence of such a knife implies that a significant portion of the original shape will probably be invisible and can be ignored during the rendering phase. This portion of course should be filtered out by B-COM.

Fig.3a shows a complex DNA structure containing more than seven thousand atoms of various types. This structure represents a trivial CSG construct, union. Compilation time for this case was only a few seconds and the picture was rendered within 10 minutes.

Fig.3b shows a version of Boolean cheese in which all the atoms of Fig.3a have been used as complements to a big sphere in which they are embedded. In order to make visible part of its interior, a complex knife defined as a cluster of two cylinders has been used. This results in a CSG construct in which all 7013 primitives are ANDed together. The total compilation time for this model was less than 35 minutes. The rendering time was less than 13 minutes, which is not much longer than for Fig.3a even though far more of the rays actually intersect the surface of an object.

Fig.3c shows another visualisation of the same model in which all atoms are clustered in a UNION and are displayed as a union with another AND cluster. These examples (and others which are not included here) show that rendering time is virtually independent from Boolean processing.

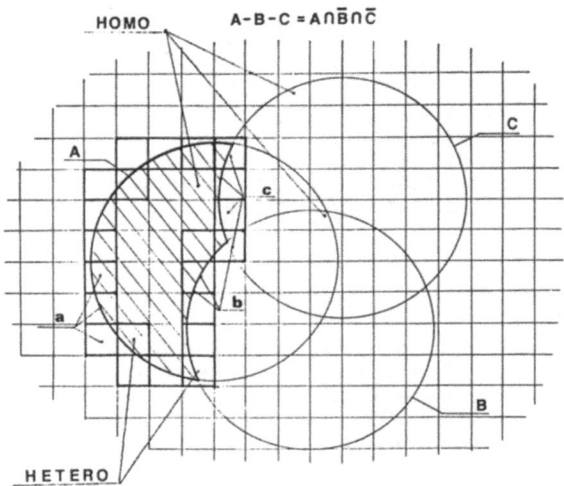

A, B, C -- primitives
a, b, c -- HETEROgeneous voxels with pointers to corresponding
           primitives.

Fig.1. Solid Boolean cluster after compilation into Spatially Enumerated
Auxiliary Data Structure (SEADS)

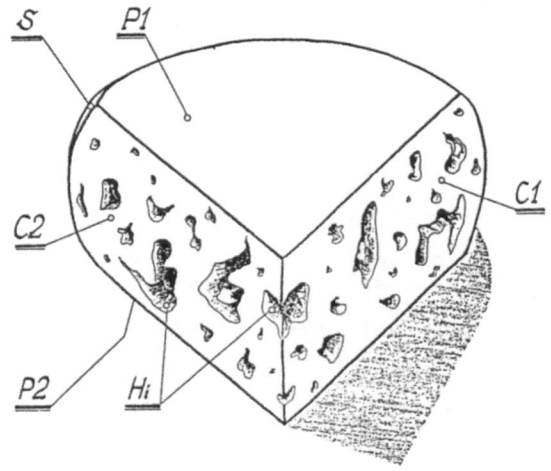

Hi (i=1,N)   -- primitives corresponding to holes in a cheese
S            -- spherical boundary of a cheese
P1, P2       -- bounding planes
C1, C2       -- cutting planes

Cheese Boolean construct:

$$S - \overline{P1} - P2 - C1 - \overline{C2} - \sum_{i=1}^{i=N} Hi = S * P1 * \overline{P2} * \overline{C1} * C2 * \prod_{i=1}^{i=N} \overline{Hi}$$

Fig.2. "Boolean Cheese"

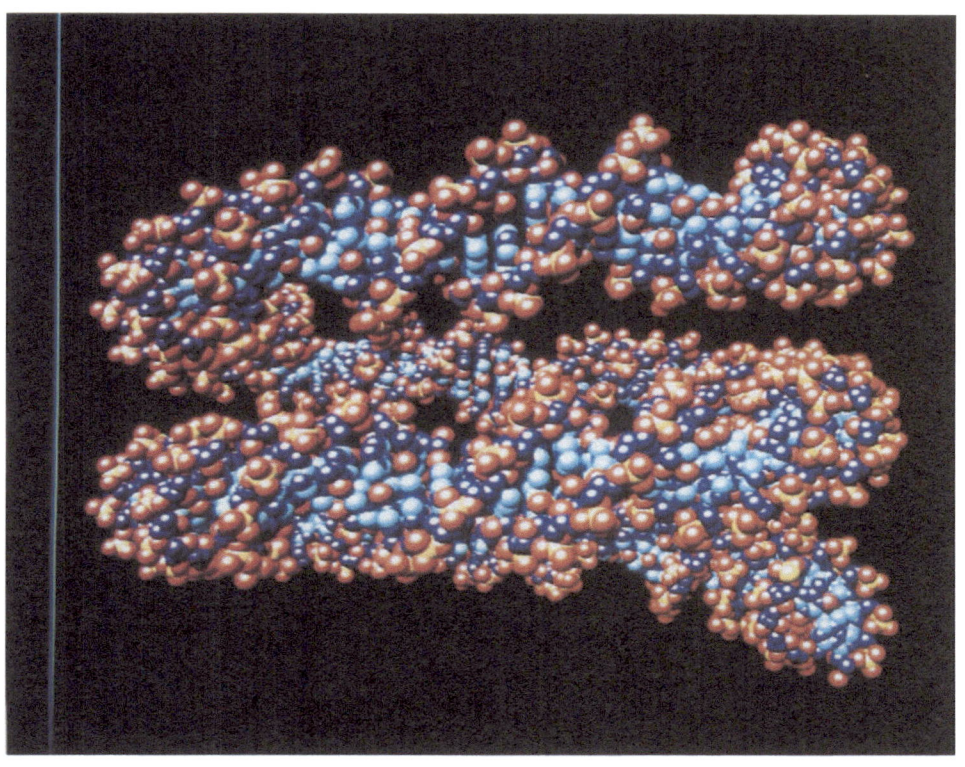

7011 atoms of various types forming a DNA molecule, evaluated and
displayed as a Boolean union cluster.
(Coordinates generated by Sussman and Trifonow).

compilation time:    7 seconds
rendering time:      9.5 minutes


Fig.3a. Spherical DNA

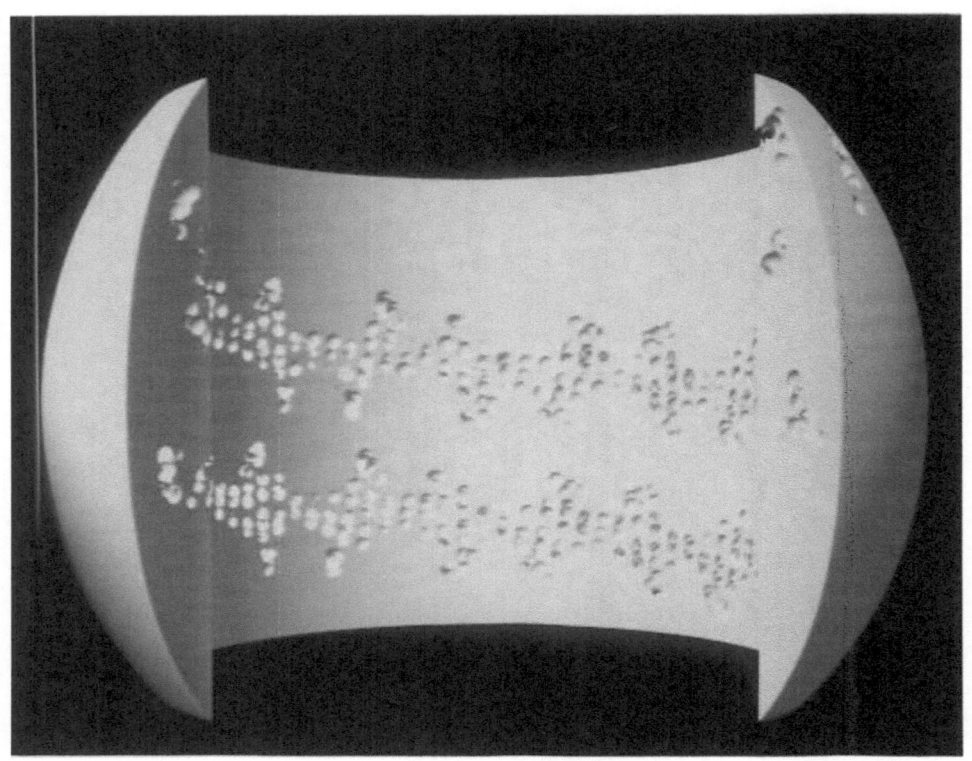

All atoms displayed in Fig. 3a, after being negated (turned into complementary mode) have been embedded in the bounding sphere. A complex knife composed from two cylinders has been used.
Shape of the object has been defined as for Boolean Cheese introduced in Fig.2:

$$S - Cc - Cm - \sum_{i=1}^{i=7011} Hi = S * \overline{Cc} * \overline{Cm} * \prod_{i=1}^{i=7011} \overline{Hi}$$

where,
S  - bounding sphere
Hi - holes corresponding to atoms in a complementary mode
Cc - cutting cylinder coaxial with sphere
Cm - another cutting cylinder with axis in front of sphere

compilation time:   34 min
rendering time:   11.5 min.

Fig. 3b. Negated spherical DNA embedded in a bounding sphere

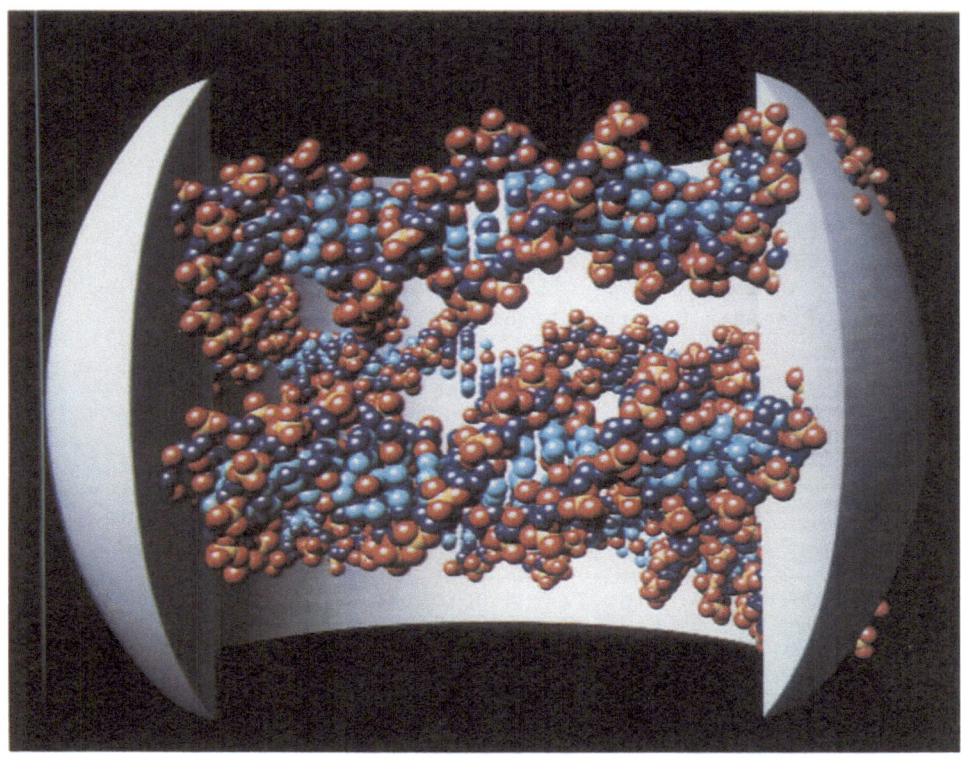

Union of Fig.3a. and a shell of Fig.3b. Shape of the object has been
defined using the following Boolean construct:

$$S - Cc - Cm + \sum_{i=1}^{i=N} Hi = S * \overline{Cc} * \overline{Cm} + \sum_{i=1}^{i=N} Hi$$

where,
S  - bounding sphere
Hi - atoms
Cc - cutting cylinder coaxial with sphere
Cm - another cutting cylinder with axis in front of sphere

compilation time:  1 min
rendering time:    11 min


Fig. 3c. Spherical DNA and Bounding Sphere

Table 1 contains timing data obtained when compiling and then rendering various numbers of atoms from the model displayed in Fig.3. The results show clearly that there is a considerable difference in the compilation time of AND and UNION clusters. This difference becomes significant in practice when the number of objects in an AND cluster is greater than 1000. This figure, however, is far above the practical requirement in virtually any application we can imagine.

Table 1.  Compilation and Rendering Timings

Compilation Time for Construct from Fig.3b.

No. of
compiled      Number of voxels along one axis
objects

|      | 10 | 20 | 30 | 40 |
|------|------|------|------|------|
| 12   | 0:00:00.23 | 0:00:01.07 | 0:00:02.91 | 0:00:07.23 |
| 52   | 0:00:00.41 | 0:00:01.40 | 0:00:03.37 | 0:00:07.63 |
| 102  | 0:00:00:67 | 0:00:01.72 | 0:00:04.35 | 0:00:08.17 |
| 202  | 0:00:02.04 | 0:00:03.32 | 0:00:05.88 | 0:00:10.01 |
| 302  | 0:00:04.20 | 0:00:05.54 | 0:00:08.03 | 0:00:13.75 |
| 402  | 0:00:06.23 | 0:00:07.58 | 0:00:10.74 | 0:00:16.08 |
| 1002 | 0:00:42.22 | 0:00:43.87 | 0:00:48.27 | 0:00:55.48 |
| 2002 | 0:03:09.80 | 0:03:07.14 | 0:03:09.94 | 0:03:17.56 |
| 3002 | 0:05:18.57 | 0:05:19.98 | 0:05:30.06 | 0:05:48.17 |
| 4002 | 0:10:11.41 | 0:10:10.26 | 0:10:23.11 | 0:10:40.12 |
| 7013 | 0:33:38.14 | 0:33:36:90 | 0:33:46.46 | 0:34:06.73 |

Compilation Time for Construct from Fig.3a.

No.of
compiled      Number of voxels along one axis
objects

|      | 10 | 20 | 30 | 40 |
|------|------|------|------|------|
| 7011 | 0:00:03.68 | 0:00:04.04 | 0:00:05.41 | 0:00:07.41 |

Rendering Time for Single Object (sphere)

No. of
rendered      Number of voxels along one axis
objects

|   | 1 | 10 | 20 | 30 | 40 |
|---|------|------|------|------|------|
| 1 | 0:04:13.14 | 0:04:24.95 | 0:04:29.68 | 0:04:34.76 | 0:04:35.72 |

Rendering Time for Object in Fig.3b.  (AND of 7013 objects)

| No. of rendered objects | Number of voxels along one axis | | | |
|---|---|---|---|---|
| | 10 | 20 | 30 | 40 |
| 7013 | 0:38:18.22 | 0:15:13.63 | 0:12:20.63 | 0:11:34.10 |

Rendering Time for Object in Fig.3a.  (UNION of 7011 objects)

| No. of rendered objects | Number of voxels along one axis | | | |
|---|---|---|---|---|
| | 10 | 20 | 30 | 40 |
| 7011 | 0:34:00.08 | 0:13:54.45 | 0:10:09.99 | 0:09:23.15 |

(NOTE:   All times are given in the format H:MM:SS.DD, hours,
        minutes, seconds and decimal fraction of a second.)

CONCLUSIONS

Requicha and Voelcker (1983) pointed out that the primacy of  boundary
and constructive representations for the curved solids  of  mechanical
engineering is likely to continue indefinitely.  They  also  suggested
that other representation schemes that might enter the charmed  circle
are (I) cell decompositions, if efficient  algorithms  are  found  for
their construction and for performing Boolean operations on them,  and
(II) hierarchical  spatial  enumerations,  e.g.  octrees,  if  special
hardware is used for manipulating them.

In our research we have tried to combine CSG with  the  first  scheme,
cell decomposition.  We believe that our developments represent a step
in the direction suggested, a step which brings solid modeling  closer
to the interactive threshold of the user.

ACKNOWLEDGMENT

The authors would like to express their gratitude to Mr. T.Tanaka  for
his assistance in coding and testing the  algorithms  presented  here,
and  for  identifying  several  special  cases  which  affect   the
completeness of the algorithms.

Dr. Nelson Max of Lawrence Livermore Laboratory provided us  with  the
DNA model used in Fig.3.1.

REFERENCES

Atherton, P.R. (1983)
A Scan-Line Hidden Surface Removal Procedure for Constructive Solid Geometry.
Computer Graphics, Vol.17, No.3

Brown, C.M. (1982)
PADL-2: A Technical Summary.
IEEE Computer Graphics and Applications, Vol.2, No.2, pp. 69-84

Fujimoto, A. et al. (1985)
Accelerated Ray Tracing.
CG Tokyo '85

Glassner, A.S. (1984)
Space Subdivision for Fast Ray Tracing.
IEEE Computer Graphics and Applications, Vol.4, No.10

Hashimoto, N. et al.
TIPS-1 '77 Version SYSTEM MANUAL.
Computer Aided Manufacturing - International, Inc.

Requicha, A., Voelcker, H. (1983)
Solid Modeling: Current Status and Research Directions.
IEEE Computer Graphics and Applications, Vol.3, No.7

Roth, S.D. (1982)
Ray Casting for Modeling Solids.
Computer Graphics and Image Processing, No.18, pp. 109-144

Sato, H. et al. (1985)
Fast Image Generation for Constructive Solid Geometry Using a Cellular Array Processor.
Siggraph '85

Sears, K.H. et al. (1984)
Set-Theoretic Volume Model Evaluation and Picture-Plane Coherence.
IEEE Computer Graphics and Applications, Vol.4, No.3

Whitted, T. (1980)
An Improved Illumination Model for Shaded Display.
Communications of the ACM, Vol.23, No.6

Wyvill, G., Kunii, T.L. (1985)
A Functional Model For Constructive Solid Geometry.
The Visual Computer Vol.1, No.1, pp.3-14

Akira Fujimoto is a director of the Computer
Graphics Software Division of Graphica Computer
Corporation, a company that produces computer
graphics and image processing systems.  His
research interests include computer graphics for
raster-scan devices, applications of computer
graphics in scientific and engineering analysis,
and CAD.
Fujimoto received an ME in mechanical engineering
from the Technical University Szczecin (Poland)
and from the University of Tokyo, where he
subsequently obtained his PhD.  He is a member of
the Society of Naval Architects of Japan, the
Computer Graphics Society (CGS), and the GKS
Japan Committee of CGS.

Christopher G. Perrott is a chief engineer in the
Research and Development Division of Graphica
Computer Corporation.  Previously, he has worked
on airline reservations software, radar systems,
and process control in Europe and North America.
His present interests include software and
hardware for computer graphics systems.
Perrott received a BA and an MA in physics from
Oxford University.  He is a member of the IEEE.

Kansei Iwata is president of Graphica Computer
Corporation, which he founded in 1975.  From 1970
to 1975, he was employed by Iwatsu Electronic
Company, Ltd., where he was the chief of the
Electronic Circuit Research Laboratory at the
Technical Institute in 1974 and 1975.  His
research interests are related to pulse
transmission and electronic circuit design.
Iwata received his BA and PhD in electrical
engineering from Tohoku University in Sendai,
Japan.  He is a member of the IEEE and the ACM.

# Interactive Solid Modeling in HutDesign

Martti Mäntylä and Mervi Ranta

Laboratory of Information Processing Science, Helsinki University of Technology, Otakaari 1, SF-02150, Espoo, Finland

## ABSTRACT

HutDesign is a three-dimensional geometric modeler under development at the Helsinki University of Technology. HutDesign puts a special emphasis on the quality and effectiveness of the interaction between a designer and the modeler. The paper describes the interaction methodology of HutDesign and gives examples of the functions offered in the interface. The use of software tools, particularly a user interface manager, is also discussed.

Keywords: interaction, user interfaces, solid modeling, CAD.

## INTRODUCTION

For some years, solid modeling technology has been in transition from academic and other research institutions to real-world engineering usage. Yet applications of solid modeling count only for a very small percentage of the Computer-Aided Design area. While the fraction is growing, progress towards solid modeling seems to be slower than what many workers in the field have expected.

Why is this so? No doubt the most important reason is the lack of applications that wholly exploit the rigorous information contained in solid models. Few companies can earn by producing shaded pictures or calculating elementary spatial properties of solid objects, and others may regard the inherent cost of switching to solid modeling too high if these are the only new applications readily available.

There are other reasons for the slow acceptance of solid modeling technology, however. Due to the added complexity of the modeling packages, their responsiveness and user-friendliness is far beyond from what users of simpler wire-frame based design systems have learned to expect. While certain coarseness is acceptable for research prototypes, a system intended for end users must be simple and effective to use. A designer working under deadline pressures will rapidly switch to the use of line-drawing systems or the drawing board if the design system fails to provide in a silky fashion the solutions he/she needs.

This article describes our ongoing work with HutDesign, an interactive three-dimensional geometric modeler that forms the core component of Hut*, a CAD system under construction with the Laboratory of Information Processing Science at the Helsinki University of Technology.

Hut* is intended for a distributed environment consisting of graphical workstations and a local area network connecting the workstations with a server node providing the required filing and output facilities. In this operating environment, a heavy emphasis must be put on the quality of user interfaces. In the case of HutDesign, topics that must be addressed include the following ones:

(1)      Conceptual simplicity: The interface must comply to current engineering prac-
         tices where the user mainly works in terms of several two-dimensional views of
         the object modeled. The interface must be based on drafting-like operations.

(2)      Functionality: The functionality available to the user must be compact, snappy
         and to the point.

(3)      Consistency: Operations available in the interface must use uniform techniques
         for naming, identification, creation, processing, and display of the objects mani-
         pulated.

(4)      Efficiency: The interface must be capable of using the facilities available in
         the workstation to a reasonable extent. In our case, these facilities present
         themselves as a windowing system including mouse input, pop-up menues, and
         icons.

(5)      Error tolerance: The interface must be supportive to a casual user. For in-
         stance, it must include on-line help and a general UNDO command for fast er-
         ror recovery.

To cope with these problems, all Hut* applications are based on a set of software tools. In
particular, all user interfaces are based on a user interface development tool, HutWindows
(Koivunen 1985), to guarantee the uniformity of user interfaces across the system. Modeling
functions of HutDesign are based on the algorithms of the Geometric WorkBench (Mäntylä
1985). The implementation environment of Hut* is BSD UNIX (tm) 4.2 and the C programming language. We have found many UNIX software tools useful in our work. In particular, HutDesign uses the compiler-compiler YACC (Johnson 1978).

The development of any interactive software system should be based on clearly understood
basic objects and their relationships. This article gives a case study of this approach, with
emphasis on a conceptually simple overall design, the separation of independent layers in the
resulting system, and the identification of useful software tools.

The article is organized as follows: First, in section 2 we outline some basic notions and issues of man-machine interaction and introduce the terminology used in the rest of the article. Section 3 discusses concepts and techniques that were used as the basis of the user interface of HutDesign (in particular, the input mechanisms of HutWindows), and section 4
gives examples of actual functions available. Section 5 indicates some of the lessons we
have learned in our project as for the choice and use of software tools such as HutWindows
and YACC. Finally, section 6 describes some extensions currently in works.


A FRAMEWORK FOR MAN-MACHINE INTERACTION


The best user interface is one that allows the user to work directly with the task he/she is
trying to solve --- that is, an interface the user can completely forget about. The user's conception of the task, the information worked on, and the operations that can be applied are
termed the user's conceptual model of the task. The purpose of the interactive system is to
let the user create a computer model of the task, i.e. a structured collection of objects, their
attributes and relationships amongst the objects that allows him/her to solve the task. In the
ideal situation, there is an exact match between the conceptual model and the data and
operations actually available in the computer model.

Unfortunately, telepathy does not belong to the input facilities available to a user interface
designer. The best the designer can do is to provide a language (textual or graphical) for
expressing the desired operations on the conceptual model, and provide feedback of the state
changes in the computer model. The feedback should allow the user to interpret the state
changes in terms of his/hers conceptual view of the task.

Hence, the user interface design problem is split into three (deeply intertwined) problems,
namely

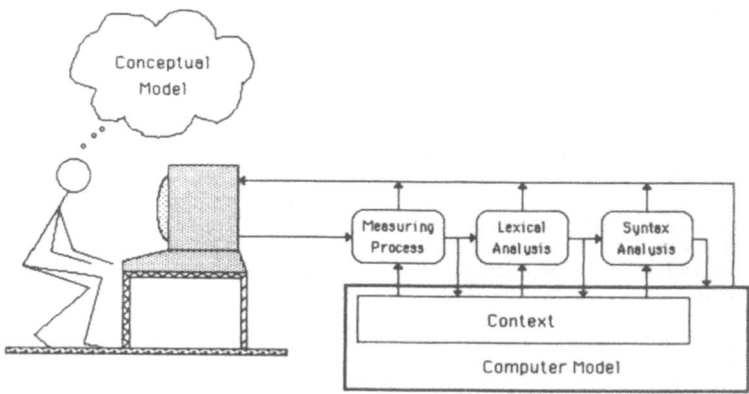

Figure 1: Framework for Man-Machine Interaction

(1)                  designing the computer model;

(2)                  designing an interaction language that supports the user's conceptual model of the task; and

(3)                  designing the feedback to be provided to the user that allows him/her to interpret the state of the task in terms of his/hers conceptual model.

In turn, the interaction language can be split in four layers:

(1)                  The <u>physical layer</u>: The physical interaction with the computer consists of primitive actions such as key hits and movements of the cursor. A measuring process implemented in hardware or system software translates user's actions into a sequence of such physical input items.

(2)                  The <u>lexical layer</u>: The physical input items are interpreted as logical items having significance for the interaction, e.g. as references to objects being displayed (picking), command names, or numerical information. This is the task of a software process called the <u>lexical analyzer</u> that transforms the sequence of physical actions into a sequence of <u>lexemes</u>. The lexical analyzer accomplishes this task by means of <u>lexical rules</u>.

(3)                  The <u>syntactic layer</u>: The lexemes of the language are grouped into a sequence of meaningful sentences of the language by a software process called the <u>syntax analyzer</u>. The analyzer works based on <u>syntax rules</u>.

(4)                  The <u>semantic layer</u>: A meaning is associated to sentences of the interaction language in terms of state changes in the computer model of the task. This is carried out by suitable <u>action procedures</u> executed at the receipt of meaningful sentences.

Observe that in principle the sequences of physical actions, lexemes, and sentences already entered by the user form a part of the state of the computer model. Hence the various interpretation processes can be guided by the past history of the interaction. Usually, the effects of the past history are grouped under the term <u>context</u> of the interaction. The context can be divided in three layers according to the three interpretation processes:

(1)    <u>Lexical</u> <u>context</u>: The interpretation of physical actions can be guided by the past history of actions. For instance, after a certain action has occured, characters typed by the user are interpreted as a character string, while otherwise they would be interpreted as function keys. Hence identical physical actions can lead to different lexical tokens depending on the lexical context.

(2)    <u>Syntactic</u> <u>context</u>: The interpretation of lexemes can be guided by the context. For instance, according to the context a character string can interpreted as a command name, an object identifier, or a numerical constant.

(3)    <u>Semantic</u> <u>context</u>: The effect of a sentence can vary according to the context. For instance, the objects worked on can partly or wholly be determined by the context. This sort of semantic context can be implemented in terms of the notion of <u>currency</u>: certain objects are considered to be "current" ones, and operations whose target objects are not explicitly specified work on the current ones.

The context of many interactive systems includes <u>modes</u> that restrict the use or alter the effect of operations depending on the past events. However, if modes are overused, unnecessary strain is put on the user. This has led to the notion of <u>modeless programming</u> strongly featured e.g. in the user interface of the Apple Macintosh personal computer (Apple 1985).

In principle, the feedback to the user can also be divided to physical, lexical, syntactic, and semantic layers. However, the designer of a user interface can only cause certain physical feedback to occur during the interaction. The interpretation of the physical feedback on higher levels relies on the ability of the user's sensory and perceptional processes to distill meaning from the physical feedback.

A particular aspect of the feedback is the proper indication of the context information. The interface must provide sufficient clues to allow the user infer how his actions are being interpreted. For instance, if currency is exploited, any current objects should be highlighted appropriately.


## INTERACTION METHODOLOGY OF HUTDESIGN

The purpose of HutDesign is to let the user design three-dimensional solid objects. HutDesign seeks to accomplish this mission by allowing the user to "draw" in several views that contain graphical displays of the object(s). As far as possible, HutDesign tries to support this conceptual model of two-dimensional drawing.


### HutDesign WorkSpace

In HutDesign, the totality of data the user is working on is termed a <u>WorkSpace</u>, the analogy of a sheet of paper. At each point of time, exactly one WorkSpace is in the process of being manipulated; the user can switch from one WorkSpace to another.

A WorkSpace consists of several kinds of entities. The entities have attributes that determine their visual representation and the operations that can be applied to them. Structure of the HutDesign WorkSpace is visualized in Fig. 2.

First, the WorkSpace contains zero or more named zero- to three-dimensional shapes termed <u>Objects</u>. Objects are arranged as a stack <u>ObjectStack</u>, where the top of the stack is considered the "most current" Object, and the bottom the "least current" Object. Every nonempty Object has a "current point" (CP) and a "current face" (CF). Together, these entities define uniquely a hierarchy of various other current things, for instance the "current edge" CE (the line segment beginning from CP in CF in the direction of CF), and the "current loop" CL (the connected component of the boundary of CF adjacent to CP).

Objects of a WorkSpace are visible through <u>Views</u>, analogous to planar projections in a drawing. The attributes of a View include the following:

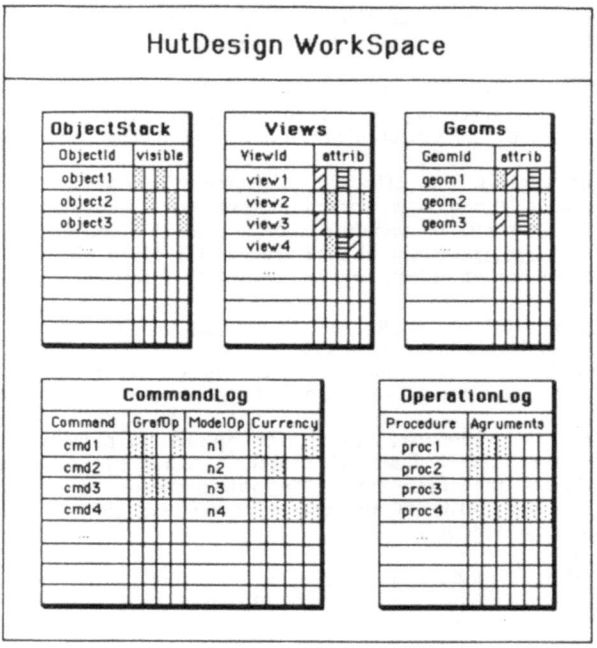

Figure 2: HutDesign WorkSpace

- a region of the screen where the View can display its contents;
- specification of a window-to-viewport two-dimensional viewing operation;
- a display list of graphical primitives currently being displayed;
- specifications of input operations available in the View and their characteristics
- specification of a three-dimensional viewing operation (projection).

To implement Views, HutDesign uses the facilities of HutWindows; the four first items of the list above are maintained by it.

Each Object is associated with a list of Views it is visible in. Hence, each Object can be visible in zero or more Views, and each View can have zero or more associated Objects. The most current Object visible in a View (if any) is considered to be the "current object" of that View.

A WorkSpace also may contain one-dimensional geometric entities termed Geoms. Geoms are three-dimensional infinite lines; they are intended to be analogous to "construction lines" in the drawing analogy. Unlike Objects, Geoms have no visibility attributes, but they are displayed in all views. Geoms are ordered into a cyclic list.

As to be detailed in the below, HutWindows transforms all user input into ASCII "commands". The command history information is stored as a part of the WorkSpace in two lists, the CommandLog and the OperationLog. The CommandLog stores one record of information on each command, including its name, arguments (if any), the currency information, and the numbers of graphical primitives and modeling procedures caused by the command. The procedures themselves are stored in the OperationLog.

HutDesign Display

The state of a HutDesign WorkSpace completely determines what should be displayed to the user to indicate the current state of the interaction process (except during state changes, i.e. while a command is being input or executed). Of course, not all details of the state can be displayed to avoid confusing visual clutter. Therefore, our current prototype version indicates the currency information of at most one Object per View, the most current one visible.

A sample HutDesign display is given in Fig. 3. The WorkSpace displayed consists of four views (three orthogonal views and one isometric view). The regions on the right (with labeled "soft" buttons) and at the bottom (with some text displayed) are maintained by HutWindows.

This WorkSpace consists of two Objects and three Geoms. The three Geoms are arranged orthogonally to indicate a local coordinate system. The current Geom is indicated by displaying it in dashed line style. One of the Objects, the triangle, is visible in two Views, the top right View (displaying a side view of the scene) and the bottom right View (displaying an isometric view of the scene). The triangle is the Current Object of both of these Views, indicated by a marker symbol at the Current Point of the triangle (the top vertex).

The other Object (slanted box) is visible in two Views, the top left View (displaying a front view) and the isometric view. This Object is current in the front view, indicated by highlighting its Current Point; however, it is not current in the isometric view. This is so because the triangle is on top of the box in the ObjectStack. Observe that the fourth View (displaying top view of the scene) has no visible Objects.

Ordinarily, detailed information on the contents of the ObjectStack is not displayed. However, the user can cause the current state of the stack to be displayed as a pop-up menu as shown in Fig. 3. If necessary, the user can make any Object the topmost one (and hence the Current Object of all Views it is visible in) by selecting the corresponding row of the menu.

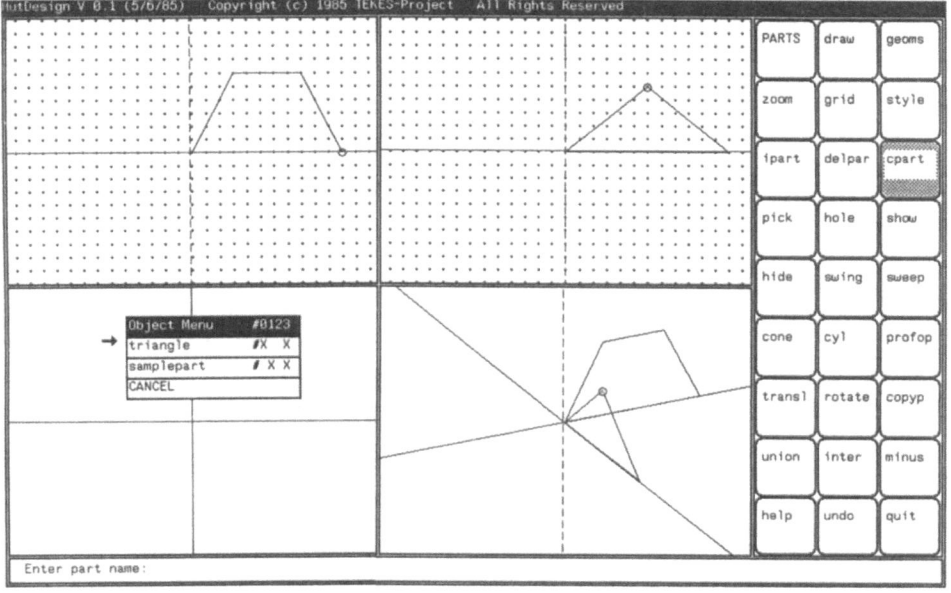

Figure 3: A HutDesign Display

Input Styles

The input styles available in HutDesign are based on the facilities offered by HutWindows. HutWindows provides mechanisms for describing tiled multiwindow displays such as Fig. 3 and the input characteristics of the windows. Figure 3 includes six HutWindows windows, namely four graphical windows (used for displaying Views), one text window (the small region at the bottom), and one icon window (the softkey region on the right).

HutWindows acts as a filter that maps the physical actions performed by the user into character strings passed to the application. Hence, commands can always be typed. In addition, HutWindows supports many other input styles specified in terms of function key definitions associated to a HutWindows window. Various input styles are available through the following kinds of function keys:

(1)     Icon selection. By hitting a key designated for this purpose, the user can jump into an icon window and select one of the icons displayed. Thereafter, the character string associated with the selected icon is passed to the application and the cursor resumes its original position.

(2)     Dynamic menu. By hitting a key designated for this purpose, the user can display a pop-up menu and select an item. After this, the character string associated with the selected item is passed to the application and the menu disappears.

(3)     Text input. By hitting a key designated for this purpose, the user can jump into a text window and type one line of text. Upon hitting the RETURN key, the string written is passed to the application and the cursor resumes its original position.

(4)     Function keys. Keys can also be plain function keys. When such a key is hit, the character string associated with it is passed to the application.

In each case, the input is considered to originate from the window the graphics cursor resided in at the moment the function key was pressed; this information is available to Hut-Design as the View Of Input (VOI) associated with each command string sent by HutWindows. When desired, HutWindows can insert the coordinates of the cursor in ASCII format into the string by associating a suitable formatting macro with a function key.

From the point of view of HutDesign, specifications of function keys, pop-up menues and icons are attribute data of a WorkSpace. These data can be modified if desired. HutDesign uses this facility for dynamically changing e.g. the pop-up menues according to the context.


OPERATIONS OF HUTDESIGN


The structure of the HutDesign WorkSpace forms the basis for the functions available to the user. In general, we have aimed at exploiting the data available in the WorkSpace, particularly the currency information, as far as possible so as to keep the interaction language simple.

The rich currency information gives HutDesign the opportunity to feature modeless operation to a high degree. HutDesign generally employs an input style where a user first selects an entity by making it current and then executes an operation to the current entity. This approach allows us to maximize the number of simple "pushbutton" commands that do not take any arguments at all.

The commands of HutDesign can be split in three categories:

(1)     Context modification: These operations allow the user to modify the currency information, i.e. to make the desired Objects, Geoms, or faces and points within an Object the current ones. They do not modify the entities themselves.

(2)     Single View operations: These operations work based on the currency informa-
        tion of one View. Usually, they modify the Current Object of that view. As
        a side effect, the currency information of that Object may be altered.

(3)     Multiple View operations: These operations work based on the global currency
        information, usually based on the ObjectStack. Usually, they modify several
        Objects and their currency information.

Context Operations

Context operations allow the user to make the appropriate entities current for further mani-
pulative operations. For instance, there are commands for moving the CP around CL
(NEXT, PREV), making an Object current by picking (PICK), making a Geom current by
picking (PICKGEOM), and so on.

To illustrate the variable input styles available, let us describe the command NEXT in
greater detail. This command makes the point following the Current Point in the Current
Face the new Current Point. The command can be given in the following ways:

- While holding the graphics cursor within the window of a View, hit the ESC
  key (the default text input key in HutDesign), and type "next". This causes the
  string typed to be sent to HutDesign.
- While holding the graphics cursor within the window of a View, push the
  center key of the mouse (the default icon input key in HutDesign). This
  causes a new cursor to appear in the icon window; while holding the mouse
  key down, use the mouse to select the icon labeled "next" and release the key.
  This causes the string "next" to be sent to HutDesign.
- While holding the graphics cursor within the window of a View, hit the key "n"
  on the keyboard. By default, "n" is defined as a function key that causes the
  string "next" to be sent to HutDesign.

These three cases are handled with the same piece of code in HutDesign; indeed, HutDesign
has no information as to how the command was given.

Single View Operations

Single view operations constitute the basic functionality of a 2-dimensional drafting system.
Hence, there are operations for making new Objects, adding and deleting lines and arcs to
Objects, editing lines and arcs, and so on. Drawing operations of several Views can be free-
ly intermixed if desired.

For instance, Fig. 4 depicts the effect of the LINE command that adds a straight line segment from the CP to a new point that becomes the new CP. This command takes two
numbers representing the projected coordinates (u v) of a point as arguments. The command
can be given in the following styles:

- Hit ESC and type e.g. "line 100 75".
- Point at (100 75), and select the icon "line" as shown in Fig. 4. This selection
  causes the evaluation of a formatting macro resulting in the string "line 100 75"
  to take place.
- Point at (100 75) and hit the key "l". As above, a macro is evaluated with
  identical results.

All commands that take coordinate arguments can be input with these styles. Irrespective of
the style used, the coordinates given are transformed to three-dimensional "world" coordinates
(x y z) according to the inverse projection operation of the View Of Input. Note that in
Fig. 4, gridding is being used to aid exact pointing. The WorkSpace displayed has just a
single View.

42

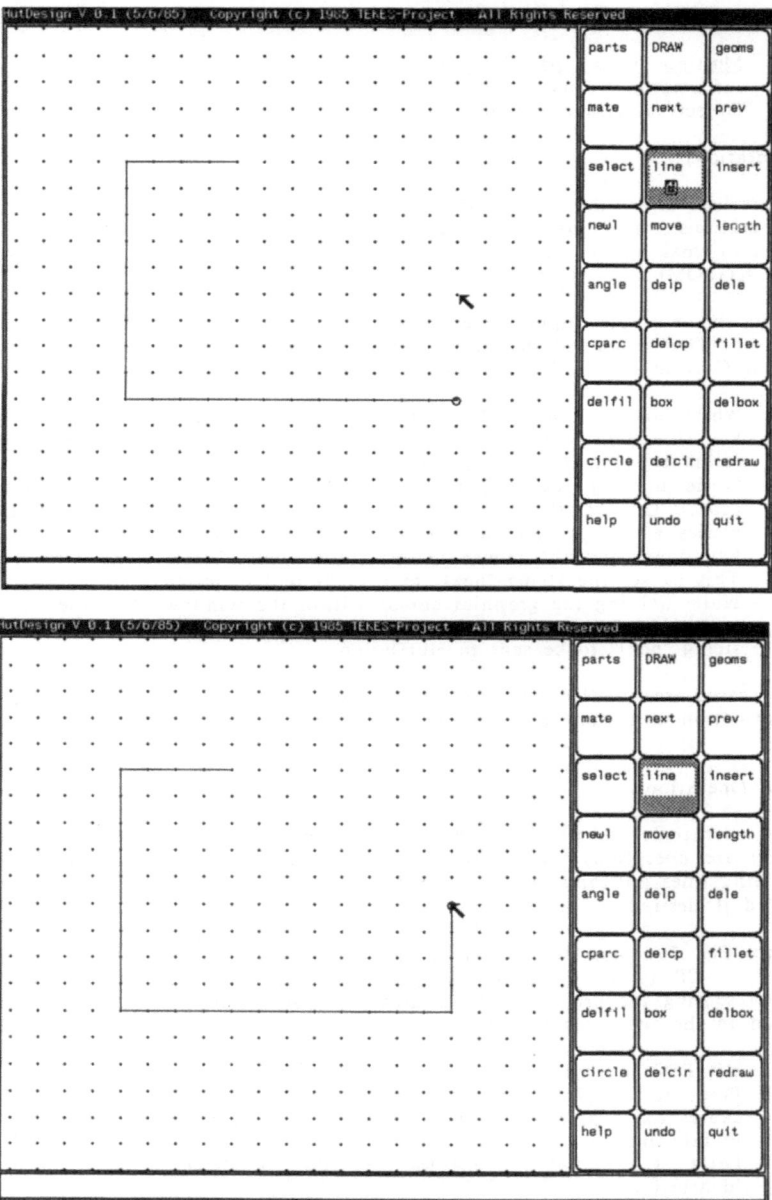

Figure 4: LINE Command

Commands that need arguments other than coordinates must be entered in a slightly more complicated fashion. For instance, Fig. 5 illustrates the FILLET command that inserts a fillet arc at a sharp corner. This command requires an argument that declares the radius of the fillet arc.

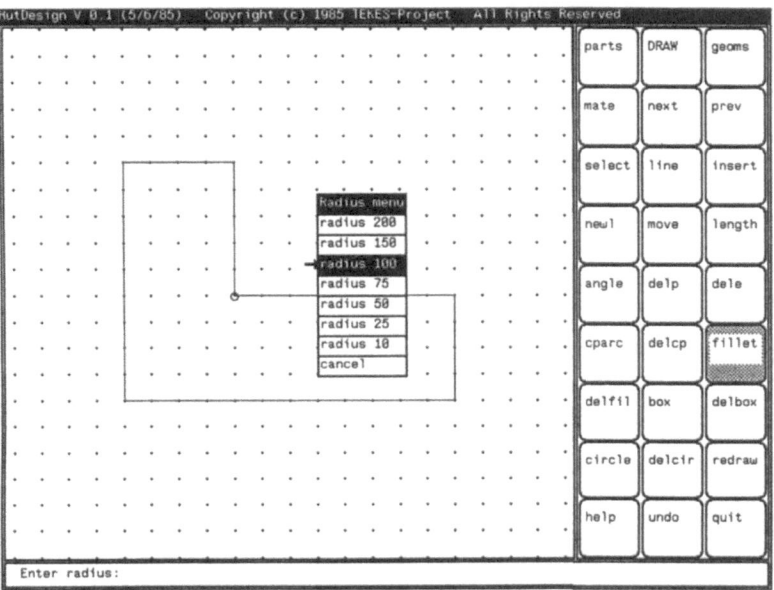

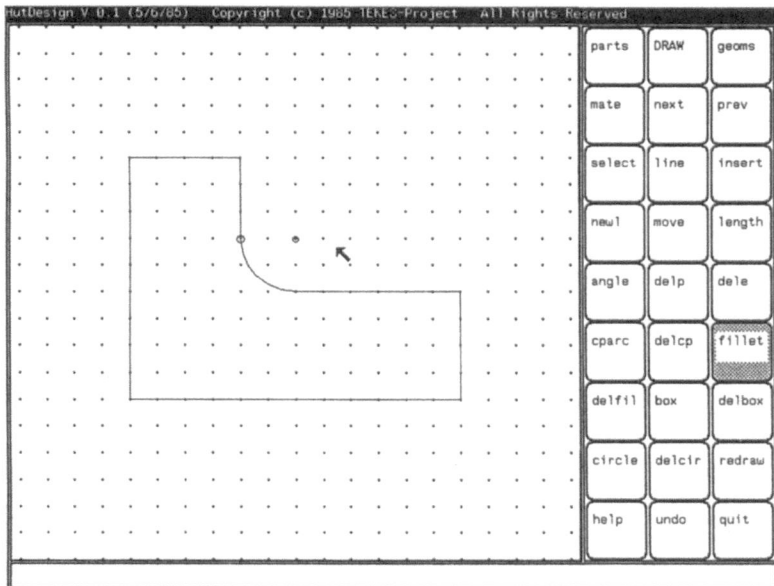

Figure 5: Fillet Construction

In this case, the following styles can be used:

    - Hit ESC and type "fillet 100". This causes a fillet arc of radius 100 to be inserted at CP.

- Select the icon "fillet". This puts HutDesign in a mode where a radius is expected. To indicate this, a prompt "Enter radius" is displayed in the text window. Now the user can type in the desired radius. Alternatively, he/she can push the left mouse key (the default pop-up menu key in HutDesign) to get a menu containing some favored radiuses, and select a suitable entry.

## Multiple View Operations

Multiple view operations form the bridge from two-dimensional constructions to three-dimensional ones. In addition to the currency of the View Of Input, they generally use the global currency information represented in the ObjectStack to locate the appropriate argument Objects.

Also in this group, HutDesign prefers drawing input to typing. Hence, instead of typing coordinates or dimensions, these data can be entered by drawing a "construction" Object which is used to calculate the desired values. To support this, many commands of this group have a variable syntax; if an argument is not explicitly given, the ObjectStack is consulted so as to locate an appropriate construction Object.

Let us consider the command SWEEP (Fig. 6) to illustrate this approach. This command sweeps a two-dimensional Object along a one-dimensional Object consisting of a single line. If the Objects are not explicitly given (e.g., if the command is invoked with an icon or with a function key), the argument objects are pulled from the context as follows:

- If the Current Object of the VOI is two-dimensional, use it as the Object to be swept. Find the most current one-dimensional Object from the ObjectStack, and use it as the construction Object.
- If the Current Object of the VOI is one-dimensional, use it as the construction Object. Find the most current two-dimensional Object from the ObjectStack, and use it as the Object to be swept.
- Otherwise (i.e., the Current Object is zero- or three-dimensional), display an error message: proper Objects cannot be found.

These rules allow the user to construct an outline in one View, and draw a line that represents the desired sweep amount and direction in another View.

In a similar fashion, Construction Objects are used to specify axes for rotational sweeping, 2-dimensional translation of Objects, rotation angles, and the parameters of various primitive Objects.

To support the conceptual model of drawing, the major construction technique of 3-dimensional Objects is the combination of two orthogonal profiles as shown in Fig. 7. To use this construction, the user draws two Objects in two Views that give the outlines of the desired 3-dimensional Object from two directions. The outlines are then combined by calculating the Boolean intersection of their extrusions.

## Miscellany

HutDesign offers a collection of commands for miscellaneous tasks such as the manipulation of WorkSpaces, Objects and Views. For instance, Views can be created, deleted, redisplayed, zoomed, and panned.

The most important operation in this group is the UNDO command. Because command history is included in the WorkSpace, all operations can be undone up to its initialization. This is implemented by applying the inverses of the basic operations stored in the OperationLog and the graphical primitives stored in display lists as guided by the CommandLog, and restoring the currency information. The details of this facility are described separately (Mäntylä 1986).

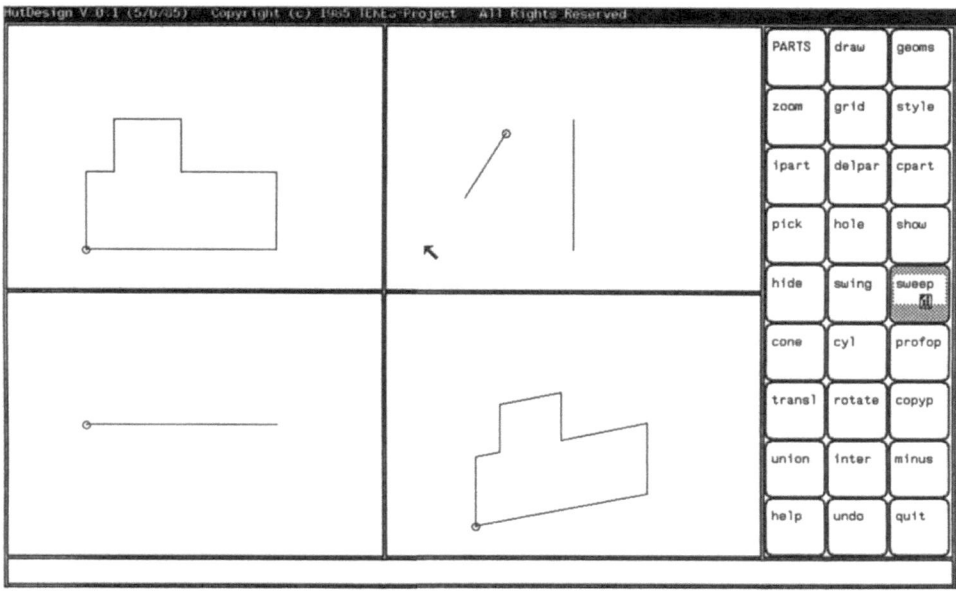

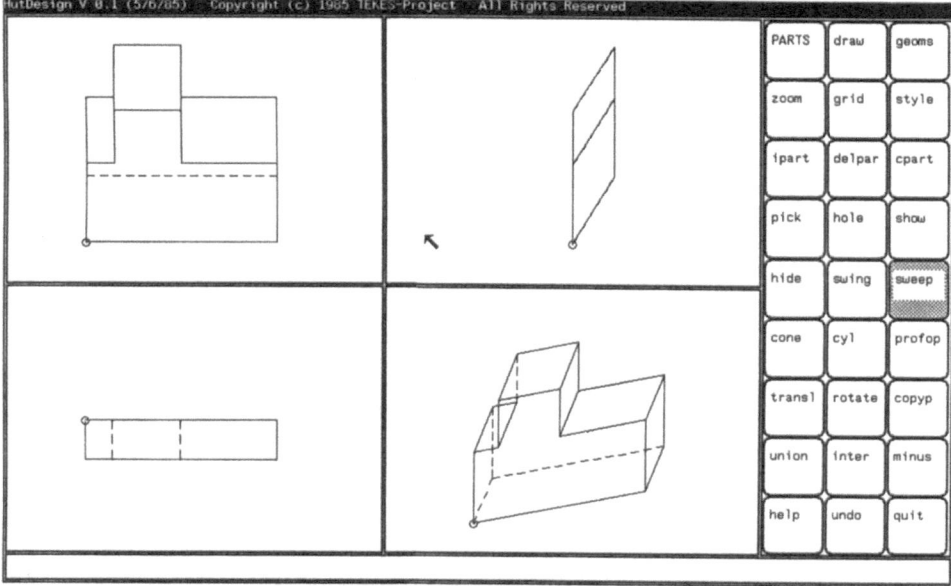

Figure 6: Sweeping

46

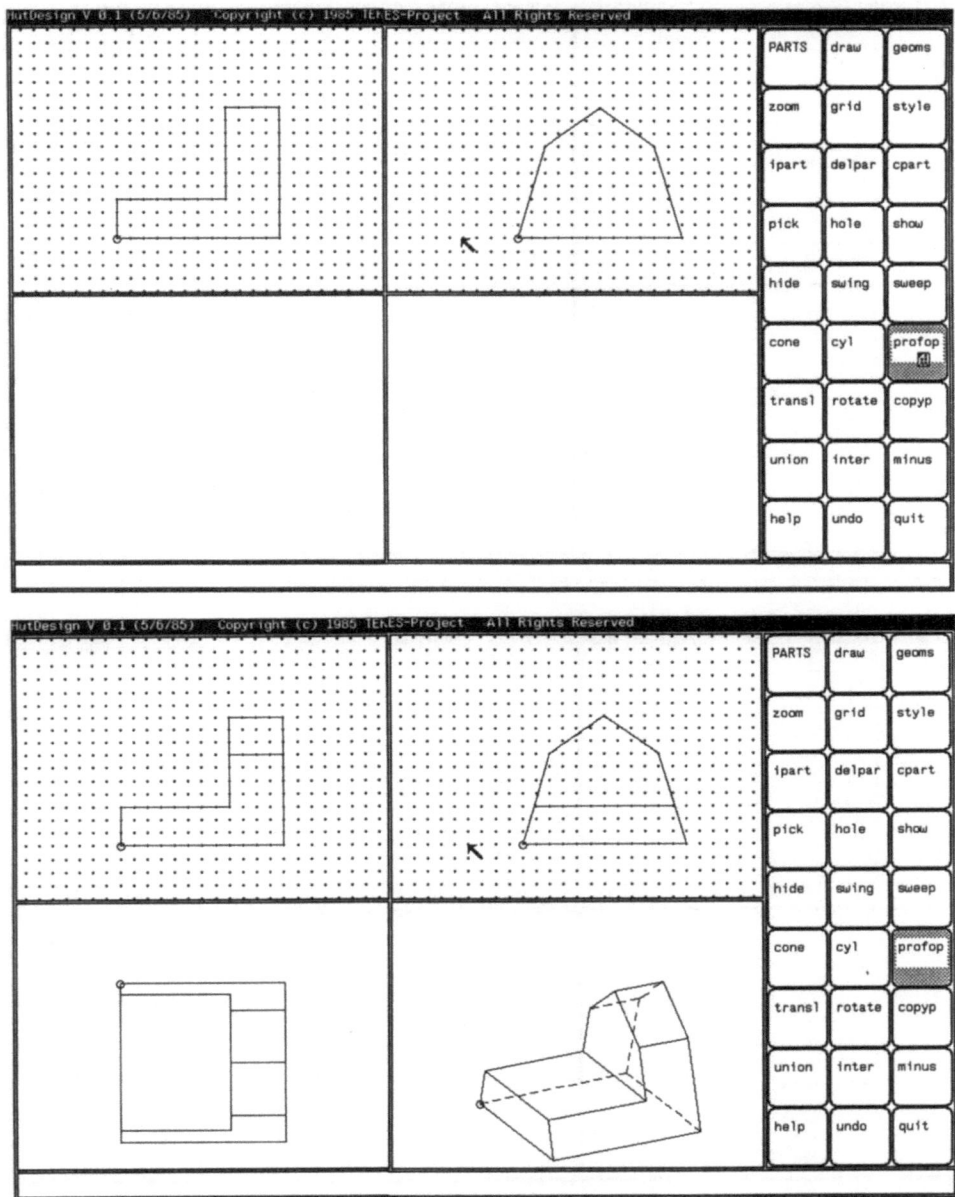

Figure 7: Profile Combination

## IMPLEMENTATION LESSONS

Without the use of software tools, HutDesign would not be what it is (in good and in bad). This section indicates some of the insights we have gained during our work on HutDesign so far.

### HutDesign and HutWindows

Clearly, the input facilities of HutWindows have had a great influence on the design of Hut-Design. The function key approach of HutWindows strongly suggests the use of argumentless "pushbutton" commands, or commands that only take coordinate arguments or arguments from some finite set of alternatives. This leads us to a rather rich context information that allows arguments to be pulled out from some "current" entities.

Whether this is a vice or a virtue is a matter of taste. Nevertheless, in our opinion the variable input styles provided by HutWindows have greatly enhanced the quality of the interaction possible with a fixed amount of effort. HutWindows has proved to be a convenient and effective tool for user interface specification.

A major feature of the HutWindows' architecture is the decision to send all user input to the application in character string format. The overhead caused by this is obvious; however, it has the advantage that HutWindows and the application can be distributed as separate processes residing in separate computers in the network. While the current prototype of HutWindows does not yet support network communication, future versions are planned to implement this.

HutWindows is designed to be relatively independent on the application using it. In fact, many useful operations can be executed locally just by HutWindows, such as zooming, panning, and redisplaying.

### HutDesign and YACC

The command parser of HutDesign was written with YACC (Yet Another Compiler-Compiler) (Johnson 1978). For a command language as simple as that of HutDesign, almost any approach could have been selected as for implementing the parser. Nevertheless, we feel there is a lot of sense in the maxim "if there is a tool for it, use it". YACC does its job very well, and we strongly recommend its use.

In the current prototype implementation, communication between HutWindows and the parser is accomplished by having HutWindows call the parser. The input string is put into a location known to the parser so that it can read the string character by character. This temporary solution makes it virtually impossible to have the parser and HutWindows execute in a coroutine fashion. Nevertheless, this difficulty will be removed in the future as the communication facility is revised.

### HutDesign and GWB

GWB is a procedure library for constructing and manipulating boundary models of solid objects. It currently supports faceted representations of solids having planar, quadric, or toroidal surfaces. For curved surfaces, exact surface data is available for accurate calculations. GWB is based on the pervasive use of Euler operators that act as the "assembly language" for higher-level algorithms such as solid primitives, sweeping, and Boolean set operations.

Euler operators and their properties are discussed elsewhere (Mäntylä 1978). As for the user interface of HutDesign, observe that Euler operators easily lend themselves to "drafting-type" operations and local modifications such as sweeping. Furthermore, each Euler operator has an exact inverse that can undo the corresponding "positive" operator. This property forms the basis of the UNDO operation of HutDesign.

## EXTENSIONS

Our work on HutDesign is an evolving one, and many extensions to the current version are being contemplated. Our modeling tools are continuously under development, and we are feeling a constant pressure of making the new procedures available also in HutDesign. Extensions of this sort include additional local operations such as the "rounding" of sharp edges, modeling facilities for surface types other than those currently available, functions for marking features and assigning attribute information to them, and modeling of static and dynamic assemblies.

Another source of extensions comes from the planned work on HutWindows. For instance, we are contemplating the inclusion of additional input styles, for instance a "desk calculator" for generating numerical input.

Last but not least, the history information of the WorkSpace can be used to support other interesting operations besides the undoing. We are contemplating a "random-access" redoing facility aimed at making the specification of repeated operations easier.

## CONCLUSION

The problems encountered while developing a three-dimensional geometric modeler are large even without the additional difficulty of providing a good graphical interface to the modeling functions. A simple and clean design of the interface can have a very positive effect on the time and effort required as for the latter.

HutDesign pursues the goal of simplicity by basing the functionality of the user interface on carefully formulated context information. While this approach certainly puts limits on the kinds of interactive operations that can be supported, uniformity of the interface can be maintained. We believe this price is worth paying.

The current design of the HutDesign WorkSpace omits many important pieces of information, such as assemblies, geometric features (e.g. dimensions and tolerances), and nongeometric attributes. In our approach, these extensions will necessarily lead to the use of new kinds of "current" entities. After this, the same principles as those followed in the design of the current operations can be followed.

HutDesign deliberately restricts its interaction styles to those supported by HutWindows. For instance, cursor tracking is not used. While this admittedly prohibits the use of certain kinds of interactiove operations, it has the benefit of enhancing the portability of HutDesign.

## ACKNOWLEDGEMENTS

The work described in this article forms a part of the project "Distributed CAD" supported by the Technological Development Center of Finland (TEKES). The authors have also been supported by the Helsinki University of Technology Foundation.

In addition to the authors, the Hut* project group currently consists of the following people: Lasse Holmström, Jussi Kanerva, Olli Karonen, Timo Ketonen, Marja-Riitta Koivunen, Reijo Sulonen, and Charles Woodward. Our sincere thanks goes to all of them for providing an exciting environment for our work, and in particular to Marja-Riitta Koivunen, the main author of HutWindows.

# REFERENCES

1. Inside Macintosh. Apple Computer Inc. 20525 Mariani Avenue, Cupertino, CA 95014, 1985.

2. Koivunen, M.-R. and Mäntylä, M. HutWindows - An Approach to User Interface Management. Proc. EUROGRAPHICS '85. North-Holland, Ams., 1985, pages 37-47.

3. Mäntylä, M. and Sulonen, R. GWB - A Solid Modeler With Euler Operators. IEEE Computer Graphics and Applications, Vol. 2, No. 7, 1982, pages 17-31.

4. Johnson, S. C. YACC - Yet Another Compiler-Compiler. Bell Laboratories, Murray Hill, N.J., 1978.

5. Mäntylä, M. Undo Support in HutDesign. To be presented at CAPE '86.

Martti Mäntylä is a senior research associate with the Laboratory of Information Processing Science at the Helsinki University of Technology, Finland; currently he also is an acting professor of Computer Science. Mäntylä received his Ph.D. in 1983 from the Helsinki University of Technology. In 1983-1984 he was a visiting scholar with the Computer Systems Laboratory at the Stanford University.

Mäntylä's research interests include computer applications in engineering, CAD, computer graphics, user interfaces, and data base management. He is a member of the ACM, the IEEE Computer Society, and the Eurographics Association.

Mervi Ranta is a research associate with the Laboratory of Information Processing Science at the Helsinki University of Technology. She is currently completing her M.Sc. degree in Computer Science at the Helsinki University of Technology. Her research interests include user interface development, computer graphics, geometric modeling and computer-aided design.

# Polygonal Subdivision of Parametric Surfaces

K. Kobori[1], M. Iwazu[1], K. M. Jones[2] and I. Nishioka[1]

[1] Computer Systems Laboratories, Sharp Corporation, Ichinomoto, Tenri, Nara, 632 Japan
[2] Corporate Design Center, Sharp Corporation, Nagaike, Abeno, Osaka, 545 Japan

ABSTRACT

This paper describes an algorithm for the polygonal subdivision of parametric surfaces. Our existing method has problems displaying trimmed surfaces with complex boundaries or surfaces with tiny holes, because parametric surfaces are divided into fine polygons of uniform size. In general, this needs relatively large memory storage for the great number of polygons.
In the method presented here, Various size of patches are generated according to the complexity of the surface bounbary. Smaller polygons are generated at only the complex boundaries of the parametric surfaces, and coarse polygons are generated at the simple boundaries of the surfaces. As a result, the method reduces the number of polygons and the computation time.


Key words and Phrases: CAD, Parametric surfaces, Polyhedra, Quad trees, Shading, Subdivision

## 1. INTRODUCTION

Color raster displays with polygon filling processors or a shading engine have appeared with advances in Computer Graphics ( C. G. ). Using these intelligent graphic displays, in the field of CAD/CAM, has made it possible to display objects using shaded images quickly. The designer can get greater understanding than that provided by 3D wireframe pictures. Currently, polygons or quadric patches are often used to model a 3D object for shaded picture generation. In either case, it is important to create a visually accurate rendering of a 3D object as quickly as possible. Figure 1 shows an example of an inadequate rendering and an adequate rendering of an object. In other words, it is necessary to convert a parametric surface into the finite polygon data to approximate a 3D object at interactive speeds.
The algorithm presented here provides an adequate approximation of a visually complex 3D object in less drawing time.
In this method, the edges of the meshes into which a surface is divided are classified into six types according to the relationship between the edges and surface boundaries. Next, the complex parts of surface boundaries are recognized automatically by these classifications, and only the complex parts are divided into fine meshes.

 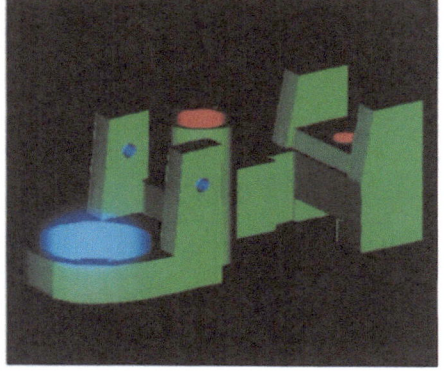

(a) Inadequate rendering          (b) Visually adequate rendering

Figure 1. Example renderings of an object

## 2. SURFACE DEFINITION

For precise algorithmic specification, we offer the following definition of an parametric surface(see Faux and Pratt[2] for further discussion of surfaces ). Surface S presented here is defined by the equation

$$S = \{P(u,v)\} \tag{1}$$
$$P(u,v) = (x(u,v), y(u,v), z(u,v)) \tag{2}$$

where $0.0 \leq u \leq 1.0$, $0.0 \leq v \leq 1.0$. $P(u,v)$ of two variables may present a point, corresponding to the component functions $x = x(u,v)$, $y = y(u,v)$, $z = z(u,v)$. $P(u_0,v_0)$ represents a position lying on the surface S provided that $u_0$ and $v_0$ are constants in the range of u and v which describe the surface.

A surface consists of a set of bounded curves and each bounded curve is given a direction such that the inside of the surface is to the left, as shown in Figure 2. A surface is divided into m×n meshes and the portion of meshes which exists inside the surface are called inner polygons ( the shaded area in Figure 2 ). Each boundary of a mesh is called a mesh edge.

## 3. CLASSIFICATION OF THE MESH EDGE

Using the relationship between a mesh edge and bounded curves, each mesh edge can be classified in one of six types shown in Table 1.

The direction of each edge is given as counterclockwise. In Table 1, the solid line

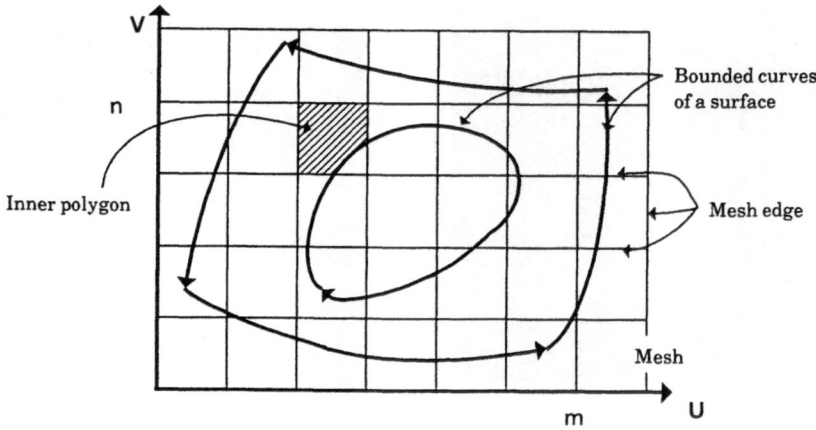

Figure 2. Definition of a parametric surface

indicates that the portion of the edge exists inside a surface and the dashed line indicates it is outside a surface. The point marked with a 'X' is an intersection point between the mesh edge and bounded curves of a surface. The dots represent the start point and the end point of a mesh edge.

The edge of type 0 is totally outside the surface, whereas the edge of type 3 is totally inside. In the case of edge type 1, the start point of the edge exists inside the surface and the end point is outside the surface.

Type 2 is the opposite situation to type 1. In the case of type 4 and 5, two or more intersection points lie on the edge.

Table 1. Type of a mesh edge

| Type | Start point of a mesh edge | End point of a mesh edge |
|------|----------------------------|--------------------------|
| 0 | •----------------------------------------------→• | |
| 1 | •————————→×----------------------→• | |
| 2 | •----------------------→×————————→• | |
| 3 | •————————————————————————→• | |
| 4 | •————→×------------→×————————→• | |
| 5 | •----------→×————————→×----------→• | |

## 4. THE ALGORITHM FOR MESH DIVISION

After dividing a suface into coarse m×n meshes of the same size, the algorithm generates a set of inner polygons to approximate the surface automatically. The meshes are subdivided into smaller meshes in order to model a complex portion of the surface. If the mesh is too complex for the decision procedure to find the inner polygon, the algorithm divides the mesh into four smaller meshes called submeshes and recurs, processing each one with the same algorithm(see discussions by Warnock and Catmull[1,6]). The criteria to decide whether or not the mesh should be subdivided are based on the relationship between a mesh edge and the bounded curves of a surface. This subdivision process is applied until this relationship is classified as simple. The algorithm involes the following three steps:

Step1)   Calculate all the intersection points between each edge of meshes and bounded curves of surfaces. The points marked with a dot in Figure 3 represent the intersection points.

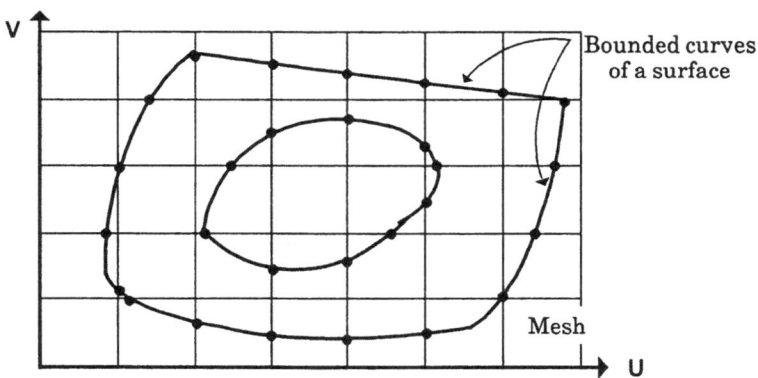

Figure 3. Intersection points between
the edges and the bounded curves

Step2)   Classify each edge of a mesh into one of six types shown in Table 1 and tag the edge with the edge type number (type 0,1,2,3,4,5).

Step3)   If the mesh has one of the following three criteria, the mesh is divided into four sub-meshes.

   Case1)   The mesh has one of the edges tagged with type 4 or 5, as shown in Figure 4(a).
   Case2)   The mesh has two edges tagged with type 1 or 2 opposite each other, as shown in Figure 4(b).
   Case3)   One or more holes are contained within the mesh, as shown in Figure 4(c).

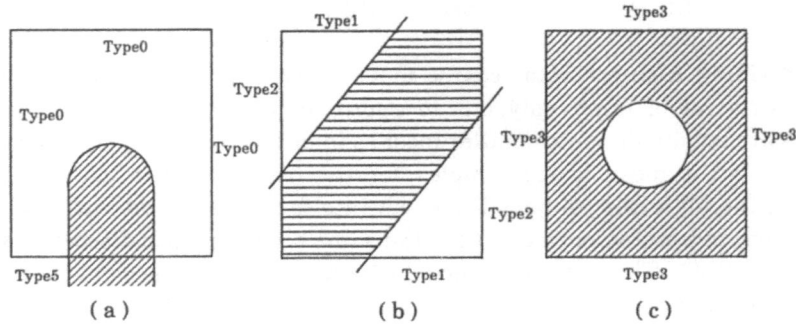

(The shaded area indicates the inner polygon.)

Figure 4. An example of the meshes which should be subdivided.

The subdivision process continues until the relationship between each new sub-mesh and the bounded curves becomes one of the five types shown in Figure 5. These are the simplest cases and inner polygons can be extracted.

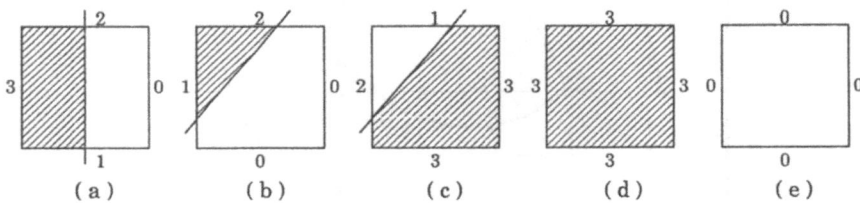

(The shaded area indicates the inner polygon.)

Figure 5. Classification of a mesh

In Figure 6, a concrete example will serve to illustrate the algorithm. After generating coarse meshes of the same size, for each mesh, the algorithm decides which of the five cases pertains. For example, the edge labeled EA1 , EA2, EA3 and EA4 of the mesh A are tagged with type 2, type3, type3 and type1 respectively. For the mesh A, the subdivision process terminates because the mesh A does not apply to the three criteria of Step3.

On the other hand, the mesh B has the edge tagged with type4 ( EB2 in Figure 6) , so that the mesh B is subdivided into four new sub-meshes labeled Bul,Bbl,Bbr and Bur, as shown in Figure 7(see discussion by Hunter and Steiglitz [4]). Further, the mesh Bul and Bbl are subdivided into four sub-meshes, because these two meshes have the edge tagged with type4. As there are no edges tagged with type4 or 5 in the new meshes generated by the second subdividision, they need not be further subdivided. For the mesh B, two subdivision steps are required to extract inner polygons. Figure 7 illustrates the process of subdivision for the mesh B of Figure 6.

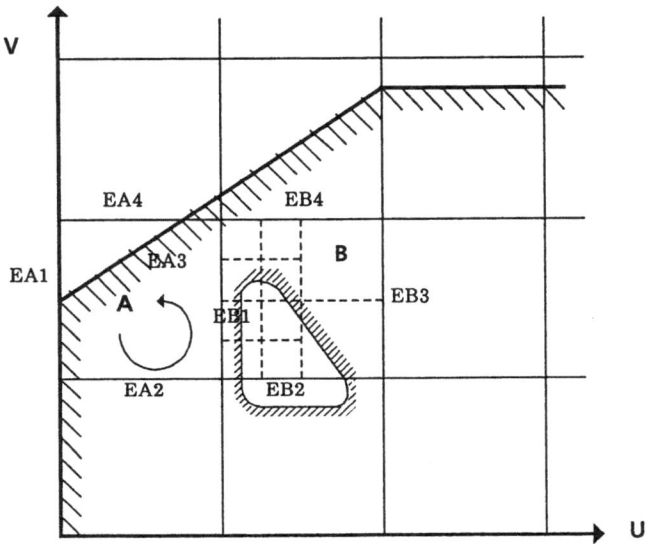

Figure 6. Subdivision of the meshes

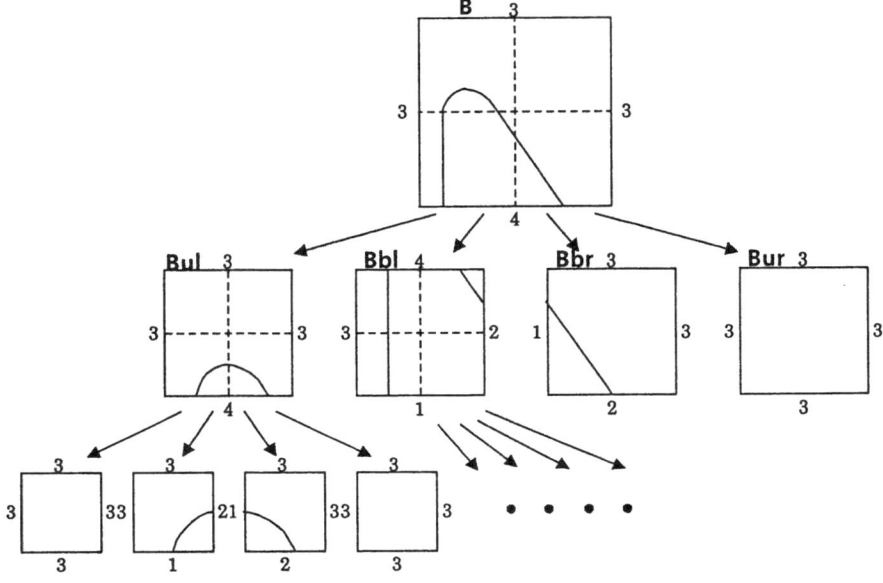

Figure 7. The process of subdivision

## 5. EXTRACTION OF INNER POLYGONS

When the subdivision algorithm completes, we can have five types of meshes as shown in Figure 5. There are no inner polygons in the mesh of type (e). If the mesh is classified as type (d), the mesh itself is considered to be the inner polygon. In case of type (a), (b) and (c), the algorithm starts at the first point of the edge tagged with type2 as the first point of the inner polygon and extracts the vertices of the inner polygon along the mesh edge in counterclockwise order. The process continues until the edge tagged with type1 is reached. As a result, we can extract all the inner polygons needed to approximate a 3D object.

## 6. EXPERIMENTAL RESULTS

Table 2 lists the execution time of the algorithm for the two examples. The subdivision algorithm reduces the excution time to less than half that of our existing method. In addition, it is obvious that the subdivision algorithm can reduce the total number of inner polygons for a given visual accuracy. In example 1 of Table 2, the existing method using 7×7 meshes resulted in an inadequate rendering as shown in Figure 8. Using the same 7×7 initial mesh size, the subdivision method presented results in the more acceptable rendering in Figure 9. With the existing method it would require 14×14 meshes (3136 polygons) to obtain a similar rendering to Figure 9. In case of example 2, Figure 10 is drawn by the method for only 10×10 meshes as the initial mesh size. However, the existing method requires 17×17 meshes ( 9826 polygons ) in order to obtain a similar rendering.

Table 2. VAX11/780 execution times and number
of polygons for obtaining a shaded picture.

|  |  | Division in unform size | | Subdivision presented here |
|---|---|---|---|---|
| Example 1 | Number of division (m×n) / surface | 7×7 | 14×14 | 7×7 ( Initial number) |
|  | Total number of polygons after division | 784 | 3136 | 856 |
|  | Execution time ( in seconds ) | 18 | 54 | 23 |
| Example 2 | Number of division (m×n) / surface | 10×10 | 17×17 | 10×10 ( Initial number) |
|  | Total number of polygons after division | 3400 | 9826 | 4303 |
|  | Execution time ( in seconds ) | 68 | 155 | 80 |

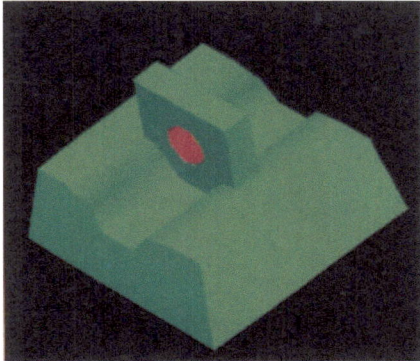

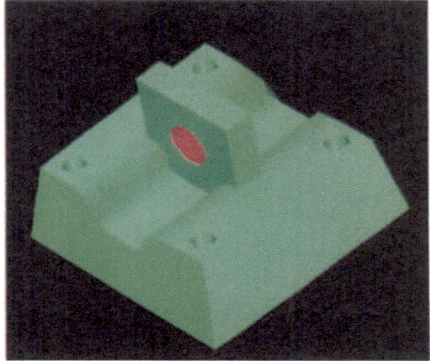

Figure 8. A shaded image
by the division of uniform size(7×7)

Figure 9. A shaded image
by the method presented here(7×7)

## 7. CONCLUSION

The performance and efficiency of the algorithm presented here is satisfactory for an interactive environment. In addition, the simplicity of the algorithm is its greatest advantage.

We have implemented the algorithm on our CAD/CAM system and have put this system to practical use for some designs. (Further description of the development of our system can be found in an earlier article.[5] Figure 11 and 12 show shaded images of a hair drier

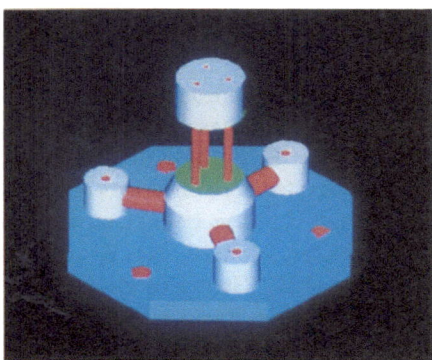

Figure 10. A shaded image by
the method presented here(10×10)

and a washing machine pulsator. The system enables a designer to evaluate design options based on these shaded representations of objects. A defined surface is divided into polygons, which are passed to a shading module with intensity values for each vertex. The shading module outputs a shaded image using the intensity interpolation method(developed by Gouraud[3]). Hidden-surface elimination is achieved with a Z-buffer algorithm.

At present, the initial division number ( m×n ) of the method is determined by designer's experience. To make the method more practical, it is being improved so that the optimum initial division number ( m×n ) can be determined automatically according to the complexity of bounded curves of a surface.

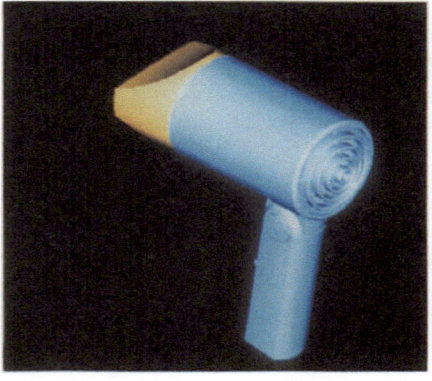

Figure 11.   An image of a hair drier

Figure 12. An image of
a washing machine pulsator

REFERENCES

1)  Catmull E (December 1974)  A Subdivision Algorithm for Computer Display of
     Curved Surfaces , Univ. Utah Computer Sci. Dept., UTEC-CSc-74-133 .
2)  Faux I D ,  Pratt M J (1979) Computational Geometry for Design and
     Manufacture. John Wiley & Sons,  pp. 89
3)  Gouraud H (June 1971) Continuous Shading of Curved Surfaces,  IEEE Trans. on
     computer, Vol. 20, No. 6, pp.623-629
4)  Hunter G M , Steiglitz K (April 1979) Operations on images using quad trees ,
     IEEE Trans. Pattern Anal. Machine Intell., PAMI-1, No.2
5)  Kobori K, et al. (1984)  Development of a total 3D CAD/CAM system for electric
     appliances, in Proc. Computer Graphics Tokyo '84 Conf.
6)  Warnock J E (1969)  A Hidden-Line Algorithm for Computer Generated Half-
     Tone Pictures, Univ. Utah Computer Sci. Dept., TR4-15

Ken-ichi Kobori received the BS and MS degrees in electronic engineering from Yamanashi University, Yamanashi, Japan, in 1973 and 1975, respectively. Since 1975 he has been with Sharp Corporation and is currently an assistant manager of the Computer Systems Laboratories, Engineering Division. His major interests are mechanical CAD and computer graphics. Kobori is a member of the Information Processing Society of Japan and the Institute of Electronics and Communication Engineers of Japan.

Masayuki Iwazu received the BS degree in information processing from Tokushima University, Tokushima, Japan, in 1983. Since 1983 he has been with Sharp Corporation and is an engineer in the Computer Systems Laboratories,Engineering Division. His major interests are CAD and computer graphics.

Kenneth M. Jones received the master of design degree in industrial design from the Royal College of Art, London in 1974. He joined Sharp Corporation in 1979 as an industrial designer at the Corporate Design Center. From 1982 to 1985 he was seconded to the Computer Systems Laboratories to participate in the company CAD development project. He is currently involved with development of CAD systems at the Corporate Design Center. His major interests are CAD for industrial design applications and computer graphics. Jones is a member of the Japanese Society for the Science of Design.

Ikuo Nishioka received the BS and MS degrees in communication engineering from Osaka University, Osaka, Japan, in 1966 and 1969, respectively, and the PhD degree in electronic engineering from Osaka University in 1981. He has been with Sharp Corporation since 1969 and is currently a general manager of the Computer Systems Laboratories, Engineering Division. His major interests are CAD and computer graphics. Nishioka is a member of the Information Processing Society of Japan and the Institute of Electronics and Communication Engineers of Japan.

# Algorithms for Automatic Mould Division Design

Jarmo T. Alander

Laboratory of Information Processing Science, Helsinki University of Technology,
SF-02150 Espoo, Finland

Abstract. Efficient algorithms to design mould division is presented. The object can consist of planar, spherical, cylindrical or conic surfaces. The more general case of sculptured surfaces is also briefly discussed. The methods and results presented can also be applied to e.g. automated assembly design and analysis.

Keywords: CAD, computational geometry, mould design.

## 1. INTRODUCTION

Currently mould division design is done by skilled person, who by cross section pictures or by some "build-in" intuition can solve this technically important and difficult problem. In this work we will first consider the geometrical aspects of 2- and 3- dimensional mould design after which we present an automatic procedure to divide moulds into separatable parts. Application of the developed theory to automated assembly is also considered.

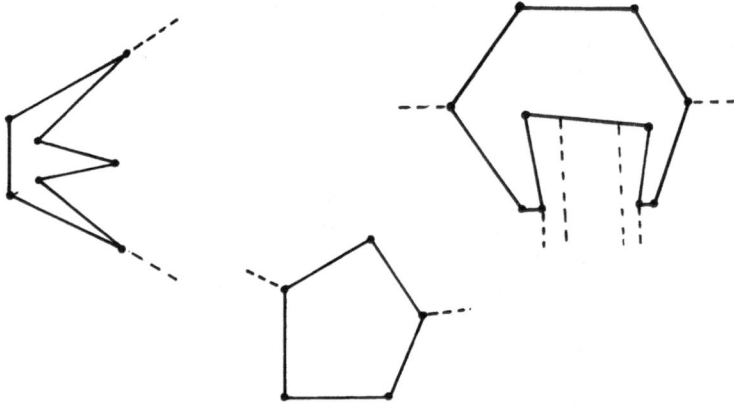

Fig. 1. Some 2-dim. mould divisions (parting lines dotted).

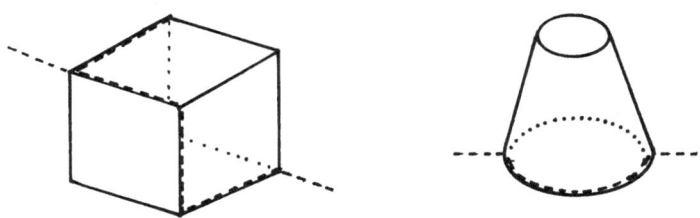

Fig. 2. Some 3-dim. mould divisions (parting lines dotted).

## 2. THE 2-DIMENSIONAL CASE

For simplicity in this chapter we will consider mould design in 2-dimensions, the results of which can be applied in production of 3-dim. prismatic objects, too. First we will examine objects consisting of polygons, after which we will briefly consider curved objects.

Definition 1: Object is a non-intersecting polygon consisting of a finite set of consecutive edges and vertices.

For practical reasons let us assume that the orientation of edges is such that when we are going forward along edges, the object is always on the left hand side.

Definition 2: Segment is a sequence of consecutive edges and vertices of an object. A segment starting from edge a and ending at edge b is denoted by a..b.

Mould parts are in principle nonintersecting and so we can omit starting and ending vertex of segments.

Definition 3: Edge angle of an edge $e_i$ is the angle between $e_i$ and the next edge $e_{i+1}$ (cf. fig. 3). The angle between edge $c_i$ and $e_j$ (i<j) is the sum (or integral) of the intervening edge angles. Let A be the minimum and B the maximum angle in segment $S = e_0..e_n$ (with respect to $e_0$). The value B - A is called the segment angle of S and denoted by a(S).

Definition 4: Let us take a segment $S = e_0..e_n$ . If we have for every segment $S_i = e_1..c_i$, $1 \leq i \leq n$ , $a(S_i) \leq 0$, while $a(c_0..c_1) > 0$ and $a(e_n..e_{n+1}) > 0$, then S is a bay segment or simply a bay (cf. fig. 4).

It is obvious that an object not having any bays is convex. And it is trivial to design mould division for a convex object. Observe, that the definition of bay is somewhat uneven as compared to the visual impression of bays.

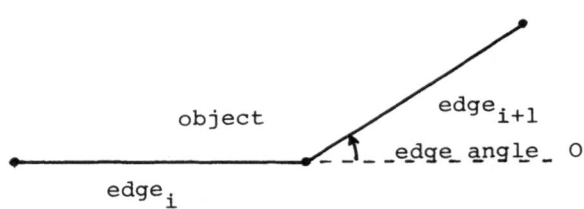

Fig. 3. Definition of edge angle.

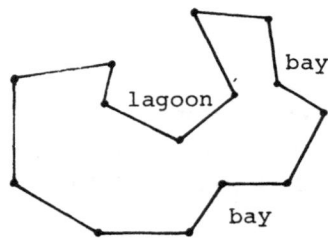

Fig. 4. An object with one lagoon and two bays.

Definition 5: Lagoon is a bay B such that $a(B) \leq -\pi$.

It is true that with care it is sometimes possible to design mould division for an object having lagoons (cf. fig. 1). However, in the following we will only consider mould design of objects without lagoons.

Definition 6: A possibly empty finite sequence $B = b_i$, (i = 1 ,..., n ), of bays is called the bay sequence of a given object C, if it contains all bays of C.

Definition 7: Pi segment of an edge $e_k$ is a segment $S = e_i..e_j$ ($i \leq k \leq j$) such that $a(e_k..e_{j+1}) \geq \pi$ and $a(e_{i-1}..e_j) \geq \pi$, while $a(S) < \pi$. The last item of Pi sequence of e is denoted by e.Pi. The segment covering all Pi segments containing edge a is called Pi hull of a and it is denoted by e.PI.

Example. The object in fig. 4 has Pi sequences n..f, g..j, k..n and m..c, d..f, g..j, k..n. For every mould segment $e..e_m$ (a segment corresponding to a mould part) we have

$$e..e_m \subseteq e.PI.$$

The following algorithm Divide_2 will part the given object C into mould segments M, if mould division is possible at all. Divide_2 returns the number of mould parts. The bays are tried to put in the middle of mould parts in order to reduce the number of mould parts.

Algorithm 1:

```
integer Divide_2(C: object, M: segment sequence )
begin comment 2-dim non-optimal mould division algorithm
        k <- 0
        S <- the bay sequence of C.
        if S empty then
                    b <- first edge of C
        else b <- largest bay of S
        if angle(b) > π then
        begin comment lagoon found
                    print("unsolvable")
                    return (k)
        end
        while not C empty do
        begin
                    take neighbours of b while total angle < π
                    M_k <- b with its legal neighbours
                    remove M_k from C and S
                    k <- k+1
                    if S empty then
                                b <- first edge of C
                    else b <- largest bay of S
        end
        return (k)
end of Divide_2
```

## 2.1. The Complexity of the Algorithm

Let n be the number of vertices in C. The number of bays $b_i$ is at most n/2. Bays can be solved and processed in time O(n). In while loop bays are retrieved in descending order, which can be done in time no more than O(nlogn).

By the decision tree model we can get a theoretical lower bound of the time complexity as follows: The mould can consists of k = 2,...,n/2 segments, which can be chosen from n edges by

$$N = \sum_{k=2}^{n/2} \binom{n}{k} = 2^{n/2} - (n/2 + 1) \quad \text{ways.}$$

A decision tree having this number of leaves must have at least $\log_2 N < n/2$ levels, i.e. the theoretical minimum time complexity of mould design algorithm is $O(n)$. So we have hope to find an asymptotically faster algorithm than the above shown.

## 2.2. Optimal Mould Design

Optimization of mould design can be done by using various criteria. We can try to minimize the number of mould parts k or we can maximize the angle of parting points in order to ease removal of mould object. Algorithm 1 may not necessarily lead to optimal mould division because it takes bays without any spatial ordering, which may force some tiny (non-Pi) segments between bay segments. It is therefore relevant to find an algorithm that can find the minimal solution of the mould division problem.

Definition 8: Rank of edge e is the minimum number of consecutive Pi segments starting from e and covering the whole object (except the parting vertices).

The minimization of k is now equivalent to finding an edge with minimum rank (Algorithm 2). The time complexity of the following simple Rank procedure is at most $O(n^2)$, which is also the worst case complexity of the total optimization algorithm. Observe, that in practice p.Pi can be found easily by starting search from the previous p.Pi edge.

Algorithm 2:

```
Rank(C : object)
begin   comment ranking of edges
        while edges left do
        begin
                e <- next edge from C
                e.rank <- 1
                p <- edge after e.Pi
                while p not in e..e.Pi do begin
                        e.rank <- e.rank+1
                        p <- edge after p.Pi
                end
        end
end of Rank
```

Practical remark: Edge e and edges p (excluding the last one) in the previous algorithm belong to the same class having equal rank value. These classes can be used to develop a less time complex partial ranking algorithm:

Algorithm 3:

```
Rank2(C : object)
begin   comment ranking of edges.
          a <- one edge of C
          A <- first edge of a.PI
          b <- edge after a
          make a node for every Pi segment that a belong to

          while b =/ A do
          begin comment link to b from previous Pi segment.
                    make link to b from such node x that have
                            x.Pi.next = b   and   x = x.Pi.first
                    b <- next edge after b
          end
          Shortest route (that covers C) in the generated graph
          gives now the optimum solution (c.f. fig. 5).
end
```

The time complexity of Rank2 algorithm is O(n) because
- a.PI and other Pi seguences need time O(n)
- the while loop needs time O(n) and
- the shortes route can be updated during
  the while loop with minimum cost.
We have found optimal and theoretically least complex mould division algorithm.

Ranking can lead to more than one solution. Further optimization can be done e.g. by choosing among those solutions that have smallest possible maximum mould segment angle, which means easiest removal of object from mould parts.

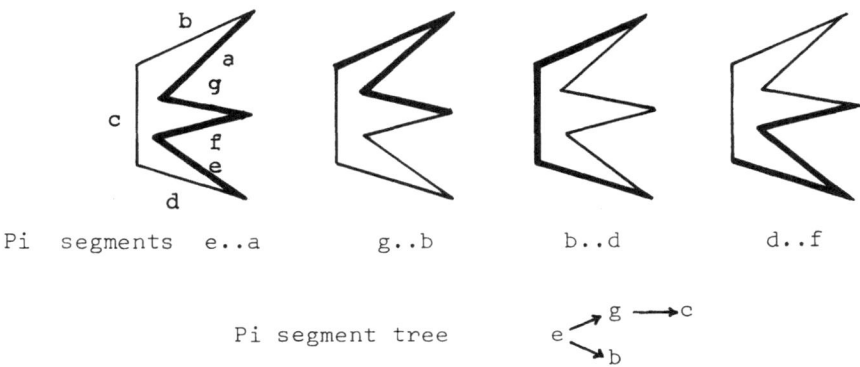

Pi  segments  e..a          g..b          b..d          d..f

Pi segment tree

Fig. 5. Partial ranking of object a..g. Pi segment tree gives two solutions: (e..a , b..d), which is optimal and (e..f , g..b , c..d).

## 2.3. Curved Objects

In the case of an object consisting totally or partly of curved edges approximate numerical methods must be used. The key problem of mould design is to find possible bays and lagoons which in terms of numerical analysis means the location of the extremal values of the normal angle.

One method to locate zeros is to use interval arithmetic methods (R. Moore, 1966 and 1979 ; S. Mudur and P. Koparkar, 1984)  A comparison of the most commonly used functional interval methods can be found in (J. Alander, 1984 or 1985).

## 3. THE 3-DIMENSIONAL CASE

The 3-dimensional mould division design is analogous to the 2-dimensional case. Let $N : C \to R^2$ be the mapping from the elements of the object to the normal angle space. The different parts of the object are mapped into different elements in angle space and vice versa in the following dualistic manner (cf. fig. 6.):

The problem of mould division in 3-dimensions reduces into geometry and topology of isocycle pieces on a (unit) ball. In case of polyhedral objects the mould design is further reduced into problems of spheric graphs as we will see later on.

| in object | in normal space |
|---|---|
| face area | point |
| edge | isocycle piece |
| vertex | area |

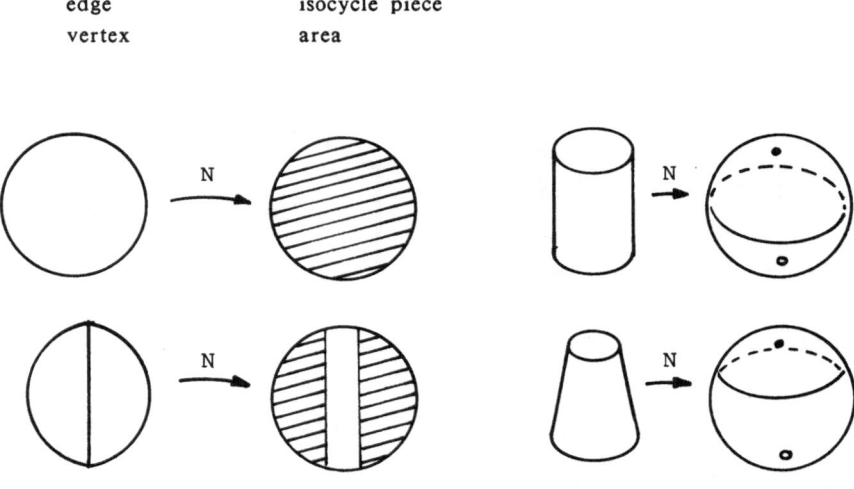

Fig. 6.  Mappings N from object space into normal angle space.

Definition 9: Valley area consists of those faces $f_i$ for which at least one of the connecting edges $e_{i,j}$ per each face are crossing (see fig. 7).

The following algorithm Divide_3 will part the given object C into mould caps M, if mould division is possible at all. Divide_3 returns the number of mould caps. The valleys are tried to put in the middle of mould parts in order to reduce the number of mould parts.

Algorithm 4:

```
integer Divide_3(C: object, M: cap sequence)
begin comment 3-dim mould division algorithm
        k <- 0
        V <- the valley sequence of C.
        if V empty then
                        b <- first face of C
        else        b <- largest valley of V

        if diameter (b) > π then
        begin comment cavity found
                        print("unsolvable")
                        return (k)
        end
        while not C empty do
        begin
                        take neighbours of b while diameter < π
                        M  <- b with its legal neighbours
                         k
                        remove b and its neighbours from C and V
                        k <- k+1
                        if V empty then
                                        b <- first face of C
                        else        b <- largest valley of V
        end
        return (k)
end of Divide_3
```

Complexity of algorithm:

The brute force method to solve all intersections of n isocycle pieces would require time $O(n^2)$. The problem can, however, be solved faster by applying the plane sweep technique of Shamos (Shamos 1976, 1978) (see fig. 8), which requires only time $O(n\log n)$.

On the other hand from the decision tree model we get a theoretical lower bound $O(n)$ for the time complexity of 3 dim. mould division algorithm as for the 2 dim. case.

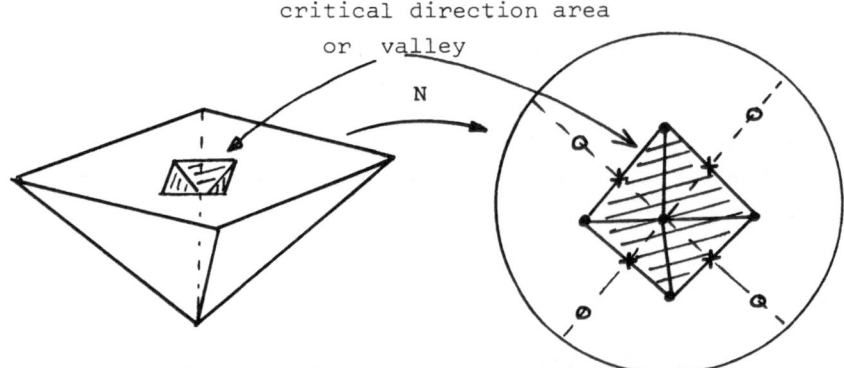

Fig. 7.  A valley area in a pyramid.

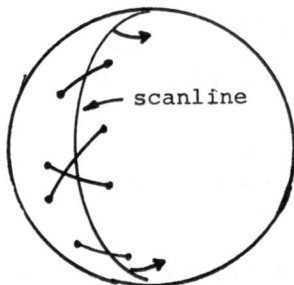

Fig. 8.  Plane sweep applied to isocycle piece intersection problem.

## 3.1. Ranking

In the 2-dim. case ranking was a very efficient way to solve optimal mould division problem and the same method also applies to the 3-dim. case although the situation is a little bit more complicated because of the 2-dim. nature of the angle geometry.

## 4. APPLICATION TO AUTOMATED ASSEMBLY DESIGN

As an application of our mould design theory we will briefly consider robot gripper design.  One way to achieve firm gripping is to use fingers, which completely fit part of the surface (grip cap) of the object to be gripped. The robot fingers are thus parts of one possible mould division of the object (see fig. 9).  It is thus easy with the above theory to check or design proper robot grippers to a given object.

Possible short range approach movements of this type of gripper relative to the given object are easily determined by intersection of the half spaces implied by the faces

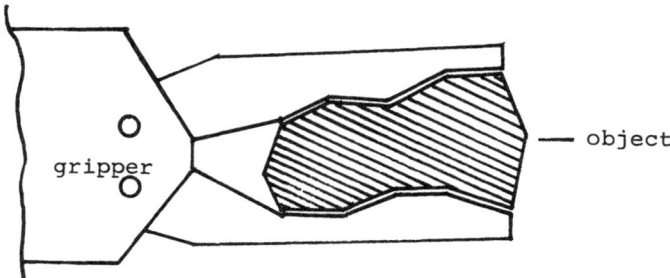

Fig. 9. Robot "mould" gripper.

of the grip cap. This information can be further used to aligning and centering analysis of the gripping which is important to correctly place and orient a more or less randomly located object.

## 5. CONCLUSIONS

Mould design algorithms for not too concave 2 and 3 dimensional objects is presented. For both dimensions and polyhedral objects the time complexity of the algorithm is O(n), where n is the number of faces. It turns out that the O(n) time complexity is also the theoretical lower bound of both problems, too.

For the mould division problem we have in many cases several possible solutions, from which we may try to find an optimal one. This problem of optimal mould design is also considered and it turns out that it can be solved without any further growth in the asymptotic complexity.

## 6. REFERENCES

R. E. Moore, Interval Analysis, Prentice-Hall, Englewood Cliffs, (1966).

S. P. Mudur, P. A. Koparkar, Interval methods for processing geometric objects, IEEE Computer Graphics & Appl., Vol. 4, 7-17, (1984).

R. E. Moore, Methods and Applications of Interval Analysis, Philadelphia, SIAM, (1979).

J. Alander, Interval arithmetic methods in the processing of curves and sculptured surfaces, Proceedings of the 6th International Symposium of Computer Aided Design and Computer Aided Manufacturing, Zagreb, (1984).

J. Alander, On interval arithmetic range approximation methods of polynomials and rational functions, to appear in Computers & Graphics, (1985).

Shamos, M. I., Computational Geometry, Dissertation, Yale University, (1978).

Shamos, M. I., Hoey, D., Geometric intersection problems, 17th Annual IEEE Symposium of Foundations of Computer Science, pp. 208-215, (1976).

Jarmo T. Alander is currently a researcher at Helsinki University of Technology. He started work there in modeling of curved surfaces and interval analysis in 1983. His research interests now include computational aspects of FMS and robotics.

Alander received his BSc and MSc in physics from the University of Helsinki in 1978 and 1983 and MSc in Engineering (Computer Science) from Helsinki University of Technology in 1985.

# Geometry in Prolog

Wm. Randolph Franklin*, Margaret Nichols**, Sumitro Samaddar and Peter Wu
Rensselaer Polytechnic Institute, Troy, NY 12180, USA

**ABSTRACT**

The Prolog language is a useful tool for geometric and graphics implementations because its primitives, such as unification, match the requirements of many geometric algorithms. We have implemented several problems in Prolog including a subset of the Graphics Kernel Standard, convex hull finding, planar graph traversal, recognizing groupings of objects, and boolean combinations of polygons using multiple precision rational numbers. Certain paradigms, or standard forms, of geometric programming in Prolog are becoming evident. They include applying a function to every element of a set, executing a procedure so long as a certain geometric pattern exists, and using unification to propagate a transitive function. Certain strengths and weaknesses of Prolog for these applications are now apparent.

**Keywords:** Prolog, Geometry, Graphics Kernel Standard

## INTRODUCTION

The fifth generation logic programming language Prolog, Clocksin (1981), Pereira (1980) appears appropriate for research in geometry and graphics. Some examples of its use in architectural design are given in Swinson (1982, 1983a, 1983b). Its use in CAD has been evaluated in Gonzalez (1984). Constructing geometric objects from certain constraints is described in Brüderlin (1985). Over the past two years, the authors of this present paper have implemented several geometric and graphic problems in Prolog using assorted machines. This paper describes the experiences, including some paradigms of programming that have appeared useful, and finally listing the advantages and disadvantages of Prolog that we have experienced.

## IMPLEMENTATIONS

Over the last two years we have implemented several graphics and geometric algorithms in Prolog, totally a few thousand lines of code, using four different Prolog interpreters on four different computers. The systems include:

| Machine | Operating System | Prolog Version |
|---------|------------------|----------------|
| IBM 3081 | Michigan Terminal System | York (U.K.) |
| IBM 4341 | CMS | Waterlog |
| Prime 750 | Primos | Salford |
| VAX 780 | Unix bsd 4.3 | UNSW |

*Until June 1986: Computer Science Division, 543 Evans, University of California, Berkeley, CA 94720, USA. Arpanet: wrf@ernie.Berkeley.EDU
** Current address: North American Philips Lighting Co., Bloomfield NJ.

The implementations include:

- Graphics Kernel Standard subset
- Convex Hull
- Planar Graph Traversal
- Big Rational Numbers
- Polygon Intersection
- Recognizing Groupings of Objects

## Graphics Kernel Standard Subset

This graphics addition to Prolog was implemented by Nichols (1985) on an IBM 4341 using Waterlog as described in Roberts (1984), under the CMS operating system. This allowed us to draw lines and so on on the 3270 graphics CRT from a Prolog program. The major problems and design decisions were as follows.

1. Waterlog, like most Prologs, lacks floating point numbers, and even four byte integers. (The latter was undocumented; large integers just didn't work.) However it has the powerful capability to be linked to programs in other languages such as Fortran. Thus we implemented a real number in Prolog as a data structure of the form real(A,B) where A and B are Prolog integers holding the upper and lower halfword, respectively, of the integer. The user never looks at A and B, but accesses the real numbers via the following Prolog procedures:

   ```
   add(A,B,C)
   dev(A,B,C)
   exp(A,B,C)
   itor(I,A)
   mult(A,B,C)
   rtoi(A,I)
   subt(A,B,C)
   ```

   that perform the obvious operations on real numbers in the stated form. Because of this modularity, the user never uses the actual form of the real number in Prolog.

2. We used the available Fortran graphics package, GSP, as little as possible, preferring to do scaling and so on in Prolog for portability reasons. GSP's limitations also prevented us from implementing variable beam intensities and the full GKS text orientation capabilities.

3. Both the long GKS names and the six character Fortran bindings are available to the user. Thus he can say either open_gks(1,1) or gopks(1,1).

4. We implemented two classes of lines: *permanent* and *backtrackable*. If the Prolog procedure that drew a backtrackable line was backtracked over, then the line would be erased. This used a feature of the graphics package GSP.

5. The lack of a *current cursor* concept in GKS eased our task since the only way to store global information such as that in Prolog would be to retract and assert it after every cursor movement. This would have been slow.

6. This is a sample Prolog routine to draw a line between two points.

   ```
   draw_to(Point_x.Point_y) :-
       erase_on_backtrack(yes),
       ifelse(deferral_mode(1, asti),
           draw1(Point_x, Point_y, 1, Key),
           draw1(Point_x, Point_y, 0, Key)),
       (True; (erase(Key), !, fail)).
   ```

```
draw_to(Point_x.Point_y) :-
    ifelse(deferral_mode(1, asti),
        draw(Point_x, Point_y, 1),
        draw(Point_x, Point_y, 0)).
```

**Draw1** is a Fortran subroutine which draws a line and returns a key which can be used to erase that line at a later time. When it is called with zero as its third parameter, the line is immediately drawn on the screen. A one in the third position enters the line segment into the data set, to be drawn when the workstation is updated.

**Draw** is a Fortran subroutine which draws a line but does not return a key. This means that the line segment cannot be erased.

The clause (true; (erase(Key), !, fail)) has no effect on the rule unless backtracking occurs, because the true goal is the only one that is encountered. However, should the Prolog proof fail somewhere after draw_to is satisfied, causing the rule to be backtracked through, then the clause (erase(Key), !, fail) will be encountered. Its effect is to call **erase**, a Fortran subroutine which will erase the line segment, and then fail, which will cause the backtracking to continue back through the proof. The cut symbol allows the rule to fail without trying to satisfy itself with the second clause.

7. Some clipping and transformations are also implemented.

8. Problems with Waterlog's not freeing trail space were never fully solved.

9. All the *ma*-level commands were implemented except some inquiry and set commands, the escape command, text rotation, and the inquire text extent command. Here are the 70 Prolog procedures that were implemented.

```
activate_workstation
adjust
allocate_and_initialize_workstation_state_list
bothin
change_state
clip1
clip2
close_gks
close_workstation
deactivate_workstation
deallocate_workstation_state_list
draw_to
error
errormsg
fill_area
find
go_to_workstation
help
initialize_gks_description_table
initialize_gks_state_list
initialize_other_state_lists
initialize_workstation_description_table
inquire_asf
inquire_clipping_indicator
inquire_current_normalization_transformation_number
inquire_current_primitive_attribute_values
inquire_current_individual_attribute_values
inquire_level_of_gks
inside
intersect
line
listadd
listdelete
```

make_adjustments
make_decision
make_transformation
member
move_to
normalize
not_both_in
open_gks
opengks0
open_workstation
plot_point
plot_point2
plot_text
point
points
polyline
polyline_
polymarker
putout
sameside
set_character_height
set_deferral_state
set_erase
set_marker_type
set_workstation_window
set_workstation_viewport
suggest
test_midpoint
test_point
test_points
text
update_workstation
wipe_out_gks_description_table
wipe_out_gks_state_list
wipe_out_other_state_lists
wipe_out_workstation_description_table

These Prolog procedures were supported by several Fortran routines and an Assembler interface.

### Convex Hull

This Graham Scan algorithm was implemented by Wu, described in (Franklin and Wu, 1985) on both the IBM 4341, and on the Prime in Salford Prolog (1984). The Salford system allows both real numbers and dynamic linking to Fortran routines. We also tested York Prolog (Spivey, 1983), which is written in Pascal. The York system has the advantage that it is portable to any machine that can compile a thousand line Pascal program that uses four byte integers. Unfortunately this did not include the official Pascal compiler available from Prime. (We have not evaluated third-party Pascal compilers for Prime computers.) We also tested York Prolog on an IBM 3081 running the Michigan Terminal System, but found the other computers' operating systems more flexible and cheaper to use.

### Boolean Combinations of Polygons

A program to perform operations such as intersection, union, and difference on two planar polygons was implemented by Franklin and Wu (Franklin and Wu, 1985) on the Prime and IBM 4341. The algorithm was by Franklin (1985). Wu first implemented a package to perform arithmetic using rational numbers in multiple precision. Each number, in life a quotient of an integer numerator and denominator, is implemented as a list of the numerator and denominator. Each of them is a list of groups of the digits of the number. For example, 123456789/987654321 is represented as [[56789, 1234], [54321, 9876]]. Rational numbers are used to avoid roundoff errors, as part of an ongoing investigation into their utility in geometry and the map overlay problem in cartography (Franklin, 1984).

## Object Grouping in Photoreconnaissance

Assume that we recognize certain objects in a photograph, and know that they tend to be grouped in clusters. However we might have failed to recognize all of the objects, and some of them might be absent. We have built an experimental system in Prolog to help (Samaddar, 1985).

## Planar Graph Traversal

At some point during an object space hidden surface algorithm, Franklin (1980), we have the set of the visible edges and must join them to find the visible polygons. This requires a planar graph traversal, sometimes called a tesselation. For example, in figure 1,

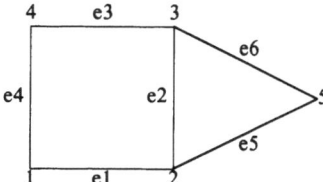

Figure 1: Finding the Faces of a Planar Graph

we are given the vertices and edges in the form

```
vert(vert-name, x-coord, y-coord)
edge(edge-name, first vertex, second vertex, angle)
```

for example

```
vert(v1, 0, 0)
edge(e1, v1, v2, 0)
```

The angle of the edge is supplied because of the difficulty of computing arctangents using only integers. The output is a set of facts of the form

```
polygon([v1, v2, v3, v4])
```

This was implemented in UNSW Prolog (Sammut, 1983) on a Vax.

## STRENGTHS AND WEAKNESSES OF PROLOG

Certain advantages and disadvantages of Prolog for graphics and geometric applications are becoming evident from these implementations.

## Advantages Of Prolog

- Prolog has same high level advantages of Lisp, as the equivalence of code and data and dynamic data allocation.

- There are the specific advantages of Prolog. Unification makes determining graph connectivity a primitive operation and in general is useful for propagating transitive properties such which occur frequently.

- The pattern matching fits with the form of expression of many algorithms. For example, our polygon combination algorithm proceeds as follows. Whenever the pattern of two edges intersecting, or one edge ends on the interior of another edge, occurs, then retract those edges and assert new smaller edges. When this pattern no longer exists, then we have a superset of the edges in the output polygon.

- Although many of the above features could be implemented in any language that is Turing equivalent, Prolog is somewhat standard so that different researchers can understand and use each others' extensions.

### Disadvantages Of Prolog

However, there are some problems with using Prolog for geometry.

- There are software engineering problems with using Prolog for a large project because of its lack of nesting in the program and databases.

- Many geometry algorithms are more natural to a forward reasoning system than a backward reasoning system. That is, we are more likely to want the output from some given input than the reverse.

- The natural way of expressing pattern matching algorithms requires us to modify a database as we are searching through it. Thus in polygon overlay, whenever we find the pattern of two edges crossing, we retract them and assert four new edges. Backtracking and redoing a database that we are modifying does not work on all Prologs.

- In general Prolog in completely unstandardized around the fringes as some tests of cuts in (Moss, 1985) show.

## PARADIGMS OF PROGRAMMING

Certain techniques have proven to be generally useful in our implementations, and may be useful to others also. They include the following paradigms.

### Set Based Algorithms

Many algorithms such as polyhedron intersection and hidden surface algorithms, Franklin (1982, 1980), are the alternation of two types of steps:

- Applying function to every element of a set, and

- Combining all the elements having a common key.

This is clearly easy in Prolog.

### Pattern Matching

The second paradigm uses pattern matching to propagate certain properties. For example, in the planar graph traversal algorithm, the edges around each vertex are found and sorted by the angle at which they leave it. Then the edges around each vertex are paired to form *corners*. These corners can be considered to be fragments of the output polygons. Whenever two fragments exist such that the last edge of one is the same as the first edge of another, then these two fragments are retracted and a single longer fragment asserted. When such a pattern no longer exists, then we have the output polygons.

### Unification

Frequently we wish to determine the closure of some transitive property, such as when we are given a set of graph edges edge(u, v), and wish to determine the connected components. We have implemented the following short algorithm that uses unification and the set processing paradigm.

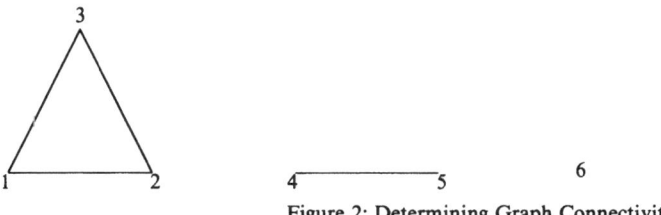

Figure 2: Determining Graph Connectivity

- Create a property list (*plist*) with one record per vertex, and the property of each vertex a free variable. For example in figure 2 we would have [[1,_],[2,_],[3,_],[4,_],[5,_],[6,_]].

- Process the set of edges and for each edge unify the free variable properties of the endpoints. After this we will have [[1,_1],[2,_1],[3,_1],[4,_2],[5,_2],[6,_3]] with one unique free variable per graph component.

- Bind a name identifying each component to the free variables in the list to give something like [[1,first],[2,first],[3,first],[4,second],[5,second],[6,third]].

A longer example of a simple hidden surface algorithm would go as follows.

- Wherever the pattern of two edges' projections' intersecting occurs, split the edges into four smaller edge segments.

- For each edge segment find the set of faces hiding its midpoint. Iff it is empty then the edge segment is visible. Draw them.

- Use a planar graph traversal algorithm such as described above to link the visible edges into polygons.

- For each polygon, find a point inside it and then find the set of faces whose projections contain the projection of that point. Find the closest such face; the polygon came from it. Color the polygon accordingly.

This illustrates all of the paradigms operating together.

## ACKNOWLEDGEMENT

This work was supported by the National Science Foundation under grant no. ECS-8351942, the Data Systems Division of the International Business Machines Corporation, and by the Rome Air Development Center under the postdoctoral development program via Syracuse University.

## REFERENCES

Bruderlin, Beat (1985) "Using Prolog for Constructing Geometric Objects Defined by Constraints," *Eurocal 85, Conference Proceedings*, Linz, Austria. Institut fü Informatik, ETH Zürich, CH-8092, Zürich, Switzerland

Clocksin, W.F. and Mellish, C.S. (1981) *Programming In Prolog*, Springer-Verlag, New York.

Coelho, H., Cotta, J.C., and Pereira, L.M. (1980) *How to Solve it With Prolog, 2nd edition*, Ministerio da Habitacao e Obras Publicas, Labatorio Nacional de Engenharia Civil, Lisboa.

Franklin, Wm. Randolph (July 1980) "A Linear Time Exact Hidden Surface Algorithm," *ACM Computer Graphics*, vol. 14, no. 3, pp. 117-123. Proceedings of SIGGRAPH'80

Franklin, Wm. Randolph (19-21 May 1982) "Efficient Polyhedron Intersection and Union," *Proc. Graphics Interface'82*, pp. 73-80, Toronto.

Franklin, Wm. Randolph (20-24 August 1984) "Cartographic Errors Symptomatic of Underlying Algebra Problems," *Proc. International Symposium on Spatial Data Handling*, vol. 1, pp. 190-208, Zürich, Switzerland.

Franklin, Wm. Randolph and Wu, Peter Y.F. (July 1985) *Convex Hull and Polygon Intersection Implemented in Prolog,* Rensselaer Polytechnic Institute, Troy, NY.

Gonzalez, J.C., Williams, M.H., and Aitchison, I.E. (March 1984) "Evaluation of the Effectiveness of Prolog for a CAD Application," *IEEE Computer Graphics and Applications*, pp. 67-75.

Moss, Chris and Fogel, Earl (June 1985) *Tests to Distinguish Various Implementations of Cut in Prolog,* Imperial College and Logicware Inc.. Reported on Usenet in Net.lang.Prolog, message-id <1742@utecfa.UUCP>.

Nichols, Margaret (August 1985) *The Graphic Kernal System in Prolog,* ECSE Dept., Rensselaer Polytechnic Institute, Masters Thesis, Troy, NY.

Roberts, Grant (1984) *Waterloo Core Prolog Users Manual (version 1.5),* Intralogic Inc., Waterloo, Ont, Canada.

Salford, University of (March 1984) , *LISP/PROLOG Reference Manual.*

Samaddar, Sumitro (August 1985) *An Expert System for Photo Interpretation,* ECSE Dept., Rensselaer Polytechnic Institute, Masters Thesis, Troy, NY.

Sammut, Claude (1983) *UNSW Prolog User Manual,* University of New South Wales (Australia).

Spivey, J. M. (March 1983) , *University of York Portable Prolog System (Release 1) User's Guide*, York, U.K..

Swinson, P.S.G. (March 1982) "Logic Programming: A Computing Tool for the Architect of the Future," *Computer Aided Design*, vol. 14, no. 2, pp. 97-104.

Swinson, P.S.G. (November 1983) "Prolog: A Prelude to a New Generation of CAAD," *Computer Aided Design*, vol. 15, no. 6, pp. 335-343.

Swinson, P.S.G., Periera, F.C.N., and Bijl, A. (July 1983) "A Fact Dependency System for the Logic Programmer," *Computer Aided Design*, vol. 15, no. 4, pp. 235-243.

Wm. Randolph Franklin is an associate professor with the Electrical, Computer, and Systems Engineering Department at Rensselaer Polytechnic Institute. For the 1985-86 academic year he is on sabbatical with the Electrical Engineering and Computer Science Department, University of California at Berkeley. His research interests include graphics, geometry, and artificial intelligence. Franklin received the BSc in computer science from the University of Toronto, and the AM and PhD in applied mathematics (computer science) from Harvard University. He is a member of IEEE, ACM, and SIAM.

Franklin's address until May 1986 is Computer Science Division, Electrical Engineering and Computer Science Department, 543 Evans Hall, University of California, Berkeley, CA 94720.

# On the Boundary of Digital Straight Line Segments

Son Pham

Department of Computer Science, School of Engineering and Computer Science,
California State University, Northridge, CA 91330, USA

## ABSTRACT

It will be proved in this paper that all digital straight segments connecting two given pixels form areas whose lower bound and upper bound are also digital straight segments. These two bounds are simply calculated and different from each other by unity in the x or y-coordinate, and their chain codes have reverse directions from each other. Hence, for practical purposes, these results can be used to define general digital straight segments as the digital arcs in this area, and also used to define the convexity and concavity of digital arcs.

*Categories and Subject Descriptors:* I.3.3[Computer Graphics]:Picture/Image Generation; F.2.2 [Analysis of Algorithms and Problem Complexity]: Geometric Problems and Computations.

*General Terms:* Digital arcs, chain codes of directions, pixel, shift, reverse, convex, concave, lower bound, upper bound, algorithms, straight line segments

## I. INTRODUCTION

On a grid a set of chain pixels is called a *digital arc*. Every pixel in the chain has exactly two neighbors in the same set, except the endpoints. If the set has infinitely many elements we call it an *infinite* chain code, otherwise we call a *finite* chain code or a *digital arc*. Hence a digital arc can be represented by either a sequence of directions from one pixel to its neighbors (Foley and VanDam 1982; Freeman 1969), or an ordered sequence of xy coordinates. Hansen (1969) and Hodes (1970) have studied the criteria necessary for a digital arc to be the digitization of a real convex arc or a real concave arc. In other words, they have studied the characterization of digital arcs digitized from the convex or concave real arcs. A well-known definition of the convexity of a real arc is that the real straight line segment connecting the two real points on the arc is under the arc. Finding a similar definition for digital convex arcs is very difficult because there are many digital straight line segments between two pixels (pixels can be called digital points). So the problem of characterizing digital convex arcs leads to the problem of characterizing digital straight line segments (Brons 1974; Chang 1971).

Numerous authors have researched this problem and studied the criteria of characterization (Arcelli and Massarotti 1975; Bresenham 1965; Pfaltz and Rosenfeld 1967; Rosenfeld 1974, 1969). The importance of the straightness of digital arcs has been studied extensively by Kim (1982) and Kim and Rosenfeld (1982). So far, three characterizations have been found. First is Freeman's criteria (Freeman 1969), second is Rosenfeld's chord property (Rosenfeld 1974), and third is Hung's absence of uneveness (Hung 1985). Most works based on these characterizations lead to complex algorithms (Brons 1974; Chang 1971; Wu 1982).

Many other works are also related to arcs such as handwritten contour analysis (Greanins *et al* 1963), convex (Sklansky 1970, 1971, 1972; Yaglom and Boltyanski 1961), contours (Montarani 1970; Morse 1968; Pavlidis 1977; Pitterway 1967; Pfaltz and Rosenfeld 1967; Ramer 1972; Reggiori 1972), and languages on grids (Brons 1974; Chang 1971; Rothstein and Weiman 1976; Rutovitz 1975; Shaw 1970; Swain anf Fu 1972; Symons 1968). In practice, digitization of straight lines might not satisfy, due to the digitization error, the criteria mentioned above. Hence, a digital arc with few errors in digitization cannot be recognized as a digital straight line segment.

How do we know when a digital arc is "nearly" a digital straight arc? To answer this question, this paper will deal only with *all* digital straight line segments between two given pixels P and Q. If the area of all digital straight line segments is calculated then a digital arc with endpoints P and Q can be defined generally as a "nearly" digital straight line segment, if it falls in the area. This general definition makes more sense if the upper bound and lower bound of the area are also the digital straight line segments between P and Q. Therefore, "nearly" digital straight line segments might not satisfy all three Freeman's criteria. Moreover, if the upper bound and lower bound of the area are determined precisely, then an algorithm for determining if a digital arc is "nearly" straight can be easily derived.

**Mathematical Notation**

The following notations are used throughout the paper.

| | |
|---|---|
| $|g|_c$ | the remainder of the integer g divided by the integer c, (g modulo c). |
| abs(x) | the absolute value of the number x. |
| $\delta = (\delta_0, \delta_1, \delta_2,..., \delta_{c-1})$ | the infinite periodic sequence ... $\delta_0, \delta_1, \delta_2,..., \delta_{c-1}, \delta_0, \delta_1, \delta_2,...,$ $\delta_{c-1}...$ |
| (g,c) = 1 | two relatively prime integers g and c. |
| $\lfloor x \rfloor$ | the greatest integer less than or equal to the number x. |
| $\lceil x \rceil$ | the smallest integer greater than or equal to the number x. |
| $P = (x_P, y_P)$ | the point P with x and y coordinates. |
| PQ | the real straight line from P to Q. |

A pixel on a grid has 8 neighbors: 2 horizontal, 2 vertical, and 4 diagonal. These 8 neighbors are numbered 0 to 7 counterclockwise. Henceforth there are 8 directions from one pixel to its 8 neighbors. Thus, the numbers 0 to 7 can also indicate directions (see Fig. 1(a)).

*Coordinates of Pixels:* An xy coordinate system can be used on a grid to locate the position of a pixel. The origin is placed at the center of a pixel. Moreover all centers of pixels have integer coordinates (see Fig. 1(b)).

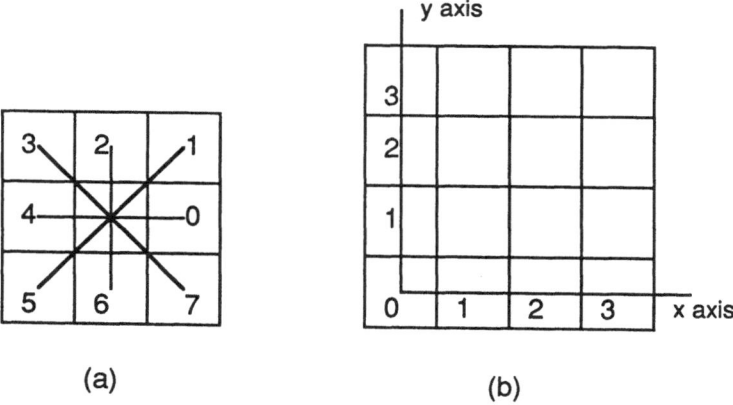

(a)                                   (b)

Figure 1    (a): 8 neighbors and 8 directions.
            (b): a xy coordinate system on a grid.

Henceforth, a chain code can be represented by one of the following two sequences:
(a)    It can be represented by the coordinates of pixel centers.    (This representation can be used for any set of pixels and is not restricted to pixels on the chain code, see the shaded area in Fig. 2(a)).
(b)    It can be represented by a sequence of directions from pixels to their neighbors. In this representation one pixel as a starting for direction should be known (see Fig. 2(b)).

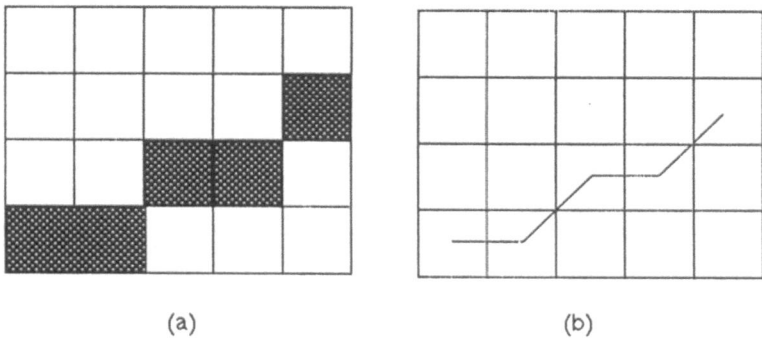

(a)                                   (b)

Figure 2    (a): a chain code in a shaded area
            (b): a chain code of directions.

## Previous Works

Freeman(1974) suggested three criteria neccessary for a chain code (represented by a set of directions) to be said digital straight line as follows:

(1) At most two basic directions are presented and these can differ by unity modulo 8.
(2) One of these values always occur singly.
(3) Successive occurrences of the principal direction singly occurring are as uniformly spaced as possible.

Several authors (Arcelli and Massarotti 1975; Bangiovanni and Zorat 1975; Bresenham 1965; Freeman 1974; Reggiory 1972; Wu 1982) have provided algorithms to digitize a drawn real line to obtain digital straight lines. Since each real line can be drawn if the slope is given, then many algorithms attempt to find the digital straight lines if rational slopes are given.

Later Rosenfeld(1966, 1968, 1969, 1970, 1973, 1974) introduced the chord property and proved that a digital arc (finite chain code) having the chord property is a digital straight line segment. In this case the chord property implies the first two Freeman's criteria. This result can be extended to the infinite chain codes, and the chord property is equivalent to the Freeman's three criteria(Rosenfeld 1974; Wu 1982). The chord property is defined as follows:

Let $\zeta$ be a finite digital arc. Let P and Q be two pixels in this arc. We say that straight line segment PQ lies near $\zeta$ if, for any real point (x, y) of PQ, there exists a pixel (i, j) in $\zeta$ such that

$$\max ( abs(i-x), abs(j-y) ) \quad < \quad 1.$$

We say that $\zeta$ has the chord property if, for every P and Q in $\zeta$, the straight line segment PQ lies near $\zeta$.

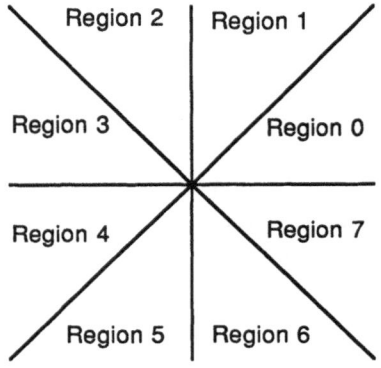

Region 0: 0 to 45 degrees
Region 1: 45 to 90 degrees
Region 2: 90 to 135 degrees
Region 3: 135 to 180 degrees
Region 4: 180 to 225 degrees
Region 5: 225 to 270 degrees
Region 6: 270 to 315 degrees
Region 7: 315 to 360 degrees

Figure 3: The 8 Different Regions of Slopes

**Recent Results** (See Appendix).

*The Chain Code Formulas:* The chain codes of directions of digital straight lines with slope g/c, (g, c) = 1, can be obtained by the following formulas. We note that the formulas are slightly different on 8 regions of slopes, and these chain codes satisfy the three Freeman's three criteria (see Fig. 3).

Region 0:  periodic sequence:   $\delta_0, \delta_1, \delta_2,..., \delta_{c-1}$

where $a_i = \lfloor g.i \rfloor_c$ , for i = 0,1,...,c;

$\delta_i = (a_i - a_{i+1} + g)/c$, for i = 0;1,...,(c-1);

Region 1:  periodic sequence: $(1+\delta_0)$, $(1+\delta_1)$, $(1+\delta_2)$,..., $(1+\delta_{g-1})$

where  $\delta_0, \delta_1, \delta_2,..., \delta_{g-1}$ is the chain code of the line with slope (g-c)/g  (see Region 0).

Region 2:  periodic sequence:   $(3-\delta_0)$, $(3-\delta_1)$, $(3-\delta_2)$,..., $(3-\delta_{g-1})$

where  $\delta_0, \delta_1, \delta_2,..., \delta_{g-1}$ is the chain code of the line with slope (g-c)/g (see Region 0).

Region 3:  periodic sequence:  $(4-\delta_0)$, $(4-\delta_1)$, $(4-\delta_2)$,..., $(4-\delta_{c-1})$

where $\delta_0, \delta_1, \delta_2,..., \delta_{c-1}$ is the chain code of the line with slope g/c (see Region 0).

Region 4:  periodic sequence:   $(4+\delta_0)$, $(4+\delta_1)$, $(4+\delta_2)$,..., $(4+\delta_{c-1})$

where   ( $\delta_0, \delta_1, \delta_2,..., \delta_{c-1}$) is the chain code of the line with slope g/c (see Region 0).

Region 5:  periodic sequence:   $(5+\delta_0)$, $(5+\delta_1)$, $(5+\delta_2)$,..., $(5+\delta_{g-1})$

where $(\delta_0, \delta_1, \delta_2,..., \delta_{g-1})$ is the chain code of the line with slope (g-c)/g (see Region 0).

Region 6:  periodic sequence: $(7-\delta_0)$, $(7-\delta_1)$, $(7-\delta_2)$,..., $(7-\delta_{g-1})$

where $(\delta_0, \delta_1, \delta_2,..., \delta_{g-1})$ is the chain code of the line with slope (g-c)/g (see Region 0).

Region 7:  periodic sequence:  $(8-\delta_0)$, $(8-\delta_1)$, $(8-\delta_2)$,..., $(8-\delta_{c-1})$

where $(\delta_0, \delta_1, \delta_2,..., \delta_{c-1})$ is the chain code of the line with slope g/c (see Region 0).

**Results of this Paper.**

Given two pixels P and Q whose centers are denoted respectively by $(x_P, y_P)$ and $(x_Q, y_Q)$. The slope of the real straight line passing these two centers is g/c where g = abs($y_Q$ -$y_P$)

and c = abs($x_Q - x_P$). Since the chain code of directions from P to Q is slightly different depending on the position of P and Q (see Recent Results), we assume throughout this paper that P is the origin (0, 0) and Q is in Region 0. The results for the cases Regions 1-7 are similar and will not be reported here in order to reduce the technical complexity of this paper.

As discussed above with slope g/c, a chain code of directions satisfying the three Freeman's three criteria can be generated by the formulas:

$$a_i = |g.i|_c , \qquad \text{for i = 0,1,...,c (in this case } a_0 = a_c = 0);$$
$$\delta_i = ( a_i - a_{i+1} + g)/c, \qquad \text{for i = 0,1,...,c-1.}$$

It is clear that the segment $\delta_0, \delta_1, \delta_2,..., \delta_{c-1}$ will connect the pixel P to the pixel Q.

With two given pixels P and Q above, how many digital straight segments are there to connect P to Q? In order to answer this question, shift and reverse operators are introduced.

The segment $\delta_0, \delta_1, \delta_2,..., \delta_{c-1}$ is a periodic sequence of the digital straight line of slope g/c and can be viewed geometrically as a path to connect a pixel to another pixel at a distance which is c pixels horizontally and g pixels vertically from the first pixel. Therefore, shift or reverse operators can be used to obtain other digital straight segments from P to Q. Let $\delta = ( \delta_0, \delta_1, \delta_2,..., \delta_{c-1} )$, the operatror shift and reverse are defined as follows:

$$\text{shift } (\delta) = \text{shift } ( \delta_0, \delta_1, \delta_2,..., \delta_{c-1} ) \quad = \delta_1, \delta_2,..., \delta_{c-1}, \delta_0;$$
$$\text{reverse } (\delta) = \text{reverse } ( \delta_0, \delta_1, \delta_2,..., \delta_{c-1} ) = \delta_{c-1},..., \delta_2, \delta_1, \delta_0;$$

If the shift operator is used multiple times, then there is a set of c different digital segments from P to Q: shift($\delta$), shift$^2$($\delta$), shift$^3$($\delta$),..., shift$^{c-1}$($\delta$), shift$^c$($\delta$). We notice that shift$^c$($\delta$) = shift$^0$($\delta$) = $\delta$. The superscript indicates the number of times the shift operator being applied. Similarly, the shift operator can be applied multiple times on reverse($\delta$) to get a set of c different digital segments: reverse($\delta$), shift(reverse($\delta$)), shift$^2$(reverse($\delta$)), shift$^3$(reverse($\delta$)),..., shift$^{c-1}$(reverse($\delta$). The two above sets are the same, i.e., reverse($\delta$) is shift$^k$($\delta$) for some k.

So far there are *c different* digital straight segments being generated. Are there any other digital straight segments from P to Q? It is rather difficult to find all digital straight segments because as a conceptual definition of digital straight segments, they are digital arcs only from P to Q of digital straight lines passing through P and Q. Therefore, we consider the set of these c different digital straight segments which form an area from P to Q.

It is proved that this area has an upper bound and a lower bound which are also digital straight line segments from P to Q. Moreover, any digital straight line passing through P and Q will have their segments between P and Q in the area. The lower bound and the upper bound are proved to be $\delta$ and r($\delta$) respectively. The upper bound is also calculated from the lower bound by one of the following two methods:
    (a) upper bound is different from lower bound by unity in some sense of y-coordinates

and
(b) upper bound chain code can be obtained from the lower bound chain code by the reverse operator.


## II.  ILLUSTRATION

Let P = (0, 0) and Q = (12, 5).  All digital straight segments connecting P to Q will be illustrated in here.  One of these segments is calculated as follows:

$$a_i = |5.i|_{12}, \qquad \text{for } i = 0,1,...,12 \text{ (in this case } a_0 = a_{12} = 0);$$

$$\delta_i = (a_i - a_{i+1} + 5)/12, \quad \text{for } i = 0,1,...,11.$$

Each direction $\delta_i$ will connect two pixels $(i, y_i)$ and $(i+1, y_{i+1})$
where

$$y_i = 0, \qquad \text{(an endpoint)}$$

$$y_i = \sum_{j=0}^{i-1} \delta_i ; \qquad \text{for } i = 1,2,...,11$$

$$y_{12} = 5, \qquad \text{(an endpoint)}.$$

We call  $\delta_0, \delta_1, \delta_2,..., \delta_{c-1}$  the sequence of directions connecting P to Q and  $y_0, y_1, y_2,...,$ $y_{c-1}$  the corresponding sequence of y-levels.  So we have the following summary table.


Table 1:    first row: the integer x-coordinates
second row: the cyclic group of modulo 12
third row: the periodic sequence of directions
fourth row: the integer y-coordinates

| i | 0 | 1 | 2 | 3 | 4 | 5 | 6 | 7 | 8 | 9 | 10 | 11 | 12 |
|---|---|---|---|---|---|---|---|---|---|---|----|----|----|
| $a_i$ | 0 | 5 | 10 | 3 | 8 | 1 | 6 | 11 | 4 | 9 | 2 | 7 | |
| $\delta_i$ | 0 | 0 | 1 | 0 | 1 | 0 | 0 | 1 | 0 | 1 | 0 | 1 | |
| $y_i$ | 0 | 0 | 0 | 1 | 1 | 2 | 2 | 2 | 3 | 3 | 4 | 4 | 5 |

↑ endpoint ... ↑ endpoint

The shift operator will generate the other 11 digital straight segments from P to Q.  These digital straight segments are listed in Table 2 with their corresponding y levels.  The reverse operator will also generate 12 digital straight  segments by reversing the 12 previous sequences.  The new 12 reverse sequences are also digital segments connecting P to Q.  They are listed in Table 3 with their corresponding y-levels.  We notice that Table 2 and Table 3 have the same digital straight segments.  In Table 2, the minimum of y-levels is at the beginning of the table, while in Table 3, the maximum is at the beginning of the table.  Figure 4 will show the lower bound and upper bound of all digital straight line segments.

**Table 2:** 12 Digital Straight Segments Connecting P to Q Generated by the Shifts
\* : the minimum of all y levels
\+ : the maximum of all y levels

| # of shift | Digital Straight Segment | The corresponding y-levels |
|---|---|---|
| 0 | 0 0 1 0 1 0 0 1 0 1 0 1 | 0 0 0 1 1 2 2 2 3 3 4 4 5 * |
| 1 | 0 1 0 1 0 0 1 0 1 0 1 0 | 0 0 1 1 2 2 2 3 3 4 4 5 5 |
| 2 | 1 0 1 0 0 1 0 1 0 1 0 0 | 0 1 1 2 2 2 3 3 4 4 5 5 5 |
| 3 | 0 1 0 0 1 0 1 0 1 0 0 1 | 0 0 1 1 1 2 2 3 3 4 4 4 5 |
| 4 | 1 0 0 1 0 1 0 1 0 0 1 0 | 0 1 1 1 2 2 3 3 4 4 4 5 5 |
| 5 | 0 0 1 0 1 0 1 0 0 1 0 1 | 0 0 0 1 1 2 2 3 3 3 4 4 5 |
| 6 | 0 1 0 1 0 1 0 0 1 0 1 0 | 0 0 1 1 2 2 3 3 3 4 4 5 5 |
| 7 | 1 0 1 0 1 0 0 1 0 1 0 0 | 0 1 1 2 2 3 3 3 4 4 5 5 5 + |
| 8 | 0 1 0 1 0 0 1 0 1 0 0 1 | 0 0 1 1 2 2 2 3 3 4 4 4 5 |
| 9 | 1 0 1 0 0 1 0 1 0 0 1 0 | 0 1 1 2 2 2 3 3 4 4 4 5 5 |
| 10 | 0 1 0 0 1 0 1 0 0 1 0 1 | 0 0 1 1 1 2 2 3 3 3 4 4 5 |
| 11 | 1 0 0 1 0 1 0 0 1 0 1 0 | 0 1 1 1 2 2 3 3 3 4 4 5 5 |

**Table 3:** 12 Digital Straight Segments Connecting P to Q
\* : the minimum of all y levels
\+ : the maximum of all y levels

| # shifts | of reversed digital straight segment | y-level of the reversed digital straight line |
|---|---|---|
| 0 | 1 0 1 0 1 0 0 1 0 1 0 0 | 0 1 1 2 2 3 3 3 4 4 5 5 5 + |
| 1 | 0 1 0 1 0 1 0 0 1 0 1 0 | 0 0 1 1 2 2 3 3 3 4 4 5 5 |
| 2 | 0 0 1 0 1 0 0 1 0 1 0 1 | 0 0 0 1 1 2 2 3 3 3 4 4 5 |
| 3 | 1 0 0 1 0 1 0 1 0 0 1 0 | 0 1 1 1 2 2 3 3 4 4 4 5 0 |
| 4 | 0 1 0 0 1 0 1 0 1 0 0 1 | 0 0 1 1 1 2 2 3 3 4 4 4 5 |
| 5 | 1 0 1 0 0 1 0 1 0 1 0 0 | 0 1 1 2 2 2 3 3 4 4 5 5 5 |
| 6 | 0 1 0 1 0 0 1 0 1 0 1 0 | 0 0 1 1 2 2 2 3 3 4 4 5 5 * |
| 7 | 0 0 1 0 1 0 0 1 0 1 0 1 | 0 0 0 1 1 2 2 2 3 3 4 4 5 * |
| 8 | 1 0 0 1 0 1 0 0 1 0 1 0 | 0 1 1 1 2 2 3 3 3 4 4 5 5 |
| 9 | 0 1 0 0 1 0 1 0 0 1 0 1 | 0 0 1 1 1 2 2 3 3 3 4 4 5 |
| 10 | 1 0 1 0 0 1 0 1 0 0 1 0 | 0 1 1 2 2 2 3 3 4 4 4 5 0 |
| 11 | 0 1 0 1 0 0 1 0 1 0 0 1 | 0 0 1 1 2 2 2 3 3 4 4 4 5 |

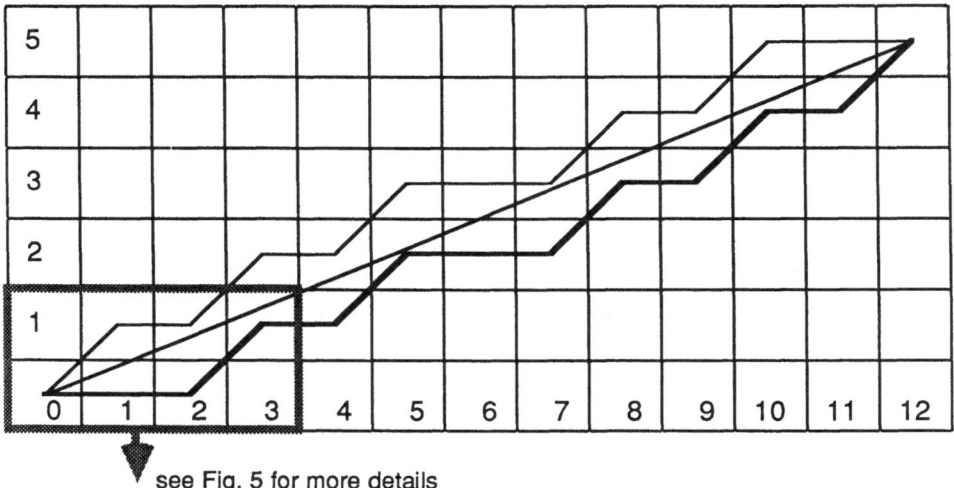

see Fig. 5 for more details

Figure 4: Area of digital straight segments from P = (0, 0) to Q = (12, 5). It is bounded by two digital straight segments **minδ** and **maxδ**.

**minδ** = (0 0 1 0 1 0 0 1 0 1 0 1),

**maxδ** = (1 0 1 0 1 0 0 1 0 1 0 0).

## III. STRAIGHT LINE SEGMENTS: SHIFT AND REVERSE OPERATORS

The operators shift and reverse and the function y-level are defined mathematically in this section. Some properties are also included.

### Shift and Reverse Operators.

We use the short notation s for the shift operator. It is a function on the Cartesian product D x D x...x D (multiplied c times) where D = {0,1,...,7} is the set of 8 directions. We also denote $s^n$ as a composite function of s being applied n times, for all positive integer n. The notation $s^0$ is considered as identity function. Here are some examples

$$s^0 (\delta_0, \delta_1, \delta_2,..., \delta_{c-1} ) = ( \delta_0, \delta_1, \delta_2,..., \delta_{c-1} ),$$
$$s^1 (\delta_0, \delta_1, \delta_2,..., \delta_{c-1} ) = (\delta_1, \delta_2,..., \delta_{c-1}, \delta_0).$$

Similarly we define the reversed operator r on the same Cartesian product D x D x...x D (multiplied c times). For example

$$r( \delta_0, \delta_1, \delta_2,..., \delta_{c-1}) = ( \delta_{c-1},..., \delta_2, \delta_1, \delta_0 ).$$

The following properties hold for s and r:

(1)  s and r are two bijections on D x D x...x D,
(2)  $r^2 = s^0$ (identity),
(3)  $r(s^k) = s^{c-k}(r)$, for all integer k.

**Y-level Function.**

For each digital straight segment in Region 0, the directions can only be 0 or 1 (as we mentioned above the discussions are similar for the other regions). Hence, the coordinates of the pixels of a digital straight segment can be constructed as partial sums of the sequence of directions. For example, the digital straight segment $\delta = (\delta_0, \delta_1, \delta_2,..., \delta_{c-1})$ has the coordinates: $(i, y_i)$, for $i = 1,2,...c-1$, where

$$y_i = \sum_{i=0}^{j-1} \delta_j$$

For completeness, let $y_0 = 0$ and $y_c = g$. Henceforth, for $i = 0,1,...,c-1$; $\delta_i$ will connect the center $(i, y_i)$ to the center $(i+1, y_{i+1})$. We call $( y_i )$ the corresponding sequence of y-levels, and denote it level($\delta$).

Some properties of y-levels are listed as follows. For every two digital straight segments $\delta$ and $\delta'$ connecting P to Q in Region 0, we have:
(1)  their corresponding sequences of y-levels are increasing,
(2)  $\delta \neq \delta'$ iff their corresponding sequences of y-levels are different.

The y-level function is convenient to define the positional order of the chain segments:
$\delta \leq \delta'$ (it is said that $\delta$ is below $\delta'$)  iff  level($\delta$) $\leq$ level($\delta'$).

This order will be used to define the upper bound and lower bound of the area of all digital straight segments from P to Q, and it will be used widely in the later proofs.

 Now we prove the following proposition which describes the relationships amongst $\delta$, s, and r.

*Proposition 1:* We have the following properties:
(1.1)  $\delta$, $s(\delta)$, $s^2(\delta)$,..., $s^{c-1}( \delta)$ are all different;
(1.2)  $r( \delta)$, $r(s(\delta))$, $r(s^2(\delta))$,..., $r(s^{c-1}(\delta))$ are all different;
(1.3)  two sets in (1.1) and (1.2) are the same, i.e.,
$\{ s^k(\delta) \mid k=0,1,...,c-1\} = \{ r(s^j(\delta)) \mid j=0,1,...,c-1 \}$.

*Proof:*  Proposition(1.2) can be derived from Proposition(1.1). So, we prove only (1.1) and (1.3).

*Proof of (1.1):* We have

$$\sum_{i=0}^{j-1} \delta_i = \sum_{i=0}^{j-1} (a_i - a_{i+1} + g) / c = (a_0 - a_j + j.g) / c$$

We extend the definition of $a_i$ for $i < c$ to the case $i \geq c$. That is $a_i = |g.i|_c$ for all integer i. Therefore $a_i = a_{i+kc}$ for all integer k and i. We have

$$\sum_{i=0}^{j-1} [s^k(\delta)]_i = \sum_{i=0}^{j-1} (a_{i+k} - a_{i+k+1} + g)/c = (a_k - a_{j+k} + j.g)/c \qquad (1)$$

We will prove $s^k(\delta) \neq s^{k'}(\delta)$ for all $k \neq k'$, by showing their corresponding sequences of y-levels are different. Applying equation(1) for k and k', we have:

$$\sum_{i=0}^{j-1} [s^k(\delta)]_i = (a_k - a_{j+k} + j.g)/c \quad \text{and} \quad \sum_{i=0}^{j-1} [s^{k'}(\delta)]_i = (a_{k'} - a_{j+k'} + j.g)/c$$

The proof of (1.1) is then reduced to find an integer j so that

$$a_k - a_{j+k} \neq a_{k'} - a_{j+k'}$$

or (by Definition of a's)

$$|g.k|_c - |g.k'|_c \neq |g(j+k)|_c - |g(j+k')|_{c'} \qquad (2)$$

Now we find an integer j to satisfy this inequality.
We have $|g.k|_c \neq |g.k'|_c$ as a result of $(g, c) = 1$. So, we can assume without loss of generality that $|g.k|_c < |g.k'|_c$. Therefore, there is a constant M less than c such that

$$|g.k|_c + M \leq c \leq |g.k'|_c + M.$$

Since a's generate the set $\{0,1,...,c-1\}$, i.e., $\{|g.j|_c \mid j = 0,1,...,c-1\} = \{0,1,...,c-1\}$, therefore we select an integer $j_0$ so that

$$M = |g. j_0|_c.$$

We have

$$||g.k'|_c + j_0.g|_c = |g.k'|_c + |j_0.g|_c - c$$
$$||g.k|_c + j_0.g|_c = |g.k|_c + |j_0.g|_c$$

and their difference is

$$||g.k|_c + j_0.g|_c - ||g.k'|_c + j_0.g|_c = |g.k|_c - |g.k|_c + c.$$

This implies that inequality (2) is valid for this $j_0$.

*Proof of (1.3):* To prove $\{\delta, s(\delta), s^2(\delta),..., s^{c-1}(\delta)\} = \{r(\delta), r(s(\delta)), r(s^2(\delta)),..., r(s^{c-1}(\delta))\}$, we need to prove only $r(\delta) = s^k(\delta)$, for some integer k. So, we prove the following proposition.

*Proposition 2:* There exists an integer k so that $r(\delta) = s^k(\delta)$.

*Proof:* We have by definitions of $\delta$, r, and s:

$$\sum_{i=0}^{j-1} [r(\delta)]_i = \sum_{i=0}^{j-1} [\delta_{c-1-i}] = (a_{c-j} - a_c + jg)/c = (a_{c-j} + jg)/c$$
$$\text{(we note that } a_c = a_0 = 0)$$

$$\sum_{i=0}^{j-1} [s^k(\delta)]_i = \sum_{i=0}^{j-1} [\delta_{k+i}] = (a_k - a_{k+j} + jg)/c$$

Hence, the problem is reduced to find an integer k, independent of j, so that $a_{c-j} = a_k - a_{k+j}$, for all $j = 0, 1,..., c-1$. It is equivalent to prove with $j = 1,...,c-1$ (case $j = 0$ is evident)

$$|g(c-j)|_c = |g.k|_c - |g(k+j)|_c \qquad (3)$$

We prove this equation as follows: since $(g,c) = 1$, therefore all $a_i$; $i = 0, 1,..., c-1$ are all different and form the set $\{0,1,...,c-1\}$. Hence, there exists an integer $k_0$ so that
$$a_{k0} = c-1, \quad \text{i.e.,} \quad |g.(k_0)|_c = c-1.$$
This $k_0$ is the candidate for the above equation (3). Indeed, with $k_0$, the right-hand side of the equation (3) is calculated as

$$|g.(k_0)|_c - |g.(k_0+j)|_c = c-1 - |(c-1) + g.j|_c$$

Because $|g.j|_c > 0$, for all $j = 1,2,...,c-1$, we have

$$|(c-1) + g.j|_c = (c-1) + |g.j|_c - c = -1 + |g.j|_c.$$

Hence

$$|g.(k_0)|_c - |g.(k_0+j)|_c = c-1 - (-1+|g.j|_c) = c - |g.j|_c$$

which is equal to the left-hand side of (3). QED

## IV. LOWER BOUND AND UPPER BOUND DIGITAL STRAIGHT SEGMENTS

In the previous sections, we constructed c different digital straight segments from the pixel $P = (0, 0)$ to the pixel $Q = (c, g)$, where $(g, c) = 1$. These c segments are shifted from each other and one of them is $\delta = (\delta_0, \delta_1, ...,\delta_{c-1})$. Let **miny** and **maxy** be respectively the minimum and maximum of all these c corresponding sequences of y-levels, i.e.,

$$(\text{miny})_i = \text{minimum } \{(\text{level } s^k(\delta))_i \mid k = 0,1,...,c-1\}$$
$$(\text{maxy})_i = \text{maximum } \{(\text{level } s^k(\delta))_i \mid k = 0,1,...,c-1\}$$
$$\text{miny} \le \text{level}(s^k(\delta)) \le \text{maxy}, \quad \text{for all k.}$$

We will prove in this section that **miny** and **maxy** are also two corresponding y-sequences of $\delta$ and $r(\delta)$ respectively. In other words, we have the following property:
$$\delta \le s^k(\delta) \le r(\delta), \quad \text{for all } k = 0,1,...,c-1.$$
Moreover, **miny** and **maxy** are different by unity except for the endpoints, i.e.,

$$(\text{maxy})_0 = (\text{miny})_0 = 0,$$
$$(\text{maxy})_i = (\text{miny})_i + 1, \quad \text{for all } i = 1,2,...,c-1,$$
$$(\text{maxy})_c = (\text{miny})_c = g.$$

*Proposition 3:* We have the following order

$$\delta \leq s^k(\delta), \qquad \text{for all } k = 0,1,...,c\text{-}1.$$

(This proposition hence implies that $\delta = \min\delta$).

*Proof:* For all $j = 0,1,...,c\text{-}1$ the sum of the first j terms (from index 0 to index j-1) of the code is calculated as follows:

$$\sum_{i=0}^{j-1} \delta_i = \sum_{i=0}^{j-1} (a_i - a_{i+1} + g)/c = (a_0 - a_j + j.g)/c = (-a_j + j.g)/c \qquad (4)$$

Similarly, the new code being shifted k times (any integer k) from the code $\delta$ will have the sum of the first j terms (from index 0 to index j-1) being calculated as follows:

$$\sum_{i=0}^{j-1} [s^k(\delta)]_i = \sum_{i=0}^{j-1} [\delta_{k+i}] = \sum_{i=0}^{j-1} (a_{i+k} - a_{i+k+1} + g)/c = (a_k - a_{k+j} + jg)/c \qquad (5)$$

To prove $\delta = \min\delta$, it is sufficient to show that $\delta$ is lower than any of its shiftings i.e., to show the value in (4) is less than the one in (5) for all j and k. Simply it is equivalent to show

$$a_j + a_k \geq a_{j+k} \quad \text{for all j and k.}$$

We prove this inequality as follows: by the definition of a's we have $a_j = |g.j|_c$ and $a_k = |g.k|_c$. Therefore there exists m and n so that

$$g.j = a_j + mc \quad \text{and} \quad g.k = a_k + nc$$

Hence, $g(j+k) = (a_j + a_k) + (m+n)c$. Therefore,

$$a_{j+k} = |g(j+k)|_c = |a_j + a_k|_c \leq a_j + a_k. \qquad \text{QED}$$

*Proposition 4:* $\max\delta = r(\delta)$.

*Proof:* The proof is similar to the one to prove $\delta = \min\delta$. We can calculate the following equalities.

$$\sum_{i=0}^{c-1} \delta_i = c \qquad (6)$$

$$\sum_{i=0}^{c-j} [r(\delta)]_i = c - \sum_{i=0}^{j-1} \delta_i = c - (a_0 - a_j + j.g)/c \qquad (7)$$

$$\sum_{i=0}^{c-j} [s^k(r(\delta))]_i = c - \sum_{i=0}^{j-1} \delta_{i+k} = c - (a_k - a_{k+j} + j.g)/c \qquad (8)$$

To prove $\max\delta = r(\delta)$, it is sufficient to show that $r(\delta)$ is greater than any of its shiftings because $\{s^i(\delta)|i=0,...\} = \{r(s^i)|i=0,...\}$, i.e., to show the value in (7) is less than in (8) for all j,k. Again, the problem is reduced to prove $a_j + a_k \geq a_{j+k}$, for all j, k which was proved in the proof of $\delta = \min\delta$.                                                                        QED

*Proposition 5:*  The following equations hold

[level $(\max\delta)]_{j-1}$ = [level $(\min\delta)]_{j-1}$ + 1,   for all j = 1, 2,..., c-1.

[level $(\max\delta)]_{c-1}$ = [level $(\min\delta)]_{c-1}$ and [level $(\max\delta)]_0$ = [level $(\min\delta)]_0$, (case j=1, or c).

*Proof:* We have for all j = 1,2,...,c-1

$$\sum_{i=0}^{j-1} (\max\delta)_i \quad = \sum_{i=0}^{j-1} [r(\delta)]_i \ = \ (a_{c\text{-}j} - a_c + j.g) / c \ = \ (a_{c\text{-}j} + j.g) / c$$

$$\sum_{i=0}^{j-1} (\min\delta)_i \quad = \sum_{i=0}^{j-1} \delta_i \ = \ (a_0 - a_j + j.g) / c$$

The difference of the two above is $(a_{c\text{-}j} - a_j)/c$.  To prove the equality we need to show that

$$a_{c\text{-}j} + a_j = c, \text{ for all } j = 1,2,...,c\text{-}1.$$

Indeed, if we let $u = |g.j|_c$ then for any j = 1,2,...,c-1, we have g.j = u+mc for some m.
Hence, g.c - g.j  = -u + (g-m)c. Therefore $|g.c - g.j|_c$ = c - u   or   $a_{c\text{-}j} + a_j = c$.
For the special case j = 0 or j = c, we have  $a_{c\text{-}j} + a_j$ = $a_c + a_0$ = 0.                 QED

## V.  AREA OF ALL DIGITAL STRAIGHT SEGMENTS

In this section, we will prove that the area of all digital straight segments from P to Q is bounded by two digital straight segments **min$\delta$** and **max$\delta$** (i.e., between $\delta$ and r($\delta$)). In other words, we will prove that for any digital straight line passing P and Q, and denote its segment from P to Q by $\delta'$, then the following orders are valid.

$$\delta \le \ \delta' \le r(\delta).$$

In order to prove this property, we will show that:

(a) First, the real line segment PQ is completely inside the area bounded by **min$\delta$** and **max$\delta$**.
(b) Second, there is no other digital straight line segment from P to Q having at least one pixel outside the area.  In other words, we will show that, as a result of (a) and the chord property, a digital straight segment from P to Q having one of its pixels outside the area will not have the chord property.

*Theorem 1:* We have the following properties:
(1.1) There are no center points of **min$\delta$** and **max$\delta$**  on PQ, i.e.,

$$\frac{\sum_{i=0}^{j-1} \delta_i}{c} \ \neq \ \frac{g}{c} \quad \text{and} \quad \frac{\sum_{i=0}^{j-1} [r(\delta)]_i}{c} \ \neq \ \frac{g}{c}$$

(1.2) The real straight segment PQ is above **min$\delta$**, i.e., the real straight segment PQ is above the real broken segment formed by connecting the centers

$$(0, 0), \qquad \{ (j, \sum_{i=0}^{j-1} \delta_i) \mid j = 1,..., c\text{-}1\}, \qquad \text{and} \qquad (c, g).$$

(1.3) The real straight line PQ is below **max$\delta$**, i.e., the real straight segment PQ is below the broken real segment formed by connecting the centers:

$$(0, 0), \qquad \{ (j, \sum_{i=0}^{j-1} [r(\delta)]_i \mid j = 1,..., c\text{-}1 \}, \qquad \text{and} \qquad (c, g).$$

*Proof of Theorem(1.1):* Suppose there is an integer j, (j > 2) so that

$$\frac{\sum_{i=0}^{j-1} \delta_i}{c} = \frac{g}{c}$$

Therefore, by the definition of $\delta_i$'s we have $(-a_j + j.g) / (j.c) = (g/c)$ or $(-a_j + j.g) = g.j$ Hence $a_j = 0$, i.e., $j = 0$ or c. Therefore, a contradiction occurs. We conclude that there are no center points of **min$\delta$** on PQ.

Similarly, there are no center points of **max$\delta$** on PQ, and the proof is similar to the one above. Indeed, suppose there is an integer j, (j < c) such that

$$\frac{\sum_{i=0}^{j-1} [r(\delta)]_i}{c} = \frac{g}{c}$$

Therefore, by the definition of $\delta_i$'s we have $(a_{c-j} - a_c + j.g) / (j.c) = (g/c)$ or $a_{c-j} = 0$. Hence $c\text{-}j = 0$ or c, i.e., $j = 0$ or c. Therefore a contradiction occurs.

*Proof of Theorem(1.2):* We will show that every real point $R = (x_R, y_R)$ on the real straight segment PQ, the value $y_R$ is greater than $y'_R$ , where $(x_R, y'_R)$ is on the broken segment formed by connecting the centers (see Fig. 5 for more details)

$$(0, 0), \qquad \{ (j, \sum_{i=0}^{j-1} \delta_i) \mid j = 1,..., c\text{-}1\}, \qquad \text{and} \qquad (c, g).$$

It is equivalent to prove that for the point R with $x_R = 1, 2,..., c\text{-}1$,

$$y_R \geq \sum_{i=0}^{j-1} [\delta_i], \tag{9}$$

The reason we reduce the proof only to the R with integer coordinates $x_R$ is that if two points R, S are under R', S' in the sense that $x_R = x_{R'}$, $x_S = x_{S'}$, $y_R \leq y_{R'}$, and $y_S \leq y_{S'}$, then the real straight segment RS is under R'S'.

Now we prove inequality (9):

For $j = 1, 2,..., c-1$, we consider the centers

$$\left( j, \sum_{i=0}^{j-1} \delta_i \right) \quad \text{and} \quad (j, y_R).$$

We have

$$\sum_{i=0}^{j-1} \delta_i = (-a_j + j.g) / c \leq j.g/c,$$

and since R is on PQ, then $y_R / j = g/c$. Hence $y_R = g.j/c$ which makes the inequality (9) holds. $\qquad$ QED

*Proof of Theorem(1.3):* Similarly, to prove PQ is under **maxδ**, we consider the center points of **maxδ**:

$$\left( j, \sum_{i=0}^{j-1} (\mathbf{max\delta})_i \right) ; \; j = 1, 2, ...,c-1$$

and the real point $R = (j, y_R)$ on PQ, and we need to prove

$$\sum_{i=0}^{j-1} (\mathbf{max\delta})_i ) \geq y_R$$

Indeed,

$$\sum_{i=0}^{j-1} (\mathbf{max\delta})_i = \sum_{i=0}^{j-1} \delta_i + 1$$

$$= (c - a_j + j.g) / c$$

$$\geq (j.g) / c$$

$$= y_R \qquad\qquad \text{QED}$$

## No Digital Straight Segment Outside the Area.

We will prove in this section that there are no digital straight line segments which fall outside the area bounded by **minδ** and **maxδ**.

*Theorem 2:* All digital straight segments from P to Q are in the area bounded by **minδ** and **maxδ**.

*Proof:* Let LINE be a digital straight line passing through the pixels P and Q (i.e., the LINE contains P and Q). Therefore, LINE satisfies the Rosenfeld's chord property. Consider the segment of LINE between P and Q. We want to prove that this segment is inside the area mentioned above. We will prove by a contradiction.

Assume that this digital straight segment is not inside the area, then there is a pixel, say $S = (x_S, y_S)$ of this segment outside the area. We have two cases: S is under **minδ** and S is above **maxδ**. We prove the case S is under **minδ**; the proof of the other case will be omitted because of its similarity.

Case S is under **min$\delta$**: We will show that LINE doesn't satisfy the chord property for a contradiction. More precisely we will show the point R = ($x_R$, $y_R$) with $x_R$ = $x_S$ on the real straight segment PQ has a distance to LINE greater than 1. That is, we will show that for all points (i, j) of LINE

$$\max \{ abs(i - x_R), \ abs(j - y_R) \} \geq 1.$$

(The quantity on the left hand side of inequality is the distance between (i, j) and R = ($x_R$, $y_R$). Since LINE can only have two directions 0 and 1, the next pixel after S cannot be above the pixel S' = ($x_S$+1, $y_S$+1). Since S is under **min$\delta$** hence S' cannot be above **min$\delta$**. (It is possible that S' is on **min$\delta$**).

Similarly, the pixel before S, cannot be above the pixel S" = ($x_S$-1, $y_S$) we need only to prove

(1) dist(R, S) $\geq$ 1
(2) dist(R, S') $\geq$ 1
(3) dist(R, S") $\geq$ 1

Indeed, because S is strictly under **min$\delta$** and PQ is strictly above **min$\delta$** therefore abs($y_S$- $y_R$) > 1. Hence dist(R, S) > 1. Since S" and S have the same y-coordinates, dist(R,S") is greater than or equal to 1. Similarly R and S have the same x-coordinates and $x_{S'}$ = $x_S$ + 1 therefore dist(R, S') $\geq$ 1. QED

## VI. CONVEX ARCS AND CONCAVE ARCS

In the previous sections, we proved that given two pixels with centers P = ($x_P$, $y_P$) and Q = ($x_Q$, $y_Q$), the area containing all digital straight segments from P and Q can be determined by its lower bound and upper bound. These two bounds are also digital straight line segments from P to Q, and they are proved to be $\delta$ and r ($\delta$) respectively.

The reason for the bound $\delta$ (resp.r( $\delta$ )) to be called lower bound (resp. upper bound) is that it has the smallest (resp. largest) y-coordinates among all digital straight segments from P to Q i.e., for all digital straight segments $\delta'$ from P to Q we have

$$level( \delta ) \leq level( \delta' ) \leq level(r( \delta )),$$

where level( $\delta$) denote the y-coordinates of $\delta$.
So, we can define the order relationships among all digital straight segments from P to Q as follows:

$$\delta' \leq \delta" \quad iff \quad level( \delta') \leq level( \delta")$$

for all digital straight segments $\delta'$ and $\delta"$.

Up to this section, we refer digital straight segment from P to Q as a segment between P and Q of a digital straight line which satisfies three Freeman's criteria or the Rosenfeld's chord property. It is clear that in the area bounded by $\delta$ and r( $\delta$ ), there are many digital arcs from P to Q without the Rosenfeld's chord property or the three Freeman's criteria. So, we redefine digital straight segment from P to Q as follows.

## General Definition of Digital Straight Line Segment.

A digital arc from P to Q is a digital straight segment if it is inside the area bounded by $\delta$ and $r(\delta)$, i.e., let $(j, y_j)$ be a pixel-center point of this digital arc, then

$$(\sum_{i=0}^{j-1} \delta_i) \;\leq\; y_j \;\leq\; (\sum_{i=0}^{j-1} \delta_i)$$

Hence a digital straight arc does not necessarily satisfy the Rosenfeld's chord property or all the three Freeman's criteria. But it lies between two bounds satisfying this chord property or these criteria. For a practical purpose, a digital arc lying between two bounds can be detected, hence it is also said to be equivalent to either the lower bound or the upper bound.

The lower bound and upper bound digital straight segments are also useful in defining convex and concave arcs.

## Definition of Convex and Concave Arcs.

Given a digital arc $\alpha$ :

(a) It is called digital convex arc if $\delta_{PQ} \leq \alpha_{PQ}$, for every P, Q in $\alpha$, where $\alpha_{PQ}$ denotes a sub-arc of $\alpha$ from P to Q, and $\delta_{PQ}$ denotes the lower bound digital straight line segment from P to Q.

(b) It is called digital concave arc if $\alpha_{PQ} \leq r(\delta_{PQ})$, for every P, Q in $\alpha$,

where $r(\delta_{PQ})$ denotes the upper bound digital straight line segment from P to Q.


## VI.   IMPLEMENTATION: NEW ALGORITHM

In this section, a new algorithm for digital straight line segments will be introduced. It is well-suited to implementation in hardware or on simple microprocessors because it avoids multiplications and divisions.

First, a new algorithm will be introduced, and then compared with the Bresenham's algorithm.

## New Algorithm.

Given two pixels with centers $P = (0, 0)$ and $Q = (c, g)$, the lower-bound digital straight segment $(\delta_0, \delta_1, ..., \delta_c)$ connecting P to Q is given by the formulas:

$a_i = |g.i|_c$ and $\delta_i = (a_i - a_{i+1} + g)/c$, for $i = 0, ..., c$.

The algorithm which is based strictly on these above formulas will require the modulo and division operators. To avoid these operators, we use the following results to produce an algorithm, requiring neither divisions nor multiplications.

(1) For $i = 0,1,...,c-1$,

$$a_i - a_{i+1} = -g \quad \text{or} \quad \text{(case 1)}$$
$$\qquad\qquad c-g. \quad \text{(case 2)}$$

(2) $a_0 = 0$,

$$a_1 = |a_0 + g|_c$$

.
.
.

$$a_{i+1} = |a_i + g|_c = \begin{array}{ll} a_i + g, & \text{if } a_i + g < c \quad \text{(case 1)} \\ \\ a_i + g - c, & \text{if } a_i + g \geq c \quad \text{(case 2)} \end{array}$$

(3) Case 1 produces Direction 0
Case 2 produces Direction 1

```
(* all variables are integer *)
a := 0;  y := 0;  x := 0;
for i := 1 to c do
   begin
     if a + g < c
       then anext := a + g
       else anext := a + g - c;
     if a-anext = -g
       then begin  write('direction0');  y := y;   end
       else begin  write('direction1');  y := y+1; end;
     a := anext;
     x := x+1;
     plot(x,y);
   end;
```

The above algorithm can also be reduced by merging two if statements and omitting the variables a and anext.

```
(* all variables are integer *)
x := 0;  y := 0;  e := c-g;
for i := 1 to c do
   begin
      if e > 0
        then e := e-g
        else begin
                e := e+c-g;
                y := y+1
             end;
      x := x+1;
      plot(x,y);
   end;
```

## Bresenham's Algorithm.

The Bresenham's algorithm constructs a digital segment of the centers to PQ in the following sense. For all centers of the same x-coordinates, the one closest to the real line PQ will be selected (see Fig. 5). To express it mathematically, we let $R = (i, y_R)$ be a point on the real line PQ, with an $i$, then $y_R/i = g/c$ or $y_R = (g/c).i$. The selected center $(i, j_0)$ is the one among the centers $\{(i, j) \mid j=0, \pm1,...\}$ and it is closest to R.

The following is the Bresenham's algorithm to construct these above closest centers.

```
(* e is real; all other variables are integer *)
x := 0;  y := 0;  e := (g/c);
for i := 1 to c do
  begin
    If e > 0.5
      then begin y := y+1; e := e-1+(g/c); end
      else e := e+(g/c);
    x := x+1;
    plot(x, y);
  end;
```

To avoid multiplications and divisions by multiplying e by 2*c, the above algorithm can be modified to be as follows:
```
(* all variables are integer including e *)
x := 0;  y := 0;  e := g+g-c;
for i := 1 to c do
  begin
    if e > 1
      then begin  y := y+1;  e := e+g+g-c+c;  end
      else  e := e+g+g;
    x := x+1;
    plot(x, y);
  end;
```

**Discussion.**

(1) The new algorithm can be interpreted as to find the highest centers under the real line segment PQ in the following sense: for all centers under PQ and of the same x-coordinates, the one with the largest y-coordinate will be selected (see Fig. 4). We express this mathematically as follows: let $R = (i,y_R)$, with an integer $i$, be a real point on the real segment PQ, then a center to be selected is

$$(i,\lfloor y_R\rfloor) \quad \text{or} \quad (i,\lfloor (g/c).i\rfloor) \tag{10}$$

These centers will form the lower-bound of all digital straight segments from P to Q. Similarly, the centers

$$(i,\lceil (g/c).i\rceil), \quad \text{for all integer } i \tag{11}$$

such that $x_P \le i \le x_Q$, will form the upper bound of all digital straight segments.

(2) In contrast with the new algorithm, the Bresenham's algorithm will select the closest centers to PQ. In other words, in every pair of the centers in (10) and (11), a closest center will be the one with a less truncation, i.e., we select $(i, \lfloor (g/c).i\rfloor)$ in the case $(g/c).i - \lfloor (g/c).i\rfloor < 0.5$, and select $(i, \lceil (g/c).i\rceil)$ otherwise.

(3) The centers in Bresenham's algorithm will also form a digital straight segment. This segment is a lower bound up to a number of shifts. The number of shifts varies

depending on the positions of P and Q (more precisely, it depends on the slope of the line connecting P to Q). These results are not proved in this paper.

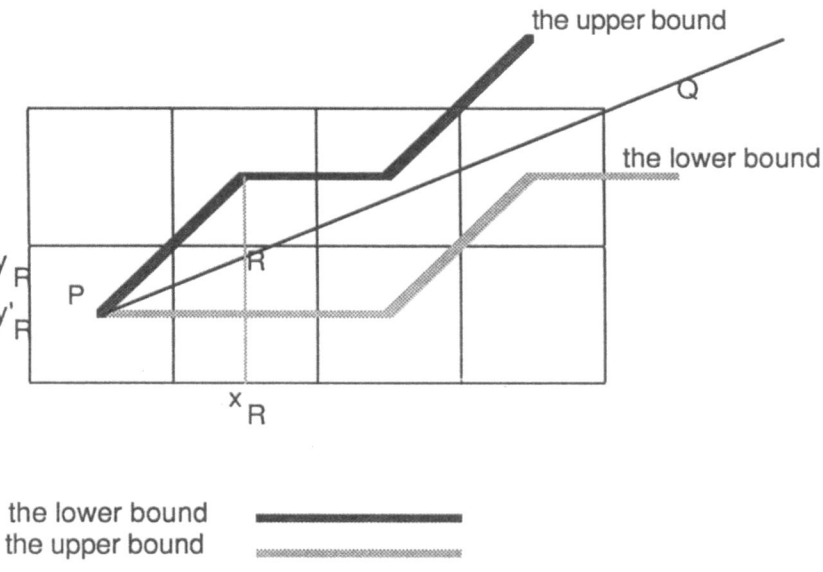

Figure 5: The Lower Bound and the Upper Bound of all Digital Straight Line Segments

## VI SUMMARY

In the paper, the area of all digital straight line segments between two given points has been reported. The boundary of the area includes the upper bound and lower bound which are proved also to be digital straight segments. All digital arcs connecting these two given points and falling in the area are called "nearly straight" digital segments. Moreover, when a digital straight line is found, the others can also be found by a number of shifts. Therefore, in order to make an unique representation of digital straight lines passing two points, we group all these straight lines together as an equivalence class. In other words, two digital straight lines are in the same class iff they are shifted from each other.

On the other hand, in order to detect digital straight arcs, we need to show that they fall in one class. Of course, such digital straight arcs might not satisfies Freeman's three criteria even though they are bounded by digital straight line segments. For example, the digital arc 0102001010020 is in the area of Fig. 4. Henceforth a correction on digital arcs "nearly straight" can be made to have "real straight" digital arcs.

## APPENDIX: FORMULAS FOR DIGITAL STRAIGHT LINES

This appendix discusses digital straight lines being represented by chain codes of directions. First it defines mathematically Freeman's three criteria, especially the third criterion ( we call it the uniformly distributed property) for characterization of digital straight lines. Then it provides and proves a simple formula to find the chain code of a straight line with given rational slope.

### Introduction.

Freeman(1970) provided a method to obtain chain codes of straight lines, and also suggested three criteria for chain codes to represent digital straight lines. The three criteria are stated as follows:

(1)  At most two basic directions are present and these can differ by unity.
(2)  One of these values always occurs singly.
(3)  Successive occurrences of the principal direction occurring singly are as uniformly spaced as possible.

The first two criteria can be easily expressed mathematically and the third one is somewhat fuzzy (Pavlidis 1977), and all these criteria need a formal proof.

### Freeman's Criteria and Uniformly Distributed Property

Some notation and definitions are needed.

*Definition 1:* A sequence $(\delta_i)$ is said to be binary on $\{x, y\}$ if $\delta_i = x$ or $\delta_i = y$ for all i, where x and y are fixed integers.

*Definition 2:* A sequence $(\delta_i)$ is said to cyclic or periodic if there is a constant integer c so that $\delta_i = \delta_j$ for all i and j with i = j mod c. The smallest value c is called the periodicity of the sequence.

*Definition 3:* A binary sequence $(\delta_i)$ on $\{x, y\}$ is equally distributed on x if the number of consecutive y's bounded by two x's is a constant k or k+1. In other words, there exists a constant k so that for all i < j such that $\delta_i = \delta_j = x$ and $\delta_m = y$ for all i < m < j: (j-i) = k or (k+1). If (j - i) = 1 then we say that direction y occurs singly.

A sequence equally distributed on y is defined similarly.

*Freeman's First Two Criteria:* Based on definitions, the first two criteria of Freeman can be expressed as follows. The sequence ( $\delta_i$) is

(1) defined on $\{x, y\}$ with abs(x-y) ≤ 1 (at most two basic directions)
(2) and equally distributed on $\{x, y\}$ with at least one direction occurring singly.

*Definition 4:* A sequence ( $\delta_i$) is called *uniformly distributed on x* if for any two segments of the sequence starting and ending with x and having the same number of x occurrunces, the lengths of two segments differ by at most one unit. Mathematically this property is described as follows: If $\delta_i \delta_{i+1}... \delta_j$ and $\delta_{i'} \delta_{i'+1}... \delta_{j'}$ are two arbitrary segments with

(1) $\delta_i = \delta_j = \delta_{i'} = \delta_{j'} = x$

(2) cardinality$\{ k \mid i < k < j$ and $\delta_k = x \}$ = cardinality$\{ k' \mid i' < k' < j'$ and $\delta_{k'} = x \}$

then abs$( (j-i) - (j'-i') ) \leq 1$.

The definition of *uniformly distributed on y* is defined similarly. For convenience, we call *uniformly distributed on both x and y* as *uniformly distributed*. It is true that if a sequence is uniformly distributed, it is also equally distributed.

*Freeman's Third Criterion:* Freeman's third criterion is the uniformly distributed property (on both x and y) with abs$(x - y) \leq 1$.

*Definition of Digital Straight Line:* A sequence $(\delta_i)$ represents a digital straight line if it satisfies the following properties:
(1) it is defined on two direction x and y with abs$(x - y) \leq 1$;
(2) it is equally distributed on both directions in which one of them occurs singly;
(3) and it is uniformly distributed.

## Formulas for Digital Straight Lines

We will state a theorem to construct the chain code of straight lines with slope g/c. We restrict the theorem only for the case $(g, c) = 1$ and $0 < g < c$. The other cases will be discussed later.

*Theorem 1.* Given a slope $(g/c)$ with $0 < g < c$ and $(g, c) = 1$. The periodic sequence $\ldots \delta_0 \delta_1 \ldots \delta_{c-1} \delta_0 \delta_1 \ldots \delta_{c-1} \ldots$ is a digital straight line where the $\delta_i$'s are calculated by the following formulas: for all integer i,

$$a_i = |g.i|_c$$
$$\delta_i = (a_i - a_{i+1} + g) / c.$$

Moreover, the sequence has only two directions 0 and 1, and there are $(c-g)$ direction 0 and g direction 1 in the period $\delta_0 \delta_1 \ldots \delta_{c-1}$.

*Note:* The formula in Theorem 1 is nearly equivalent with Equation 12 in the paper of Dorst and Smeulders (1984). The formula in Theorem 1 was based on the linearly conditions, where as the result in Dorst and Smeulders (1984) was derived from the digitization.

## Proof of Theorem 1

To prove Theorem 1, we need to prove that the periodic chain code $\delta_0 \delta_1 \ldots \delta_{c-1}$ satisfies Freeman's three criteria. In this section we assume that $0 < g < c$, i.e., the line with slope g/c is in the first octant. First, we show that the sequence has at most two basic directions 0 and 1 for Freeman's first criterion. Secondly, we show that the sequence is equally distributed on both directions and the length of 0's between two 1's is $\lfloor c/g \rfloor$ or $\lfloor c/g \rfloor -1$, and the length of 1's between two 0's is $\lfloor c/(c-g) \rfloor$ and $\lfloor c/(c-g) \rfloor - 1$. Depending on the conditions $2.g < c$ or $2.g > c$ these lengths imply that one of the two directions occurs singly. In the special case $2.g = c$, both directions occur singly, i. e., it is the sequence 01. Finally for Freeman's third criterion, we prove that the sequence is uniformly distributed.

## Freeman's First Criterion: at Most two Directions

*Proposition 1:* the values $a_i$, $i = 1, 2,...c$ are all different.

*Proof:* If $a_i = a_j$ with $i \neq j$ and $i, j \leq c$, then $|g.i|_c = |g.j|_c$. Therefore $|g.(i-j)|_c = 0$ or $c$ divides $g.(i-j)$. Since $(g, c) = 1$, therefore $c$ divides $(i-j)$. But $i \neq j$ and ($i$ and $j < c$), therefore $i = j$ which is a contradiction. $\hfill$ QED

*Proposition 2:* The following equation holds for all i: $a_i - a_{i+1} = -g$ or $(c - g)$.

*Proof:* Let $u = |g.i|_c$, then we have $u < c$ and $a_i - a_{i+1} = u - |u + g|_c$. We prove the preposition by considering all possible cases of $(u+g)$.

case 1: $\quad u + g < c$ (hence $|u + g|_c = u + g$).

$\quad\quad$ Therefore $a_i - a_{i+1} = u - (u + g) = -g$.

case 2: $\quad u + g \geq c$ (hence $|u + g|_c = c - (u + g)$).

$\quad\quad$ Therefore $a_i - a_{i+1} = u - (c - (u + g)) = c - g$. $\hfill$ QED

*Theorem 2:* The sequence $(\delta_i)$ has at most two basic directions. More precisely, $\delta_i = 0$ or 1 for all i.

*Proof:* From the definition of $\delta_i$ in Theorem 1, we have $\delta_i = (a_i - a_{i+1} + g) / c$. If $a_i - a_{i+1} = -g$ then $\delta_i = 0$. If $a_i - a_{i+1} = c - g$ then $\delta_i = 1$. $\hfill$ QED

## Freeman's Second Criterion:  Equally Distributed Property

Let $\delta_i, \delta_{i+1},..., \delta_{i+u+1}$ be a segment which has no direction 1 except for two endpoints, i.e., $\delta_i = \delta_{i+u+1} = 1$ and $\delta_{i+1} = \delta_{i+2} = ... = \delta_{i+u} = 0$ ( by the result of Theorem 2). Therefore we have the following equations:

$$\text{Equation I(1):} \quad a_i - a_{i+1} = (c - g)$$
$$\text{Equation I(2):} \quad a_{i+1} - a_{i+2} = (-g)$$

.

.

.

$$\text{Equation I(u+1):} \quad a_{i+u} - a_{i+u+1} = (-g)$$
$$\text{Equation I(u+1):} \quad a_{i+u+1} - a_{i+u+2} = (c - g)$$

The following proposition 3 will be proved and used to proved the equally distributed property of the sequence $(\delta_i)$ on direction 1. The indices i and u are fixed throughout this proposition. The idea in this proposition is to prove that u is the largest number to hold the inequality $a_{i+1} + u.g < c$ (see the pattern of Equation I(1) to I(u+2)). With this result, the upper bound and lower bound for u can be found and force u to have at most two values.

*Proposition 3:* The following inequalities hold

$\quad\quad\quad$ 3.1: $a_{i+1} < g$

$\quad\quad\quad$ 3.2: $a_{i+1} + u.g < c$

$\quad\quad\quad$ 3.3: $a_{i+1} + (u + 1).g \geq c$.

*Proof of 3.1:* We prove by a contradiction. Assume that $a_{i+1} \geq g$. Therefore Equation I(1) implies $c - g \leq a_i - g$. Hence $a_i \geq c$ which is a contradiction.

*Proof of 3.2:* Adding Equations I(2) through I(u+1), we have $a_{i+1} - a_{i+u+1} = -u.g$. Hence $a_{i+u+1} = a_{i+1} + u.g$. But $a_{i+u+1} < c$, therefore $a_{i+1} + u.g < c$.

*Proof of 3.3:* Adding Equations I(2) through I(u+2), we have $a_{i+1} - a_{i+u+2} = -u.g + (c-g)$. Hence $a_{i+u+2} = a_{i+1} + u.g - (c-g)$. But $a_{i+u+2} \geq 0$, therefore $a_{i+1} + u.g - (c-g) \geq 0$ which is the inequality 3.3. QED

*Theorem 3:* The sequence $(\delta_i)$ is equally distributed on direction 1.

Proof: By Proposition 3, we have

$$\frac{(c - a_{i+1})}{g} - 1 \leq u < \frac{(c - a_{i+1})}{g}, \quad \text{where} \quad a_{i+1} < g \tag{1}$$

To prove the number u has at most two values for all i we consider all possible cases of $(c - a_{i+1}) / g$.

Case 1: $(c - a_{i+1}) / g$ is an integer. Denote this integer k, then $c = k.g + a_{i+1}$. But $a_{i+1} < g$ by Proposition 3, hence $a_{i+1}$ is the remainder of the division c/g. Moreover, k $= \lfloor c/g \rfloor$. Hence by (1), $u = \lfloor c/g \rfloor$.

Case 2: $(c - a_{i+1}) / g$ is not an integer. Let k also be $\lfloor c/g \rfloor$. Therefore $c = k.g + r$, where r, which is less than g is the remainder of the division c/g. Substituting c $= k.g + r$ in the inequality (1), we have

$$k + \frac{(r - a_{i+1})}{g} - 1 \leq u < k + \frac{(r - a_{i+1})}{g}, \quad \text{where} \quad a_{i+1} < g$$

Of course r is not equal to $a_{i+1}$, otherwise $(c - a_{i+1}) / g$ would be an integer, which is a contradiction our assumption of this case. Therefore if $r > a_{i+1}$ then $u = k$ or if $r < a_{i+1}$ then $u = k-1$. QED

Similarly we can prove that the sequence $(\delta_i)$ is equally distributed on direction 0, and the number of 1's between two 0's is either $\lfloor c/(c-g) \rfloor$ and $\lfloor c/(c-g) \rfloor - 1$. In the following we will construct similar notations and results to prove the equally distributed property on 0.

Let $\delta_j, \delta_{j+1}, ..., \delta_{j+v+1}$ be a segment which has no direction 1 except for two endpoints, i.e., $\delta_j = \delta_{j+v+1} = 0$ and $\delta_{j+1} = \delta_{j+2} = ... = \delta_{j+v} = 2$ ( by the result of Theorem 2). Therefore we have the following equations:

| Equation J(1): | $a_j - a_{j+1} = (-g)$ |
| Equation J(2): | $a_{j+1} - a_{j+2} = (c-g)$ |

.

.

.

| Equation J(v+1): | $a_{j+v} - a_{j+v+1} = (c-g)$ |
| Equation J(v+2): | $a_{j+v+1} - a_{j+v+2} = (-g)$ |

The following proposition 4 will be proved and used to proved the equally distributed property of the sequence $(\delta_i)$ on direction 0. The indices j and v are fixed throughout this proposition. The idea in this proposition is to prove that v is the largest number to hold the inequality $a_{j+v+1} + v.(c-g) \leq c$ (see the pattern of Equation J(1) to J(v+2)). With this result, the upper bound and lower bound for v can be found and force v to have at most two values.

*Proposition 4:* The following inequalities hold
  4.1: $a_{j+v+1} < c-g$
  4.2: $a_{j+v+1} + v.(c-g) \leq c$
  4.3: $a_{j+v+1} + (v+1).(c-g) > c$.

*Proof of 4.1:* We prove by a contradiction. Assume that $a_{j+v+1} \geq g$. Therefore Equation J(v+2) implies $c - g - a_{j+v+2} \leq -g$. Hence $a_{j+v+2} \geq c$ which is a contradiction.

*Proof of 4.2:* Adding Equations J(2) through J(v+1), we have $a_{j+1} - a_{j+v+1} = v(c-g)$. Hence $a_{j+v+1} + v(c-g) = a_{j+1} < c$.

*Proof of 4.3:* Adding Equations I(1) through J(v+1), we have $a_j - a_{j+v+1} = v(c-g) - g$. Hence $a_j = a_{j+v+1} + v.(c-g) - g$. But $a_j \geq 0$, therefore $c \leq a_{j+v+1} + (v+1).(c-g)$, (by adding the number c to both sides).          QED.

*Theorem 4:* The sequence $(\delta_i)$ is equally distributed on direction 0.

*Proof:* By Proposition 4, we have

$$\frac{(c - a_{j+v+1})}{c-g} - 1 < v \leq \frac{(c - a_{j+v+1})}{c-g}, \quad \text{where} \quad a_{j+v+1} < c-g \tag{2}$$

To prove the number v has at most two values for all i we consider all possible cases of $(c - a_{j+v+1})/(c-g)$.

Case 1: $(c - a_{j+v+1})/(c-g)$ is an integer. Denote this integer k, then $c = k.(c-g + a_{j+v+1})$. But $a_{j+v+1} < c - g$ by Proposition 4, hence $a_{j+v+1}$ is the remainder of the division $c/(c-g)$. Moreover, $k = \lfloor c/(c-g) \rfloor$. Hence by (2), $v = k = \lfloor c/(c-g) \rfloor$.

Case 2: $(c - a_{j+v+1}) / (c - g)$ is not an integer. Let k also be $\lfloor c/(c-g) \rfloor$. Therefore $c = k \cdot (c-g) + r$, where r, which is less than c-g is the remainder of the division $c/(c-g)$. Substituting $c = k \cdot (c-g) + r$ in the inequality (2), we have

$$k \cdot + \frac{(r - a_{j+v+1})}{c - g} - 1 \; < \; v \; \leq \; k + \frac{(r - a_{j+v+1})}{c - g}$$

Of course r is not equal to $a_{j+v+1}$, otherwise $(c - a_{j+v+1}) / (c - g)$ would be an integer, which is a contradiction our assumption of this case. Therefore if $r > a_{j+v+1}$ then $v = k$ or if $r < a_{j+v+1}$ then $v = k-1$. QED

To summarize Theorems 3 and 4, we proved that the sequence $(\delta_i)$ is equally distributed on both directions 0 and 1. The length of 0's between two 1's ican only be $\lfloor c/g \rfloor$ or $\lfloor c/g \rfloor$ - 1, and the length of 1's between two 0's is $\lfloor c/(c-g) \rfloor$ and $\lfloor c/(c-g) \rfloor$ - 1. Now we prove the single occurrence of one of two directions.

*Theorem 5:*  If $2 \cdot g \leq c$, then direction 1 occurs singly.
If $2 \cdot g \geq c$, then direction 0 occurs singly.
If $2 \cdot g = c$, then both directions 0 and 1 occur singly.

*Proof:* We prove only the first case. The other cases can be prove similarly. Assume $2 \cdot g \leq c$. We need to prove u, constructed in Theorem 3, is not equal to 0. Indeed if $u = 0$ then either $\lfloor c/g \rfloor = 0$ or $(\lfloor c/g \rfloor - 1) = 0$. Either case will lead to a contradiction. One implies that $c < g$ and the other implies $c < 2g$. QED

## Freeman's Third Criterion: Uniformly Distributed Property

*Theorem 6:*  The sequence $(\delta_i)$ is uniformly distributed.

*Proof:* We will prove the sequence is uniformly distributed on direction 1. For direction 0, the proof is similar. Given two segments, say $\delta_i \delta_{i+1} \dots \delta_j$ and $\delta_{i'} \delta_{i'+1} \dots \delta_{j'}$ such that both segments start and end with direction 1 (i. e., $\delta_i = \delta_j = \delta_{i'} = \delta_{j'} = 1$), and they have the same number of occurrences of direction 1. We will prove that
$$(j - i) = (j' - i') \pm 1.$$
Let m be the number of 1's in each segment. By proposition 2 we have m equations of the form $a_k - a_{k+1} = (c - g)$ and (j-i)-m equations of the form $a_k - a_{k+1} = (-g)$ for the first segment. Adding all these equations except the first one, we have
$$a_{i+1} - a_{j+1} = (m - 1)(c - g) + (j - i - m)(-g).$$
Similarly for the second segment, we have
$$a_{i'+1} - a_{j'+1} = (m - 1)(c - g) + (j' - i' - m)(-g).$$
Therefore their difference between these above two equations is
$$a_{i+1} - a_{j+1} - (a_{i'+1} - a_{j'+1}) = (j - i - (j' - i'))(-g).$$
By Proposition 3.1, we have $a_{i+1} < g$, $a_{j+1} < g$, $a_{i'+1} < g$, and $a_{j'+1} < g$. Therefore, (all $a_i$'s are non negative) $(j - i) - (j' - i') = \pm 1$ or 0. QED

We have discussed digital straight lines of slopes g/c with $(g, c) = 1$ and $0 < g < c$. I. e., the digital straight lines are in the first octant. We now discuss the other cases where abs(g) > abs(c), or abs(c) > abs(g), and prove that the results for the other octants can be derived from the previous results by simple transformations.

*Theorem 7:* The digital straight line of the straight line with slope g'/c' with g' > c' > 0 and (g', c') = 1 is the periodic sequence $(\delta_0 + 1)\ (\delta_1 + 1)\ ...\ (\delta_{c-1} + 1)$, where the periodic sequence $\delta_0\ \delta_1\ ...\ \delta_{c-1}$ is the chain code of the straight line with slope g/c with g = (g' - c') and c = g'.

*Proof:* Given g' > c' > 0 and (g', c') = 1. Let g = (g' - c') and c = g', then g < c and (g, c) = 1. Therefore the chain code of the line with slope g/c can be obtained by Theorem 1. We denote this sequence as $\delta_0\ \delta_1\ ...\ \delta_{c-1}$. Moreover this sequence satisfies Freeman's three criteria, asdoes that sequence $(\delta_0 + 1)\ (\delta_1 + 1)\ ...\ (\delta_{c-1} + 1)$. To complete the proof of the theorem, we verify that the sequence $(\delta_0 + 1)\ (\delta_1 + 1)\ ...\ (\delta_{c-1} + 1)$ is the chain code of the line with slope g'/c'. Indeed, the possible directions in $\delta_0\ \delta_1\ ...\ \delta_{c-1}$ are 0 and 1, therefore the possible directions of $(\delta_0 + 1)\ (\delta_1 + 1)\ ...\ (\delta_{c-1} + 1)$ are 1 and 2. Moreover the slope of the sequence $(\delta_0 + 1)\ (\delta_1 + 1)\ ...\ (\delta_{c-1} + 1)$ is the following ratio:

$$\text{slope of \# of } (\delta_i + 1) = \frac{\text{\# of 1's in } (\delta_i + 1)\ +\ \text{\# of 2's in } (\delta_i + 1)}{\text{\# of 1's in } (\delta_i + 1)}$$

$$= \frac{\text{\# of 0's in } (\delta_i)\ +\ \text{\# of 1's in } (\delta_i)}{\text{\# of 1's in } (\delta_i + 1)}$$

$$= c/(c - g)$$

$$= g'/c' \qquad \text{QED}$$

From Theorems 1 and 7, the digital straight lines with other slopes can be generated and be proved similarly (see Recent Results for a summary of formulas of chain codes in different regions. )

**Acknowledgment:** *The author is grateful to Professors M. Barnes and R. Hogan, and H. Pham for their careful reading of the manuscript. He also wishes to thank anonymous referees for pointing out errors in the manuscript and bringing several references to his attention. Appreciation is expressed to Professor A. F. Ratcliffe, Dean of the College of Engineering and Professor J. Motil, Chairman of Department of Computer Science for their support. He would also like to acknowledge the help of Sally Gamon in preparing this paper.*

## REFERENCES

Arcelli, C. and Massarotti, "Regular Arcs in Digital Contours," Computer Graphics Images Processing, Vol. 4, 1975, pp. 339-360; Erratum, Vol. 5, 1976, p. 280.

Arcelli, C. and L. Cordella, "Concavity Point Detection by Iterative Arrays," Computer Graphics Image Processing, Vol. 3, 1974, pp. 34-47.

Bongiovanni, F. Luccio and A. Zorat, "The Discrete Equation of the Straight Line," IEEE Trans. on Computers, Vol. C-24, 1975, pp. 310-313.

Bresenham, J. E., "Algorithm for Computer Control of a Digital Plotter," IBM Systems J., Vol. 4, 1965, pp. 25-30.

Brons, R., "Linguistic Methods for the Description of a Straight Line on a Grid," Computer Graphics Image Processing, Vol. 3, 1974, pp. 48-62.

Chang, S. K., "Picture Processing Grammar and its Applications," Information Science, Vol. 3, 1971, pp. 121-148.

Dorst Leo and Smeulders A. W. M., "Descrete Representation of Straight Lines," IEEE Transactions on Pattern Analysis and Machine Intelligence, Vol. PAMI-6, No. 4 July 1984, pp. 450-463.

Foley, J. D. and A. Van Dam, "Fundamentals of Interactive Computer Graphics," Addison-Wesley Publishing Company, 1982.

Freeman, H., "Techniques for the Digital Computer Analysis of Chain-encoded Arbitrary Plane Curves," Proceeding Natl. Elect. Conf., Vol. 17, 1961, pp. 421-432.

Freeman, H., "A Technique for the Classification and Recognition of Geometric Patterns," Proc. 3rd Intl. Congress on Cybernetics, Namur, Belgium, 1961, pp. 348-368.

Freeman, H., "On the Encoding of Arbitrary Geometric Configurations," IRE Trans. Elect. Comput., Vol. EC-10, 1961, pp. 260-268.

Freeman, H., "Boundary Encoding and Processing," Picture Processing and Psychopictorics, B. S. Lipkin and A. Rosenfeld, Eds., Academic Press, New York, 1970, pp. 241-266.

Freeman, H., "Computer Processing of Line-Drawing Image," Computing Surveys, Vol. 6, 1974, pp. 57-97.

Freeman, H., "On the Digital Computer Classification of Geometric Line Patterns," Proc. Natl. Electron. Conf., Vol. 18, pp. 312-324.

Freeman, H., "A Scheme for the Efficient Encoding of Graphical Data for Communication and Information Processing," Proc. 16th Intl. Congress on Electronics, Rome, 1969, pp. 341-348.

Greanias, E. C., et al., "The Recognition of Handwritten Numerals by Contour Analysis," IBM J. Res. Dev., Vol. 7, Jan. 1963, pp. 14-21.

Hansen, B. J., "Recognizing Convex Blobs by Computer," M. S. Thesis, School of Engineering, University of California, Irvine, 1969.

Hodes, L., "Discrete Approximation of Continuous Convex Blobs," SIAM J. Appl. Math., Vol. 19, 1970, pp. 477-485.

Hung S. H. Y. and Kasrand T., "On the Chord Property and Its Equivalences," Proc. 7th ICPR, July 30-Aug.21 1984 Montreal pp. 116-119.

Hung, S. H. Y., "On the Straightness of Digital Arcs," IEEE Trans.on Pattern Analysis and Machine Intelligence, Vol.PAMI-7, No. 2, March, 1985, pp. 203-215.

Kim, C. E., and A. Rosenfeld, "Digital Straight Lines and Convexity of Digital Regions," IEEE Trans. on Pattern Analysis and Machine Intelligence, Vol. PAMI-4, 1982, pp.149-153.

Kim, C. E. "On Cellular Straight Line Segments," Computer Graphics Image Processing, Vol. 18, 1982, pp. 369-381.

Montanari, G. U., "A Note on Minimal Length Polygonal Approximation to a Digitized Contour," Comm. Asso. Comput. Machinery, Vol. 13, 1970, pp. 41-47.

Montanari, G. U., "On Limit Properties in Digitization Schemes," J. Asso. Comput. Machinery, Vol. 17, 1970, pp. 348-360.

Morse, S., "A Mathematical Model for the Analysis of Contour-Line Data," J. ACM, Vol. 15, 1968, pp. 205-220.

Pavlidis, T., "Structural Pattern Recognition," New York: Springer-Verlag, 1977.

Pitterway, M. L. V., "Algorithm for Drawing Ellipses or Hyperbolae with a Digital Plotter," Computer J., Vol. 10, 1967, pp. 282-288.

Pfaltz, J. L. and A. Rosenfeld, "Computer Representation of Planar Regions by their Skeletons," Comm. Asso. Comput. Machinery, Vol. 10, 1967, pp. 119-125.

Ramer, U., "An Interative Procedure for the Polygonal Approximation of Plane Curves," Computer Graphics Image Processing, Vol. 1, 1972, pp. 244-456.

Reggiori, "Digital Computer Transformation for Irregular Line Drawings," Technical Report 403-22, New York University, 1972.

Rosenfeld, A., "Digital Straight Line Segments," IEEE Trans. on Computers, Vol. C-23, 1974, pp. 1264-1269.

Rosenfeld, A., "Picture Processing by Computer," N. Y. Academic Press, 1969.

Rosenfeld, A., "Connectivity in Digital Pictures," J. Asso. Comput. Machinery, Vol. 17, Jan. 1970, pp. 146-160.

Rosenfeld, A., "Arcs and Curves in Digital Pictures," J. Asso. Comput. Machinery, Vol. 20, 1973, pp. 81-87.

Rosenfeld, A. and J. L. Pfaltz, "Sequential Operations in Digital Picture Processing," J. ACM, Vol. 13, Oct. 1966, pp. 471-494.

Rosenfeld, A., "Distance Functions on Digital Pictures," Pattern Recognition, Vol. 1, 1968, pp. 33-61.

Rothstein and C. Weiman, "Parallel and Sequential Specification of a Context Sensitive Language for Straight Line Grids," Computer Graphics Image Processing, Vol. 5, 1976, pp. 106-124.

Rutovitz, D., "An Algorithm for In-line Generation of a Convex Cover," Computer Graphics Image Processing, Vol. 4, 1975, pp. 74-78.

Shaw, A. C., "Parsing of Graph-Representable Pictures," J. ACM, Vol. 17, No. 3, 1970, pp. 453-481.

Sklansky, J., "Measuring Concavity on a Rectangular Mossiac," School of Engineering, Univ. of California, Irvine, Technical Report TP-71-4, Sept. 1971.

Sklansky, J., "Recognition of Convex Blobs," Pattern Recognition, Vol. 2, Jan. 1970, pp. 3-10.

Sklansky, J., R. L. Chazin and B. J. Hansen, "Minimum-Perimeter Polygons of Digitized Silhouettes," IEEE Trans. Comput., Vol. C-21, March 1972, pp. 260-268.

Swain, P. H. and K. S. Fu, "Stochastic Programmed Grammars for Syntactic Pattern Recognition," Pattern Recognition, Vol. 4, No. 1, 1972, pp. 83-101.

Symons, M., "New Self-Organizing Pattern Recognition System," IEE, London, Eng., July 1968, pp. 11-20.

Yaglom, I. M. and V. G. Boltyanski, Convex Figures, New York, Holt, Rhinehart and Winston, 1961.

Wu, L. D., "On the Chain Code of a Line," IEEE Trans. on Pattern Analysis and Machine Intelligence, Vol. PAM I-4, No. 3, May 1982, pp. 347-353.

Chapter 2
# Rendering

# Soft Objects

Geoff Wyvill[1], Craig McPheeters[2] and Brian Wyvill[2]

[1] Department of Computer Science, University of Otago, Box 56, Dunedin, New Zealand
[2] Department of Computer Science, University of Calgary, 2500 University Drive,
 N.W. Calgary, Alberta, Canada

ABSTRACT

We introduce the concept of soft objects whose shapes change in
response to their surroundings. Established geometric modelling techniques exist to handle most engineering components, including 'free
form' shapes such as car bodies and telephones. More recently, there
has been a lot of interest in modelling natural phenomena such as
smoke, clouds, mountains and coastlines where the shapes are described
stochastically, or as fractals.

None of these techniques lends itself to the description of soft objects. This class of objects includes fabrics, cushions, living
forms, mud and water. In this paper, we describe a method of modelling
such objects and discuss its uses in animation.

Our method is to represent a soft object, or collection of objects, as
a surface of constant value in a scalar field over three dimensions.
The main technical problem is to avoid calculating the field value at
too many points. We do this with a combination of data structures at
some cost in internal memory usage.

Key words: soft objects, geometric modelling, computer animation.

INTRODUCTION

The Graphicsland project group (Wyvill, B. 1985a) at the University of
Calgary has developed an organised collection of software tools for
producing animations from models in three dimensions. The system allows the combination of several different kinds of modelling primitive
(Wyvill et al 1985b). Thus polygon based models can be mixed freely
with fractals (Mandelbrot 1983, Fournier 1982) and particles (Reeve
1983) in a scene. Motions and camera paths can be described, and animations generated. Note that we do not include the use of a two dimensional 'paint' system. Our objective is always to construct views
of a full three dimensional model.

An important class of objects in the everyday world is soft. That is,
the shape of the object varies constantly because of the forces imposed on it by its surroundings. A bouncing ball is a simple example:
as it strikes the ground, it flattens. The smoothly covered joints of
animals change shape with seamless continuity, and liquids mould themselves to their surroundings and even break into separate droplets.
Even apparently rigid objects deform in some cicumstances. Trees, for
example, bend in the wind.

To date, there seems to have been few attempts to model __soft__ objects
for computer graphics. Possibly, this is because __soft__ objects are less
important in engineering. But it is also true that much effort in
computer graphics has been directed to producing still pictures and
you cannot tell that an object is __soft__ until it moves. Clouds (Gardner
1985) and particles (Reeve 1983) come close, but there is nothing in
either of these papers which deals with the interaction of particles
with surrounding objects.

We have been experimenting with a general model for __soft__ objects which
represents an object or collection of objects by a scalar field. That
is a mathematical function defined over a volume of space. The object
is considered to occupy the space over which the function has a value
greater than some threshold so the surface of the object is an iso-
surface of the field function. That is a surface of constant function
value within the space considered.

This is not a new idea. The technique is described by James Blinn
(1982), and used to create models of molecules. He also suggests other
applications and describes a direct rendering technique using an
elegant set of sorted lists. Ken Perlin (1985) has used a modification
of Blinn's method to represent 'stochastic' shapes. We, however, are
interested in simpler shapes which we can __move convincingly.__

By suitable choice of field function, we can represent a wide variety
of shapes conveniently and, in principle, any shape somehow. For this
paper we concentrate on simple functions based on proximity to given
data points. We achieve animation by specifying the motions of these
key points, without otherwise altering our function.

Strictly speaking, the word 'field' refers to a particular set of
values distributed across space at some time. Thus the value of
'field' at some point $\langle x,y,z \rangle$ is found by evaluating the function
$f(x,y,z)$. In what follows we use the words 'function' and 'field' more
or less interchangeably.

In this paper we describe our choice of function and the data structures which enable us to construct the surface quickly. In the near
future we will also report on the techniques for moving the key points
for some simple models.


SPACE FUNCTION OR FIELD


We want to construct a function which will enable us to represent arbitrary shapes when we plot the iso-surfaces. The function is therefore going to depend on a set of given key points. We assume that the
key points are independent. That is, we treat them like particles in a
cloud. They are all alike and the field value at a point in space
depends only on the proximity of key points. (These assumptions are
arbitrary. One can easily imagine a function of key points which includes some knowledge about relations between points. The points could
be ordered, for example, and a function value calculated by interpolation between adjacent point values.)

For our models we want the field to be continuous. For some models, we
may use hundreds, thousands or even tens of thousands of key points.
So it is important that we do not have to inspect every key point
whenever we wish to calculate a field value. Therefore we use a function which is not influenced by any point beyond a certain distance
away. This distance is known as the radius of influence, R. Again, ar-

bitrarily, we make the field value due to several nearby points equal to the sum of the values due to each point. This is the very simplest way to combine the effect of many points and it seems to work well enough.

By definition, the contribution to the field made by any key point beyond its radius of influence, R, is zero. The contribution at the position of the point itself will be some maximum value (we use 1.0) and we would like to arrange that the field drops smoothly to zero at R. If we express this contribution to the field as a function C of r, the distance from the key point, these requirements can be expressed in terms of the values of the function at the point, r=0.0, and at the radius of influence r=R.

$$C(0.0) = 1.0 \qquad C'(0.0) = 0.0$$
$$C(R) = 0.0 \qquad C'(R) = 0.0 \qquad\qquad [1]$$

where C' is the derivative of C with respect to r. These conditions are sufficient to define a unique cubic function for C:

$$C(r) = \frac{2r^3}{R^3} - 3\frac{r^2}{R^2} + 1 \qquad\qquad [2]$$

The field at any point <x,y,z> is then the sum of C(r) calculated for each key point within R. This field function turns out to be quite satisfactory but a little slow because calculation of r requires a square root. We eliminate the need for this by using a cubic in r squared and adjusting the coefficients to make it approximate the original function C. A cubic in r squared is guaranteed to have C'(0.0)=0.0, so we can add another condition: C(r)=f, for some chosen values r,f. We use r=R/2 and f=0.5 and this is close enough to the original function to make no difference in practice. Our field function is thus:

$$C(r) = a\frac{r^6}{R^6} + b\frac{r^4}{R^4} + c\frac{r^2}{R^2} + 1 \qquad\qquad [3]$$

where the values of a,b,c are found by solving equations [1] together with the condition c(R/2)=0.5. Approximately:

$$a = -0.444444$$
$$b = 1.888889$$
$$c = -2.444444 \qquad\qquad [4]$$

This function is shown graphically in Fig. 1.

Blinn (1982) used an exponential function for his field based on the known field of electron density around an atom. Our function is similarly shaped and has the desirable property of dropping to zero at the radius of influence, R. It is also very cheap to calculate, needing only three additions and five multiplications.

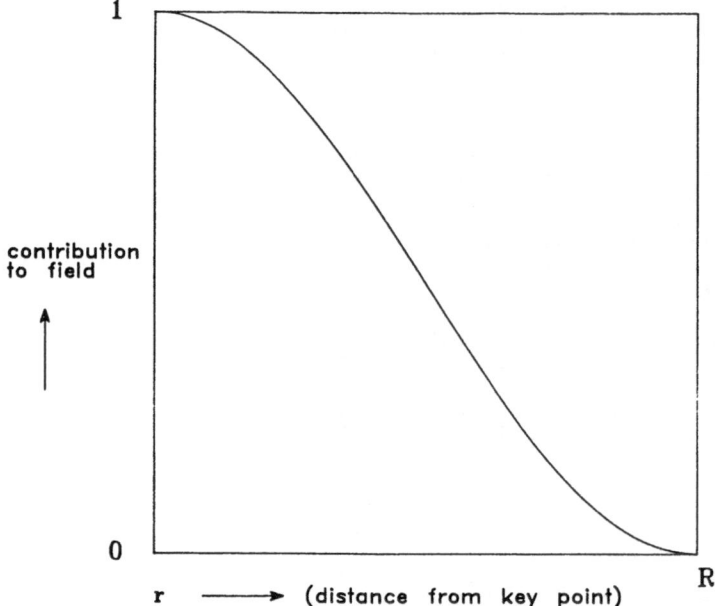

Fig. 1: Field Contribution as a function of radius.

## DEFINING THE ISO-SURFACE

Having established a definition of the field, we must choose a field value for the iso-surface. Clearly the field due to a single key point will be symmetrical about the point and any iso-surface in that field will be a sphere. Suppose we choose a function value, <u>magic</u>, and plot the iso-surface connecting all points whose field value equals <u>magic</u>. Now consider the field due to two key points in the same place. It is still symmetrical and an iso-surface for value <u>magic</u> in this field will be a sphere of larger radius than the iso-surface in the field due to one point. We have chosen <u>magic</u> so that this larger sphere has exactly twice the volume of the other.

This choice is intended to suit the modelling of liquids, to provide a reasonable effect when two droplets merge. Other choices are possible as are other functions for the field. Finding functions appropriate to particular applications is a research project in its own right. For our purposes, the above is used throughout.

## PRODUCING THE SURFACE

The surface defined in this way, by a collection of data points, is very general. It is not even necessarily connected and in order to make a picture, we first convert it to a more tractable form. We have chosen to use a simple polygon mesh for this purpose.

We construct the mesh in two distinct stages. Imagine that the part of space occupied by the surface is divided by a three dimensional grid into small cubes. First we find all the cubes which are intersected by the surface and then we construct the polygons in each cube.

To find the cubes intersected by the surface without scanning the whole of a large three dimensional grid, we take advantage of the knowledge that all our key points are enclosed by some part of the surface. For each key point, starting at the nearest grid point, we calculate the field at a succession of adjacent grid points along one axis until we encounter a point whose field value is less than magic. This point and the previous one form the endpoints of one edge of a cube which is intersected by the surface. This process gives us a set of 'seed' cubes such that every disconnected component of the surface intersects at least one seed cube.

Each seed cube shares faces with six neighbours. Starting at the seed cubes, we examine each cube's neighbours to see whether or not it is intersected by the surface. If a neighbour is intersected then we look at its neighbours and so on until all of the cubes intersected by the surface have been found. This completes the first stage.

In the second stage, we have only to deal with cubes which are intersected by the surface. For each cube we have eight values which are the field values at its vertices. From these we construct a set of polygons which are part of the iso-surface. The previous stage has sorted out all the cubes intersected by the surface, so when we put these polygons together we have a representation of the surface.

To complete the description we must explain the data structure used in the first stage and the logic used in the second.


Data Structure

There are two distinct problems, each handled by a structure using a hash table.

The first problem is to be able to calculate the field value at any point efficiently. This means that we must avoid inspecting key points which are too far away to affect the result. We do this by dividing our space into cubes, and sorting the key points according to which cubes they occupy. We only need to look at key points which occupy cubes which are close to the point where we are finding the field. The data structure for this is shown in Fig. 2.

The key points are represented by a linked list of triples of floating point values, $\langle x,y,z \rangle$. These are grouped spatially into cubes of side R, where R is the radius of influence (defined above). All the triples in such a list belong to one group. These 'large' cubes are used only for finding the field value. They are not the same as the cubes used later to construct the polygons.

The group is represented by a pointer to such a list and a triple $\langle l,m,n \rangle$, where $\langle l*R, m*R, n*R \rangle$ represents the 'low' vertex of a cube of side R, containing one or more key points. The 'low' vertex is the bottom-south-west corner, or, more formally, the vertex of least $\langle x,y,z \rangle$. The groups are also elements of a linked list.

Key points are accessed via a hash table. A hash address is calculated from the $\langle l,m,n \rangle$ triple. This is used as an index in the table. The table entry contains a pointer to a linked list of groups. To access

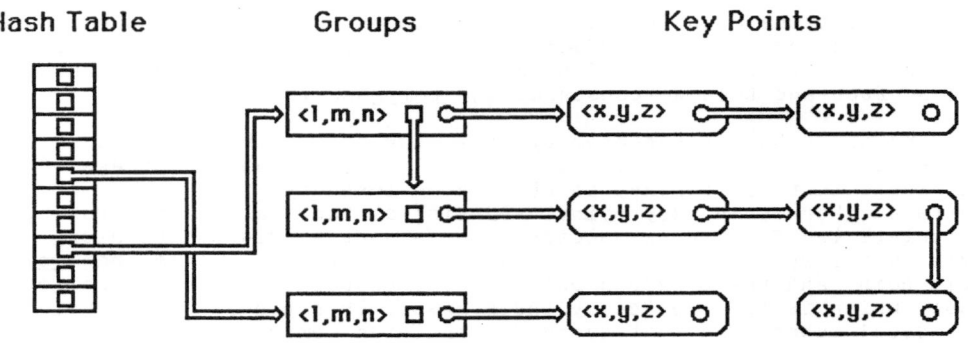

Fig. 2: Data structure for efficient access to key points.

all the key points in a given group, we first find the list of groups
from the hash table. Then search down the list of groups until we find
one which matches our starting values of <l,m,n>. This group contains
the pointer to the appropriate list of key points.

Any cube in space has twenty six neighbouring cubes. To find the field
value at <x,y,z>, we must examine every key point within a distance R
of <x,y,z>. These points must lie within the same cube as <x,y,z> or
in one of its neighbours. Using this hash table and linked structure
we can quickly check the twenty seven possible groups and thus calculate the field without inspecting every key point.

In doing this, we are inspecting all the key points within a volume of
space:

$$V = 27 R^3 \qquad\qquad [5]$$

but all the points we are interested in lie in a sphere of radius R
and volume:

$$W = \frac{4}{3} \pi R^3 \qquad\qquad [6]$$

By making our groups represent smaller cubes, and searching a larger
collection of 'neighbours' we can find the field by inspecting fewer
points. But when the number of points in each group is small, this is
wasteful because of the time taken to search more neighbouring cubes.
The maximum possible saving is a factor of seven and the extra work
for searching more cubes goes up rapidly. In our models, the key
points are not crowded within the radius of influence and the field at
any point usually depends on less than thirty key points. Our simple
strategy is thus justified.

Our second problem is to avoid recalculating field values as we find
the little cubes which intersect the surface. This is done with a
second hash table, Fig. 3. We are only interested in calculating the
field at grid points which are the vertices of our little cubes. It is
convenient, therefore, to represent these points by integers i,j,k

## Hash Table    Vertex Quintuples

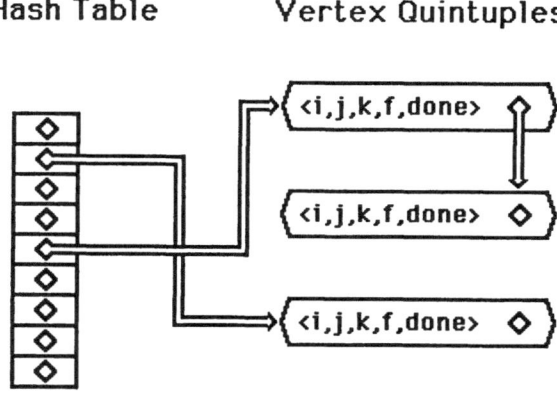

Fig. 3: Data structure for cube vertices.

where i*d,j*d,k*d are the actual co-ordinates of the point and d is the grid spacing. Each vertex is represented by a quintuple <i,j,k,f,done> and these are linked in a list for access through the hash table. 'f' is the field value for the vertex and the meaning of 'done' is explained below.

To access the quintuple representing a given vertex, a hash code is calculated from its i,j,k values. This is used as an index in the table and the table entry contains a pointer to a linked list of vertices. This list must be searched to find the particular vertex. When a vertex is referred to for the first time, the search fails. In this case the field value, f, is calculated and a new vertex is linked into the list. Each vertex is shared by as many as eight cubes but its field value need be calculated only once. Subsequent references will find it stored in the structure.

To trace all the cubes intersected by the iso-surface, it is necessary to mark those cubes which have already been processed. For this purpose, each vertex is also considered to represent the cube of which it is the 'low' vertex. The flag 'done' within the vertex is made TRUE to indicate that this cube has been dealt with.

The algorithm for finding all cubes on the surface from a seed cube can now be described. Observe the numbering of the cube vertices in Fig. 4. The low vertex of the cube is numbered 0 and this is the vertex <i,j,k>. Consider the four vertices 0,4,6,2. These are shared by the cube <i-1,j,k>. If the field values of these vertices are all greater than the iso-surface value or if they are all less, then the surface does not pass through the face 0,4,6,2. If some of the values are greater and some less than the iso-surface value, the surface does pass through the face and the cube <i-1,j,k> must be processed if this has not already been done. To process a cube, first its 'done' flag is made TRUE and then a pointer to the low vertex of the cube is entered in a queue. More precisely:

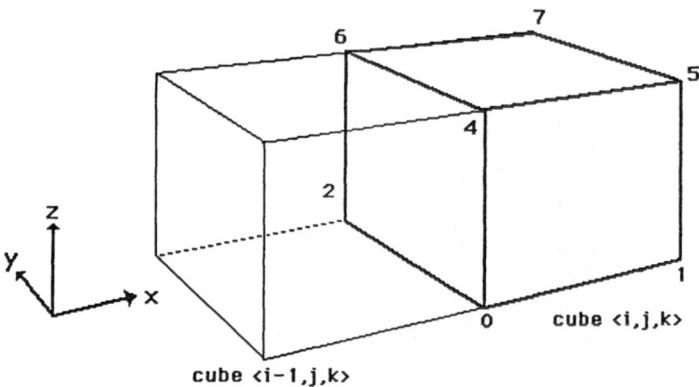

Fig. 4: Neighbouring cubes.

```
begin Set seed cube's done flag to true.
   Add seed cube to the queue.
   while queue is not empty do
      begin Remove one cube from the queue.
         for each face of cube do
            begin if surface intersects face then
               begin select neighbour cube for that face.
               if neighbour's done flag is not true then
                  begin Set neighbour's done flag to true.
                  Add neighbour to queue.
                  end
            end
         end
      Pass vertices and values for cube to second stage.
      end
end
```

The Hash Functions

Most of the space is empty. That is to say that the cubes which intersect our soft object's surface represent a small fraction of the total. Similarly, the group cubes of side R which contain key points
are few compared with the number of such cubes in the region of space
we are dealing with. If this were not so, we would find no advantage
in using a hash table. We would simply store points in an array. So
our hash function must have an even distribution for points which are
geometrically close together. In both of our tables, the hash function
maps a triplet to an address. For a table of size l*m*n we map <i,j,k>
to:
(rem(i,l)*m+rem(j,m))*n+rem(k,n)
where rem(x,y) is the remainder when x is divided by y. We use
l=m=n=16 and the function is calculated quickly by logical operations.
A more sophisticated function might be appropriate for some applications but we have found no reason to change it.

The Second Stage: Generating the Polygons

In this part of the process, we are given the field values at the vertices of a cube in the mesh and we must construct polygons which represent the part of the iso-surface which intersects that cube.

Firstly we find points which approximate the intersection of the iso-surface with the edges of the cube. Then we connect these to make the polygons. To avoid ambiguity we refer to these points as 'intersections'. The word 'vertex' is reserved for vertices of the cube. A vertex whose function value is greater than magic, we call hot, and a vertex whose function value is less than or equal to magic we call cold. Vertices whose field value is exactly magic, present minor complications. (We have to take special action to avoid generating polygons of zero size.)

Suppose two adjacent vertices p,q have field values $f_p, f_q$. If q is hot and p is cold, then:

$$\frac{magic - f_p}{f_q - f_p} \qquad\qquad [7]$$

is taken as the distance from p to the intersection of the iso-surface with pq. Although this 'linear interpolation' is not the true intersection, it is much cheaper to calculate and, provided the cubes are small enough that the polygonal approximation to the surface is reasonable, it is good enough. Note that this calculation is consistent across adjacent cubes which share edges.

The process by which we connect these points is fairly complex, so we start with an example. Figure 5(A) shows a cube with only one hot vertex. Clearly the intersecting iso-surface is approximated by a single triangle. In Fig. 5(B), there are two adjacent hot vertices and we have a quadrilateral. In Fig. 5(C), there are two non-adjacent hot vertices and the polygon is a hexagon which encloses both of them. Why do we choose this hexagon rather than two triangles, Fig. 5(D)? In effect, we are electing to link the two hot vertices and separate the two cold ones. Whether to link the hot or cold vertices in this case is decided by examining the values of the field. The value at the centre of the face is approximately the mean of the four vertex values. If this value is greater than magic we link the hot vertices.

Each intersection is uniquely associated with one edge of the cube. So we can label an intersection by the pair of vertices <p,q> between which it lies. The possible configurations of one face of the cube are shown in Fig. 6. When the number of hot vertices in this face is four or zero, no polygon edges are created: cases A,B. When the number of hot vertices is one or three, a single edge is created: cases C,D. For two hot vertices we have case E: create one edge; case F: create two edges linking hot vertices; and case G: create two edges linking cold vertices. These created polygon edges are represented by ordered pairs of intersections. That is pairs of vertex pairs. In the diagram, the order is indicated by the arrows.

These polygon edges are stored in an array, indexed by the first intersection. The second intersection is always the same as the first intersection of some other edge, so we can form a polygon by tracing the natural successors of each edge until we return to the edge we started at.

The algorithm follows:

```
for each edge of cube, <p,q> do
    if p is hot and q is hot or p is cold and q is hot
    then create intersection <p,q>;
```

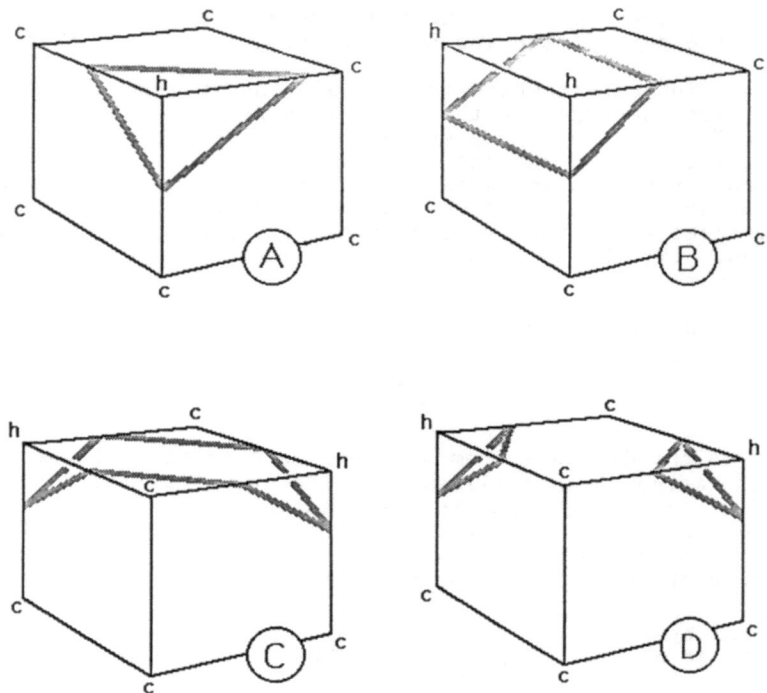

Fig. 5: Cubes with one and two hot vertices.

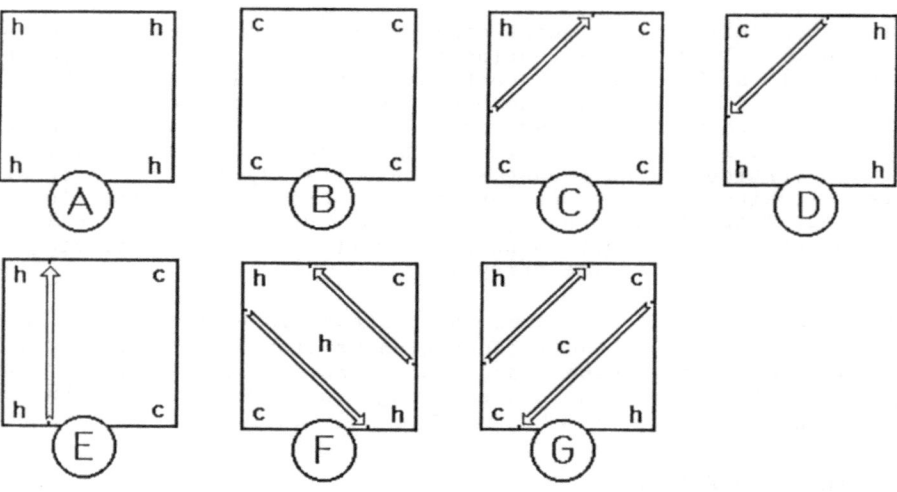

Fig. 6: The seven different cases for connecting intersections.

```
          for each face of cube do create edges according to Fig. 6;
          while edges remain do
             begin start:=any edge; polygon:={start};
                   remove start from edge array;
                   next:=successor of start;
                   while next <> start do
                      begin polygon := polygon + {next};
                            remove next from edge array;
                      end;
                   output polygon
       end
```

The polygons are not, in general, planar. So we divide them into triangles by connecting each intersection to a centroid as follows:

Given an ordered set of points (polygon vertices):

$$p_i = \langle x_i, y_i, z_i \rangle, \; 0 < i < n \qquad [8]$$

the centroid is:

$$C = \langle \frac{1}{n}\sum_{i=0}^{n-1} x_i, \frac{1}{n}\sum_{i=0}^{n-1} y_i, \frac{1}{n}\sum_{i=0}^{n-1} z_i \rangle \qquad [9]$$

For n>3 we can divide the polygon into triangles:

$$\langle p_{i-1}, p_i, C \rangle, \; 0 < i \leqslant n-1$$

and
$$\langle p_{n-1}, p_0, C \rangle \qquad [10]$$

This method of triangulation doesn't work for polygons in general, but it seems to be alright for polygons generated by this algorithm.


ANIMATING THE OBJECTS


The shape of a _soft_ object is entirely determined by the positions of the key points. So we describe its motion and shape changes by moving key points only. A general principle we have adopted for natural animation is to use a physical simulation rather than interpolate between key frames. Traditional fairing techniques can be viewed as an attempt to do this without performing the calculation needed for simulation. In this paper we describe only a few examples.


EXAMPLES OF APPLICATION


Figure 7 shows two droplets merging in stages. This is quite pleasing in animation. The droplets are modelled by single key points with R=2.0. The distance, r, between the two key points is shown for each stage.

Figures 8 to 10 are frames from an animation of a _soft_ object sliding down steps. The object is roughly shaped as the letters of _Soft_ and these distort smoothly as they slide down.

Figures 11 and 12 show the letters of _Soft_ rising from a trough of bubbling _soft_ material. The background in Fig. 11 features fractal mountains and rolling hills. These are part of the solid scene and show how the _soft_ objects have been incorporated into the _Graphicsland_ system.

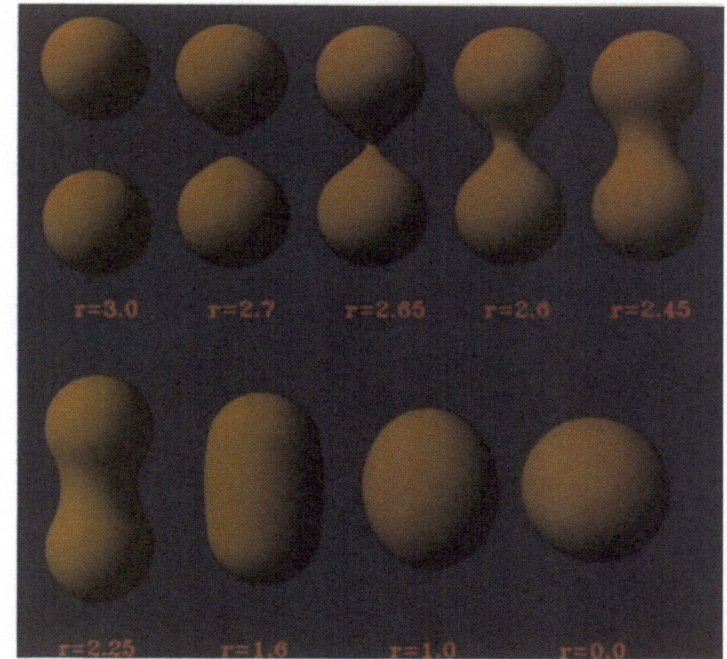

Fig. 7.

Fig. 8.

Fig. 9.

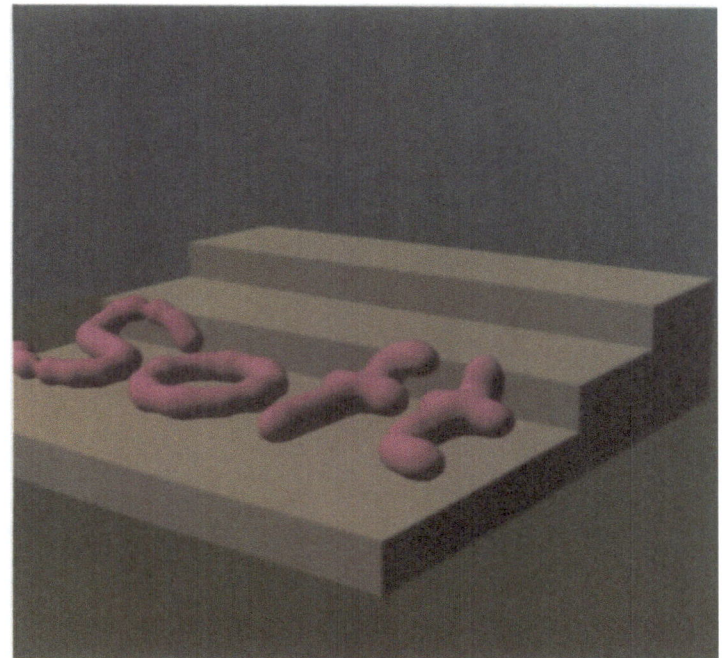

Fig. 10.

Fig. 11.

Fig. 12.

# DISCUSSION

Our modelling technique has proved to be a convenient tool in computer animation. So far, we have concentrated on one very simple method of making our field functions and there are many other possibilities which are worthy of investigation. The field can be generated by arbitrary functions permitting the modelling of mathematical surfaces. Our field function can be modified by extra terms which are not related to the key points. This can be used to make objects deform in special ways. For example, if we add a surface held to a negative field value, objects can be made to vanish bit by bit as they approach the surface, and to reappear on the other side. If we make a 'hole' in the surface, an object approaching the hole appears to squeeze through it.

We have represented our surfaces by polygon patches. This is because the Graphicsland system already offered us versatile display tools for this kind of model. It would clearly be a good idea to use bicubic or conic patches instead and we are planning some experiments to do this. We have not followed Blinn's technique (1982) of rendering the surface directly, because we wanted to produce objects which we could easily incorporate into Graphicsland. Also, our models can contain a very large number of key points and most of them are not near to any surface. This is particularly true of models of liquids. The polygon generating algorithm is particularly efficient in this case because the 'hidden' key points do not have to be known to the rendering algorithm.

We are, however, experimenting with a ray-tracer which renders the field directly. In this case, we use our surface following algorithm to construct a boundary of cubes which contains the iso-surface.

Even when we have a superior rendering technique for these surfaces, an efficient generator of polygon patches will be useful. Graphicsland does not yet offer interactive graphical development of animations, because it takes too long to render the scenes. We are introducing a new feature to produce very fast rendering of scenes at greatly reduced quality. For this purpose we expect to continue to need a polygonal representation.

Our soft objects are reasonably quickly generated. The letters and contents of the trough in Fig. 11 took about eight minutes per frame on a VAX11/780 computer to generate the polygons. This is much less than the rendering time for 512 by 512 pixels using a z-buffer algorithm.

# ACKNOWLEDGEMENTS

The JADE project at the University of Calgary has been particularly supportive. This work and Jade is supported by the Natural Science and Engineering Research Council of Canada.

## REFERENCES

Blinn J (1982) "A Generalization of Algebraic Surface Drawing"
ACM Transactions on Graphics, 1, 235.

Fournier A, Fussel D, and Carpenter L, (June 1982) "Computer Rendering
of Stochastic Models" CACM, 25, 6, 371-384.

Gardner, G (July 1985) "Visual Simulation of Clouds" SIGGRAPH 85,
Computer Graphics, 19 (3) 297-303.

Mandelbrot B (1983) "The Fractal Geometry of Nature" W.H. Freeman and
Company. (First Edition 1977).

Perlin K (July 1985) "An Image Synthesizer" SIGGRAPH 85,
Computer Graphics 19 (3) 287-296.

Reeves W (April 1983) "Particle Systems - A Technique for Modeling a
Class of Fuzzy Objects" ACM Transactions on Graphics, 2, 91-108.

Wyvill BLM, McPheeters C and Garbutt R (July 1985a) "A Practical 3D
Computer Animation System" The BKSTS Journal (British Kinematograph
Sound and Television Society), 67 (6) 328-332.

Wyvill BLM, McPheeters C and Novacek M (July 1985b) "Specifying
Stochastic Objects in a Hierarchical Graphics System" Proc. Graphics
Interface 85, Montreal.

Geoff Wyvill graduated in physics from Jesus College
Oxford and started working with computers as a
research technologist with the British Petroleum
Company.  He gained MSc and PhD degrees in computer
science from the University of Bradford where he
lectured in computer science from 1969 until 1978.
He is currently senior lecturer in computer science
at the University of Otago and has been working
at the University of Calgary, as Visiting Professor,
while on sabbatical leave.  He is on the editorial
board of The Visual Computer.

# The Simulation of Natural Features Using Cone Tracing

David B. Kirk

Raster Technologies, Inc., 2 Robbins Road, Westford, MA 01886, USA

ABSTRACT

The method of ray tracing with cones is used to area sample objects for properly filtered rendering. Methods for generating anti-aliased reflections and refractions distorted by normal vector perturbation (bump-mapping) are developed to simulate the appearance of rippled water surfaces. The sampling aperture of the cones is distorted to anti-alias the reflections and refractions properly. A calculated texture function is used as a diffusion map for transparent surfaces to simulate the visual effect of diffuse, soft-shadowed cloud layers.

General Terms: Algorithms

Additional Keywords and Phrases: texture-mapping, anti-aliasing, ray tracing, cone tracing, image synthesis

## INTRODUCTION

Ray tracing is an elegant, although computationally intensive, approach to realistic image generation. Optical features such as shadows, reflections, refractions, and lighting may be modeled in an integrated fashion, yielding images of perhaps higher quality than any other method. The major drawback to ray tracing is the tremendous amounts of time required to render complicated scenes, either of many objects, or of complex primitives.

The actual shading and lighting calculations take up a relatively small amount of the computation time, often as little as 5 percent (Whitted 1980). The bulk of computational time is consumed by calculations of ray/object intersections. To properly filter the image, one must supersample, which increases the number of intersection calculations as the number of source (eye-origin) rays increases. Even with clever adaptive supersampling, the solution to the anti-aliasing problem is a lot of CPU time. As has been shown by Kajiya (1983), the number of intersection calculations is proportional to the product of the number of rays and the number of objects. The use of a spatially enumerated data structure, such as octrees, or a grid of 'voxels', can reduce the number of intersection calculations, by allowing the rays to be traced through the space, and not the entire list of objects (Fujimoto 1985).

An extension of rays to include a spread angle and virtual origin (Amanatides 1984) allows a ray tracer to area sample the scene using a cone instead of an infinitely thin ray. Amanatides (1984) developed the concept of generalizing rays as cones. He described methods for the intersection of cones and spheres, infinite planes, and planar polygons, as well as ideas for future investigation of cones. This generalization of rays allows sampling to be done at the pixel display resolution, with filtering being accomplished by evaluation of partial coverage of the cones. Any primitives which may be ray traced are candidates for conical ray tracing, given the development of an appropriate algorithm for each.

The constantly expanding list of primitives which are reasonable for ray tracing now includes twisted superquadrics (Barr 1984), volume densities (albedo cloud models) (Kajiya and Von Herzen 1984), Steiner patches (Anderson and Sederberg 1984), fractals (Kajiya 1983), parametric patches (Kajiya 1982), and others. Most of these primitives are well suited for modelling manufactured objects, but are of little use for natural phenomena. Particle systems (Reeves 1983) as used for trees, grass and fire are ill-suited for ray tracing, due to the large number of items, however simple, which are involved.

Stochastic databases, such as fractals (Voss 1983, Carpenter, et al. 1982), particle systems (Reeves 1983), and graftals (Smith 1984), are splendid methods for generating artificial detail which has the quality of appearing natural. The problem that they present for ray tracing is precisely this level of detail which is their greatest advantage for realism. Kajiya's (1983) clever nested subdivision extents for fractals reduce the scale of the problem considerably, to about 3.2 hours for a 256 x 256 aliased image. Still, ray tracing execution time grows with the number and complexity of objects, so that rendering something with many pieces is inefficient. A ray tracer is better equipped to handle complicated appearances than to render large and/or complicated databases.

This suggests that methods which cause simpler objects to appear more complex in the final images are more likely to be useful for fast ray tracing. Texture mapping, for perturbing the color, normal vector, and other surface or mass properties, is a method which has been used to great effect for other image generation algorithms. Some specific work has been done attempting to generate calculated texturing functions to realistically simulate the appearance of rough detail in terrain, and detail in clouds (Gardner 1984). Through the use of conical ray tracing, proper sampling of these textures has become even simpler. To avoid aliasing, one must not attempt to represent information with a frequency of greater that half the sampling frequency (the Nyquist number). With a calculated texture, one need not, and must not, calculate terms of higher frequency than can be faithfully represented, or aliasing will result. A cone intersection contains the information of exactly what frequencies can be displayed without aliasing, so that cones and calculated textures work very well together.

This paper presents one way of using conical ray tracing to properly filter images, while attempting to maximize simplicity and speed. A method of pre-calculating parameters for fast edge filtering is also described. Several methods are presented for adding a reasonable amount of detail to the scene without greatly increasing the number of objects. A construction is described for anti-aliasing bump-mapped or otherwise distorted reflections or refractions, to add surface features to simple primitives. A construct for generating cloud-like objects from planes is shown.

CONE INTERSECTIONS

One of the most useful parts of cones is the knowledge, at any given point, of the exact area the sample contains. This is due to the fact that intersection with a cone can produce a fractional coverage instead of a simple binary (hit / did not hit) answer that one gets from simple ray intersections. A description of the intersection algorithm for cones and spheres is now presented, partly from Amanatides (1984). The intersection test has two parts: a quick binary (hit / did not hit) test, and a partial/complete coverage calculation for the 'hit' case. The point P on the cone centerline ray which is nearest to the sphere is calculated, along with the distance D between the point P and the center of the sphere. For a simple ray/sphere intersection, the distance D is compared with the sphere radius R, but cones are slightly more complicated. The value S must be calculated (Eq. 1) to take the spread angle of the cone into account. The first term of S is the width of the cone at point P, and the second term allows for intersections at points other than at the nearest point on the sphere (Fig. 1).

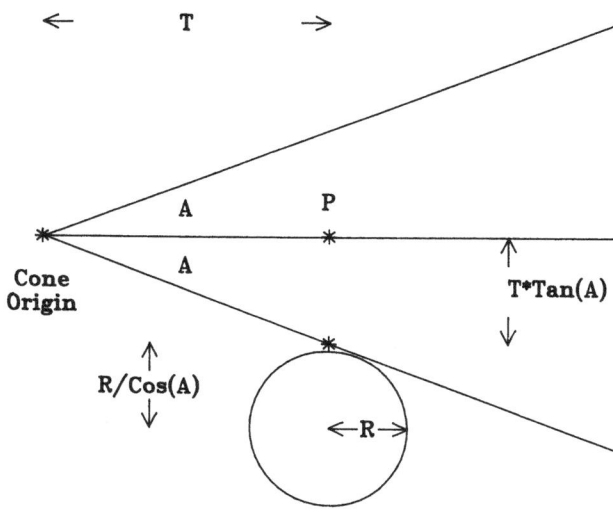

**Figure 1.**

$$S = T * Tan(A) + R / Cos(A) \qquad [1]$$

Where T is the distance between the cone origin and the point P, and A is the spread angle. If S is less than D, then there is no intersection. Also, if the point P is behind the cone origin (T is negative), then Eq. 1 cannot be used, but if the magnitude of T is greater than the sphere radius R, then the sphere and cone do not intersect. If the magnitude of T is less than the sphere radius R, the cone origin must be checked to see if it is inside the sphere. If so, the cone coverage is complete, since the cone originates inside the sphere.

The fractional coverage information allows for simple determination of the frequencies to filter out (or avoid generating) in stochastic databases, since the size of the area which intersects the cone is exactly the sample size. The area-sampling character of cones comes from the fact that the intersection determines an area, not just a binary flag. This area is inherently the size which has been sampled. Any stochastic features smaller than twice this size cannot be correctly represented, so the cone intersection area directly determines the level of detail to generate.

The importance of local surface curvature is also easily ascertained, since the size of the cone at the area of the intersection can be compared to the magnitude of the change in the surface normal across that area. This is important, since if the surface normal changes greatly across the cone intersection area, a given sample may not be an accurate representation of the contents of that area. In this case, a number of point samples may be taken within the cone area, and averaged together to obtain a good representative sample.

Even with cones and multiple point samples, complexity is a problem, since with high degrees of curvature or sharp edges it may be difficult to choose a representative sample (Amanatides 1984). This problem has not been completely successfully addressed, although sampling errors near edges can be reduced by avoiding choosing representative samples exactly at surface edges. This involves comparing the distance to the surface edge with the size of the cone at that point. If the distance to the edge of the surface is less, the sample can be chosen at a point further away from the edge, but still inside the cone area. Also, with more advanced primitives, the already difficult ray/object intersection may become worse. More complicated objects such as Steiner patches, B-spline surfaces, and superquadrics, which already require iterative methods for ray intersections, have yet to be investigated for use with cones.

## TABLE-BASED FILTERING

Filtering edges of primitives can be accomplished a number of different ways. In a simple ray tracer, adaptive supersampling with an appropriate post-process filtering step is the common method (Whitted 1980). With conical ray tracing, since an area is being sampled, some sort of calculation of the partial coverage of the cone must be performed, and then the filtering may be done similarly as for a simple ray tracer. Amanatides (1984) suggested the use of a polynomial to determine partial coverage for a sphere, and direct calculation for planes and polygons, but did not provide the details. One way that this could be accomplished is to evaluate the area by performing a piecewise integration, as shown in Fig. 2. This is straightforward and effective, but represents a lot of calculation if it must be done at each partial intersection.

For both spheres and planar primitives, the percent coverage can be precalculated for a range of values and stored in a table. This is done by actually performing exact intersection calculations between cones and the primitives for a range of sizes and separation distances, and storing the results in a table. For spheres, the relevant parameters are: R1 - the radius of the sphere, R2 - the radius of the cone at the intersection, and D - the distance between the centerline ray of the cone and the sphere center. It is useful to combine these in some way, since a 3-dimensional table becomes quite large very quickly. The author has found

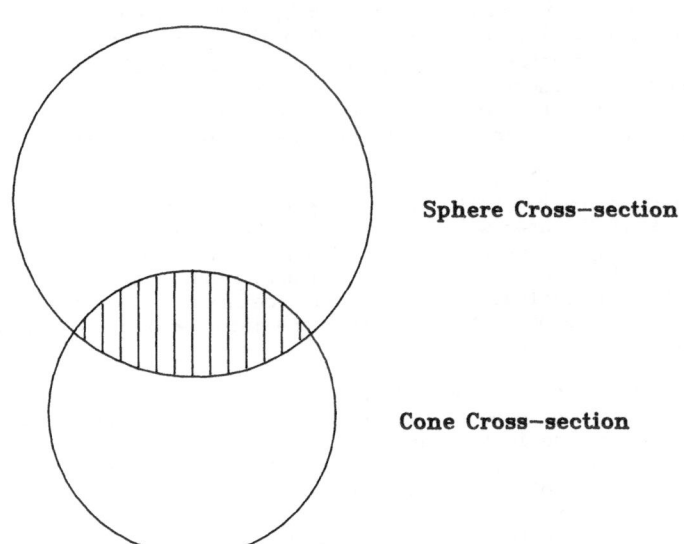

Sphere Cross-section

Cone Cross-section

**The Area of the Intersection is the Sum
of the Areas of the Quadrilaterals.**

**Figure 2.**

empirically that these values may be reduced to two quantities which affect the amount of coverage. One is the ratio R1/R2, and the other is the function D/(R2+R1). A plane is simply the limit as R1 becomes much greater than R2, so the same table of values may be used for planes.

A filtering function, such as a cosine-squared filter (used for images in this paper), may be incorporated into the table, so that the resultant values are pre-filtered. Distances greater than the desired filter radius have a weighting of zero. This is accomplished by convolving the area of the intersection with the function W = cos**2(D/FR * pi/2), where W is the weight for a given point, FR is the filter radius, and D is the distance from the cone centerline. The convolution is approximated by breaking the cone into small areas (rectangular) and taking a summation of the weighting W calculated for each area which is filled. This is done once for each cone/sphere intersection. Distances greater than the filter radius are not evaluated. Each total is normalized so that a completely covered cone has a summation equal to exactly 1.0 (Eq. 2).

$$W = \sum_{i=1}^{n} Cos**2(Di/FR * pi/2) * Ai \qquad [2]$$

$$Wn = W \ / \ Wcovered$$

Where the values being summed represent small areas of the cone which are filled, Di is the distance from the centerline for each area, Ai is the area, W is the weighting for a given fractional coverage, Wcovered is the weighting obtained if the cone is completely covered. Wn is therefore the normalized weighting so that a completely covered cone has a 100 percent weighting.

Since the errors introduced by poor approximations of coverage in the table lie near the outer edge of the filtering function, their weighting is relatively low, and has little effect on the results. Support of this is found by considering two facts. First, the nature of the cosine-squared filter is that it falls off to zero at the edges, so area calculation errors at the edges are weighted less than in other places. Second, the nature of the intersection of a cone and a sphere is such that the cross-section is the intersection between two circles. The error introduced by a small change in one of the radii (the cone or the sphere) is greater at the outer edges. This error is offset by the low weighting from the filter. Therefore, only a small number of table entries are needed for high-quality anti-aliasing. The images in this paper were generated using a table of 8 values of R2/R1 by 32 values of D/(R2+R1) as shown in Table 1. Increasing the number of table entries in D/(R2+R1) generates slightly more smoothly diffused shadows and reflections, but is barely discernible at 512 x 512 resolution. Figure 3.1 shows the use of an 8 x 32 table and Fig. 3.2 shows the use of an 8 x 64 table.

## BUMP-MAPPED REFLECTIONS AND REFRACTIONS

A well-known method for imparting detailed interest to simple primitives is 'bump-mapping', or normal vector perturbation (Blinn 1978). This method has been used to great effect for many scenes, but has not enjoyed much favor among ray-traced images. Many ray traced images exhibit color texture mapping, since this does not affect the resolution of the rays, only the resultant color. By altering the normal vector, one may introduce changes in what the rays intersect, resulting in wide variations in the desired sampling resolution. Complete supersampling is unquestionably too slow, and adaptive supersampling may get bogged down in details which are really too small or high frequency to be desirable to reproduce.

Using conical ray tracing, one is able to distort the sizes and spread angles of the cones in areas of high 'curvature' to properly sample the distorted reflections

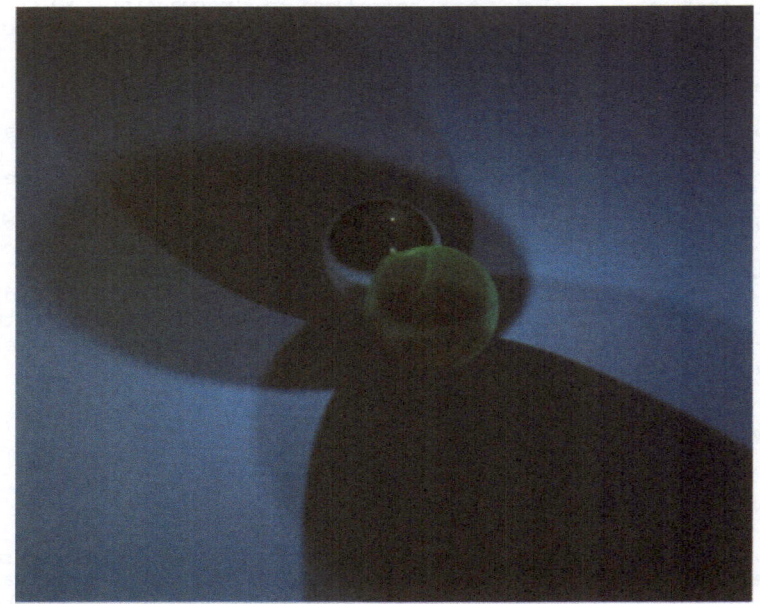

Figure 3.1.

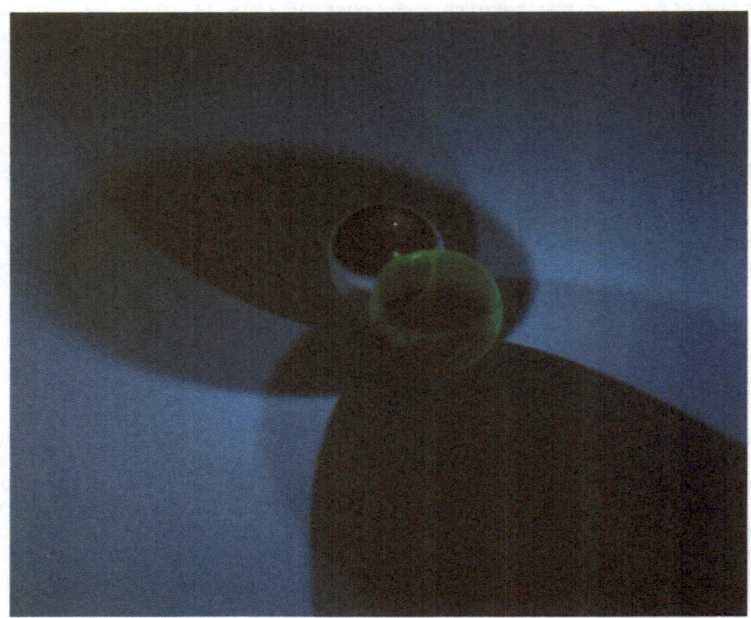

Figure 3.2.

Table 1.

R2/R1

| D/(R1+R2) | .1250 | .2500 | .3750 | .5000 | 1.000 | 2.000 | 4.000 | 8.000 |
|---|---|---|---|---|---|---|---|---|
| .0176 | .0498 | .1915 | .3923 | .6106 | .9997 | .9999 | .9999 | .9999 |
| .0352 | .0494 | .1904 | .3881 | .6014 | .9978 | .9989 | .9990 | .9990 |
| .0527 | .0485 | .1860 | .3805 | .5872 | .9927 | .9961 | .9967 | .9969 |
| .0703 | .0475 | .1808 | .3694 | .5686 | .9831 | .9892 | .9904 | .9907 |
| .0879 | .0448 | .1745 | .3548 | .5422 | .9682 | .9789 | .9816 | .9827 |
| .1055 | .0458 | .1677 | .3374 | .5155 | .9467 | .9612 | .9650 | .9662 |
| .1230 | .0432 | .1614 | .3180 | .4838 | .9190 | .9394 | .9457 | .9484 |
| .1406 | .0407 | .1517 | .2971 | .4509 | .8836 | .9075 | .9152 | .9178 |
| .1582 | .0387 | .1409 | .2744 | .4137 | .8426 | .8725 | .8832 | .8879 |
| .1758 | .0350 | .1308 | .2508 | .3756 | .7939 | .8257 | .8376 | .8420 |
| .1934 | .0346 | .1179 | .2282 | .3379 | .7415 | .7781 | .7930 | .7998 |
| .2109 | .0316 | .1089 | .2041 | .2998 | .6822 | .7186 | .7339 | .7399 |
| .2285 | .0283 | .0964 | .1780 | .2609 | .6220 | .6615 | .6793 | .6877 |
| .2461 | .0259 | .0863 | .1544 | .2279 | .5568 | .5937 | .6107 | .6178 |
| .2637 | .0221 | .0743 | .1327 | .1946 | .4937 | .5317 | .5504 | .5595 |
| .2813 | .0209 | .0647 | .1112 | .1649 | .4278 | .4614 | .4781 | .4853 |
| .2988 | .0175 | .0535 | .0916 | .1372 | .3671 | .4000 | .4175 | .4263 |
| .3164 | .0150 | .0438 | .0761 | .1120 | .3059 | .3333 | .3479 | .3544 |
| .3340 | .0129 | .0355 | .0612 | .0896 | .2522 | .2778 | .2923 | .2999 |
| .3516 | .0100 | .0272 | .0468 | .0697 | .2000 | .2200 | .2312 | .2363 |
| .3691 | .0086 | .0213 | .0354 | .0520 | .1568 | .1744 | .1850 | .1908 |
| .3867 | .0065 | .0155 | .0264 | .0390 | .1165 | .1293 | .1366 | .1400 |
| .4043 | .0047 | .0115 | .0186 | .0273 | .0854 | .0958 | .1024 | .1061 |
| .4219 | .0035 | .0078 | .0124 | .0186 | .0578 | .0646 | .0686 | .0704 |
| .4395 | .0021 | .0047 | .0080 | .0121 | .0384 | .0434 | .0468 | .0487 |
| .4570 | .0015 | .0030 | .0051 | .0073 | .0224 | .0252 | .0268 | .0275 |
| .4746 | .0008 | .0014 | .0026 | .0039 | .0126 | .0144 | .0156 | .0164 |
| .4922 | .0004 | .0008 | .0012 | .0018 | .0056 | .0063 | .0067 | .0068 |
| .5098 | .0002 | .0003 | .0005 | .0006 | .0023 | .0026 | .0028 | .0030 |
| .5273 | .0000 | .0001 | .0001 | .0002 | .0005 | .0005 | .0005 | .0005 |
| .5449 | .0000 | .0000 | .0000 | .0000 | .0001 | .0001 | .0001 | .0001 |
| .5625 | .0000 | .0000 | .0000 | .0000 | .0000 | .0000 | .0000 | .0000 |

Perturbed Normal Vectors

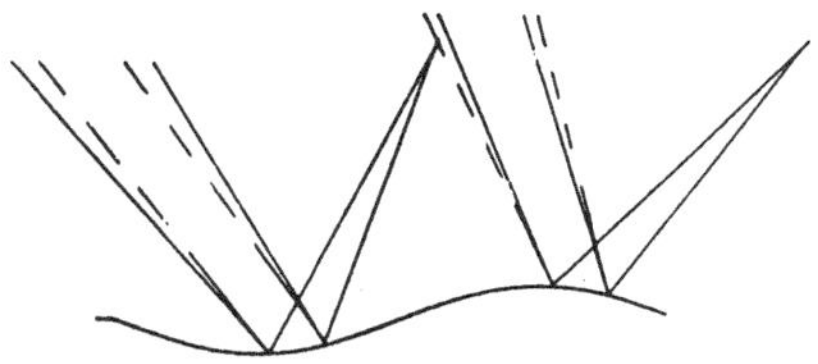

Simulated Surface showing
Normal Reflected Cones (solid)
Distorted Reflection (dashed)

Figure 4.

or refractions (fig. 4). The curvature, estimated using local differences in normal vectors, determines the amount to spread or squash the cones. The new cone spread angle is determined by the incident cone spread angle plus the angular difference between the normal vectors at the cone centerline intersection and the cone edge. The new cone origin is then calculated using the incident cone origin offset along the cone centerline ray to the point where the new spread angle indicates. This is actually extrapolating where the cone 'must' have originated, given the radius at the intersection, the centerline ray, and the new spread angle.

Figures 5.1, 5.2, and 5.3 show two spheres suspended over a surface with reflective properties similar to clean water. Figure 5.1 shows no distortion, figure 5.2 shows 10 percent weighted 'bump-mapping', and figure 5.3 shows 20 percent weighting. The distorted reflections are anti-aliased as well as the other features, since the reflected cones are distorted to match the local changes in the normal vector at the distortion. The texturing function used is a summation of sine wave products, as shown in Eq. 3 (Gardner 1984). Gardner's work involves simulation of terrain and clouds using texture-mapping on quadric surfaces. Gardner uses summations of sine wave products to produce an easily calculated texture with a known frequency content. His work with texturing functions led to well-behaved and easily calculated textures, which are used in this work.

$$T(X_s, Y_s, Z_s) = \sum_{i=1}^{n} C_i \frac{Sin(W_i * X_s + PX_i) + 1}{2} \times$$

$$\sum_{i=1}^{n} C_i \frac{Sin(W_i * Y_s + PY_i) + 1}{2}$$

[3]

Where $PX_i$ and $PY_i$ represent phase shift functions. From Gardner (1984), defining $PX_i$ as a sinusoidal function of $Y_s$ and $PY_i$ as a sinusoidal function of $X_s$ produces natural looking patterns for low values of n (4 is used in figures 5.x).

Figure 5.1.

Figure 5.2.

Figure 5.3.

Figures 6.1, 6.2, 6.3, and 6.4 show two spheres floating underneath a surface with reflective and transmissive properties chosen to simulate clear water. The weightings for the percent of normal vector perturbation are 0, 10, 20, and 30. The texturing function is the same as that in figures 5.x, based on 4 sine wave products, with various phases and amplitudes. The refractions are anti-aliased to match the distortion from the texture-mapping.


DIFFUSION-MAPPED 'CLOUDS'

Another property which may be parametrically mapped onto a simple surface is the amount of light that the surface diffuses. This diffusion weight is described as follows: a fraction of incoming light is transmitted, and the remainder is divided between being absorbed (disappears), and being radiated unidirectionally (diffused). Figure 7. describes this relation. A plane with this property modulated by a calculated texture gives an appearance similar to a soft cloud with a small amount of light absorption, and mostly diffuse radiation. These diffusion mapped primitives cast fuzzy shadows, diffuse views of objects behind them, and are simple to calculate, being simply planes. The intersection calculation between a cone and a plane is now described. The centerline ray of the cone is intersected with the plane. If the intersection point is behind the cone origin, then we must check to see if the spread angle of the cone is greater than the angle the plane makes with the ray centerline. If the cone spread angle is greater, then the cone intersects the plane, even though the centerline intersection is behind the cone origin (Fig 8.1). If the intersection point is in front of the cone origin, then the cone definitely intersects the plane, and the angle between the cone centerline and the plane normal must be computed to determine if the cone coverage if partial or complete. If the computed angle is less than 90 degrees plus the cone spread angle, then the coverage is partial (Fig 8.2). The area of the partial coverage is calculated by reducing the problem to a two-dimensional intersection between the cone cross-section, a circle, and the plane's projection to the horizon, a line.

The area may be calculated as a polynomial, as the sphere-cone intersection was earlier. The alternative, as presented here, is to use the table-based filtering as described above, treating a plane as the limit of an infinitely large sphere.

The method of diffusion mapping is not restricted to use with planes, although planes were the author's choice due to the simplicity of the calculation for planes and the complexity of the visual effect even with simple primitives. A number of planes at different positions can give a convincing replica of cloud layers, which may move separately, and shadow and diffuse each other.

Figures 9.1 and 9.2 show diffusion-mapped cloud replicas. These show six cloud layers of varying 'densities', from two different views. The blue band at the bottom of figure 9.2 shows the actual color of the background sky. These objects can be moved smoothly, shadow other objects in the scene, and may have any other properties that other ray traced objects have.

All images were computed on a Prime-750 at 512 x 512 by 24-bits and were photographed on a Raster Technologies Model One/25-S using a Dunn Instruments 631 camera. Figures 5.1, 5.2, 5.3 took approximately 20 minutes of CPU time each. Figures 6.1, 6.2, 6.3, and 6.4 took about 40 minutes each, and figures 9.1 and 9.2 took approximately 50 minutes of CPU time.


CONCLUSIONS

The area sampling character of cones is very useful and is a very powerful tool for proper sampling. Each cone carries with it the proper sampling aperture at any given distance, which makes cones an attractive method to combine with texture mapping of all kinds. With or without cones, texture mapping of various surface properties adds much to ray tracing appearance, without the computational drain of physically more complex databases.

Figure 6.1.

Figure 6.2.

Figure 6.3.

Figure 6.4.

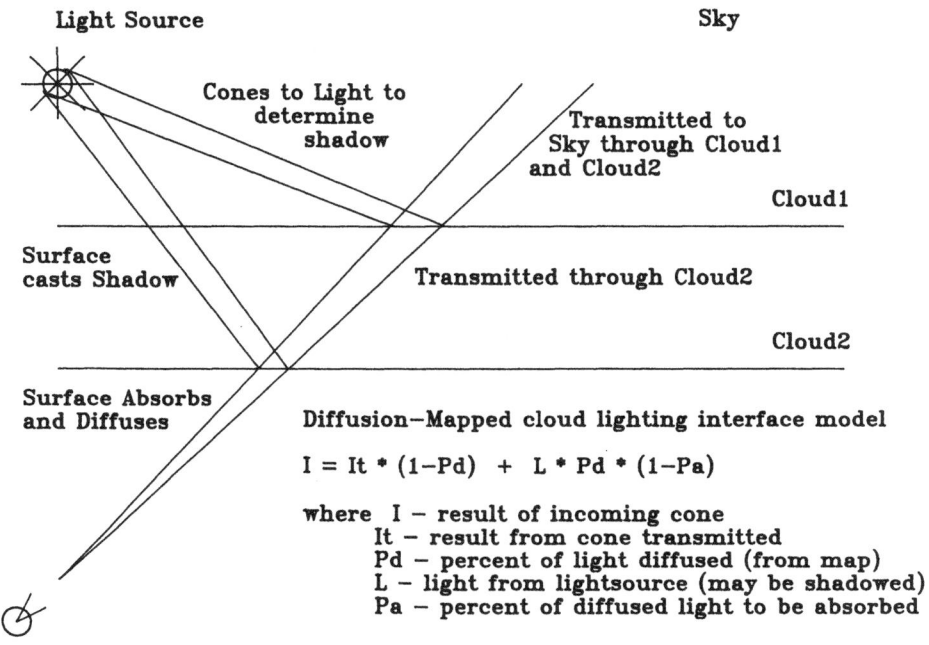

**Light Source**　　　　　　　　　　　　　　　**Sky**

Cones to Light to
determine
shadow

Transmitted to
Sky through Cloud1
and Cloud2

Cloud1

Surface
casts Shadow

Transmitted through Cloud2

Cloud2

Surface Absorbs
and Diffuses

Diffusion–Mapped cloud lighting interface model

$$I = It * (1-Pd) + L * Pd * (1-Pa)$$

where  I – result of incoming cone
　　　　It – result from cone transmitted
　　　　Pd – percent of light diffused (from map)
　　　　L – light from lightsource (may be shadowed)
　　　　Pa – percent of diffused light to be absorbed

**Eye Point**

Figure 7.

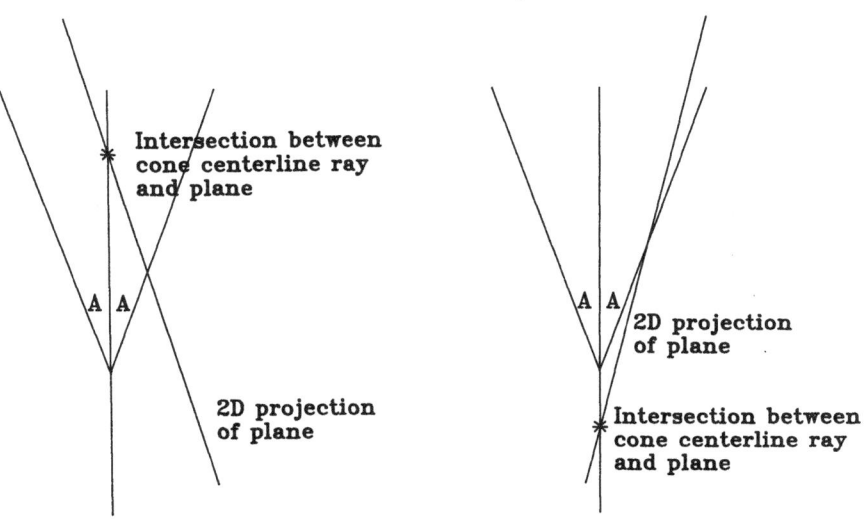

Intersection between
cone centerline ray
and plane

A A

2D projection
of plane

A A

2D projection
of plane

Intersection between
cone centerline ray
and plane

Figure 8.1　　　　　　　　　　　　　　　Figure 8.2

Figure 9.1.

Figure 9.2.

At some point, however, one must degenerate to point sampling, even if only to evaluate a representative color and intensity for a surface. Also, some types of primitives may not lend themselves easily to intersecting with cones, so point sampling may be used cooperatively with area samples to integrate the best features of both. When choosing a representative sample result from the lighting model, a point sample is chosen. The choice is always the point at which the cone centerline intersects the primitive, unless that line does not intersect the primitive, in which case another point must be used. The representative sample is then chosen to be a point which is equidistant from the cone surface and the point on the primitive which is nearest to the cone centerline. All textures are area-sampled to be properly anti-aliased. Texture-based primitives are particularly well-suited to complex simulation with ray/cone tracing.


FUTURE IDEAS

If diffusion-mapped clouds are also given the property of refraction with chromatic aberrations, a convincing replica of a sunset may be possible.


REFERENCES

Anderson, D. C., and Sederberg, T. W., "Ray Tracing of Steiner Patches", Computer Graphics, Vol. 18(3), July 1984, pp. 159-164.

Amanatides, J., "Ray Tracing With Cones", Computer Graphics, Vol. 18(3), July 1984, pp. 129-135.

Barr, A., "Global and Local Deformations of Solid Primitives", Computer Graphics, Vol. 18(3), July 1984, pp. 21-30.

Blinn, J. F., "Simulation of Wrinkled Surfaces", Computer Graphics, Vol. 12(3), August 1978.

Gardner, G. Y., "Simulation of Natural Scenes Using Textured Quadric Surfaces", Computer Graphics, Vol. 18(3), July 1984, pp. 11-20.

Fournier, A., Fussel, D., and Carpenter, L., "Computer Rendering of Stochastic Models", Communications of the ACM, Vol. 25(6), 1982.

Fujimoto, A., and Iwata, K., "Accelerated Ray Tracing", CG TOKYO '85.

Hanrahan, P., "Ray Tracing Algebraic Surfaces", Computer Graphics, Vol 17(3), pp. 83-90, 1983.

Hecht, E., and Zajac, A., Optics, Addison Wesley Publishing Company, Reading, Massachusetts, 1974.

Kajiya, J. T., "Ray Tracing Procedurally Defined Objects", Computer Graphics, Vol. 17(3), pp. 91-102.

Kajiya, J. T., "Ray Tracing Parametric Patches", Computer Graphics, Vol. 16(3), pp. 245-254.

Kajiya, J. T., and Von Herzen, B. P., "Ray Tracing Volume Densities", Computer Graphics, Vol. 18(3), July 1984, pp. 165-174.

Reeves, W. T., "Particle Systems: a Technique for modeling a class of fuzzy objects", ACM Transactions on Graphics, Vol. 2(2), 1983.

Smith, A. R., "Plants, Fractals, and Formal Languages", Computer Graphics, Vol 18(3), July 1984, pp. 1-10.

Voss, R., "Fourier Synthesis of Gaussian Fractals: 1/f Noises, Landscapes, and Flakes", Tutorial on State of the Art Image Synthesis, SIGGRAPH 1983.

Whitted, T., "An Improved Illumination Model for Shaded Display", Communications of the ACM Vol. 23, 1980, pp. 343-349.

David B. Kirk is currently a Senior Engineer at Raster Technologies, Inc., where he is involved in 3D graphics display controller development and image synthesis research. His areas of technical expertise include parallel and dataflow computer architectures, 3D geometry, and shaded rendering algorithms. He is a member of the ACM, SIGGRAPH, and SIGART. He received his BSc and MSc in Mechanical Engineering from Massachusetts Institute of Technology in 1982 and 1983.

Kirk's address is Raster Technologies, Inc., 2 Robbins Road, Westford, Ma, 01886, USA.

# Shadows for Bump-Mapped Surfaces

Nelson L. Max

Lawrence Livermore National Laboratory, P.O. Box 808, L-301, Livermore, CA 94550, USA

ABSTRACT

Bump mapping produces realistic shading by perturbing normal vectors to a surface, but does not show the shadows that the bumps cast on nearby parts of the same surface. In this paper, these shadows are found from precomputed tables of horizon angles, listing, for each position entry, the elevation of the horizon in a sampled collection of directions. These tables are made for bumps on a standard flat surface, and then a transformation is developed so that the same tables can be used for an arbitrary curved parametrized surface patch. This necessitates a new method for scaling the bump size to the patch size.

Key Words

Bump mapping, normal perturbation, wrinkled surface, horizon, shadows, parametrized surface, shading, illumination, texture table.

## INTRODUCTION

James Blinn (1978) showed how to simulate wrinkled surfaces by perturbing the normal vector, without moving the surface itself. This method, popularly known as "bump mapping," has since been widely applied to generate realistic images (Whitted 1978, Bloomenthal 1985).

The input to Blinn's algorithm is a bump function $F(u,v)$ of the surface parameters, stored as a two-dimensional table indexed by u and v. The wrinkled surface is formed by moving the parametrized surface $\vec{P}(u,v)$ an amount $F(u,v)$ in the direction of the surface normal $\vec{N}$. Assuming F is small compared with $\vec{P}$, and using differential calculus and some vector identities, Blinn arrived at a simple formula for the new normal $\vec{N}'$ as perturbed by the effect of the wrinkles. (See section 3 below.)

If this perturbed normal is used in a shading model, realistic highlights and reflections can be generated. A shading model which removes the contribution of a light source when the normal $\vec{N}'$ points away from it can also simulate self-shadowing of the bumps. However, no shading model which uses only $\vec{N}'$ can account for shadows cast by one bump on another. Near the edge between the illuminated and self-shadowed regions of a surface, where the normal is almost perpendicular to the light source direction, the bumps should cast long shadows which are important in making the rendering look realistic.

To simulate the cast shadows, a separate shadow map is needed for every light source direction. Since two angles are needed to specify a light source direction, it would seem that a two-parameter family of tables would be required. However, due to the special nature of the bump function, we will see in the following two sections that a one-parameter family of tables is

sufficient. In the figures here, this parameter was sampled at only eight
values, demonstrating that it is possible to generate good bump shadows with only
eight extra numbers per texture entry, besides the bump height F(u,v).

## 1. THE SUNSET MODEL

Imagine sunset at the equator on the spring equinox, when the sun appears to move
in a vertical line towards the western horizon. Assume bumps on the earth, i.e.,
mountains, are defined by a single-valued bump function F(u,v), so that there are
no tunnels or overhanging cliffs. Then once a given point on the terrain becomes
covered by the shadow of a mountain, it will remain in darkness until the next
morning. Therefore, to specify the shadow texture for every instant during the
afternoon, it is only necessary to specify the time of sunset for each point on
the terrain. This sunset time is determined by the angle of elevation of the
western horizon, as viewed from a given terrain point. The horizon elevation
angle is the maximum angle of elevation from the given point to any other terrain
point located directly to its west. If the function F(u,v) is tabulated with
rows going west to east, only a single row of data is needed to find this maximum
angle.

In computing the elevation angle, we assume a flat earth and do not take into
account the extra lengthening of the shadows due to the curvature of the earth.
In general, we will not know in advance the shape or curvature of the
parametrized surface around which the bump texture will be wrapped, so we must
precompute the shadows as if the surface were flat. Whenever F(u,v) is small
compared to the curvature of $\vec{P}$(u,v), this will give a good approximation to the
shadows on the curved parametric patch $\vec{P}$(u,v). (See section 4 below.)

## 2. STANDARD FLAT PATCHES

Assume given a flat patch $\vec{P}$(u,v) = (u,v,0), for $0 \le u \le 1$, $0 \le v \le 1$, with surface
normal $\vec{N}$ = (0,0,1), and a non-negative bump function F(u,v). Then the wrinkled
surface Q is Q = {(u,v,w)| $0 \le u \le 1$, $0 \le v \le 1$, w = F(u,v)}. Let $\vec{L}$ be a unit vector
from a point on the patch in the direction towards a light source. In spherical
coordinates with the pole along the Z axis, $\vec{L}$ = (sin$\varphi$ cos$\theta$, sin$\varphi$ sin$\theta$, cos$\varphi$).
Here, $\varphi$ is the angle $\vec{L}$ makes to the normal $\vec{N}$, and $\theta$ is the angle of the projection
of $\vec{L}$ on the (X,Y) plane, measured from the X axis. (Because of the convention
for spherical coordinates, the horizon elevation angle discussed above is
actually $90° - \varphi$).

For each fixed $\theta$, we may imagine the sun setting in a vertical plane with $\varphi$
increasing from 0° to 90°. As above, the horizon angle in the direction
corresponding to $\theta$ completely determines the shadow pattern for any sun vector $\vec{L}$
in this plane. Let ß(u,v, ) be a table of horizon angles, indexed by the surface
parameters u, and v, and the angle $\theta$.

This table is the one-parameter family of texture tables promised in the
introduction. It is customary to use from 64 to 512 sampling values for u and v,
since the bump function F(u,v) is handled as a raster image. However, it is
often sufficient to sample $\theta$ at only eight different values: 0°, 45°, 90°, 135°,
180°, 225°, 270° and 315°. These correspond to E, NE, N, NW, W, SW, S and SE for
a sunset direction, and the horizon angle ß can easily be found using rows,
columns, or diagonals of the bump function table. This coarse sampling in $\theta$
still permits the shadows to move smoothly because we interpolate the sunset
angle ß between two adjacent tabulated $\theta$ values, and then compare the result with
the actual sun angle $\varphi$ to determine whether a point is in shadow. If we instead
computed two shading intensities, including shadows, and then interpolated
between them, we would see one shadow fade out and the other fade in, which would

look less convincing. If the bump map consists of long ridges, as in the figures here, then at the worst case angle of 22 1/2°, the shadows are shortened by cos 22 1/2° = .93, so the error is only 7%. With 16 samples, the worst error would be 2%. Of course, if the texture consists of isolated narrow peaks, the errors will be more obvious.

## 3. SCALING FOR CURVED PATCHES

Let $\vec{P}(u,v)$ be be a parametrized surface, and $F(u,v)$ be a bump function, both defined for $0 \le u \le 1$ and $0 \le v \le 1$. Following Blinn (1978), we can take $\vec{P}_u$ and $\vec{P}_v$ to be the tangent vectors (partial derivative vectors) in the u and v direction, $\vec{N} = \vec{P}_u \times \vec{P}_v$ to be the surface normal, and $\vec{P}' = \vec{P} + F\,\vec{N}/|N|$ to be the perturbed surface. After dropping terms of first order in F, Blinn finds

$$\vec{P}_u' = \vec{P}_u + F_u\,\vec{N}/|N|,$$

$$\vec{P}_v' = \vec{P}_v + F_v\,\vec{N}/|N|,$$

and then

$$\vec{N}' = \vec{P}_u' \times \vec{P}_v' = \vec{N} + D,$$

where

$$\vec{D} = (F_u\,\vec{N} \times \vec{P}_v - F_v\,\vec{N} \times \vec{P}_u)/|N|$$

is the perturbation of the normal due to the bumps.

Blinn next interprets this perturbation as a rotation of the normal $\vec{N}$ by an angle $\tan^{-1}(|D|/|N|)$ about the axis $\vec{A}$ perpendicular to $\vec{N}$ and $\vec{N}'$. He remarks that if a patch is made twice as large, $\vec{N}$ will be multiplied by 4 but $\vec{D}$ only by 2, so the normal will be rotated less, causing an undesired flattening of the bumps.

His solution is to find the rotation angle from a standard flat unit-sized patch, as in section 2 above, and then determine only the axis of rotation from the geometry of the actual patch. However, the resulting shading may not correspond to any physical surface.

For example, suppose the bump function is defined by the pyramid ABCDE of height 1/2 as shown in Fig. 1. Each of the slanted faces of the pyramid slopes by 45°.

The patch $\vec{P}(u,v) = (2u,v,0)$ stretches the u direction by 2 but leaves v unchanged. Blinn's scale adjustment would keep the slopes of 45°, resulting in inconsistent heights for the center vertex. As shown in Fig. 2, E' has height 1/2, but F' has height 1.

It should theoretically be possible to determine a 3-D shape from its shading (especially if there are two light sources of different colors), but nobody has ever noticed any visually unreasonable effects due to Blinn's scaling algorithm. However, the situation in Fig. 2 is clearly inadequate if shadows are to be determined, so we use an alternate scaling method. We define a perturbed surface $\vec{P}''$ by

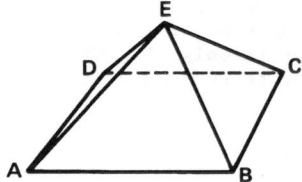

Fig. 1. A piecewise-linear bump function defined for $0 \leq x \leq 1$ and $0 \leq y \leq 1$. It takes the value 0 at the corners of the squares ABCD, and the value 1/2 at the center. The sides slope at 45°.

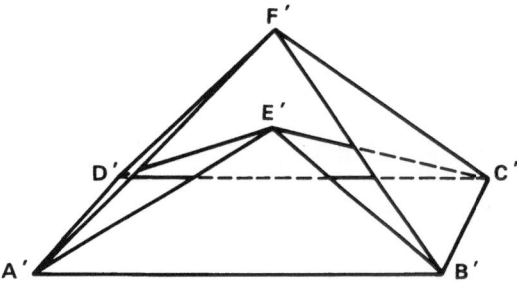

Fig. 2. The bump function of figure 1, stretched over the rectangle A'B'C'D', with $0 \leq x \leq 2$, and $0 \leq y \leq 1$, and taking the value 0 on the corners. If the sides must slope by 45°, there are two inconsistent positions E' and F' for the center.

$$\vec{P}'' = \vec{P} + F \, \vec{N}/|N|^{1/2}$$

Now, if the surface is scaled up by a factor of 2, $\vec{N}$ will be scaled up by 4, but $\vec{N}/|N|^{1/2}$ will be scaled up only by 2 and the apparent shapes of the bumps will be unchanged. If only u is stretched by a factor of 2, some regions will become more steeply sloped, and some less. As shown in Fig. 3, E'' has a compromise height of $1/2 \sqrt{2}$.

With this adjustment, the approximation for $P_u''$ and $P_v''$ become

$$\vec{P}_u'' = \vec{P}_u + F_u \, \vec{N}/|N|^{1/2}$$

and

$$\vec{P}_v'' = \vec{P}_v + F_v \, \vec{N}/|N|^{1/2}$$

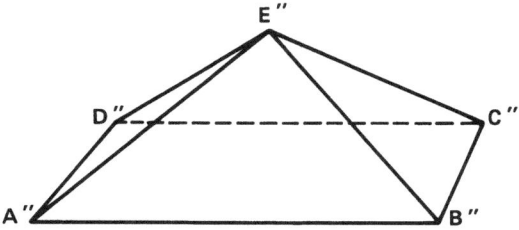

Fig. 3. The bump function of figure 1, stretched over the same rectangle as figure 2, but with center vertex E″ of height $1/2\sqrt{2}$. The face A″E″D″ has slope less than 45°, and the face A″E″B″ has slopes greater than 45°.

and the perturbation D″ becomes

$$\vec{D}'' = (F_u \, \vec{N} \times \vec{P}_v - F_v \, \vec{N} \times \vec{P}_u)/|N|^{1/2}.$$

Now consider the skew transformation $\vec{P}(u,v)=(u + v, v, 0)$. In this case $\vec{P}_u = (1,0,0)$ and $\vec{P}_v = (1,1,0)$, so $\vec{N} = \vec{P}_u \times \vec{P}_v = (0,0,1)$. The bumps will still keep their original height, which is appropriate because the skewing transformation does not change the surface area.

## 4. LIGHT VECTOR TRANSFORMATION

We saw in section 2 how to compute shadows for a wrinkled surface Q defined on a standard flat patch, and in section 3 how to define a wrinkled surface $\vec{P}''$ corresponding to a curved patch $\vec{P}$. Now we will look for an affine transformation B which brings Q to a position which approximates $\vec{P}''$ at the point $\vec{P}''(u_0, v_0)$. The affine transformation B is made up of a linear transformation C and a translation. We need to have

$$B(u_0,v_0,0) = \vec{P}(u_0,v_0)$$

$$B(u_0,v_0,F(u_0,v_0)) = \vec{P}''(u_0,v_0)$$

$$C(1,0,0) = \vec{P}_u(u_0,v_0)$$

$$C(0,1,0) = \vec{P}_v(u_0,v_0)$$

$$C(0,0,1) = \vec{N}/|N|^{1/2}$$

Therefore,

$$B(u,v,w) = (u-u_0) \, \vec{P}_u(u_0,v_0) + (v-v_0) \, \vec{P}_v(u_0,v_0)$$

$$+ \, w \, \vec{N}/|N|^{1/2} + \vec{P}(u_0,v_0).$$

If the curvature of $\vec{P}(u,v)$ is small, in a sense to be discussed in section 5, then the transformed standard bump surface $B(Q)$ is close enough to the wrinkled patch $\vec{P}''$ for the purpose of shadow computation. Since an affine transformation takes straight lines to straight lines, the point $(u_0, v_0, F(u_0, v_0))$ on surface $Q$ will be in shadow from a light in direction $\vec{K}$ if and only if the point $\vec{P}''(u_0, v_0)$ on surface $B(Q)$ is in shadow from a light in direction $C(\vec{K})$.

Therefore, if $\vec{L}$ is the direction from point $\vec{P_0}'' = \vec{P}''(u_0, v_0)$ to the light source, we can take $C^{-1}(\vec{L})$ to be the light direction on our standard bump surface $Q$, and compute the shadow as in section 3. The matrix for the linear part $C$ of $B$ is made up from the three vectors $\vec{P}_u(u_0, v_0)$, $\vec{P}_v(u_0, v_0)$, and $\vec{N}/|N|^{1/2}$.

The angles $\varphi$ and $\theta$ are computed from the components of $C^{-1}(\vec{L})/|C^{-1}(\vec{L})|$, a horizon angle $\beta$ is computed by interpolation in the tables $\beta(u, v, )$, and the point $P_0''$ is in shadow if $\varphi > \beta$. Note that this method will also work for light sources at a finite distance or even inside the field of view. In these cases, the light source direction $\vec{L}$ should be recomputed at each surface point, as it should with any other finite-light-source shading model. If multiple light sources are used, the inverse matrix $C^{-1}$ need be computed only once per surface point.

It is also possible to use the angles $\varphi$ and $\beta$ to create penumbers for a circular area light source like the sun. Since $\varphi - \beta$ represents the angle of the sun's center below the horizon, the visible fraction of the sun is a function of $\varphi - \beta$, which can be used to multiply the contribution of the shading from the sun illumination. If $\delta$ is the apparent angular diameter of the light source ($1/2°$ for the sun), let $\alpha = (\beta - \varphi)/(\delta/2)$.

Then by integration or plane geometry area formulas, the visible fraction of the sun is

$$f(\alpha) = \begin{cases} 0., & \alpha \leq -1 \\ .5 + (\sin^{-1}\alpha + \alpha\sqrt{1 - \alpha^2})/\pi, & -1 \leq \alpha \leq 1 \\ 1., & 1 \leq \alpha \end{cases}$$

This function can be tabulated, and used to determine the shading of the penumbra. It will give an accurate answer for the case of a shadow cast by a horizontal ridge in the bump map, but will be slightly inaccurate for sloping bump profiles, because $\varphi - \beta$ measures an angle in a plane perpendicular to the original surface, not perpendicular to the bump profile. Also, the transformation $C^{-1}$ can take a round sun into an elliptical one, so $\delta$ should be taken to be the angular extent of the ellipse in the $\beta$ direction.

The method of bump mapping as described by Blinn (1978) does not effect the profile of a surface, only its shading. Therefore when a polygonal or smooth-surface based hidden-surface/shadow-casting algorithm is applied for inter-surface occlusion and shadows, the shadows cast by bumpy surfaces will not appear bumpy. Rob Cook (1984) describes a generalization of bump maps called displacement maps, which can change the profile of a bumpy surface. Such displacement maps might also be capable of casting bumpy shadows from one surface to another, if the shadow algorithm of Williams (1978) were used.

## 5. EFFECTS OF SURFACE CURVATURE

Shadows from bumpy profiles are difficult, and not treated here. However, it is easier to cast the shadows of a smooth profile on the nearby bumps belonging to the same surface, taking into account its curvature. This should add to the realism of textures with scattered small bumps on an otherwise smooth surface.

The left side of Fig. 4 shows a section curve S of a surface $\vec{P}''$, made by the plane T containing the normal $\vec{N}$ and the light source direction $\vec{L}$ at a point $\vec{P}_0 = \vec{P}(u_0, v_0)$. There is an isolated bump which moves $\vec{P}_0$ to $\vec{P}_0''$ by an amount $h = |N|^{1/2} F(u_0, v_0)$. We want to find the condition for the line from $\vec{P}_0''$ in the direction $\vec{L}$ to be tangent to the surface P at the profile point Q.

To second order, the section curve S is approximated by a circle with center C, whose radius R, is the radius of curvature of S. The curvature of S is $k = 1/R$. It can be computed from the first and second partial derivative vectors $\vec{P}_u$, $\vec{P}_v$, $\vec{P}_{uu}$, $\vec{P}_{uv}$, and $\vec{P}_{vv}$, and the angle $\theta$ found at the end of

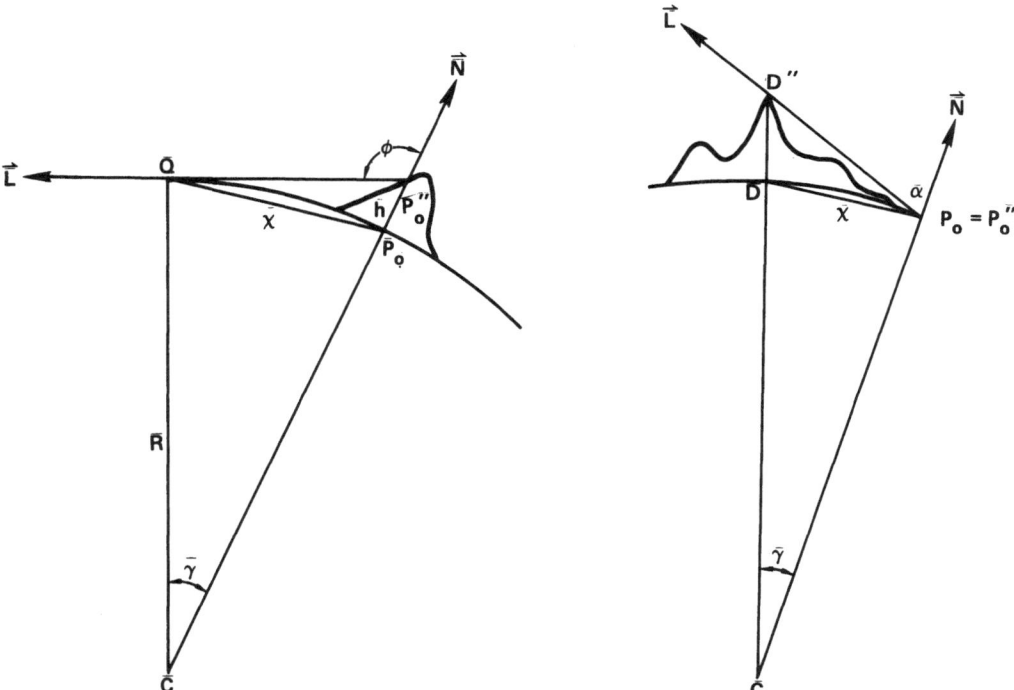

Fig. 4. Left: a section of the surface $\vec{P}''(u,v)$ in a plane containing the normal and light-source direction at $\vec{P}_0$. The illuminating ray is just tangent to the surface at Q. Right: A similar section with the illuminating ray just passing the top D" of a bump of maximum height, and making an angle of $\propto$ with the surface normal.

section 4, which defines the direction of the section plane T. To second order, $h \cong k\, x^2/2 = x^2/(2R)$, where x is the distance from P to the tangency point Q, and $\gamma \cong x/R$, where $\gamma$ is the central angle $QCP_0$ on the approximating circle. Eliminating x, we find $x \cong \sqrt{2Rh}$ and $\gamma \cong \sqrt{2h/R}$.

Recall that $\varphi$ is the angle between $\vec{N}$ and $\vec{L}$. Angle Q $P_0$"C is the supplement of angle $\varphi$ and the complement of angle $\gamma$, so $\varphi = 90° + \gamma$. Thus $\gamma$ measures the tilt of the horizon below the 90° angle which would be expected if the surface P were flat. So if we replace the estimated horizon angle ß from our table by ß' = ß + $\gamma$, the same test as before will apply: The point $\bar{P}_0$" is in shadow whenever $\varphi$ß'. If the surface is concave $\gamma$ should be subtracted from ß instead. These adjustments of ß have the effect of lengthening shadows on convex surfaces and shortening them on concave surfaces, but not necessarily by the correct amount.

We can also use the curvature of the section S to determine the relative error in the length of the shadows, caused by the curvature of the surface. Suppose a light source at an angle $\alpha$ with $\vec{N}$ casts a shadow from D" to $P_0$". The right side of Fig. 4 shows the worst case, where the points $P_0$ and $P_0$" are equal, because $F(u_0, v_0) = 0$, but at D, F takes on its maximum value G, and DD" = $G\,|N|^{1/2}$.

If the angle $\alpha$ is small, then angle D"D$P_0$ is approximately a right angle, and angle DD"$P_0$ is approximately equal to . Thus x is approximately DD" $\tan\alpha = G\ N^{1/2} \tan\alpha$. As above, the change in the height of the bump due to the curvature is approximately $.5\, k\, x^2$. So the relative change in the bump height is $.5\, k\, x^2/(G|N|^{1/2}) = (.5/R)\, G|N|^{1/2} \tan^2\alpha$. This is also equal to the relative change in the shadow length. Thus, the affinely transformed surface B(Q) discussed in section 4 is sufficiently close to the actual surface P" if $k\, G\ |N|^{1/2} \tan^2\alpha$ is small. The errors due to surface curvature will be greatest for grazing illumination, when $\tan^2\alpha$ is large.


6. ANTI-ALIASING


The comparison of the angle $\varphi$ with the horizon angle ß is an all-or-nothing test, so the shadows computed by this method will have jagged edges. To eliminate these jaggies, we can compute by interpolation the values of $\varphi$ and ß at the four corners of each pixel and use the method of Duff (1985), Fig. 1, to determine the fraction of the area where $\varphi >$ ß. This will only work if all four corners of the pixel belong to the same patch, in which case the four values of $\varphi$ and ß can be reused for adjacent pixels.

The above method is appropriate if the projected size of the pixel on the bump map is small compared to the spatial frequency of the bumps, so that most pixels will contain only one shadow edge, or none at all. If the pixel covers several squares of the texture, it may be better to assume $\varphi$ is constant, interpolate ß only in the $\theta$ direction for each (u,v) map entry in the pixel's projection, and count the number of entries where $\varphi >$ ß. A superior method, which would also cure aliasing in the bump shading, would use several tables for the bump function, of successively coarser resolution, as suggested by Williams (1983). Finally, the penumbra calculation in section 4 above will tend to smooth the shadow edges even if the penumbra itself is too narrow to be visible.

# 7. RESULTS

Figures 5, 6 and 7 show shadows on tree bark, formed by the methods above. In figures 5 and 6, the bump textures for tree bark were mathematically defined periodic functions on a 256 x 256 grid. In the horizon tables, the angle ß was scaled to fit into 8 bits, and the values for ß in the eight directions at each grid point were packed into a single 64 bit word on the Cray-1. In figures 5 and 6, the left side shows the results of Blinn's algorithm, and the right side shows the algorithm presented here. Notice that with Blinn's algorithm, parts of the bark whose perturbed normal points towards the light source are brightly illuminated, even though they are hidden from the light source by the rest of the cylinder. In Fig. 5, the shapes of the shadows give visual cues which are important in understanding the shapes of the bumps.

It took the Cray-1 18 seconds to compute the bump and horizon maps for the bark of Fig. 6, and 11 seconds to render fig., right, at 512 x 512 resolution, using these tables. For contrast, Fig. 6, left, took 6 seconds. These images are not anti-aliased.

In Fig. 7, the bump texture for the bark was measured by Bloomenthal (1985) from a plaster cast of maple bark. On the left, a point light source was simulated causing aliasing at the high contrast shadow edges. On the right, a large disk was used for the sun, creating a penumbra, as discussed in section 4. This gives a softer edge to the shadow, and removes the "jaggies."

Figure 8 shows a view of the moon, with a bump texture formed by randomly adding craters of random size. Note the shadows cast from one rim to the other, on craters near the terminator of the sunlit region. A sun of angular diameter 1 1/2° was used, giving realistic penumbras.

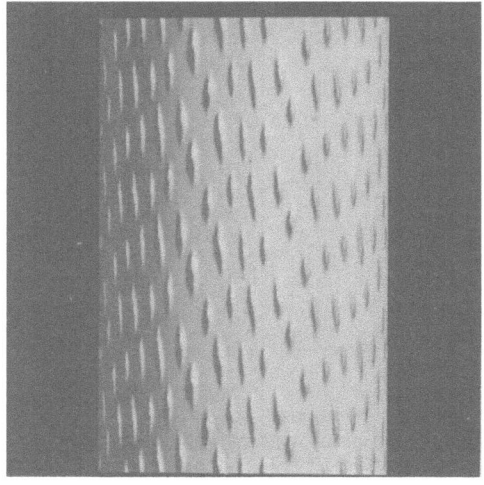 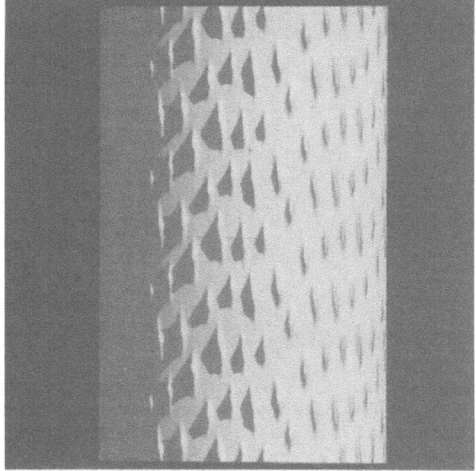

Fig. 5. A bump-mapped image of a tree trunk with a blister pattern on its bark. Left, with only normal perturbation, and right, with shadows.

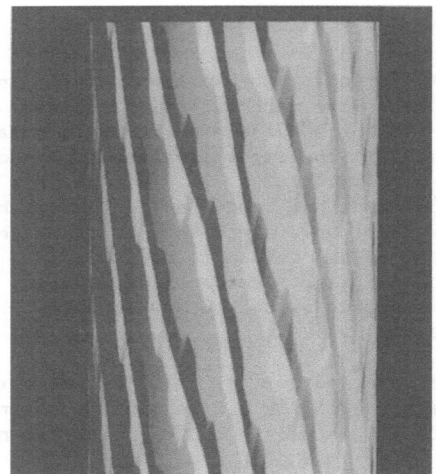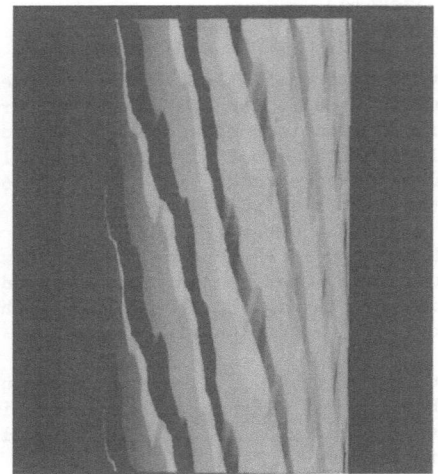

Fig. 6. A bump mapped image of a tree trunk, using a mathematically defined bump height function for the bark. Left, with only normal perturbation, and right, with shadows.

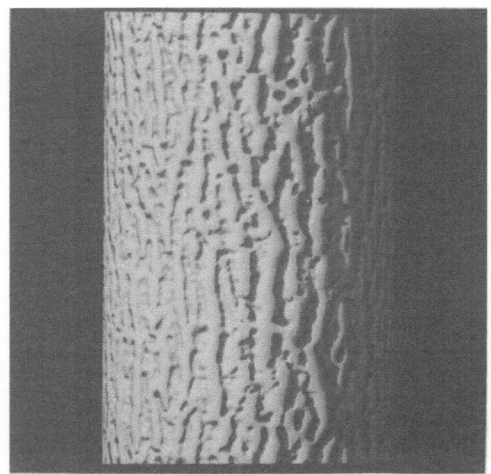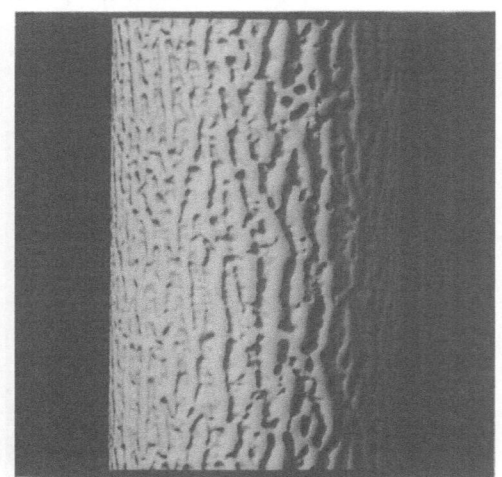

Fig. 7. An image of a tree trunk, with an actual bump map taken from Bloomenthal (1978). The ambient light in the shadowed region was taken as coming from the same direction as the sun, but with only 7% intensity, so the normal perturbation still gives texture to the shadowed areas, unlike figures 5 and 6.

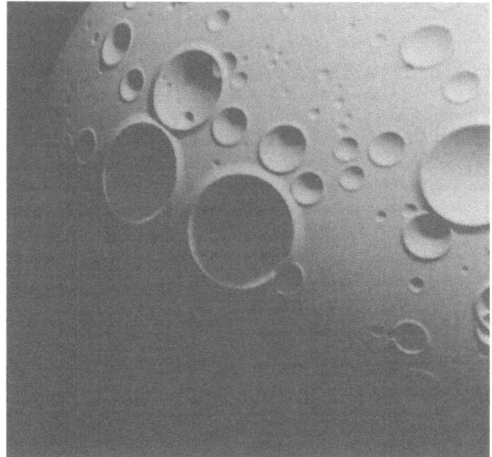

Fig. 8. A crater texture pattern on the moon, with the shadow illuminated by 7% "earthshine".

ACKNOWLEDGEMENTS

I would like to thank Maria Lopez for typing this manuscript and Charles Grant for carefully reading it and suggesting the penumbra computation. This work was performed under the auspices of the U.S. Department of Energy by Lawrence Livermore National Laboratory under contract number W-7405-Eng-48.

REFERENCES

Blinn JF (1970) Simulation of wrinkled surfaces. Computer Graphics, 12 (n.3):
286-292

Bloomenthal J (1985) Modelling the mighty maple. Computer Graphics 19 (n.3):
305-311

Cook RL (1984) Shade trees. Computer Graphics 18 (n.3): 223-231

Duff T (1985) Compositing 3-D rendered images. Computer Graphics 19 (n.3): 41-44

Whitted T (1980) An improved illumination model for shaded display. CACM 23:
343-349

Williams L (1978) Casting curved shadows on curved surfaces. Computer Graphics
12 (n.3): 270-274

Williams L (1983) Pyramidal parametrics. Computer Graphics 17 (n.3): 1-11

**Nelson Max** is a computer scientist at the Lawrence
Livermore National Laboratory, California and currently
also a visiting lecturer at the University of California.
He received his BA in mathematics at John Hopkins
University in 1963 and his Ph.D. in mathematics at
Harvard University in 1967. His research interests
include computer representation of molecular surfaces
and interactions and realistic reprensentation of
national phenomena in computer graphics. Max has several
award-winning films to his credit.

# Chapter 3
# Visual Interface and Languages

# Interaction with IBS
## An Icon-Based System

M. Erradi[1] and C. Frasson[2]

[1] Département de mathématiques et d'informatique, Université de Sherbrooke, Sherbrooke, QC, J1K 2R1, Canada
[2] Département d'informatique et de recherche opérationnelle, Université de Montréal, C.P. 6128, Succ. "A", Montréal, QC, H3C 3J7, Canada

ABSTRACT

IBS is an interactive graphical query language based on icons. It allows direct manipulation of objects dealing with pictorial data as well as alphanumeric data. In this paper we point out the interaction techniques between users and database systems. We present an overview of IBS and illustrate how queries are formulated in a medical context.

KEYWORDS

Database query languages, interaction techniques, icons, graphics and pictures, user interface.

INTRODUCTION

Availability of database systems, display editors, word processing systems and other software on micro-computer permitted access to a new class of users. These are non specialized users who generally wish a ready to use and simple system which does not require technical knowledge. The interface progressively evolved with database systems and particulary with the relational model (Astrahan 1976), (Chamberlin 1980), (Zloof 1975). It is difficult or impossible for conventional query languages (Date 1982), designed for storage, retrieval, and manipulation of alphanumeric data to express queries such as "Give the name of the person whose stomach looks like the one on the screen". Thus, in the last few years, pictorial query languages were designed as augmented conventional query languages (Chang and Fu 1981). Several experiments were done towards the integration of textual and pictorial data (Tang 1981), (Crosby 1984).

However, users, especially novel ones, need flexible user interfaces to express their needs. Thus, a fundamental step for enhancement of man-machine communication is presented in (Chang and Fu 1980b), (Herot 1980), (Frasson and Erradi 1985). A user interface using interactive techniques, like the mouse, pop-up menus, multiple windows and bit-mapped displays, enables users to directly and easily perform their tasks (Schneiderman 1983). We will discuss the advantages of visual representation of data. Then we will show how IBS allows a direct interaction using those techniques.

GRAPHICAL INTERACTION AND ICONS

Interest in graphical interfaces was not really emphasized before the beginning of the eighties when two forces converged: new developments in graphics and image processing, and the availability of new interactive facilities.

The advantage of a graphical query language was first noted by Zloof with OBE (Query-By-Example) (Zloof 1975). A query may be built up in any order the user likes which is important because the perception of a problem and the solution are generally different for different users. When an end-user understands his own needs, he wishes a direct and visual interaction with the computer. He wants to query without having to worry about procedural details. CUPID (McDonald and Stonebraker 1975), implemented on top of a predicate calculus language, is another graphical language in which the user builts queries by light-pen manipulation of a set of symbols. Recent introduction of new functionalities such as multiple windows, selection and manipulation of objects with a mouse, pop-up menus and bit-mapped displays, allow defining and using icons for various purposes.

An icon is an image or pattern which bears a natural ressemblance to that which it represents (Tanimoto 1976). So images are easily learned, remembered and recalled as single units of information. It is commonly acknowledged that human knowledge is based on visual perception. An image is more explicit and representative of a domain than several hundred of words describing its contents.

An important aspect of human behavior is that it is possible to understand the meaning of an image at a glance, which is not the case of one page of alphanumeric data even in a structured form. An image that represents a real-world object will help not only the specialist to formulate and communicate thoughts faster and better, but will also aid the novice. Images express information concerning the spatial disposition of objects, their appearance, their texture and their composition.

Another important fact is that it is not always necessary to consider a complete and precise image of an object to understand the meaning of the underlying information. An icon can be sufficiently expressive. The international system of road signs is an example of icons that everybody can easily understand. In various domains (medecine, chimestry, mechanic, traffic control...) icons are used for communicating with groups of users.

Taking in account this capability of the human brain to process picture more efficiently than text we designed (Erradi and Frasson 1985) an interactive system based on icons: IBS (Icons-Based System). The approach is similar to that of QPE (Chang and Fu 1980) but instead of using a tabular form of query formulation, we use icons to sketch a graphical example of a possible answer, including graphical and textual data. Answers can also be given by the system under iconic or textual form.

IBS CONCEPTS

IBS is based on an iconic interface through which it is possible to define and manipulate both conventional and pictorial data. Icons are used to represent objects and their characteristics. They also constitute means of indexing and a simplified representation of actual images which can be retrieved and associated with textual information. IBS allows the user to express his queries by a direct and visual interaction with the computer without having to worry about procedural details. Two types of objects will be considered: iconic and textual entities.

An iconic entity represents an object having iconic or textual characteristics. A textual entity represents an object with only alphanumeric characteristics. For instance, a lung is an iconic entity characterized by some diseases and diagnosis. Diseases can be represented by icons while diagnosis are textual comments.

The conceptual environment of IBS is based on an object oriented interface composed of:
  - a set of objects familiar to the user
  - a set of commands which can be performed on the objects.

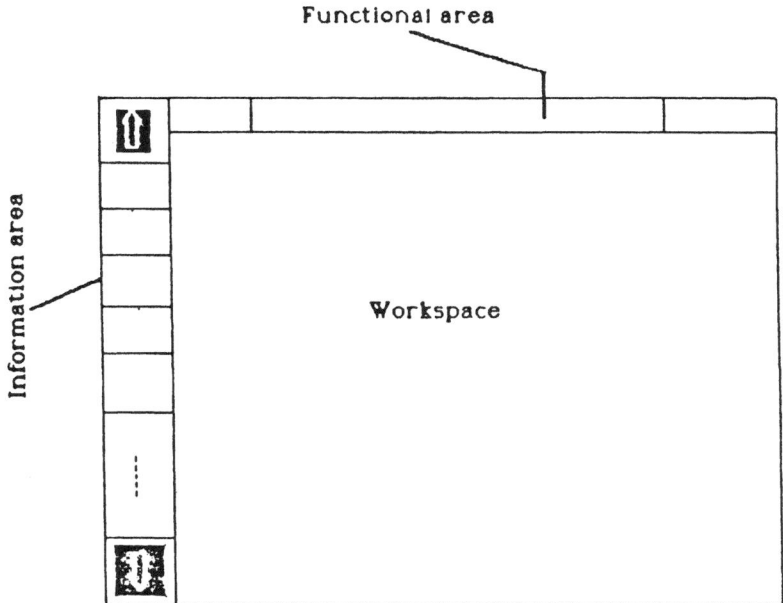

Fig. 1 : The interface areas

The screen is divided into three areas (Fig. 1):

- A workspace area where the objects selected can be manipulated through a window,

- an information area where the various iconic characteristics can be scrolled,

- a functional area which contains classes of commands to be performed on the objects.

The selection of an object is done by direct manipulation (pointing on the icon and clicking on a mouse, for instance) which will bring the object into the workspace for further manipulations.

When an alphanumeric object is activated, all the attributes, in relational model terms (Date 1982), are displayed in the workspace for eventual manipulation. When an icon is activated it appears in the workspace while its associated characteristics fill in the information area as shown in Fig. 2, where we have lungs with diseases such as cancer, bronchopneumonia, perforation, oedema. Other characteristics can appear via scrolling.

Iconic representation provides facilities to show the existing relationships among different objects. Icons representing the objects are interrelated by graphical lines which symbolize existing relationships. Fig. 3 shows a simple model concerning patients and organs such as lungs, stomach, teeth. Diseases can affect patients' organs. It is possible to draw different relationships which will be distinguished by differents labels.

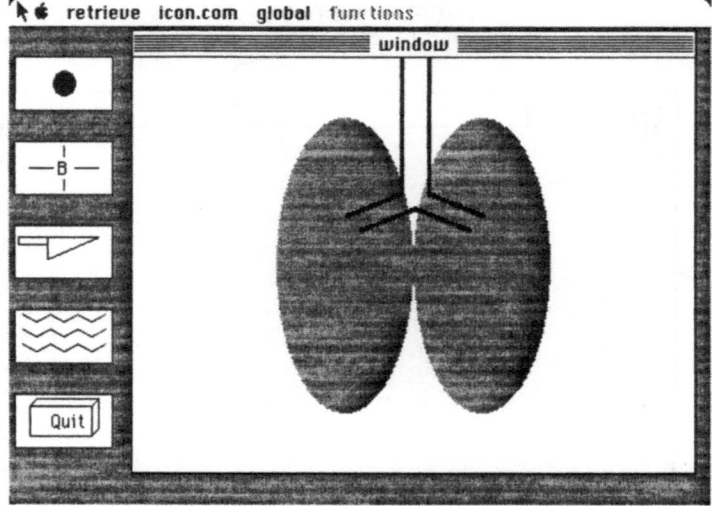

Fig. 2 : An object with some characteristics

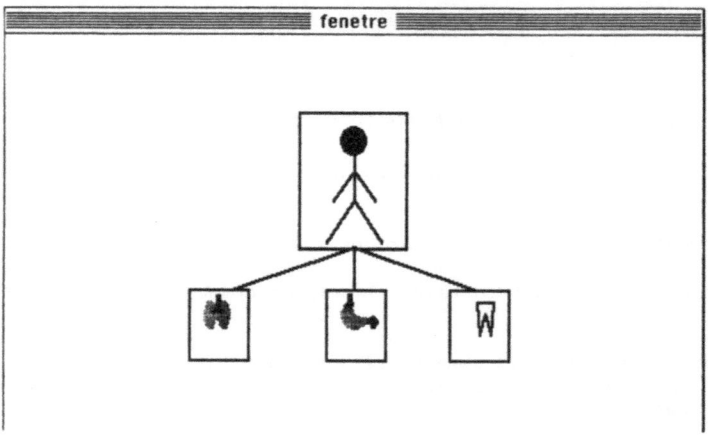

Fig. 3 : An iconic data model

Notice that nothing in the model specifies whether the objects involve alphanumeric or image data. The type of data associated with the object will appear when selected, and similarly for the meaning of relationships.

IBS ARCHITECTURE

The architecture of IBS is shown on Fig. 4.

We first distinguish a set of primitive objects which are used to build the environment of an application. We have there a set of basic icons designed to represent different objects which can be general (a human, a part of the body, a hospital information desk) or specific (a physician, a medical treatment, a disease,...). Icons can be extracted from this set, modified or built up from scratch using an icon editor. The corresponding commands are grouped into the pop-up menu called "icon.com" shown in Fig. 2.

We also have a set of commands capable of retrieving or manipulating the objects, such as SEARCH LIKE an object with the same criteria as those of the object which is displayed on the screen, HIDE elements of the object present in the workspace, LINK, which binds a set of selected instances of an object to another object... All these commands are described in (Frasson and Erradi 1985). Here, we will use a subset of these commands for illustrating the process. Also, a subset of the commands can be extracted for an application.

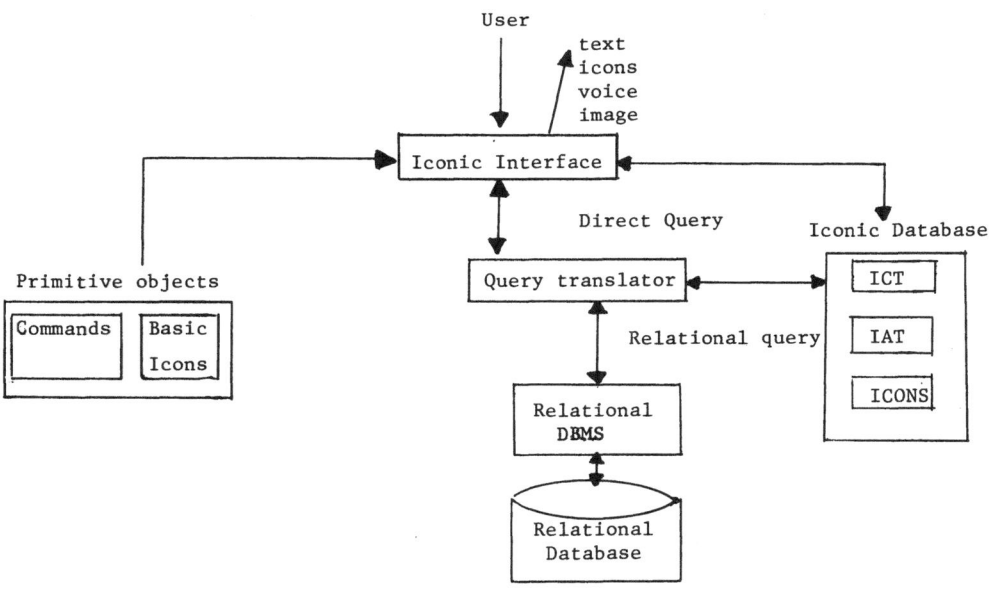

Fig. 4 : Architecture of IBS

An example of such a subset is shown on Fig. 6.

The iconic interface was described above. Notice that the iconic interface comprises of the different objects and commands with which the user is concerned, but also the areas of interaction where objects and commands are displayed.

The iconic database is composed of two iconic tables, the iconic correspondance table (ICT) and the iconic associative table (IAT), and a database of all icons used by the applications. ICT contains all the surrogates (*Grosby* 1984) of the icons (Icon-Id). These surrogates are symbolic addresses of the icons in secondary memory. They are associated with their respective textual meaning (the name of the icon) as indicated on Fig. 5. Notice that there is no difference in this table between an iconic entity and an iconic characteristic since all objects are considered as icons only.

| Icon-id | Icon-name |
|---------|-----------|
| I1 | Lungs |
| I2 | Stomach |
| I3 | Cancer |
| I4 | Pneumonia |
| I5 | Heart |
| I6 | Gastric-Ulcer |
| I7 | Tooth |
| I8 | Duodenal-Ulcer |

ICT

| Icon-id | Sub-Icon-Id |
|---------|-------------|
| I1 | I3 |
| I2 | I6 |
| I2 | I3 |
| I1 | I4 |
| I2 | I8 |

IAT

Fig. 5 : The iconic database

The IAT connects an iconic attribute to the iconic entity for which it is a characteristic. For instance cancer (I3) and pneumonia (I4) can affect Lungs (I1).

The Query translator receives a query (direct query) as a succession of events of interaction and translates it into a relational query. We will see examples of such events later. Data input to the query translator are composed of icons, commands, alphanumeric data and positions of icons. The iconic database is used to substitute textual data with iconic data. The result of the translation consists in a QBE-like-table where attributes are automatically filled with the previous values. Then, the relational query is issued to the relational DBMS and the database.

The answers are recomposed in a reverse way. Thus, relational tuples are converted into iconic or textual representation and given to the user through the iconic interface.

MANIPULATIONS USING ICONS

In this section, we will show how IBS allows users direct manipulation of objects leading to the formulation of a query on the database. To illustrate the following discussions, we will consider a medical context with a simple relational model concerning patients organs (stomachs, lungs) and treatments received.

- PATIENT (Pat-Id, name, address, phone, birth-date)

- LUNGS (Pat-id, Lung-dis-id, disease, diagnosis, date, xl,yl, width)

- STOMACH (Pat-id, Stom-dis-id, disease, diagnosis, date, xl,yl, width)

- TREATMENT (Pat-id, dis-id, treat-desc, start-date, end-date, physician)

- PICTURE (Pat-id, dis-id, Frame)

The PATIENT relation contains information identifying the patient. The LUNGS and STOMACH relations are defined on the same domains: the identification number of the patient, the identification number of the disease (a surrogate), the disease description and the diagnosis issued from a visit of the patient, the date of the visit, the position (coordinates) of the disease and the width of a region where the disease occurs.

The TREATMENT relation contains a description of a treatment (treat-desc) received by a patient (pat-id) for a disease (dis-id), with the starting-date and the end-date of the treatment and the name of the physician who recommanded it.

Finally, the PICTURE relation gives the frame number of the actual image containing the disease (the image may or may not exist).

Let us consider now the following queries:

Q1:   Give the name of the persons having a cancer in their left lung.

Q2:   Show lungs and diagnosis of 25 years old patients having a duodenal ulcer in their stomach.

Q3:   Give the name of the person whose stomach looks like the one on the screen.

Q4:   Display all images corresponding to the given stomach.

We know that such queries cannot be solved using conventional query languages because we are using pictorial examples. So, we will show how these queries can be formulated in IBS. We suppose that, for all these queries, we start from the iconic model indicated on Fig. 3.

Q1:   To illustrate this query we decompose the manipulation according to different successive events. In fact, once a user has a minimal training of the interface these events are performed with ease and fun. Pointing and clicking are performed with the mouse. These two combined actions will be referred to as "select". The user:

  - selects the icon representing lungs (the lungs appear into the workspace area and simultaneously their characteristics fill in the information area as in Fig. 2),

  - drags the "cancer" icon over to the left lung (Fig. 6), (the position on the lung is automatically calculated by the system). A function ("functions" command) is provided to specify the range of retrieval. The user can specify a value (corresponding to the width attribute in the relations), or he can choose a region (a lung for instance) by pointing to it.

  - selects the "LINK" command from the pop-up menu (Fig. 6). The iconic model is displayed again in the workspace for further selections to be linked to the previous choice. At this stage the query translator has automatically translated the events into the following equivalent QBE table:

| Lungs | Pat-id | Lung-dis-id | disease | diagnosis | date | X1 | Y1 | width |
|-------|--------|-------------|---------|-----------|------|----|----|-------|
|       |        |             | cancer  |           |      | x1 | y1 |       |

  - selects the PATIENT icon. The textual attributes of a patient appear in the workspace and the user selects the name attribute (Fig. 7),

  - selects the "SEARCH" command to start the retrieval process.

At this stage the equivalent QBE table would be:

| Lungs | Pat-id | Lung | dis-id | disease | diagnosis | date | X1 | Y1 | width |
|-------|--------|------|--------|---------|-----------|------|----|----|-------|
|       | X      |      |        |         | cancer    |      | x1 | y1 |       |

| Patient | PAT-id | name | adress | phone | birth-date |
|---------|--------|------|--------|-------|------------|
|         | y      | P    |        |       |            |

Q2:  In a similar way, the user selects the stomach icon and drags the duodenal
     ulcer icon (Fig. 8) on to the stomach (notice that integrity constraints can
     easily be implemented to avoid placing a duodenal ulcer into the stomach).
     Then the user selects the "LINK" command which displays the objects having a
     relationship with the stomach (Fig. 3). Selecting the patient icon shows the
     patient's attributes and the birth date is inserted (Fig. 9). After selecting
     the "LINK" command, then a lung icon, the user initiates the retrieval process
     by activating the "SEARCH" command. A example of results including the diag-
     nosis is given in Fig. 10. An additional characteristic of IBS is its
     capability to output textual data like diagnosis by voice. The interest is
     that more complete comments can be added to a simple displayed diagnosis.
     This capability can be activated by selecting the "COMMENT" command shown in
     Fig. 12.

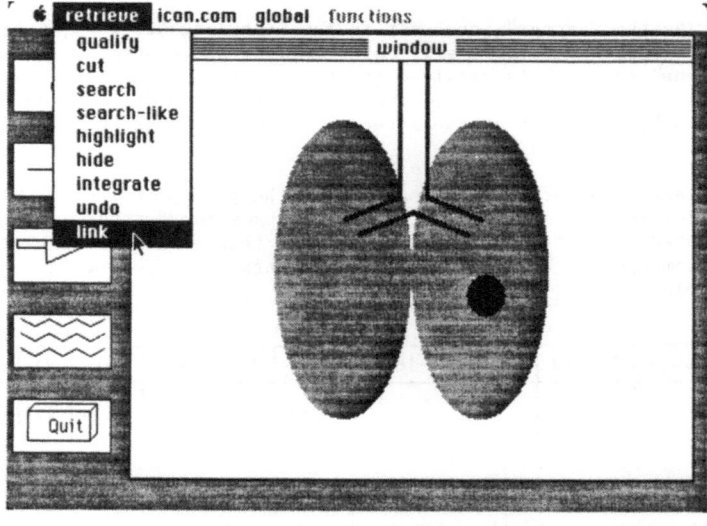

Fig. 6 : A Search Pattern

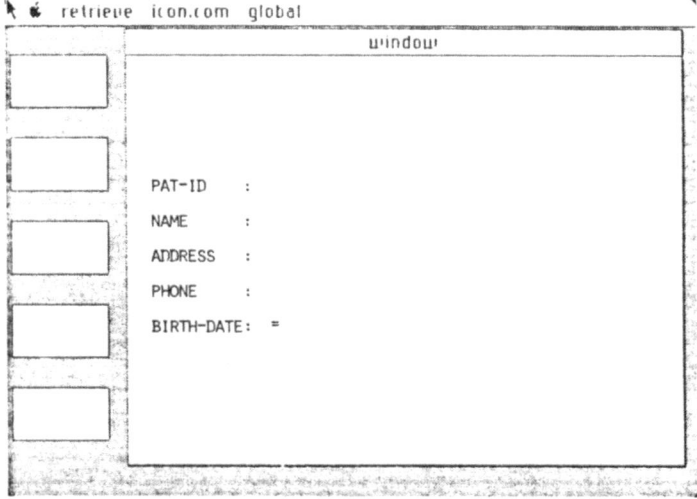

Fig. 7 : Attributes of the PATIENT relation

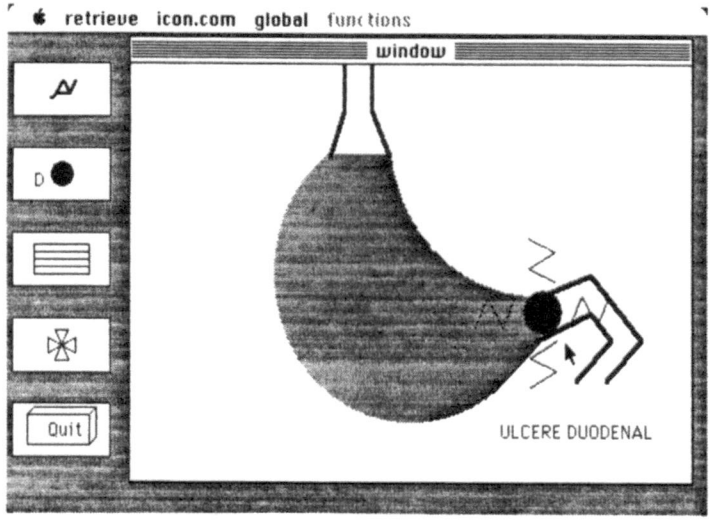

Fig. 8 :

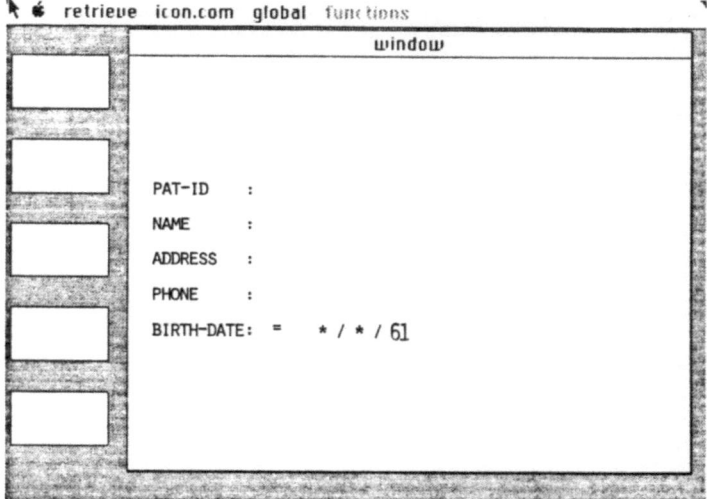

Fig. 9 :

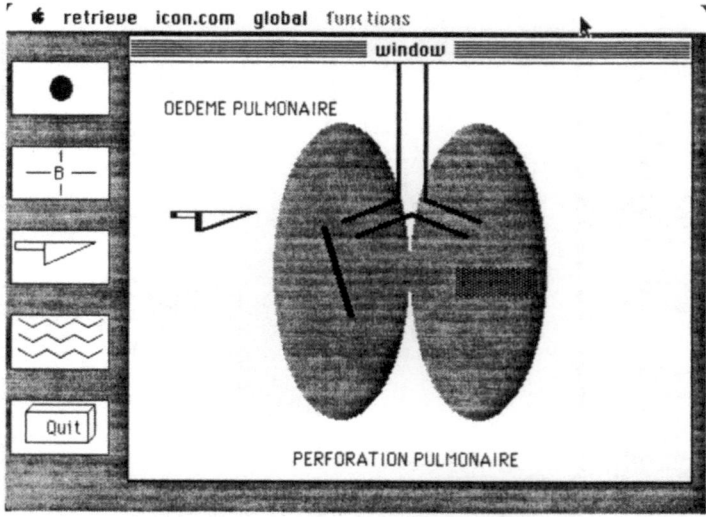

Fig. 10 :

Q3: In this query a certain stomach, having cancer and mucosity, is displayed on the screen (Fig. 11). The user selects the "SEARCH LIKE" command to find identical instances. Then, after the selection of "LINK" command and patient icon the user selects the patient's name and the "SEARCH" command.

Q4: This query is immediate. Having, for instance, the organ represented in Fig. 12 we select the "IMAGE" command within the global pop-up menu and obtain the ·corresponding actual images.

Other capabilities are provided in IBS. They encompass the main functions which exist in QPE. However actual images are not automatically converted into icons (as sketches in QPE). An interesting aspect in IBS is that icons are used both as a support for expressing queries and as a means to visually represent the different characteristics stored in a relational database. In that case icons are reconstructed from the relational tuples.

CONCLUSION AND FUTURE WORK

An iconic interface has been presented. The system we have designed is intended for users interested in the of "what you see is what you get" principle. Some aspects of the present system have been implemented on a Macintosh micro-computer, in Mac-Forth language, using file access techniques, and also in C language. The C language has been selected for integration with a relational system, operation currently being implemented on a Sun.

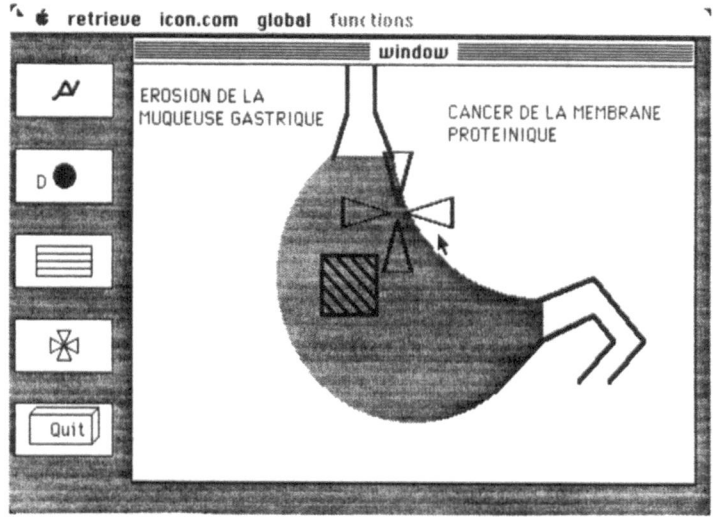

Fig. 11 :

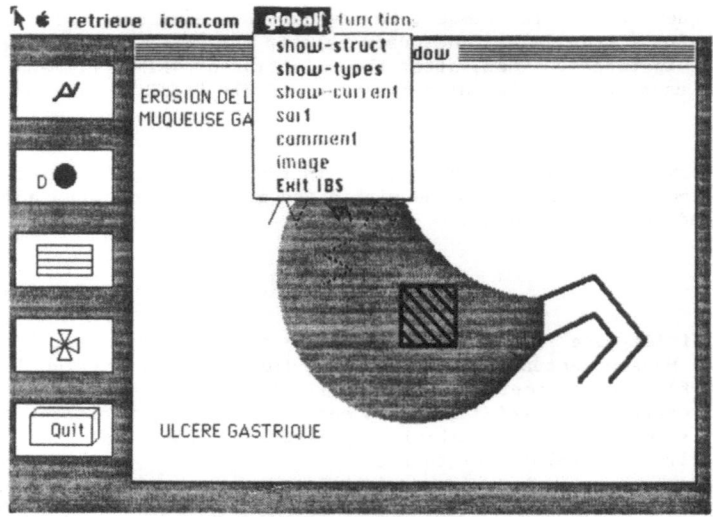

Fig. 12 :

ACKNOWLEDGMENTS

This work was supported by NSERC under grant A0196. We would like to acknowledge the numerous students who have contributed to the first stages of implementation of the project: S. Decarie, C. Blouin, D. Funke, S. Michel, P. Marchand. Several suggestions and remarks by the referrees were very appreciated. Finally we would like to thank Pierre McKenzie for his critical review.

REFFRENCES

Astrahan MM et al (1976)  System R: a relational approach to database management. ACM trans. on Database system, Vol 1, No 2.

Chang NS, Fu KS (1980)  Query-By-Pictorial-Example.  IEEE transaction on software engineering, Vol SE-6, No 6, pp 519-524.

Chang NS, Fu KS (1981)  Picture query languages for pictorial database systems. Computer, IEEE, pp 23-33.

Chamberlin D (1980)  A summary of user experience with SQL data sublanguage. Proc. International conf. on databases, Aberdeen, Scotland.

Date CJ (1982)  An introduction to database systems.  The systems programming series, 3rd edition, Addison-Wesley, Reading, Mass.

Frradi M, Frasson C (1985)  A Forth-based iconic interface.  Proceedings 1985 Rochester Forth Conference, June 12-15.

Frasson C, Erradi M (1985) An Icon Based Language for application in medicine. Document de travail no. 158. Département d'informatique et de recherche opérationnelle, Université de Montréal.

Frasson C, Frradi M (1985) Graphics interaction in databases. Proceedings Graphics Interface '85, May 27-31.

Crosby W (1984) Toward a data model for integrated pictorial databases. Computer Vision Graphics and Image Processing 25, Academic Press, pp 371-382.

Herot CF (1980) Spatial management of data. ACM transaction on database systems, pp 493-513.

McDonald N, Stonebraker (1975) Cupid, the friendly query language. Proceedings of ACM Pacific Conference, San Francisco.

Shneiderman B (1983) Direct manipulation: a step beyond programming languages. Computer, IEEE, pp 57-69.

Tang GY (1981) A management system for integrated database of pictures and alphanumeric data. Computer Graphics Image Processing 10, 270-286.

Tanimoto SL (1976) An iconic/symbolic data structuring scheme. Pattern recognition and artificial intelligence, Academic Press, pp 452-471.

Zloof MM (1979) Query-By-Example language design consideration. Infotech status of the art report: Man/computer communication, Vol 2, pp 356-363.

Mohammed Erradi is currently lecturer in Computer Science at the University of Sherbrooke. His research interests include database systems, (graphics interaction) and computer communications.
Erradi received his Analyst Engineer degree in computer science from INSEA (MOROCCO) in 1982, and an M.Sc. degree in Computer Science from the University of Montreal in 1985 where he is a PHD student in Computer Science.
He is an ACM member.

Claude Frasson is Professor in Computer Science at the University of Montreal. His research interests include database systems, performance, user interfaces, expert systems, computer-assisted education. He has authored numerous articles and a book on databases. Frasson worked at IBM Research in La Gaude France, then he joined the University of Tunis and later the University of Nice as Professor. He was also consultant for ADI (Ministry of Industry, Paris).
Frasson received his Ph.D. in Computer Science in 1974 and a "doctorat d'Etat" in 1981 from the University of Nice. He is member of ACM and AFCET.

# GEO
## Graphics System with Editable Objects

Peter Wisskirchen

Gesellschaft für Mathematik und Datenverarbeitung mbH, Schloss Birlinghoven,
D-5205 St. Augustin, Federal Republic of Germany

Summary: *The Computer Graphics Standard GKS does not support complex segment structuring and editing facilities. With the dissemination of very powerful workstations and devices, there is a need for GKS-extensions with multilevel segment structures and editable objects. One approach to a specification of such a system is PHIGS, the Programmer's Hierarchical Interactive Graphics Standard. In the following we will present an alternative to PHIGS called GEO (Graphics System with Editable Objects). GEO is upwardly compatible to GKS in a very natural way. In addition, naming of graphics objects can be provided in terms of application oriented aspects.*

Key Words: *graphics utilities, graphics standards, GKS, PHIGS, object-oriented systems, Smalltalk-80*

## 1. Motivation

### 1.1 GKS-Extensions

The Computer Graphics Standard GKS [ANSI84, ENDE84] does not support high level segment editing facilities. In GKS segments can be named, deleted and inserted, highlighted, etc. However, the content of a segment cannot be changed after a segment has been closed. In addition to that, GKS supports only a one-level segment hierarchy. With the dissemination of very powerful workstations and devices, there is a need for GKS-extensions with multilevel segment structures and editable objects.

One approach to a specification of such a system is PHIGS, the Programmer's Hierarchical Interactive Graphics Standard, which is still under development [ANSI85]. In the following we will present an alternative to PHIGS called GEO (Graphics System with Editable Objects), which has essentially the same basic functionality as PHIGS. GEO differs from PHIGS in its naming and segment editing mechanism, and it appears to be more upwardly compatible with GKS.

The main advantage is that the PHIGS-concept of integer element pointer is unknown to GEO, and that the application programmer can name graphics objects in *his* or *her* application-oriented model.

Although the basic idea can be realized for all procedure-oriented languages, we have formulated the GEO-functions in Smalltalk-80. The Smalltalk-80 syntax provides a very elegant way to express functions concerning high-level objects (here: elements of graphics segments) and functions (messages) operating on them. We are also using Smalltalk-80 for an experimental implementation which is under way.

## 1.2   The Functional Specification PHIGS

The Programmer's Hierarchical Interactive Graphics Standard (PHIGS) is a functional specification of the interface between an application program and its graphics support system. PHIGS supports "multilevel/hierarchical structuring of graphics data, a high degree of interactivity, rapid modification of graphics data and the relationships among the data, applicability to a diverse application family, minimality of functionality while producing an effective standard."[ANSI85]. PHIGS graphics data is organized into units called structures. Structures can be related to each other hierarchically. The hierarchy is modeled by an acyclic directed graph. Structures contain structure elements such as output primitives, attribute selections, viewing selections and so-called application-specific data (non-graphical data used by an application program). A structure is organized as a one-dimensional array (linear list). The PHIGS structure editing operations are essentially deletions and insertions of structure elements at a position described by an (integer type) element pointer. It is possible to insert so called label-elements into a structure; this allows limited referencing facilities independent of the "integer-type"-naming over element pointers.

In [WISS85] we have criticized the PHIGS approach. Our main point was that editing structures via element pointers produces structure clashes between application-oriented naming and the PHIGS referencing concept. This leads to the need to manage two hierarchies and to establish a bridge between them, to be built by the application programmer. With GEO we propose a constructive alternative of a graphics system with high-level editing functions.

## 2.   Basic Design Criteria for GEO

## 2.1   Preliminary Remarks

The object-oriented concepts and programming in Smalltalk-80 are described in [GOLD83].

The main characteristics of object-oriented systems are the following:

— The basic construct in object-oriented systems is the *object*.

— Its behavior is described by the *class-definition*; besides that objects may contain instance specific information.

— Classes are described by *messages* which can be received by their instances and by *methods* which are used for processing them.

— Providing a framework of subclassing and superclassing, object-oriented systems allow *inheritance* of common behavior (methods and variables) within the class hierarchy. In addition, individual behavior of a subclass can be defined by adding new methods and by *overriding* default inherited methods.

Remark: Defining classes in object-oriented systems can be seen in analogy to the definition of abstract data types. However, the inheritance concept of object-oriented systems goes beyond the usual mechanisms for defining abstract data types. This concept of inheritance would be very useful for an *implementation* of GEO. Because we concentrate here only on *specification* aspects of the GEO functionality, our concept is also applicable to languages supporting abstract data types. Even in the case of classical languages the GEO-concept can be formulated, but not in the same elegant way.

## 2.2   Definition and Insertion of Segment Elements

Segment elements (called structure elements in PHIGS) are the basic graphics objects such as output primitives, attribute selections, viewing selections which should be inserted in segments (called structures in PHIGS). In PHIGS and GKS, creation and insertion of segment elements is one atomic action. We will break this action down into two different steps. Firstly, we will define totally instantiated objects. Then we will insert these objects into open segments:

We use the basic class Array for the creation of two one-dimensional sequences psequx and psequy of length n for the definition of the class **Pointsequence**. Then we create objects of this class by

**(1)    vertices ←PointSequence px: pSequx py: pSequy** .

(The message to **PointSequence** has the *message pattern* **px:py:** and *message content* **pSequx** and **pSequy**). For a predefined class Polyline, we can create by

**(2)    poly ←Polyline new: vertices**

a graphics output primitive.

Remark: The class membership and value of the "return-value" of the object, on the left side of ← is defined by the receiver of the message i.e. **PointSequence** in example (1).

The object **poly** created in (2) can now (one or more times) be used for the insertion into graphics segments:

**(3)   Segment insert: poly.**

Our main idea is to apply the ⟵-referencing mechanism also for naming of elements, while inserting them into segments:

**(3')   polyinSegm ⟵ Segment insert: poly .**

Now, the above action is marked, and can be referenced if editing should be required later on.

## 2.3   Segment Editing

For segment editing we will support functions for deletions, modification and insertion of all segments' elements. We split up the segments elements into two classes: *Labeled* elements named as in (3') can be changed later on an individual basis; *anonymous* elements as in (3') cannot be changed individually, but they can be affected by more general actions such as deletions between labeled objects.

## 2.4   Inheritance of Attributes

We use exactly the same principle for the inheritance of attributes as in GKS. Attributes such as current transformation, linestyle, color etc. are inherited by the environment. The environment is changed during run-time by attribute setting functions of GKS in a *sequence which is defined by the temporal order in which these functions are called by the application program.* This sequence is completely defined by the application programmer using constructs of the host language like loops or branches. We should note that the inheritance of attributes in PHIGS is defined by the sequence of the structure elements ordered by an integer type element pointer; i.e. besides the control flow, an additional sequentialization mechanism has been added by PHIGS.

## 2.5   Structuring of Graphics Data

We will support the same structuring of graphics data as in PHIGS: Segments (called structures in PHIGS) can be related to each other hierarchically. The hierarchy is modeled by an acyclic directed graph. We propose also the same traversal and posting concept as in PHIGS.

Although we differ from PHIGS in the way that we edit segment elements, we correspond with its functionality. We will show the advantage of the proposed GEO naming mechanism by means of examples.

## 3. An Example for Segment Editing

We show the main specifications by means of examples. In the example we construct a segment (#house). Later on, #house is reopened and changed by typical editing operations. We assume that we have defined the required polylines for the construction of our house by respective objects (contour, door, window) in analogy to (2).

(5)     Segment new: #house

{Creation of a new segment. We name it by the symbol #house (and not by the —-mechanism) because naming is mandatory. }

(6)     Segment insert: contour

(7)     Segment insert: door

(8)     windowtr1 — Execute object: window under: transf1

(9)     rightWindow— Segment insert: windowtr1

(10)    windowtr2 — Execute object: window under: transf2

(11)    leftWindow — Segment insert: windowtr2

(12)    Segment close

At this point, we have constructed a segment with name #house. Only (9) and (11) have been "arrowed" by —- and can be changed later on an individual basis, whereas (6) and (7) are anonymous segment elements. We will now change our house in the following way: The right window should be deleted, and the left window should be changed to another shape which we assume to be predefined by windnew.

(13)    Segment reopen: #house

(14)    rightWindow delete

(15)    window2 — Execute object: windnew under: transf2

(16)    newWindow modifyby: windowType2left

(17)    Segment close

## 3.1 Comparision with PHIGS

The above example shows that segment naming and editing appears quite natural. How does the analogue example look like if we are using PHIGS?

Let's assume that the integer element pointer (i.e. the PHIGS-reference) of the right window (analogue to (9)) is 3, and that of the left window (analogue to (11) is 4. After deletion of the right window (analogue to (14)), PHIGS changes the element pointers of all successive segment elements. Therefore, the application programmer must implement a mechanism for keeping in mind that in our example the element pointer of the left window has been changed from 4 to 3, because 3 must be used as parameter for the PHIGS operation, analogue to (16).

It should be noted that PHIGS offers also another possibility: the insertion of so-called label elements *between* segment elements. It appears to us as a rather complicated way to do simple things. In our example, four labels would be necessary to be included (before and after (9) and (11)).

## 4. Additional Editing Operations

Besides the fundamental editing operations there exist some additional ones for achieving the same functionality as PHIGS. We will briefly describe some of these:

(18)    name2 — name1 delete

{Deletion of name1 and creation of an empty element name2, which can be refilled later on.}

(19)    a deleteupto: b

{Deletion from a up to b. Note, that the ordering relation is given by the temporal order as outlined in 2.4!}

(20)    a2 — a1 insertafter: poly

{Insertion of poly with label a2 after a1.}

## 5. Remarks to GEO-Language Binding

The functional specification of GEO does not require an object-oriented environment. However, a language binding for a classical language as Fortran would be less elegant. Because there is no direct naming facility for high level objects all information has to be "transmitted" over strings, to be inserted into parameter lists, i.e.

**(21)**    CALL POLYLINE-WITH-NAME(XA,YA,N,'POLY')

**(22)**    CALL SEGMENTINSERT('NAME','POLY')

for the generation of a labeled segment 'POLY' with label 'NAME'.

## 6.  Conclusions

We have shown by examples how the GEO proposal works. We are presently implementing the main concepts as a pilot version, using the Smalltalk-80 environment. It should be noted that we agree with the PHIGS-functionality in its general aspects. We see GEO as are more abstract specification that can (but not must) be implemented on top of PHIGS. In that case the job of bridging between the general GEO-naming concept and PHIGS's integer element pointer concept would be that of the manufacturer of the graphics kernel, and not a task left back to the group of applications programmers.

## 7.  Acknowledgements

The author thanks his colleagues D. Bolz, R. Kolb, K. Kansy, and S. Smith for their support and for valuable discussions.

## 8.  References

ANSI84     AMERICAN NATIONAL STANDARDS INSTITUTE: *"Graphical Kernel System"*; ANSI, New York, Dec. 1984.

ANSI85     ANSI/X3H31: *"Programmer's Hierarchical Graphics System"*; ANSI, New York, Aug. 1985.

ENDE84     G. ENDERLE, K. KANSY, G. PFAFF: *"Computer Graphics Programming"*; Springer-Verlag, Berlin Heidelberg New York Tokyo 1984.

GOLD83     A. GOLDBERG, D. ROBSON: *"Smalltalk-80: The Language and its Implementation"*; Addison-Wesley, Reading, Mass., USA (1983).

WISS85     P. WISSKIRCHEN: *"Towards Object-Oriented Graphics Standards"*; in EUROGRAPHICS'85, North Holland, Amsterdam, 391-400 (1985).

**Peter Wisskirchen** is a director of the Institute for
Applied Information Technology of the Gesellschaft fuer
Mathematik und Datenverarbeitung in St. Augustin, near
Bonn, West Germany. His research interests include
computer graphics, generalized man-machine communication, and integrated office information systems.
He coordinates a number of research projects in these
areas, where a common theme is the attempt to utilize
a so-called "Knowledge-based" approach. He has
authored numerous publications in computer graphics
and integrated office systems.

Wisskirchen is chairman of the special interest
group in Graphics Systems within the German scientific
and professional computing organization, "Gesellschaft
fuer Informatik" (GI). He also coordinates the
computer graphics activities of West Germany's
large-scale national research centers of the Arbeits-
gemeinschaft der Grossforschungseinrichtungen (AGF).

Wisskirchen is one of the pioneers in the definition of the computer graphics
standard GKS. He was the first German delegate in the ISO Working Group "Computer
Graphics" ISO TC97/SC5/WG2, and was a member of the first editorial subgroup,
chaired by J. Encarnacao, which produced the early specifications for GKS.

Wisskirchen received his Ph.D. in Mathematics from the University of Bonn in 1969.

# A Pixelated Design Medium

Ranjit Makkuni

XEROX Palo Alto Research Center, 3333 Coyote Hill Road, Palo Alto, CA 94304, USA

*ABSTRACT.    This paper illustrates the use of pixelated structures as a representational medium through which design may be accomplished. In this medium, compositions are constructed from parts called pixels which are very simple. Methods to generate a design vocabulary from these parts, and establish relationships between parts to construct compositions are brought together in the framework of formal languages.*
*Keywords: design medium, pixelation, motifs of composition, formal languages, cellular automata.*

## INTRODUCTION

Representations store the markings that index a designer's thought process. In a traditional design medium, these markings are formed by tracing a drawing instrument over a drawing surface. The quality and the characteristics of these markings depend upon:
1) the physical properties of the drawing surface and the physical construction of the drawing instrument, and
2) techniques by which the physical properties of a medium are manipulated to the designer's expressive advantage by gestural movements, such as the manner in which a designer handles an instrument to strengthen or bring out the character inherent in the physical properties.

The physical properties and techniques, hence create an environment whereby a designer's ideas can flourish and may be judged by how best a designer is able to transmit ideas in one's head to the markings on a representational medium, and how easy it is for a designer to interpret, evaluate, refine and reorganise the markings. Just as traditional media are characterised by the physical properties and techniques, the materials of computing exist in:
1) the machine processable knowledge structures that we employ, and
2) techniques that manipulate these knowledge structures.

Different knowledge structures will elucidate different design properties, and the selection of the design medium is important in the transmission, evaluation and the development of an idea. This paper will consider a pixelated knowledge structure which is built from component parts that are very simple, and examine the nature of techniques that manipulate this structure in the development of a class of compositions.

-------------------------------------------------------------------------------------

* Author's present affiliation and address: XEROX Palo Alto Research Center,
  Palo Alto, CA 94304.

# PIXELATION OF COMPOSITIONS

A pixelated knowledge structure views compositions in terms of an assemblage of parts. It decomposes compositions into small atoms or cells that encode special properties that define the state of a part. The process of decomposing compositions into its parts is called pixelation. In a two dimensional composition the simplest unit of decomposition is a pixel, where a pixel is a coordinate pair in a two dimensional Cartesian coordinate system with which some additional information is associated, (X,Y,<information>). An approach that can represent two dimensional compositions as pixelated assemblages has been shown by March (1976) and applied by Mitchell (1977) and Eastman (1977). In this pixelated representation of two dimensional compositions, the additional information associated with the pixels specified an occupancy state that determined whether a pixel was empty or occupied.

Similarly, any three dimensional form may be dissected into a number of thin layers along the dimensioning vectors of the three axes that define an object's lengths, widths and heights. Dissections taken horizontally are equivalent to plans and dissections taken vertically similar to sections. When these dissections are applied together, unique cellular spaces emerge. These cellular spaces are termed voxels, and a voxel may be viewed as a quadruple in a three dimensional Cartesian coordinate system with which some special properties are associated. The special properties associated with a voxel could include its occupancy state, colours, textures, materials, or even objects of increasing structure that are circumscribed in a voxel space.

The minimum grating or lattice that uniquely contains an object, and the contents of the voxels created by this grating, form the rudimentary design variables in the composition of voxelated assemblages; and a particular design can be represented by assigning values to these variables. In the representation of rectilinear compositions, voxels may be viewed as cubic solids (Fig. 1a), or they may be interpreted as polyhedra in the composition of wedged and bevelled shaped form (Fig. 1b). With the specification of additional properties, voxels may be interpreted into any object of interest. The phrase 'object of interest' is used to refer to the careful and restricted interpretation of voxels into objects of structure; and lies opposed to the universe of all possible designs determined by the Cartesian product of the ranges of the rudimentary design variables. More abstractly, it requires the designer to specify:
1) vocabulary elements by interpreting voxels as objects of increasing structure; and
2) define relationships between the elements of the vocabulary to construct the motifs of composition. These will be dealt with in the subsequent section.

# MOTIFS OF COMPOSITION

## Vocabulary

A vocabulary is a collection of carefully generated objects of interest termed vocabulary elements by a designer. In a voxelated lattice, a vocabulary may be constructed by considering voxels or subsets of voxels, applying the operations of union, intersection and difference to them, and later interpreting resultant voxel clusters into objects of interest. Steadman (1973,1975) and March (1976) have demonstrated an algebra that generates rectilinear dissections and polyominoes that may be viewed as edge connected pixels or face connected voxels.

Typically, the interpretation of a voxel into an vocabulary element requires the parametric input of the dimensioning and proportioning properties of the object in a voxel space. These parameters form a receptacle for a designer's input, and when values are assigned to the parameters, a particular instance of the object is constructed. Figure 2 illustrates a simple example of various instances of an arched vocabulary element that lies embedded in a voxel space. Here, the description of an arch was computationally constructed by the interpolation of polygons whose vertices lie on points that define segments of the outer and inner arcs of an arch. Each arc has a center, a starting and finishing angle, two polar radii and two equatorial radii.

## Rules of Composition

Once the elements of a designer's vocabulary are established, the next step is to specify how different elements in the vocabulary relate to each other in order to construct the motifs of composition. Motifs of composition may be characterised by the existence of particular kinds of symmetries in the perception of compositions due to the existence of particular relationships between instances of vocabulary elements. Simple motifs are the positioning relationships between instances of vocabulary elements: positioning vocabulary elements coaxially produces bi-laterally symmetrical compositions and concentrically produces compositions with point symmetry.

In a voxelated composition three kinds of relationship forming processes are possible:
1) an additive process occurs when all the voxels in the composition are initially empty and a designer builds up a composition by repeatedly adding instances of vocabulary elements;
2) a subtractive process occcurs by removing parts from a composition;
3) a substitution process replaces one instance with another in a voxelated composition.

The formation of relationships towards a composition can be viewed as the rules of composition, and expressed as productions. Productions take the form $a \text{---} \rangle b$. where the left hand side of the production, $a$, specifies the conditions under which the production can be applied, and the right hand side, $b$, specifies the result of its application. The application of a rule of composition requires a starting voxel structure on which a rule can apply, and when the state of computation is frozen at any time step, it is called a composition at that generation of the rule application.

Similarly, Fig. 3a illustrates a voxelated rule of composition that transforms a mass of stone into a system of pillars and ribs, and the third generation of its application on an initial cubic voxel. The resulting composition appears fractal in nature (i.e., the structure is identical at different magnifications) since the right hand side of the production is also a structure of voxels that again allows the left hand side of the production to apply (Fig. 3b). Figure 4 illustrates the application of a production in a voxel lattice that is presented as an assemblage of layers. The expansion of the voxels after a rule aplication shows the data base amplification property inherent in productions since the resultant is expressed in the same layered representation as the operands.

In the previous example, the production rule applies uniformly to all the voxel sites. In order to manipulate only particular parts of a composition, or control the locality of a rule application, a rule of composition needs the additional encoding of regulations that specify the context under which a production can apply. An example of a controlled rule application on a starting 3x3x3 lattice of voxels to produce a design option for a house in a corner lot is illustrated in Fig. 5. First an initial mass that represents the total volume of a corner lot is specified. Then it is dissected into a 3x3x3 lattice of stones and the rule is applied to varying sites in this lattice so that the designer is able to exploit the diagonal axes of a cube during the rule application. Figure 6 shows a dimensioning variation of the corner house obtained by assigning different values to the dimensions of the resulting voxel structure.

## Formal Languages

The process of defining a vocabulary, a set of relationships between instances of vocabulary elements, and rules of compositions expressed as productions provide a framework for the specification of compositions within a particular syntactical structure. In this framework a particular composition is regarded as an instance of the language employed by a designer. Different systems that define formal languages exist, such as fractals by Mandelbrot (1983), graftals by Smith (1984) and shape grammars by Stiny and Gips (1972). Although they all share a common process of implementation (i.e., they employ a starting symbol, a vocabulary of symbol strings and productions which rewrite symbol strings), they address different representations. The following section will present a model known as cellular automata that elucidates systems containing identical components, and will examine its potentials as a grammatical device in a voxelated lattice.

## CELLULAR AUTOMATA

A cellular automaton, as adapted from Wolfram (1984), consists of a lattice of inter-connected voxels, with each voxel being interpretable into one of a finite set of $k$ possible instances of vocabulary elements. The system evolves over time, with the new instance of a vocabulary element specified by a fixed rule in terms of previous vocabulary elements at a distance of $r$ or less on each side.

In the simplest case, a one dimensional cellular automaton consists of a line of inter-connected pixels, each having a value between $0$ and $k$ and denoted by different colours. At each time step the new value of a pixel is determined by a rule that specifies the new value based on its old value and the values of pixels in some neighbourhood of it. In essence, a one dimensional cellular automaton may be created by the input of the following parameters:
1) the range of values a pixel can take;
2) the neighbourhood of pixels that influence a pixel;
3) the initial sequence of the starting line of pixels;
4) a rule code (if $range = \{0....k\}$ and $neighbourhood = 1$ (nearest neighbours) then there are $(3*k + 3)$ number of $mapping\ rules$).

An evolution or a pattern of cellular automata is constructed by stacking lines of pixels below each other as it evolves through time, and studying emergent patterns. The first line of pixels represent the starting sequence, the last line represents the terminal sequence and all other time steps represent non-terminal sequences. Patterns are classified based upon spatial and temporal entropies: the spatial entropy describes the set of pixel sequences that can occur at a particular time step; the temporal entropy describes the sequence of pixels attained with time by a single pixel site in the cellular automaton evolution.

According to Wolfram (1984), cellular automata fall under four classes of behaviour:
1) pattern quickly dies out leaving a homogenous state;
2) pattern consists of a sequence of simple structures;
3) pattern leads into an apparently chaotic but with varying degrees of structure (Fig. 7a);
4) patterns lead into complex localised structures that are long lived (Fig. 7b).

Similarly, a two dimensional cellular automaton consists of a grid of pixel sites, with each site being occupied or empty. By stacking the pixel sequences obtained at various time steps over each other, it can be shown that the design option shown in Fig. 5 may be generated by a two dimensional cellular automaton.

The classification of cellular automata is also based on the ability to predict the value of a pixel at any given time step if the starting sequence and the rules are known. The effects of the variation in the starting sequence of pixels on the pixel values at a future time step are shown below :
1) class 1 does not affect the pixel values;
2) class 2 changes a predictable region of pixel values;
3) class 3 changes a region of increasing size of pixel values;
4) class 4 is unpredictable, except by explicit simulation.

Figure 7 illustrates two patterns generated by varying the parameters of a one dimensional cellular automaton evolution. They illustrate the ranges of predictability in the emergent patterns: Figure 7a shows patterns that result into predictable and self-similar fractal configurations; Figure 7b illustrates unpredictable, complex and long lived structures. Extensive reading on the classification of the spatial and temporal entropies of cellular automata are available in Wolfram (1984) and Toffoli (1984).

Based on the predictability, the state associated with the initial pixel values propogates only a finite distance in classes 1&2, but may travel an infinite distance in classes 3&4. If we are to restrict the universe of pixel sequences, a class 2 cellular automaton is preferred over class 1 since class 1 becomes homogenous over time. Thus, a class 2 cellular automaton is a grammar whose rules represent transformations for a particular pixel value based on pixel sequences that precede it. The rules of a class 2 cellular automaton are equivalent to productions that define rewriting rules for strings of pixel values, and the terminal and non-terminal sequences are equivalent to the instances or words in a language. The following example will present applications of a class 2 cellular automaton that will delineate pixelated options in a design language.

## EXAMPLES

Figures 8 and 9 illustrate plans, elevations and sections of a project that constructs the concept of reincarnation. The facade is formed by the disposition of cloud-like pavillion forms on a labyrinth of stone. Alongside each pavillion is a stairway and a water-cascade that represent mountains and rivers respectively. The waterfall and the stone wall rest over a pool at the lowest level which represents the ocean. Together, the ocean, the clouds, the rain and the rivers symbolises the endless cycle in nature, and which in turn confirms the symbols of endlessness, fertility and reincarnation. In this example, a pavillion form will be separated, and a class 2 cellular automaton used to generate alternative pavillion forms analogous to the construction process of an artisan laying stones (voxelated vocabulary elements) in courses over each other.

A pavillion is a cloud like mass of stone from which arched openings are carved out. The first step in the enumeration process required the pixelation of this pavillion into vocabulary elements, and for the purposes of this example, they were simplified to consist of an empty voxel, a solid voxel, and instances of voxels interpreted as parametric vocabulary arches and curved forms (Fig. 10). These were constructed by the methods of parametric vocabulary generation outlined earlier.

The next step required the definition of the parameters of a class 2 cellular automaton by the specification of:
1) the minimum number of voxel sites in a line of inter-connected voxels;
2) a minimum distance (time steps) that informs the system when and how to clip a cellular automaton configuration by a cloud profile (a cloud profile is characterised by the disposition of semi-cylindrical forms at the upper envelope of a cloud);
3) the ground state or the starting sequence of values;
4) cellular automaton rules that determine the values of new voxels based on sequence of voxel values in the neighbourhood of a previous time step.

The initial sequence of voxel values together with the class 2 rules determine the characteristics of the configurations that become periodic with time, and typically consists of a sequence of simple structures. Generally, three kinds of rule systems were employed to regulate the positioning of voxel values with time. They produced:
1) patterns that move diagonally across voxel sites (Fig. 13&15);
2) patterns with no displacement (Fig. 11);
3) patterns that are symmetrical about a particular voxel site (Fig. 12).
Combinations of these patterns may be produced by employing many rule systems for an evolution (i.e., rule systems would change depending upon the combination of patterns desired over time).

The rule system need not apply to all the voxel sites and a designer could also specify the voxel sites that remain passive to a rule application. Such sites are termed quiescent sites and may respond to a different rule system. Figure 14 shows the use of quiescent states that enable scaling properties by the redefinition of a cluster of voxels that lie embedded in a larger voxel. Also, quiescent states will allow a designer to break the regularity in the patterns as illustrated in Fig. 14&15. Hence, by the specification of quiescent sites, the resultant cellular automaton configuration from a evolution is subjected to modulation whereby a designer could vary, substitute elements in, or re-organise the configuration to break the symmetry or regularity inherent in certain class 2 patterns.

A class 2 cellular automaton provides a grammar that composes vocabulary elements in a voxelated lattice towards a pavillion form. Here a sequence is implied where the definition of a vocabulary element precedes the definition of a grammar. Also in this example, instances of vocabulary elements are assumed to be rigidly encased in a cubic voxel space whose dimensions fix the dimensioning properties of the vocabulary elements. However, the design parameters (including dimensioning) of an instance of a vocabulary element may depend upon design properties of another instance and the first instance can inherit properties or receive information that can assign its design variables from a second instance. Here, a communication network of design information exists between instances in a lattice, and these encode knowledge about dependencies and inheritance characteristics of design properties.

If a designer specifies the dependencies, then a cellular automaton grammar can be used only to construct a compositional topology map (data structure map), that could be later subject to interpretation by the enforcement of dependencies and inheritance characteristics on the map. Also, knowledge about dependencies and inheritance helps to preserve the conventions by which design options may be later decomposed and interpreted. With this knowledge, and for any generated topology map, a designer can examine, vary and refine the design properties of vocabulary elements to explore and observe variations in the perception of compositions, and is an area for future research .

## DISCUSSION

Within the framework presented in this paper, a design process may be viewed as the composition, evaluation and selection of a design option in a language that satisfies a set of design objectives. In a pixelated representation, cellular automata provide the generative machinery to construct compositions within a particular language by transforming a simple input into an amplification of the level of design choice. An interpretation algorithm may later ascribe semantic properties to these descriptions of design options, assess and order their quality based on some selection criteria. Although the examples presented in this paper illustrate the rich array of choices available to a designer, it leaves a question unanswered: how should this framework be integrated into traditional practice?

Traditional practice is characterised by an initial phase during which the objectives of the project crystallise and a designer formulates an initial intuitive response. If this intuitive response can be paraphrased into the formalisms for grammar provided in this paper, then a designer can explore a greater variety of design options that make up his language. Alternatively, it may be conceivable that in the future there may exist some intelligent receptor that parses a designer's intuitive response into a language. The designer's role is to vary the formal properties of a language, enumerate design options, assay their interpretations and select an option that meets a set of pre-determined objectives. This may begin by an experimental 'generate and test' process, subsequently progress into a refined process when a designer understands the potentials of a language, and finally evolve to a stage that calls for the modification of the existing language or the invention of a new language.

The strength of a pixelated medium lies in the ability to structure a composition and instrument interaction and process through parts that are very simple. The examples provided in this paper illustrate the compositional diversity that is possible through a simple pixelated assemblage. It presents us an opportunity to explore and express our compositional intentions.

Fig. 1a. Voxels interpreted as cubic cells.
Fig. 1b. Voxels interpreted as polyhedra.

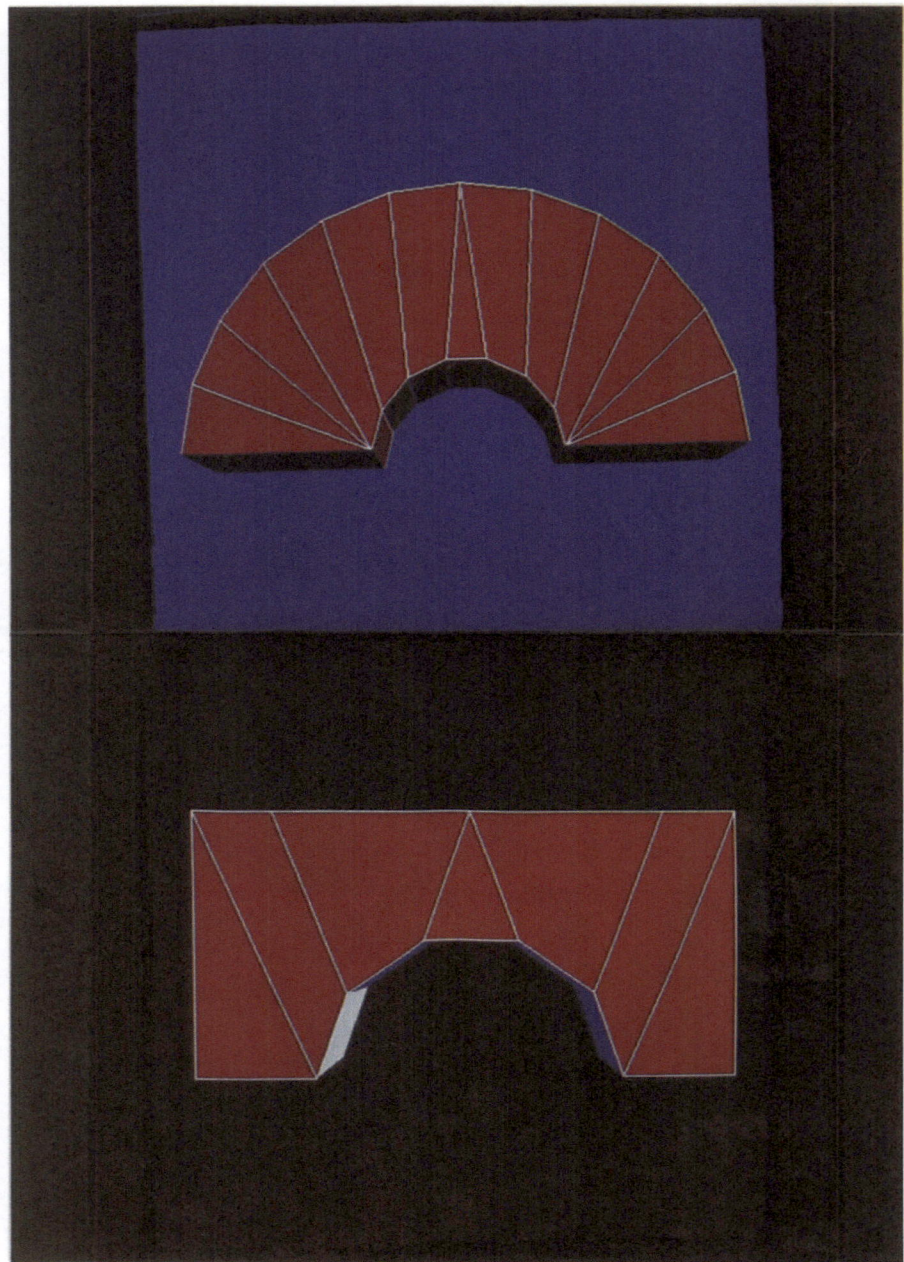

Fig. 2. Parametric vocabulary arches constructed by interpolating between varying segments of the outer and inner arcs.

Fig. 3a. Voxelated rule of composition expressing the transformation of a mass of stone into a system of pillars and ribs.
Fig. 3b. Third generation of the rule application on a cubic voxel.

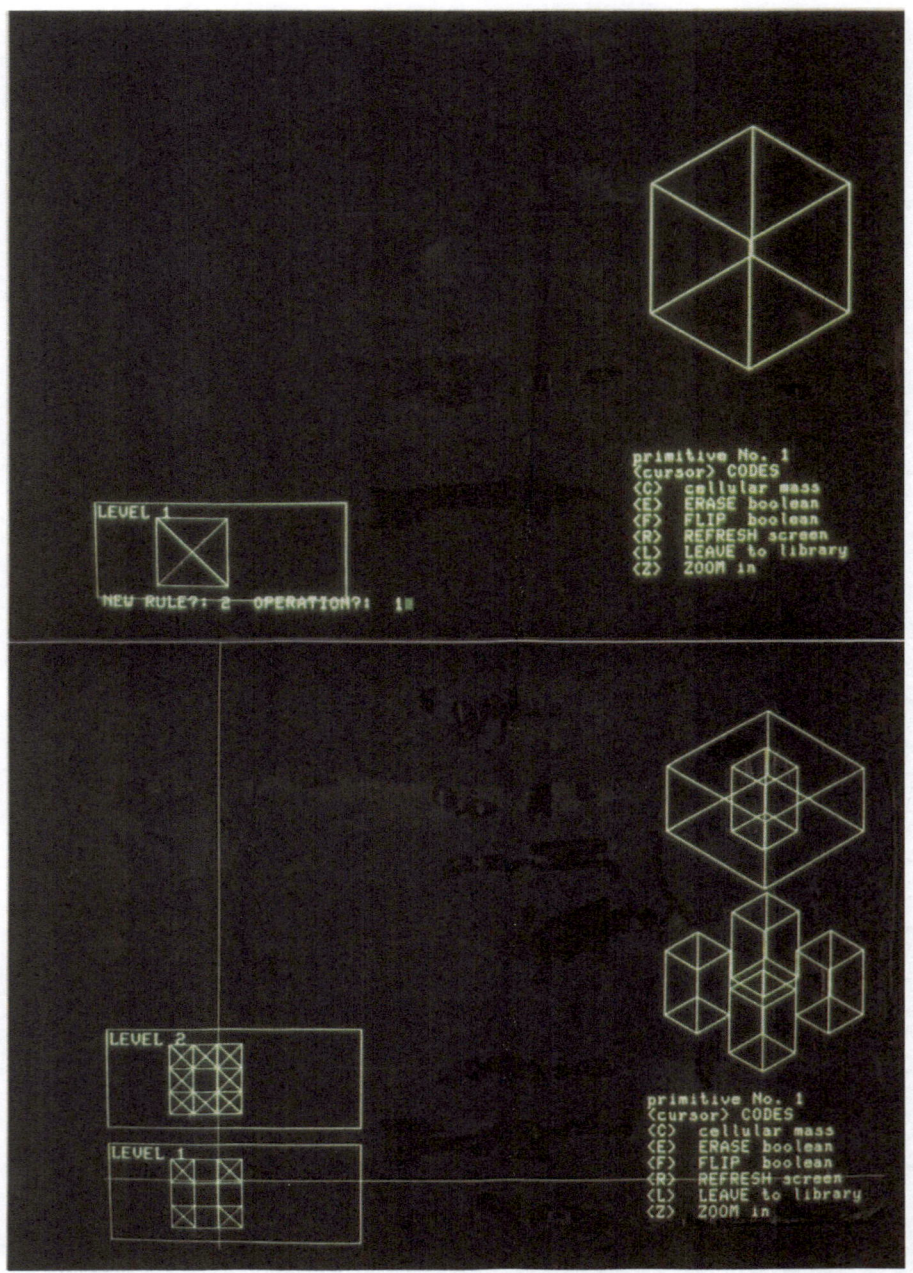

Fig. 4. Layered presentation of a voxelated assemblage before and after the rule application.

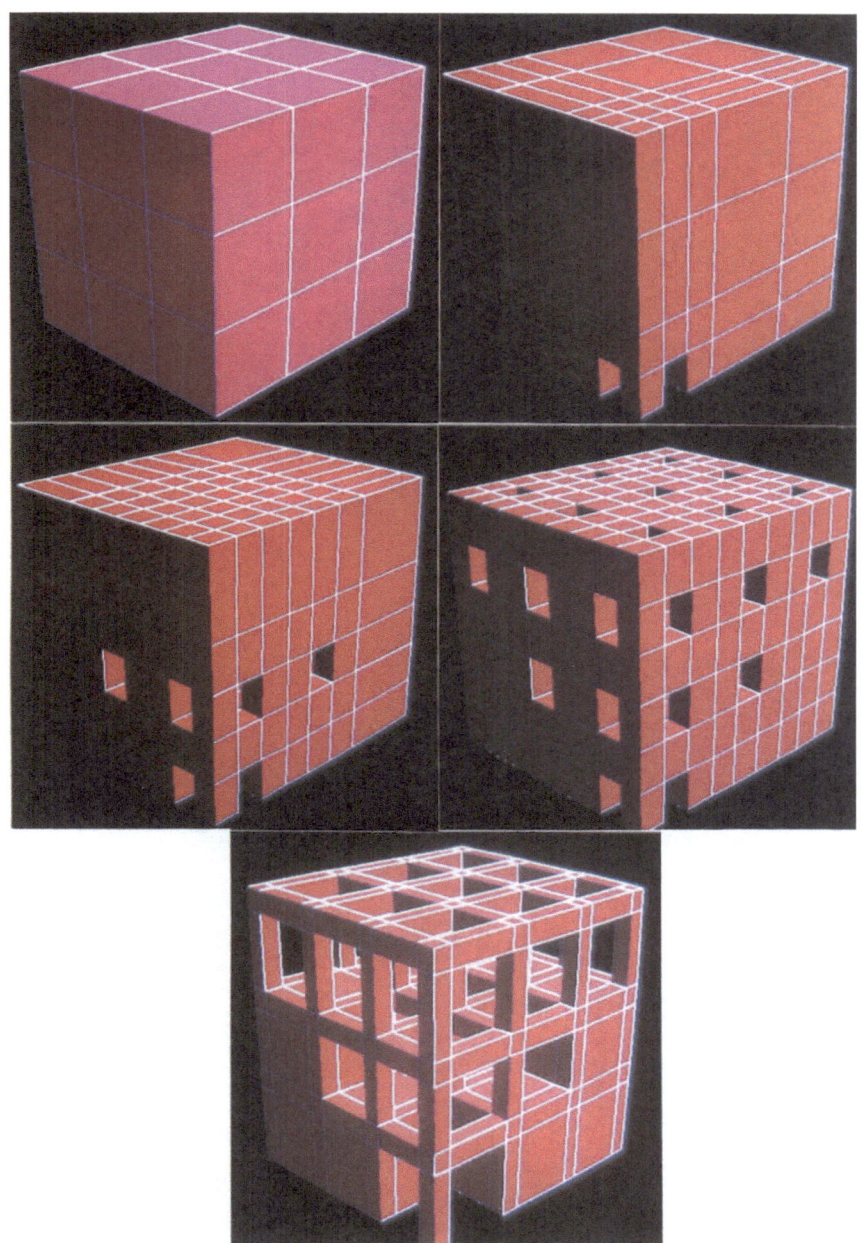

Fig. 5. Derivation of an option for a house on a corner lot by controlled rule applications.

Fig. 6. House on a corner lot and a dimensional variation.

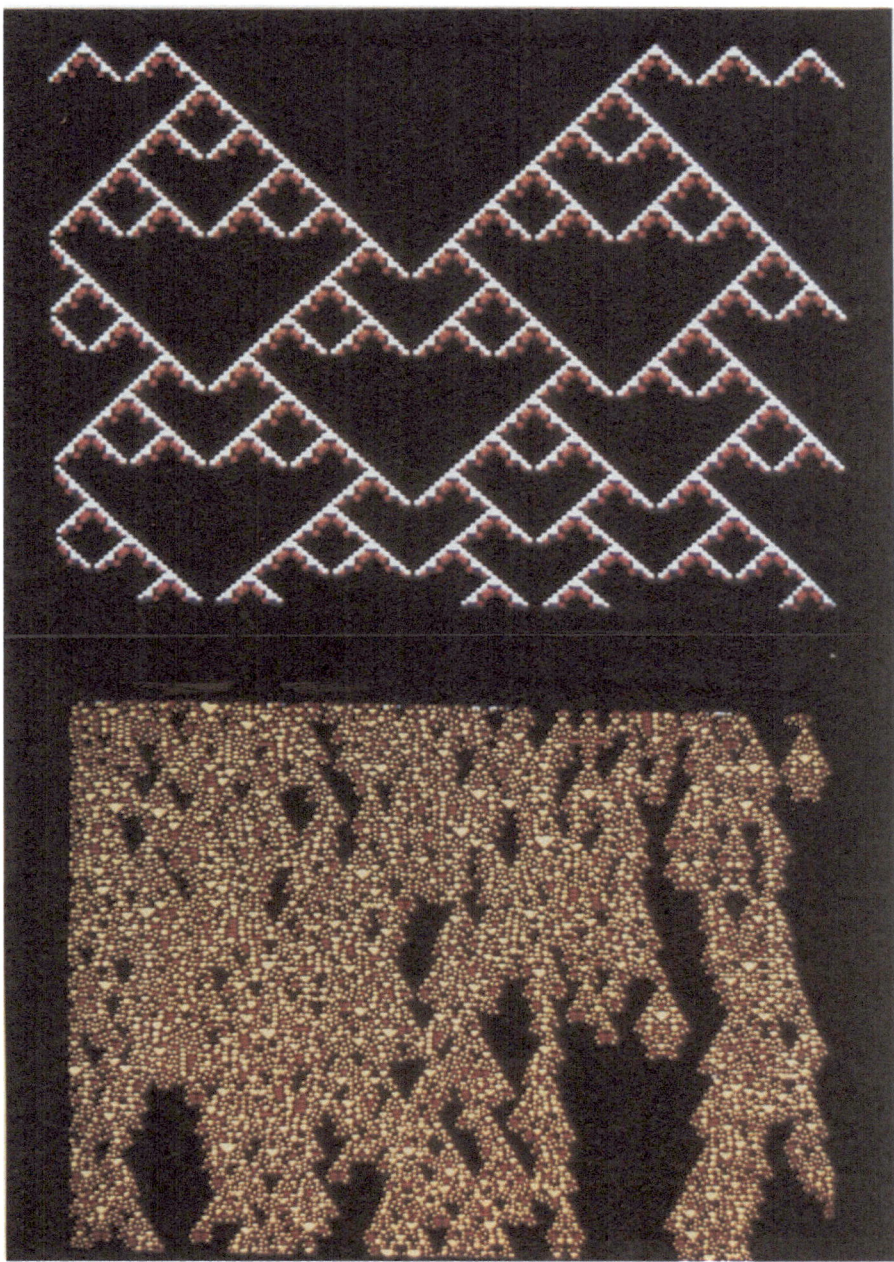

Fig. 7a. Self similar configurations, and
Fig. 7b. Complex and longlived patterns produced by a cellular automaton evolution.

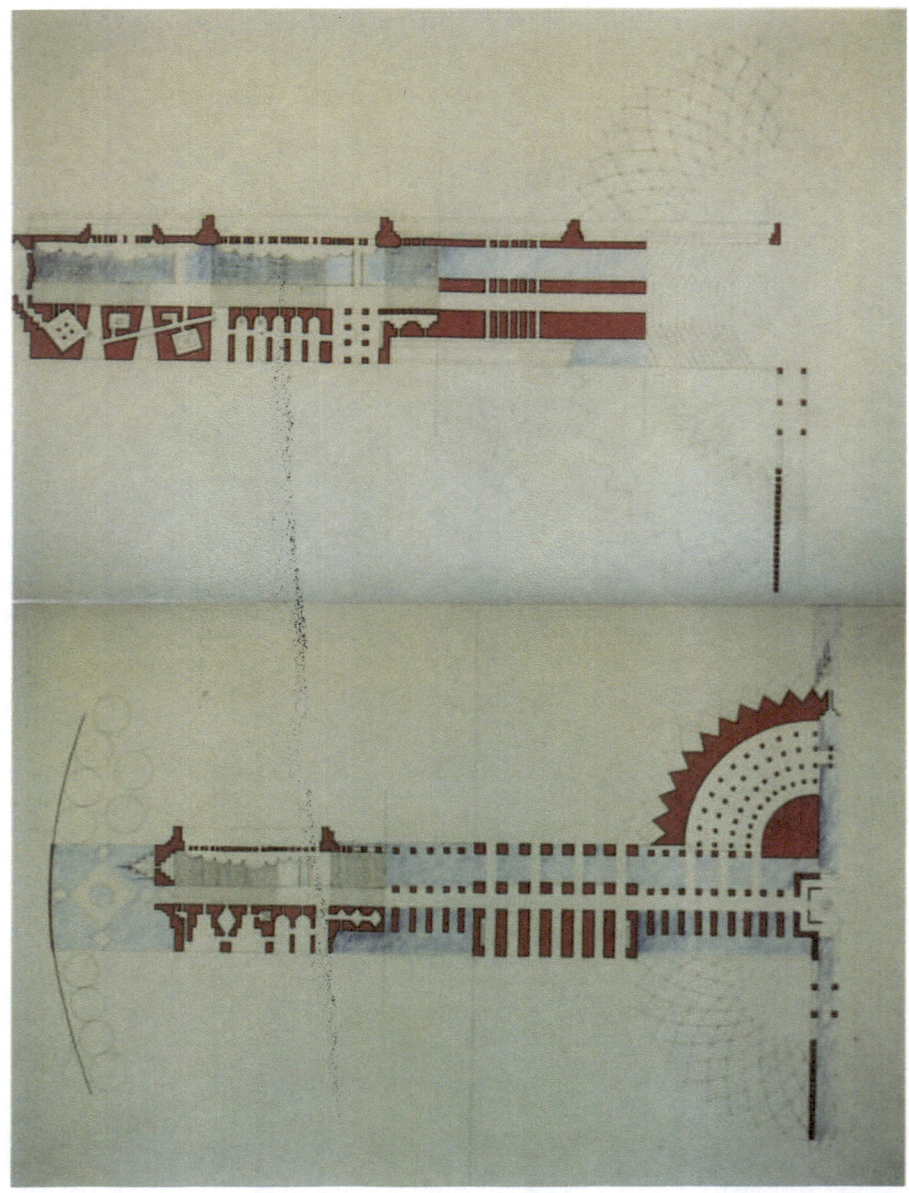

Fig. 8. Plans of the project that constructs the concept of reincarnation.

Fig. 9. Elevations and sections showing the disposition of cloud-like pavillion forms on a labyrinth of stone.

Fig. 10a. Cloud like pavillion form.
Fig. 10b. Pixelation of a pavillion into vocabulary elements: parametric arches, curved forms, etc..

Fig. 11. Pavillions with horizontal and vertical positioning of vocabulary elements.

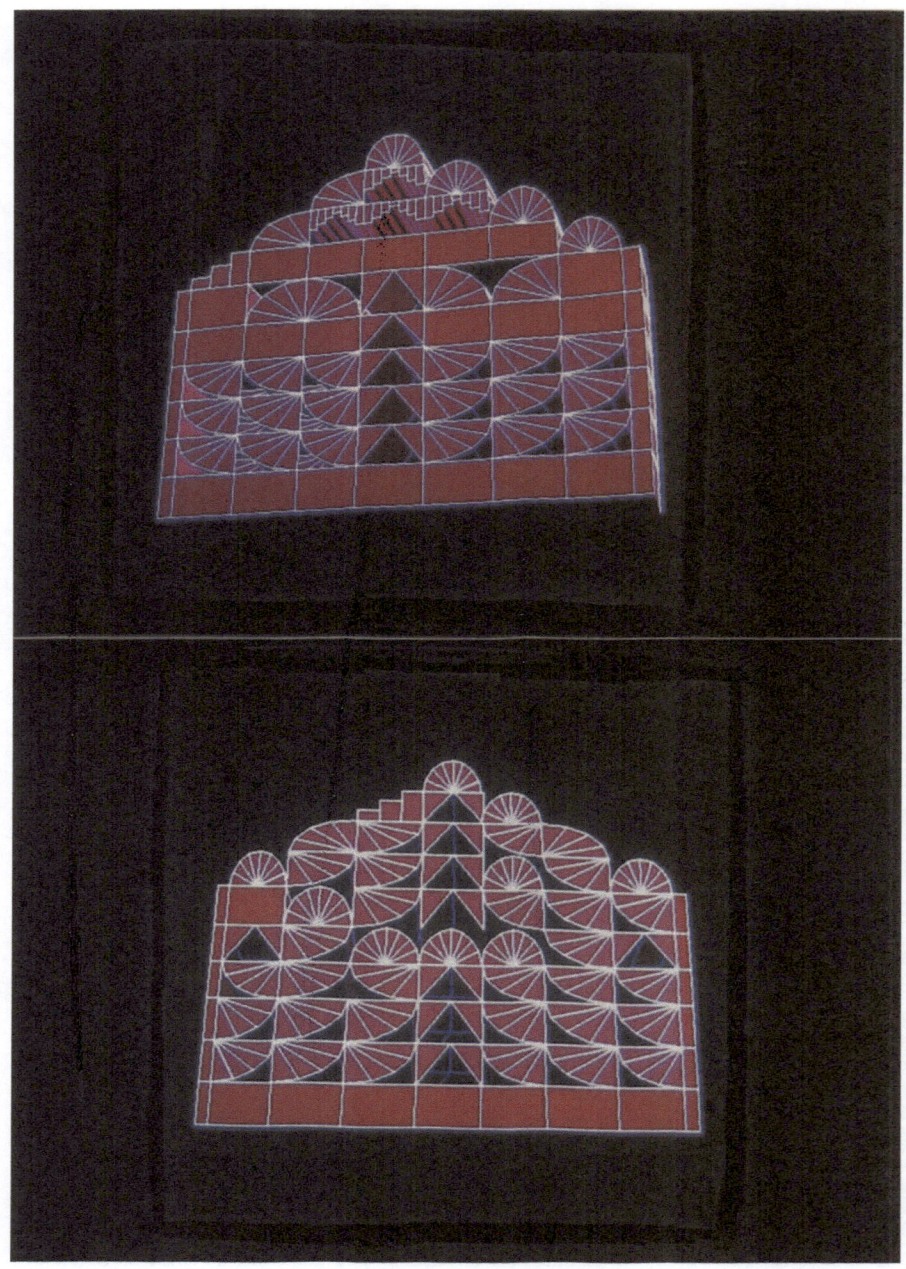

Fig. 12. Pavillions with bi-lateral symmetry.

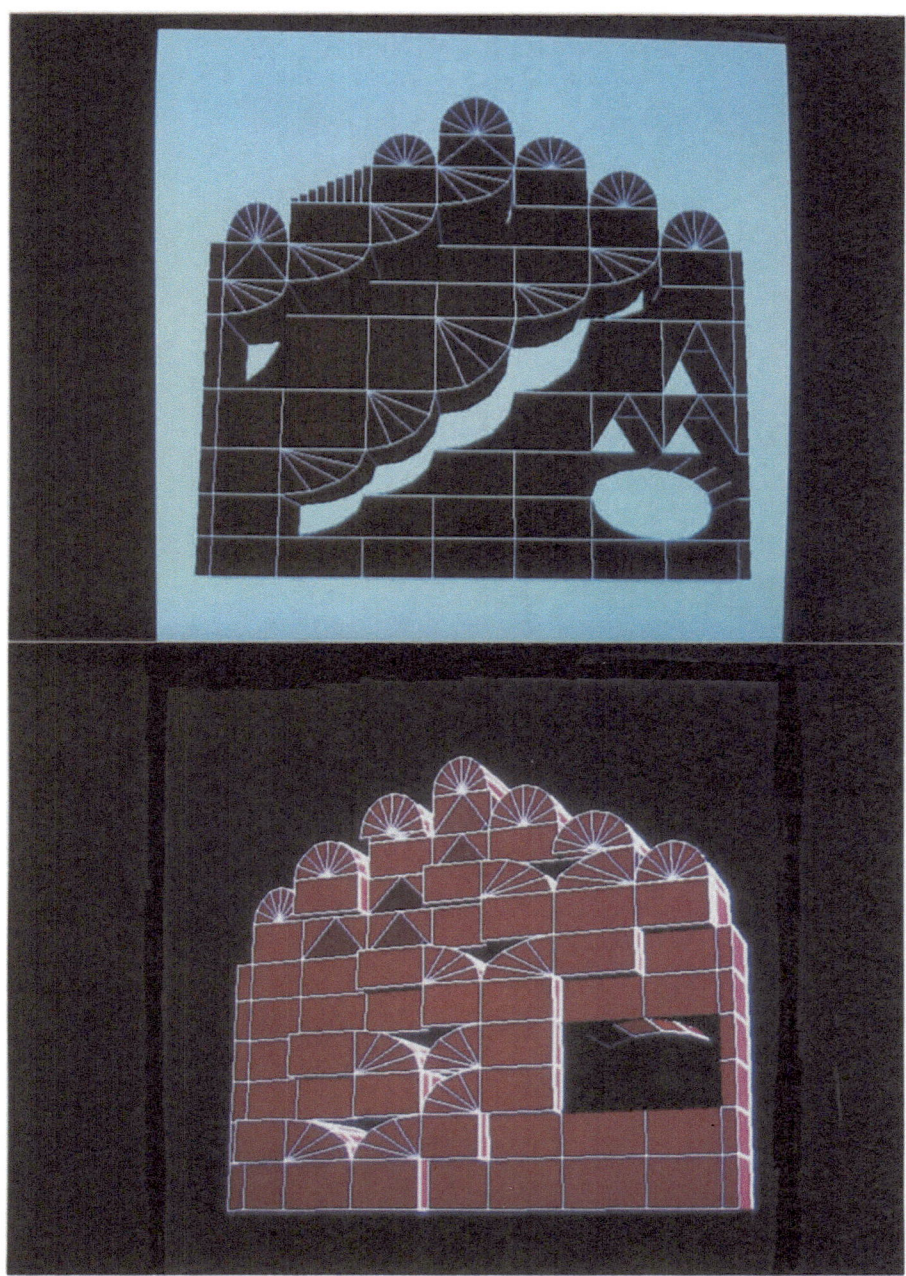

Fig. 13. Pavillions showing diagonal movement of vocabulary elements.

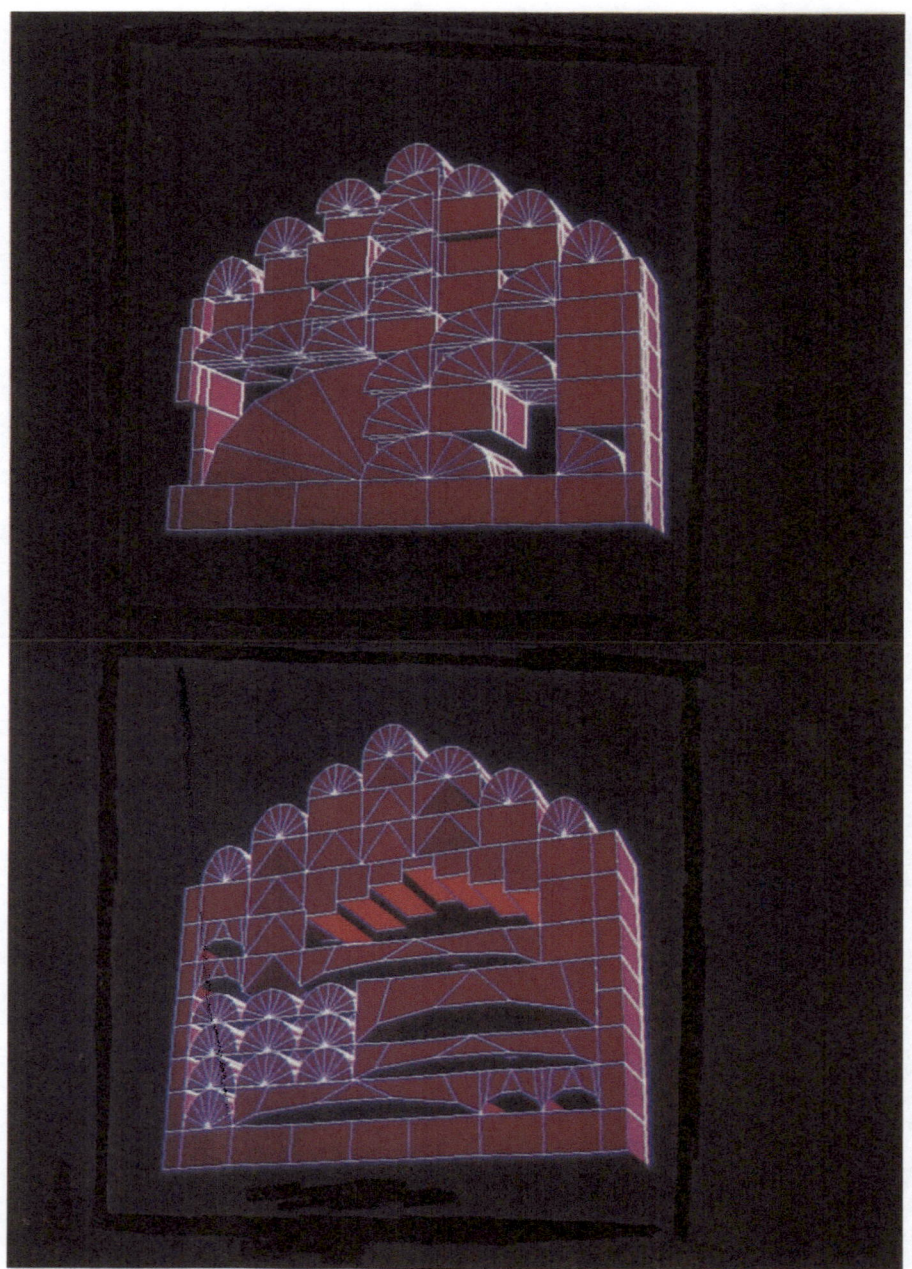

Fig. 14. Pavillions showing the use of quiescent states that enable scaling properties by the redefinition of a cluster of voxels that lie embedded in a larger voxel.

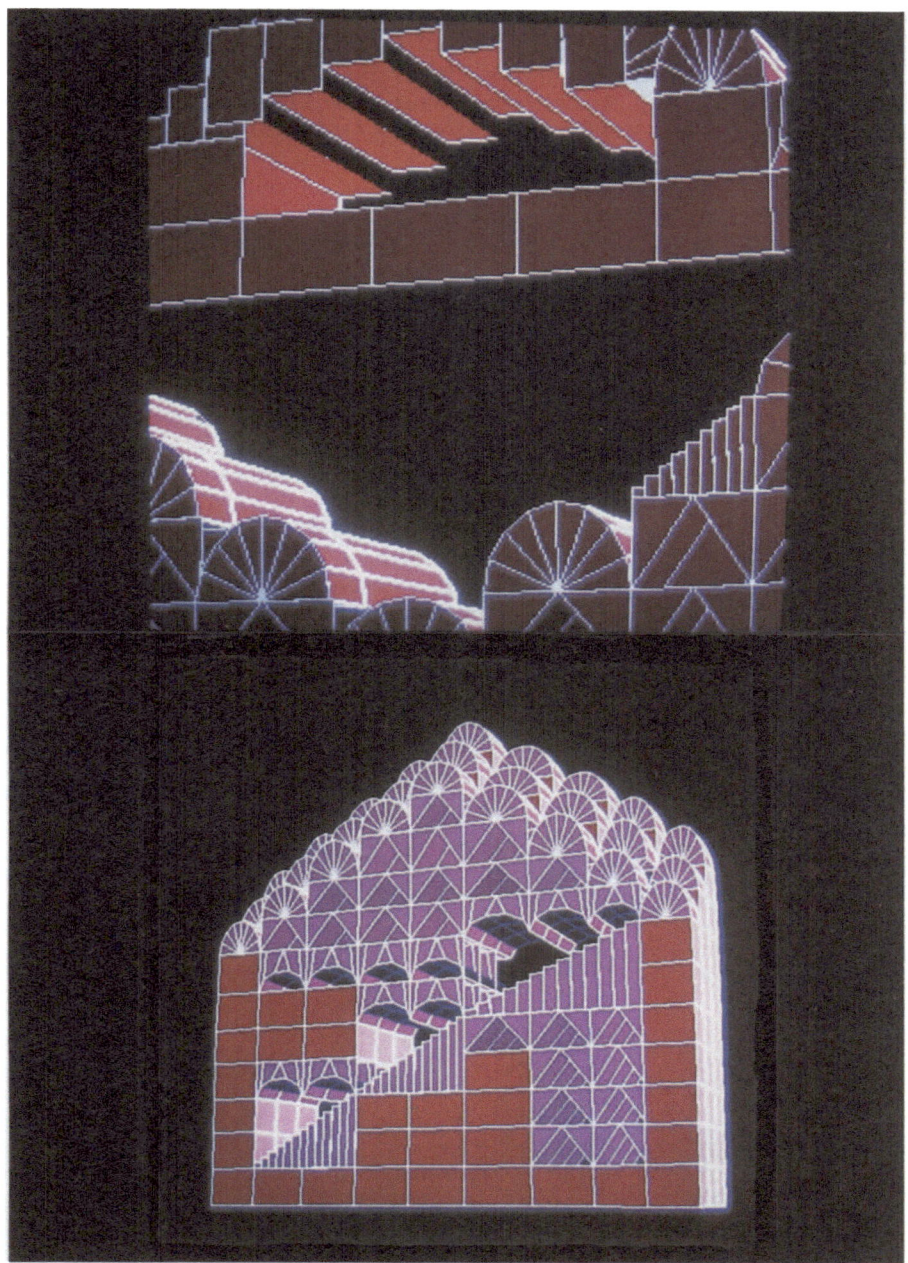

Fig. 15. Pavillions.

# REFERENCES

March, L. (1976) The Architecture of Form. Cambridge University Press, Cambridge.

Mitchell, W. J. (1977) Computer Aided Architectural Design. Petrocelli Charter, New York.

Eastman, C. (1977) A Survey of Geometric Modeling. Institute of Physical Planning, Pittsburgh.

Steadman, P. (1973) Graph-Theoretic Representation of Architectural Arrangement. Architectural Research & Teaching, vol.2. no.3.

Steadman, P. (1975) Biological Analogy in Architecture and Design, Ph.D thesis. University of Cambridge, Cambridge.

Mandelbrot, B. (1983) The Fractal Geometry of Nature. W.H. Freeman & Co., San Fransisco.

Smith, A. R. (1984) Plants, Fractals & Formal Languages. SIGGRAPH 84, Computer Graphics 18,3.

Stiny, G. & Gips, J. (1972) Shape Grammars and the Generative Specification of Paintings and Sculpture. Information Processing 71: 1460-1465.

Wolfram, S. (1984) Universality and Complexity in Cellular Automata. Physica D 10, North Holland Physics Publishing Co., Amsterdam: 1-35.

Toffoli, T. (1984) Cellular Automata as an Alternative to Differential Equations. Physica D 10, North Holland Physics Publishing Co., Amsterdam: 117-127.

Codd, E. F. (1968) Cellular Automata. Academic Press Inc., New York.

Mitchell, W.J. (1984, 1985) personal communication, lectures.

Makkuni, R. (1985) Experiments on a Grid, M.Arch thesis. University of California, Los Angeles.

**Ranjit Makkuni** is currently a researcher in Design Methodology at the XEROX Palo Alto Research Center, Palo Alto. His research interests include the exploration of video and computing as a design medium, the design of expressive design environments, and the preservation and revitilisation of craft in the third world.

Before getting involved with computers, he worked on building low cost rural housing in India. Makkuni received his B.Arch. in Design Theory and Methods from the University of California, Los Angeles.

# A New Graphics User Interface for Accessing a Database

C.T. Wu

Department of Computer Science, Code 52, Naval Postgraduate School, Monterey, CA 93943, USA

## ABSTRACT

A new graphics user interface for accessing a database is proposed in this paper. Our proposed graphics user interface *GLAD* (*G*raphics *LA*nguage for *D*atabase) achieves a high degree of 1) descriptiveness by graphically displaying a database schema and offering help whenever users need it, 2) ease of learning by maintaining a consistent interaction method and minimizing the number of different concepts that users have to learn, 3) power to express a complex query by adopting a QBE-like query specification method, and 4) ease of using by allowing users to formulate a complex query in many different ways. The paper first reviews the previously proposed graphics user interfaces, and then describes the initial design of GLAD and provides a sample session to illustrate its features.

## INTRODUCTION

With the wider use of database management systems, more different types of users will be accessing a database. These users range from very sophisticated users, such as database administrators and system designers, to naive users, such as secretaries, clerks, and casual users of databases. A "canned" menu-driven query system, where each choice in the menu is a specific query such as "list all customers with outstanding balance," is a common user interface for the naive users. Problems with the canned menu-driven query system are that it can only be used by the naive users (it is too tedious for the sophisticated users) and that it has very limited querying capability (users can only ask what the menu provides). Sophisticated users normally access a database by using a special query language, such as SQL and Quel. These query languages can be used very effectively to form ad hoc queries against a database. Although these languages are non-procedural

This research was initiated while the author was affiliated with Northwestern University, Evanston, IL. The research is partly funded by the Naval Postgraduate School Research Foundation Program.

(that is, you specify *what* you want and not *how* to get it), we cannot reasonably expect naive users to learn a query language and become proficient enough to access the database by using it. In this paper, we will explore the use of graphics as a method of interface to a database that is acceptable to both sophisticated and naive users.

A good user interface capable of supporting both sophisticated and naive users must have the following characteristics:

(1) It must be descriptive. It must show what kinds of data (employee, department, equipment, etc) are stored in the database and how they are related to each other. In a database term, we call such a representation of data and their relationships the *database schema*. Also, it should provide help (i.e. describe more about the database) if requested by users.

(2) It must be powerful. Users must be able to express a complex query by using it.

(3) It must be easy to learn. Naive and uninitiated users should be able to master the interaction method quickly and start accessing the database with a short learning period.

(4) It must be easy to use. It must be easy enough to use so that users rarely make erroneous queries and can formulate complex queries simply and speedily. Also, users should be able to specify a same query in different ways; they should not be forced to remember a particular way to pose a query.

Query languages of currently available database management systems are lacking in all of the characteristics except (2).

There are generally three different approaches in developing a good user interface. They are a natural language interface, a modified query language interface, and a graphics interface. A natural language interface [BOGU84, WALTS78] is primarily developed for the naive users, and therefore, it may not be suitable for more sophisticated users. Pros and cons for using a natural language interface as a database access method are presented in [PETR76]. The second approach, a modified query language interface [KORT84, MACG85], employs a syntax similar to a regular query language but with more simplied syntax and enriched semantics. It is intended for both sophisticated and naive users. These two approaches fulfill characteristics (2), (3), and (4) with varying degree of success but they both are not at all descriptive. In this paper, we explore the viability of the third approach, a graphics interface, as a possible user interface that possesses all four characteristics of a good user interface. It should be noted that it is not our intention to analyze and compare three different approaches in this paper. Rather, our objective here is to explore the possibility of a graphics user interface.

We first review the previously proposed graphics user interfaces in the next section. We then describe our proposed graphics user interface called *GLAD*(*Graphics LAnguage for Database*) in Section 3. A sample session is used to illustrate the features of GLAD. In Section 4, we discuss how the GLAD interface holds the aforementioned four characteristics fo a good user interface. We conclude the paper by mentioning some possible future research.

## REVIEW

We review the previously proposed graphics user interfaces in this section. Most of these are developed for a particular database model, namely the relational database, where the data (employee, department, etc.) and their relationships (employee works for department, etc.) are both represented as a table (more formally called a *relation*).

QBE (Query-By-Example) [ZLOO77] and CUPID [MCDO74] are the earliest work in using graphic objects as a tool for accessing database. The graphic object in QBE is a table skeleton. A user specifies a query by requesting a table skeleton for the desired table and filling the entries. The graphic objects in CUPID are rectangles, circles, and so forth. A user specifies a query by connecting appropriate objects. Both interfaces display the result of a query in a tabular form. They are easy to learn and use, but CUPID is limited in its power and both CUPID and QBE are not descriptive. Other approaches similar to QBE, but with better semantics, are reported in [LARS84, SUGI84]. These new approaches are better than the first two, but they still lack in descriptiveness.

SDMS (Spatial Data Management System) [HERO80] is essentially a relation browser. Contents of a relation are displayed on the screen as graphic objects. For example, an icon of ship (one for destroyer, one for aircraft carrier, etc) is used to represent each ship (content) in the table. A user can move the cursor to the desired icon and zoom it to retrieve more detailed information about that ship. SDMS is powerful as a relation browser because a user can move the cursor and zoom and unzoom the data in the table represented as graphic objects. However, a user cannot, with "move cursor", "zoom", and "unzoom" operations, formulate complex queries that access more than one table nor see the database schema of the whole database. SDMS, therefore, has characteristic (3) and does not possess characteristics (1), (2), and most of (4).

TIMBER (Text, Icon and Map Browser for Extended Relations) [STON82] is another relation browser. but unlike SDMS, it is capable of browsing icons. maps, text, and normal fixed-format relations. It has greatly extended the capability of SDMS; but it still fails to possess characteristics (1), (2), and (4) satisfactorily.

GUIDE (Graphical User Interface for Database Exploration) [WONG82], which uses the Entity/Relationship diagram to describe the database, is the only graphics user interface that is descriptive. It also uses a hierarchical subject directory so that a user can locate the desired part of the database expediently.

The feature of GUIDE that makes it easy to use is its capability of allowing users to compose queries in a piecemeal fashion and providing feedback (i.e. answer) to a partially composed query. Piecemeal querying is similar to the separate compilation technique of program development, where, instead of writing a program as one piece, you compile modules separately and finally compose a whole program by integrating these modules. To a certain degree GUIDE has the other two characteristics also. However, we observe the lack of relation browsing capability, use of two screens (one for schema representation and another for query result), lack of aggregate functions, and use of two separate diagrams (Entity/Relationship diagram and subject directory) for representing a database schema as weak points of GUIDE.

In this paper, we propose a new graphics user interface GLAD which can be viewed as a synthesis of aforementioned graphics user interfaces. By incorporating their good features and eliminating their weak points, we believe that GLAD has achieved a higher degree of descriptiveness, ease of learning and using, and power.

## DESCRIPTION OF GLAD

We now describe the features of GLAD. A sample session is provided to present a concrete example to illustrate the features described here. Specifically, we show how the user can retrieve the answer to "List all classes that deal with the subject of probability and that are taken this quarter (Fall '85) by the students who are majoring in Computer Science and whose gpa's are better than 3.5."

Figure 1 is the GLAD diagram for a university database schema. Users directly manipulate this graphical display of database schema to query about it and retrieve data stored in it.

Figure 2a shows the hierarchical structure of GLAD commands (not all commands are shown here). A detailed description of these commands and a complete specification of GLAD can be found in [ADCO86]. The top level menu is shown in Figure 2b. Menu will be placed on one part of a screen. Exact position is not yet determined, but we anticipate to position it either on the top or on the right hand side of a screen. Associated with each command is a positive integer which corresponds to the special function key number. A user can select the command by first moving the mouse to the desired operation and then clicking the mouse button. A user can also select the command by pressing the corresponding function key or typing the command name. Depending on the type of a command, a user must then select an argument(s) that a desired command will be executed on. In GLAD, a user may reverse the sequence of interaction, that is, a user selects argument(s) first and then selects the command.

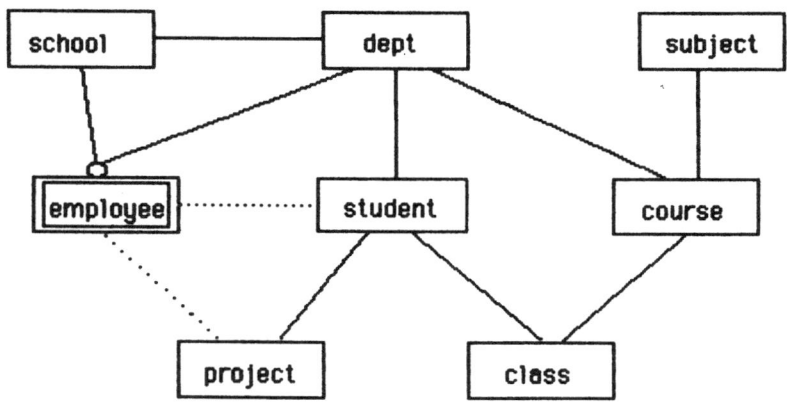

University Database

**FIGURE 1**

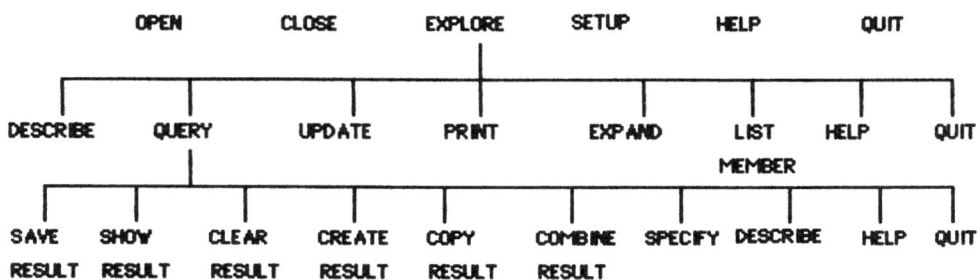

a) Hierarchical structure of commands

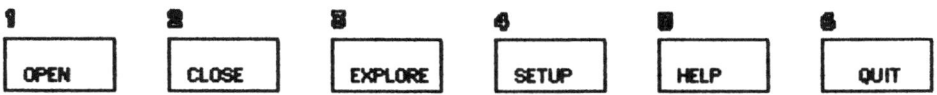

b) Top level menu

**FIGURE 2**

Database schema is depicted as a collection of objects and relationships (or associations) among objects. An object is an *aggregation* of (sub)objects. We do not define the term object here; we intuitively view an object as a "thing" (both tangible and intangible) that exists. For example, student object could be an aggregation of name, address, ssno, gpa, and dept (sub)objects. An aggregate object is represented as a rectangle in a GLAD diagram (see Figure 1). A user can see the sub(objects) of an aggregate object by EXPANDing it (see Figure 3). Notice that the dept object is not shown in the expanded student object because it is not an atomic object. Only first four objects are *atomic*; that is, they are an aggregation of exactly one system-defined or a user-defined *base* object (string, number, enumeration, subrange and boolean). Since the dept object is an non-atomic aggregate object, say, an aggregation of name, set of students, set of courses, and school, it was not shown in the expanded student object. Each non-atomic object in the database is displayed, and an association between objects is represented as a solid line between these objects (see Figure 1). Notice that the non-atomic object dept is shown as a separate rectangle in Figure 1. Database designer (or user) can modify the setup so a non-atomic object is not displayed.

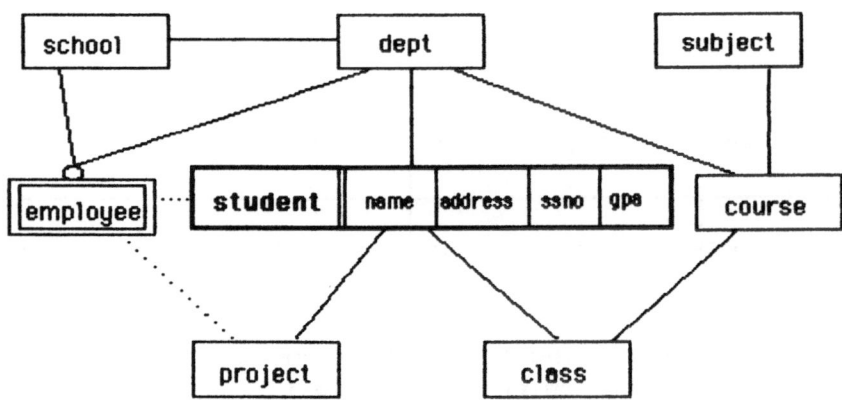

Expanded student object

**FIGURE 3**

Individual objects, such as faculty, secretary, and technician, can be grouped together to form a *generalized* object, say, employee. Faculty, secretary, and technician objects are called *specialized* objects of employee. Generalization abstraction can be characterized as a IS-A relationship (faculty IS-A employee, etc.).

Generalized object is represented in a GLAD diagram as a nested rectangle (see Figure 1). A user can expand the nested rectangle and view the specialized objects (see Figure 4). These specialized objects can themselves be the generalized objects of yet further specialized objects. Faculty object, for example, is a generalized object of full, associate, and assistant professors.

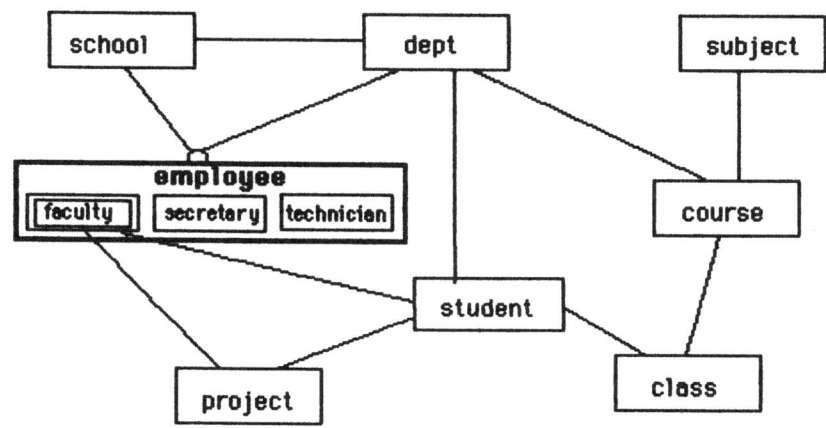

Expanded generalized object

**FIGURE 4**

We have already mentioned that an association between objects is represented as a solid line in a GLAD diagram. When one or both of the associated objects are specialized objects, a dotted line is used. Figure 5 shows how the dotted lines are used in a GLAD diagram. We see in Figure 1 that a specialized object of an employee object is related to a project object. By EXPANDing it, we realize that the faculty object is the one related to the project object (see Figure 4).

Either i) specialized object of A is related to B or
ii) specialized object of B is related to A or
iii) specialized object of A is related to specialized object of B.

If a user is interested in this relation, he can either expand A and/or B, or prompt GLAD to describe the relationship between A and B. This is a very important point; GLAD only provides more information when asked, it will not force information on a user.

**FIGURE 5**

An aggregate object can have a disjunctive association, which means that an object can have either one (sub)object or another. We use a small circle to show a disjunctive association. In Figure 1 we can notice that an employee belongs either to a department or to a school.

Each data item stored in a database is an information about some object. For example, data item [bruce springsteen, n. j., 123-45-6789, 3.2, music] is an information about student, and it is *classified* as a student object. We call each data item of an object a *member* of that object, and a user can list the members of the object by choosing the LIST MEMBER command (see Figure 6). In Figure 6 the result cannot fit in a window and therefore, only seven subject matters are displayed in the window. A user can browse the data by moving the small square vertically or by positioning the mouse at the arrow and pressing the mouse button. A user also has an option of enlarging the whole window to display more subject matters simultaneously.

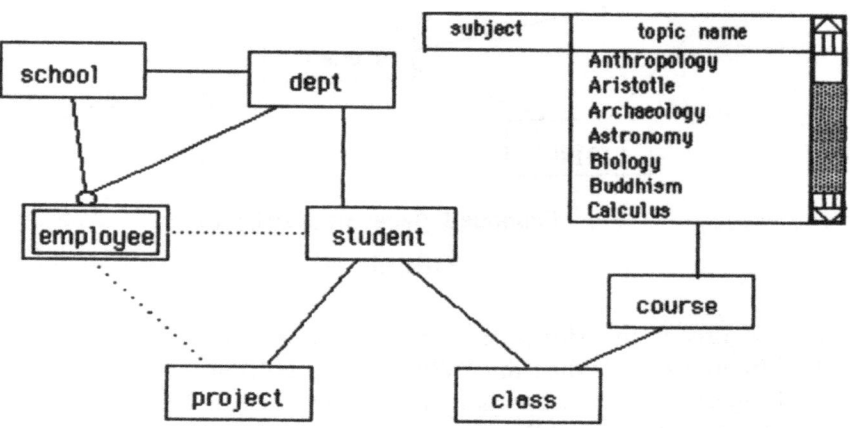

**Listing members of a subject object**
**FIGURE 6**

If a user is a first-time user or an infrequent user, then he probably needs to first inquire about the meaning of different objects and relationships shown in the GLAD diagram. For example, if he likes to know about the semantic of the relationship between the student and class objects, he selects the DESCRIBE command and a solid line between these objects (see Figure 7).

To get the answer to the query, the user enters the QUERY mode by selecting the QUERY command. Third level menu is now displayed on the screen. He decomposes the query into two part: one that lists all courses that deal with probability and another that lists all classes taken Fall '85 quarter by the Computer Science students whose gpa's are better than 3.5. He may, of course, decompose in other ways. The user SPECIFYs the subject (see Figure 8), the course (see Figure 9), and the line connecting the two to get the result of the first subquery.

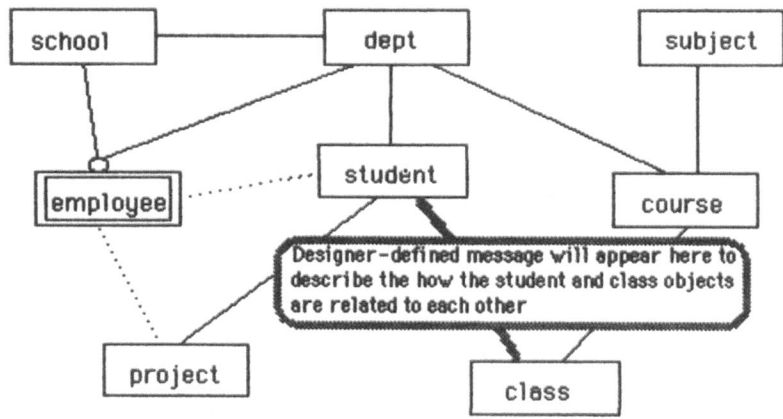

Description box for the relationship
between student and class objects

**FIGURE 7**

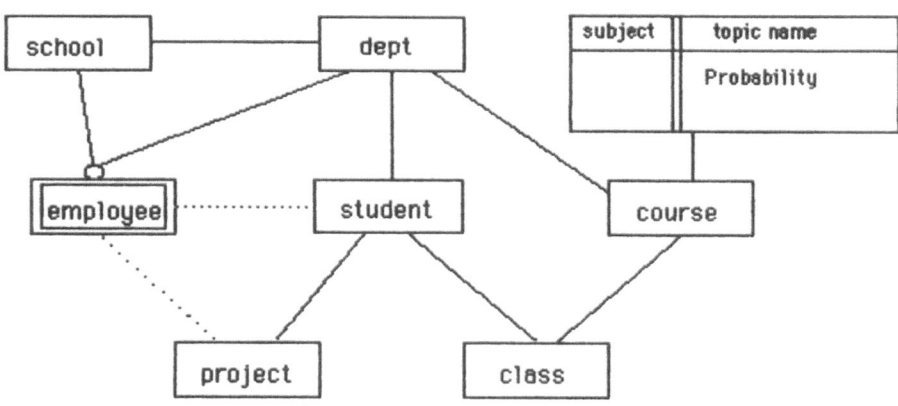

Specifying the desired topic "probability"

**FIGURE 8**

To actually get(retrieve) this intermediate result, the user issues the CREATE RESULT command (see Figure 10). Notice that the result icon and the subject and course objects are shaded identically. He can now request SHOW RESULT to verify that the intermediate result is what he wants. Similar to the LIST MEMBER command, the SHOW RESULT command will allow users to browse the intermediate result. The SHOW RESULT command gives an immediate feedback to users enabling the early detection of erroneous query specification. As users become more proficient, they can bypass the SHOW RESULT command. Having these two separate commands, GLAD can give a help to the naive users (if

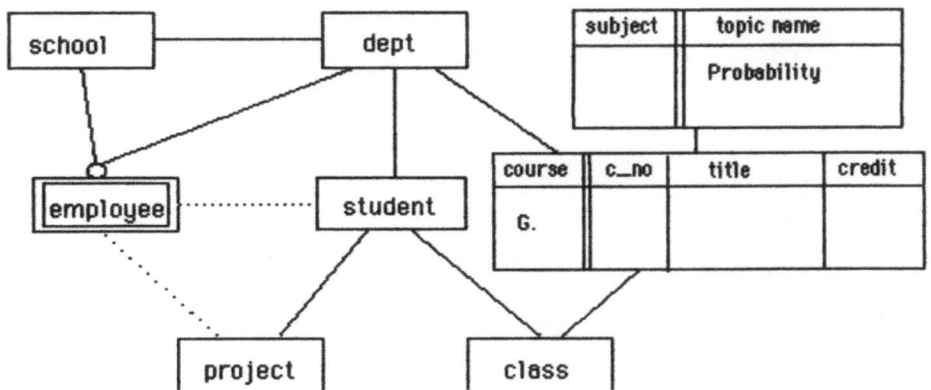

Request to retrieve (G.) all information on course
is made in the course object query skeleton

**FIGURE 9**

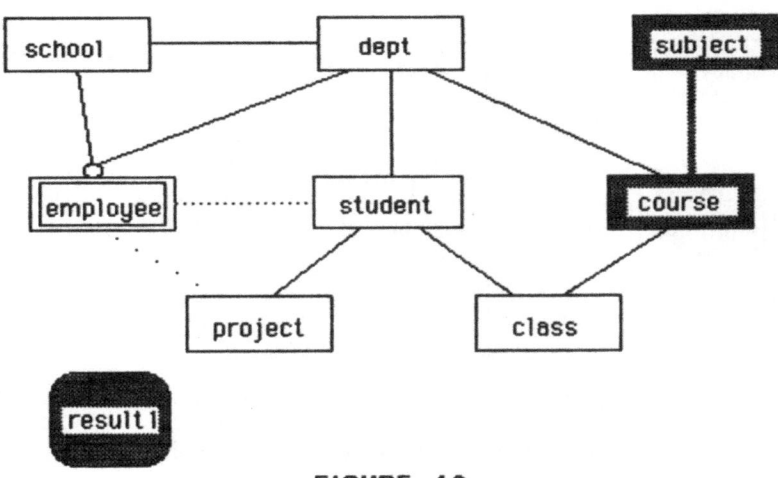

**FIGURE 10**

asked) by providing an immediate feedback, but it will not force such help to the sophisticated users. By going through the similar query specification, the user creates the result for the second subquery (see Figure 11).

When a user formulates many subqueries, he may forget what the (sub)results were about. He may prompt GLAD to describe them. For example, the description of

> contains class information where
> dept.name = 'Computer Science' and
> student.gpa > 3.5

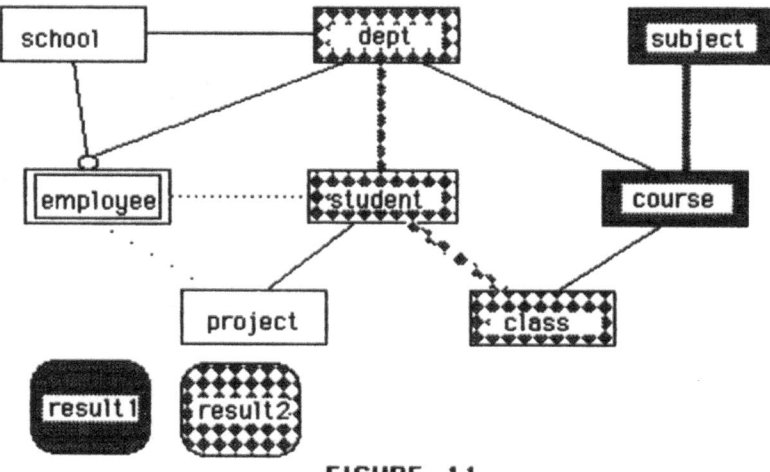

**FIGURE 11**

will appear under **result 2** if the user requests to DESCRIBE **result 2**. A user may change the environment by executing the SETUP command so the description of a result is displayed automatically.

Finally, the user retrieves the complete answer by combining two (sub)results by executing the COMBINE RESULTS command (see Figure 12). If the user desires to have a permanent copy of the answer, he can save the answer by selecting SAVE RESULT.

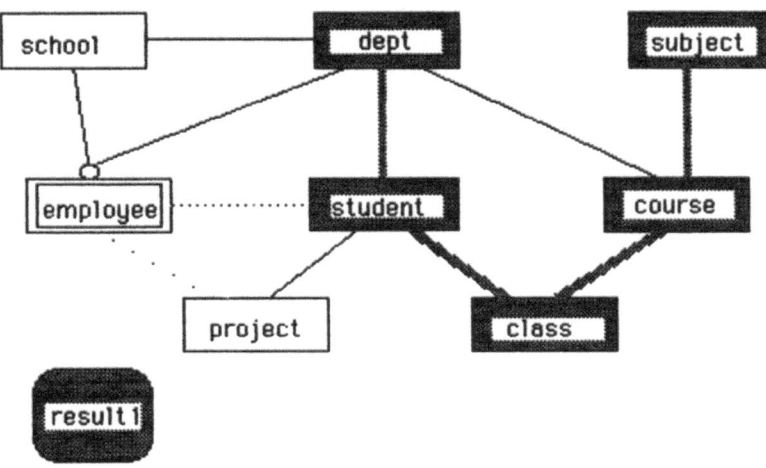

**FIGURE 12**

## ANALYSIS OF GLAD

In this section, we show that GLAD possesses four characteristics of a good user interface mentioned in the Introduction Section by analyzing its features.

### GLAD is descriptive

GLAD displays a diagram of the database schema. This GLAD diagram is semantically rich, which means that it is capable of capturing a real world semantics (how the information stored in the database are related to each other) naturally and precisely. Conventional data models, such as relational, network, and hierarchical data models are semantically poor compared to new data models, such as SDM, TAXIS, E/R, etc data models. A GLAD diagram is applicable to any particular semantic data model, because it provides an elegant diagrammatic representation of real world abstraction concepts those semantic data models employ. The abstraction concepts supported by GLAD are aggregation, generalization and classification.

### GLAD is easy to learn

The number of concepts a user has to learn in order to access a database via GLAD is few, and the interaction method is consistent throughout the interface. Circle, regular and nested rectangles, and line are the only concepts that a user need learn to understand the GLAD diagrams. Moreover, the HELP and DESCRIBE commands are always available to a user. The interaction method is also very straightforward. A user can select a command either by using the mouse, by pressing the function key, or by typing the command name. After selecting a desired command, a user then selects an argument(s) that the chosen operation will be executed on. In GLAD, a user may reverse the sequence of interaction, that is, a user selects argument(s) first and then selects the operation. This flexibility helps users learn the interaction method easily because they only have to learn the one most natural to them.

For more complex retrieval operations, QBE-like interface is used. The notable difference between ours and the original QBE is that ours does not need the use of variables for queries involving more than one objects (relations in the original QBE). The results of various psychological studies that demonstrate the QBE's ease of learning and using are well documented in [THOM75]. By avoiding the use of variables and by displaying the database schema, we believe ours is easier to learn and use.

## GLAD is powerful

GLAD's power to express a complex query is a direct consequence of adopting a QBE-like interface for specifying a query. QBE is relationally complete, which guarantees that it is capable of expressing any query that can be expressed in relational algebra or relational calculus. This relational completeness is a general criteria used to prove the expressive power of a query language. Because GLAD has inherited all the querying capabilities of QBE, GLAD is also relationally complete.

## GLAD is easy to use

GLAD's flexibility of allowing a user to formulate a query in different ways and in incremental, piecemeal fashion makes it easy to use. By allowing a user to pose a query in different ways, it appeals to the wider range of users. If there is only one way to pose a query, it probably would not appeal to all users, because the allowed query specification may be too difficult to the naive users or may be too cumbersome for the sophisticated users. Each user has his own preferred way of specifying a query, and the user interface should allow different ways of specifying the same query as much as possible.

Incremental query specification would also appeal to the wide range of users. Rather than writing the specification for a complete query and executing it, GLAD users can retrieve the result of the complete query in a piecemeal, incremental manner. A user formulate the complete query by first (mentally) decomposing the query into smaller subqueries. After specifying each subquery correctly, he combines them to retrieve the result for the complete query. By this way, a user can formulate a complex query in an expedient manner with very few errors.

Ability to browse the result also improves the ease of use. The result may actually contain more than what a user really wanted. Instead of reformulating the query, the user can simply browse through the result. If the user wants to save the correct result, then he can delete the unwanted records while browsing through the result.

## CONCLUSION

We have provided in this paper a description of our initial design of GLAD. We believe our proposed graphics user interface is very descriptive, easy to learn and use, and powerful. Its flexible interaction method makes it an ideal candidate for a user interface that appeals to a wide range of different types of users. Separate subject directory such as the one used in GUIDE is not necessary in our graphics user interface because the generalization concept incorporated in the GLAD diagram functions as a subject directory.

We have already initiated an implementation effort by using the NBI workstations with graphics terminals. We anticipate that the majority of the features described in this paper will be implemented in the next six months. Our implementation goal is to make it portable and independent of any particular DBMS. In other words, we would like to make our graphics user interface adaptable as a front-end for any DBMS.

Our future research includes the addition of a dynamic help, a more flexible querying capability, a diagrammatic representation of a recursive relation, and a non-normal form display of an object and result.

In the initial design and implementation, the HELP command only provides a static help since it only gives the description of the other commands listed in the menu. We would like to add to the HELP command a dynamic help capability which remembers the sequence of commands issued by the user and which offers a helpful suggestion when the erroneous command is requested or when the confused user asked "what to do next." We also would like the future GLAD versions to have a capability of providing error messages more meaningful than the rudimentary ones available in the initial implementation.

In order to specify a query that accesses more than one object, a user now has to select all objects involved (by moving the mouse to them) and issues the SPECIFY commands. We would like to add a feature that allows users to pose a multi-object query without selecting all objects. Instead, they select an object, issue the SHOW CONNECTED OBJECT commands within this object, and place the specifications in the expanded table skeleton.

There are cases where an object is related to itself. For example, a part object is related to itself in the relationship subpart: that is. a part is a subpart of another (larger) part. Query specification method for such recursive relations is discussed in [HEIL85]. They extended a QBE format and used a regular (i.e. non-graphic) terminal. We would like to add a nice diagrammatic representation of a recursive relation to the GLAD diagrams and, more importantly, develop an associated querying method for a recursive relation that is simple and easy to use.

Finally, we would like to utilize a non-normal form [KAMB83, KITA79] for displaying members of object and members of result. An object that has a set of related (sub)objects can be best represented in a non-normal form (see Figure 13), and we would like to have such a non-normal form display in the future versions of GLAD.

| student | class |
|---------|-------|
| Pascal  | CS 101 |
| Pascal  | MATH 2A |
| Pascal  | CS 200 |
| Galileo | CS 101 |
| Galileo | MATH 120 |
| Newton  | CS 121 |

| student | class |
|---------|-------|
| Pascal  | CS 101 |
|         | MATH 2A |
|         | CS 200 |
| Galileo | CS 101 |
|         | MATH 120 |
| Newton  | CS 121 |

a) Normal tabular display          b) Non normal tabular display

**FIGURE 13**

## REFERENCES

[ADCO86]   Adcock, J. K. Design of a graphics interface package for a database program. M.S. Thesis, Naval Postgraduate School (in preparation).

[BOGU84]   Boguraev, B. K. and Jones, K. S. A natural language front-end to data bases with evaluative feedback. In *New Applications of Databases*, Gardarin, G. and Gelenbe, E., Eds., Academic Press, London, 1984, 159-182.

[HEIL85]   Heiler, S. and Rosenthal, A. G-WHIZ, a visual interface for the functional model with recursion. In *Proceedings of 11th Conference on Very Large Data Bases*, (Stockholm, 1985), 209-218.

[HERO80]   Herot, C. F. Spatial management of data. *ACM Transactions on Database Systems*. Vol 5, No 4 (Dec. 1980), 493-514.

[KAMB83]   Kambayashi, Y., Tanaka, K. and Takeda, K. Synthesis of unnormalized relations incorporating more meaning. *Information Sciences*. Vol 29 (1983), 201-247.

[KITA79]    Kitagawa, H. and Kunii, T. L. APAD: An application-adaptable database systems -- Its architecture and design. In *Data Base Design Techniques II: Physical Structures and Applications*, G. Goos and J. Hartmanis, Eds., Springer-Verlag, New York, 1979, 320-344.

[KORT84]    Korth, H. F., Kuper, G. M., Feigenbaum, J., van Gelder, A., and Ullman, J. D. System/U: A database system based on the universal relation assumption. *ACM Transactions on Database Systems*. Vol 9, No 3 (Sept. 1984),331-347.

[LARS84]    Larson, J. A. The forms pattern language. In *Proceedings of IEEE International Conference on Data Engineering* (Los Angeles, 1984), 183-191.

[MACG85]    MacGregor, R. M. ARIEL -- a semantic front-end to relational DBMSs. In *Proceedings of 11th Conference on Very Large Data Bases*, (Stockholm, 1985), 305-315.

[MCDO74]    McDonald, N. and Stonebraker, M. CUPID - the friendly query language. Memo ERL-M487, ERL, University of California, Berkeley, CA, October, 1974.

[PETR76]    Petrick, S. R. On natural language based computer systems. *IBM Journal on Research Developments*. Vol 20, No 4 (July, 1976), 314-325.

[STON82]    Stonebraker, M. and Kalash, J. TIMBER: A sophisticated relation browser. In *Proceedings of 8th Conference on Very Large Data Bases* (Mexico City, 1982), 1-10.

[SUGI84]    Sugihara, K., Miyao, J., Kikuno, T. and Yoshida, N. A semantic approach to usability in relational database systems. In *Proceedings of IEEE International Conference on Data Engineering* (Los Angeles, 1984), 203-210.

[THOM75]    Thomas, J. C. and Gould, J. D. A psychological study of query by example. In *Proceedings of the National Computer Conference* 44, (1975), 439-445.

[WALT78]    Waltz, D. L. An english language question answering system for a large relational database. *Communications of ACM*. Vol 21, No 7 (July, 1978), 526-539.

[WONG82]  Wong, H. K. T. and Kuo, I. GUIDE: graphical user interface for database exploration. In *Proceedings of 8th Conference on Very Large Data Bases* (Mexico City, 1982), 22-32.

[ZLOO77]  Zloof, M. M. Query-by-example: a data base language. *IBM Systems Journal*, 4 (Dec. 1977), 324-343.

C. Thomas Wu received his Bachelor of Arts in Mathematics from San Diego State University in May, 1975. In August, 1983, he received his Ph.D. in Computer Science from University of California, San Diego.

From September, 1983 to June, 1985, he was associated with Northwestern University, Evanston, IL as Assistant Professor in the Department of Electrical Engineering and Computer Science. In June, 1985, he joined the faculty of Naval Postgraduate School as Associate Professor in the Department of Computer Science.

His research interest includes all aspects of database system, especially the semantic data modelling, user interface, new applications, database design, and physical database organization. He is a member of Association of Computing Machinery and IEEE Computer Society Technical Committee on Data Engineering. He was a referee for IEEE Transaction on Software Engineering, Information Sciences, IEEE Computer Magazine, and numerous conferences.

[WGM82] Wong, H. K. T. and Kuo, I. (1982), GUIDE: Graphical user interface for database exploration. In *Proceedings of the 8th Conference on Very Large Data Bases (Mexico City)*, 1982, 22-32.

[ZL00??] Zloof, M. M. Query by example and office automation, pp. 18-? *Computer*, 1 (May 1977), 324-35?.

# Chapter 4
# Visual Data Bases

# Solid Modeler with Assembly Representation Tables

Takashi Hasegawa and Naomasa Nakajima

Faculty of Engineering, University of Tokyo, Hongo, Bunkyo-ku, Tokyo, 113 Japan

ABSTRACT

We, the authors, have developed our own Solid Modeler with Assembly Representation Tables (SMART) with the aim of improving the functions to
represent the assembly composed of many components which has been lacking in the existing solid modelers.  SMART has also such a characteristic
as applying the relational database to itself, which allows the commercial database adopting mainly the relational database to be utilized
with easy interchangeability.

SMART has a hierarchical data structure which has the data called "top"
as top level and some "ASSEMBLY"'s on the levels beneath the "top".
Also it has "OBJECT" and "PRIMITIVE" furthermore beneath the said levels, and each of these also has the data "RELATION" which represents the
relationship between lower-ranking level data.  And they all link to each
other in a ring structure.

On the relational database (RDB), SMART consits of four relations, i.e.
ASSEMBLY, OBJECT, PRIMITIVE, and RELATION, and the individual relation
has its own attribute as column data such as the tuple number, lower-
ranking level tuple number, initial number of relation, etc. as shown
below.

[Key word: CAD/CAM, database, CIM, assembly]

## 1. INTRODUCTION

In general, commercial databases have been being achieved a remarkable
development for years as a huge system in today's industry and their
data structure has already been established.  On the contrary, engineering databases are still on their way to develop and none of their
structure is established yet.  As the result, great distance is at present noticed with regard to the management between these two groups of
databases.  It is however assumed that a proper measure to utilize the
said two groups of databases with interchangeability is required, in
order to realize a total production system.  In the meantime, above all
with reference to an engineering database system which is to be used in
CAD system, it has such characteristics as shown below.
  (1) A two and three dimensional geometric model becomes a kernel of
      the database.
  (2) The database system is composed of different types of data such
      as illustrations, shapes, and text information.
  (3) Changes which are beyond the frame of the predefined database
      scheme are created.
It is extremely difficult to realize all these characteristics just with
the help of commercial databases.  However a relational database has,

among the databases which have already been put to practical use as commercial database, some merits such as easy comprehension, non-procedural features, data independence, etc. [1]. A data model, PICCOLO, proposed by Kunii et al. [2] is a model which can represent pictures with expansion of the relational model and constitutes a feature to be capable of representing both physical and logical pictures with the use of the same model by classifying the general picture representation into them. With our SMART, the logical picture is a specialty to be dealt with. However we are inclined to determine that we should take up the concept of PICCOLO and adopt the relational database as database. With reference to the database we have in mind however, our aim is to carry out the hierarchical assembly representation. Accordingly the data model becomes tree structure and the order of tuple identifiers will therefore be under consideration in due course, where a peculiar difference from PICCOLO is distinguished.

In general, it is conceived that the solid modeler is a very useful utensil in a step of working out various kinds of machine design, especially in the case of shape design utilizing CAD/CAM. However it cannot be said that the assembly representation performance which the modeling system possesses is a satisfactory one. The aims of our study are (1) to expand the data model of the existing solid modelers into such structure with which the assembly representation can be accomplished in order to ensure the possibility of building up the integrated database and (2) to make up Solid Modeler with Assembly Representation Tables where such data as the assembly or other such structure can be stored upon the relational database.

## 2 ASSEMBLY REPRESENTATION

### 1) Existing Study concerning Assembly Representation

As we have earlier stated, we have to deal with a two and three dimensional geometric model as one of the characteristics of the database in a CAD system. In order to store the information which an actual three dimensional object possesses onto the data upon the database of the CAD system, two conversions, i.e. objects into a geometric model and a geometric model into a database are required. As geometric models, we have shape information which has been being dealt with for years in the existing solid modelers such as B-rep., CSG, etc. and another kind of information which displays the relationship between components and is supposed to be dealt with in mainly SMART. Recently several types of research of data model with which the assembly can be dealt with have been prosecuted taking account of computer-integrated manufacturing (CIM). Although Location Graph contrived by Eastmann [3] is of the graph structure which links objects with relative coordinate conversion matrices among respective local coordinates, it does not yet have any concept of an assembly as hierarchical structure.

World Model contrived by Liebermann and Wesley [4] as data structure of a system for automatic assemblying reveals the relationship among aggregates and sub-parts, using graphs. This can either represent the assemblies of several levels or obtain the distinguishable relationship among objects. Also the relative relationship between two objects including join and inclusion relation, e.g. one is another's sub-part, is depicted with the aid of the same graph as well. Since both relationships are represented with the same graph, we find it rather difficult to sound out, for example, such a matter how the assembly is fabricated from subparts. Also, since not a few pointers become necessary to cover the vertexes which correspond to individual nodes in the graph, it is diffi-

cult to store the data upon the relational database with the fixed
length.

Lee [5] proposes a data model which can represent hierarchically an assembly by introducing Virtual Link, revealing the relationship of the
data between two objects. In this model however, there is no pointer
corresponding to the hierarchy on the lower-ranking level beneath the
assembly. Therefore no retrieval for objects of the hierarchy on the
lower-ranking level can be conducted without passing through the above-
mentioned Virtual Link.

Accordingly, there is a possibility that overlapped retrieval will be
accidentally prosecuted in such a case when sub-parts are required to be
retreived sequentially. In addition, the data are liable to be overlapped and the efficiency of the memory region is susceptible to aggra-
vation, if a trial to store the data upon the database is made without
providing the said model with any rectification. To make the matters
worse, there is also a probability that no guarantee to be free from
contradiction when they are renewed is afforded against the data. Thus
we have come to a conclusion that the model is not adequate enough to be
used for the database.

Since FD (feature description) data model has been developed by Takase [6], Ishida [7], et al. with the database utilizing a frame form
taking LISP into account, its data are of the variable length and it has
such conspicuous features as being available for any types of data as a
frame in the same method, being liberated from such nuisances as defining the data model beforehand, etc. Judging from a viewpoint of treatment of the shape data, the model is of the structure easy to deal with.
However it is next to impossible for the model to be incorporated in the
relational database.

  2) Structure of Assembly Representation Tables

In SMART, a data model called ART (assembly representation tables) has
been conceived. This has such four types of data, i.e. ASSEMBLY,
OBJECT, PRIMITIVE, and RELATION, and B-rep. data is also attached to
them. In connection with PRIMITIVE, it represents the primitive in solid modelers. In the meanwhile, OBJECT represents an object composed of
the primitive. In other words, an objective body dealt with by a usual
solid modeler corresponds to this OBJECT, which positions PRIMITIVE as a
member of the ring structure for CGS representation data. Furthermore
ASSEMBLY data represent an assembly composed of several kinds of
OBJECT, and since it has in itself the data called "level", the ASSEMBLY
on the upper-ranking level has a ring structure to which the ASSEMBLY on
the lower-ranking level belong as a member and the lowermost ASSEMBLY
has a ring structure with OBJECT as its member. In accordance with such
a process, ART becomes the structure having an assembly with the dummy
data called "top" on the uppermost level. Illustrated in Fig. 1 is the
hierarchical structure of ART. An arrow on the end of the dotted line
indicates a pointer directed to the member, whereas an arrow on the end
of the solid line denotes a pointer forwarded to the next data. As can
be deduced from the Figure, although a special pointer is used when
transfer is made toward the lower hierarchy, none of peculiar pointer is
employed when transfer is done toward the upper hierarchy in case of
dealing with one-sided ring structure. Accordingly, individual data
themselves should have the data revealing their own hierarchy (class).
However, since their own way how to be treated is determined with regard to the data of respective hierarchy on account of this adversely
affecting feature, the structure is a one adequate for an object-

oriented treatment system. That is to say, if we have a procedure applicable for the data of the class as database (although it might be very difficult for such data to be realized upon the relational database), it is made clear that no person is required to be aware of the procedure beforehand in a step of preparing the application.

Next, the RELATION data are a member of ASSEMBLY or OBJECT, and they reveal the relationship between two types of the data belonging to any of ASSEMBLY, OBJECT, or PRIMITIVE on the lower-ranking level which are the said relation data. The relatinship among the optional pieces of data groups is shown by the plural number of RELATION. Following such procedures, the number of pointers which RELATION possesses can be fixed at 2. Illustrated in Fig. 2 is an example of the ring structure in which an owner is ASSEMBLY and members are OBJECT. The Figure reveals that the owner has two types of ring structure (double ring structure). With the aid of this structure, search can be performed with regard to not only the data on the lower-ranking level but also the relationship with which they are composed of, without repetition.

Moreover OBJECT has a pointer guided toward the winged-edge data. Shown in Table 1 is the composition of the individual data.

## 3. DATA STORAGE IN THE RELATIONSHIP DATABASE

With SMART, pattern data have been represented with the use of the four relations of ASSEMBLY, OBJECT, PRIMITIVE, and RELATION. The meaning and role those relations have are quite the same as those referred to in Chapter 2. Therefore we herewith designate names of the attribute which the individual relations actually possesses, without furnishing detailed explanation.

ASSEMBLY
      member:      first number of OBJECT
      relation:     first number of RELATION

OBJECT
      address:     (for work)
      assembly:    number of owner
      primitive:   first number of PRIMITIVE
      relation:     first number of RELATION

PRIMITIVE
      address:     (for work)
      category:    category of PRIMITIVE
      object:      number of owner
      vector11
         :        local coordinate
      vector23
      position1
         :        position
      position3
      value1
         :        main attribute
      value3

RELATION
      category:    category of RELATION
      ownerc:     class of owner
      ownern:     number of owner
      member1:    one related data
      member2:    the other related data

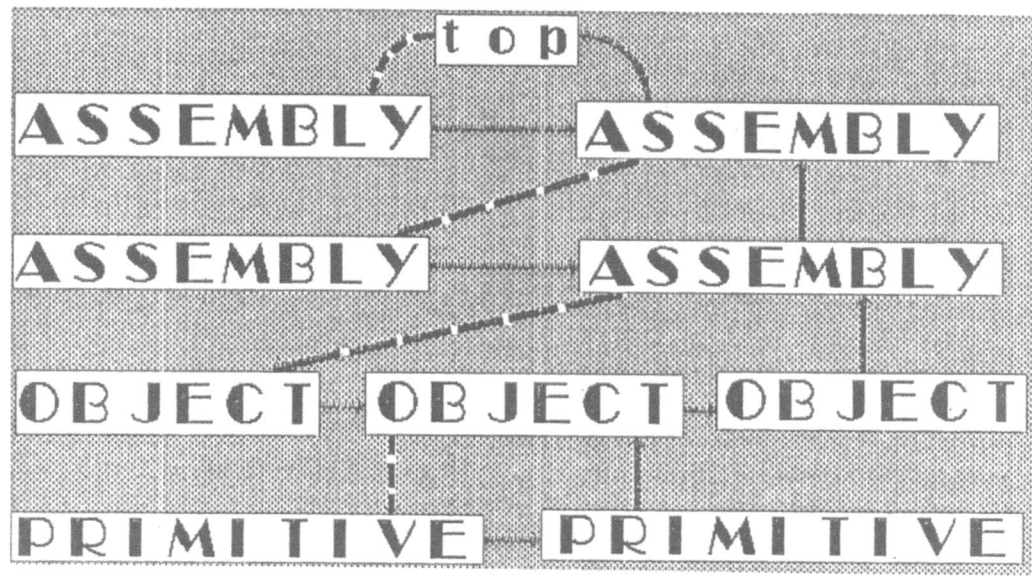

Fig.1   The hierarchical structure of ART

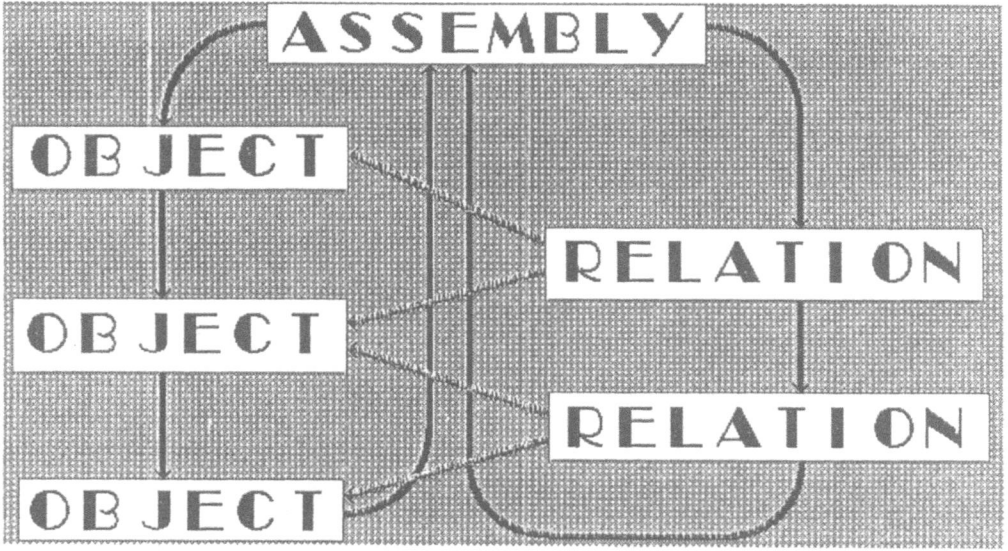

Fig.2   Double ring structure with pointers

Table 1  Construction of Data

```
top
     class:      "h"
     next:       pointer to ASSEMBLY

ASSEMBLY
     class:      "a"
     next:       pointer to next ASSEMBLY
     member:     pointer to lower-level member
     prelation:  pointer to RELATION
     name:       name of ASSEMBLY
     level:      level of ASSEMBLY
     astruct:    method of solving attribute (*)
     avalue:     value of attribute (*)

OBJECT
     class:      "o"
     next:       pointer to next OBJECT
     member:     pointer to PRIMITIVE
     prelation:  pointer to RELATION
     pvert:      pointer to vertices
     pedge:      pointer to edge
     pface:      pointer to face
     pstruct:    method of solving attribute (*)
     pvalue:     value of attribute (*)
     name:       name of OBJECT

PRIMITIVE
     class:      "p"
     next:       pointer to next PRIMITIVE
     category:   category of PRIMITIVE
          "c":   cylinder; "r" rectangular prism
     pvec[3,2]:  local coordinate
     ppos[3]:    position of origin of local coordinate
     pstruct:    method of solving attribute (*)
     attr[3]:    main attribute (size)
     pvalue:     value of attribute (*)

RELATION
     class:      "r"
     next:       pointer to next PRIMITIVE
     category:   category of RELATION
          "t":   touch;    "j": join;    "h": making hole
     member[2]:  two related OBJECT or ASSEMBLY
     pstruct:    method of solving attribute (*)
     attr[2]:    main attribute
     pvalue:     value of attribute (*)

(In SMART Ver. 1.0, the data marked (*) is not supported.)
```

## 4. AN EXAMPLE

Illustrated in Fig. 3 is an example obtained by utilizing SMART. This is a result of procedures executed by creating two rectangular prisms and a cylinder, transferring horizontally the cylinder, making a hole, and combining the two rectangular prisms. Shown in Table 2 are the data of the solid data stored upon dBASE-Ⅱ which are represented by employing functions of SMART.

## 5. CONCLUSIONS

1) SMART (Solid Modeler with Assembly Representation Tables) has been developed on relational databases (RDB).
2) Owing to the double ring structure of assembly database, easy data dealing for a solid modeler on RDB has been attained.
3) A possibility of RDB as common integrated database including the data for commercial and engineering purposes has been confirmed.

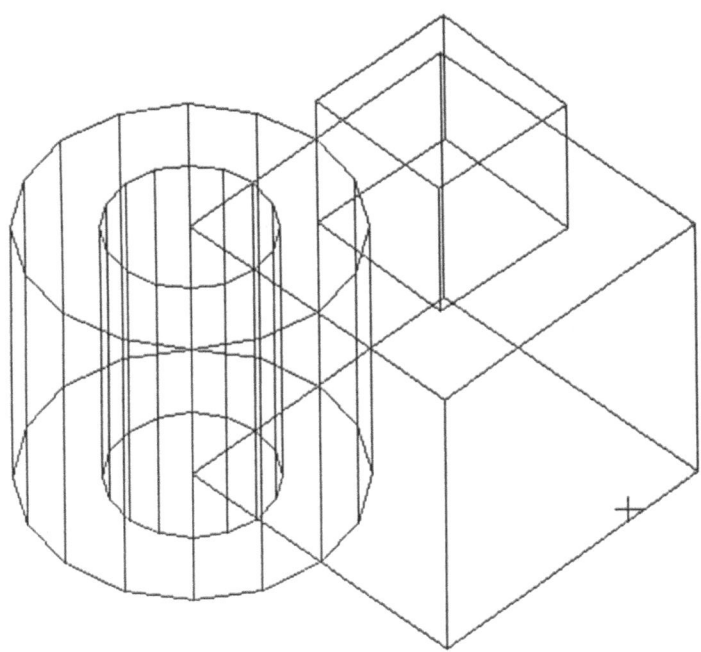

Fig.3  An example of simple assembly

Table 2  SMART data list

---

```
* ASSEMBLY #1 *

+ OBJECT #1 +
 ----- hole PRIMITIVE #1 into PRIMITIVE #2

  . PRIMITIVE #1 .  CYLINDER

    radius = 50.000000, height = 200.000000

  local co-ordinate
    0.000000,0.000000,-1.000000
    0.000000,0.000000,0.000000
    0.000000,0.000000,0.000000

  position
    x = 0.000000, y = -120.000000, z = 100.000000

  . PRIMITIVE #2 .  CYLINDER

    radius = 100.000000, height = 200.000000

  local co-ordinate
    0.000000,0.000000,-1.000000
    0.000000,0.000000,0.000000
    0.000000,0.000000,0.000000

  position
    x = 0.000000, y = -120.000000, z = 100.000000

* ASSEMBLY #2 *

+ OBJECT #2 +
 ----- join PRIMITIVE #4 onto PRIMITIVE #3

  . PRIMITIVE #3 .  RECTANGULAR PRISM

    xsize = 200.000000, ysize = 200.000000, zsize = 200.000000

  local co-ordinate
    1.000000,0.000000,0.000000
    0.000000,1.000000,0.000000
    0.000000,0.000000,1.000000

  position
    x = 0.000000, y = 0.000000, z = 0.000000

  . PRIMITIVE #4 .  RECTANGULAR PRISM

    xsize = 100.000000, ysize = 100.000000, zsize = 100.000000

  local co-ordinate
    1.000000,0.000000,0.000000
    0.000000,0.000000,-1.000000
    0.000000,1.000000,0.000000

  position
    x = 50.000000, y = 50.000000, z = 150.000000
```

---

APPENDIX 1

"SMART Ver. 1.0" is a three dimensional solid modeler developed by us with the intention of pursuing the earlier-stated research of us, and it has the functions shown below.
(1) Creation (rectangular prism / cylinder) of primitive
(2) Exchange of objects to be operated
(3) Join of objects
(4) Hole making with objects (penetrated / not penetrated)
(5) Transfer of objects (horizontal transfer / rotational transfer)
(6) Touch among individual objects
(7) Storage of pattern data upon the relational database
(8) Output of pattern data from the relational database
Also, the plural number of the objects can be dealt with in a combined form by assemblying them. Furthermore, the plural number of assemblies can be dealt with in a combined form as the assemblies on the upper-ranking level and hierarchy.

Hardware we used:  NEC PC-9801 (8087) as host computer
                   PC-KD551 as CRT display
                   MS mouse as subsidiary instrument

Software we used:  MS-DOS as OS
                   dBASE-II as relational database
                   Optimizing C86 & MASM as language for development
                   C to dBASE & EGR98-CSV as utility

APPENDIX 2

In order to sharply distinguish a polyhedral-body-approximated cylinder from a polygonal pillar similar to a cylinder, an improved winged-edge data model is used. In SMART, rings of all the faces and edges protruding from OBJECT are hierarchized and new data called RFACE (real face) and REDGE (real edge) are settled for the sake of easy dealing of curved surfaces and curved lines. Furthermore faces and edges which are settled to attain approximation are dealt with in a combined form of curved surfaces and curved lines by enrolling them as members in the ring structure of RFACE and REDGE.

REFERENCES

[1] M. Managaki, "Relational Database and CAD", Computer Today No. 7, May 1985 (In Japanese)
[2] K. Yamaguchi, T.L. Kunii, "PICCLO Logic for a Picture Database Computer and its Implementation", Reprinted from IEEE Transactions on Computers Vol. C-31, No. 10, Oct. 1982
[3] C.M. Eastman, "The Design of Assemblies", SAE Technical Paper Series, Feb. 1981
[4] M.A. Wesley, L.I. Lieberman, D.D. Grossman, etc., "A Geometric Modeling System for Automated Mechanical Assembly", IBM J. RES. DEVELOP. Vol. 24, No. 1, Jan. 1980
[5] K. Lee, D.C. Gossard, "A hierarchical data structure for representing assemblies: part 1", CAD, Vol. 17, No. 1, Jan./Feb. 1985
[6] H. Takase, N. Nakajima, "A Language for Describing Assembled Machines", Proc. of ISDS, PP600-605, 1984
[7] T. Ishida, H. Minowa, N. Nakajima, "Detection of Unanticipated Function of Machines", Proc. of ISDS, PP21-26, 1984
[8] F. Yamaguchi, T. Tokieda, "A Solid Modeler with a 4*4 Determinant Processor", CG and Applications (IEEE), April 1985

Takashi Hasegawa is a graduate student of information engineering at the University of Tokyo.
His research interests include database for CIM and Computer Aided Instruction for CAD/CAM education.
He received BE from the University of Tokyo in 1986.

Naomasa Nakajima is a professor of mechanical engineering for production at the University of Tokyo, where he has been teaching CAD/CAM and engineering design, and directs the research of graduate students and research associates in knowledge base CAD/CAM system and CAD/CAM education system. His research interests include not only CAD/CAM and computer graphics but also systems design for autonomous energy system, autonomous building and welfare apparatus.
He received a BE, a MS and a PhD from the University of Tokyo in 1964, 1966 and in 1969 respectively. He is a member of IEEE and Computer Graphics Society.

# Visual Business Graphics Query Interface

Kuan-Tsae Huang

IBM T.J. Watson Research Center, P.O. Box 218, Yorktown Heights, NY 10598, USA

## Abstract

Due to the relatively inexpensive availability of displays and printers, graphic interfaces are increasingly playing an important role in analyzing stored or computed data. The integration of graphical data presentation and computerized databases is thus becoming important for the professional end user. This paper describes the design of a visual business graphical interface for office applications. A visual programming approach for creating a business graphic query and generating business graphics is presented. It provides a flexible interface between graphics applications and database. The system enables professionals who are non-programmers to generate the desired graphical presentation of data from database without the help of a professional programmer.

## 1. Introduction

Although computer graphics has been in existence for many years, the high cost of displays and output equipment prevented these systems from being popular to a large number of users. In recent years, the combination of falling prices of raster color displays, memory, and processor and output devices have contributed to the significant progress in computer generated graphics for business applications [1]. The data for those business graphics are normally generated from various data bases of business departments, such as marketing, manufacturing, accounting, finance, etc. This data and its graphic representation play a major role in the process of management decision making.

As computers become directly available to the management echelon of an organization, it is becoming clear that: first, the interaction with the computer must be straight forward, namely that for most cases there is no need for the intervention of a professional programmer. Second, users must have easy, dynamic access to local and corporate data bases. By dynamic we mean an on-line, up-to-date version of the data. Third, is that the professional himself can generate various graphs from this on-line data.

Currently, there are a number of graphic software packages in the marketplace that can generate various kinds of graphs from retrieved or analyzed data. These packages can generally be classified into two categories: First, there are those packages which supply a set of subroutine libraries. The user formulates programs by supplying data and calling the subroutines with appropriate parameters to generate the graphs. Certainly, for a user to use these packages he/she must be a professional programmer. Secondly, are those standalone software packages which provide the use of commands and menus for specifying features of the desired graph. In most of these packages, the user has to supply the values of the data to the system directly, lacking a dynamic link to a local or central database. Furthermore, once the graph is generated, the need to modify colors, scales, titles, etc., on the output screen may require cumbersome manu manipulations.

This paper describes a method for a non-programmer-professional to directly generate graphics from a stored database system. These graphics are restricted to the domain of business graphics, e.g., various bar graphs, pie graphs and histograms. In addition, the output of these graphics can be itself stored as a new object in the database and retrieved at a later time. This paper is organized as follows: In Section 2 we give a short overview of the Office-by-Example (OBE) system environment [5], which is being developed at IBM Thomas J. Watson Research Center. In Section 3 we describe the visual interface for business graphics query and the interactive editing facility for modifying the generated output. In section 4, we compare the interface of the integrated softwares on the market with our approach. The conclusion and future research is stated in section 5.

## 2. OBE System Environment

The non-procedural business graphics interface has been implemented as part of Office-By-Example (OBE)[5]. OBE is a two-dimensional language and system which attempts to mimic manual procedures of business and office systems. OBE is a superset and natural extension of the Query-By-Example (QBE) database management system [6]. QBE, a relational database system, is an IBM product that is used in many applications. OBE, on the other hand, is a research project of office information system currently in various stages of architecture and development.

The OBE system has the QBE relational database management system as its base. It attempts to combine and unify aspects of office activities such as data retrieval, report writing, business document processing and electronic mail, etc. It supports manipulation of objects such as:

* Tables(database relations).
* Documents(e.g., text, memos, reports, and forms).
* Windows(stored OBE program, i.e., sets of operations).
* Menus(list of execution commands).
* Graphic objects(e.g., bar charts, scatter charts).
* Image objects(e.g., pictures, signature).

The programming style of OBE is the same as that of QBE: direct programming within two-dimensional pictures of business objects. The data objects in OBE include tables, letters, menus, forms, reports, charts, graphs, and images. These objects can be manipulated on the screen in a very flexible manner. Each object can be displayed, moved, copied, and scrolled within a single window [program]. It can also be stored, retrieved, and updated to and from a database. The users are able to manipulate objects and text within the objects by using expand, erase, copy, move, scroll, locate, zoom and pushdown functions. In addition, the users can easily customize a variety of menus for them- selves or others, so that one need not know more about the system than to point at menu selections that have been designed especially for them. It is expected that QBE users will require very little additional training to be able to use OBE. OBE had been implemented for both VM and PC DOS in various stages running at various terminals (IBM 3270 series terminals, 3270 PC and PC/XT, etc.). The business graphics interface was fully implemented in VM version and partially implemented in PC version.

# 3. Direct Visual Interface for Business Graphics Query

Two fundamental concepts of QBE language that has been carried over into the design of graphics query interface are to program directly on the user-desired objects and the use of example elements to map data among database tables. The example elements are variables to allow users to program within fields of different objects. They are used to perform a wide variety of operations such as cross-referencing between fields by entering identical example elements in two or more fields of the same or different objects; formulating conditions of field values (e.g. __A+__B>100); moving data from one object to another; and deriving new fields (e.g. put __A+__B in a new field). In QBE, the database tables are the user-desired objects. For business graphics query, we follow the same approach by creating pictographical object for each type of business graphics. To create a graphics query, We use example elements to link data between database tables and graphics objects.

A direct visual programming interface can be best described by examples. In this section, we will use examples to illustrate the functions and features of our design. We first describe the visual interface of graphics objects and the direct programming concept of the graphics query. Then, by using examples we show the flexibility and easiness of creating different graphics queries.

## 3.1 Pictographical Objects for Business Graphics

Graphical programming environment is an approach that would make it possible for a person to converse with computer rapidly through the power of a graphical interface. The important idea of depicting abstractions graphically has been applied to many areas, such as general programming environment, computer aided design and computer aided instruction, etc.

Following the same approach, a pictographical programming object is created for each business graphics type. Within each pictographical object, a pictorial form of the kind of business graphics is shown along with the colored fields to allow the user to fill in example elements for data linkage. The pictorial form of the object enables the user to feel like he is operating on the object of interest and to expect the output graphics resulting from his direct programming action. The colored fields of the pictographical object allow user to specify the color and spatial relationships among data of example elements directly. An input pictographical object is very similar to it's output graphic object. This use of the similar objects as both input and output entities is an essential feature in representing the behavior of an object in such a way that the user expects it to be.

Figure 1 shows an example of vertical bar graphics input object and output object. All the colored fields of both vertical and horizontal bar area in the input object are used as input programming area. The color of the field where the example element is putted is the color to be plotted for the data linked by that example element. If the user specifies example elements one on top of the other in the vertical bar area, the resulting graphics will be a stacked bar graphics with corresponding colors. On the other hand, if the example elements are putted into the horizontal bar area, the resulting graphics will be a parallel bar graphics. In figure 1, this query example is to plot the marketing, operating and R and D expenses of the company GF in the stack bar chart by year. The lower left object in this figure is the graphics query object. The user links the data from the EXPENSE table to the graphics query object through example elements. In order to generate stack bar chart, we put __M, __O and __R in the vertical color fields. The output graphics in the lower right object of the figure shows the bars plotted for expense daa from marketing in red, operating in green and R and D in yellow. Because the expense data for the graphics will be plotted by year, we put down __Y in the yellow field under the x axis to link to the EXPENSE table.

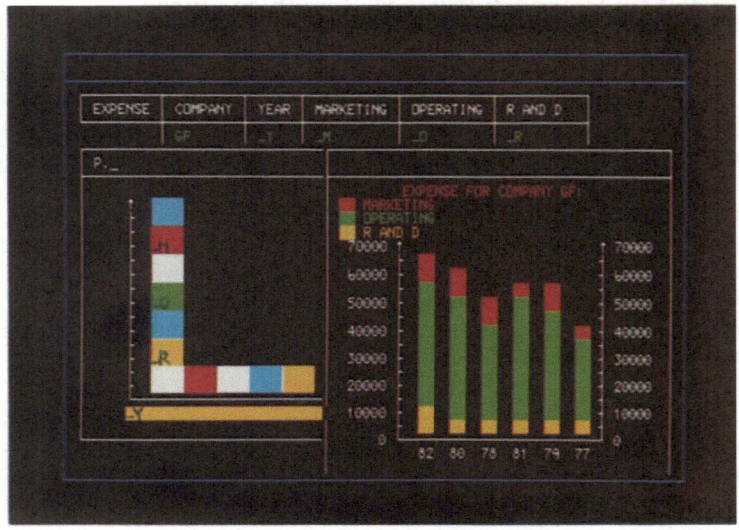

Figure 1. An example query of vertical bar graphics

The system supports nine types of business graphics. They are line graph; surface graph; scatter graph with linear, logarithmic, exponential regression optional; pie graph; vertical bar graph; horizontal bar graph; curve graph; histogram graph with normal curve fitting; and statistical graph. Figure 2 and Figure 3 show examples of other types of output graphic objects. In addition, the system has a "GRAPH MENU" object to allow user to select the graphics type from this menu object. Figure 4 shows the "GRAPH MENU" object.

## 3.2 Creating Business Graphics Query

We use the following example to illustrate how a user in our system can create a query for business graphics. Suppose we want a horizontal bar graphics showing hardware and software sales for the year 1983. Further, suppose that we have a database table containing hardware and software sales per state per calendar quarter. An OBE program to generate the graphics is illustrated in Figure 5.

In OBE, SUM. is an aggregate operator to sum or total multiple values. G. is a group__by operator on data within objects. Because the table contains the sales data for each quarter, to plot the sums of the hardware and software sales grouped by state (over the quarters of the year 1983), the user has to specified SUM.__HW and SUM.__SW in the data field area and G.__S in the field for vertical axis. In this example, G.__S which has __S serves as a link between the graph and the field STATE of the SALES table means group the data according to state. It can be interpreted as "for each state". The SUM.__HW and SUM.__SW example element expressions specify the variables corresponding to the horizontal bars. The spatial relationship and field colors of these two example elements in the input object specifies the two bars will be shown in parallel with the corresponding color in the output graph. Thus, the output graph will have a hardware sales bar and a software sales bar parallely shown for each state. Figure 3-2 is the output graph of this example.

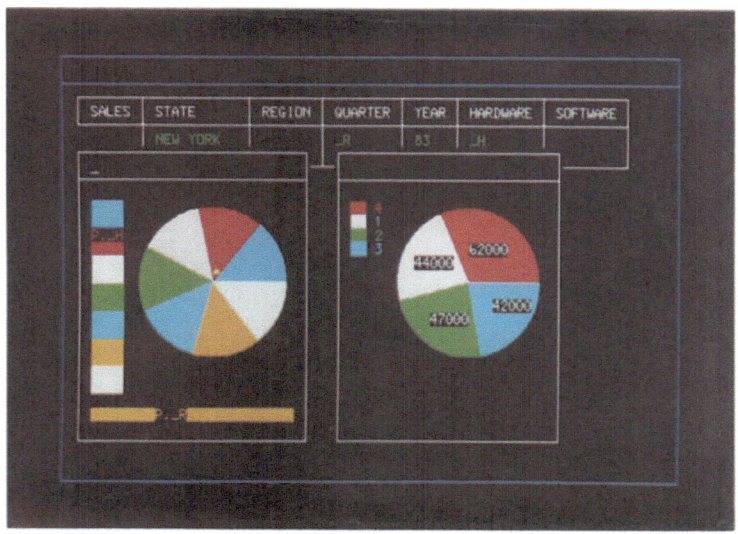

Figure 2-1.   Pie chart with data shown on the graph

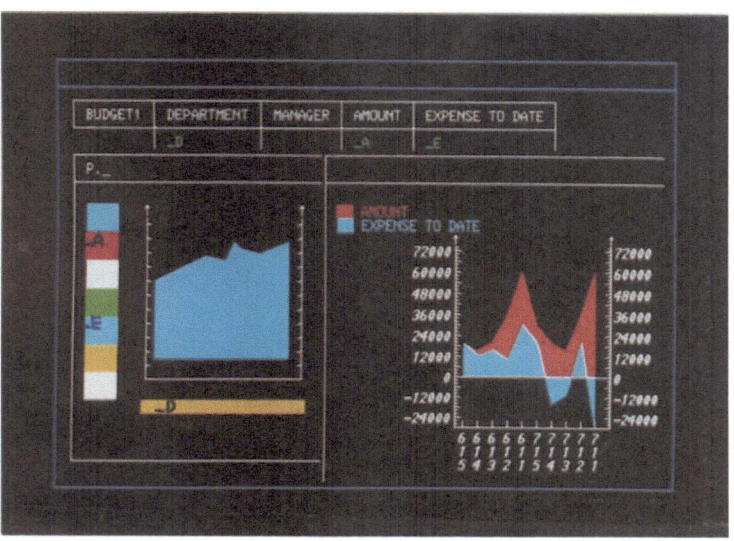

Figure 2-2.   Surface chart

Figure  2.   Examples of Business Graphics

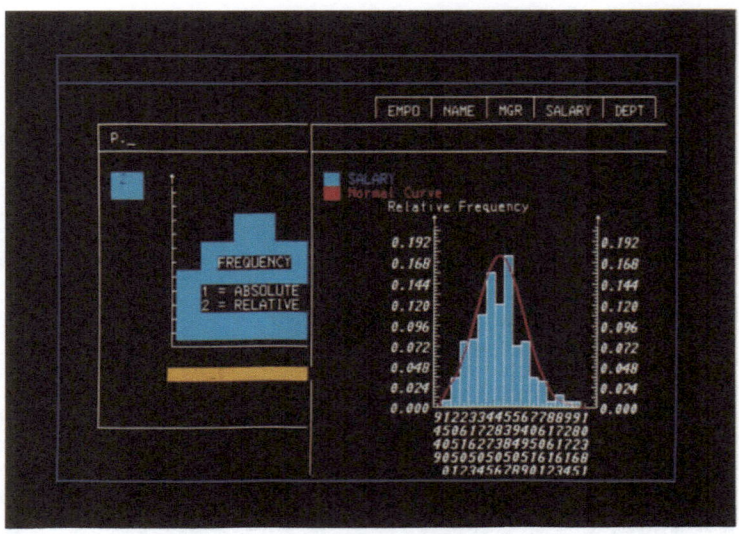

Figure 3-1.    Histogram with normal curve fitting

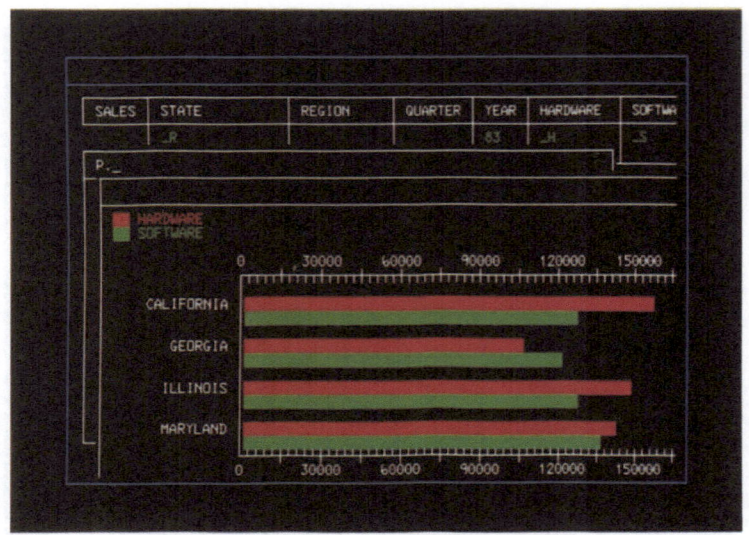

Figure 3-2.    Horizontal bar chart

Figure  3.    Examples of Business Graphics

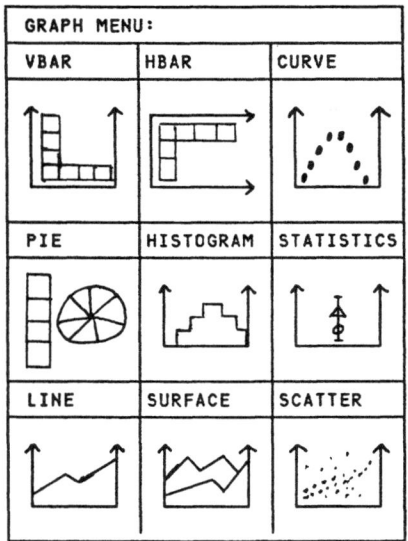

Figure 4. Graph Menu Object

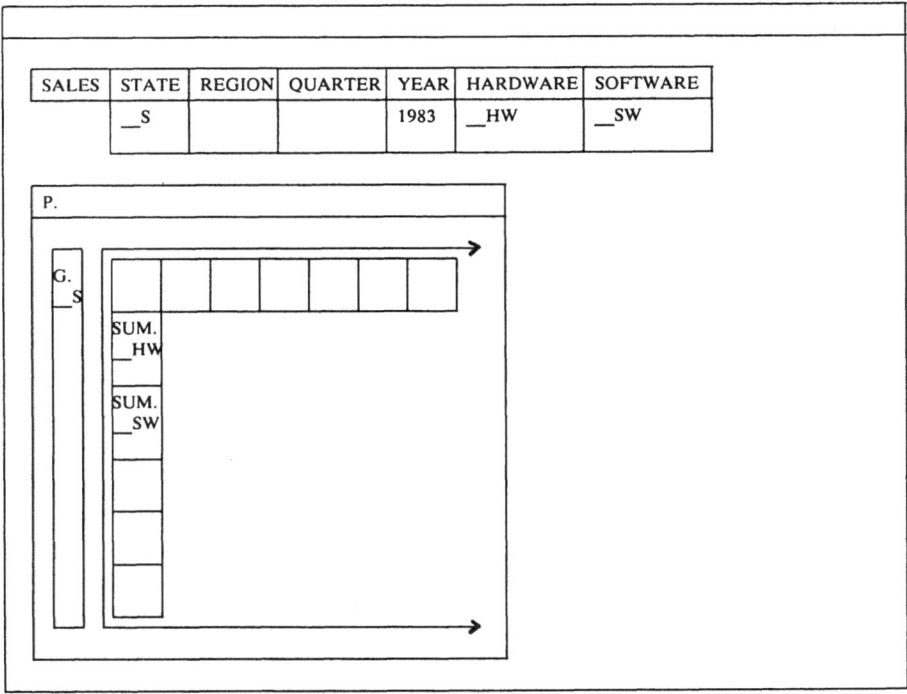

Figure 5. Query for generating a horizontal bar graphics

### 3.3 Creating Different Business Graphics Queries

In our system, the user can request business graphics with different sets of data by slightly revising an existing query. The above example shows the query for generating horizontal bar graphics of both hardware and software sales of 1983 by states. Suppose the user also wants to generate the horizontal bar graphics of both hardware and software sales of 1983 by regions. In spite the fact that the two graphics use the same set of data and they differ only in the variable of the base axis, the user of many integrated softwares existing on the market, such as Symphony [4], has to go through a sequence of menus to generate such a new graphics. In our system, to generate such a graphics by region, the user simply modifies the example element __S in the field of STATE to the field of REGION and reprocesses the query. The reason of such tremendous saving of effort for generating different graphics using the same set of data in our system compare to other system is because of the integration of database for data sharing. All QBE query language capability can be used to create graphic queries, such as using condition box to specify constraints, using arithmetic operators to create formula for derived data, etc.

### 3.4 Interactive Graphics Editing

Having generated the output graph on the screen, the user can edit it interactively in a very flexible manner. Examples of editing functions for graphic objects are: to modify the width or spacing of all bars by pressing a single function key; to change the vertical scale by expanding or shrinking the vertical coordinate; to modify the bar colors by change the color areas in the legend; to add the headings, footings and comments by typing text strings into the object directly, to highlight a pie segment of the pie graphics by moving the segment slightly apart from the whole pie. etc. The edited graphics objects can be either stored in the database for future use or superimposed into other text or image objects.

All the operations use the same set of function keys described in the OBE language section above. Their behaviors are dependent on their cursor position and and the content of their pointing objects. Readers are referred to [2] and [3] for the details of graphics of OBE system.

## 4. Comparison with Integrated Softwares on the Market

Within last two years, many integrated softwares for microcomputer such as Symphony from Lotus Development Corporation, Framework from Ashton-Tate, and Enable from the Software Group have emerged. Most of the integrated softwares that are popularized on the market have the ability to create graphs from and to perform database functions on the data stored in the spreadsheet cells. Although the integration has made the process of generating the business graphs relatively easy, it still requires an amount of time to go through the menus to generate the desired graphs. In this section, we will compare the process of generating graphs of this non-procedural visual interface approach with other package's approach by the following example task.

Assume we have a database table for salary information with attributes (Name, Dept, Base Salary, Commission, Gross Salary). Consider the following task of generating a vertical bar graph showing base salary, commission and gross salary of employees in the TOY department whose commission exceeds their base salary, with the names sorted in alphabetical order.

In other package currently on the market, the user has to go through the following steps to generate the desired graphs:

A. Sorting the records
   1. specify sort key
   2. execute sort
B. Executing the query and copying result to an output table
   3. specify selection criteria
   4. copy column headings to blank area of worksheet
   5. specify output range
   6. extract records to output range
C. Creating the graph
   7. chose graph type
   8. specify ranges to be graphed
   9. specify color
   10. specify legend labels
   11. specify title
   12. specify x-axis label

Each step may involve with several menu selection processes. The sequence of menu operation is very tedious and time consuming. Any small change resulting in the user's query may end up to repeat the same sequence of menu processes performed by the user before.

With our non-procedural visual interface for business graphics, the user can perform the same task by simply calling three objects to the screen and putting the example elements into the objects to generate the business graphics query. Figure 6 shows the corresponding query in our system. AO. is the ascending operator. AO.__N under the x axis in the figure specifies the bar graphs will be plotted in the ascending order of the employee name. The reader can see the distinct difference of user interface of our system with other integrated softwares on the market.

## 5. Conclusion and Future Research

We have presented here a non-procedural approach for creating a business graphic query and generating business graphics. This approach provides a flexible interface between graphics applications and database. Both statistical data and graphical data are stored in the same database with uniform interface. The statistical data can be used not only for graphical applications but also any other business applications like reports, forms, etc. The graphical data is stored in object-oriented graphical structure manner such that the manipulation of the constructing components of the graphics can be easily done. Its advantage is that users who are non-programmers can write non-procedural programs to directly pull data from large corporate databases and generate and edit the graphs interactively. The elegant, two-dimensional programming approach of Query-By-Example and Office-By-Example, as was shown in this short example, makes the formulation of such graphics programs easy and straight forward.

The extension of this non-procedural approach to generate multiple graphics report can be done easily. If the user put another example element on the first row of the graphic template, for example, an example element link to the department, then after processing this query the system will generate a graphics object for each department which have data from the resulting query. The generating of multiple graphics can be extended to the hierarchy of several example elements in the ordering of their appearance.

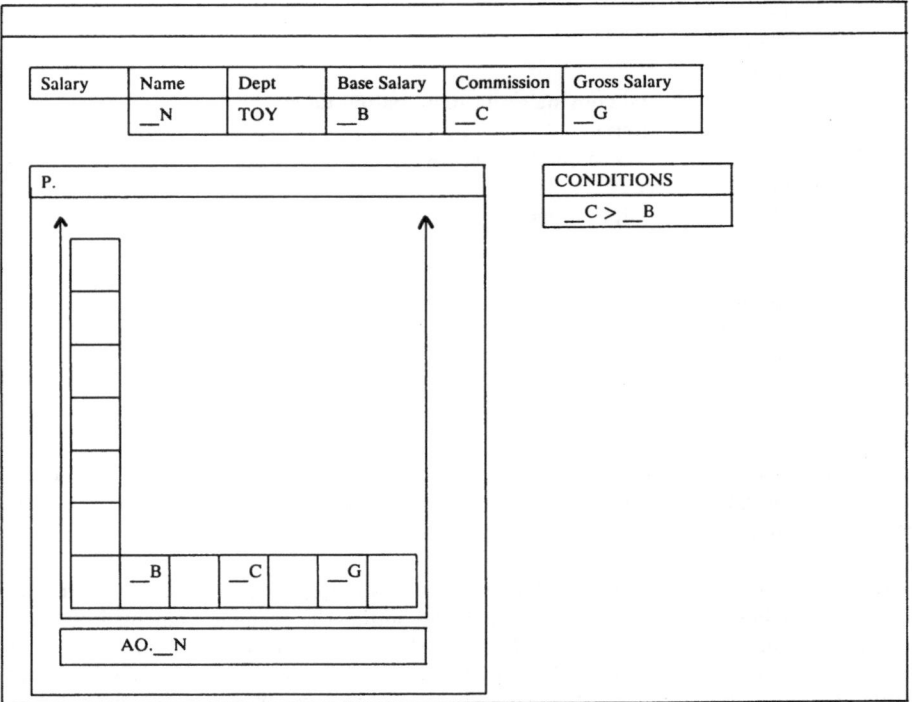

Figure 6. The corresponding visual query for the graphics

Several other directions to extend the non-procedural feature of current system to graphics application are possible. Such as, different sizes of fonts; automatically and intelligently select graphics type based on the pattern, type, and domain of the business and statistical data; Map graphics for geographic information; and 3-dimensional business graphics, etc. Further research of the above directions is needed in order to enable office workers to view and produce business graphics interactively for their daily business activities.

The interface of this paper also presented a visual programming language [7] for business graphics and database. Our approach provides a two dimentional progrogramming interface which take advantage of spatial relathionship and colors of the screen. The syntax and semantics of this visual programming language is quite different from the conventional linear language. Although the domain of this visual programming language is limited, we are extending the concept to more general domain of programming language and better graphical interaction. Our current research activities not only center on the syntax and semantics of visual programming language but also on the issues of object modularity, reusability and interconnection.

# Acknowledgements

I would lile to thank members of OBE project for their stimulated discussion. Al Khorasani and Paula Sweeney helped the implementation of graphics package in VM version. Vas Putcha implemented part of it in PC version. Guy Hochgesang contributed the window manager. Relational Database in OBE are desinged by Art Ammann, Tony Bolmarcich, Ravi Krishnamurthy, Vance Waddle, Gary Sockut, and Kyu-Young Whang. Special thank for the management support from Patricia Goldberg and Moshe Zloof.

# References

[1] W. C. House, "Interactive Computer Graphics Systems" Petrocelli Books, Inc., 1982.

[2] K. T. Huang and M. M. Zloof, Business Graphics Interface to Databases, Proceeding of Graphics Interface'84, Ottawa, Canada, June 1984 pp. 29-34.2.

[3] K. T. Huang and P. Sweeney, A User's Guide to OBE Graphics and Images, Internal report, IBM Watson Research Center, 1985.

[4] Symphony user manual, Lotus Development Co.,Cambridge, Mass., 1984.

[5] M. M. Zloof, "Office-By-Example: A Business Language that Unifies Data and Word Processing and Electronic Mail", IBM Systems Journal, Vol. 22, No. 3, 1982, pp. 272-304.

[6] M. M. Zloof, "Query-By-Example", AFIPS Conference Proceedings, National Computer Conference 44, 1975, pp. 431-438.

[7] N. C. Shu, "Visual Programming Languages: A dimensional analysis", Proc. of Symp. on New Directions in Computing, Trondheim, Norway, Aug. 1985.

**Dr. Kuan-Tsae Huang is currently a manager of workstation graphics project at IBM T. J. Watson Research Center. He was working on Office-By-Example, an integrated office system project since joined IBM at 1982. His research interests are in the areas of databases, office automation, computer graphics, expert systems and visual programming language. Huang received his B.S. in Mathematics from National Taiwan Normal University in 1974, M.S. in Applied Mathematics from University of Illinois at Urbana-Champaign in 1979 and Ph.D. in Electrical Engineering and Computer Sciences from MIT in 1983. He is the chairman of symposium and conference of ACM SIGSMALL/PC special interest group and member of ANSI graphics standard committee.**

# The Geo-Graph Simulation System
## Towards Dynamic Use of a Geomatic Data Base

T. Couesnon[1], D. Laurent[1] and S. Motet[2]
Institut de Topologie et de Dynamique des Systèmes[1] and Institut Géographique National[2],
Associé au CNRS, 1, rue Guy de la Brosse, 75005–Paris, France

ABSTRACT

This paper describes an interactive use of a Geographic Data Base. The user is free
to move over the entire map or select a particular zone where graphical transformations can be processed. It is possible also to change continuously the point of view
and add or suppress specific informations (electric networks, houses).

GGSS is a powerfull tool allowing to open a window on a large numerical Data Base in
order to produce synthetic and graphical outputs of landscape. It is used to simulate
landscape topography seen at constant height.

KEY WORDS

Geographic Data Base, Relief, Planimetry, Simulation.

INTRODUCTION

Geomatic data base, i.e. data bases in which information bearing on altimetry and
planimetry (roads, rivers, agglomerations, woods,...) has been gathered in numerical
form, are being developed in the United States, Japan, Canada,... (3)(9)(11) In
France, the Institut Géographique National (IGN), the state agency in charge of map
production, is currently implementing a major terrain data base that will be made
available to outside organizations. (1)

The evolvement pace has already quickened. Geomatic Data Base are at the heart of
many applications in computer-aided design or in decision-making aids in a wide variety of fields such as rural and urban planning, installation of communication networks, public works, military projects,...

Computer graphics is an essential component of a Geomatic Data Base Management System. This is easily explainable because, designwise, geomatic data (altimetry, planimetry) are pictorial data bearing on points or objects in space (3D) that consequently must be described, located, and placed in their environment. So, the best
way of interacting with a Geomatic Data Base Management System (GDBMS) is to realistically and dynamically display geomatic data onto a screen. The goal is to have a
simulation tool that lets relief and planimetry be simulated from internal geomatic
data structures, i.e. it allows synthesizing static and dynamic geomatic pictures
from the Geomatic Data Base according to a variety of criteria.

This is the general aim of the Geo-Graph Simulation System (GGSS) currently being
developed at Paris VII University in a joint project with the Institut Géographique
National. The Geo-Graph Simulation System (GGSS) is implemented on an Evans and
Sutherland Multi-Picture System connected to a VAX-11/780.

The procedures made available to the user of the GGSS are intended for :

a. the dynamic 3D simulation of a static terrain zone, i.e. clearly marked off and fixed during processing

    1. Geo-Graph Relief (GGR) exclusively displays the relief of a terrain while displaying contour levels (constant altitude lines) or zones that are lighted or shaded according to their position with respect to the sun, the terrain is seen according to the position of the viewer who can move within a zone.

    2. Geo-Graph Planimetry (GGP) displays the relief and the planimetrical elements defined by the user.

b. Geo-Graph Travelling (GGT) simulates the travels of a viewer within the data base, i.e. in real time, it shows the relief or the relief and the planimetry as seen by the viewer travelling over or above the terrain along a well-defined path.

Point a.1. has already been discussed in various papers. (10)(7)(8) The general functions of GGSS, its components, the nature of the problems that have arisen, the thinking behind solutions that have been adopted, and the current results of our work are presented hereafter.

GENERAL CHARACTERISTICS OF THE GEO-GRAPH SIMULATION SYSTEM (GGSS)

Geographic Data

Relief data result from the overlap of two stereographical aerial pictures and cover ca. 15 square kilometers. The corresponding topographic file contains all information visible on the pictures (roads, RR tracks, woods, rivers, dwellings,...). Data input is achieved by digitizing x,y coordinates and the altitude of these elements by specialized hardware.

Roads, dwellings, lots and other topographical elements (a point inside a zone, a water tower,...) are represented by single points or by sets of connected vectors (polylines). To every element is associated a data validation code and two parameters to subsequently indicate the position, width or height of a given element.

Interactivity

The Geo-Graph Simulation System provides the user an opportunity for genuine interaction with the system in the choice of simulations and displays of representations.

Interaction is ensured by the menus. This choice is not original, but it fully suits complex command languages. However, menus are generally static. Indeed, the task-scheduler, i.e. the module devised to manage interruptions, depends on the texts enclosed in the menu boxes and on the tasks associated with each box.

This is why we have elaborated a task scheduler generator. This generator, which results from precompilation of the call sequence uses a simple language to describe menus and actions. It generates a distributor specific to the command language. In particular, it creates menu display orders and instructions for plugging into the various tasks.

GEO-GRAPH ARCHITECTURE

The Geo-Graph Simulation System architecture is derived from its assigned functions (Fig. 1).

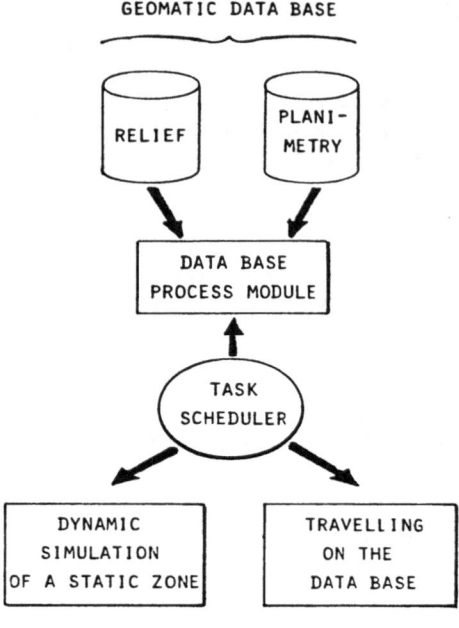

GEOMATIC DATA BASE

RELIEF    PLANI-
          METRY

DATA BASE
PROCESS MODULE

TASK
SCHEDULER

DYNAMIC          TRAVELLING
SIMULATION         ON THE
OF A STATIC ZONE  DATA BASE

Geo-Graph Relief and
Geo-Graph Planimetry    Geo-Graph Travelling    Fig. 1. Geograph Functions.

It includes :
- the task scheduler which, as we have seen, insures and supervizes the communication between the user and the system
- an access module to the geomatic data base which manages the research procedures
  necessary to extract input data by the simulation module
- the simulation modules consist of :
  • a simulation dynamic sub-module of a patch of land (Geo-Graph Relief and Geo-
    Graph Planimetry)
  • a simulation displacement sub-module which insures the travelling on the geoma-
    tic database (Geo-Graph Travelling).

GEO-GRAPH : SIMULATION OF A STATIC TERRAIN ZONE (3D)

Geo-Graph Relief Simulation (GGR)

The simulation and display of the relief involve  drawing an rigid solid from a
particular numerical representation of the relief. This is a two-step process :

1. A creation procedure that generates a 3D display list containing only constants
   representing coordinates for the solid extracted from the Geomatic Data Base

2. A display procedure that transforms this list into a screen image ; through man-
   made interaction, different realistic views of the object can be obtained from
   data provided by the user.

Two types of representation encompassing the various solutions adopted for the representation of the relief of a terrain on an internal level can activate these procedures : a digital terrain model and a contour drawing (Fig. 2) :

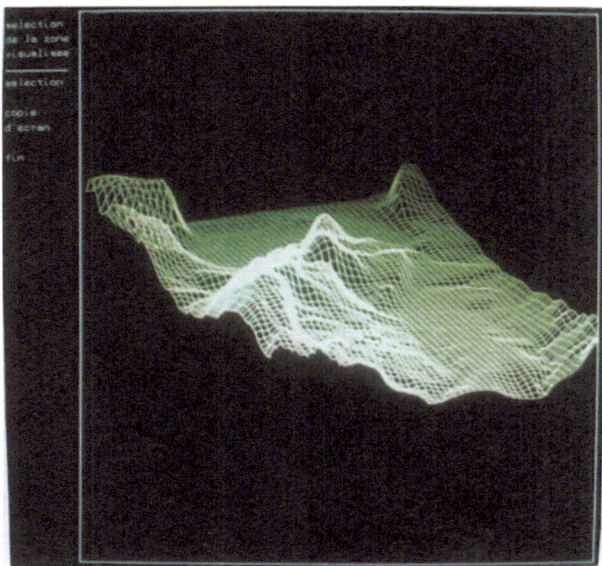

Fig. 2. A block diagram representing a digital terrain model is a matrix whose coefficients are altitudes. The block diagram is depicted as a gridwork in which the nodes are related to the DTM elements and to the user's viewpoint (static or dynamic).

A certain number of functions are available to the user : shading, hidden faces, contour levels generation.

The points are stored in a stack. A contour is represented by a filing containing the address in the stack with the first point, the number of points and color-related information. The elements in the stack are ordered for each contour from the first to the last point. So there is no ambiguity (Fig. 3).

There are two types of contours, depending on whether they are defined by 3D or 2D curves. The entire object is described by the chain of contour filings. Access to this object is gained via a "first" pointer on the first contour.

Creation procedures. *Shading*. The operator can interactively choose the position of the sun defined by the angle of the horizon and the zenithal distance. This procedure makes it possible to shade the block diagram or the curve contour levels (Fig. 4).

*Hidden faces*. This procedure is an adaptation of standard procedures (5) but aims at producing a sharper picture, retaining only those pieces of the grid which are wholly visible while discarding all the others.

Another procedure detects hidden faces from a contour drawing or from a DTM. It can be applied to lines showing altitude.

*Contour levels*. The aim of contour drawing is the generation and display of constant altitude lines. Each line is displayed immediately after being created, so progress in calculations can be assessed (Fig. 4).

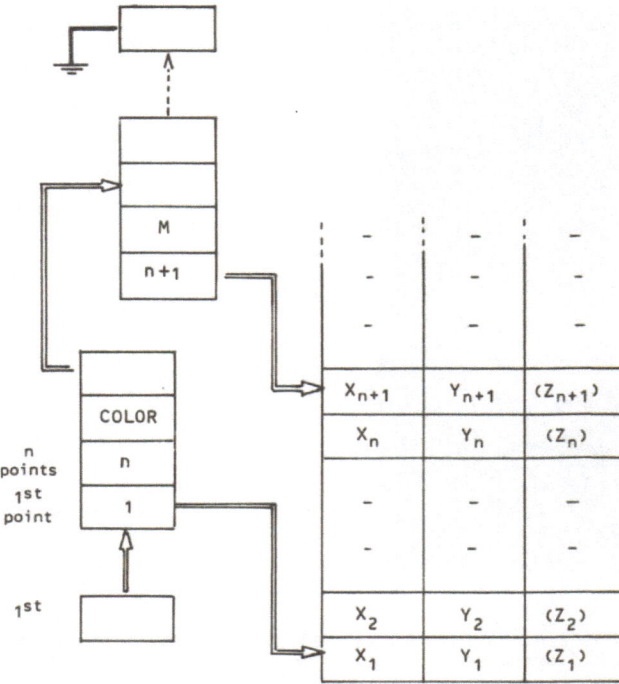

Fig. 3. Contour-drawing data structure. The points (x,y,z) are stored in a stack. A contour drawing is represented by a linked list in which each node contains the address in the stack of the first point, the number of points, and color-related information. The elements in the stack are ordered for each contour from the first to the last point.

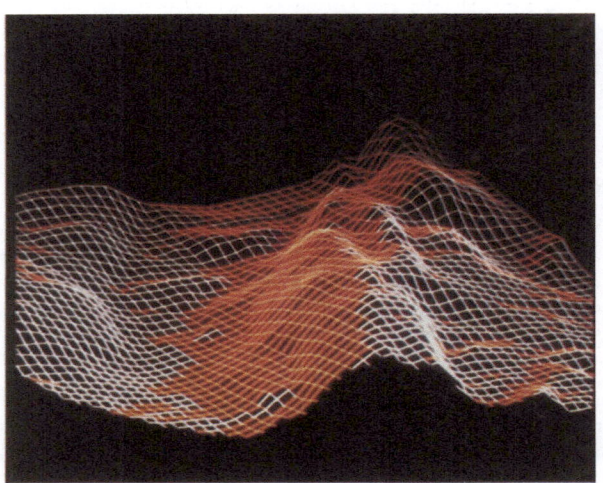

Fig. 4. Zones shaded from an imagery sun are calculated. Lines lying in these zones are darkened. The user can choose the position of the sun by selecting the angle of the horizon and the zenithal distance.

Algorithms for the production of contours on a triangular mesh are described by Heap. (6) The algorithm in our system is recursive. For a given triangle containing a contour line, the next triangle continuing the same line is determined. (2)

The problems posed by this algorithm lie in the topology of specific cases. Contour lines must not get lost in plane zones and must not backtrack once they have crossed a horizontal edge ; for instance, by entering one triangle and leaving the adjacent triangle.

Display Procedures. Two display procedures are provided. The first display procedure gives a view devoid of perspective (to infinity). Potentiometers make it possible to interactively display close-up and rotations from a line vertical to the terrain and the horizontal axis of the screen. The second display procedure gives a view from any point on a terrain. The position of this point can be modified interactively. Close-up and rotation potentiometers can also be used.

Geo-Graph Planimetry (GGP)

In the extension of our work on relief, we have studied simulations on the entire planimetry. The structuring of the functions in transformations and display procedures is preserved. However the functions are different. The transformations are few. They offer a better image. They are limited to the selection of themes and of the zone to be visualised.

However, the display functions are more elaborate. The improvements aim notably at obtaining more realism and clearness by the interactive amplification of the relief.

Thematic Selection. In view of the volume of data contained in topographical files, it is interesting (as stated in paragraph 1) to be able to choose a certain type of information. A procedure for the selection of information according to their nature by entering a computer code specific to these elements has been implemented. There are over 100 different codes grouped into six main topics (roads, RR tracks, rivers, lots, dwellings, inside points).

For example, a user wishing to display paths and parcels, will enter the codes of the path and parcelled lots using add mode ; on the other hand, a user seeking all information other than that pertaining to paths and parcelled lots will enter the same codes, but using suppression mode (Fig. 5).

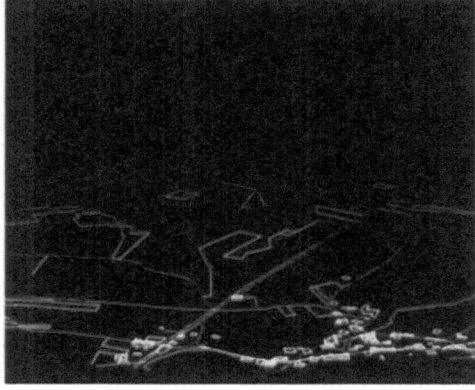 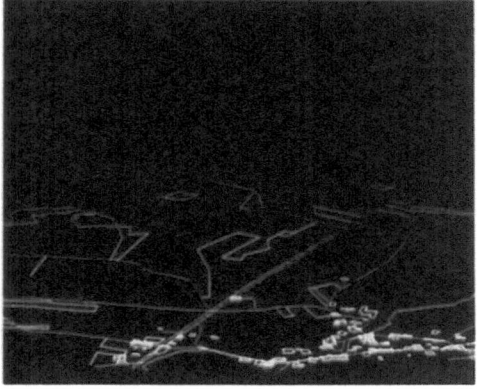

Fig. 5. Planimetry and relief views of a region of the map indicating : 1) all information, 2) information other than that pertaining to parcelled lots.

*Spatial Selection.* Maps are carved into squares by extracting information (points, vectors and characteristics) from the topographical file inside the area marked off by each one of these windows.

The selected map-carving method involves the direct calculation of the points where each vector intersects the sides of a window without prior processing or precoding. Successive application of comparison tests makes possible the elimination of points or vectors outside the clipping window and the retention of vectors lying inside the window, while at the same time making possible the processing of vectors intersecting the sides of a window : a vector passing through one or two sides of a window.

This standard method is very efficient in the case at hand, because vectors are generally very small compared to the sides of the clipping window, and any advantage that methods involving precoding might present regarding speed of calculation is reduced.

Simulation Procedure

Simulation procedures provide the user with the same functions as the "Geo-Graph Relief" display procedures. It is possible to zoom or rotate the 3D image. To increase realism of the simulation, one other function is available.

Relief Amplification and Magnification. Outside mountainous regions, relief varies slightly with ground distance, although altitude is measured in decimeters and distance in meters. Thus, it is sometimes usefull to artificially increase altitude variation in order to get a better perception of the relative height of the displayed elements.

This amplification given by a scale factor applied on altitude only is equivalent to an asymetric magnification along the vertical axis. This operation is realized by the matrix multiplier of the graphic station. The user is free to change at anytime the magnitude of the relief by turning a dial selected for this purpose.

GEO-GRAPH : TRAVELLING ON A GEOMATIC DATA BASE

Trajectory Definition

The movements of an observer at ground level on a 3D map are obtained by placing the current point in the center of the screen and by unrolling the landscape from back to front once it has been correctly orientated in the direction imposed by the trajectory (Fig. 6). The vision of landscape on the screen is simular to the vision provided by a camera pivoting around the vertical axis and translated by X, Y and Z at the moving current point. Landscape moves up or down respectively as the altitude decreases or increases. In space coordinates these operations are composed of an inverse translation of the altitude and coordinates of the current point followed by an inverse rotation in the map plane (Xc, Zc) equal to the angle formed between the perpendicular to the screen (Zc) and the current moving vector (Fig. 7).

Tilting. Because of the extented calculations required for hidden lines removal and the impossibility to apply them in real time on graphic representations used, it is desirable to be able to fly over the map keeping a constant view angle towards the ground. This allows a better vision of the landscape and diminues (in particular) undesirable effects caused by the transparency of the representation. Note that this effect is slightly reduced by the "depth cueing process", decreasing beam intensity with increasing distance. The vision of the landscape after tilting corresponds to the vision of an observer located further back than the current point and flying over the landscape at a fixed height. The fly over, at constant altitude from the map following a well determined trajectory amounts to the rotation around the horizontal axis once the previous transformations have been applied (Fig. 8).

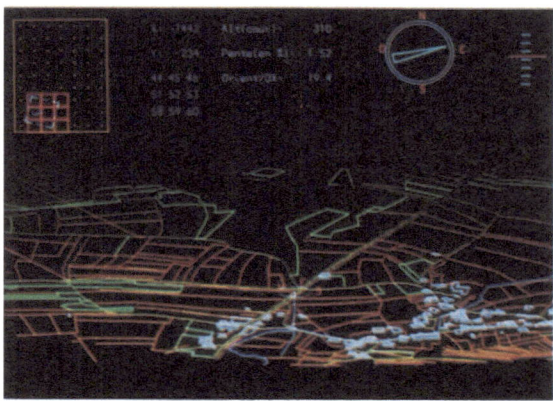

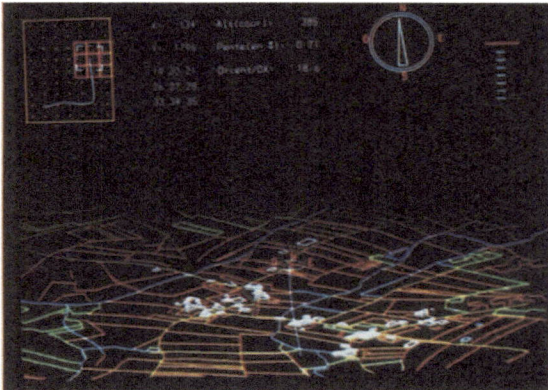

Fig. 6. Travelling on the Data
Base Relief and Planimetry.
The photos 1 and 2 give the position of the observer on two
points on the trajectory. In the
right hand corner a compass per-
menantly indicates the orientation of the landscape according
to movements along the trajectory (blue line). An altimeter,
schematized by graduations, moves
vertically and indicates variations of slope.

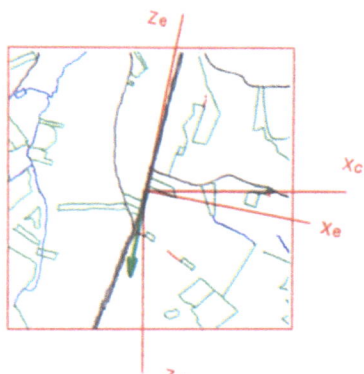

The map is rotated around a vertical
axis passing through the current point
accordingly to the displacement vector

The current point is translated
to the center of the screen

Fig. 7. Movement along the trajectory.

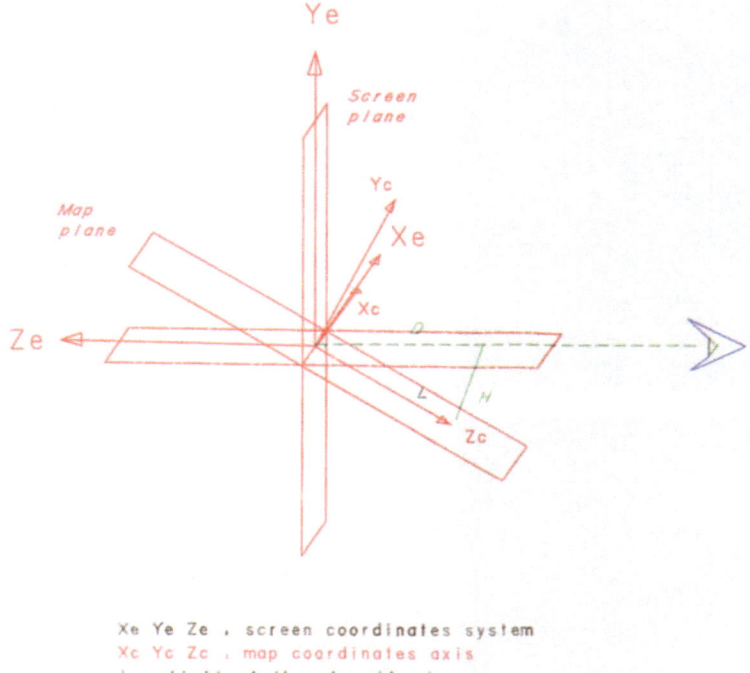

Xe Ye Ze , screen coordinates system
Xc Yc Zc , map coordinates axis
L . limit of the visualized zone
H . current point altitude
D . distance from the observer to the current point

Fig. 8. Fly over the map at constant altitude.

Trajectory Determination. Constant animation along a determined trajectory must be done with a time base. For reasons particular to the hardware we use, it is not possible to produce animation using the time provided by the computer clock. However, in giving greatest place to the execution speed of a MPS task on the VAX (increase of priority, suspension of the other processes), it is possible to approach a calculation configuration simular to a real time machine where we need pay no attention to the variations of time taken to reply to the request between the graphic processor and the VAX.

The time base can thus be replaced by a movement base or increasing movement along the trajectory. This assumes that the updating time of the image is the same for each new image.

Choice of the Displacement Base. In the above hypothesis where the transition from one image to another is supposed to happen in the same elapse time -this is still possible if the elapse time is sufficiently increased- the impression of deplacement at constant speed is obtained by displaying consecutively views from locations equally separated on the trajectory. A segments division algorithm cutting the trajectory into equal parts has been realized. After processing the definition points of the polyline are not necessarily conserved.

Dividing the trajectory into equal segments is done in two steps. First of all, we assign a length to the unit base segment so that the real unitary displacement vector (displacement used for animation) is a multiple of the unit base segment. The division into unit base segments is executed beginning at the first end of each of the vectors constituing the polyline. Then we procede with a fittering or elimination of points inside the unitory displacement vectors and we obtain in this way N regularly spaced points (N is equal to the initial number of points multiplied by the ratio of the length of the unitory displacement vector over the length of the base unit segment). The spacement errors, on the definition points of the polyline level are as a result limited to a value lower than the unit base segment.

Smoothing Trajectory. The preceding treatment gives a control of the speed movement along the trajectory but does not improve significantly the angulous character of the trajectory. Data input being done manually without any particular constraints, the trajectory associated to the roads and rivers has a broken line aspect. Simulation of movement on these path lines is jerky and not realistic. In order to prevent this, it is necessary to perform a smoothing of the trajectory ; a smoothing erasing irregularities and rounding off angles while keeping equidistance between points.

A simple method based on subdivising initial segments into parts and calculating new points from the position of neighbouring points has been used. It consists firstly of dividing each segment of the polyline into three equal parts and then calculating the 3(N-1)+1 new points from the initial 3N points (Fig. 9).

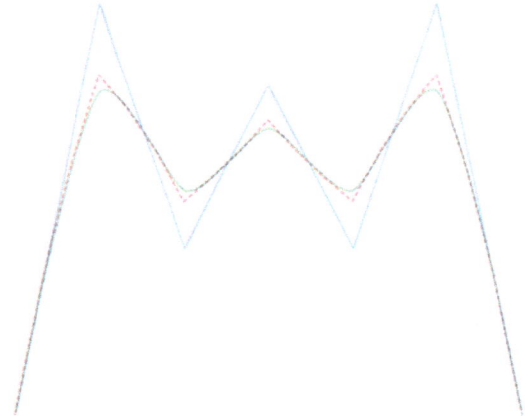

Fig. 9. Broken line (initial polyline). Dotted line (subdivision). Broken line (3rd subdivision).

Geomatic Data Base Visualization

The preceding procedures allow simulation of movement but the displacement zone is limited.

In fact, this zone is identical to the visualized zone and it is not possible to extend this visualized zone because the size of the display list is limited. More particularly the buffer refresh time must be small enough to prevent blinking.

Travelling Zone and Display Zone. To permit large displacements on the map, we have differentiated the displacement zone from the visualized one. A zone extractor is now necessary to make the link between the two zones.

Modelization of the Displacement Zone

The displacement zone is split up into small square zones. Graphic information contained in each zone is translated into commands directly absorbed by the graphic station. These are, in fact, 3D display lists, stored in the computer host memory they can be adressed separately through a two dimensional array (using the axis X and Y) (Fig. 10). All of this structure together constitutes the Display Data Base.

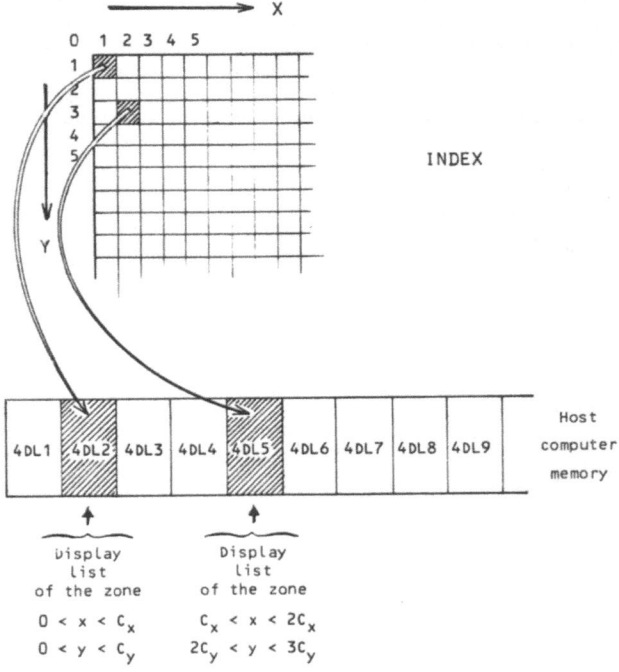

Fig. 10. Structure of the display data base. The dimensions of the squares are $C_x$ and $C_y$.

Bearing in mind that six bytes are needed to encode a 3D point or vector and that each command (color, line texture, flashing) occupies four bytes, memory capacity needs grow quickly with the size of an area. However, with a 500 K bytes memory, it is possible to memorize all information bearing on an area ten times bigger than the area displayed by a fixed zone simulation system.

Extraction

The visual zone is any orientation square centered on the observer's position. The extraction zone is calculated for each displacement. This zone is a body of squares containing the visualized zone (Fig. 11). It is a rectangular surface containing the extremes of the visual zone.

By increasing the number of squares and thus reducing the size of each square, we improve the ratio between the visualized zone and the extracted zone and in this

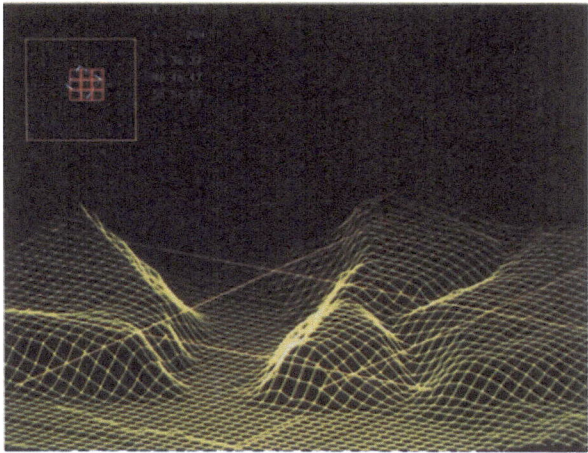

Fig. 11. Relief view. The visual zone is indicated in the upper right corner by the dotted blue square centered on the points X and Y. The extraction zone is defined by the red squares. The number of the 9 squares extracted are displayed in blue.

way we decrease the clipping charge which allows the visualized zone to be increase (Fig. 12).

However, the calculations of the mailing function and the transfer time increase with the number of display lists, which brings us back choosing a small number of squares (n = 9 or 16).

The index of the Data Base Display allows access to the mailing lists which are sent to the Graphic Process. The latter executes a hardware clipping which erases the vectors not belonging to the visualized zone (Fig. 13).

Applications

We applied this algorithm to a relief map and a planimetry map respectively. For the relief map the dimensions of the displacement zone are 260 x 180 units. The squares are 20 x 20 units. Thus we create 13 x 9 display lists representing the small units. We set ourselves a field of 25 units. 3 x 3 to 4 x 4 display lists are thus extracted for each interaction.

In planimetry, the displacement zone studied ranges to 3 500 meters in X and to 4 500 meters in Y. In using 500 x 500 m squares, we create 63 display lists (occupying 350 K bytes). The extraction zone being limited to 3 x 3 squares allows continuous vision of a surface (0.5 x 1.414) = 0,7 km.

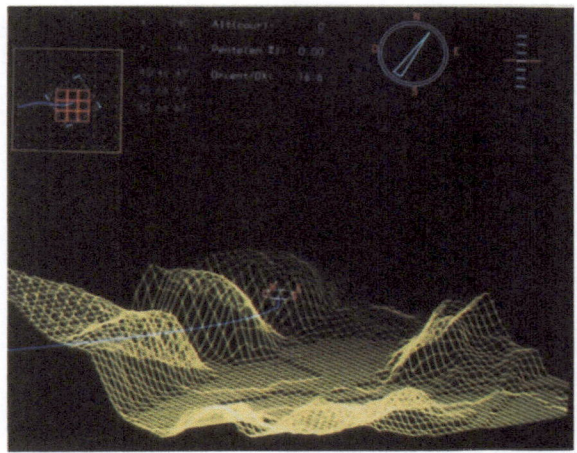

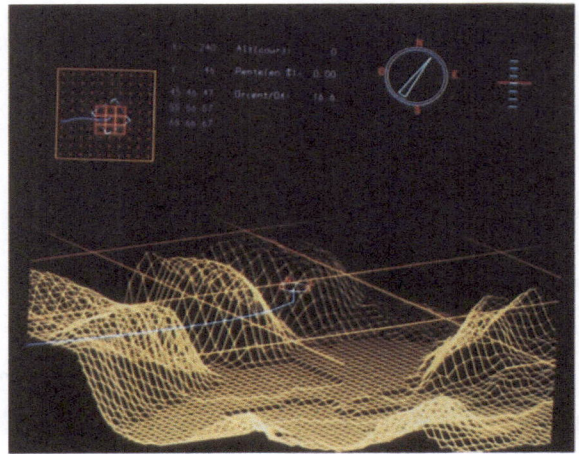

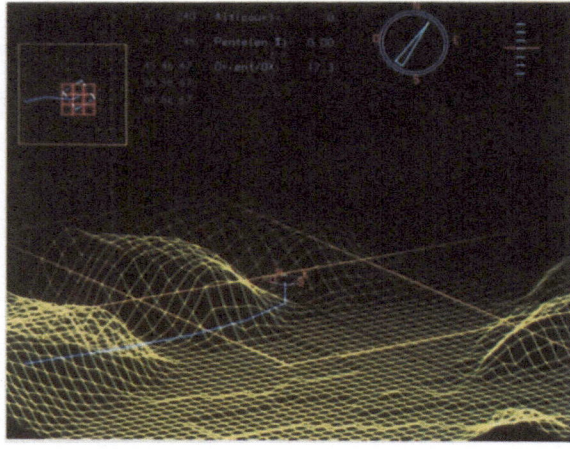

Fig. 12. Relief view. The visualized zone centered on the point X = 240 and Y = − 46 of a size :
- greater than the extraction zone
- equal
- inferior.

In the views below, the extraction zone consists of 9 squares, the size of the visualization window must not exceed 1.414 times the edge of a square. If we want the same ground surface displayed on the screen whatever the orientation of the zone to be observed.

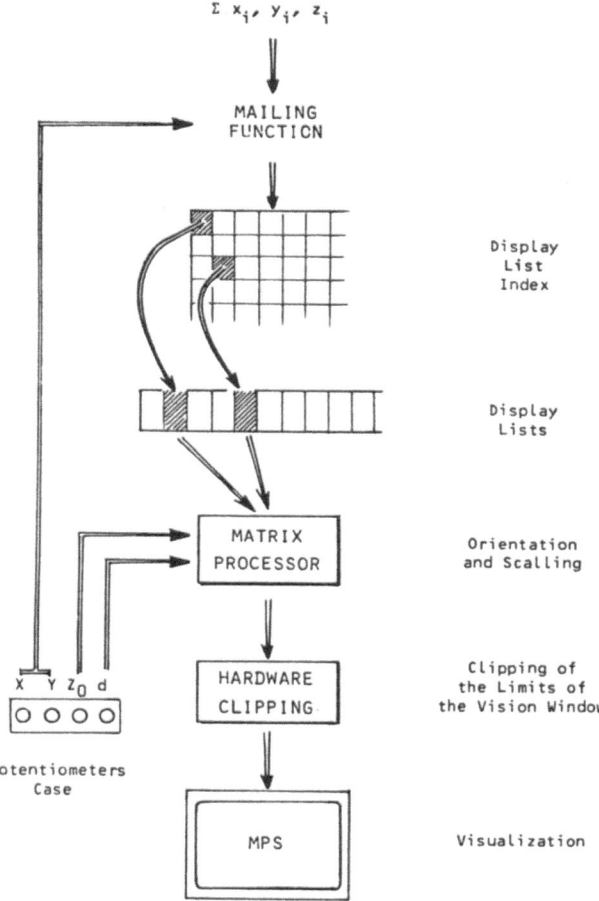

Fig. 13. Extraction from the Display Data Base.

CONCLUSION

The Geo-Graph System permits a genuine interactivity in the selection of scenes and view points. It gives access to a vast zone and the most varied topographic information and formes a basic tool to exploit interactively and dynamically a Geographic Data Base. Its use is simple and may be extended to other applications focusing on the visualization of surface which can be represented by altitude matrixes for example : study of energy surfaces and conformational surfaces in chemistry, dynamic visualization of the tridimensional histogram. (4)

We are studying a more realistic example of topography by replacing the polylines representing the objects by synthetic schematic representations. For example, we obtain a more realistic image of houses by using regular polydedrons. We can also replace the lines representing a road by a double line.

Our interest also is to take into account both the geomatic and the topology of the geographic data. In the near future we expect to travel over the Data Base by networks (roads, rivers). The trajectory will be determined only by the start and end nodes.

REFERENCES

Bernard A (1982) Digitization of Relief Data and Exploitation of Digital Terrain Model at IGNF. In: Actes d'Auto-Carte V

Boissonat JD (1984) Geometric Structures for Three-Dimensional Shape Representation. ACM Trans on Graphics 3,4: 266-286

Borrel J (1981) Computer Graphics : The Next Step in On-Line Retrieval. In: Fourth International On-Line Information Meeting, London, Dec. 1980, Lerned Information, Oxford, p 31

Dubois JE, Laurent D, Weber J (1985) Chemical Ideograms and Molecular Computer Graphics. The Visual Comput 1: 49-64

Foley JD, Van Dam A (1982) Fundamentals of Interactive Computer Graphics. Addison-Wesley, Reading, Mass.

Heap BR (1972) Algorithms for the Production of Contour Maps over an Irregular Triangular Mesh. In: National Physical Laboratory, Report NAC10

Laurent D, Motet S (1984) Géomatique : Un système de simulation graphique du relief (3D). In: Cesta (ed) Proceedings du 1er Colloque Image, Biarritz, 21-25 mai 1984, Paris

Laurent D, Motet S (1984) Geomatic : A 3-D Graphic Relief Simulation System. IEEE Comput 17,12: 25-30

Nagy G, Wagle S (1979) Geographic Data Processing. ACM Comput Surv 11,2: 139-181

Motet S, Laurent D (1985) Geomatic : a 3-D Graphic Relief Simulation System. In: Kunii TL (ed) Frontiers in Computer Graphics, Proceedings of Computer Graphics Tokyo'84, Springer Verlag, Tokyo, Berlin, p 146

Kanakubo T, Nonomura K (1980) The Use of 'Digital National Land Information' : Present State and Future Possibilities. In: Data for Science and Technology, Proc Seventh International Codata Conference, Pergamon Press, New York, p 161

Thierry Couesnon is an engineer of the CNRS working at the Institut de Topologie et de Dynamique des Systèmes at Paris VII University. He has developped components of a search and retrieval Chemical Information System and has been involved in graphical applications on different systems. He received is MS degree in 1976 from the University of Paris VII. His current interests include molecular modeling and computer graphics.

Daniel Laurent is a professor in computer science at the Institut de Topologie et de Dynamique des Systèmes at Paris VII University. He received his PhD from University of Paris in 1971 and has been involved in the design and development of the Description, Acquisition, Retrieval, Computer-aided Design system, a chemical information system that fonctions as an expert system besides providing data storage and retrieval. His current interests are graphic systems and topological data banks.

Serge Motet, a 1978 graduate of the Ecole Polytechnique, is currently preparing a PhD on geographic data bases at Paris VII University. He is an engineer at the Institut Géographique National and a research associate at the Institut de Topologie et de Dynamique des Systèmes.

Questions concerning this article can be addressed to Laurent at the Institut de Topologie et de Dynamique des Systèmes, Université Paris VII, 1, rue Guy de la Brosse, 75005 - Paris, France.

Chapter 5
# Computer Animation

# Integrating Key-Frame Animation and Algorithmic Animation of Articulated Bodies

L. Forest, N. Magnenat-Thalmann and D. Thalmann

MIRA Laboratoire, HEC/IRO, Université de Montréal, Montréal, Canada

## ABSTRACT

Most authors distinghish between two types of three-dimensional computer animation: key-frame animation and algorithmic animation. Our main goal is the integration of the different techniques. Motion is controlled by joint angles which must vary according to the values calculated by BODY-MOVING, a parametric key-frame system. However, it is also possible to have one or more angles following an algorithmic law. This approach has great advantages. Most of the angles may be controlled by the keyframe process, which is less expensive in fact; however more realistic effects may be performed on selected angles.

**keywords**: keyframe animation, interpolation, actor, subactor

## INTRODUCTION

Most authors (Hanrahan and Sturman 1985; Parke 1982; Magnenat-Thalmann and Thalmann 1985; Steketee and Badler 1985; Zeltzer 1985) distinghish between two types of three-dimensional computer animation: key-frame animation and algorithmic animation.

### Key-frame animation

Keyframe animation consists of the automatic generation of intermediate frames, called inbetweens, based on a set of key-frames supplied by the animator. There are two fundamental approaches to keyframe animation:

1. The inbetweens are obtained by interpolating the keyframe images themselves. This technique is called **image-based keyframe animation** by Steketee and Badler (1985) and **shape interpolation** by Zeltzer (1985). This is an old technique, introduced by Burtnyk and Wein (1971). A linear interpolation algorithm produces undesirable effects such as lack of smoothness in motion, discontinuities in the speed of motion and distorsions in rotations. Alternate methods have been proposed by Baecker (1969), Burtnyk and Wein (1976), Reeves (1981), Kochanek and Bartels (1984). According to Stekettee and Badler (1985), there is no totally satisfactory solution to the deviations between the interpolated image and the object being modeled.

2. A way of producing better images is to interpolate parameters of the model of the object itself. This technique is called **parametric keyframe animation** by Parke (1982) and Steketee and Badler (1985) and **key-transformation animation** by Zeltzer (1985). In a parameter model, the animator creates keyframes by specifying the appropriate set of parameter values, parameters are then interpolated and images are finally individually constructed from the interpolated parameters.

### Algorithmic animation

In this kind of animation, called algorithmic animation by Zeltzer (1985) and modeled animation by other authors (Lansdown 1982; Magnenat-Thalmann and Thalmann 1985), motion is algorithmically described. Physical laws are applied to parameters of the human figures (e.g. joint angles). Control of these laws may be given by programming as in ASAS (Reynolds 1982) and MIRA (Magnenat-Thalmann and Thalmann 1983) or using an interactive director-oriented approach as in the MIRANIM (Magnenat-Thalmann et al 1985) system. With such an approach, any kind of law may be applied to the parameters. For example, the variation of a joint angle may be controlled by kinematic laws as well as dynamic laws. This latter approach has been recently introduced by several authors (Badler 1984; Armstrong and Green 1985; Armstrong and Green 1985a; Wilhelms and Barsky 1985).

## A comparison of methods

The various methods have advantages and disadvantages and may be compared using several criteria as shown in Fig.1.

| | animation quality | CPU time | human intervention | versatility | source of difficulty |
|---|---|---|---|---|---|
| shape interpolation | depends on the number of key-frames | depends on the number of points and the type of interpolation law | very long lack of creativity | very bad | often unrealistic except with many key-frames or a complex interpolation law |
| parametric interpolation | depends on the number of key-values | depends on the number of parameters | shorter more creative | better | to find the best parameters |
| kinematic algorithmic animation | depends on the laws, but often unrealistic | depends on the laws, but not very expensive | may be difficult depends on the human interface | very good | realistic laws are not so easy to find |
| dynamic algorithmic animation | very realistic | very expensive | may be limited | good | complete dynamics-based models are too expensive for large sequences |

Fig.1 A comparative table of animation methods

From this table, it is clear that no one model is superior to all the others. In particular, methods which are efficient (low CPU time) do not provide a very realistic animation except when human intervention is very important (e.g. shape interpolation many key-frames).

Our approach is based on an integration of several methods. For non-human animation, our experience has shown that the best approach is algorithmic animation as in the director-oriented animation system MIRANIM. For human animation, we have decided to emphasize an approach based on parametric key-frame animation. However, as we believe that only an integrated method may provide animation quality and efficiency, we have developed an approach for integrating the various methods.

In summary, our principle is as follows:

**if** parametric animation is possible
**then** use it
**else if** kinematic algorithmic animation is acceptable
    **then** use it
        **else** use algorithmic animation based on dynamic analysis
            or robotics

## Our practical approach

In MIRALab., the main animation system we used is the extensible director-oriented MIRANIM system. The system is mainly based on three components:

1) the object modelling and image synthesis system BODY-BUILDING
2) the director-oriented animation editor ANIMEDIT
3) the actor-based sublanguage CINEMIRA-2 (Magnenat-Thalmann and Thalmann 1985a)

MIRANIM has been recently interfaced with the multiple-track animator system MUTAN (Fortin et al 1983), an image-based 3D key-frame system, designed in 1983. A new system has now been designed and implemented: BODY-MOVING; this is a parametric key-frame animation system in which human bodies are mainly controlled by joint angles.

The following sections describe BODY-MOVING and how it is interfaced to the MIRANIM system. In particular, we show how a 3D character may be articulated simultaneously by keyframe animation and algorithmic animation.

## THE PARAMETRIC KEY-FRAME ANIMATION SYSTEM BODY-MOVING

BODY-MOVING is an interactive program that allows the user to build any sequence of motion for a given 3D character. Actually, motion is controlled by 50 joint angles as shown in Fig.2.

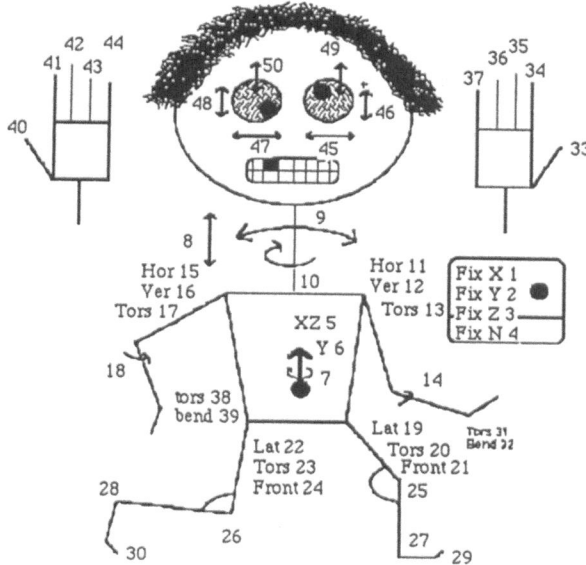

Fig.2 The joint angles

A keyframe is specified by modifying values for these angles from the previous keyframe in the sequence. Corrections may be done vertically for any keyframe, or horizontally for a given parameter in each keyframe. The animator may look at parameter values for any keyframe or interpolated frame. He/she also may obtain a wire-frame view of the human bodies for any frame. Fig.3 shows a table of the available commands in the main menu:

| | |
|---|---|
| [1] create a new sequence | [2] modify the current sequence |
| [3] read a sequence from a file | [4] write a sequence on a file |
| [5] interpolate the current sequence | [6] show the inbetweens |
| [7] create wire-frame figures | [8] show the current sequence |
| [9] create the dimensions of a human | [10] show the body points |
| [11] horizontal correction | [12] move a key-position |
| [13] add a key-position | [14] remove a key-position |
| [15] terminate the session | |

Fig.3 The BODY-MOVING commands in the main menu

For each parameter, interpolation may be computed linearly or using bicubic splines.

**fixed point**

There is a parameter called " fixed point ", it allows the user to center the given point at the position <FixedX,FixedY,FixedZ>. When the limbs move, the effect is to move the complete character. During a sequence, the fixed point may change location. For example for a walk, the fixed point changes from one foot to the other foot. Fig.4 shows an example with the key-values and Fig.5 displays the interpolated figures.

**faces**

Faces are also parameterized, but an independent and arbitrary number of key-values may be given for each parameter. This approach is different from the approach used for the body and limbs, because body motions require more global coordination than facial motions. An example of face is shown in Fig.6.

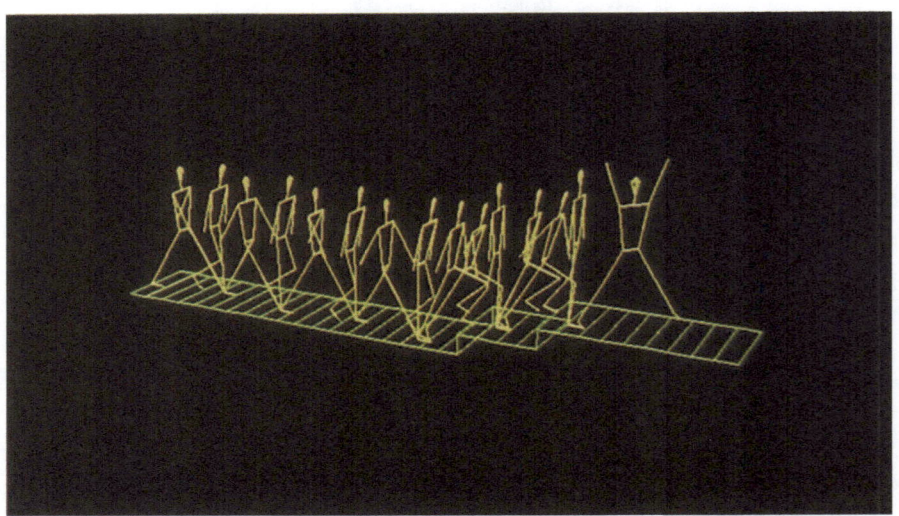

Fig.4 Walk: Key-values

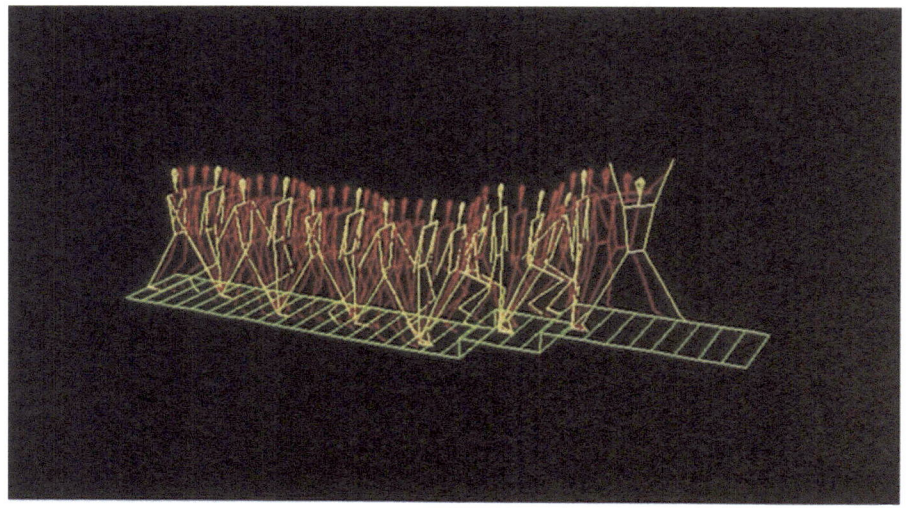

Fig.5 Walk: Key-values and inbetweens

Fig.6 A human face

# THREE-DIMENSIONAL SHADED BODIES AND CLOTHES

Once the motion of the 3D character is designed, the character needs to be covered with surfaces. For this, we try to completely separate the topology of the surfaces from the wire-frame model. This means that parts of the human bodies may be designed using ruled surfaces such as revolution surfaces, free-form surfaces or 3D reconstructed surfaces obtained from digitized projections. Fig.7 shows a wire-frame model (7a) with two different sets of surfaces (7b and 7c). Our system transforms the surfaces according to the wire-frame model assuring an automatic continuity between the different surfaces. This correspondance is based on a changing of reference systems independent of the segment length. This means that for the same set of surfaces, several bodies of different sizes may be obtained according to the segment length in the wire-frame models. Fig.8 shows the different segment lengths.

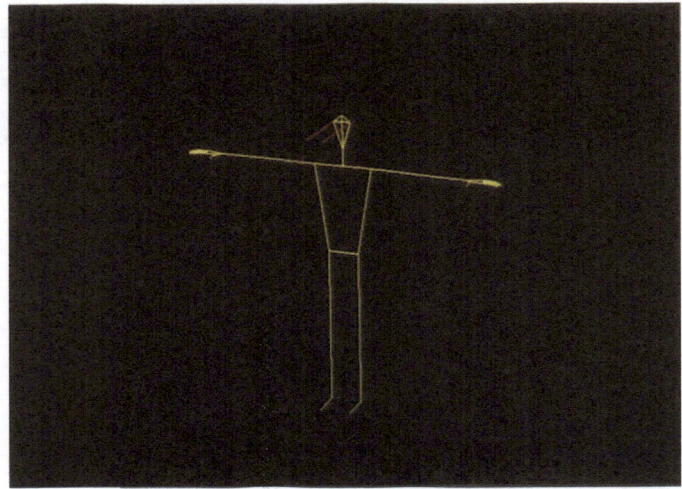

Fig.7a A wire-frame model

Fig.7b A surface body

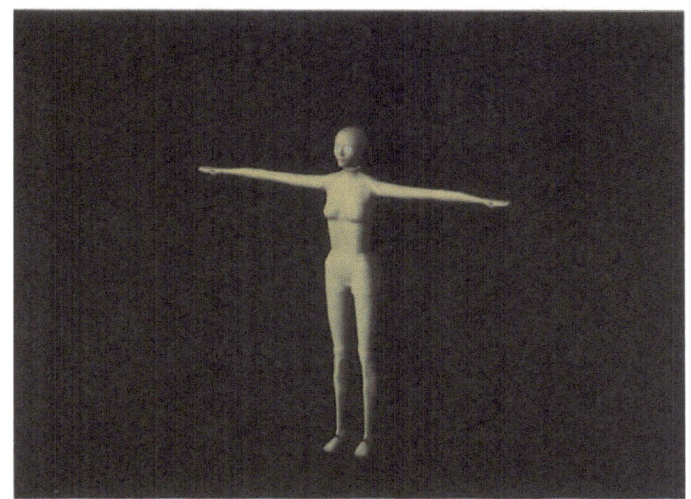

Fig.7c A surface body

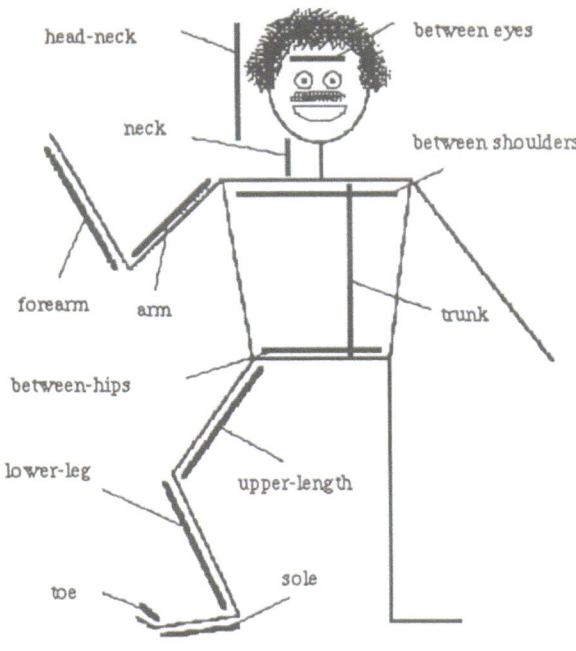

Fig.8 segment lengths

For example consider a point between the elbow and the wrist; when we change the reference system, it is important to notice that both parts may be bent and/or twisted. This means that the surface must be extended on the external side of the elbow and twisted at the wrist, while preserving continuity. The principle is shown in Fig.9.

## Reference system A

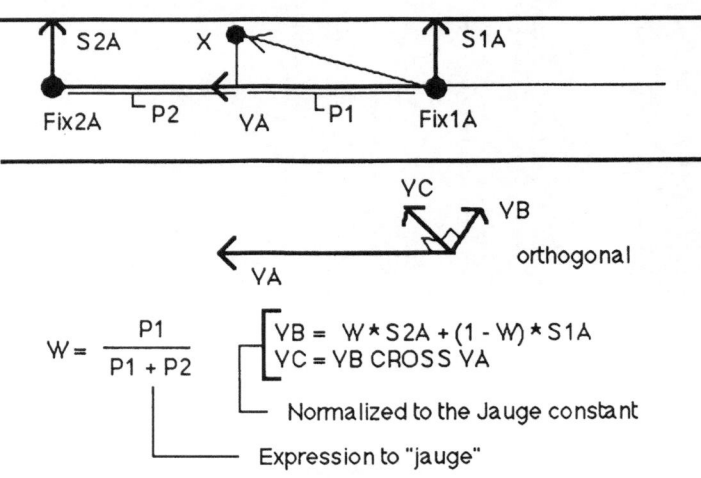

$$W = \frac{P1}{P1 + P2}$$

$$VB = W * S2A + (1 - W) * S1A$$
$$VC = VB \; CROSS \; VA$$

Normalized to the Jauge constant

Expression to "jauge"

## Reference system B

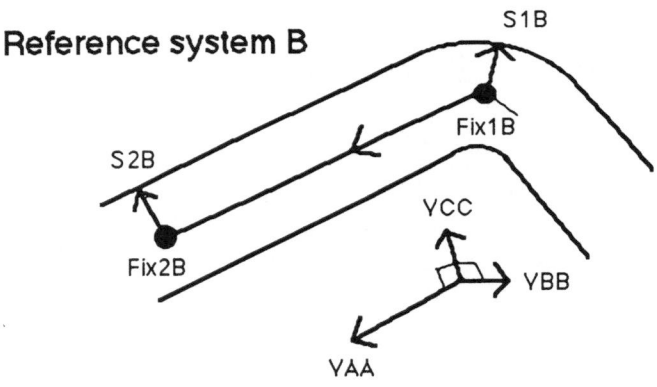

Fig.9

With such an approach, it is also possible to build a "wardrobe" for any 3D character. This process may be accelerated by using the following methodology:

1. take a copy of the character
2. cut all necessary parts using a clipping algorithm
3. scale by a factor 1+e to be sure that the clothes cover the body.
4. color the clothes and/or use image mapping or 3D bump mapping to texture the clothes

## Implementation considerations for an integration

The system BODY-MOVING written in the language MIRA-SHADING (Magnenat-Thalmann et al 1984) allows two kinds of output files:

1. files of wire-frames figures for all frames
2. sequence files consisting of key-positions

In the first case, the animation may be seen using a very little CINEMIRA-2 program consisting of an animation block which reads at each frame the corresponding wire-frame figure and display it using the current ANIMEDIT camera parameters. This approach is especially useful to preview the animation using a real-time playback based on the zoom-pan-scroll technique. Another CINEMIRA-2 program transforms wire-frame figures into surfaces using the strategy described previously.

Sequence files are used for two purposes:
1. To allow interactive editing with BODY-MOVING
2. To allow the integration of techniques

Our approach to the integration of the different techniques is as follows: the joint angles must vary according to the values calculated by BODY-MOVING, but it is also possible to have one or more angles following a law defined in the ANIMEDIT editor or programmed with the CINEMIRA-2 sublanguage. This integration has been performed using the following strategy. An interface module has been written in CINEMIRA-2 , so that any human body designed with BODY-MOVING is considered as a subactor in ANIMEDIT. This subactor has 50 real parameters, grouped in 17 3D vector parameters where each component is an angle. Each vector parameter is identified by a name; for example LEFTSHOULDER is the 3D vector that controls the motion of the shoulder. If there is no law defined for this parameter, the interpolated values are taken. If there is a law defined for the parameter, this law is applied and values computed by interpolation are ignored.

This approach has great advantages. Most of the angles may be controlled by the key-frame process, which is less expensive in fact; however more realistic effects may be performed on selected angles. For example, laws based on dynamics may be applied using similar equations to those described by Armstrong and Green (1985, 1985a). Of course, to obtain an angle  following a law based on the dynamic analysis, dynamic properties like masses, forces, inertia matrices and torques have to be supplied. In our case, intrinsic properties of bodies like masses and moments of inertia will be given  at the creation of the surfaces in BODY-BUILDING. Forces and torques have to be specified as parameters of the laws in ANIMEDIT. A simpler example where a law is preferable to a key-frame calculation is when the motion is periodic (like the angle of a hand when a character waves).

**With our approach, expensive computations are performed only when absolutely necessary.**

The integration approach has another important application: the relation between ANIMEDIT actors and human characters generated by BODY-MOVING. The typical case is when the value of a parameter (angle) of the human character have to be derived from data for an actor. For example, the ANIMEDIT actor is a ball and the human character receives the ball on the head. In this case, the motion of the character has to be controlled using data about the ball. To solve this case, our approach is to predefine functions which return at any frame the value of any parameter.

A human body may be considered as a subactor and it is dependent on an actor which may be transformed in ANIMEDIT by a list of global transformations like translation, rotations, shear, scale, color transformation, flection, traction. Several actors like these may participate in the same scene with other actors implemented using only algorithmic animation, cameras, lights and decor (Magnenat-Thalmann et al 1985). Fig.10 and 11 show an example.

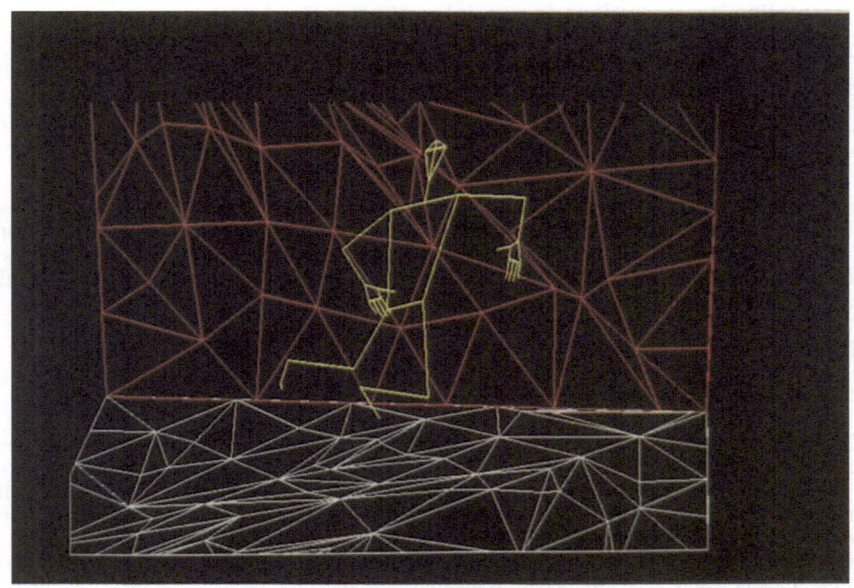

Fig.10 A motion with a wire-frame figure

Fig.11 The same motion with a surface figure

## Acknowledgements

The authors would like to thank Ann Laporte who revised the English text. The research was supported by the Natural Sciences and Engineering Council of Canada, the Art Council of Canada and the Government of Quebec.

## References

Armstrong WW, Green M (1985) **The Dynamics of Articulated Rigid Bodies for Purposes of Animation**, The Visual Computer, Vol.1, No4, pp.231-240.

Armstrong WW, Green M (1985a) **Dynamics for Animation of Characters with Deformable Surfaces**, Computer-generated Images (Eds. N Magnenat-Thalmann and D Thalmann), Springer Tokyo Berlin Heidelberg New York, pp.203-208.

Badler NI (1984) **Design of a Human Movement Representation Incorporating Dynamics**, Technical Report, Department of Computer and Information Science, University of Pennsylvania.

Baecker R (1969) **Picture-driven Animation**, Proc. AFIPS Spring Joint Computer Conf., Vol.34, pp.273-288.

Burtnyk N, Wein M (1971) **Computer-generated Key-frame Animation**, Journal of SMPTE, 80, pp.149-153.

Burtnyk N, Wein M (1976) **Interactive Skeleton Techniques for Enhancing Motion Dynamics in Key Frame Animation**, Comm. ACM, Vol.19, No10, pp.564-569.

Fortin D, Lamy JFL, Thalmann D (1983) **A Multiple Track Animator System for Motion Synchronisation**, Proc. ACM SIGGRAPH/SIGART Interdisciplinary Workshop on Motion: Representation and Perception, Toronto, pp.180-186.

Hanrahan P Sturman D (1985) **Interactive Animation of Parametric Models**, The Visual Computer, Vol.1, N04, pp.260-266.

Kochanek D, Bartels R (1984) **Interpolating Splines with Local Tension, Continuity and Bias Tension**, Proc. SIGGRAPH '84, pp.33-41.

Landsdown J (1982) **Computer-aided Animation: a Concise Review**, Proc. Computer Graphics '82, Online Conf., pp.279-290.

Magnenat-Thalmann N, Thalmann D (1983) **The Use of High Level Graphical Types in the MIRA Animation System**, IEEE Computer Graphics and Applications, Vol. 3, No 9, pp. 9-16.

Magnenat-Thalmann N, Thalmann D (1985) **Computer Animation: Theory and Practice**, Springer, Tokyo New York Berlin Heidelberg.

Magnenat-Thalmann N, Thalmann D (1985a) **Controlling Evolution and Motion using the CINEMIRA-2 Animation Sublanguage**, Computer-generated Images, Springer Tokyo Berlin Heidelberg New York, pp.249-259.

Magnenat-Thalmann N, Thalmann D, Fortin M (1985) **MIRANIM: An Extensible Director-Oriented System for the Animation of Realistic Images**, IEEE Computer Graphics and Applications, Vol. 5, No 3, pp. 61-73.

Magnenat-Thalmann N, Thalmann D, Fortin M, Langlois L (1984) **MIRA-SHADING: A Language for the Synthesis and the Animation of Realistic Images**, Frontiers in Computer Graphics (Ed, TL Kunii), Springer Tokyo Berlin Heidelberg New York, pp.101-113.

Parke FI (1982) **Parameterized Models for Facial Animation**, IEEE Computer Graphics and Applications, Vol.2, No9, pp.61-68

Reeves W (1981) **Intbetweening for Computer Animation Utilizing Moving Point Constraints**, Proc. SIGGRAPH '81, Vol.15, No3, pp.263-269.

Reynolds CW (1982) **Computer Animation with Scripts and Actors**, Proc. SIGGRAPH'82, pp.289-296.

Steketee SN, Badler NI (1985) **Parametric Keyframe Interpolation Incorporating Kinetic Adjustment and Phrasing Control**, Proc. SIGGRAPH '85, pp. 255-262.

Wilhelms JP, Barsky BA (1985) **Using Dynamic Analysis to Animate Articulated Bodies such as Humans and Robots**, Computer-generated Images (Eds. N Magnenat-Thalmann and D Thalmann), Springer Tokyo Berlin Heidelberg New York, pp.209-229.

Zeltzer D (1985) **Towards an Integrated View of 3D Computer Animation**, The Visual Computer, Springer, Vol.1, No4, pp.249-259.

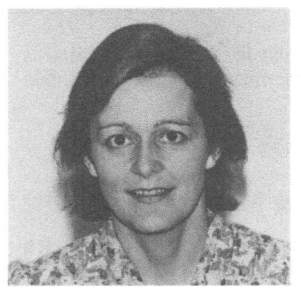

**Nadia Magnenat-Thalmann** is professor of communication and computer science at the graduate business school of the University of Montreal. From 1977 to 1979, she taught computer science at the University Laval in Quebec. During the 1983 academic year, she was a visiting professor at the University of Geneva. Her research interests include the design of graphical interfaces, business graphics, computer animation, and knowledge-based graphical systems. She has written and edited several books and research papers in various application areas of computer science, and she was producer and codirector of the computer-generated films Dream Flight and Nirvana. She served as general chairperson of the Graphics Interface 85 Conference. A member of the Council of Science and Technology of the Government of Quebec and of the Council of Science and Technology of the Canadian Broadcasting Corporation, she also serves as a director of the Computer Graphics Society in Canada.

Magnenat-Thalmann received a BSc in psychology, an MSc in biochemistry, and a PhD in quantum physics and computer graphics from the University of Geneva.

**Daniel Thalmann** is professor and director of the MIRA computer graphics laboratory at the University of Montreal. He has taught at the Swiss Federal Institute of Technology and at the University of Nebraska and has been a research member of the Computer Graphics Group at CERN. His research interests are computer graphics, computer animation, and the design of programming languages. He has published over 40 papers in these areas and is coauthor of eight books, including Computer Animation: Theory and Practice. He was codirector of two computer-generated films, Dream Flight and Nirvana. Thalmann served as program chairman of the Graphics Interface 85 Conference and is a member of the editorial board of "The Visual Computer". He is a director of the Canadian Man-Machine Communication Society and is a member of the IEEE Computer Society, ACM, Eurographics, and SIGGRAPH.

Thalmann received his diploma in nuclear physics and his PhD in computer science from the University of Geneva.

# Molecular Shape Embedding in a Grid Stage Modelling and Animation

J-E. Dubis, S.Y. Yue and J-P. Doucet

Institut de Topologie et de Dynamique des Systèmes, Associé au CNRS, 1, rue Guy de la Brosse, 75005 – Paris, France

ABSTRACT

A computer system is proposed for bi or tri-dimensional graphic display of various structural shapes (molecular bodies) and property shape representations (one electron properties, electrostatic potential...).  Calculation spaces, linked to molecular coordinates, are jointly handled within a unique representation space structured as a 3 D stage or grid Box.  The Box fixed coordinates ensure Boolean and geometric operations through interactive graphic sub-systems.  Direct images, sub-images and composite images can be generated, as well as processed data and/or images.  The polymodelling system presented – POLYMOD – leads to rapid and original animation operations on modelizations based on lengthy calculations.

KEY WORDS

Representation Space, Molecular Polymodelling, 3 D Grid Stage, Boolean Operations, Composite Images.

INTRODUCTION

Chemistry and biology play particular and fascinating parts in our view of the world.  To the infinitely large where actions are slow and serene and distances are immense but where objects are real, we must oppose an infinitely small or microscopic world where actions are coherent but undergo accidents and distances are very short and the size of objects so very small that it is difficult for the mind to compare them to ordinary macroscopic objects and actions.

AN IMAGINARY WORLD

This world is that of atoms, molecules and electrons.  In order to elucidate molecular actions we must be able to imagine each molecule and to actually see it animated.  On an imaginary stage, we must be able to produce a symbolic show and see the play of inert matter and of biological matter.  Molecules have physical shapes, but even their properties must be evoked visibly.  Their molecular actions are based on recognition of their associated shapes, and we must penetrate these forms of dialogue.  The astronomer can travel into the cosmos, the architect can see the house he plans, but the chemist does not see molecules and scarcely even perceives macromolecules.

## THEORETICAL SHAPES

To help elucidate the nature of this molecular world, we have gradually built representations of its component parts. For example, molecules are endowed with generic forms by theories or by inferences. These forms are either symbolic or considered as "real", subject to certain approximations. Their physical retrieval is important, and their representation is essential. Diagrams and formulas are vital parts of our molecular knowledge. This is why molecular computer graphics (MCG) has become the indispensable complement and interpreter of the molecular world. (1)

This began with the birth of the first formulas, perceived as true ideograms, and the process was speeded up in rapid evolution. This kept pace with the evolution of ever more detailed scenarios of basic chemical concepts hidden by lengthy listings but shown ever more visually both by the imagery of theoretical concepts and by some more trivial imagery used in computer aided conception.

## MCG BIRTH AND ASPECTS

From the inception of computer graphics, chemistry has been an ideal field for demonstrating potential uses of graphic systems both on the static and on the dynamic levels. It began essentially with biological macromolecules (MAC program, 1966). (2) From the start, the difficulty of exchanging molecular information led chemists to translate graphic formulas into a language and thereby into systematic words, but with the DARC System, (3-5) we proposed as of 1966 that all documentation operations be centered on questions and answers in graphic form. This was achieved by creating graph matrices of formulas and DARC topological codes. Users communicate by interactive graphic input and output with large data bases situated halfway between alphanumerical data bases and picture data bases. (6,7) However large the file, this only involves one limited aspect of molecular chemistry, using only a tiny part of the multiple representations needed to take into account all properties of the world of matter. Nowadays, the complex situations that call upon MCG are conveniently approached by structural representation of chemical shapes as well as by property shape representation. Both of these now rely on complex graphic logistics and can be associated with heavy computing "downstream".

## SOURCES OF MOLECULAR INFORMATION AND MCG

The structural shapes of molecules and the shapes translating their properties are either obtained theoretically (Quantum Mechanics, Molecular Mechanics) or experimentally (X rays, NMR, reactivities) but according to variable approximations. We thus dispose of a very large variety of situations to be translated, in particular by graphics in order to work interactively. "Perceiving solutions and intuiting certain comparisons are recognized assets of viewing problems by computer graphics. More directly, computer graphics must make it possible to have certain fixed situations fly by swiftly on the screen when desired, to catch those key moments of perception or intuition in man-machine interaction when a particular image or view of things gives rise to a new, creative idea". (8)

Color improves the manipulation of data, but the situation is usually inextricable because of too much available information present (distances, angles, surfaces, local sites...). The graphic display would be overloaded if suitable tools were not created to handle various types of information by locating them clearly and very rapidly visualizing only those needed at a given time. MCG provides these illuminating outputs (cueing, zooming, clipping operations). These, however, are only useful means of manipulating the molecular "marionettes". (9) The latter are animated by various programs and, in order to coherently integrate their action potential, the "marionettes" and their controls must be located on a convenient stage.

Such a stage should be well equipped for assistance, in particular to enhance communication between the various representations that will act in the play.

A 3 D WORKING SPACE : a graphic stage or BOX

Such a stage is presented in our Polymod System planned to deal with the interaction of multiple modelling based on various representations. This specific tool cannot be dissociated from the general graphic and computational molecular management system in which it is strongly integrated. Such an organized 3 D working space can be considered as a working BOX or a 3 D Window for Molecular Graphics (WMG) or a 3 D FRAME, in which various molecular representations can be precisely embedded. If their molecular dimensions are too large, the BOX can be used to scan a large molecule, like a protein, through its controlled displacement in the structure.

Two types of situation lead to different uses.

- In a static mode the (3 D) WMG has been planned to carry out geometric and Boolean operations on one or several structures (bodies and property shapes).

- In a dynamic mode simulations are planned to study interactions by animation.

We should note that this type of 3 D space is organized to handle information concerning shapes generated by numerical data. It must also, however, interactively visualize geometric or topological shapes, whether derived or secondary. In this case, it produces, on request, numerical information concerning distances, surfaces, volumes or relations. Only images of syntheses provide unique facilities for various animations. For example, the three dimensional visualization of two neighboring analgesics is sufficient to point out their conformational differences (Fig.1), while their two dimensional formulas only reveal the presence, apparently minor, of a methyl group. This example also stresses the importance of the simple shape for the virtual operation of superposing molecules. The visual result would be uninteresting if the representation were too rich, like space-filling representations.

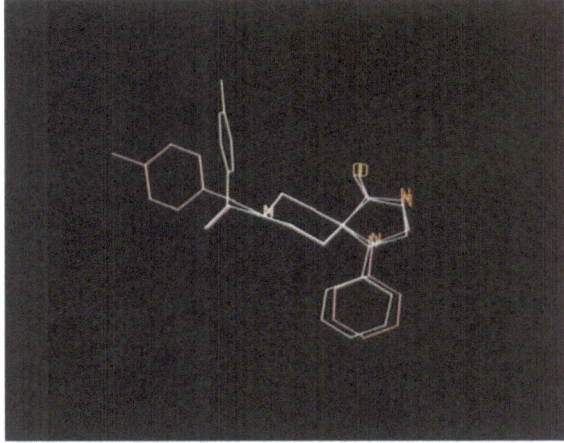

Fig. 1. Partial superposition of 2 neighboring analgesic drugs.

CHEMICAL SHAPES AND THEIR BASIC ORGANIZATION

a) Structural shapes or bodies

Various representation levels can be attained by Computer Graphics. The simplest modelizations show the molecule according to the general organization laws of its constituting elements (atoms) endowed with a shape and with specific metrics in certain standard states.

Ball-and-stick or wire type representations allow one to rapidly seize the nature of atoms according to their colors and their geometric relations, while space-filling models aim at a more realistic representation or molecular volumes. The surface resulting from the union of atomic Van der Waals radii is accepted as a symbolic representation of molecular shape and volume. (10)

Such representations are valuable for specifying the geometric characteristics of structural shapes, such as in the study of drug-receptor interactions. These problems are generally linked to a search for privileged geometries (preferential conformations), for the isolated molecule or when the receptor's approach induces conformational modifications on the molecule.

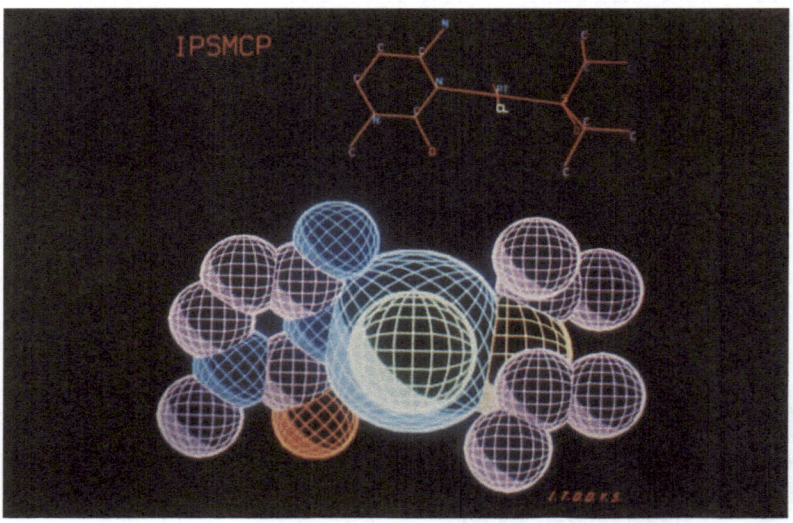

Fig. 2. Wire type and space filling representation of a Platinum Complex Compound.

For biological macromolecules, too complex for all of their component atoms to be individualized, primitives (prefabricated standard symbols) relieve the difficulty of complete representations by various simplifications of descriptive structural primitives (amino acids of proteins are coded symbolically by three letter initials) or by pictorial primitives (ribbon, cylinder, specter...). These condense the essential morphological characteristics. Other methods are computer techniques such as the use of local windows or zooming effects (Fig. 3).

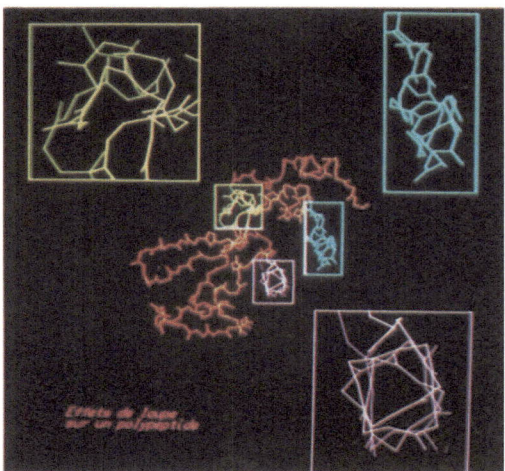

Fig. 3. Magnifying effects and extracting parts of a polypeptide. Spiral form, full face, violet colored.

PROPERTY SHAPES

One of the basic advantages of molecular graphics is to be able to superpose onto the symbolic structural shape of the molecule, property shapes characterizing its behavior with regard to the surrounding environment (solvent, biological, receptor.. .).

Indeed the adequacy of topological or topographical forms and of chemical or biological activity can be approached by geometrical structural representations (space filling models or Van der Waals surfaces) but also by means of properties (mainly electronic) characterizing the molecular sensitivity to external perturbations.

The hydrophilic nature is often sketched out with only the nature of the atoms involved as a starting point, but more often quantum chemistry electronic indices are used to define and foresee behavior in interacting systems. Thus, electronic density or superdelocalizability define the spatial localizations of electrons. Charge distribution in the molecule creates an electrostatic potential in its neighborhood, and this is what a receptor or a binding site may perceive. (11,12)

Electron-deformation densities (difference of electronic densities between the molecule and its supposedly isolated constituting atoms) play a particular part insofar as they can be compared to experimental crystallographic measures. (13) Contrary to the magnet which is itself visible while its action is invisible but materialized by iron filings, for the molecule, synthetic images reveal two realities, invisible but known thanks to theory and experimentation.

POLYMOD APPROACH

The Polymond approach developed by us allows for diverse and flexible displays of molecular behavior functions. It is conceived for bi or tri-dimensional visualization of electronic properties (such as molecular electrostatic potential). It also handles geometric structural descriptors (distances, surfaces, volumes...).

One important step involves immersing the molecule or molecules studied in a unique representation space (R). This space is designated here by an orthogonal lattice : the box (other shapes can be envisaged with specific applications in mind: docking, intercalation...). It is structured by a tri-dimensional grid or network whose nodes constitute observation points (points for calculating the property sought for). When the threads of this network are known according to the three reference axes, the position of the observation points is unambiguously fixed in the representation space by index triplets $(i,j,k)$ ordered $(i$ = 1st point according to direction X...). For medium size molecules, a 100 x 100 x 100 grid with a 0.2 Å thread seems a good compromise between computer time cost and desired precision.

Procedures for changing coordinates ensure correspondences between associated (R) and (C) spaces :

- Representation Space (R) defines the observation points and is used for local handling and for creating and manipulating images,
- Calculation Space (C) is linked to the system of initial molecular coordinates for each molecule studied.

Defining this unique (R) representation space makes it possible to use various data obtained in different referentials and facilitates comparative studies of molecules. This solution is well adapted for carrying out simple operations controlled by graphic sub-systems.

It has already been proposed elsewhere (14) to immerse a molecule in a virtual space, in association with binary coding, in order to calculate with Boolean operators the form or volume of molecules considered as matter filled bodies and represented by Van der Waals radii. In our POLYMOD framework, we also work with the quantitative electronic information (i.e., through representations which do not require systematic recourse to heavy programs of Quantum Mechanics before each new visualization).

Our approach is sketched in figure 4. The arrows show the direction taken by the principal input items (molecular coordinates...) towards the basic treatment steps :

- creation of GEO Box file through BOX GENERATOR
- molecular wave function calculations
- correspondence operations between R et C spaces, and calculating electronic properties,
- local treatments, constructing and handling images.

QUANTUM CALCULATION AND EVALUATING ELECTRONIC PROPERTIES

Wave functions are calculated at the STO 3G level with the GAUSSIAN 80 program (version D). (15) Molecular coordinates can be supplied by crystallographic results, energy minimization calculations (search for preferential conformations) or, more simply, can be deduced from standard values of bond lengths and angles.

At a point P in the neighborhood of the molecule, the Molecular Electrostatic Potential measures the electrostatic energy between this molecule and a unitary positive point charge situated at P and used as a probe. This Potential can be considered as "what a positively charged reagent feels when it approaches the molecule". It is, therefore, generally recognized as an index of quantitative reactivity for such interactions. (11)

$$V(P) = -\int \frac{\rho(P')}{r_{PP'}} \, d\tau(P') + \sum_\alpha \frac{Z_\alpha}{r_{P\alpha}}$$

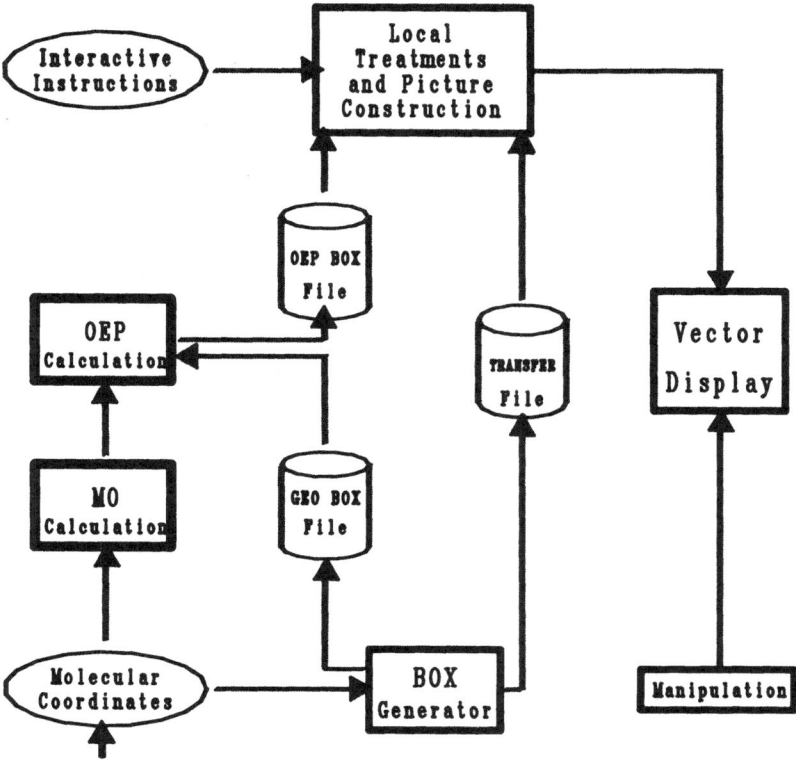

Fig. 4. Schematic diagram of the POLYMOD System.    (arrows indicate the main data flow).

The first term (summed up over all nuclei) represents the nucleus-point charge repulsion ($Z_\alpha$ is the charge of the nucleus, $r_{\alpha P}$ is the distance from the nucleus to the point charge).  The second term (where the integral is evaluated over the entire space) takes care of the electron-point charge attraction.  ($\rho(P')$) is the electron density at a point $P'$, $r_{P'P}$ is the distance point P-charge.

CALCULATION AND REPRESENTATION SPACES

The initial data are constituted by molecular geometry.  This defines the calculation space (C) used to evaluate wave functions and electronic properties.  At this stage, geometry optimizations or interactive rotations for a better disposition of the molecular skeleton are possible.  Then the Representation space (R) is fixed by choosing an observation window (the "box").  The given thread  according to three edges of the box enables one to create the tridimensional network of observation nodes structuring this space.

A "Box generation" program ensures correspondences between the two spaces C and R.
It specifically defines space R with regard to the reference mark linked to the
initial molecule (C space) and, inversely, it makes it possible to immerse the molecule (defined in C) in R. It then translates the observation node coordinates
(marked in R) in the calculation space C (reference mark linked to the molecular
coordinates).

A "GEO BOX" file is thereby constituted, showing for each observation node, ordered
in R according to the value of the triplets (i,j,k), its coordinates in the calculation space C. A second "TRANSFER" file contains the characteristics of the box
(number of points and threads according to the three dimensions), and the molecular
coordinates transformed in space R - data needed to localize the molecule in R.

The "GEO BOX" file is given to the program that calculates the property sought for
(in this case, for the MEP, the GAUSSIAN 80). The retrieved results (potential
values) are collected in the OEP BOX file in the form of a list of OEP values, ordered according to the sequence of triplets (i,j,k) characterizing the observation
nodes. This file is then transmitted to the Graphic Construction and Local Treatment part.

This organization makes it possible to keep the geometric parameters of the molecular skeleton and the set of quantitative information associated with the representation space points in the two files : TRANSFER and OEP BOX. It is thus possible to generate various images and to carry out local treatments without retur-
ning to clumsier programs of quantum mechanics. Greater flexibility is achieved.


BUILDING DIRECT AND COMPOSITE IMAGES

After reading the TRANSFER and OEP BOX files, two main procedures take place : one
represents the molecular skeleton localized in the box, from the data in the TRANS-
FER file ; the other handles OEP data. Interactive instructions enable one, through
    the IGL operators, to create image files in a format adapted to the graphical
output device.

Various types of representation are possible. Direct images include 2 D or 3 D
visualizations : isometric surfaces or isometric 2 D line maps. Composite images
deal with simultaneous and various representation of a part of the isometric surfaces and of a planar map. A rough diagram of this image building is shown in
figure 5.

Some interactive instructions associated with various visualization possibilities
(details here for the MEP) are specified in Table I.

The option "Set a point to visualize a part of isopotential surface" is used to
simultaneously represent a map (planar) and a part of an isopotential surface. The
point chosen indicates which part of the surface, on one or another side of the map,
is to be kept in the visualization. In the option "set a plane", various possibilities are offered so as to easily determine, by referring to the atom positions,
the plane in which one desires an isopotential map. The number of contours desired
and the chosen values of the property are also fixed by the user.

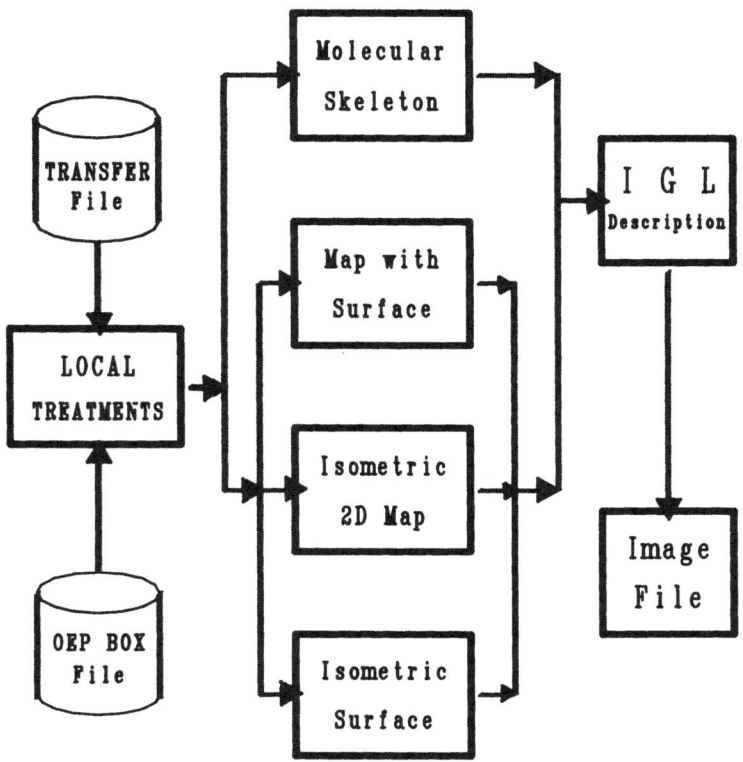

Fig. 5. Schematic diagram of the picture construction part. Data coming from OEP BOX File and TRANSFER File can be previously manipulated via Local Treatments (IGL = Interactive Graphic Library).

Table 1 : Principal conversational instructions and utilizations

| Definition | Utilization * | | |
|---|---|---|---|
| Set a value of surface | 1 | | 3 |
| Set a plane | | 2 | 3 |
| Set a number of contours | | 2 | 3 |
| Set a value of contour | | 2 | 3 |
| Set a point ... a part of surface | | | 3 |

\* Utilizations1, 2, 3 refer to the display of isometric surfaces, planar isometric contours, planar isometric contours with a part of surface.

DRAWING ISOMETRIC SURFACES AND CURVES

Graphic representation of isopotential surfaces or curves is obtained thanks to a
three step Computer Aided Design process (via polygon building)

1. property interpolation between the grid nodes

2. search for next property points

3. ordering junction of points

This process organizes data according to a plane (or a series of parallel planes).
This plane can be parallel to the sides of the box or not. In the plane, we find
a bidimensional grid associated with the tridimensional grid of the box. The relevant data of this working plane are then stored in two buffers or temporary files.
One contains the property values retained on this 2D grid ; the other retains the
third coordinate of the plane points, information from the TRANSFER file and the
parameters needed for the drawing (number of contours, associated values...). The
retrieved data from these procedures are transmitted to the Graphic Edition part
to constitute image files.

To draw 2D isopotential outlines in a given plane, the imprint of the 3D grid is
defined on this plane. A test is carried out to choose the best resulting 2D grid
for MEP calculation ; then a loop of the CAD process is carried out for each outline desired.

To completely trace an isopotential surface, we examine the sections of the box –
obtained by intersection planes parallel to the reference sides XY, YZ, ZX (we use
a technique of loops according to each one of the variables X, Y, Z). Two buffers
are created for each plane. Then the CAD procedure is used to draw the outlines,
according to the chosen values. At the end of the loop, the tridimensional surface
is complete.

The third type of image file (plane plus a part of 3D surface) corresponding to
composite images is obtained from the two preceding algorithms. The plane map part
is called first. Then the choice of a point of the space (see Table 1) shows which
part of the equipotential surface is to be retained. Thus, the corresponding points
of the MEP can be identified. The surface algorithm is then called to draw the corresponding envelope.

Some of the system's possibilities are illustrated in figure 6. The results are
visualized on a vector display (Evans & Sutherland Multi Picture System) connected
to a VAX 11/780 computer. The color photographs reproduce 3D representations of the
molecular electrostatic potential of neuromediators $\gamma$ amino-butyric acid (GABA) and
Muscimol. (16)

The yellow outline corresponds to a repulsive positive potential of 100 kcal/mole
representing the body of the molecule. The red outlines visualize the negative
potential zone at -100 Kcal/mole characterizing the privileged approach zones for
an electrophilic reagent or binding site.

Clipping allows us to discover potential surfaces from within leading to a better
seizure of localization in space. It also specifies the molecular skeleton.

Photograph 6c corresponds to a composite image comprising an isopotential map in a
plane bisecting group $COO^-$, and the 3D surfaces of repulsive potentials (100 Kcal)
in yellow as well as the neutral zone in blue are maintained above this plane. The
molecular skeleton is visible in the lower part of the photograph.

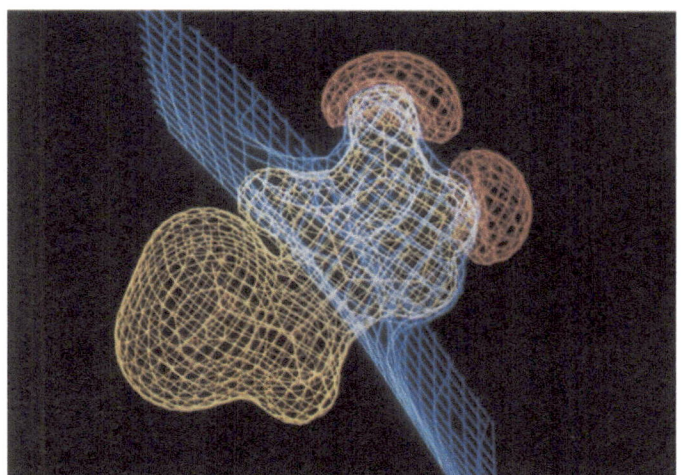

a)

Fig. 6. Representations of MEP. Display of isometric surfaces (yellow: repulsive 100 Kcal potential ; red : attractive -100 Kcal, blue : neutral surfaces) for a) MUSCIMOL and b) GABA Clipping allows for visualization of a part of the molecular skeleton, c) composite image : Planar map + 2D surface.

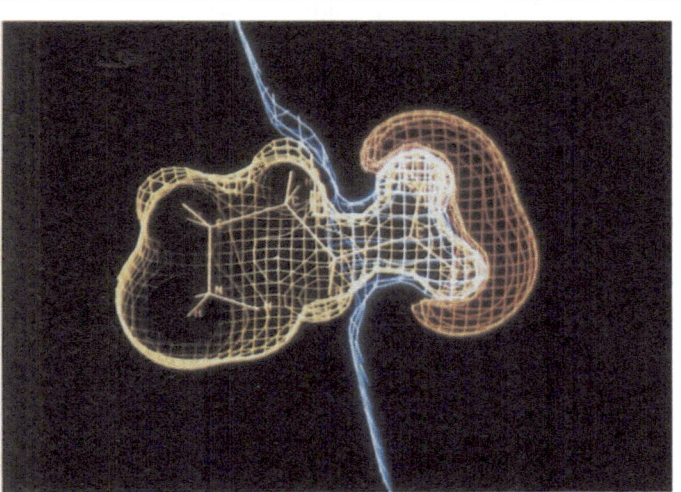

b)

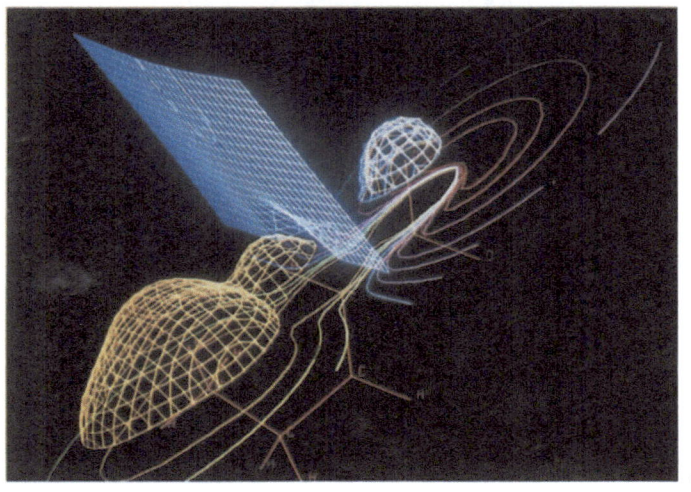

c)

LOCAL TREATMENT AND BOOLEAN OPERATIONS

The image files thus created correspond to tri-dimensional descriptions. One can, therefore, take advantage of all the possibilities offered by graphic sub-systems for interactive manipulation : translation, rotation, zoom, clipping...

Local handling is proposed for pattern recognition. In the unique representation space (R), the immersion of different molecules, superposed starting from their interactively chosen anchoring points, is carried out. These procedures are useful for elucidating molecular interaction or for studying coherent families of structures.

The usual geometric operations are either carried out directly or via the grid with the help of ordered tensors to manage the elementary operations of union, intersection, complementarity, all controlled by <u>Boolean operations</u>.

For each structure studied, the procedure is to examine, on each observation node, the value of the property studied (or the existence of a fixed conditions). A combination of elementary logical operations makes it possible to retain those valid nodes defining the relevant area for the property. This area is then visualized by communicating the node file (i, j, k) chosen to the graphic construction part.

With the help of the grid, this treatment provides an approximate but rapid solution for quantitative geometric information (surface, volume, accessible surface) linked to the molecular forms. It also makes possible an easy comparison between localization areas associated with discrete values of electronic properties.

Smoothing procedures then enable one, by consulting in return the initial numerical information (OEP box file), to substitute, for the mesh of selected nodes, continuous traces that improve the graphic presentation.

These treatments are particularly useful to characterize properties closely linked to molecular topography : e.g., searching for the common part of a set of structures in a population (population focus) cr determining the <u>trace</u>, imprint of the population set. Examples of immediate application are the study of steric factors with regard to chemical interaction processes, or geometric deformations regarding a reference structure or an "average compound" in a family.

Several previous treatments : Minimum Steric Difference, (17) or the DRAGO approach, (14) attacked this problem on the level of geometric descriptors : form, distance, volume,... Our POLYMOD approach includes these possibilities and extends the range of application to electronic properties more directly linked to chemical or biological reactivity.

Examples of Boolean operations are given in Fig. 7 reproducing planar section of negative potential zones (-100 Kcal/mole) for $\gamma$ amino-butyric acid and its tetrazole analogue. In figure 8 the corresponding attractive potential surfaces are superposed in a 3 D visualization pointing out a quite different electron delocalization in these systems. Such displays providing insight into common privileged zones of electrophilic interactions for related compounds, are valuable for obtaining information concerning the actual receptor shape.

By permitting interactive treatments of limited perturbations, this methodology constitutes a privileged tool for the dynamic study of molecular interactions : approach of rigid molecules or inducing mutual deformations among them.

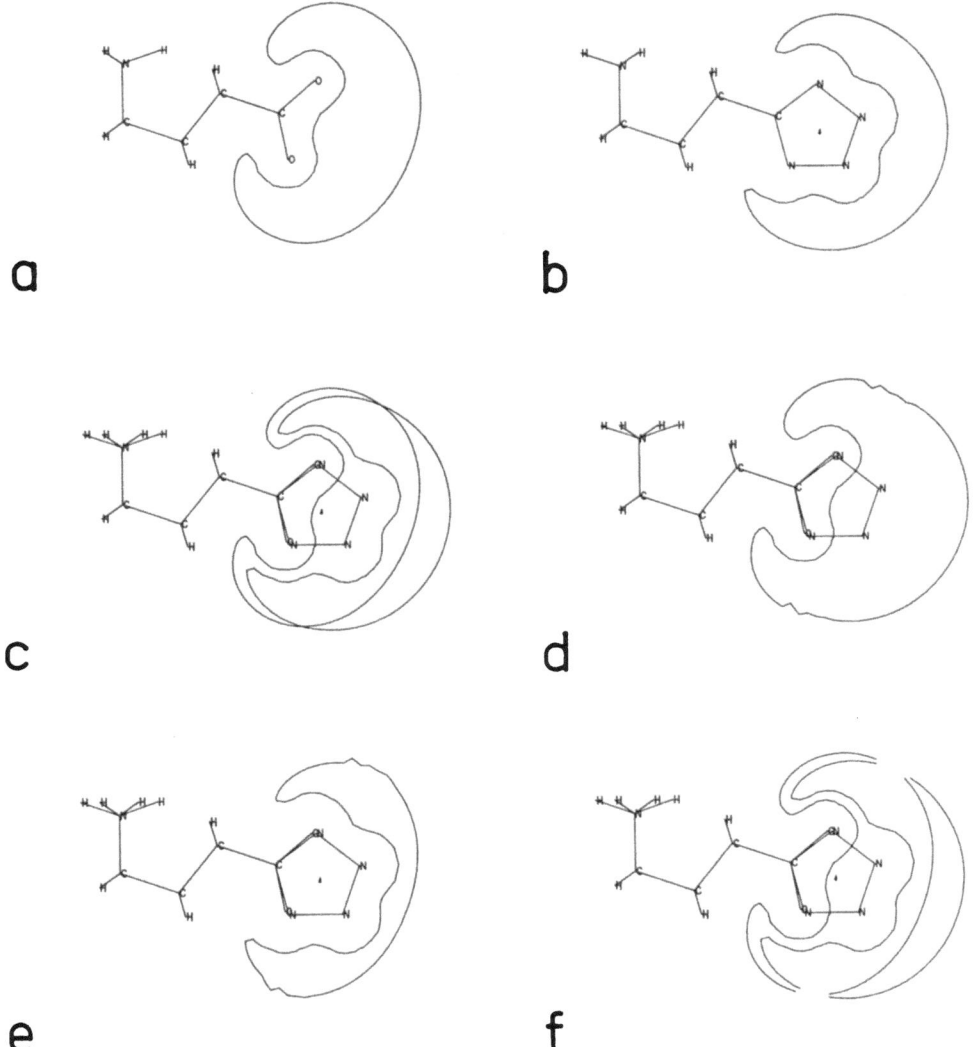

Fig. 7. Local treatments via Boolean operators : Planar map of electrostatic potentials neighloring neuromediators. (CNDO approximation).
Isopotential lines at -50 Kcal/mole for γ amino butyric acid and tetrazol analogue
are represented in Figure a,b and superposed in Figure c. Figures d,e and f correspond to union, intersection and complement (residual part belonging to one molecule
but not to their common part) : the threshold was set at ± 5 Kcal.
Calculations being made with standard bond lengths and angles, the skeletons are
strictly coïncident in the acyclic part. For purpose of illustration, the proto-
nated amino groups are rotated.

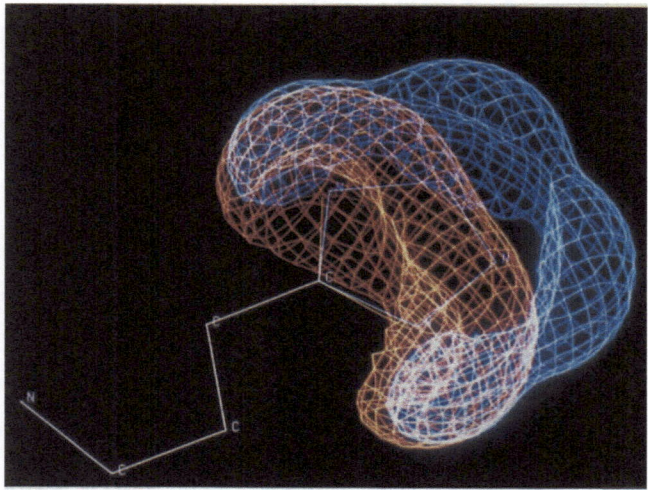

Fig. 8. Superposition of STO-3G MEP surfaces (attractive -100 Kcal) for GABA (red) and tetrazole analogue (blue). As previously, calculations are made with standard geometry.

## OUTLOOK

The POLYMOD approach opens the way for similarity searching in Structure-Activity Relationships. Off stage manipulations in the POLYMOD BOX provide flexibility with regard to chemical objects (bodies and properties). However, for similarity and animation scenarios, the usual QSAR functions must also be worked out inter-actively in the local discrete mode.

We are presently developing an algorithmic approach to proximity relationships of non bonded sites, as well as a heuristic approach to local stereoelectronic cons-traints in molecular interactions.

## REFERENCES

Dubois JE, Laurent D, Weber J (1985) Chemical Ideograms and Molecular Computer Graphics. The Visual Comput 1: 49-64

Levinthal C (1966) Molecular model-building by computer. Sci Am 6: 42-52

Dubois JE, Laurent D, Viellard H (1966) Système de documentation et d'automatisation des recherches de corrélations (DARC). Principes généraux. CR Acad Sci Paris 263C: 764-768

Dubois JE (1974) DARC system in chemistry. In: Computer representation and mani-pulation of chemical information. Wipke WT, Heller S, Feldmann R, Hyde E. (eds) John Wiley, New York, pp 239-263

Dubois JE (1976) Ordered chromatic graph and limited environment concept. In: Balaban AT (ed) Chemical applications of graph theory. Academic Press, London, pp 330-376

Bonnet JC, Dubois JE (1979) The DARC pluridata system: the 13C NMR bank. Anal Chim Acta 112: 245-252

Sobel Y, Dagane I, Carabédian M, Dubois JE (1985) Specific features of scientific data banks. Proceedings of the Ninth International CODATA Conference, Glaeser Jerusalem, (in press)

Dubois JE (1984) DARC creative data to meet the challenge of the fifth generation in chemistry. Proceeding International Conference on Information and Knowledge. ICIK. 3-10 March 1984, Tokyo

Lesk AM (1977) Macromolecular Marionettes. Comput Biol Med 7: 113-129

Max NL (1984) Computer representation of molecular surfaces. J Mol Graph 2: 8-13

Quarendon P, Maylor CB, Richards WG (1984) Display of quantum mechanical properties on Van der Waals surfaces. J Mol Graph 2: 8-13

Scrocco E, Tomasi J (1973) Electrostatic molecular potential as a tool for the interpretation of molecular properties. Top Curr Chem 42: 95-170

Roch M, Weber J, Williams AF (1984) Electronic structure and spectroscopic properties of chronium (V), molybdenium (VI), and niobium (V) tetraperoxide. Inorg Chem 23: 45-71

Marsili M, Floersheim P, Dreiding AS (1983) "Generation and comparison of space-filling molecular models" Comput Chem 7: 175-181

Chandra Singh U, Kollman P 'Gaussian 80 UCSF Program' QCPE 446

Schlewer G, Wermuth CG, Chambon JP (1984) Analogues tetrazoliques d'agents Gaba-mimétiques. Eur J Med Chem Chim Ther 19: 181-186

Chiriac A, Chiriac V, Ciubotariu D, Holban S, Simon Z (1983) Minimal Steric Difference (MTD) . Study for flexible molecules: substituted acetic acids derivatives with auxinic activity. Eur J Med Chem 18: 507-513

Jacques-Emile Dubois is Professor of Physical Organic Chemistry and Chemical Informatics at the University of Paris VII and Director of the Institute of Topology and Systems Dynamics (ITODYS). In 1947 he received his Ph.D. from the University of Grenoble. He developed, as of 1957, a strong interest in chemical informatics. As early as 1963, this led to his pioneer work on the DARC Topological System and the subsequent development of EURECAS, the DARC on line service utilizing the CAS file. He chaired the IUPAC Interdivisional Committee on Machine Documentation in the chemical field (1969-1977) and is presently Vice-President of CODATA. He founded several chemical information agencies, such as the Centre National de l'Information Chimique (CNIC) and the Association for Research and Development in Chemical Informatics (ARDIC).

Jean-Pierre Doucet is Professor of Physical Chemistry at the Institute of Topology and Systems Dynamics (ITODYS) at Paris VII University. He received his Ph.D. from the University of Poitiers in 1964 and has been involved in the development of expert systems in the DARC chemical information system: Description, Acquisition, Retrieval and Computer Aided Design System. His current interests are computational chemistry and molecular modelling.

Shi Yi Yue, a 1982 graduate of Jilin University, is currently preparing a Ph.D. on molecular modelling at Paris VII University. He is a research associate at the Institute of Topology and Systems Dynamics (ITODYS).

Chapter 6
# Graphics Software/Hardware Architecture

# Dynamic Display of Heart Potential Images with Parallel Processing

Norio Akamatsu

Department of Information Science, Tokushima University, Minami-Josanjima-cho, Tokushima, 770 Japan

ABSTRACT

Body surface potential mapping has been shown to improve the diagnostic accuracy of certain cardiac electrophysiological disorders. In order to display heart potential distribution maps dynamically in color graphic, we have developed a high-speed data acquisition and presentation system based on double parallel processing technique. The data presentation system consists of 16 parallel processing elements. Each processing element includes a local CPU and arithmetic processing unit (APU). Double parallel processing can be accomplished between the local CPU and APU in each processing element. By applying this double parallel processing technique we can achieve the dynamical display of heart potential distribution with good precision. Clinical application of this electrocardiographic mapping system should significantly increase the understanding of certain heart diseases. These double parallel computations may be adapted for use in other fields of computer graphics.

## 1. INTRODUCTION

Diseases of heart and circulatory system represent the most common and serious health problem in contemporary society. The measurement of electrocardiographs (ECGs) have been found to be useful and effective for diagnosis and prediction of abnormalities of heart (Goldman 1970). Since the heart potential distributes all over the body surface, sometimes the standard ECG recording results in the omission of useful data that might appear at other points, especially, right chest and back surface. With the development of body surface potential mapping equipment, the heart potential distribution on the entire chest surface as well as on the back can be observed. Many researchers have drawn the body surface isopotential maps (BS-map) at a particular sampled time (Ambroggi, Taccardi and Macchi 1976; Taccardi 1963). But, the time history of the heart potential distribution contains significant and important information on electrocardiac phenomenon ( Vincent, Abildskov, Burgess, Millar, Lux and Wyatt 1977; Sugenoya et al. 1977). It is necessary for diagnosis of heart disease to display the change of the body surface potential maps sequentially. There was no satisfactory equipment that could dynamically present the body surface potential distribution. However, a lot of data processing is necessary for precise presentation of surface potential maps. Since our ability of visual pattern recognition is not so poor, low-quality maps may offer us confused information occasionally. If investigators would miss the delicate variation of potential maps, it might be serious problem for diagnosis. Moreover, in order to make the best use of afterimage phenomenon of eye and graphic display, we must display at least a couple of maps on color graphic terminal during one second. Therefore, a high-speed data processing system should be necessary for dynamic presentation of potential maps.

However, the digital implementation of dynamic display of heart potential images has been difficult (or impossible) since an amount of the body surface ECG data exceeds a single computer bound. Consequently, the quest for fast processing has resulted in a strong push for the development of parallel processors. In order to realize smooth movement of potential contour lines with good precision, we have developed a high-speed data presentation system. The data presentation system consists of 16 parallel computer elements and a color graphic display. Each parallel processing element include a CPU, RAMs and an arithmetic processing unit (APU). During execution of arithmetic program in the APU, a CPU in the parallel processing element can independently execute the next command to be processed prior to receive the END flag from the APU. We call it a double parallel processing technique. By applying such double parallel processing to ECG data, we can accomplish a dynamic display of body surface potential distribution maps with good precision.

Fortunately, the ECG data extracted from a human body surface have an efficient parallel computation structure. During generation of potential map data, ECG data movement among the parallel processing elements is unnecessary. Therefore, prior to parallel computation ECG data are only transmitted simultaneously to all the parallel processing elements.

The graphic display terminal is designed as an intelligent terminal with its own CPU (Z80B) and large memory for image storage. Since the memory address is sequentially incremented by TTL logic, the heart potential maps can be displayed in high-speed. Precise surface potential maps can be continuously displayed by swapping of its two-pages video-RAM. Functions such as slow-motion, reverse display, and map expansion are also provided. Dynamic display of potential maps can express heart potential distribution and its variation as a function of time. The dynamic presentation of heart potential distribution maps should contribute to the reliable and accurate diagnosis of heart diseases. In this paper, the hardware and software technique for displaying the potential maps are described.


## 2. MATHEMATICAL FRAMEWORK AND COMPUTATIONAL METHOD

The composite electrodes are placed in a two-dimensional grid arrangement across the front and back of a human torso to form a 16X8 rectangular array. By using the composite electrodes the body surface potential distribution can be quickly measured (Akamatsu and Mori 1980, 1984). We denote ECG measured by the electrode whose position is the i-th row and j-th column as

$$V_{ij}(t) \qquad \begin{array}{l} (i = 1, \dots , M) \\ (j = 1, \dots , N) \end{array}$$

First, we shall arrange this data stored in a memory to draw heart potential maps by newly-developed parallel processing computers. In many cases, ECG is almost periodic in time, then we here assume the following periodicity for simple explanation;

$$V_{ij}(t) = V_{ij}(t + T) \qquad (1)$$

where T is a period of t. Therefore, the repeated display of potential maps during time interval T can offer us medically significant information.

After applying interpolation procedure to $V_{ij}(t)$, the heart potential distribution can be expressed by the following equation:

$$v = f(x,y,t) \qquad (2)$$

where

$$1 \leq x \leq M$$

$$1 \leq y \leq N$$

$$0 \leq t \leq T$$

Although the function $f(x,y,t)$ should be represented in three-dimensional space, we have no method except for displaying in two-dimensional surface and observing its variation as a function of time. Hence, we shall show the body surface potential distribution in color graphic display.

The ECG data stored in disk possess a special structure that the data at a time $t_i$ is independent of the one at any time $t_j$ ($t_i \neq t_j$). Hence, the data for drawing potential maps at time t do not affect the other data at all. This fact suggests that the data processing is highly suitable for parallel computation, because of no data exchange among the parallel processing elements.

Let $T_0$ and $T_{mn}$ be a starting time and ending time of potential map presentation respectively. During the time interval $T=[T_0,T_{mn}]$, the potential maps are dynamically displayed with high resolution. The time interval T is uniformly divided into mn time units. Then, a time sequence $\{T_i\}$ is generated for satisfying

$$T_{mn} - T_0 = mn[\ T_i - T_{(i-1)}]$$

$$(i=1,2,\ldots,mn)$$

The following sets of time sequence $\Sigma$ for explaining parallel computation by n parallel processing elements is considered.

$$\Sigma = \{ \Pi_0, \Pi_1, \Pi_2, \ldots, \Pi_{m-1} \} \tag{3}$$

where

$$\Pi_0 = [\{\Phi_0\}]$$

$$\Pi_1 = [\{\Phi_1\}, \{\Phi_2\}, \ldots, \{\Phi_n\}]$$

$$\Pi_2 = [\{\Phi_{n+1}\}, \{\Phi_{n+2}\}, \ldots, \{\Phi_{2n}\}]$$

$$\vdots$$

$$\Pi_i = [\{\Phi_{(i-1)n+1}\}, \{\Phi_{(i-1)n+2}\}, \ldots, \{\Phi_{in}\}]$$

$$\vdots$$

$$\Pi_{m-1} = [\{\Phi_{(m-2)n+1}\}, \{\Phi_{(m-2)n+2}\}, \ldots, \{\Phi_{(m-1)n}\}]$$

$$\Pi_m = [\{\Phi_{(m-1)n+1}\}, \{\Phi_{(m-1)n+2}\}, \ldots, \{\Phi_{mn}\}]$$

$$T_{mn+i} = T_i \qquad (i=1,2,\ldots,n)$$

$$\Phi_0 = \{ T_1, T_2, \ldots, T_n \}$$

$$\Phi_{(j-1)n+1} = \{ T_{jn+1}, T_{(j-1)n+2}, T_{(j-1)n+3}, \ldots, T_{jn} \}$$

$$\Phi_{(j-1)n+2} = \{ T_{jn+1}, T_{jn+2}, T_{(j-1)n+3}, \ldots, T_{jn} \}$$

$$\vdots$$

$$\Phi_{(j-1)n+k} = \{ T_{jn+1} , T_{jn+2} , \ldots , T_{jn+k} , T_{(j-1)n+k+1} , \ldots , T_{jn} \}$$

$$\Phi_{jn} = \{ T_{jn+1} , T_{jn+2} , T_{jn+3} , \ldots , T_{(j+ )n} \}$$

$$(j = 1, 2, \ldots , m)$$

At first, the state $\{\Phi_0\}$ is loaded. Then, the ECG data sampled at $T_1$, $\ldots$, $T_n$ are parallelly and independently processed in the n parallel processing elements. The computational result for drawing the potential map at $T_1$ is transmitted from the first parallel processing element to the first page of the graphic display. The next state $\{\Phi_1\}$ is loaded to transfer the ECG data sampled at $T_{n+1}$ from the host computer. And the computed result for drawing the potential map at $T_2$ is transmitted from the second parallel processing element to the second page of the graphic display. The graphic display terminal can swap the two page memories for exchanging the map data. The states $\{\Phi_2\}$, $\{\Phi_3\}$, $\ldots$, $\{\Phi_{(m-1)n}\}$ is sequentially execurted in the same way. After the process at the state $\{\Phi_{(m-1)n}\}$ is finished, the processing state returns to the initial state $\{\Phi_0\}$. Such process may be repeated before the host computer receives interruption command from the investigator.


## 3. IMPLEMENTATION

BSMAP program has been implemented at ECG Laboratory of Tokushima University by using a parallel processing system. The data analysis and presentation program requires high-speed processing. Consequently, all the programs are written in assembly language in order to eliminate inefficiencies that would have been present if high-level languages had been used. BSMAP is composed of two separate modules GETECG and DRAWMAP.

### 3.1 GETECG subsystem

An interactive dialogue based on menu selection is used to simplify user input. Thus, a series of choice is displayed and selection is made by the cursor. The cursor movement is controlled by the joystic or mouse.

(i) Analogue input

In order to measure the heart potential in a patient's skin surface, composite electrodes, as shown in Fig. 1, is developed. The composite electrodes have been constructed in our laboratory as where no equivalent commercial product was available (Akamatsu and Mori 1980, 1984).

(ii) A/D converter and data storage

ECG signals extracted from a subject's surface are simultaneously digitized by 128 A/D converters. Since a multiplexer is not used, there is no delay among 128-channels. A block diagram of ECG data acquisition subsystem is shown in Fig. 2.

ECG data from A/D converters can be stored in a disk file, which contains the sample number, the time elapsed from the onset of QRS complex and the sampling rate.

## (iii) Data display

Individual waveform of ECG can be displayed by color-graphics during or after the ECG measuring phase. The user has the facility to inspect and get ECGs again if the obtained result is not good.

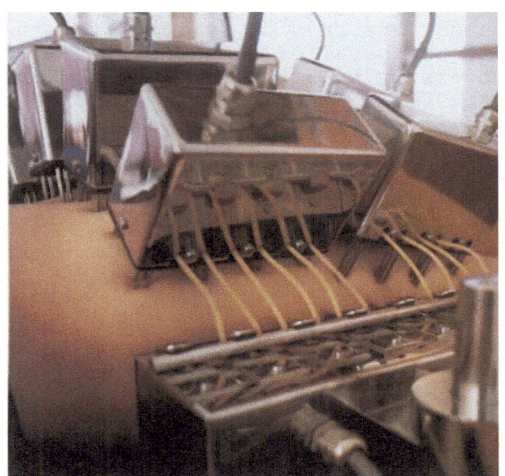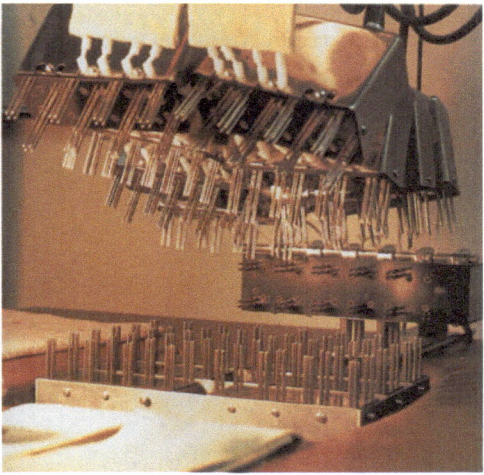

Fig. 1 A newly-developed composite electrodes for body surface mapping.

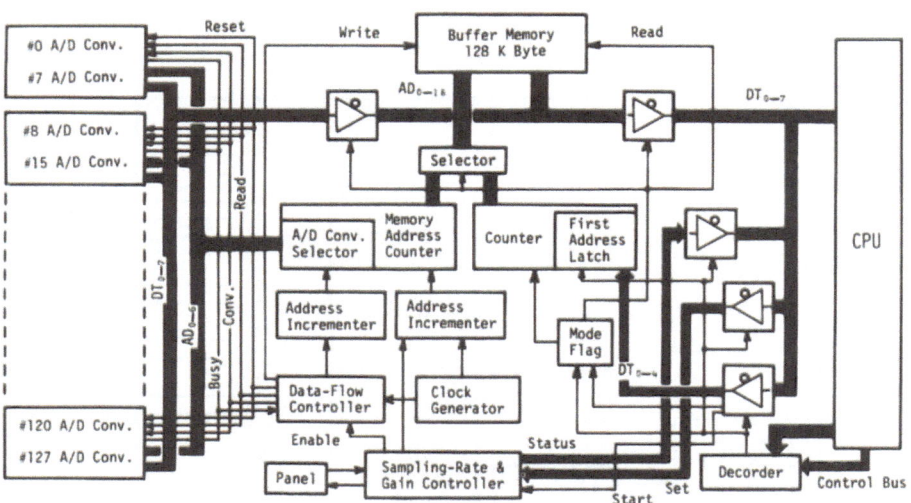

Fig. 2  A block diagram of ECG data acquisition subsystem.

## 3.2 DRAWMAP subsystem

The ECG data structure indicates that the i-th BS-map data has no relation to the j-th one (i=j). Therefore, the i-th BS map data is assigned independently to the i-th computer board. Hence, this parallel processor is belong to a distributed data system. Prior to parallel processing the ECG data are uniformly distributed to all the parallel processor boards by the host computer. Taking a special structure of ECG data and realization of smooth movement of contour lines with good precision into consideration, we have developed a parallel processing system which uses an array of sixteen micro-computer boards. A block diagram of the parallel computer system is shown in Fig. 3. Each parallel processing board include a CPU, RAMs and an arithmetic processing unit (Am 9511). A block diagram of the parallel processing board is shown in Fig. 4. Figure 5(a) shows a photograph of parallel computer system. And a photograph of each parallel processing board is shown in Fig. 5(b).

The graphic display terminal is designed as an intelligent terminal with its own CPU (Z80B) and large memory for image storage. Since the memory address is sequentially incremented by TTL logic, the heart potential maps can be displayed in high-speed. Precise surface potential maps can be continuously displayed by swapping of its two-pages video-RAM.

### Program for interpolation

When time is fixed at $t_0$, we obtain the following heart potential matrix.

$$\begin{bmatrix} V_{11}(t_0) & V_{12}(t_0) & \cdots & V_{1N}(t_0) \\ V_{21}(t_0) & & & \vdots \\ V_{M1}(t_0) & V_{M2}(t_0) & \cdots & V_{MN}(t_0) \end{bmatrix}$$

This matrix represents the spartially discrete potential distribution at time $t_0$.

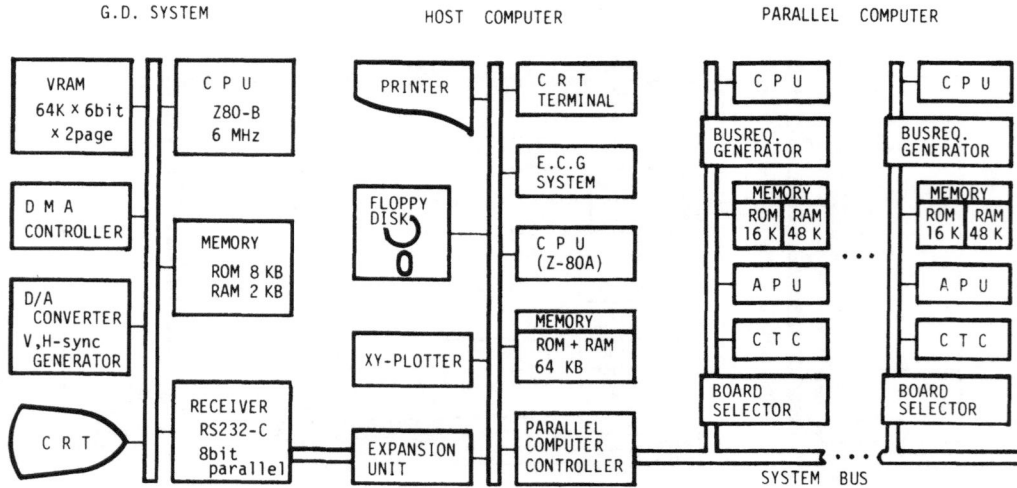

Fig. 3  A block diagram of parallel computer system.

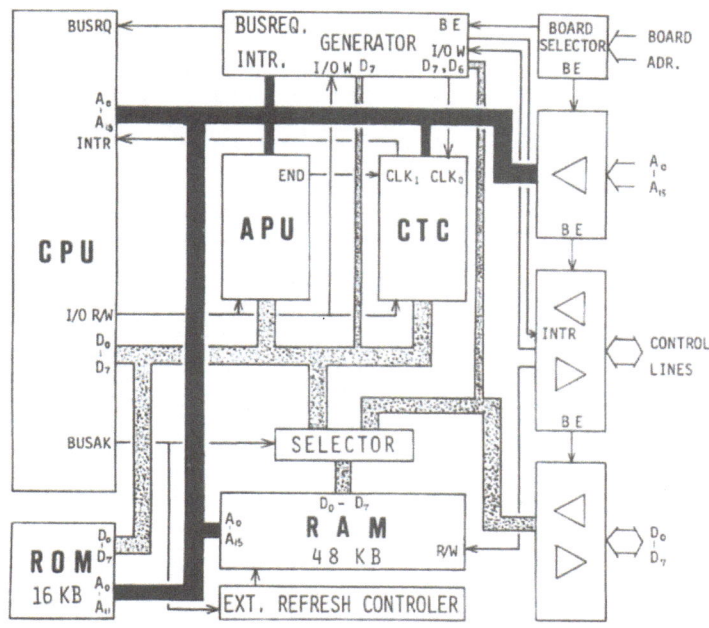

Fig. 4   A block diagram of parallel computer board.

Fig. 5(a)   A photograph of parallel   Fig. 5(b)   A photograph of parallel
            computer system.                       computer board.

The electrode grid being rather coarse, some scheme is necessary for interpolating the potential within each fundamental square. Many body surface mapping systems have used only the four corner voltages to obtain the interpolated values. But, in this case the grobal style of the drawed maps is unnatural and not so beautiful. Hence, we have used cubic spline function in the two-dimensional space to create interpolated data. This interpolation is divided into two stages, taking into consideration of computation time. First, we apply a two-dimensional cubic spline function as a coarse interpolation, because the computation time to calculate the minute spline function is too much. So, to realize a high-speed display, we are compelled to use linear interpolation procedure in the fine pixel. However, judging from the displayed maps, the difference of interpolated results between by the cubic spline function and the linear one is so small as undistinguishable in the locate area of image. The heart potential at a point $(x,y)$ has to be estimated from the array of measured potentials. If we let $i = \lfloor x \rfloor$, and $j = \lfloor y \rfloor$, be the integer parts of $x$ and $y$, then the body surface voltage $V(x,y)$ can be estimated by the cubic spline interpolation. A program for the interpolation is shown in Fig. 6. Quality of dynamically displayed maps was found not to be impaired, however, the fine pixels data are generated by using interpolation and scan-conversion algorithm.

## Program for APU

In order to obtain high-quality body surface potential maps, we encounter many numerical computations, for example two-dimensional

Program INTERPOLATION

```
begin
    SET_STACK_POINTER;
    INITIALIZE_PARALLEL_COMPUTER;
    SET_UP_CTC;
    Go_Flag := false;
    repeat
        while Go_Flag := false goto WAIT
        Go_Flag := false;
        INPUT_START_TIME;
        TRANSFORM_DATA_FROM_BINARY_TO_FLOATING;
        SELECT_SPLINE_INTERPOLATION
            "F" :  FAST_INTERPOLATION
            "P" :  PRECISE_INTERPOLATION
        end
        PRODUCE_GRAPHIC_COMMAND;
        REQUEST_DMA_TRANSFER;
    until_Mode_Flag := n
end;
```

Fig. 6  A program for interpolation.

spline interpolation. Therefore, if only one computer processes a great deal of ECG data by step-by-step algorithm, long processing time is necessary. Hence, one APU (Am9511) chip is mounted in each parallel computer board for the purpose of high-speed execution of arithmetic operation. During execution of arithmetic program, the local CPU in the parallel processing element can independently transfer the address which indicates the memory location of the next data into the HL and/or DE resistors prior to receive the END flag from the APU. This is, of course, a kind of parallel processing executed in APU and CPU. Such local parallel processings are also done in all the parallel processing elements almost simultaneously. These double parallel processings can achieve a high-speed numerical computation about 32 times faster than Z80 single processor system.

Since a small amount of the extracted ECG data before applying some interpolations is easy for partition, the data broadcasting time is not so long. Then, the host computer partitions ECG data and distributes them to the parallel processors. When the computation in one parallel processing element finished, the command is

Program  MAP

```
begin
    repeat
        NEXT_FILE := false
        SEARCH_ECG_DATA_FILE;
        SELECT_ECG_DATA_FILE;
        LOAD_INITIAL_DATA;
        repeat
            INPUT_COMMAND;
                if NEXT_FILE := true then break
            for REC_NO := n downto 0  do  LOAD_ECG_DATA
            for REC_NO := n downto n-16  do
                TRANSFER_ECG_DATA;
            for REC_NO := n-16 downto 0  do
            begin
                while Interrupt_Flag := false goto WAIT
                INTERRUPT_HANDLING;
                TRANSFER_GRAPHIC_COMMAND;
                    if Mode_Flag := true then
                        GRAPHIC_DISPLAY_MODE
                    TRANSFER_ECG_DATA_TO_PARALLEL_COMPUTER;
            end
        until_Mode_Flag := nn
    until_Mode_Flag := mm
end;
```

Fig. 7  A program for drawing heart potential distribution maps.

transmitted from the parallel processing element to the graphic display, the graphic display collects the processed results for drawing the body surface potential map. After the data transmitted from the local processor to the graphic display is finished, the host computer receives the END command from the parallel processor. Then, the new ECG data are distributed from the host computer to the parallel processing element where the data transmission has finished processed. A program for drawing heart potential distribution maps is shown in Fig. 7. If a coarse interpolation procedure for high-speed data processing is used, the dynamically displayed potential maps are not suitable for diagnosis because of their discontinuous movements.

## 4. SAMPLE RUN

Serial potential distribution maps with high-resolution can be dynamically displayed without any pause. As a result, we can see the repeated display of the body surface potential maps, until the host computer is interrupted by receiving an END command from the investigator.

We have developed two kinds of the dynamic presentation of heart potential distribution as shown in Fig. 8. Figure 8(a) shows one example frame of the isopotential maps which can be displayed four maps during one second as maximum speed in the color graphic display. The potential levels are displayed as different colors. The timing of the displayed frame is labeled in two ways: 1) the time in msec from QRS onset is displayed below each map, and 2) the time within the heart cycle is shown on the bottom trace. The potential values (relative to a Wilson Central Terminal) are represented by colors. A potential of zero is displayed as dark green as indicated by the "0" on the color scale. Increasing positive values of potential are displayed as light green, yellow and red as indicated by the positive sign on the color scale. Decreasing negative values of potential are displayed blue and dark blue in the same way. The peak positive and peak negative potential values (in millivolts) are shown at their locations as marked by a "+" and "-" sign, respectively. Figure 8(a) indicates the onset of recognizable breakthrough appearing near the mid-sternal line, at the level of the fourth sterno-costal joint. The potential of the closed region displayed by blue color falls rapidly as the apical depolarization is completed (Flowers, Horan, Sohi, Hand and Johnson 1976). In the subsequent stages of ventricular activation the upper minimum moves progressively from the right sub-clavicular region toward the mid-sternal minimum. The two minima finally merge together and the potential niche is formed. The location and time course of some simultaneous maxima and minima are almost continuously represented by the dynamic display of the three-dimensional maps which are parallelly processed by the 16 micro-computers. The values of maxima ad minima in the potential map can be displayed on user's request. In Fig. 8(b), we can see the isometric projection grids at 32 msec after onset of the QRS complex. In isometric projection form, outward bulges represent positive potential, while inward bulges or sinks indicate negative expression (Olliff, Horan and Flowers 1972). In order to recognize distinct variations of isometric projection grids, the inclined angles T and H of the zero-potential plane can be discretely changed by the displayed menu selection. And display speed can be controlled by the joystick or mouse.

The dynamic display of maps not only contributes information from more body surface sites, but also has an advantage of presenting simultaneous comparison and contrast of potential at these many different locations.

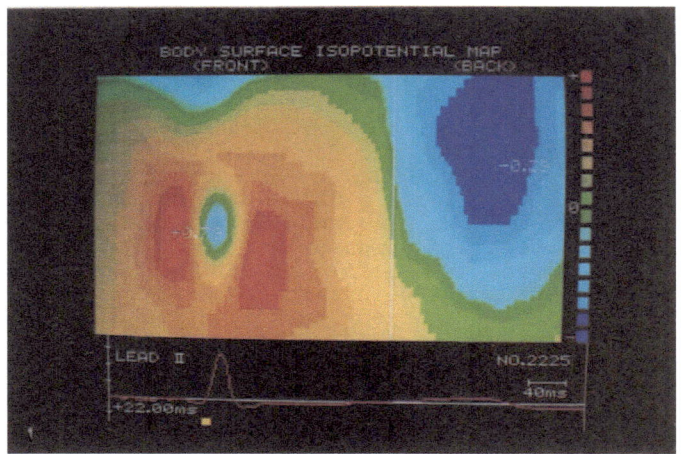

Fig. 8(a)  One example frame of displayed body surface
isopotential maps.

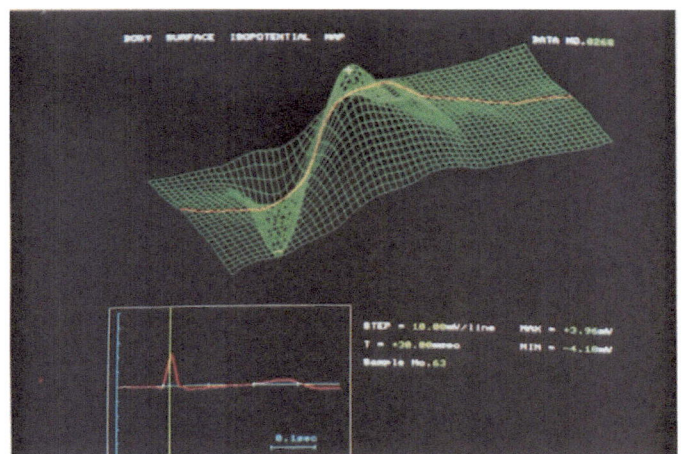

Fig. 8(b)  One example frame of displayed isometric projection grids
of heart potential distribution.

# 5. CONCLUSION

Despite the progressive speed of many recent computers, many area of computer applications, such as image processing, computer graphics and computer simulation of large-scale systems, are limited by computation speed. In order to overcome these limitations, parallel processing system should be used for displaying dynamic presentation of visual images (Haynes, Lau, Siewioreck and Mizell 1982). Therefore, we have developed a high-speed data presentation system which consists of 16 parallel computer boards and color graphic display. Each parallel processing board contains arithmetic processing unit (APU). Parallel processing can be accomplished between the local CPU and APU in each processing board. By using this double parallel processing technique, the cardiac potential distribution can be dynamically displayed. Without such double parallel computations, it is impossible to continuously display high-resolvable surface potential maps with a system based on off-the-shelf micro-processors components.

The time history and particularly the slow motion display of the spacial distribution of heart potential presents important information regarding certain cardiac electrophysiological disorders. In order to realize smooth movement of contour lines with good precision, we have developed a high-speed data presentation system. The graphic display terminal is designed as an intelligent terminal with its own CPU (Z80B) and large memory for image storage. Since the display terminal contains two pages of video-RAM, precise surface potential maps can be continuously displayed by page swapping. Functions such as slow-motion, reverse display, and map expansion are also provided in the parallel processing system. The ability to observe the global changes in a surface potential map through the entire cycle of a heart beat will make fast, accurate, and reliable diagnosis of the electrical cardiac condition possible. The time history and particularly the slow motion display in the selected time interval presents precise information regarding the electrical activity of the heart. The isometric projection grids of heart potential maps present a three-dimensional visualization of positive potentials as peaks and negative potentials as valleys or dips below the zero-potential plane. We have found that such dynamic display of medical images contains invaluable information beyond our imagination. The dynamic presentation of heart potential distribution may contribute to the reliable and accurate diagnosis of certain cardiac diseases. This system is directly related to the practical need to accomplish the dynamic display of heart potential maps. The developed technique of double parallel processings may be adapted for use in other fields involving spatially distributed, time-varing potentials, e. g., electrocephalography, chemical process, etc.

Since the ECG data have a special structure that there are no common data among the body surface potential maps, data exchange among the computer boards during parallel processing is unnecessary. The performance of parallel processing is quite good, because of the balanced load on each computer board. In conclusion, efficiency and performance of parallel processing is greatly depend on the data structure to be processed.

REFERENCES

Akamatsu N, Mori H (1984) Body surface multi-electrode for inverse
    problem in electrocardiography and its application. Trans IECE Japan
    J67-C:104-111
Akamatsu N, Mori H (1980) A computerized technique for body surface
    isopotential and topological maps. IEEE 1980 IECI Proc:361-366
Ambroggi LD, Taccardi B, Macchi E (1976) Body-surface maps of heart
    potentials. Circ 54:251-263
Flowers N C, Horan LG, Sohi GS, Hand RC, Johnson JC (1976) New
    evidence for inferoposterior myocardial infarction on surface
    potential maps. Am J Cardiol 38:576-581
Goldman MJ (1970) Principles of clinical electrocardiography. Lange
    Medical Publications.
Haynes LS, Lau RL, Siewioreck DP, Mizell DW (1982) A survey of highly
    parallel computing. Computer 15:9-24
Olliff BC, Horan LG, Flowers NC (1972) Correlative analysis of
    vectorcardiograms and serial instantaneous surface potential maps in
    normal young men. Am Heart J 83:780-789
Sugenoya J, et al. (1977) Body surface potential distribution
    following the production of right bundle branch block in dogs.
    Effects of breakthrough and right ventricular excitation on the body
    surface potentials. Circ 55:49-55
Taccardi B (1963) Distribution of heart potentials on the thoracic
    surface of normal human subjects. Cir Res 12:341-352
Vincent GM, Abildskov JA, Burgess MJ, Millar K, Lux RL, Wyatt RF
    (1977) Diagnosis of old inferior myocardial infarction by body
    surface isopotential mapping. Am J Cardiol 39:519-515

**Norio Akamatsu** was born in Tokushima, Japan, on September 9, 1943. He received the B.S. degree in electrical engineering from Tokushima University, Tokushima, Japan, in 1966, and the M.S. and Ph.D. degrees in electrical engineering from Kyoto University, Kyoto, Japan, in 1968 and 1974, respectively.

From 1971 to 1974 he was an Associate Lecturer of Electrical Engineering at Tokushima University. Since 1975 he has been an Associate Professor at the Department of Information Science of Tokushima University. His research interests are nonlinear phenomena in biomedical fields and their representation by using computer graphics technique.

Akamatsu is a memeber of the Institute of Electronics and Communication Engineers of Japan.

Akamatsu's address is Department of Information Science, Faculty of Engineering, Tokushima University, 2-1, Minami-Josanjima-cho, Tokushima, 770 Japan.

# The Single Array Approach to Engineering and Maintenance of CAD Software

Yehuda Shiran

SILVAR-LISCO/NCA Corporation, 3250 Jay Street, Santa Clara, CA 95054, USA

ABSTRACT:   The industry trend towards usage of workstations  in  the
electronic  design  process  motivates  CAD  vendors  to  port  their
software from traditional minis and mainframes to a collection of new
hardware  and  operating systems.  This paper deals with the software
engineering methodology  to  make  this  process  easier.   The  main
contribution  of this paper is showing how a single-array structuring
of a code and a run-time memory allocation can make the  porting  and
maintenance  tasks  fast  and  thus  inexpensive.  The methodology is
demonstrated via a compiler implementation.

KEYWORDS:   Software    engineering,    FORTRAN,    Run-time    memory
allocation,   Software   Portability  and  maintainability,  Hardware
description language, Relational database.

INTRODUCTION

Only a few software vendors can afford developing their products  for
a  specific  target  machine.   Most companies port their software to
many different machines and operating systems.  The accelerated usage
of  engineering  workstations has increased the diversity of hardware
and operating systems that the software developer  must  accommodate.
When porting a code, there are 2 main issues to consider:

1.  How can the code be structured so it will be fast to install
    on different computers/operating systems?

2.  How will the memory and storage limitations of the different
    computers affect the program's capabilities?

The contribution of this  paper  relates  mainly  to  FORTRAN  codes.
Although  a  very  old programming language, FORTRAN is still popular
among application programmers.  On the Apollo's DOMAIN computer,  for
example,  95%  of  the available application packages (about 140) are
written in some  dialect  of  FORTRAN  (Apollo  1983).   FORTRAN  has
several deficiencies which modern langugaes are avoiding.  This paper
shows how to solve this problems in  FORTRAN  and  its  contribution,
therefore,  is  directed  towards  those vendors and programmers that
must program in FORTRAN (the reasons are not  addressed  here).   The
paper  demonstrates  how  a  FORTRAN code can be engineered to assure
fast porting, easy maintenance and an efficient usage of the  machine
resources.

This paper is presented in a top-down fashion. First, the deficiencies of the old approach are detailed; Secondly, the advantages of the new approach are presented. Then it shows how one can apply the methodology to 3 different types of databases. A compiler program (MDL) is used to demonstrate the last two (more complex) implementations. The paper ends with a comparison between the new MDL compiler and the old version of it. The limitiations of the new approach are also included.


THE OLD APPROACH


FORTRAN has the following critical limitations:


Data Structure; The only data structure is the array.


Memory Allocation; The memory is allocated statically and must be defined at compile time.


For ease of programming, programmers tend to use many arrays to do the computations. This approach makes the program difficult to port and maintain because:


Turnaround Time; Sometimes the customer needs to change the size of the arrays. The vendor would be contacted if the source code is not provided or if the user is not familiar enough with the code to do the modifications. The need for the vendor's assistance makes the turnaround time very long (usually over a week).


Memory Usage; The memory is not used efficiently. Some arrays are fully populated but others are only partially filled. This overallocation of the memory tends to overload the system and decrease its performance.


Array-Dimension Adjustments; In extreme cases, when more memory is not available to the program, adjustments must be made. In order to be able to handle a large database on such a machine, some arrays need to be lengthened and others need to be shorten. This adjustment is usually done in a trial-and-error fashion and as such is very expensive in programmer's time.


Coordination; The change of array sizes is usually accompanied by other changes in the declaration portion or in the initial assignment of variables. Since all these changes must be coordinated with each other, this step may be very difficult and tedious, especially when the documentation is not precise.


THE SINGLE-ARRAY APPROACH


Most of the above problems may be solved by using a single array. When a change in the memory allocation is needed, only 2 entries are modified: the dimension declaration and the size constant. Memory usage is more efficient and no adjustments are needed when the database is large - there is only one array which can be as long as the available memory.

The Single-Array approach may be applied to homogeneous data as well as to heterogeneous and compound types.

HOMOGENEOUS SINGLE-ARRAY IMPLEMENTATION

Cases where there is only one type of information entity are included in this category. Each entity is an independent data unit and there is no explicit relationship between the different elements of the database. Assuming that each entity is implemented by a single record, then the database is modified by changing existing records, by adding new ones or by deleting others. For this type of database, a fixed number of elements of the array are allocated for each record. Figure 1 shows how to apply this approach for a simple CAD application: geometric database. Every record represents an edge and has 8 fields: 7 attributes and one pointer to another edge

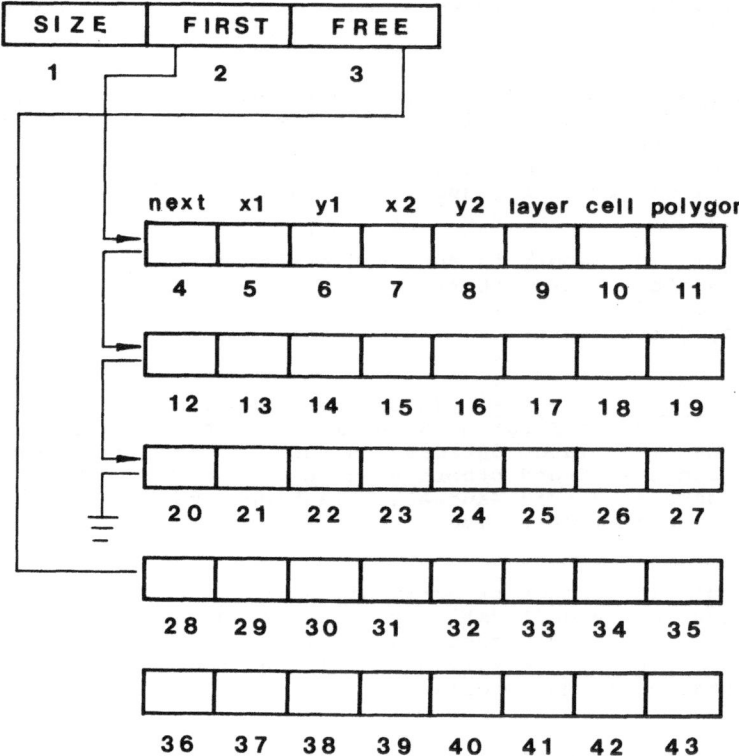

Figure 1. A Single-Array implementation of a homogeneous database (a simple geometric one). The information entities (records) are identical in nature.

record. Depending on the algorithms used, more pointers or other attributes may be added. Notice the first 3 elements of the array: they enable the passing of the array address to a subroutine as the only argument. Some additional information, such as an index for fast searching, may be built into the single array.

To illustrate the application of the Single-Array approach to non-homogeneous databases, a compiler for Hardware Description Language (HDL) is presented as an example.


AN EXAMPLE - COMPILER IMPLEMENTAION - OPENING REMARKS


The compiler is designated to process a description of an electronic chip in an English-like language. This language is called MDL - Master Design Language. As in a programming language preprocessor (C, m4, Ratfor), the description is based on macro definitions. Each macro has a content part and an interface part.

The MDL description can be considered as a relational database, as described by Wiederhold (1983), with the following entities:

Macro's Definition; A definition of a macro usually contains a description of a subcircuit. It may consist of calls to other macros or instances of primitive devices such as transistors, capacitors and resistors.

Macro's Interface Definition; This part contains the definition of the parameters passed to the macro when it is called from another macro.

Macro's Instance Reference; This is the call to a macro from within another macro. The details of this instantiation includes the actual arguments passed to the called macro.

There is a nested relation between the Macro's Definition Entity and each of the other two. The Macro's Definition Entity owns its Interface Definition and its Instances. These instances will be referred to as the children of their father macro. Each Instance references a macro or a primitive device and therefore there is a reference relation between the Instances and the Macro Definitions. This may seem to cause a circularity in the database but it is accepted, since this is an integrated database, not just one view of it. Figure 2 shows the connections between the entities. An ownership connection represents the nested relations and a reference connection represents the reference relation. In Fig. 2 the conventions of Wiederhold (1983) are followed.

HETEROGENEOUS SINGLE-ARRAY IMPLEMENTATION


In this category the database is not homogeneous as in Fig. 1. The record is not uniform as it is in the geometric database and there is

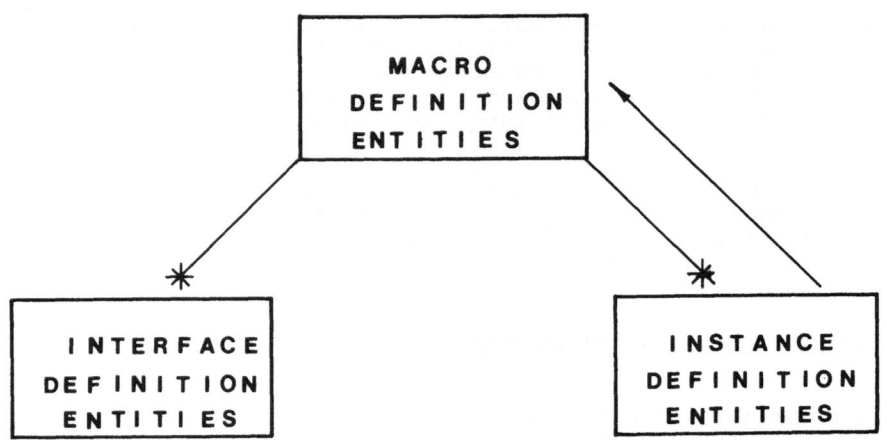

Figure 2. The MDL compiler as a relational database. Similar in
structure to programming language preprocessors such as m4, Ratfor
and C.

a dependency between the different entity types. The dependency is
such that none of the entity types can exist by itself. This case is
handled by dividing the single array into two parts:

Random Pool; The bottom part (low index values) which will store
random data elements (strings).

Stack;The top part which will store a structured representation of
the database. This usually consists of pointers to the Random Data
Pool at the bottom of the array, or to other pointers in the top
part, see Fig. 3. The Pool Top and the Stack Top are constantly
updated while loading the data into the array.

Figure 4 shows the implementation of the MDL compiler in a single
array. The entity concept is implemented by a physical record and
the connection is translated into a pointer.
The Stack region is populated by 3 types of records: Macro Records,
Interface Records and Content Records. The Macro Record and the
Content Record point to elements of both the Stack and the Random
Pool. The Interface Record points to the Random Pool only. The
Random Pool stores packed strings which begin with the character
count. It also stores Primitive Device Records.

COMPOUND SINGLE-ARRAY IMPLEMENTATION - HASH TABLES

In an application like a compiler, there is a need for a fast
searching algorithm. Common to such problems is the use of hash
tables. The MDL compiler program first builds the Random Pool and
the Stack and then starts processing the data. A lexicon between

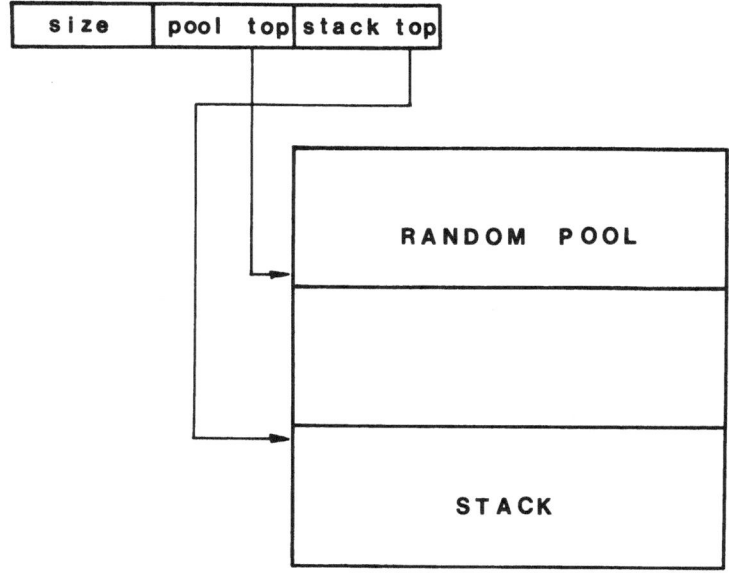

Figure 3. A Single-Array implementation of a heterogeneous database (compiler). The information entities are not all of the same type. The Random Pool contains strings which have corresponding pointers in the Stack. The Stack contains a structered representation of the database - pointers to the Random Pool or to other entries in the Stack.

variable-length (optionally user-defined) node names (similar to variable names in programming languages) and compiler-assigned integer numbers (similar to addresses) is needed during this process. This lexicon is implemented by a hash table in the free space between the Random Pool and the Stack. Using an open hashing methodology and assuming n nodes are accommodated, 3 zones are formed:

Hash Zone; Will have 1.5n entries, each entry needs 2 words: one for pointing to the Lexicon Zone and one for pointing to the Overflow Zone. The required size is therefore equal to 3n.

Overflow Zone; Will have 0.5n entries, 2 words per entry as the Hash Zone. The required size is therefore equal to n.

Lexicon Zone; Consists of variable length Lexicon Records, each holding a name (packed and begins with the character count), a node number and some other data values. The average node name is 12 characters long, so 3 array elements per name are needed (32 bit long memory word). Adding the character count, the node number and one additional data value the total comes up to 6 elements per record. The required size of the zone is therefore equal to 6n.

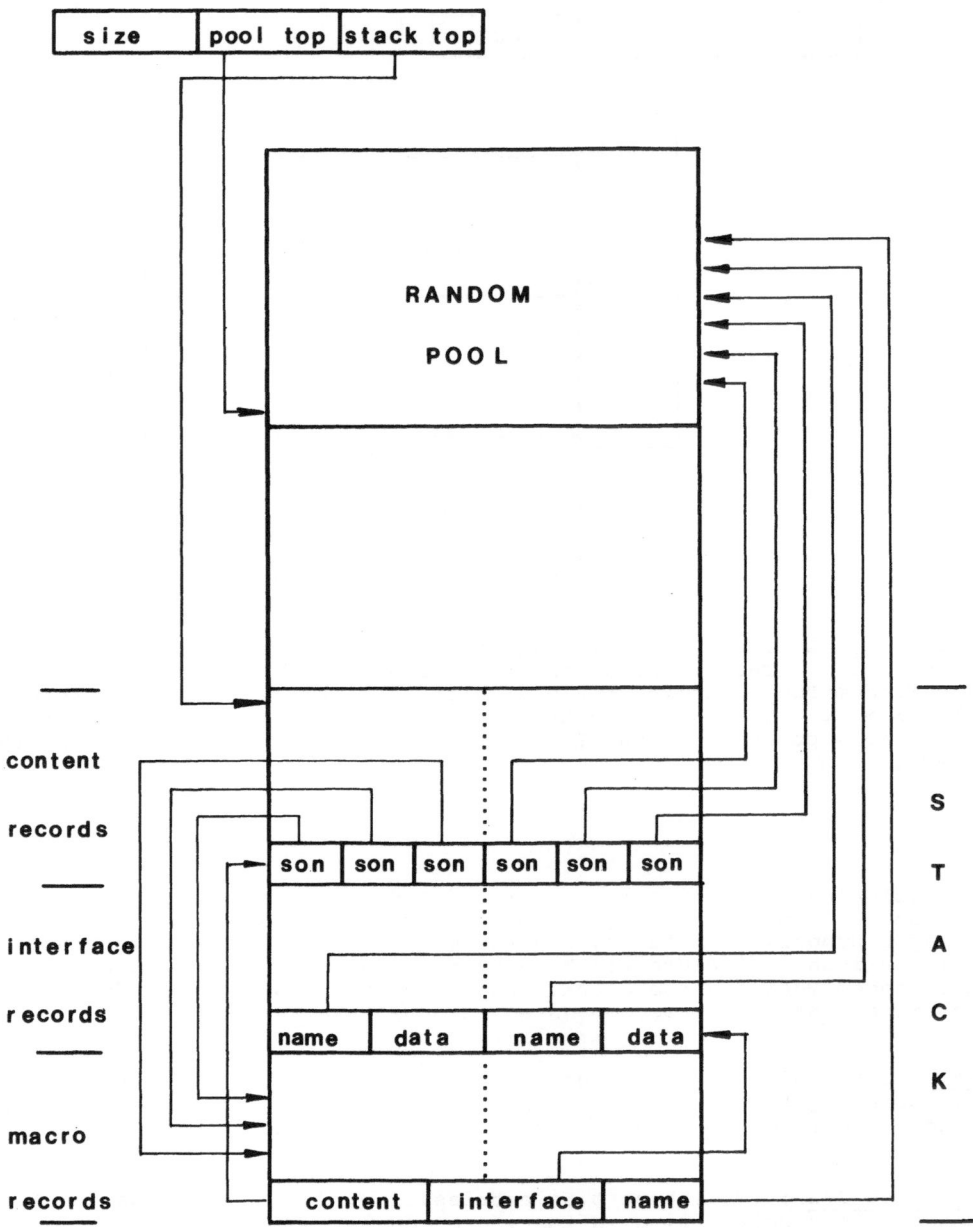

Figure 4. A Single-Array implementation of the MDL compiler. The Stack contains 3 different types of information entities.

The total size needed for the three zones is therefore $3n + n + 6n = 10n$. Knowing the size of the free space left between the Random Pool and the Stack, the accommodation of our lexicon ($n$), can be calculated. Figure 5 shows the structure of the array.


## MAIN MEMORY - EXTERNAL MEMORY TRADEOFFS


When the database is homogeneous in nature, the program can partition the data so it will be accommodated by the allocated memory. The data which cannot be handled by the main memory may reside on the disk. When the database is heterogeneous in nature, it is much more difficult to divide-and-conquer the problem, due to the dependencies among the units of information. External files are used in the processing of the lexicon of the MDL compiler. After loading the Random Pool and the Stack, as many nodes as there is space available for them are processed. When the program runs out of space (in either the Overflow Zone or the Lexicon Zone) the Lexicon Records are written to an external file and the processing of the next batch of nodes begins. On every space overflow, a new file is opened and the Lexicon Records are output. After the processing of the whole database is completed, each file is sorted by node name and then the external files are merged using a K-way merge method, as explained by Aho et al. (1983).


In this method the entries from all the input files are systematically interleaved. Consider the files as pop-up stacks, each sorted in an ascending order. Every time an entry is to be read, the smallest name among those on the top of their stacks needs to be found. To avoid resorting after each time an entry is popped from one of the stacks, a priority queue is used to keep track of the sort order among those top elements. The queue is constantly updated after each read operation, accommodating the new entry which replaces the one just popped. The smallest name always heads the queue and is ready for its removal.
Figure 6 illustrates the K-way merge and the priority queue. The smallest name is on top of file #3 and is going to be read into the main memory.


By implementing a tradeoff between main memory and external memory, the porting task becomes even easier. The program will automatically use external memory when it runs out of main memory. This advantage is extremely helpful in the workstation market, where the available main memory is smaller than on the traditional minis and mainframes.


## RUN-TIME MEMORY ALLOCATION


The Single-Array approach brings the porting and maintenance tasks down to a modification of two constants in the code, as explained above. Sometimes, the user does not have the source code to do those changes. If he tries to contact the vendor, the turnaround time might be over a week. The solution is to implement a run-time memory allocation on those machines that can support it. The scheme can be implemented by calling a system routine (like LIB$GET_VM on VAX), by a C subroutine which calls the C function malloc or even by writing an assembly subroutine to do it. The amount of memory needed can be input by the user or estimated by the program itself according to the

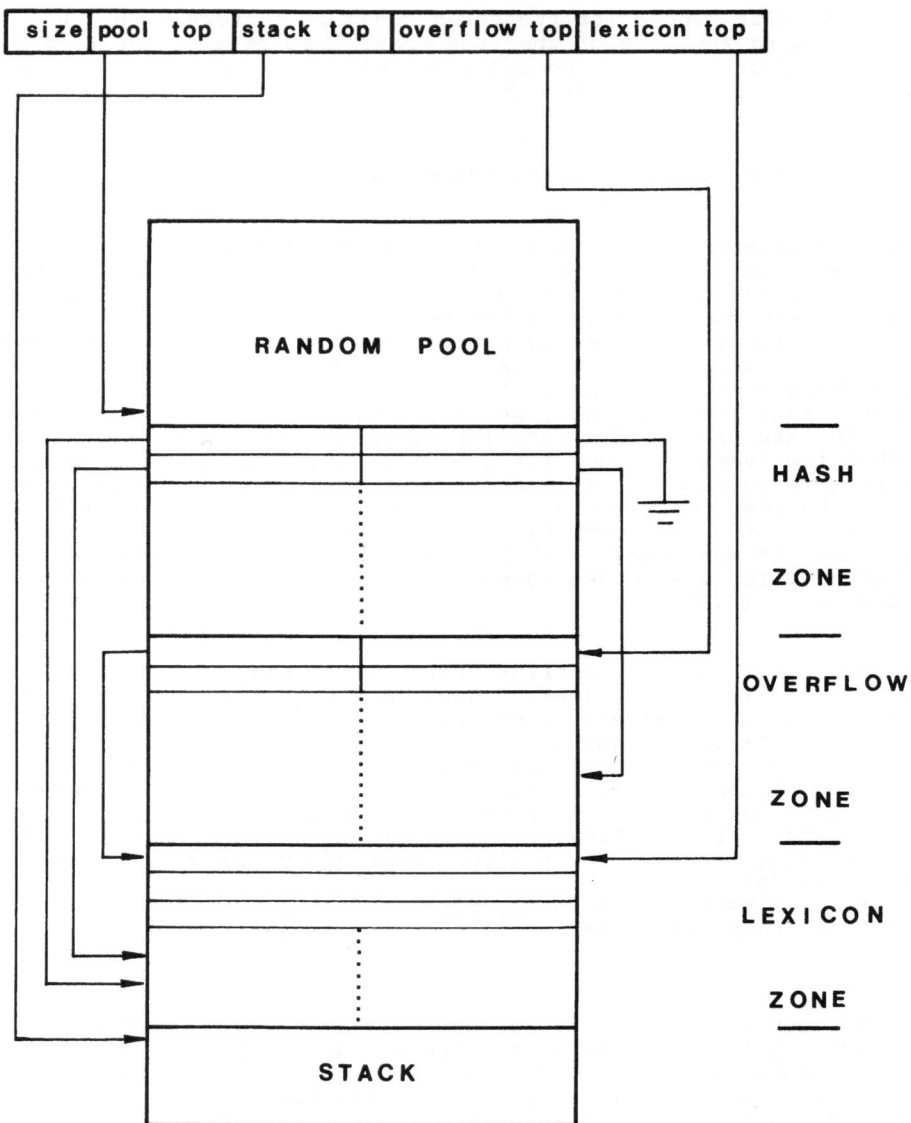

Figure 5. A Single-Array implementation of a hash table. The Hash Zone, the Overflow Zone and the Lexicon Zone fully span the space between the Random Pool and the Stack.

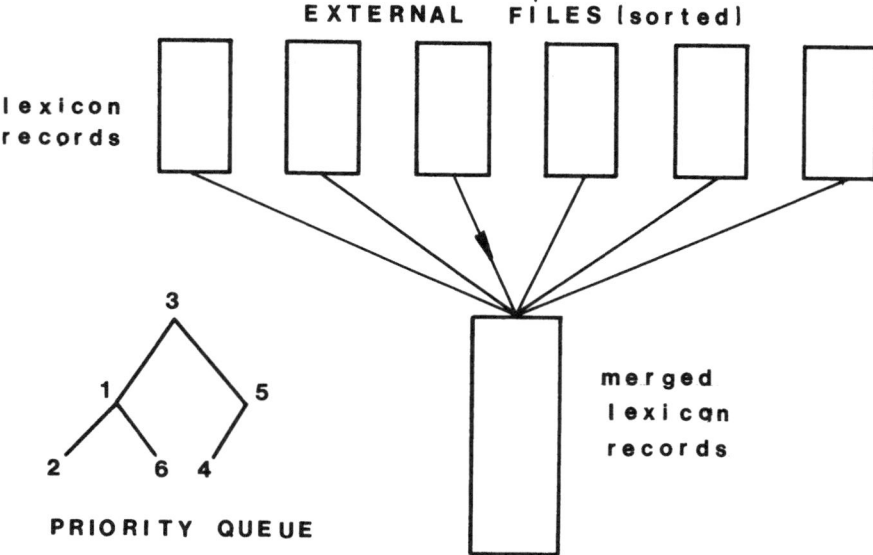

Figure 6. K-way merge of lexicon records. A priority queue is keeping the sort order of the top elements and is updated after the the smallest element is popped from the external file (#3).

input database size. The user can now extend the program capability to the limit: He can allocate all the memory available on a particular machine and change this allocation without having the source code. Another benefit of the run-time memory allocation is that the user can adjust the allocation to the problem at hand. This way he can use the resources much more efficiently.

AN EXAMPLE - COMPILER IMPLEMENTATION - CLOSING REMARKS

The old MDL compiler was written in FORTRAN using 6 two-dimensional arrays and 14 one-dimensional arrays, all allocated at compile-time. Whenever an array storge accommodation was exceeded, the customer had to wait at least 1 week to get a new object module with an increased size of that array. Sometimes the process became an iterative one since there was no way to determine the required size except by trial-and-error. This scheme did not work at all on small computers. The memory limitation forced the programmer to decrease a couple of arrays when an increase in other was needed, making the iterative process even more complex. In fear of overflowing the arrays, the program always used disk storage for the Lexicon processing, even if the main memory could have handled it. Because of the fixed size of the arrays, the user-defined node names were limited to a maximum lenght of 10 characters.

In the new MDL compiler there is only one array and the user has a control over its size. The trial-and-error method for sizing that array is sometimes needed (the program first tries to estimate the

size of the array according to the size of the input MDL
description), but the user can do it by himself and does not need the
vendor's assistance. There are no adjustments to make for small
computers; The main memory is always used first, and only when its
limitation is exceeded is the Lexicon processing using the disk
storage. Since the node names are stored in a single
(one-dimensional) array, there is no limit on the length of the
user-defined identifiers - they are packed and then stored in the
next free spot of the Random Pool, while a pointer to it is stored in
the Stack.

## LIMITIATIONS OF THE APPROACH

The single array approach has some apparent disadvantages:

Extra code complexity; Since a significant amount of the code must
be devoted to the maintenance and use of pointers, the resulting code
will generally by much less transparent to the reader. This problem
is solved by using a FORTRAN preprocessor, very similar to the C
preprocessor. The preprocessor allows hiding much of this
"bookkeeping" details by the capability of grouping lines of code
inside different macros and then calling these macros from within the
main program or from other macros.

Machine-dependency; The run-time memory allocation scheme is
machine-dependent. This problem is addressed in the same way as
other machine-dependent operations (such as I/O routines) are handled
- a special file with the machine-dependent routines is being
included by the FORTRAN preprocessor. Such a file is created for
every machine supported by the vendor.

Execution time; The execution time is longer due to additional
"bookkeeping" tasks and pointer address calculations. This penalty
is offset by the gain of the new approach. As mentioned above,
external memory is used only when the main memory cannot accommodate
the large database. The old MDL compiler always used external memory
and therefore was slower, even when the database was small. Overall,
the new MDL compiler is more than 10 times faster than the old
program.

Different data types; Since the array can be only of a specific data
type, referencing data of different type is more complex. Using two
buffers and the FORTRAN EQUIVALENCE statement can solve the problem.
One buffer will be used to address the elements and the other buffer
will be used to process the values as being of different data type.

## SUMMARY

A code can be made much easier and less expensive to port and
maintain by using two basic methodologies:

Single-Array Structure; This approach can be implemented for
homogeneous databases (like geometric) as well as for compound ones

(like compilers). The disadvantages of the new approach are either offset by the advantages or else are overcome by using a FORTRAN preprocessor.

<u>Run-Time Memory Allocation</u>; It is desired to have a run-time memory allocation scheme. Since FORTRAN does not support it, the scheme will be borrowed from the operating system or from a different programming language. For those computers that cannot support any run-time memory allocation, the traditional FORTRAN static allocation will be used. In order to make this installation-dependency easy to handle, the run-time memory allocation scheme is instantiated only once.

REFERENCES

Aho AV, Hopcroft EJ, Ullman DJ (1983) Data Structures and Algorithms. Addison-Wesley, Reading Menlo Park London Amsterdam Don Syndey.

Apollo Computer inc. (1983) Catalogue of applications for the DOMAIN.

Day BD, Warren WK (1985) The Integration of Design and Test. VLSI DESIGN 6(3):46-52.

Girczyc FE, Buhr AR, Knight PJ (1985) Aplicability of Subset of ADA as an Algorithmic Hardware Description Language for Graph-Based Hardware Compilation. IEEE Transactions on Computer-Aided Design 4(2):134-142.

Goksel KA et al. (1984) A VLSI Memory Management Chip: Design Consideration and Experience. IEEE J. of Solid State 19(3):325-328.

Johnson B, Crowley J. (1984) Software Standard Eliminates CAD Interface Problems. Int. Cir. Magazine 2(7):46-51.

Maruyama F, Fujita M. (1985) Hardware Verification. IEEE COMPUTER 18(2):22-32.

Maynard DE (1985) VHSIC Database and Database Management system Requirement. VLSI DESIGN 6(2):94-96.

Wiederhold G (1983) Data Base Design. McGraw-Hill, New York.

**Yehuda Shiran** is a Member of Technical Staff at SILVAR-LISCO/NCA Corporation, Santa Clara, California. Before then, he was a research programming consultant at EPRI - Electric Power Research Institute, Palo Alto, California. From 1975 to 1980 he held a technical position with the Israeli Ministry of Defense. His current research areas of interest are IC design verification, silicon compilation, computational geometry, supercomputers in engineering applications and fluid dynamics.

Shiran received his BSc and MSc in Mechanical Engineering from the Technion - Haifa, Israel in 1975 and 1980. He received his MS in Electrical Engineering from Stanford University in 1984 and is currently a Ph.D candidate at Stanford University.

# The Integration of Computer Graphics and Image Processing Techniques for the Display and Manipulation of Geophysical Data

I. Chakravarty[1], B.G. Nichol[1] and T. Ono[2]

[1] Schlumberger-Doll Research, Old Quarry Road, Ridgefield, CT 06877-4108, USA
[2] Nippon Schlumberger K.K., Fuchinobe, Sagamihara, Kanagawa, 229 Japan

## ABSTRACT

Data measurements whose distribution constitutes a regular 3D grid are becoming increasingly common in many application areas relating to the scientific, engineering and medical fields. To efficiently visualize any inherent structure or spatial relationships that may exist in this type of data, a user must have the ability to interactively enhance, manipulate and display the data. In this paper we examine the requirements for developing such a software environment for use with 3D data arrays, and then describe a prototype system that illustrates the use of the techniques developed for seismic data analysis.

## INTRODUCTION

A 3D array of data, where every location in the array contains a measured value, arises in many engineering and medical applications such as in seismic analysis and computer-axial tomography. In these applications, the value at each location in the array corresponds to a physical measurement such as energy or density. The acquired data may be inherently 3D or may be construed as 3D when multiple 2D data slices are successively placed together to form a 3D array. An essential component in the interpretation of the 3D data array is the ability to manipulate and display the data in a manner such that the size, shape and extent of features in the data can be easily visualized. The objective of this paper is to describe a system that combines the manipulation of 3D data array with 3D computer graphics and image processing techniques for data display and image enhancement.

There are several aspects of the problem of manipulating 3D array data which pertain to both the software and hardware architecture. First, in many practical applications, the magnitude of the 3D data is so large that simple operations such as displaying or rotating the data are time-consuming on a general purpose computer. Since the data is often larger than the physical memory of a minicomputer, a major bottleneck in the manipulation is the large number of disk accesses that have to be performed in order to read the data from disk and process the data for an operation. Consequently, to facilitate real-time interaction there is considerable interest in the development of specialized hardware for 3D data manipulation (Meagher 1982), (Goldwasser 1984). Second, the display and processing of 3D data requires a combination of techniques utilizing both 3D graphics and image analysis. Thus, the software environment in a system designed for interacting with 3D data must be able to efficiently accommodate both image synthesis and analysis operations within the same hardware architecture.

Third, in order to access large amounts of data from a host computer for real-time interaction, it is necessary to minimize the transmission time. Thus any system developed for the purpose of manipulating 3D array data must either contain large amounts of local memory for storing the entire data set or must be able to decode a compact representation of the data prior to any manipulation. This last requirement has stimulated a great deal of interest on the optimum representation of 2D and 3D data in a computer for fast access and manipulation (Burt 1982), (Hardas and Srihari 1984). Although individual graphic systems and image processing systems abound, it is important to note that it is the ability combine all these operations into a single system that is of importance.

In this paper we address the problem of developing a specialized processor for the interaction and manipulation of 3D array data. By a specialized processor we mean a graphics subsystem containing local processors, closely coupled to a host computer, enabling the subsystem to perform a variety of functions independently and in parallel with the host system. We have three primary objectives in the development of such a subsystem. They are (i) to ensure a high-level of performance and interactivity for manipulation and display of 3D array data, (ii) to ensure extendibility so that new application algorithms can be easily added to the existing subsystem, and (iii) to ensure flexibility so that the processing sequence can be easily changed to accommodate a diverse set of requirements.

We first present a brief overview of the current techniques for visualizing 3D array data and then describe the system and the software tools that we have developed for this application. Although the examples described in this paper illustrate the use with seismic data, the concepts and techniques presented are equally applicable to any 3D array data set.

## TECHNIQUES FOR VISUALIZATION OF 3D FEATURES

Current techniques for visualizing 3D features can be categorized into two major classes: surface oriented and volume oriented. In the first technique, 2D slices of the data, accessed along one of three primary axes, are displayed and features of interest delineated either manually or through some pattern recognition technique. The boundaries of these features are then reconstructed into a 3D surface by correlating the features derived from successive slices of the data. Once the surfaces are reconstructed they may be displayed, cross-sectioned, and manipulated using efficient 3D graphics rendering algorithms (Atherton 1981). There are several variations to this approach notable among which is the use of color encoding to display successive slices of 3D data (Farrell 1983) and the reconstruction of discrete surfaces directly from the 3D data (Udupa 1982). This technique of reconstructing surfaces from 2D slices has been used successfully in several medical imaging applications (Herman and Liu 1979).

The second approach is based on a volumetric representation where the original data is thresholded and the resulting binary data is converted into an octree representation. Specialized hardware can then be used for real-time display and efficient cross-sectioning capabilities inherent in the octree representation. If the thresholding, connectivity analysis and conversion of the data into an octree representation can be done very fast then one can, in effect, selectively reconstruct 3D features derived from several densities of the 3D data array (Meagher 1984).

The major disadvantage of the surface oriented approach is that the reconstruction of the surfaces is difficult because the features are restricted to three orthogonal directions. Furthermore, once the surfaces are reconstructed, it is difficult to correlate the accuracy of the reconstruction with the actual features in the 3D data because it is difficult to cross-section the data along an arbitrary path. The major disadvantage of the volume oriented approach is the need to "binarize" the data which significantly decreases the information content and makes it difficult to see subtle features and textures in the data. Moreover, the inability to combine either conventional wire-frame representations with the 3D data or image enhancement techniques to improve the quality of the data for display within the same framework presents a problem in any practical application (Meagher 1984).

## SPECIFICATIONS FOR MANIPULATING 3D DATA

The objective in manipulating and visualizing 3D data is to identify features of interest and build a model that reduces the data array into its essential geometric components. This reduced representation can then be used for further computation, simulation or for interpretation.

To begin we first define the notion of 3D data array and illustrate some typical data retrieval requirements. In Fig. 1 we illustrate a 3D data array where each location in a 3D array contains a numerical value. In computer-axial tomography the numerical value is a measure of density whereas in seismic data the numerical value is a measure of reflected acoustic energy. Accessing the data along one of the three primary axes is the most obvious way of indexing into the data. If the data is linearized and stored on disk then the most efficient way to retrieve the data is along the axis of linearization. Access along any other axis would cause excessive page thrashing and becomes a bottleneck in any general purpose computer.

A typical data access operation is to retrieve a planar non-axial slice, that is, a slice specified along an arbitrarily oriented plane as shown in Fig. 2. Special cases of data access include the ability to take a planar slices along an arbitrary path (Fig. 3) and along a vertical plane (Fig. 4).

In order to generate the image shown in Fig. 4 given a 3D data array as shown in Fig. 1, three different types of operations are required. First, a data retrieval operation returns a 2D array of values, from the 3D array, that corresponds to the desired slice. Second, the 3D coordinates of the data array and the verticies of the non-planar slice are then transformed and projected to the screen coordinates. Third, the 2D array of values must then be resampled (interpolated or decimated) to fit the polygons projected on the screen.

In order to quantify requirements we have divided the class of functions into three categories:

1. Data Access - The data access tools are concerned with three types of operations. They are:

(i)    the encoding and decoding of data (so that the transmission time between the host computer, where the data resides, and the workstation is minimized),

(ii)   the retrieval operations that allow access to a 3D data volume along any arbitrary path, and

(iii)  sampling operations that either interpolate or decimate the data depending upon the resolution of the data and the size of the viewports on the workstation.

2. Data Analysis - The data analysis tools are concerned with three types of operations:

(i)    interactive enhancement of data through the use of image processing techniques,

(ii)   automatic tracking and detection of features, and

(iii)  correlation and reconstruction of features in the 3D data volume.

3. Data Display - The data display tools can be categorized into four classes. They are:

(i)    display of 2D image data,

(ii)   display of 3D wire-frame objects,

(iii)  display of solid objects with hidden surfaces removed,

(iv)   overlay of image data with 3D objects.

Based on the enumeration above it becomes clear that there are two classes of algorithms being detailed. The first class of algorithms is the display, manipulation and interaction of coordinate data. This type of data has traditionally been represented with structured display lists. The second class of algorithms is the display, manipulation and interaction of raster data. This type of data is less structured and has traditionally been associated with a frame-buffer. Typically, a user application may use both types of operations, for example, a parametric patch may be defined by a set of coordinate points

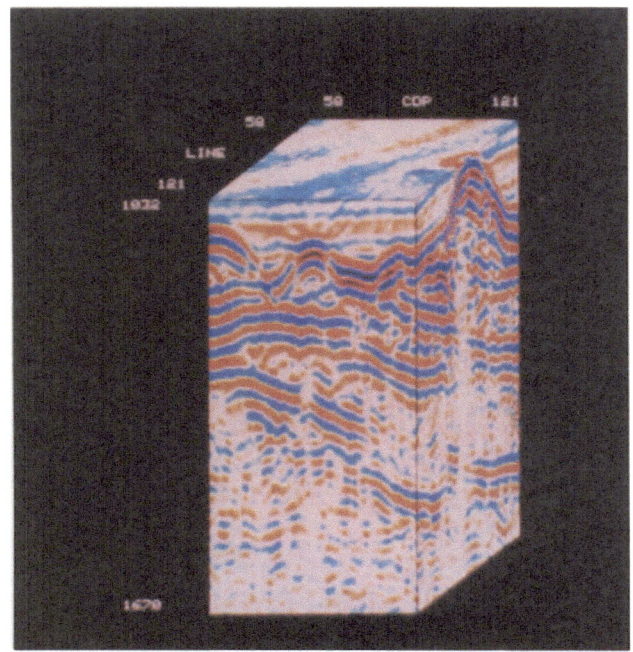

Fig. 1. Three-Dimensional Seismic Data
Array with 64 lines, 64 CDPs, and 320 time-slices.

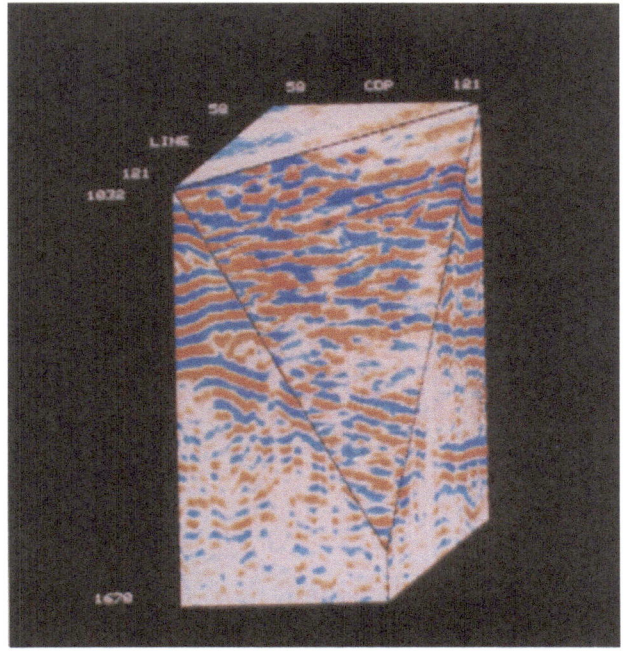

Fig. 2. An Arbitrarily Oriented Planar Slice.

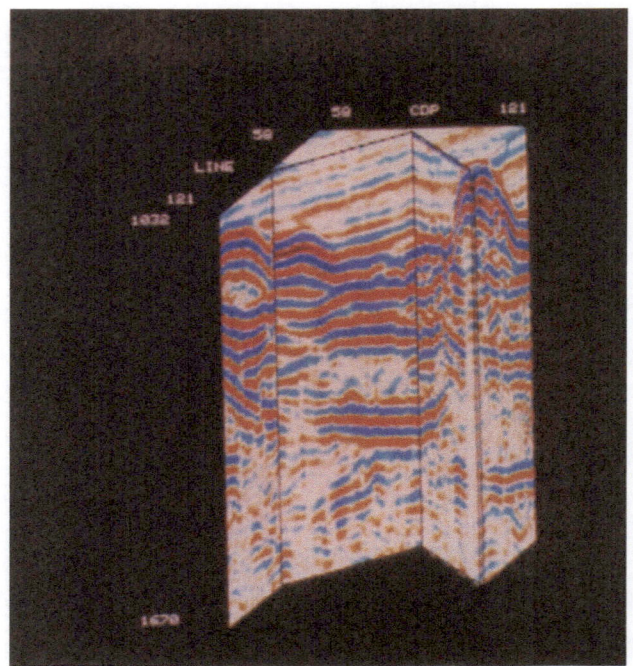

Fig. 3. An Arbitrary Path Cut-Away View.

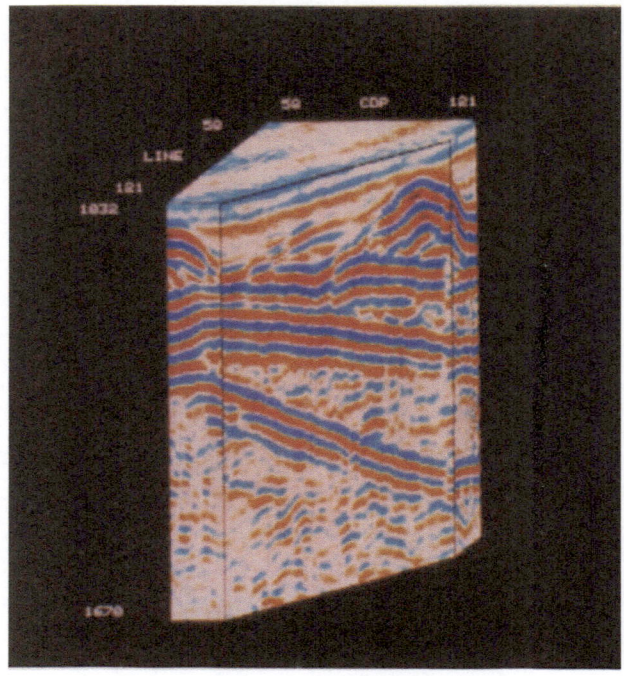

Fig. 4. A Horizontal Plane Cut-Away View.

but the rendering may use a raster based subdivision technique. The objective of this system is to provide a uniform mechanism supporting both types of algorithms within the same framework.

## OVERVIEW OF THE SYSTEM

The framework for manipulating the 3D data is built around the Adage 3000 hardware. The graphics subsystem is comprised of three major computing components:

(i) a 32-bit wide bipolar bit-slice processor (BPS)

(ii) a 4x4 matrix multiplier accumulator (MA)

(iii)a Motorola M68000 microprocessor (MPC).

All three computing components are programmable by the user and can be synchronized to perform a specified task. The system contains 3M bytes of image memory organized into a 512 x 1536 x 32 bit deep image. Of this total memory only a 512 x 512 x 24 section is visible at any one time. All components of the system, including the image memory, are connected to a single bus, called the *Adage bus*. The host computer for the system is a VAX 11/750. A detailed description of the hardware architecture can be found in Adage RDS 3000 Users Manual (Adage 1982).

### General Design Principles

The general design of the system relies upon the ability to decompose a complex application function into a sequence of primitive microcoded operations. These primitive operations are then performed by the bit-slice processor in the graphics subsystem. The decomposition of an application function into a set of primitive operations is performed by the host computer, that is, a single function call may generate a sequence of interconnected primitive operations. These primitive operations are encoded into a linear display list, transmitted to the bit-slice processor and stored in local memory within the graphics subsystem. The bit-slice processor then executes each command sequentially, independent of the host computer. The bit-slice processor may also invoke other computing devices within the system such as the matrix multiplier to perform a specified task concurrently with the bit-slice processor. The software allows parallel operation of the host computer and the graphics subsystem.

The key features in the system are the following:

1. *Microcode Libraries*: We have developed several specialized microcode libraries each of which perform tasks related to an application area. Since the amount of microcode memory available is limited, a microcode library is loaded from a host computer disk depending upon the task to be executed. This approach makes it possible to alter the functionality of the system and also permits additions to the primitive operations. The microcoding has been done in a high-level language similar in characteristics to 'C' (Icross 1984).

2. *Image Memory*: We have partitioned the 3M bytes image memory so that only a portion is used for display. The rest of the memory is dynamically reconfigured and used as temporary storage by the bit-slice processor. In addition, the host computer disk is used to save the state of the image memory depending upon the application. The ability to use the image memory as a temporary storage area for menus, texture maps, z-buffer, double buffering, data decoding and a scratch area for the bit-slice processor has proven to be a valuable asset.

3. *Process Encapsulation*: We have isolated the algorithms executed by the bit-slice processor from the input and output of data with the intent that we do not differentiate between a 3D image synthesis operation and an image analysis operation. Thus, the input data to a series of processing steps may reside either in a display list in the local memory of the bit-slice processor, or in a sec-

tion of the image memory. Likewise, the output may be scan-converted for display or may be written back to another area of the image memory. This flexible structure allows us to intermix image synthesis and image analysis operations within a single display list structure.

4. *Microcode Context Switches:* The ability to stop the bit-slice processor and save the state of the system plays an important role in microcode context switching. This allows us to view the computing elements in the graphics subsystem as a specialized processor that can perform a variety of operations ranging from data access to image filtering. In addition, an application program can also read back the result of a computation performed by the bit-slice processor or the matrix multiplier. Thus, a transformation composed in the graphics subsystem may be read back by the host computer. This enables the host computer to perform the same transformations as the hardware multiplier and pass the results of the transformation to a host resident routine. These tools allow the user to use the processing power of the graphics subsystem selectively with a host resident application program.

## IMPLEMENTATION

In this section we describe the software architecture implemented to satisfy the requirements stated earlier. We describe the key features in the system and conclude the section with several examples illustrating the use of such a system.

### Software Hierarchy

There are four levels of hierarchy in the software as shown in Fig. 5. The lowest level interface to the graphics subsystem are the communication programs that address the hardware components. The microcode libraries form the next level in the hierarchy. These libraries are binary dumps of the microcode modules that are executed by the bit-slice processor. In addition to binary microcode dumps, the libraries contain the symbol table indicating the physical location of the microroutines in the binary file. At the third level is the display processor which controls the decomposition of an application function into primitive operations and for loading the appropriate microcode library to execute the specified task. Finally any application software resides above the display processor and provides function calls for image synthesis, data-access and image-analysis operations. From a user standpoint, however, the decomposition of functions and the subsequent switching of microcode is completely transparent. The software described uses several microcode libraries developed by Adage Inc. as part of the Seismic 3000 (Seismic 1984) and Solid 3000 (Solid 1984) packages and have been integrated into our framework.

### Software Reconfiguration Of Pipeline

Most existing graphics and image processing systems utilize a hardwired pipeline to speed the throughput of arithmetic operations that are performed repeatedly. Although the hardware implementation results in significant gain in efficiency (Clark 1982) it is inflexible and does not permit experimentation with new algorithms.

The approach we have taken here is to sacrifice the throughput in exchange for flexibility. The reconfigurability is based on our ability to link together a variety of microroutines into modules. These modules are dynamically loaded into the microcode memory depending upon the operation to be performed.

A microcode module is a program that resides entirely in the microcode memory of the bit-slice processor. Input to the program is usually a pointer indicating where data and parameters required to execute the module reside. Likewise, output from the module is also a pointer which indicates the

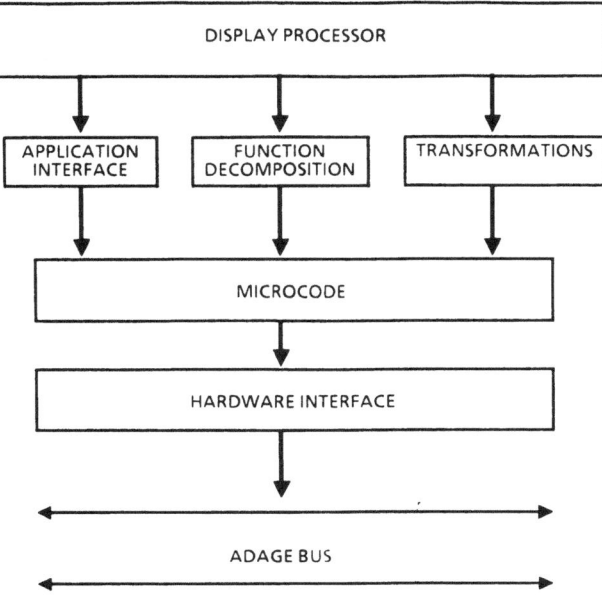

Fig. 5. The Software Hierarchy.

location of the output data. This data may be placed either in the scratch-pad memory, a working area for the bit-slice processor, or the frame-buffer memory depending upon the operation. Several microcode programs can be chained together by passing the output of one microroutine to the input of another microroutine. Note, however, that since there in only one processor involved, each microroutine in the chain is executed sequentially.

A typical example of such a chain where several modules are used to generate an image is shown in Fig. 6. In order to display the wire-frame model one needs to execute transformation (modeling and projection), clipping, and scan-conversion algorithms to render the line-drawing. In order to convert the line drawing into a shaded object, the output of the clipper needs to be routed to a z-buffer algorithm which renders the individual polygons. This re-routing of the output can be accomplished in one of two ways. We can either (i) create (compile and link together) a new microcode module that comprises all of these individual operations, or (ii) we can switch microcode modules after the clipping operation and bring in a z-buffer module for rendering. In terms of effort, the first technique requires more system level programming than the second. Typically, we will experiment with the second method and implement the first technique when we are sure of the utility of the function.

Display List Structure

The display list structure is a linear display list (Foley and Van Dam 1982) that is executed by the bit-slice processor. Although the application data structure may be complex, in order to display an image the contents of the application data structure must be transformed into a linear display list. The conversion of the high-level commands from the application program into a set of low-level microcode calls is performed on the host computer. These microcode calls contain the address of the microroutine to be executed and parameters needed for the execution (Fig. 7).

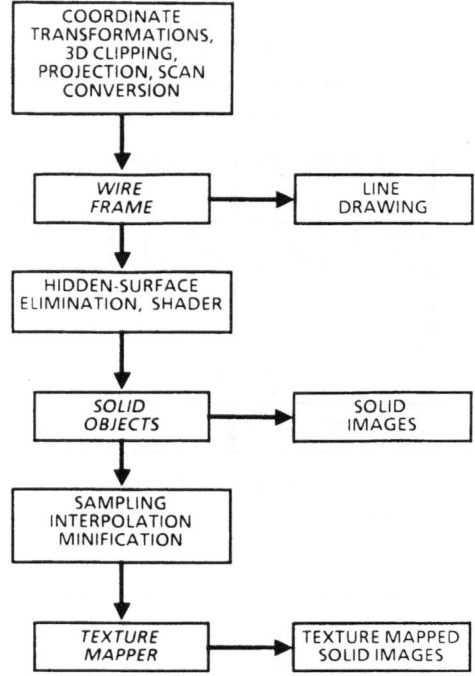

Fig. 6. Three-Dimensional Display Pipeline.

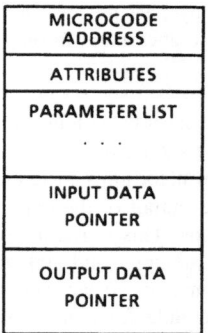

Fig. 7. Display List Structure.

The display list controller is the main program that interprets the display list and jumps to the micro-routine to perform the specified task. The display list controller resides in the microcode memory and waits for a display list packet to be shipped from the host computer. When such a packet arrives, the controller will decode the address of the microroutine and jump to the specified location and begin executing the routine. This routine is then responsible for extracting the parameters and data from the display list structure. This scheme permits an arbitrary number and location of parameters and data for the microcode routine (Fig. 8).

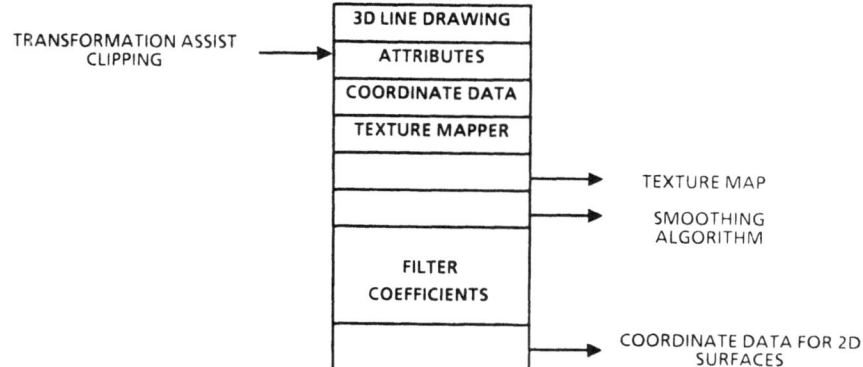

Fig. 8. Intermixed Image Synthesis and Analysis Display List Structure.

The general display list structure allows us to intermix synthesis and analysis programs. A typical example where such intermixed operation is a necessity is shown in Fig. 9 where a section of the 3D seismic cube has been enhanced so that the user can track a feature in more detail. The feature being tracked is shown as a red line superimposed on the imagery.

Graphical And Image Viewports

Although considerable effort has been made in the past to map text and 2D graphics into viewports, relatively little progress has been made in combining 3D graphics with image data in a viewport. In our implementation the concept of a window, which maps part of a 3D object space within a viewport, scales both image data and 3D coordinate data in a consistent manner. Thus, when a large image is to be displayed onto a small area on the screen, the image is scaled (resampled) to fit the viewport. This allow the user to map features delineated from a slice of the 3D data volume into a 3D display at the same scale.

Other attributes of a viewport remain consistent with both image and coordinate data. For example, a color map associated with different viewports will apply to both types of data. Multiple graphical and image viewports can co-exist on the same display screen. The contents of the graphical viewports can be dynamically updated to provide real-time rotation, scaling and translation. Fig. 10 exemplifies several possible viewport attributes: image data, graphical data, with individual lookup tables. Fig. 11 shows several image processing viewports including scaling, histogram equalization, edge enhancement, power spectrum, and a 3D graphical viewport displaying a plot of the power spectrum.

EXAMPLE

In this section we describe an example utilizing many of the system capabilities described. This example is an illustration of how such a system is used in interpreting 3D seismic data. The concepts and techniques presented are, however, equally applicable to any 3D array data set.

The science of interpretation for oil exploration is a rapidly changing domain. Interpreters apply past experience, physical principles, and supplemental information (such as geological and geophysical data) to predict the empirical relations between the measurements and the geological environment. We

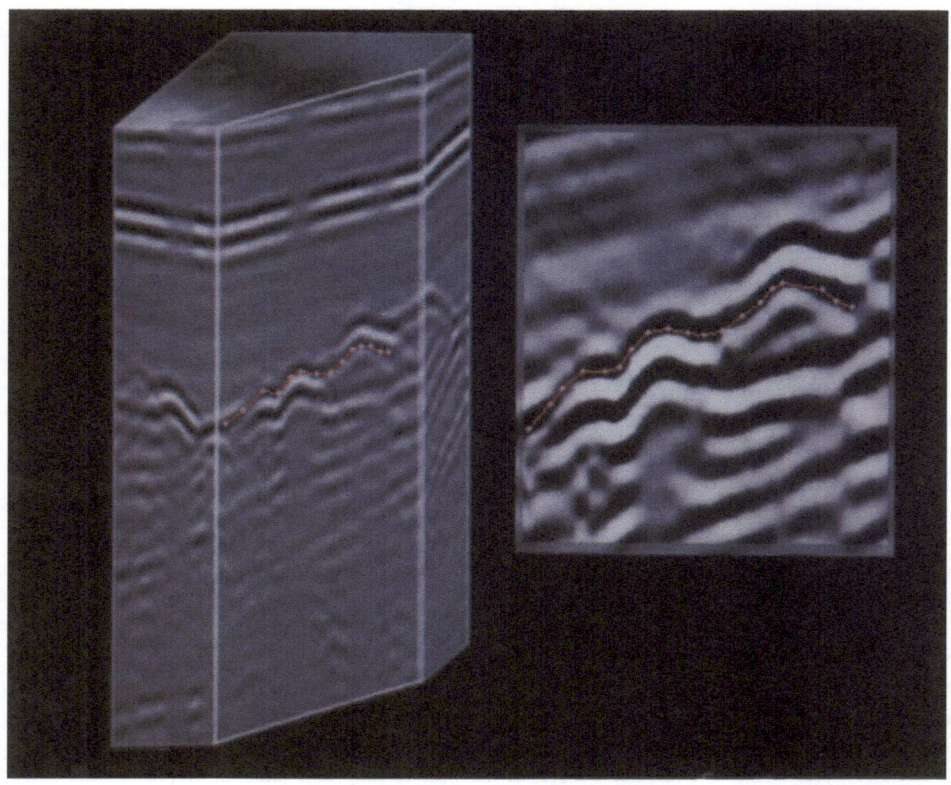

Fig. 9. Image Enhancement for Feature Tracking.

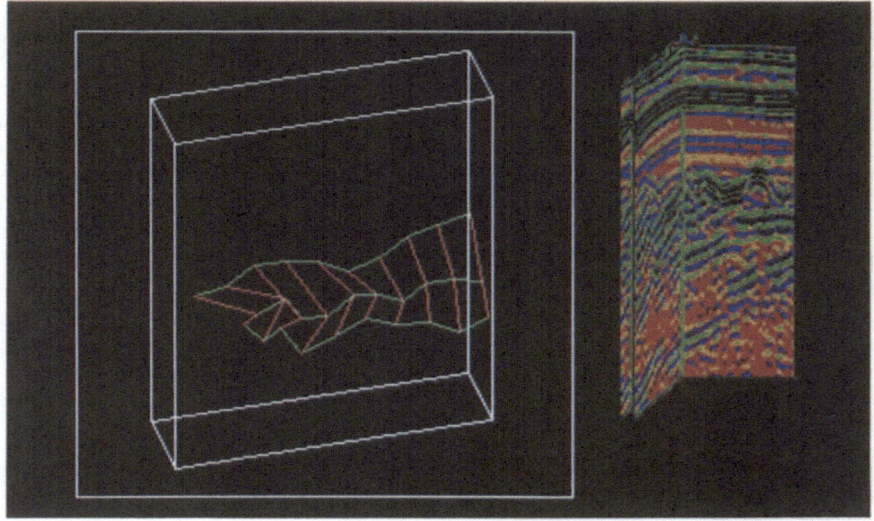

Fig. 10. Simultaneous Image and Graphical Viewports for Surface Reconstruction.

Fig. 11. Image Processing Viewports.

describe here some of the steps of geophysical interpretation using the 3D seismic data shown in Fig. 1. The goal is to isolate surfaces and potential traps that indicate the presence of formations which may be oil bearing.

To obtain a spatial description of the major structures, it is best to begin with a LINE cross-section (X-axis) where features of interest (horizon lines indicating a reflecting surface) can be delineated easily. Then, this horizon is tracked across the survey to determine its extent and shape. In tracking the horizon, more confidence is placed on those features that are visible across several seismic slices. At this stage we also identify the main faults.

Next, the features picked from the entire survey need to be correlated making sure that all LINE (X-axis) and CDP (Y-axis) crossections are geometrically consistent. This is a very powerful check on the correctness of the interpretation but often problems occur. It is useful to make a rough schematic map of the main structural features at this stage. In Fig. 12 and Fig. 13 the LINE and CDP seismic sections used for picking horizons are illustrated. The black lines represent the intersection of the two slices along the LINE and CDP axis. Fig. 14 shows the horizon surface formed from the picked horizons.

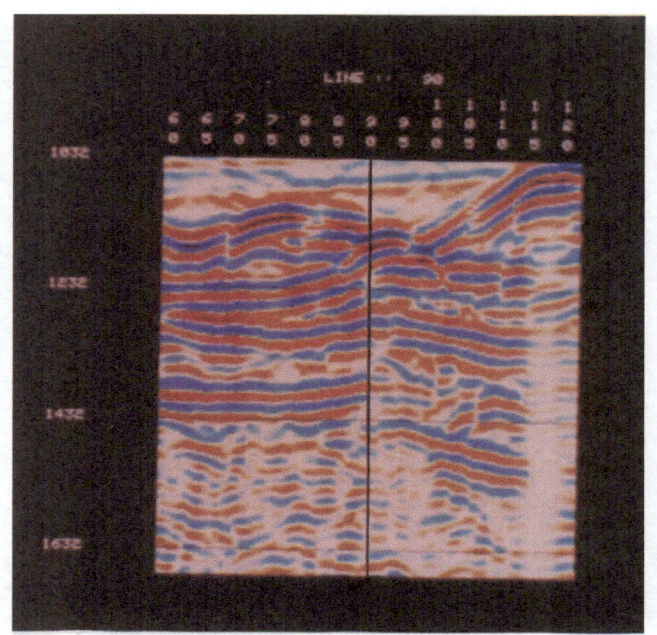

Fig. 12. Line Section 90 Of Seismic Cube.

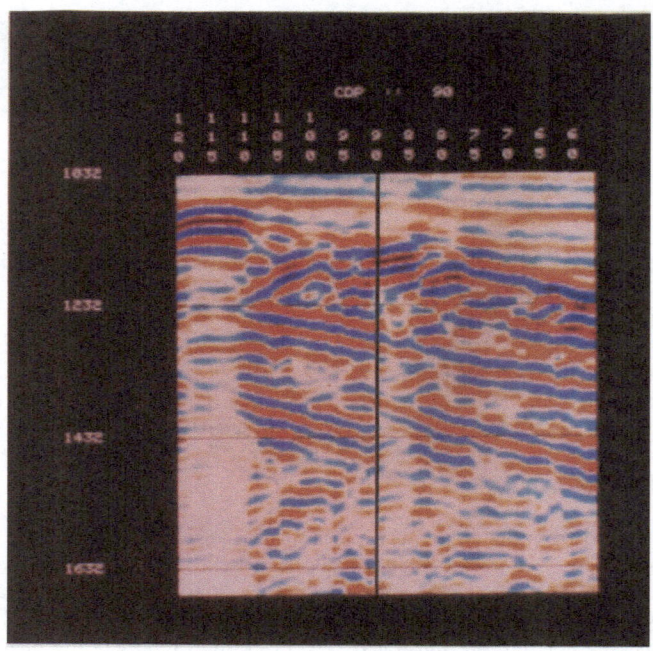

Fig. 13. CDP Section 90 Of Seismic Cube.

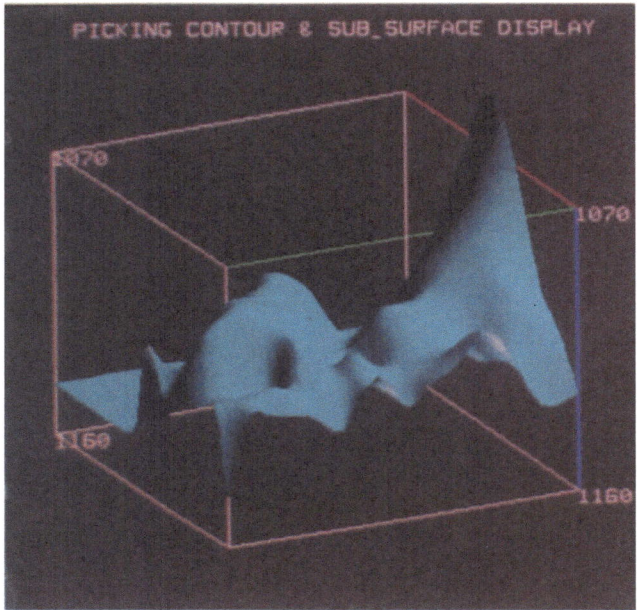

Fig. 14. Reconstructed Horizon Surface picked from LINES 58-121, CDPs 58-121, and Times 1032-1670 ms.

The next stage is to produce a contour surface of two-way-time (a slice along the third axis is time) for each horizon that was picked by the interpreter. Before contouring the values it is useful to mark all the faults on the map and decide how to connect them together, making sure that faults on maps of different horizons are coincident.

Given two-way-time slices for various horizons and the average velocities between the formations, it is in principle simple to multiply the times by the velocities to arrive at depth of the reflecting horizon. This process is repeated for each horizon thus building a geometric model of the sub surface terrain. These depth values can then be posted and contoured in the same way as the two-way-time values. Figure 15 shows the depth contour surface obtained by picking two-way-time slices.

The primary product of a geophysical interpretation of the 3D seismic cube is a series of maps, two-way-time maps, depth contoured maps, and in some cases, isopach maps. Isopachs may be constructed by subtracting the time or depth values to two different horizons at each CDP. They are often useful in assessing the history of sedimentary deposition. In oil prospecting, these maps are then annotated to indicate the presence of prospective highs, or other potential hydrocarbon traps. In mining and engineering investigations, important features such as faults, steep dips, structural axes, pinchouts or interval thickness variation are likely to be the important features which need highlighting on the finally drafted maps.

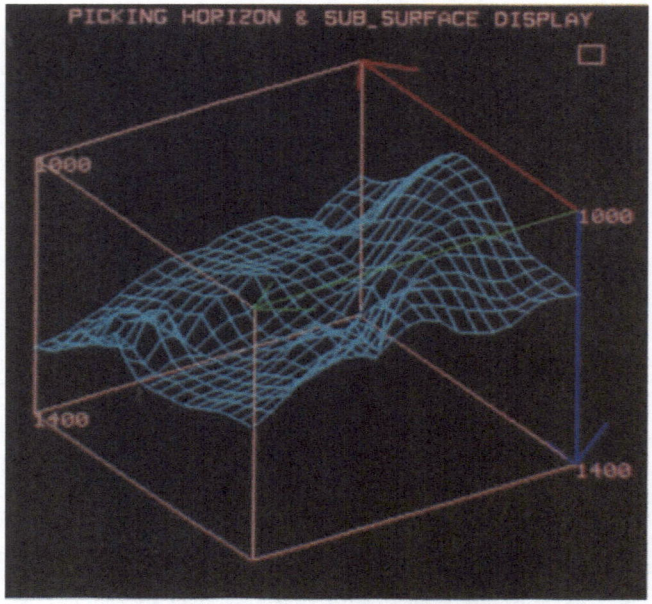

Fig. 15. Contour Surface Formed By Picking Contours From Time-slices 1600-1130ms, Lines 58-121, and CDPs 58-121.

## CONCLUSION

As the acquisition of 3D data arrays become important in many applications, the ability to view, manipulate and enhance this data interactively in a workstation becomes increasingly essential. In this paper we have defined the necessary capabilities for interacting with 3D data arrays and described a system designed to display and manipulate the data in close to real-time.

From a software standpoint we have attempted to develop a system that combines image synthesis and image analysis functions within the same hardware and software framework. By microcoding a set of primitive operations the system is interactive and allows a flexible environment for experimentation. The functionality of this system can be continually enhanced by adding more microroutines as specific tasks in the manipulation of 3D data become well-defined. Several of the obvious functions for manipulating 3D data have been implemented in the system described. It is increasingly clear that even these rudimentary functions provide a very useful set of tools for analyzing and interpreting the 3D data, and that in the future these functions can be enhanced to meet requirements of the user.

ACKNOWLEDGMENT

The Display Processor was implemented at Schlumberger-Doll Research by Ingrid Carlbom, Indranil Chakravarty, Henry Moreton and Baldev Singh. The authors gratefully acknowledge the use of the Display Processor for building the framework described in this paper. The authors would also like to thank Dr. Peter Will, Director, System Science Department, Schlumberger-Doll Research and Mr. Philippe Lacour-Gayet, Director, Reservoir Modeling, Nippon Schlumberger for their support and encouragement during the course of this research.

REFERENCES

Adage (1980) Adage RDS 3000 Users Manual, Adage Inc., Boston, MA.

Atherton PR (1981) "A Method of Interactive Visualization of CAD Surface    Models on a Color Video Display," *Computer Graphics*, 15, 279-287.

Burt PJ (1982) "The Pyramid As A Structure For Efficient Computation", Image    Processing Laboratory Technical Report IPL-TR-038, Rensselaer Polytechnic    Institute, Troy, NY.

Clark JH (1982) "The Geometry Engine: A VLSI Geometry System for Graphics",    *Computer Graphics, 16*, 3, July 1982, 127-133.

Farrell EJ (1983) "Color Display and Interactive Interpretation of 3D Data", *IBM    Journal of Research and Development*, Vol. 27, No. 4, July 1983.

Foley JD and A Van Dam (1982) *Fundamentals of Interactive Computer Graphics*,    Addison-Wesley Publishing Company, Reading, MA.

Goldwasser SM (1984) "A Generalized Object Display Processor Architecture",    *IEEE Computer Graphics and Applications*, Oct. 1984, pp. 43-55.

Icross (1984) "Icross-3000 Programming Reference and Guide", Intermetrics, Inc.,    Cambridge, MA.

Hardas DM, Srihari SN (1984) "Progressive Refinement of 3-D Images Using    Coded Binary Trees: Algorithms and Architecture", *IEEE Transactions On Pattern Analysis and Machine Intelligence*, Vol 6, No. 6, Nov. 1984.

Herman GT, HK Liu (1979) "3D Display of Human Organs from Computer    Tomograms", *Computer Graphics and Image Processing*, Vol. 9, 1-21.

Meagher DJ (1982) "Geometric Modeling Using Octree Encoding", *Computer    Graphics and Image Processing*, No. 19, 129-147.

Meagher DJ (1984) "Interactive Solids Processing for Medical Analysis and Planning", Proceedings of National Computer Graphics Association Conference.

Seismic (1984) SEISMIC 3000 Software Package, Rev 1.4, Adage Inc., Raleigh,    N.C.

Solid (1984) SOLID 3000 Software Package, Rev 1.4, Adage Inc., Raleigh, N.C.

Udupa JK (1982) "Interactive Segmentation and Boundary Surface Formation for    3D Digital Images," *Computer Graphics and Image Processing*, No. 18, 213-235.

**Indranil Chakravarty** is a member of the professional staff at Schlumberger-Doll Research, Ridgefield, Connecticut. His research interests lie in the areas of computer graphics, image processing, and computer architecture.

Prior to joining Schlumberger-Doll Research, Chakravarty was on the staff of the Electrical, Computer and Systems Engineering Department and the Image Processing Laboratory at Rensselaer Polytechnic Institute in Troy, New York.

Chakravarty received his BS in electrical engineering from New York University and the M.Eng and PhD degrees in computer and systems engineering from Rensselaer Polytechnic Institute. He is a member if IEEE, ACM, Sigma Xi and the New York Academy of Sciences. He also serves as the Category Editor for Pattern Recognition and Image Processing for ACM Computing Reviews.

**Bruce Nichol** is an associate member of the professional staff at Schlumberger-Doll Research, Ridgefield, Connecticut. His current research interests are in geometric modeling, computer graphics, and three-dimentional image processing.

Prior to joining Schlumberger-Doll Research, Nichol was a memeber of the Digital Image Analysis Laboratory staff at the University of Massachusetts at Amherst, where he designed software for image processing and acted as a private consultant for the image processing and computer graphics community.

Nichol received his BS degree in Software Engineering from the University of Massachusetts at Amherst. He is currently completing requirements for a MS degree in Computer Science at the Polytechnic University in New York. He is a member of IEEE and ACM, SIGGRAPH.

**Tomoyoshi Ono** is a project leader in Reservoir Modeling Engineering at Nippon Schlumberger KK. His current interests include the technologies of computer graphics and artificial intelligence.

Prior to his current position, Ono was a group leader of Institute of JUSE at Tokyo, where he worked at the Toshiba R&D Center from 1978 to 1982. In this capacity he was involved in the development of parallel processing architectures for Pattern Information Processing Systems, a large scale project sponsored by Agency of Industrial Science and Technology. Ono also has experience in the design of CAD system and graphical workstations.

Ono received a MS in applied mathematics in 1969 from National Tsing-Hua University (Taiwan), and an ME in compter science in 1977 from Yamanashi University (Japan). He is a member of ACM, IEEE, and Computer Graphics Society.

# Applications of the 4×4 Determinant Method and the TRIANGLE PROCESSOR to Various Interference Problems

Fujio Yamaguchi[1], Takaomi Tatemichi[2] and Ryoji Ebisawa[2]

[1] Department of Mechanical Engineering, Waseda University, Nishiohkubo, Shinjuku-ku, Tokyo, 160 Japan

[2] SEIKO Instruments and Electronics Co., Akanehama, Narashino, Chiba, 275 Japan

Abstract

In the beginning the paper reviews the 4×4 determinant method and the TRIANGLE PROCESSOR proposed by one of the present authors. The 4×4 determinant method makes it possible to unify various types of interference problems by computing some 4×4 determinants. The TRIANGLE PROCESSOR is a hardware processor based on the 4×4 determinant theories, which accelerates the processing speeds of these programs.

The paper reports the experimental results of the TRIANGLE PROCESSOR to four types of interference problems, which include set operations in solid modeling, hidden line elimination, visible surface detection using a ray tracing method and mass property computations.

The results are considered to be very satisfactory.

[Keywords]
Interference problems, Geometric Modeling, Solid Modeling, Hidden Line Elimination, Visible Surface Detections, Mass Property Computations, Computer Aided Design, Graphic Processor, Geometry Engine

## Introduction

One of the present authors has proposed a 4×4 determinant approach to many types of interference problems which include set operations in solid modeling, hidden line elimination, visible surface detec-tion, ray tracing picture generation, mass property computations and so on[1]. He showed that many types of basic geometric processing, such as classification tests, triangulations, intersections, containment tests, depth priority tests and so on, can be performed by computing some 4×4 determinants. Furthermore he proposed a hardware processor (TRIANGLE PROCESSOR) based on the 4×4 determinant theories[1],[2],which accelerates the processing speeds of these programs.

In this paper we, first of all, review the 4×4 determinant method and the TRIANGLE PROCESSOR and then report the trial TRIANGLE PROCESSOR and some results of its applications to set operations in solid modeling, hidden line elimination, visible surface detection by a ray tracing method and mass property computations. The results are considered to be very satisfactory. It is expected that the TRIANGLE PROCESSOR will be implemented in very large -scale integrated hardware and will play important roles in various applications of computer graphics and geometric modeling.

# A Review of the 4×4 Determinant Method and the TRIANGLE PROCESSOR[1],[2]

Let us constitute a 4×4 determinant by using four points in homogeneous coordinates. Let us represent a point $V_A$ as $(X_A, Y_A, Z_A, w_A) \equiv (w_A X_A, w_A Y_A, w_A Z_A, w_A)$ and three vertices of a triangle as $V_0 (X_0, Y_0, Z_0, w_0) \equiv (w_0 X_0, w_0 Y_0, w_0 Z_0, w_0)$, $V_1 (X_1, Y_1, Z_1, w_1) \equiv (w_1 x_1, w_1 y_1, w_1 z_1, w_1)$, $V_2 (X_2, Y_2, Z_2, w_2) \equiv (w_2 x_2, w_2 y_2, w_2 z_2, w_2)$ in a counterclockwise order, seen from the exterior side of the triangle (Fig.1). We denote a 4×4 determinant constituted by these four points in homogeneous coordinates by $S_{A012}$ as shown in (1). That is,

$$S_{A012} \equiv \begin{vmatrix} X_A & Y_A & Z_A & w_A \\ X_0 & Y_0 & Z_0 & w_0 \\ X_1 & Y_1 & Z_1 & w_1 \\ X_2 & Y_2 & Z_2 & w_2 \end{vmatrix} \qquad (1)$$

$$= X_A \cdot N_x + Y_A \cdot N_y + Z_A \cdot N_z - w_A \cdot D \qquad (2)$$

$$= w_A \cdot \{(x_A - x_P) \cdot N_x + (y_A - y_P) \cdot N_y + (z_A - z_P) \cdot N_z\} \qquad (3)$$

where $x_P$, $y_P$, $z_P$ represent ordinary coordinates of a point on the triangle plane.

$$N_x = \begin{vmatrix} Y_0 & Z_0 & w_0 \\ Y_1 & Z_1 & w_1 \\ Y_2 & Z_2 & w_2 \end{vmatrix} \quad N_y = \begin{vmatrix} Z_0 & X_0 & w_0 \\ Z_1 & X_1 & w_1 \\ Z_2 & X_2 & w_2 \end{vmatrix} \quad N_z = \begin{vmatrix} X_0 & Y_0 & w_0 \\ X_1 & Y_1 & w_1 \\ X_2 & Y_2 & w_2 \end{vmatrix} \quad D = \begin{vmatrix} X_0 & Y_0 & Z_0 \\ X_1 & Y_1 & Z_1 \\ X_2 & Y_2 & Z_2 \end{vmatrix} \quad (4)$$

$$V_A (X_A, Y_A, Z_A, w_A)$$

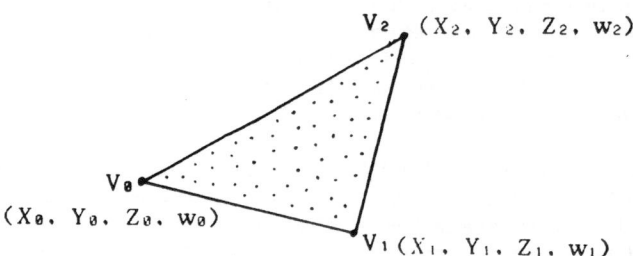

Fig.1  A Point and a Triangle in Homogeneous Coordinates

$[N_x \ N_y \ N_z]$ is a normal vector of the triangle $V_\theta - V_1 - V_2$. $S_{A\theta12}$ represents a signed volume of a parallelpiped and is expressed as follows(Fig.2).

$$S_{A\theta12} = H_{A\theta12} \cdot B_{\theta12} \qquad (5)$$

where $H_{A\theta12}$ and $B_{\theta12}$ are the scaled height and scaled base area respectively and expressed in the following.

$$H_{A\theta12} = k_h \cdot h_{A\theta12}, \quad B_{\theta12} = k_b \cdot b_{\theta12} \qquad (6)$$

where $k_h$ and $k_b$ are scale factors for the height $h_{A\theta12}$ and for the base area $b_{\theta12}$. Fig.2 shows a case where all the $V_A$, $V_\theta$, $V_1$ and $V_2$ are finite points (that is, $w_A, w_\theta$, $w_1, w_2 \neq 0$). In this case $h_{A\theta12}$ is the perpendicular distance from $V_A$ to the triangle $V_\theta - V_1 - V_2$ and $b_{\theta12}$ is the area of a parallelogram made by $V_\theta$, $V_1$, $V_2$ and $k_h = w_A$, $k_b = w_\theta w_1 w_2$. As for $h_{A\theta12}$ and $b_{\theta12}$ in the other cases, refer to Yamaguchi[2].

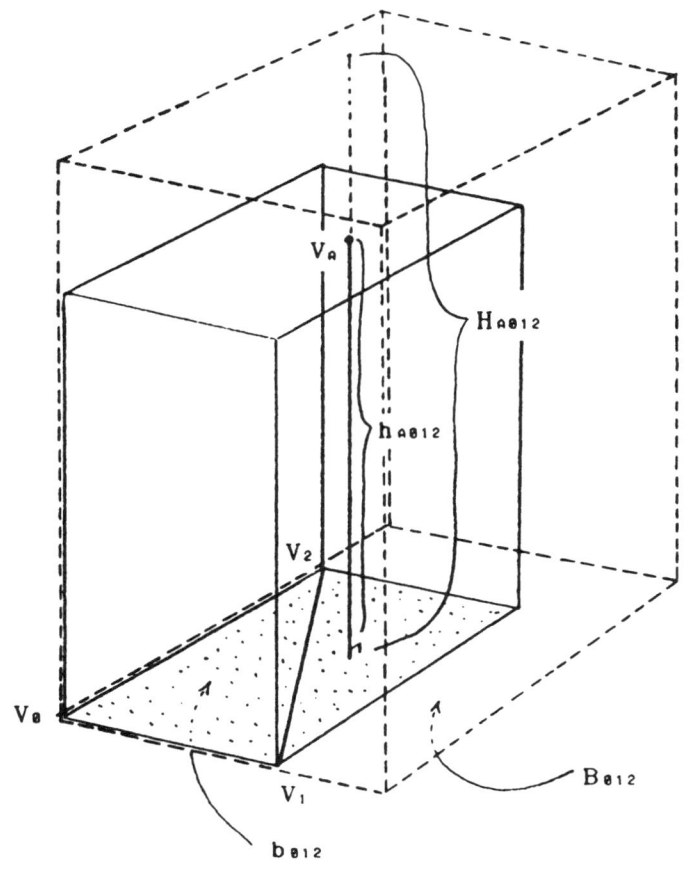

Fig.2 Geometric Implications of the 4×4 Determinant

(All the $V_A$, $V_\theta$, $V_1$ and $V_2$ are finite points)

Formerly we had used $S_{A012}$ in processing various types of interference problems. Recently we have used $H_{A012}$ in place of $S_{A012}$. $H_{A012}$ can be handled more easily than $S_{A012}$ because $H_{A012}$ has length dimension while $S_{A012}$ has volume dimension.
In computing $H_{A012}$, $B_{012}$ is calculated first and then $H_{A012}$ is derived by dividing $S_{A012}$ by $B_{012}$. We call this division normalization of the $4 \times 4$ determinant.

The following two properties of $H_{A012}$ are utilized in the $4 \times 4$ determinant method.
①The sign of $H_{A012}$ determines the half space in which $V_A$ exists with respect to the triangle $V_0 - V_1 - V_2$ plane.
That is,
- $[ (\text{Sign}(k_h) = \text{Sign}(k_b)) \cap (H_{A012} > 0) ]$
  $\cup [ (\text{Sign}(k_h) \neq \text{Sign}(k_b)) \cap (H_{A012} < 0) ]$

    $V_A$ exists in the exterior half space of the triangle.

- $H_{A012} = 0$

    $V_A$ exists on the triangle plane.

- $[ (\text{Sign}(k_h) \neq \text{Sign}(k_b)) \cap (H_{A012} > 0) ]$
  $\cup [ (\text{Sign}(k_h) = \text{Sign}(k_b)) \cap (H_{A012} < 0) ]$

    $V_A$ exists in the interior half space of the triangle.

②The absolute value of $H_{A012}$ is proportional to the perpendicular distance from $V_A$ to the triangle $V_0 - V_1 - V_2$ plane.
In computing an intersection point, the following formula holds between a line segment $V_A - V_B$ and a triangle $V_0 - V_1 - V_2$. Suppose $V_A$, $V_B$, $V_0$, $V_1$ and $V_2$ are represented in homogeneous coordinates. The intersection point $P = (X, Y, Z, w)$ is given in the following.

$$P = V_A + \frac{H_{A012}}{H_{A012} - H_{B012}} \cdot (V_B - V_A) \qquad (7)$$

The ordinary coordinates $(x, y, z)$ are obtained by $x = X/w$, $y = Y/w$, $z = Z/w$.

By making use of these two properties, we can perform various types of geometric processing such as vertex and edge classification tests, triangulations, intersections, containment tests, depth priority tests.

Based on the $4 \times 4$ determinant theories the TRIANGLE PROCESSOR performs one of the followings, according to the "K" number specified.

- (k=0): Intersection test of two triangles $V_0 - V_1 - V_2$ and $V_A - V_B - V_C$ (general)

- (K=1): Intersection test of two triangles $V_0 - V_1 - V_2$ and $V_A - V_B - V_C$ not on a plane

- (K=2): Intersection test of two triangles $V_0 - V_1 - V_2$ and $V_A - V_B - V_C$ on a plane

- (K=3): Intersection test of a triangle $V_0 - V_1 - V_2$ with a line segment $V_A - V_B$ (general)

- (K=4): Intersection test of a triangle $V_0 - V_1 - V_2$ with a line segment $V_A - V_B$ not on the triangle plane

•(K=5):Intersection test of a triangle $V_0 - V_1 - V_2$ with a line segment $V_A - V_B$ on the triangle plane

•(K=6):Intersection test of two line segments, $V_0 - V_1$ and $V_A - V_B$

•(K=7):Containment test of a point $V_A$ in a triangle $V_0 - V_1 - V_2$

•(K=8):Side test (half space test) of a point $V_A$ with respect to a triangle $V_0 - V_1 - V_2$

The outputs of the above tests,i.e.,intersection status,intersection coordinates and characteristic values about input data are recorded IST,COT and CVT tables respectively.

## The TRIANGLE PROCESSOR

### System Configuration

AS shown in Fig.3,the TRIANGLE PROCESSOR is composed of assembly programs executed on the PC 9801F personal computer and a special purpose hardware unit.

(1)PC 9801F:a 16 bit personal computer (Nippon Electric Co.) working with the TRIANGLE PRO-CESSOR in MS-DOS environment.
(2)APPLICATION PROGRAMS:higher level programs utilizing the TRIANGLE PROCESSOR
(3)PASCAL INTERFACE:interface program between application programs and the TRIANGLE PRO-CESSOR
(4)Main Processor:assembly language program performing main processing other than numerical computa tions.
(5)DRIVER PROGRAM:interface program with TP ARITH MODULE
(6)TP ARITH MODULE:microprogrammed processor performing numerical computations of $4\times4$ determinants,normal vectors and intersection points.

### TP ARITH MODULE

The hardware configuration is shown in Fig.4.
(1)MICRO PROGRAM:this includes RAM,pipeline registers,sequencer and diagnostic processor
(2)IFIFO:32 bit,16 stage FIFO for receiving command from main processor
(3)OFIFO:32 bit,16 stage FIFO for outputting computational results to main processor
(4)REG FILE:32 bit,256 word register file(3 operands can be specified)
(5)FMUL:pipelined,32 bit floating point multiplier(5MFLOPS)
(6)FALU:pipelined,32 bit floating point adder and subtracter(5MFLOPS)
(7)ALU:32 bit integer operation ALU for address computation
(8)ADR REG:address register for RAM and LUT
(9)RAM:memory for input data and computation results
(10)LUT:memory for 1/X,1/SQRT(X)

### Various Data

(1)PC 9801F
    CPU(i8086)・・・・・・・・・・・・・・・・・・・・・・・・8 MHz
    FPP(i8087)・・・・・・・・・・・・・・・・・・・・・・・・8 MHz
    PASCAL INTERFACE+MAIN PROCESSOR・・・Approx. 10 Kbytes
    DRIVER PROGRAM・・・・・・・・・・・・・・・・・・・・Approx. 400 bytes
    OPERATING SYSTEM・・・・・・・・・・・・・・・・・・MS-DOS

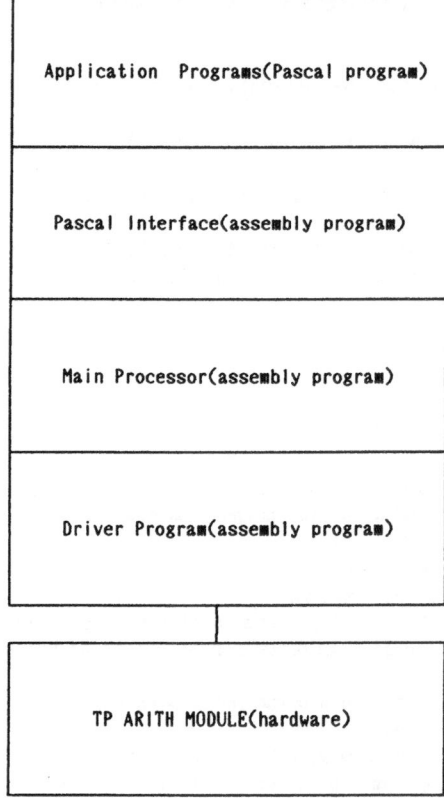

Fig.3  The System Configuration of the TRIANGLE PROCESSOR

(2)TP ARITH MODULE
     MACHINE CYCLE••••••••••••••••••••••2 MHz
     MICROPROGRAM•••••••••••••••••••••••Approx. 800 steps
     REG FILE••••••••••••••••••••••••••72 words
     RAM•••••••••••••••••••••••••••••••256 words

**Results of the Applications of the 4×4 determinant theories and the TRIANGLE PROCESSOR**

We tested the effectiveness of the 4×4 determinant method and the trial TRIANGLE PROCESSOR
by applying them to four types of applications, which are implemented in the CAD/CAM system
FREEDOM. These  applications are  set operations in solid modeling, hidden line elimination
,visible surface detection by a ray tracing method and mass property computations.  Table 1
shows object program size of each application program, which employs the 4×4 determinant
method.  It seems clear that the sizes of the application programs are very  compact  since
the processing method is unified. In the following  we compare the processing times between
with- and without-the TRIANGLE PROCESSOR in the personal  computer  9801F(Nippon Electric Co.
)+8087 environment.

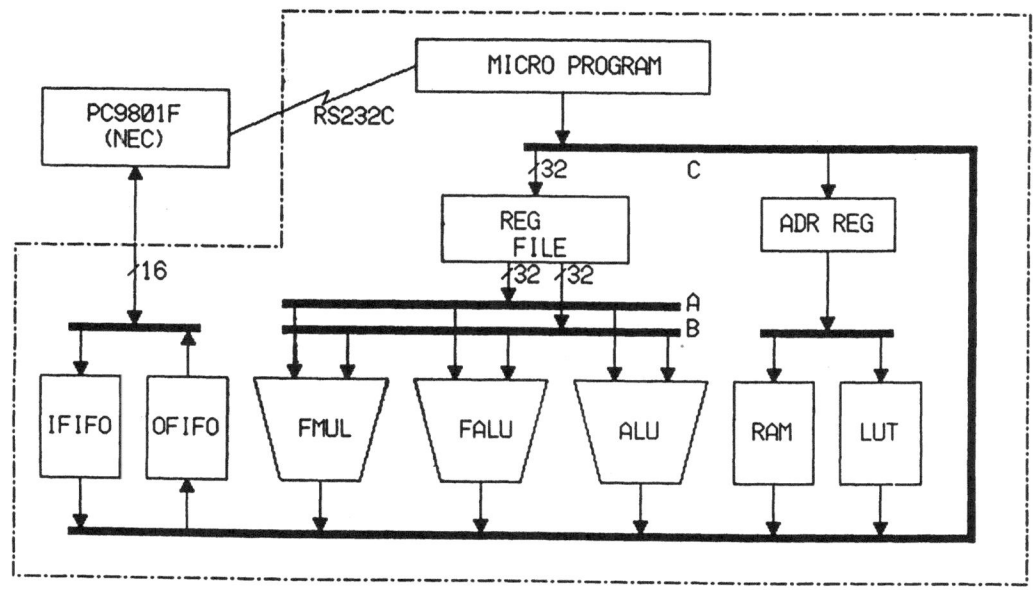

Fig.4  The Hardware Configuration of the TRIANGLE PROCESSOR

Table 1  Object Program Sizes of Application Programs Based on the 4×4 Determinant Method

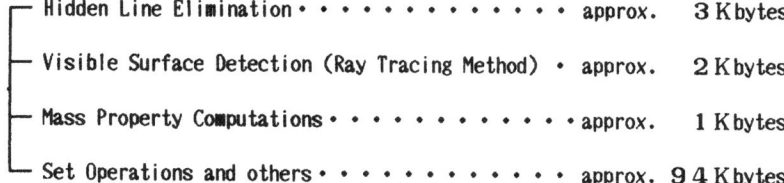

- Hidden Line Elimination · · · · · · · · · · · · · · approx.   3 Kbytes

- Visible Surface Detection (Ray Tracing Method) · approx.   2 Kbytes

- Mass Property Computations · · · · · · · · · · · ·approx.   1 Kbytes

- Set Operations and others · · · · · · · · · · · · approx. 9 4 Kbytes

## Set Operations in Solid Modeling

As for the fundamental algorithm  for set operations using the 4×4 determinant  method,
refer to the author's other articles[3],[4].  In order to facilitate comparison, the shapes
to be operated on were chosen to exactly the same one that were used in Tanaka's experiment
[5].  That is, subtraction operations  were done between  two regular prisms as illustrated
in Fig.5. The results are  shown in Fig.6. From the results the  solid modeler FREEDOM with
the  trial TRIANGLE PROCESSOR can perform the operation five to six times more quickly than
without the TRIANGLE PROCESSOR.   From our measurement, about 85% of  the total processing

time can be processed and shortened by the TRIANGLE PROCESSOR in this example. This number indicates the limit of processing time improvement ratio is about 7 when an ideal TRIANGLE PROCESSOR is used with the PC 9801F computer. We can understand that the trial TRIANGLE PROCESSOR displays its power almost fully in this case. Table 2 shows other experimental data.

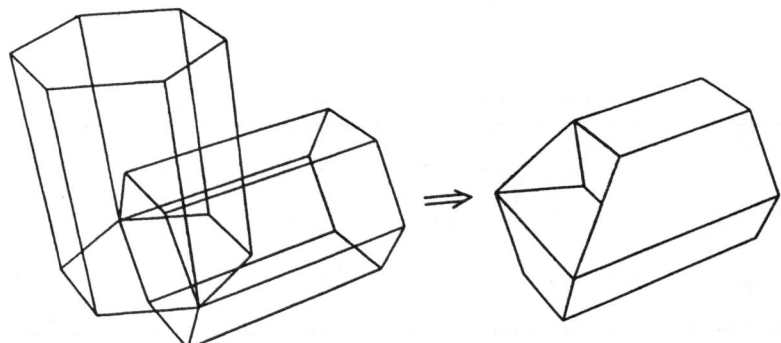

Fig.5    Subtraction Between Two Regular Parallelepipeds

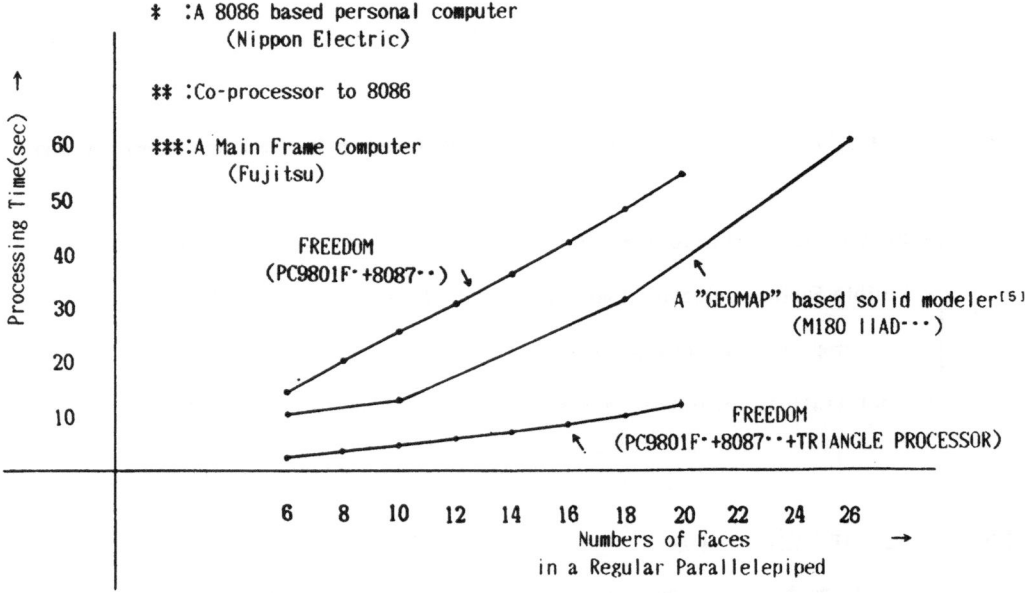

Processing Time versus Number of Faces

Fig.6   An Application of the TRIANGLE PROCESSOR and the 4×4 Determinant Approach to Solid Modeling

Table 2    Numbers of $4 \times 4$ Determinants Computations and
Calls of Types of Processing in the TRIANGLE PROCESSOR

| Numbers of Faces in Prism | Numbers of $4 \times 4$ Determinant Computations | Numbers of Calls of Types in TRIANGLE PROCESSOR | | |
|---|---|---|---|---|
| | | k = 0 | K = 8 | K = 9 |
| 6 | 3,761 | 100 | 81 | 19 |
| 8 | 5,287 | 140 | 107 | 26 |
| 10 | 6,685 | 177 | 133 | 34 |
| 12 | 8,001 | 212 | 159 | 42 |
| 14 | 9,389 | 249 | 185 | 50 |
| 16 | 10,849 | 288 | 211 | 58 |
| 18 | 12,381 | 329 | 237 | 66 |
| 20 | 13,985 | 372 | 263 | 74 |

## Hidden Line Elimination

Prior to processing, all the polygons are triangulated by the TRIANGLE PROCESSOR and each edge is tested against each triangle for occlusion. In this case the algorithm treats the problem as an intersection problem between a line segment and a special tetrahedron (a triangular prism) constituted by the given triangle and a point at infinity in the eye direction. The experimental results concerning the objects illustrated in Fig.7 are shown in Table 3. The improvement ratio of the processing speed gained by the TRIANGLE PROCESSOR is apprroximately four. 89% of the total processing time can be processed by the TRIANGLE PROCESSOR. This means that the improvement ratio could be raised to 9.9 with an ideal TRIANGLE PROCESSOR. In hidden line elimination the types of processing used in the TRIANGLE PROCESSOR are K=3 and K=8. These types perform less $4 \times 4$ determinant computations than K=0 and the times for data transfer and for sign tests influence the improvement ratio.

Table 3    Hidden Line Elimination

| | Numbers of $4 \times 4$ Determinant Computations | Numbers of Calls of Types in TR. PROCESSOR | | Processing Time (sec) | |
|---|---|---|---|---|---|
| | | K = 3 | K = 8 | Software Simulator | TRIANGLE PROCESSOR |
| 1 | 1992 | 298 | 64 | 7.31 | 1.71 |
| 2 | 4226 | 687 | 104 | 15.60 | 3.86 |

## Visible Surface Detection by a Ray Tracing Method

Visible Surface detection was done by using a ray tracing method. The results concerning the objects illustrated in Fig.7 are shown in table 4. The ratio of the improvement of the processing time gained by the TRIANGLE PROCESSOR is approximately five. 95 % of the total processing time can be processed and shortened by the TRIANGLE PROCESSOR. The times for data transfer and for sign tests influence the improvement ratio.

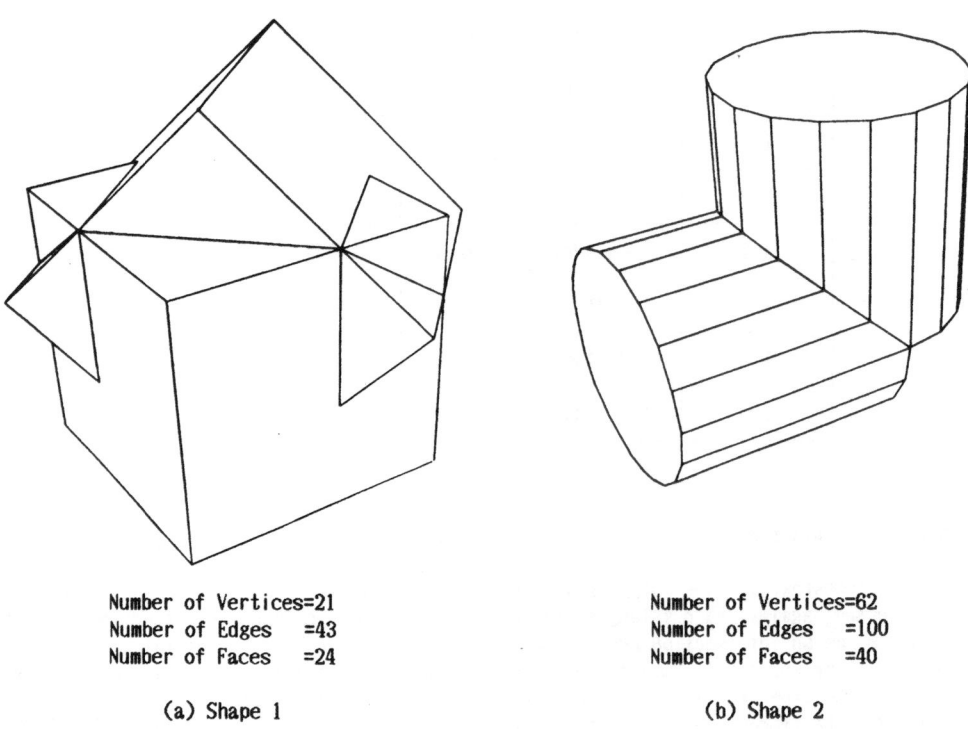

| Number of Vertices=21 | Number of Vertices=62 |
| Number of Edges =43 | Number of Edges =100 |
| Number of Faces =24 | Number of Faces =40 |

    (a) Shape 1          (b) Shape 2

Fig.7 Shapes for the Tests of Hidden Line Elimination,
Visible Surface Detection and Mass Property Computations

Table 4    Visible Surface Detection

|   | Numbers of 4×4 Determinant Computations | Numbers of Calls of Types in TR. PROCESSOR (K=3 only) | Processing Time | |
|---|---|---|---|---|
|   |   |   | Software Simulator | TRIANGLE PROCESSOR |
| 1 | 343,984 | 57,320 | 18min29s | 3min28s |
| 2 | 429,558 | 71,519 | 23min39s | 4min36s |

## Mass Property Computations

According to the method proposed by Lien and Kajiya[6], a polygonal area can be determined by successively taking three vertices and a point at infinity in the outward normal vector and computing 4×4 determinants constructed by the four points. Similarly, the volume and moment of inertia of a polyhedron can be determined by successively taking three vertices and some fixed point and computing 4×4 determinants made by the four points. The results concerning the objects shown in Fig.7 are shown in Table 5. These computations require simple repetition of the K=8 processing in the TRIANGLE PROCESSOR. The programming for mass property computations become extremely simple. The improvement ratio of the processing time gained by using the TRIANGLE PROCESSOR is only 2.5 in this case while the estimated limit of the ratio with an ideal TRIANGLE PROCESSOR is approximately 10. The time for data transfer affects the improvement ratio significantly in this case because the processing type of the TRIANGLE PROCESSOR is only K=8 and the type performs only one 4×4 determinant computation while it requires as many as 16 32-bit data transfer.

Table 5    Mass Property Computations

| | Numbers of 4×4 Determinant Computations | Processing Time(area or volume) | |
|---|---|---|---|
| | | Software Simulater | TRIANGLE PROCESSOR |
| Shape 1 | 38 | 0. 24sec | 0. 09sec |
| Shape 2 | 120 | 0. 74sec | 0. 28sec |

## Conclusions

We list up some advantages gained by the 4×4 determinant approach and the TRIANGLE PROCESSOR to interference problems.

(1) Unified processing is made possible to various types of interference problems, where we mean by "unified" triangle processing in a broad sense, 4×4 determinant computations and use of the TRIANGLE PROCESSOR.

(2) Algorithms become simplified to many applications because face geometry is confined to a triangle in a broad sense.

(3) Algorithms are speeded up in many applications if the TRIANGLE PROCESSOR is used. Almost all of geometric processing can be done in 4×4 determinant forms and accordingly dealt with by the TRIANGLE PROCESSOR. Many multiplications in computing a 4×4 determinant computation could be done in a parallel way and furthermore some determinants relevant to some processing could also be computed in a parallel way. If the TRIANGLE PROCESSOR is implemented in very large-scale integrated hardware a number of the TRIANGLE PROCESSORs could be used to accelerate processing speed in some applications such as ray-tracing picture generation.

(4) There are a number of routines common to many applications because the processing method is unified.

(5) Processing can be done in homogeneous coordinates from the very beginning of modeling operations to the very last of displaying process, because the intersection formula is valid in homogeneous coordinates.

（6）Anomalous cases such as  a very small triangle  or very narrow  triangle can also  be handled just in the same way as in ordinary cases.

（7）Precise processing can be performed by manipulating the scale factors $w_b$ and $w_h$.

（8）Axis independent processing can be done.

（9）Geometric processing can be separated from other types of processing.

From the experiments we have done on  such applications as set operations in solid modeling , hidden line elimination,ray tracing picture generation and mass property computations, it has become more and more clear that various types of interference problems can be processed in a unified way by employing the 4×4 determinant approach and quickly by using the TRIAN-GLE PROCESSOR.  We would like to investigate to extend the applicability of the 4×4 determinant approach and  the TRIANGLE PROCESSOR  to other interference  problems  such as  more general ray tracing problem, robotics interference problems, clipping and  so on, which  we have not experienced.

As for the TRIANGLE PROCESSOR, there are  some problems to be solved. First, data transfer takes considerable  time in some applications.   More tight  integration of the  TRIANGLE PROCESSOR with the computer is desired  than the present  programmed I/O method.  Secondly , there are  many sign  tests performed by  assembly routines  of the 9801F  personal comp-uter.  This time  is  also desired  to  be processed and shortened in hardware. Thirdly, the TRIANGLE PROCESSOR is implemented on a 300mm×450mm board. This size is a little too large.

The authors expect  that in the future large-scale integrated TRIANGLE PROCESSORs will play important roles as basic elements in various geometric processing.


## References

[1]Yamaguchi,Fujio(1985) A  Unified  Approach  to Interference  Problems  Using a  Triangle Processor,SIGGRAPH'85  Conference    Proceedings,Vol.19,No.3

[2]Yamaguchi,Fujio(1986) Theoretical  Foundations  for the 4×4  Determinant  Approach  in Computer Graphics and Geometric Modeling,Submitted to SIGGRAPH'86 for presentation.

[3]Yamaguchi,Fujio & Toshiya Tokieda(1984) A Unified Algorithm for Boolean Shape Operations IEEE Computer Graphics and Applications,Vol.4,No.6

[4]Yamaguchi,Fujio & Toshiya Tokieda(1985) A Solid Modeler with a 4×4 Determinant Process-or,IEEE Computer Graphics and Applications,Vol.5,No.4

[5]Fujii,Tanaka & et al.(1983) Development of  a Solid  Modeling  CAD System, Symposium  on GRAPHICS and CAD, Information Processing Society of Japan

[6]Sheue-ling Lien and James T. Kajiya(1984) A Symbolic Method for Calculating the Integral Properties of Arbitrary Nonconvex Polyhedra,IEEE Computer Graphics and Applications,Vol.4, No.10

**Fujio Yamaguchi** is now an professor with the department of Mechanical Engineering at Waseda University, Tokyo, Japan. Between 1952 and 1961 he was with the department of industrial design at Kyushu Institute of Design. From 1978 to 1979, he was a visiting associate professor at the computer science, University of Utah, and taught computer graphics there. His research interests include computer graphics and geometric modeling.

Yamaguchi received the degree of the doctor of engineering from Waseda University. He is a member of the Japan Society of Mechnical Engineers, the Japan Society of Precision Engineering and Information Processing Society of Japan.

Chapter 7

# Mechanical and General Purpose CAD/CAM

# On Design of a Robot with Three Legs by Computer Graphics

Takanori Sumi[1], Yooichiro Ban[2] and Hiroshi Mieno[2]

[1] Technology Center, ANRITSU Corporation, Onna, Atsugi, Kanagawa, 243 Japan
[2] Faculty of Science and Engineering, Science University of Tokyo, Yamazaki, Noda, Chiba, 278 Japan

ABSTRACT

A three-legged robot is proposed here in this paper, and the motion of the robot is simulated on a color CRT screen by computer graphics. A structural model of the robot in a computer is presented in a form of a diagram. Some modules in the robot's model has been implemented and demonstrated by graphical simulation. In addition, a few problems on an advanced robot are discussed and an idea for the future robot is suggested.

## 1. A ROBOT WITH THREE LEGS

Two legs are enough for a human being to keep balance of his body and to move himself around. This is because he has a sophisticated neuron system which collects the information from many sensors in the body, processes them, and controls verious parts of the body to let him take actions.

In this paper, we concentrate our interest in an advanced robot which is capable of doing something in a catastrophical situation, e.g., fire or radioactive hazards, where no one can work or keep himself stay even for a short time. Then question arises: How many legs are necessary for this kind of robot? To answer this question, the following requirements are satisfied for concerning the robot's legs.

First of all, the robot must be stable during his work at the site. Second, he has to move and to change his location, although the ground of his active area is not always expected to be as flat as a drive way. Usually there must be a number of obstacles, such as rocks, broken furniture and so on, scattered on the ground of the site. So the robot has to be able to move from one location to another avoiding these obstacles. Third, the ground itself could be on the tilt. Fourth, there could be some door-way which is so narrow that the robot has difficulty of passing through. Therefore, the type of robots which we concern here should have some flexibility of moving himself around the disastrous area.

As the legs (moving devices) for the advanced robot of this type, wheels or caterpillars are not feasible, partly because these moving devices are not so flexible in such a strict condition, and partly because the robot need not move fast. Two legs are not enough for the robot to keep himself in balance because his body is not stable in the direction which is perpendicular to the line through apexes of two legs. So each leg must not touch the ground at a point, but through at least three points or with a plane like a foot of a man. In this case, however, a strong pibotting joint like an ankle of human legs has to be built in the legs, and to be sensitively controlled with many sensors to keep balance of the body. This mechanism becomes very complicated and expensive to keep them stand. So two legs are not enough for the advanced robot.

It is obvious that too many legs are disadvantageous for the flexibility of the robot and for its economy. Apexes of three legs makes a triangle plane which gives the stability to the body of the robot as far as the center of gravity of its body stays inside the triangle. Therefore, the number of legs which is necessary and sufficient for the advanced robot should be three.


## 2. GRAPHICAL SIMULATION


Computer graphics system is able to give us an opportunity to trace the motion of the robot and to analyze its behavior by computer simulation. Therefore, experiments are accomplished on the computer's CRT screen prior to constructing the robot in hardware. In order to design the robot, this becomes a very useful tool to estimate how its features work.

Figure 1 shows the robot with three legs discussed here, which is displayed on a color CRT by a computer graphics system. A view from the top is also shown in Fig. 2 in which a black dot indicates the center of gravity of the robot. The robot is said to be stable as far as the black dot stays inside a triangle which is formed by the apexes of its three feet. Thus the black dot indicates stability of the robot as it is taking actions.

A block diagram, which shows how a real robot machine functions as a system, is shown in Fig. 3. The robot machine itself is shown by block 1, which is able to take actions by commands. Block 2 indicates a pattern recognition sensor which inputs a scene through a camera and processes the image of the scene. An object in the scenery might be picked up from the input image, for instance, and the sensor could measure the distance of the object from the robot. Block 3 is an artificial intelligence which analyzes the information from the sensor of block 2, and makes a decision how the robot should react or respond to the object. Block 4 is a command generator which interprets the action of the robot into a sequence of commands which determines the movement of the robot's mechanical parts.

A model of the robot in computer graphics is a creature who lives inside a computer's world, and emerges in front of us only through its CRT screen. In this case, a way of talking to the computer model is realized through its keyboard. There are several commands which controlles actions of the robot. When commands are input to the system through the keyboard, the robot on the CRT screen behaves just like a real robot by a simulation software in which robot's behavioral commands are predefined.

A block diagram of Fig. 4 explains the model of the robot in computer graphics system. Block 3 and 4 are the same as those in Fig. 3, respectively. When the command generator of block 4 issues a command for the robot to take a certain action, a simulation software I of block 5 interprets the command into a sequence of graphic commands. In block 5, the robot then changes its shape and position in the graphic display of block 1. The effect of the robot's action is calculated in a simulation software II of block 2, and data obtained in block 2 is sent to block 3 as information from the sensor of the robot. This simulation is very useful not only for a hardware design of robots but also for its software design.

At present we have implemented the command generator (block 4) and the simulation software I (block 5) on the personal computer, i.e. NEC's 9801. In order to simplify the three dimensional graphic simulation, the wire frame modeling was employed instead of the solid modeling, because the solid modeling is extremely time consuming for its calculation. Even though the center of gravity of the robot cannot be calculated accurately without the solid modeling, the wire frame modeling is suitable for the personal computer as far as interactivity of the system is concerned.


## 3. A VISION SENSOR FOR AN ADVANCED ROBOT


Advanced features are required for a robot's eye, so called "vision sensor", which should include pattern recognition. Since a scenery from the robot's eye changes as the robot moves, the vision sensor must analyze the dynamical change of input images and process them in real time. In order to realize this vision sensor, there are many problems to be solved.

One of the problems is dynamical analysis of changing scenery. This makes the vision sensor different from a traditional static image processor. If the vision sensor finds a moving object in its eye, it has to be able to distinguish which one is moving, the object or the robot itself. The sensor must also recognize whether the object is approaching or moving away from the robot, and estimate how fast it moves. Suppose there is an object which changes its shape as time goes. There is another problem arising. It is quite difficult for the sensor to determine whether a shapeless object like liquid is leaking or a solid object collapsing. These analyses have to be done within a short time, because the system needs additional time to make a decision what counter-action should be taken to this situation. Therefore, the vision sensor itself must have pre-processing mechanism of the input image. This is an significant problem to be solved in the near future.

It is also required for the advanced robot to make scene analysis. A two-dimensional floor map in a building is given to the robot in advance, and is stored in a knowledge base of artificial intelligence of the system. However, if the robot is standing in a corridor inside the building, for example, he can only see a view of the three dimensional world in stead of a two-dimensional floor map. There are walls standing around, ceilings at a top, and another corridor across its path. Thus the system must translate three-dimensional view into the two-dimensional floor map. Then it becomes possible that the translated floor map due to a robot's input image is compared to the map in the knowledge base, and that the system is able to identify its own location on the building's floor map.

As the simulation software II (block 2) in Fig. 4, a simplified model of scene analysis has been tested in a primitive way as follows: A simple floor map of a T-shaped corridor and photo image at its cross point are given in the first place. The photo image is characterized by a set of line segments of its contrast edge. As the robot moves, then the number of segments and the angles between them are expected to change continuously. So a few monitoring points from a starting point to the cross point are selected, and scenes at these points are given to the system. Then the simulation software II compares an input image to the expected one at the goal, i.e., the cross point.

Accepting an image of a world which a robot is paying attention to, he understands the world only from his point of view. This robot may be called 'a first person robot'. Then one can imagine another kind of robots which processes an input image and objectively recognizes the surroundings including the robot himself. 'A third person robot' is the one of this kind. So the robot is able to consider himself as one of the objects. Moreover, the other kind of robot can be conceivable, that is to say, 'a second person robot', which realizes the situation from a second personal point of view. For instance, consider a rescue robot which goes into the scene of a fire and takes one of the wounded from a flaming house. Under these circumstances, this robot is expected to think of the wounded person and to treat him as if the robot were the wounded person himself.

## 4. SUMMARY

The three-legged robot proposed here has been studied and simulated by computer graphics. For the advanced robot, its functional and economical conditions are fullfilled by features of three legs. The model of the robot system in computer graphics has been also investigated. Two software modules has been implemented: one is displaying the robot on the CRT screen, and the other for a part of the sensor of scene analysis.

The vision sensor which includes pattern recognition has serious problems to be solved, while more advanced functions are expected for it. Artificial intelligence seems to be one of the promising solusions which we do not discuss here in this paper. We leave a detailed discussion about this for another opportunity.

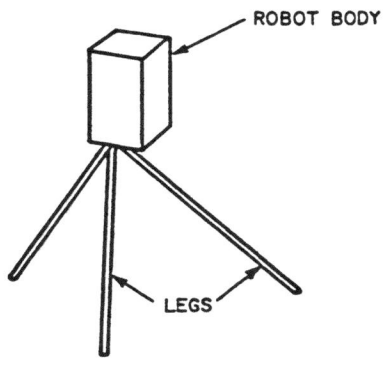

Figure 1

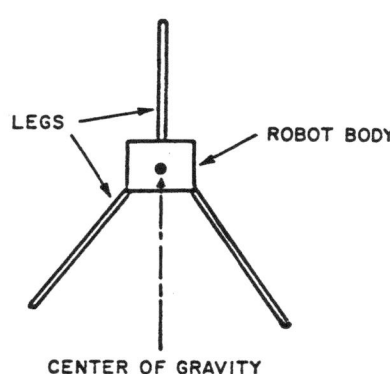

Figure 2

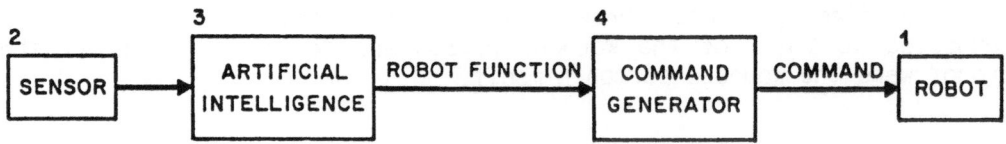

Figure 3

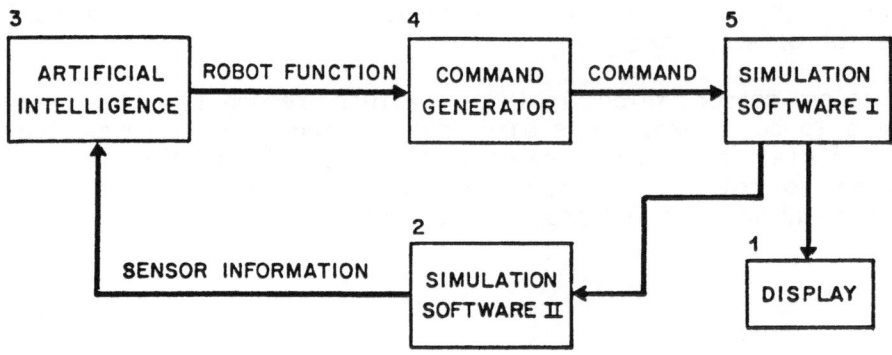

Figure 4

REFERENCES

Kobayashi A, Nakamura K (1983) Rescue robot for fire hazards.
    Proceedings of International Conference on Advanced Robotics: 91-98
Mieno M (1983) Function analysis of both arms and algorithm for
    mechanization. 1st Symposium on the Robotics Society of Japan:
    103-104

**Takanori Sumi** was graduated from Science University of Tokyo, Japan, in 1975 and received the M.S. degree in Theoretical Physics from University of the Pacific, Stockton, CA, in 1977.

After doing some graduate work in Physics at the Johns Hopkins University, Baltimore, MD, he was employed as a research scientist at ANRITSU CORPORATION, Atsugi, Japan in 1981. At present he is a chief engineer of CAD system in the same company.

His current research interests include group theory, fazzy theory, image processing, computer grpahics, and VLSI CAD system.

**YOOICHIRO Ban** is a graduate student in the Department of Industrial Administration at the Science University of Tokyo. His research interests include the medical system and the robot engineering. He published a paper, "Color Blindness Tests by Color Graphic Display" in "CG Tokyo '85".

**Hiroshi Mieno** is professor of information science at the Science University of Tokyo. He has authored 18 information and computer system books. His research interests include pattern recognition, computer graphics, general information system design and personel management expert systems.

His address is Department of Industrial Administration, Faculty of Science and Technology, Science University of Tokyo, Noda, Chiba, Japan.

# High Performance CAD System with Full Automatic Dimensioning and Multi-Modeling Features Based on Engineering Workstation

Junji Hashimoto, Hirokazu Fukushima and Wataru Kowaguchi

Department of Computer Graphics, Hitachi Software Engineering Co., Ltd., Onoe-machi, Naka-ku, Yokohama, 231 Japan

ABSTRACT

XCAD(expansible CAD system) is a high performance CAD system which supports superior features based on the new ideas and techniques. The system is designed for mechanical drawings and it is implemented on UNIX[1] based engineering workstations. This paper describes the following new ideas and techniques :

(1) expansible and flexible inverse Polish notation language (kain, 1972)
(2) full automatic dimensioning
(3) multi modeling
(4) masking

which allow users to produce drawings more efficiently.

KEYWORDS

CADD, inverse Polish notation, automatic dimensioning, multi modeling, and masking

## 1. INTRODUCTION

As the processing power of microprocessors is rapidly increasing, the engineering workstation offers powerful high-speed interactive graphics and network capability. Since it provides enough power to process complex calculation for CAD systems, it is becoming possible to implement various features which were not forecasted to work on small systems.

The XCAD system we implemented has some superior features such as easily expansible and flexible command language, powerful automatic dimensioning, multi-modeling, and masking which are not seen in other CAD systems. This system is general purpose CAD, but it is intended especially for the mechanical field.

---

1 UNIX operating system was developed and is licensed by AT&T Bell labs.

## 2. SYSTEM CONFIGURATION

### 2.1 Hardware configuration

This system consists of engineering workstation, graphics display of CORE standard with tablet and cursor, and A1 size xy plotter as shown in Fig. 1. Because of easier transplantation, we chose UNIX based engineering workstation with C language. XCAD needs at least 2 mega bytes RAM and 20 mega bytes hard disk.

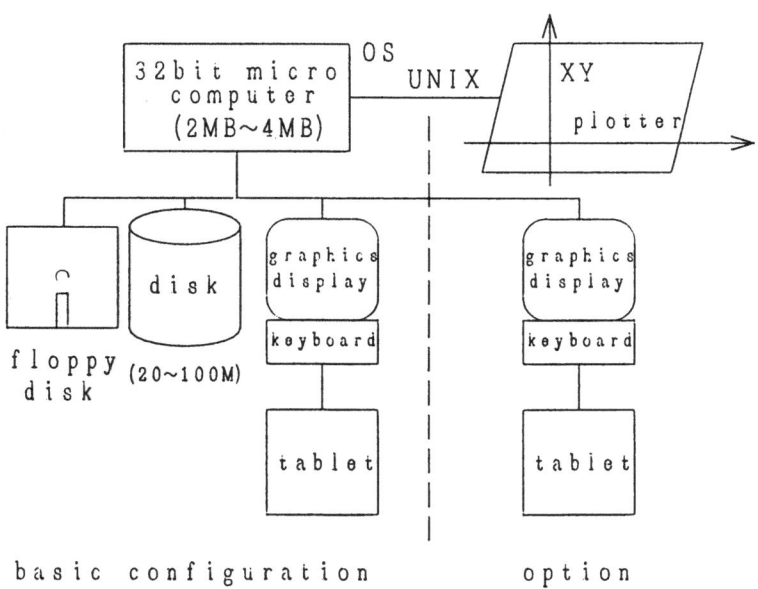

Fig. 1. Hardware configuration of XCAD

### 2.2 Software Diagram

Figure 2 shows the software diagram of XCAD. The XCAD software consists of the drawing software and the utilities software. The drawing software is for creating and editing primitives interactively while the utilities software is for file management and plotter output.

## 3. COMMAND INTERFACE

In most other CAD systems, commands are entered in a manner where most frequently used primitive operations are empirically selected. A given set of command tends to become larger to cover more variety of users and yet is not able to fulfill a particular user's or user group's needs.

UNIX SYSTEM V

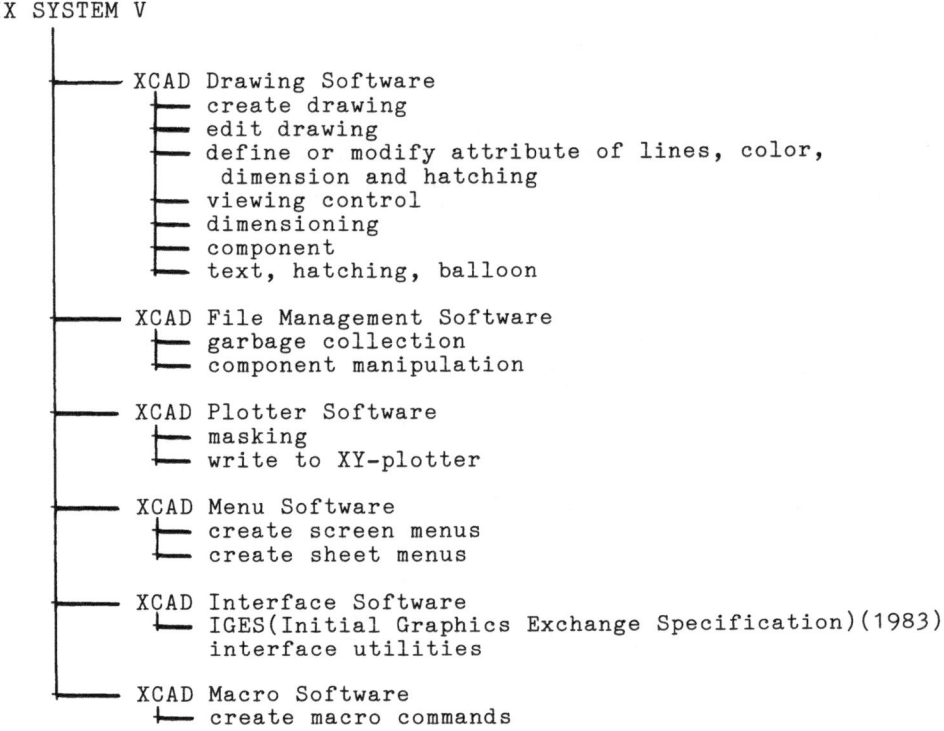

```
├──── XCAD Drawing Software
│        ├── create drawing
│        ├── edit drawing
│        ├── define or modify attribute of lines, color,
│        │    dimension and hatching
│        ├── viewing control
│        ├── dimensioning
│        ├── component
│        └── text, hatching, balloon
│
├──── XCAD File Management Software
│        ├── garbage collection
│        └── component manipulation
│
├──── XCAD Plotter Software
│        ├── masking
│        └── write to XY-plotter
│
├──── XCAD Menu Software
│        ├── create screen menus
│        └── create sheet menus
│
├──── XCAD Interface Software
│        └── IGES(Initial Graphics Exchange Specification)(1983)
│             interface utilities
│
└──── XCAD Macro Software
         └── create macro commands
```

Fig. 2.  Software Diagram of XCAD

Also, these commands, which have been historically defined, are not necessarily clear: it is commonly seen that drawing operation such as draw a line, a circle, etc. are mixed with operand manipulation. Under the category of draw a circle, there could be:

(1) Draw a circle with a given center point and a radius.
(2) Draw a circle with a given center point and tangent to a given line or a circle.
(3) Draw a circle with a given center point and a point on the circle.
(4) Draw a circle with a given radius and tangent to two lines or circles.
(5) Draw a circle with a given radius, and a point on the circle, and tangent to a line or a circle.
(6) Draw a circle with a given radius and two points on the circle.
(7) Draw a circle with three points on the circle.

etc.

However, all of these are simply draw-a-circle commands. Variations exist to identify positions where the circles are to be drawn. All of these commands can be viewed as having the following two steps:

(1) To determine the identity of the circle. One basic approach of identification is to determine the center and the radius.
(2) To draw the circle of given center and the radius. Center point and radius are the elementary information of a circle in any CADD(Computer Aided Design and Drafting) primitives.

The first step can be seen as operand manipulation, while the second is actually drawing operation.

In order to draw a line, other varieties exist, where most of the operand manipulations are similar to the ones in the draw-a-circle commands.

In ordinary CADD systems, the most common set of draw-a-circle commands, draw-a-line commands, etc. are given. Because of the lack of distinction between drawing operation and operand manipulation, many combinations of drawing operations such as draw-a-circle, draw-a-line and operand manipulation operations such as define-a-point, define-a-distance must be included in a command set. Therefore the given set of commands tends to be large yet never fulfills a particular user's needs.

In XCAD command structure, the drawing operation and operand manipulation are clearly distinct.

## 3.1 Command Syntax

XCAD command syntax is based on an inverse Polish notation because Polish notation, used in other CAD systems, is not easy for operand manipulation. An example of inverse Polish notation is described in the next section, but suppose you are going to draw a circle with a given center point and a point on the circle by Polish notation language. First, you enter an operator for getting distance and enter two points.

Dis c1 c2      ----------->   r : distance between c1 and c2

Then distance, r is obtained. You take a memo of the value of r. Next, you enter an operator for drawing a circle and enter the parameters, c1 and r.

Circ c1 r      ----------->   desired circle is constructed.

This is an example without a command drawing a circle by given two points. To support this function in the ordinary way, programmers have to design and code the algorithm. But, coding makes the set of commands larger.

If you try to support this function by combining 'Circ' with 'Dis', then you have to make them nested. In Polish notation, you must enter

Circ c1 Dis c1 c2 ------->   desired circle is constructed.

In this case, just after 'c2' is entered, 'Dis' is operated and the distance is obtained. And then, using it as a radius, 'Circ' is operated and the circle is constructed. But, this method is rather difficult to use, for the order of entering commands is the reverse of the order of execution.

If you consider carefully the process of drawing in this case, you find the following sequence:

(1) You want to draw a circle with a center point and a point on the circle.
(2) You want to get distance between the points for radius of the circle.
(3) You measure the distance between points.
(4) You draw the circle with the radius.
(See Fig. 3.)

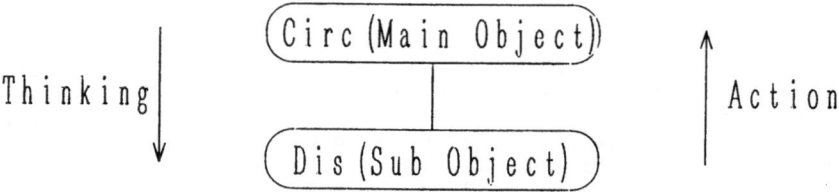

Fig. 3. Process of drawing


Thinking proceeds from main object(draw a circle) to sub object(get distance) like Polish notation. On the other hand, real action proceeds from sub object to main one. We regard CADD commands as the tools for drawing action, so we decided to use inverse Polish notation so that we can nest commands in the same order as the drawing actions.

If you consider the case in which entering commands are more nested than the previous example, you will find that the difference between the order of entering commands and the order of real manipulation is a serious problem.

To support the function by inverse Polish notation, no modification is needed for the program and user may enter commands utilizing 'Circ' or may generate a macro as described in section 3.2.

XCAD command is a set of XCAD operations and their operands. XCAD operations consist of the drawing operations, the operand manipulations and execution control. Operation is preceded by their operands.

Draw-a-line operation is preceded by two operands, starting point and ending point. Get-the-middle-of-a-line operation is preceded by an operand, a line.

Sequence of input is stacked and is executed when an operational symbol is encountered. This is a command execution. The result of a command execution can be a drawn figure, operand(s), such as a point, a coordinate, distance, etc., or a change of control.

General command list is like

a1 b1 b2 B A

where capital letters indicate operation and small letters indicate operands. Operation B is executed using b1 and b2 as its operands and generates a result, a2. Then operation A is executed using a1 and a2 as its operands.


## 3.2 Command expansibility and flexibility

Suppose a set of basic commands is given like:

    Circle:   Draw a circle with a given center and radius
              c1 r Circle

    Distance: Calculate a distance between two points
              c1 c2 Distance

    Duplicate: Duplicate an indicated operand on the stack
              n Duplicate

And a list of these commands

    c1 c2 -2 Duplicate Distance Circle   ------------ (1)

XCAD first detects command Duplicate with its operand -2 and duplicate second preceding operand to current position. Therefore the first interpretation of the list is

    c1 c2 c1 Distance Circle   --------------- (2)

where second c1 is the duplicated result of the 'Duplicate' operation.

Then the next leftmost command becomes Distance. The result of this command execution is

    c1 r Circle   ----------------------- (3)

where r is the result of the 'Distance' operation, that is the distance between c1 and c2.


The result of execution of (3) is to draw a circle with the center c1 and radius r which is the distance between c1 and c2.


If we name this list 'cop' (Circle O & P) by creating a file named 'cop.mcr' that includes text string '-2 Duplicate Distance Circle', new command is obtained to draw a circle with a given center point and a point on the circle. The new command 'cop' can now be considered exactly the same as the existing commands as shown in Fig. 4. We have just defined a new command using the basic commands.


This expansibility nature of XCAD command syntax allows the set of basic commands to be greatly reduced, which leads the reduction in size of the core part of execution code, and allows the expansion of the set of commands for the use of a particular user or a user group. In fact, most commonly used commands, as the industry learned from experience, are defined as a part of the standard XCAD command set. Users may or may not choose these pre defined commands.

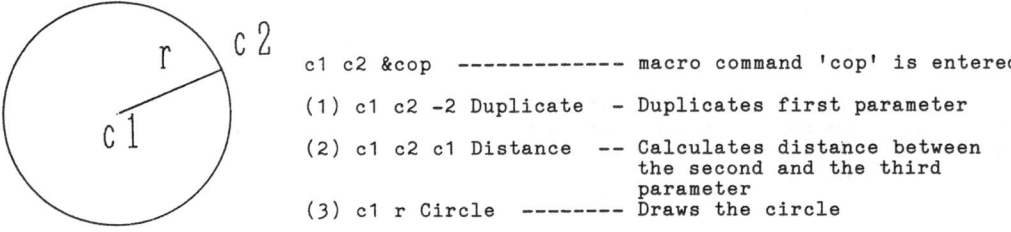

```
c1 c2 &cop ------------- macro command 'cop' is entered.

(1) c1 c2 -2 Duplicate  - Duplicates first parameter

(2) c1 c2 c1 Distance  -- Calculates distance between
                          the second and the third
                          parameter
(3) c1 r Circle  -------- Draws the circle
```

Fig. 4.  Example of the execution of a macro command

In the real drawing situation, you often encounter a non-routine procedure. In these cases, making macro is not a suitable method. XCAD command language offers you the flexibility by combining commands interactively. For example, when 'cop' is not used often, only by entering these commands in the upper example sequence instead of making macro command, you can draw a circle with a center point c1 and a point c2 on the circle.

## 3.3 Command independency

Because of the nature of XCAD command syntax, any command can be executed while part or whole operands of other commands are keyed in. Commands can be executed without disturbing others.

While selecting figures to be copied, a designer often notices his line style, color or layer are not properly attributed. While deleting auxiliary figures from the drawing, one would often notice meaningful figures are too close to distinguish from auxiliaries. Change attribute command, zooming, panning or windowing are expected to intercept the current commands: during deletion or selection, you can zoom, pan or change attribute.

In these cases, when the operator is not fully prepared to place a command, XCAD allows him to execute another command without canceling the command that he has just been going to execute.

## 3.4 Demerit of Inverse Polish Notation and Countermeasures

A demerit of using inverse Polish notation as a CAD command language is that in this language, we cannot support guidance facility that tells users one by one what parameter is needed for the command.

It is important for a command language to be easily learnable. For this, XCAD has display menu facility and help facility. By display menu facility you can call up a list of commands from index menu, and pick one of them. By using help facility you can display a command's manual. These facilities are both user definable.

# 4. FULL AUTOMATIC DIMENSIONING

A drawing consists of primitives, dimensions and texts. Primitive is a drawing element such as a line, circle, ellipse or so on. Text is a string element which appears in tables or annotations.

We in the industry have been attempting to reduce the designers' time to produce drawings by developing programs which aids the constructing of the primitives, for designers spend most of their time in doing it. But recently, the development of the program is settled for the time being and users have the desire to add dimensions and annotations easily.

Semi-automatic dimensioning function generates the dimensioning by indicating subject dimension point and the point of text to appear. On the other hand, full-automatic dimensioning function automatically generates possible dimensioning for a set of figures by indicating the set.

It is convenient to add dimensions automatically to an existing drawing. We decided on the following function and restriction concerning the full automatic dimensioning:

(1) It is possible to modify existing dimensioning easily.
(2) Full automatic dimensioning is available only for radius
    ones and ones parallel to x or y axis.

## 4.1 Algorithm of full automatic dimensioning

Primitive is lines, circles, ellipses, texts or other drawing elements which are stored in the data base of CAD system. Dimension consists of lines and texts in most CAD systems. But in this case, it is not possible to modify dimension easily, since CAD system cannot recognize dimension. Dimension should be one of the primitives although it brings complexity of the data base.

This algorithm assumes that full automatic dimensioning is available only for radius ones and ones parallel with x or y axis.

```
Procedure Full-Automatic-Dimensioning Algorithm ;
  Begin
    For each primitives in a set of figure do
    Begin
      Select the objective primitives and load them in
        memory ;                         (* See Fig. 5 *)
    End ;
    For selected objects of circle, arc, ellipse or arc of
    ellipse do
      Construct radius dimension ;       (* See Fig. 6 *)
    If user requests neglect of trimming or rounding
    corner concerning dimension then
      For each objects touched with trimming or rounding
      corner do
        Modify objective data for neglect of trimming or
        rounding corner ;                (* See Fig. 7 *)
```

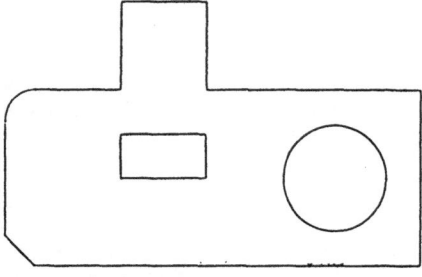

Fig. 5.  Object drawing

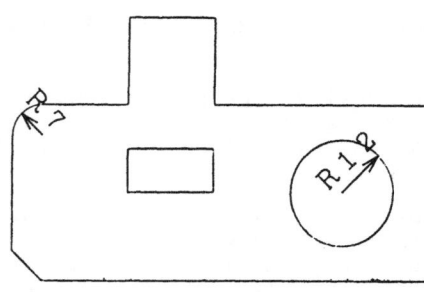

Fig. 6.  Construct radius
dimension

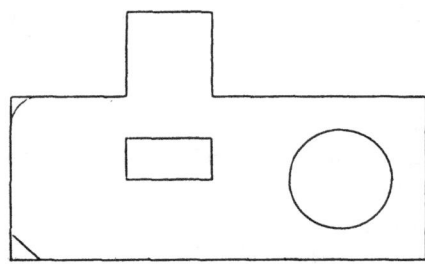

Fig. 7.  Neglect round and chamfer

```
For all objects in memory do
    Assume dimension of all objects
    (dimension for length along axes of each segment, and
    dimension for each independent point such as a center of
    a circle from the base point );  (* See Fig. 8 *)
For all dimensions in memory do
Begin                                 (* See Fig. 9 *)
  Check duplicate ;
  If duplicate is true then
  Begin
    Delete dimensioning unless two dimensions overlap ;
    Delete lead line unless two lead lines overlap ;
  End ;
End ;
Define hierarchy of dimensions (dimensions belonging to the same
outline should be in the same level. outer outline's ones should
be outer. wider ones should be outer.) ;
                                   (* See Fig. 10 *)
Construct all dimensions in the data base ;
                                   (* See Fig. 11 *)
  End ;
```

Figures, from  Fig. 5  to  Fig. 10 show the process of  full automatic
dimensioning.  Fig. 11 shows an example of completed figure with  full
automatic dimensioning.

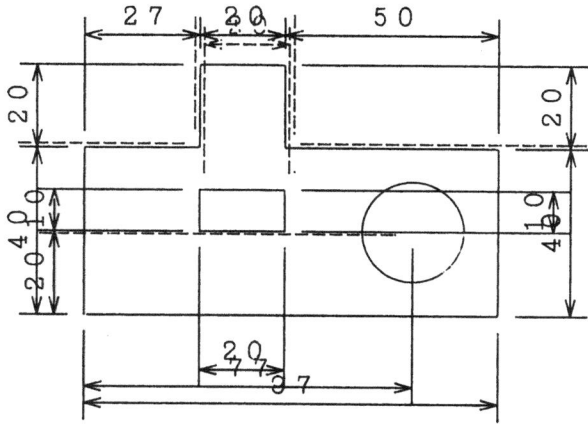

Fig. 8. Make x-y dimensions

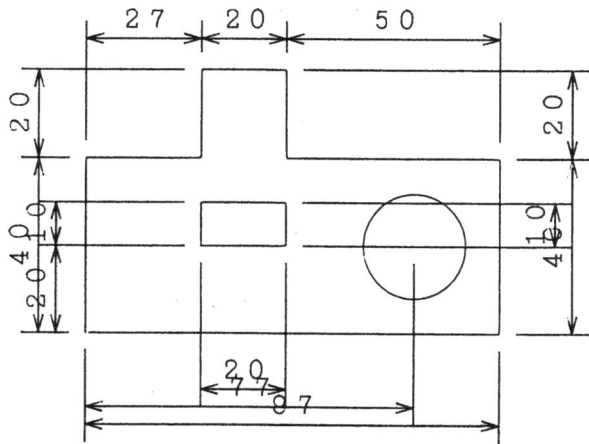

Fig. 9. Delete multiple dimension and move foot of leader line

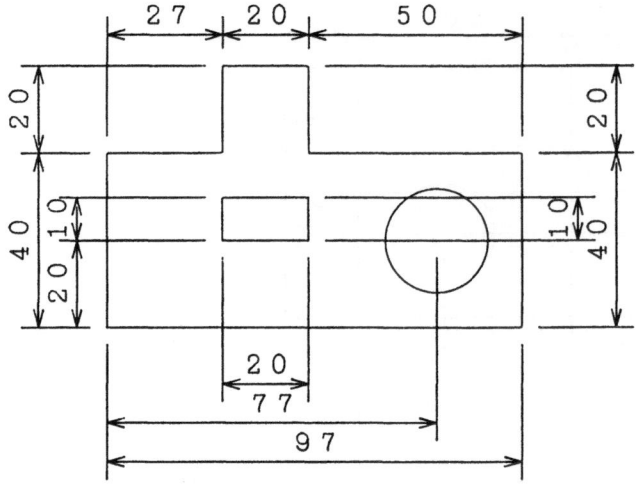

Fig. 10.   Hierarchy of dimensions

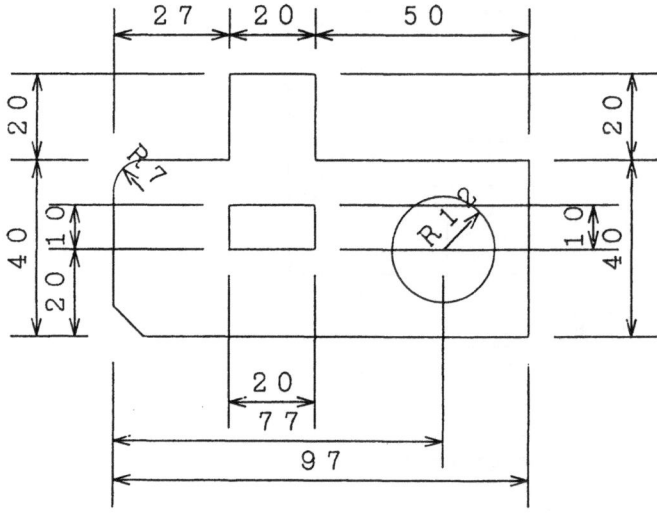

Fig. 11.   Completed figure with full automatic dimension

## 4.2 Subject to improve

The dimension modification facility of XCAD is made for a single dimension. The dimension modification facility for a set of dimensions should be made. For example, when you delete a dimension, you may want the facility that define hierarchy of remaining dimensions again.


## 5. MULTI MODELING

When a designer draws a diagram, he often uses his old diagrams. For example, he may modify an old diagram or compose old diagrams to make a new one. In these cases to make a new diagram using old diagrams effectively, it is necessary to display old and new diagrams on graphics display simultaneously and deal them. On the other hand, CAD systems available today have zooming and multi window facility. As shown in Fig. 12, zooming facility is the ability to zoom up a portion in a diagram on to a graphics display and make it easy to operate on the display. As shown in Fig. 13, multi window facility of CAD is to display zoom-up-portion without losing entire picture.

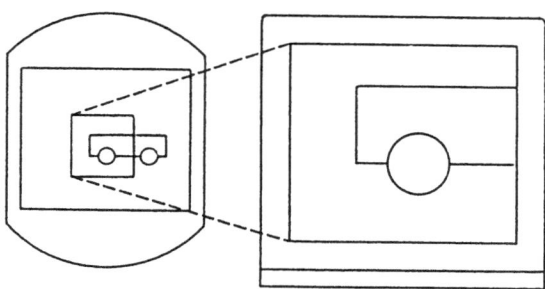

Fig. 12.  Example of zooming

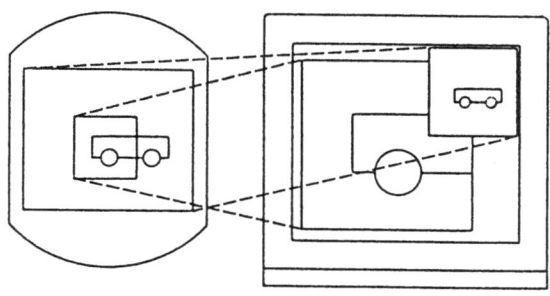

Fig. 13.  Example of multi window

We implemented multi modeling facility by enhancing this multi window facility. Multi modeling facility makes it possible to assign windows to different diagrams, display them simultaneously, and copy a primitive from one diagram to another. You can use a length of picture in a diagram to make another diagram, too.

There are multi window systems for OA(Office Automation). The idea of multi modeling resembles them. But, in those systems, each window is for an individual job such as mailing, editing, word processing and so on. Our multi modeling facility is for CAD. Drawing is drawing, not another job. Each window is for an individual data. Therefore we use windows related to different drawings.

Between windows we copy the models and parts of them, and modify them. Those models represent real products, so when they are copied, the differences of unit and zooming rate between windows are automatically adjusted.(If a model is 1 inch long in a drawing, then when it is copied to the other drawing that uses mm system, it becomes 25.4 mm long.)

Figure 14 shows an example of multi modeling. In this case, window 2 is assigned to a portion of diagram A, window 1 to the whole of A, and window 3 to the diagram B. You can operate all the pictures displayed on the graphics monitor. In Fig. 14, the picture of diagram B is picked from window 3, coordinates of window 3 and window 2 are specified, and pictures in diagram B are copied to diagram A.

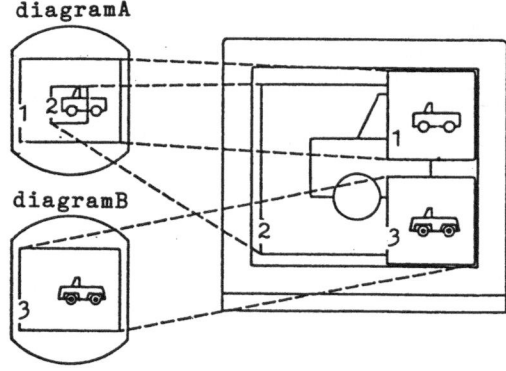

Fig. 14. Example of multi modeling

However, when you draw a line by specifing coordinates from a tablet, the line should be saved in a file assigned to the window through which the coordinates were entered. In this case, you need not specify the window number. The window number is attached to the coordinate parameter, so that the line command module can select the file to store the line. In this way, multiple diagrams are operative even in one command as shown in Fig. 15.

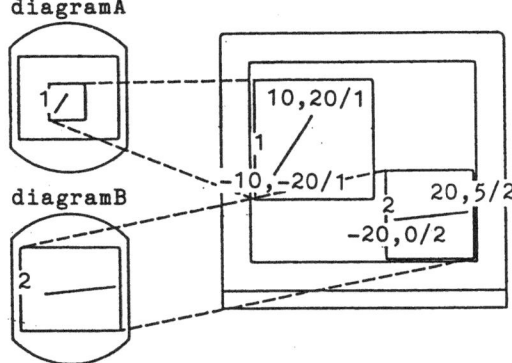

Fig. 15. Coordinates with window number

Since the picked primitive parameter also has a file identifier in it,
every translate or edit primitive command module can select the file
without explicitly specifying the window number.

As shown in Fig. 14, copy command module finds the original file name
from primitive parameters and original coordinate, and gets the object
file name from object coordinates. Because these file identifiers are
attached by system automatically, users do not need to recognize the
difference of files. Copy operations between different files are
totally the same as copy operations in a file.

6. MASKING

A component is a set of primitives grouped together into a complex
object. Once so grouped, the primitives are given a name and a user
can use this name to insert that group of primitives into his drawing
wherever he likes.

Although the use of components is very efficient for assembly drawing,
there is a problem when two or more components overlap each other.
The method of hiding a part of a component is requested in case of
overlapping as shown in Fig. 16.

The conventional way of hiding a part of a figure is, first, by
getting intersections of the overlapped area ( point 1 and 2 in the
above figure) and, second, by cutting the lines including the obtained
points and, third, by trimming the hidden lines as shown in the figure
on the right. This procedure is usually done by separate commands.

XCAD has a masking facility which erases overlapped parts of the
objects. The masking process is done in two dimensional coordinates.

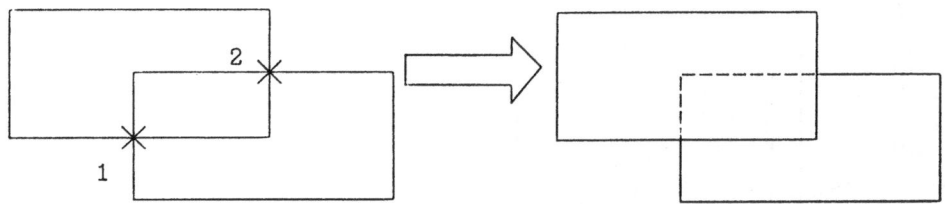

Fig. 16. Example of overlapped components

We wanted to keep data in 2 dimensional coordinate system without z axis, because introducing z axis makes the program complicated and large, so we chose the way to determine cover-covered relations according to the order of primitives made.

## 6.1 Masking process

This section shows the abstract of masking which utilizes masking primitive. A masking primitive is a filled polygon used for masking process. As shown in Fig. 17, there are three steps in masking process. First, create figure to be masked. Second, create masking primitive (hatching polygon in the figure) and erase a part of the figure using the masking primitive. Third, add overlapping figure to the position just masked.

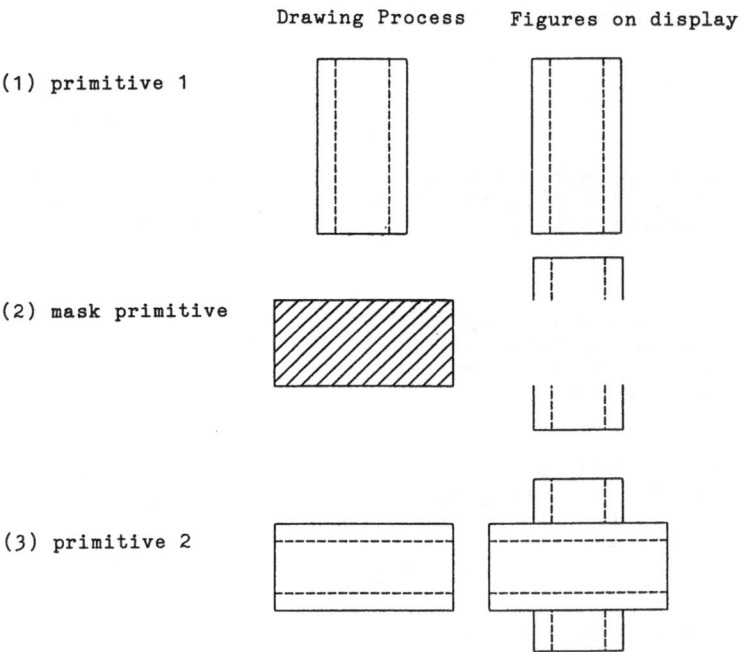

Fig. 17. Masking process

There are three following advantages for users in this masking method:

(1) The  masking  process  is  performed  fast.
(2) Masking can be cancelled easily by deleting a masking  primitive.
(3) Masking area can be moved easily by moving a masking primitive.


On the other hand,  we have to use a command that changes the order of
primitive made, to modify the cover-covered relation.

## 6.2  Plot out masked diagram

Diagrams  made by the interactive drawing program are finally  plotted
out  to X-Y plotter by a batch program.  X-Y plotter can not erase the
picture already drawn, so our batch program must trim diagrams. Figure
18 shows the way how the program trims a diagram. Every picture should
be trimmed by upper masks so, we take pictures from the top to bottom.
When  we get the mask primitive,  we add it to the mask region in  the
manner of set operation.  Every picture other than mask, is trimmed by
this  mask region.  Thus,  we get the same diagram plotted as the  one
displayed  on a graphic.  In this program,  the problem was to shorten
the  time  of calculating intersections.  We  chose  Bentley-Ottmann's
algorithm(1979)  for reporting and counting geometric intersections to
solve this problem.

(1) search a mask picture
    from top,and save it
    to mask region M.

(2) get a picture from
    top, and save it to
    D.

(3) if end of picture,
    then stop.

(4) calculate crossing
    points of region M
    and D.

(5) determine inner or
    outer segments.

(6) delete the inner
    segments.

(7) add mask picture
    to region M in the
    manner of set
    operation.

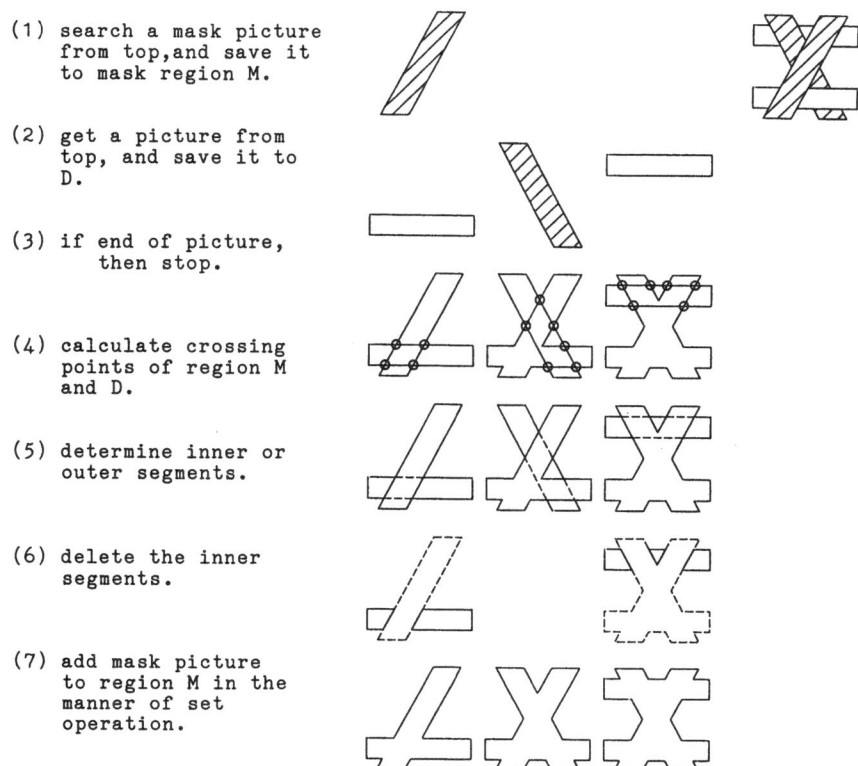

Fig. 18.  Automatic trimming for X-Y plotter

# 7. CONCLUSION

As the processing power of processors increases, CAD software must have higher features. In this paper we described four features based on new ideas and techniques:

(1) command language based on inverse Polish notation,
(2) automatic dimensioning,
(3) multi modeling,
    and
(4) masking.


The advantages of these innovations are:

(1) expansibility and flexibility of command,
(2) reduction of time to dimension,
(3) ease to use old diagrams to produce new one,
    and
(4) ease to simulate hidden line process in 2 dimensional coordinate system.

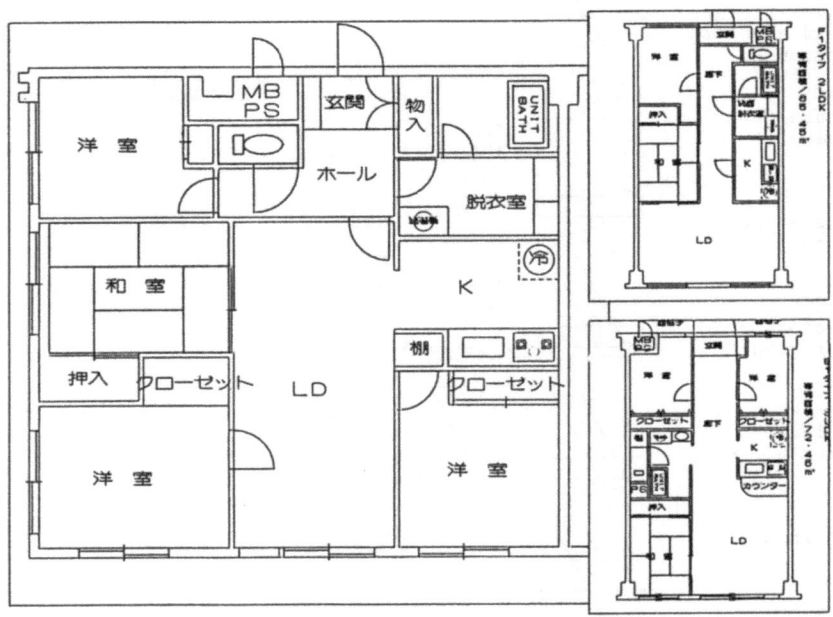

Fig. 19.  Example of multi modeling

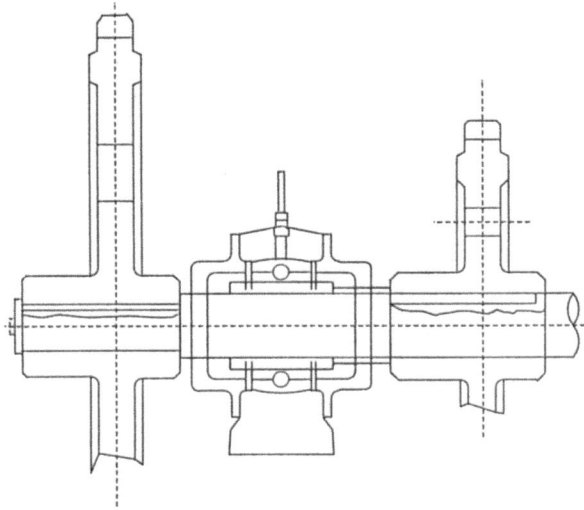

Fig. 20.   Figure before masking process

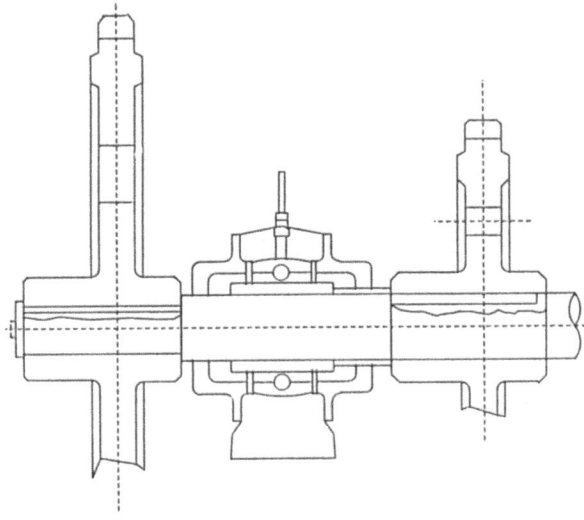

Fig. 21. Figure after masking process

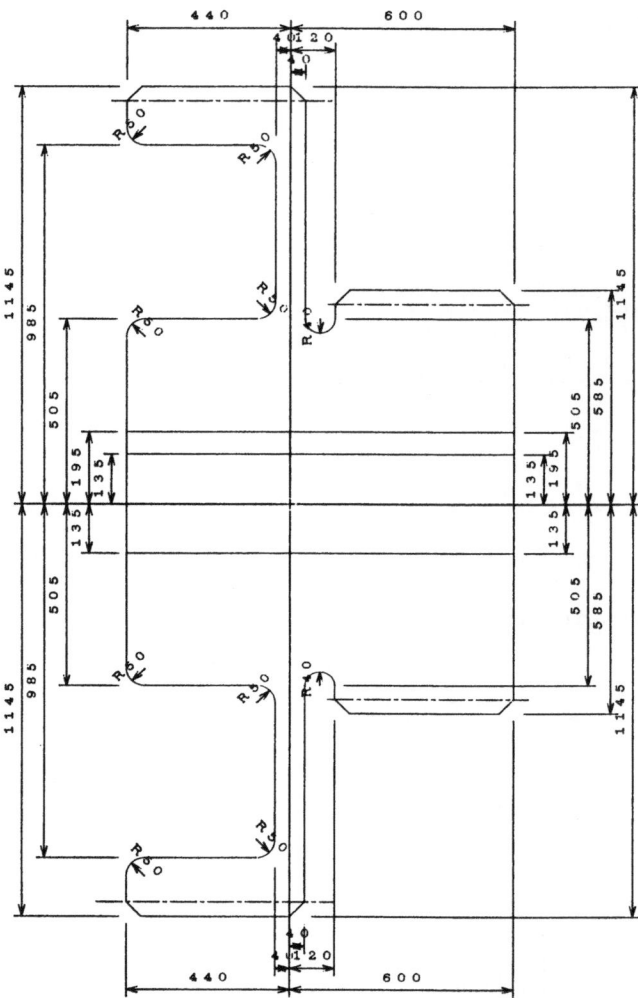

Fig. 22.   Figure with full automatic dimensioning

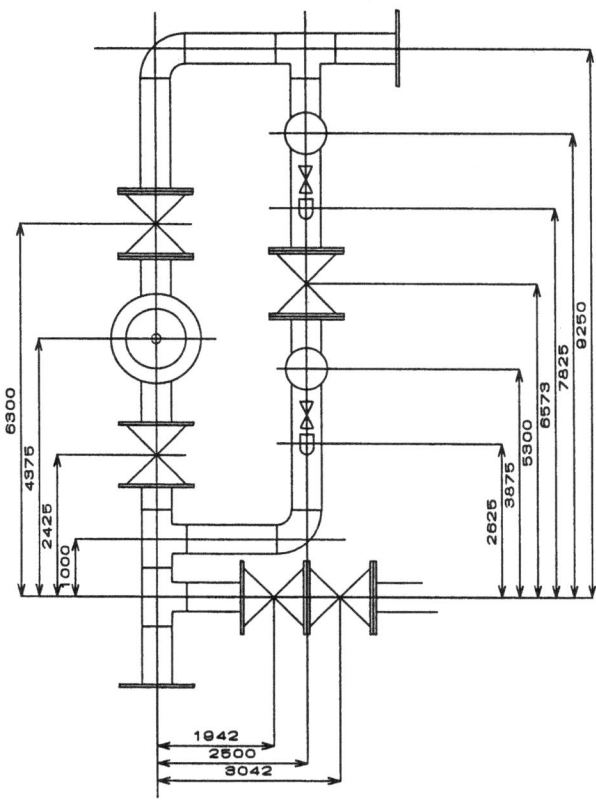

Fig. 23.  Figure with full automatic dimensioning

REFERENCES

(1983) Initial Graphics Exchange Specification (IGES) Version 2.0.
  (U.S.) National Bureau of Standards.
Asano  T  (1984)  computational  Geometry  and  Its  Applications.
  J. IPS Japan 25/3: 208-219
Bentley  JL,  Ottmann TA (1979) Algorithms for Reporting  and  Counting
  Geometric Intersections. IEEE Trans Comput C-28/9: 643-647
Kain  RY  (1972)  Automata Theory:Machines  and  Languages,  1st  edn.
  McGraw-Hill

**Junji Hashimoto**, the section manager of Computer Graphics Department in Hitachi Software Engineering Co., Ltd., has been engaged in developing software and systems related to Computer Graphics, such as application software in apparel industry, and turnkey CAD system for mini and micro computers since 1974.

He has been the chief designer of XCAD project represented in this paper. He is interested in human interface of CAD system.

Hashimoto received his BSc in physics from the University of Shinshu in 1973.

**Hirokazu Fukushima** has been the manager of Computer Graphics Department of Hitachi Software Engineering Co., Ltd. since 1966.

There he has developed software such as an operating system for mainframe computer, and medical information system.

He is now developing 2D CAD systems based on personal computers or Engineering Workstations (EWS). He is interested in 3D solid modeler system on EWS.

Fukushima, a member of Information Processing Society of Japan, received his BSc in electrical engineering from the University of Gifu in 1966.

**Wataru Kowaguchi** is an engineer of Computer Graphics Department in Hitachi Software Engineering Co., Ltd. He entered there in 1977 and since then he has been engaged in developing interactive Computer Aided Design systems based on mini- and micro-computers.

For two years, he has been designing and implementing XCAD. He is interested in man-machine interface and database of CAD system.

Kowaguchi, a member of Information Processing Society of Japan, received his BSc in mathematics from the University of Toky in 1977.

# VIRGO
## A Computer-Aided Apparel Pattern-Making System

Tsukasa Noma, Kojun Terai and Tosiyasu L. Kunii

Department of Information Science, Faculty of Science, The University of Tokyo, Hongo, Bunkyo-ku, Tokyo, 113 Japan

ABSTRACT

This paper introduces VIRGO, a new computer-aided apparel pattern-making system based on flat pattern-making. To interface design processes with manufacturing processes, VIRGO handles the entire information on flat patterns and also on guide lines or points separately from patterns. Its data definition and manipulation are formalized. It also deals with design process information as well as results of design, and it enables us to return to any stage of design through reverse operations. A graphics package generator is also developed.

KEYWORDS: apparel design, computer-aided design, computer-aided apparel pattern-making system, reverse operation, graphics package generator

## 1. INTRODUCTION

There are two ways of apparel pattern-making, that is, draping and flat pattern-making (Kopp 1976). In draping, muslin is draped on a model form and patterns are developed in three-dimensional space. On the other hand, patterns can be also developed from basic patterns called "basic slopers" through two-dimensional drawing called "flat pattern-making".

This paper describes a computer-aided apparel pattern-making system VIRGO, based on flat pattern-making. VIRGO handles the entire information on flat patterns and also on guide lines or points separately from patterns. It deals with design process information as well as results of design.

## 2. DESIGN PRINCIPLES

A computer-aided apparel pattern-making system VIRGO is designed for saving manpower in apparel design and manufacturing, which have been heavily dependent upon human labour. The development of VIRGO has the following objectives:
a) Having pattern editing functions based on flat pattern-making,
b) having interface with the manufacturing processes such as marking and cutting, and
c) dealing with design process information.

To achieve the objective a), VIRGO is designed and implemented as a two-dimensional (2D) computer-aided design (CAD) system. In general, 2D CAD systems are not for the definition of designed objects but only for drawing them. For example, such general-purpose systems do not know whether a line segment is an edge of the designed object, whereas VIRGO does. They have to know the attributes of the line segments, such as line types, line width, and colors. Although VIRGO is a 2D CAD system, its requirements are much different from those of general-purpose 2D CAD systems. To achieve the objective b), VIRGO manages the data of two-dimensional real objects, flat patterns, so as to satisfy topological integrity.


## 2.1 Pattern

Kopp and others (1976) define a pattern as what represents a piece of a garment developed in sections. In this paper, a pattern is defined as a set of pieces which form a garment, and each piece is called a part of the pattern. All patterns within their shapes include seam and hem allowances, grainline, size, notches, placement for buttons, buttonholes, pockets, etc.(Kopp 1976)

Each part of a pattern consists basically of several loops, each of which does not intersect itself. Some loops are called "seam loops", where the part is sewn or the outline of the garment exists. Others are called "allowance loops", where the part is cut out of cloth.

We will informally explain the topological restriction of the seam and allowance loops of a part.

When a part has no hole, it has one seam loop and one allowance loop. Let SA be an area surrounded by the seam loop. Let AA be an area surrounded by the allowance loop. Then AA - SA is seam allowances. It is obvious that the allowance loop encloses the seam loop.

In case of a part with holes and/or closed darts, they are formed by loops. Inversely, in such a case, the seam loops enclose the allowance loops, and they never cross. From the connectivity of a part, there never exists an "island" in the hole.

Formally we can restate the topological restriction of a part as follows:

<u>Definition</u>
    $sur(x)$ = the area surrounded by loop $x$;
    $x > y \iff sur(x) \supset sur(y)$:
        $\iff$ loop $x$ encloses loop $y$;
    $x = y \iff x > y$ and $y > x$;
    $S$ : a set of seam loops of a part;
    $A$ : a set of allowance loops of the part;

<u>Restriction</u>
    (1) $\exists! so \in S$, $\forall s \in S$, $so > s$;
        $\exists! ao \in A$, $\forall a \in A$, $ao > a$;
        $so$ and $ao$ are called a seam outer loop and an allowance outer loop, respectively.
    (2) $\forall s, s' \in S - \{so\}$, $s \not> s'$;
        $\forall a, a' \in A - \{ao\}$, $a \not> a'$;
    (3) $ao > so$;
        $\forall s \in S - \{so\}$, $\forall a \in A - \{ao\}$, $a \not> s$;
    (4) $\forall p, q \in S \cup A$, $p > q$ or $p < q$ or $sur(p) \cap sur(q) = \phi$;

Although both loops must be treated separately, we cannot assume that each part has seam loops and allowance loops. For example, a sloper has no seam allowance, since seam allowances can sometimes interfere with the proportioning and developing of design variations (Kopp 1976). Some of the patterns used in the apparel industry have only allowance loops.

## 2.2 Two-Dimensional Drawing

VIRGO is based on flat pattern-making, and its user-commands include a kind of two-dimensional drawing notation. However, in VIRGO, 2D drawing is not only for editing patterns but also for the development of slopers based on rules mainly offered by educational institutions (Bunka 1976).

In the case of 2D drawing, it is important to distinguish guide lines and points from patterns. Otherwise, for example, moving a guide line results in modifying a pattern. The earlier work (Kato 1980) does not pay attention to it.

## 3. CONCEPTUAL DESIGN

### 3.1 Data Manipulation Level

To make the system reliable and compact, actions in VIRGO are divided into two levels, a "data manipulation level" and a "command level". Actions at the data manipulation level directly manipulate the database in VIRGO. Actions at the command level call actions at the data manipulation level. Only those at the command level are available to users.

In VIRGO, objects and relations are defined as a group of sets and functions. Actions at the data manipulation level are defined as procedures composed of operations on the sets and the functions. They are described in detail in APPENDIX A.

Pattern and Part: In VIRGO, a part is a standard unit of pattern-making. Each part belongs to a pattern.

Sheet: In VIRGO, Patterns are drawn and edited on virtual drafting papers called "sheets".

There are two classes of sheets, "local sheets" and "global sheets". A local sheet is for the display of one part, and the part is drawn on the local sheet associated with it by using its local coordinate system. A global sheet is for the simultaneous display of several parts, and on the global sheet are drawn the parts associated with it. Each part is drawn in its local coordinate system and the parts so drawn are integrated in the global coordinate system associated with the global sheet.

Pattern and Environment: In VIRGO, "pattern" and "environment" are manipulated as two different types of data. The pattern is what apparel shapes consist of, and the environment is data except pattern, for example, guide lines and points.

Part Mark Attribute: Part mark attributes, such as grainline, notches, and placement of buttons, have to be defined also.

<u>Definition</u> (Part Mark Attribute)
    PMA : a set of part mark attributes;

<u>Part</u>: Here we show the definitions of parts and actions on  part  seam
as an example of data definitions and actions at the data manipulation
level.  Parts are defined as follows:

<u>Definition</u> (Parts)
    A part of a pattern p is given by:
    p = (PSV, PSL, pslf, pscf, so, PAV, PAL, palf, pacf, ao, PNP, PNS,
        pnsf, pncf, PM, pmaf, pmcf, pmdf, PIP, psif, paif, pnif, picf)
    where
        (1)  PSV  : a set of part seam vertices;
        (2)  PSL  : a set of part seam loops;
        (3)  pslf : part seam loop function:
             pslf : PSL --> $\bigcup_n$ $PSV^n$;
        (4)  pscf : part seam coordinate function:
             pscf : PSV --> $R^2$;
        (5)  so   : a part seam outer loop;
        (6)  PAV  : a set of part allowance vertices;
        (7)  PAL  : a set of part allowance loops;
        (8)  palf : part allowance loop function:
             palf : PAL --> $\bigcup_n$ $PAV^n$;
        (9)  pacf : part allowance coordinate function:
             pacf : PAV --> $R^2$;
        (10) ao   : a part allowance outer loop;
        (11) PNP  : a set of part nonloop points;
        (12) PNS  : a set of part nonloop segments;
        (13) pnsf : part nonloop segment function:
             pnsf : PNS --> PNP x PNP;
        (14) pncf : part nonloop point coordinate function:
             pncf : PNP --> $R^2$;
        (15) PM   : a set of part marks;
        (16) pmaf : part mark attribute function:
             pmaf : PM --> PMA;
        (17) pmcf : part mark coordinate function:
             pmcf : PM --> $R^2$;
        (18) pmdf : part mark direction function:
             pmdf : PM --> R;
        (19) PIP  : a set of part interpolation points;
        (20) psif : part seam interpolation function:
             psif : PSV --> $\bigcup_n$ $PIP^n$;
        (21) paif : part allowance interpolation function:
             paif : PAV --> $\bigcup_n$ $PIP^n$;
        (22) pnif : part nonloop segment interpolation function:
             pnif : PNS --> $\bigcup_n$ $PIP^n$;
        (23) picf : part interpolation coordinate function:
             picf : PIP --> $R^2$;

To manipulate the data of part seam, we need seven actions.   "Create"
and "delete" change the number of part seam loops. "Divide" and
"connect" insert and delete a vertex of a  part  seam  loop,
respectively.  These four actions alter the topology of part seam.
"Move" moves a vertex of a part seam loop.  "Add" and "remove"
transform an edge of a part seam loop. The latter three actions
change the geometry of part seam.

<u>Definition</u> (Actions on Part Seam)

```
(1)   create(1)        : create a part seam loop 1:
                        {
                                PSL <-- PSL + {1};
                                pslf(1) <-- ();
                        }

(2)   delete(1)        : delete a part seam loop 1:
                        {
                                for all v ∈ PSV
                                    pslf(1) = (.., v,..)
                                    ==> PSV <-- PSV - {v};
                                PSL <-- PSL - {1};
                        }

(3)   divide(1,v,x,y) : divide a part seam edge associated with a
                        part seam vertex v in loop 1 into two part
                        seam edges and insert a part seam vertex v':
                        {
                                (* suppose pslf(1) is
                                (v1, v2, .. ,v, v", .. ,vn) *)
                                PSV <-- PSV + {v'};
                                pslf(1) <--
                                    (v1, v2, .. ,v, v', v", .. ,vn);
                                pscf(v') <-- (x, y);
                                psif(v) <-- ();
                                psif(v') <-- ();
                        }

(4)   connect(1,v)     : connect two part seam edges and delete a
                        part seam vertex v in loop 1:
                        {
                                (* suppose pslf(1) is
                                (v1, v2, .. ,v', v, v", .. ,vn)*)
                                pslf(1) <--
                                    (v1, v2, .. ,v', v", .. ,vn);
                                PSV <-- PSV - {v};
                                psif(v') <-- ();
                        }

(5)   move(v,x,y)      : move a part seam vertex v:
                        {
                                pscf(v) <-- (x, y);
                        }

(6)   add(v,n,p[])     : add the part interpolation points p1,..,pn
                        to a part seam edge associated with a part
                        seam vertex v:
                        {
                                psif(v) <-- (p1, .., pn);
                        }

(7)   remove(v)        : remove the part interpolation points from a
                        part seam edge associated with a part seam
                        vertex v:
                        {
                                psif(v) <-- ();
                        }
```

In VIRGO, such mathematical notations help the system clearly specified.

## 3.2 Command Level

<u>Data Type</u>: In VIRGO, the following data types are used.

(1)  pattern identifier
(2)  part identifier
(3)  global sheet identifier
(4)  part seam loop identifier
(5)  part seam vertex identifier
(6)  part allowance loop identifier
(7)  part allowance vertex identifier
(8)  part nonloop point identifier
(9)  part nonloop segment identifier
(10) part mark identifier
(11) part mark attribute
(12) part interpolation point identifier
(13) local environment point identifier
(14) local environment segment identifier
(15) local environment interpolation point identifier
(16) global environment point identifier
(17) global environment segment identifier
(18) global environment interpolation point identifier
(19) coordinate value
(20) length
(21) angle
(22) number

<u>Data Queue</u>: To share and hold values and/or names, variables are often used. However that the use of variables is too difficult for our users who are apparel designers/makers and usually do not know programming. Furthermore, there are too many data types in VIRGO for such users to use the variables.

Therefore VIRGO adopts data queues. Although the programming language Forth uses stacks as a substitute for variables of other languages, queues have the advantage of keeping the input order for the same kind of data.

However data queues associated with each data type are not easy to handle. For example, suppose that
    YDEFP #A #B 1
is a command which defines a local environment point A whose coordinate value is $(xB, yB + 1)$, and that the input comes from the queues. When the state of the queue of local environment point identifiers is (A, B), the command functions well. On the other hand, if the state of the queue is (B, A), the result becomes unpredictable.

In the above example, #A is a point newly set, and #B is a base point called a basis, relative to which the other points are defined. If a data queue for #A and a data queue for #B are treated separately, users do not have to pay attention to the order of data in queues.

Therefore VIRGO adopts a data input attribute decided by semantics of the data. Each item of data has its own data type and data input attribute, and each data queue is associated with a pair of data type and data input attribute.

The classes of data input attributes are shown below.

(1)  set      the data is newly set
(2)  basis    the data is used as a basis

**Examples of Commands**: These are part of VIRGO commands, which are sufficient for understanding the rest of this paper.

(1)   XDEFP point(set) point(basis) exp(basis)
          Define point(set) at a distance of exp(basis) from
          point(basis) parallel to the x axis.
(2)   YDEFP point(set) point(basis) exp(basis)
          Define point(set) at a distance of exp(basis) from
          point(basis) parallel to the y axis.
(3)   CDEFP point(set) coordinate_value(basis)
          Define point(set) as a points of coordinate_value(basis).
(4)   DIV2P point(set) $point_1$(basis) $point_2$(basis)
          Define point(set) as a middle points of the line segment from
          $point_1$(basis) to $point_2$(basis).
(5)   DIV3P $point_1$(set) $point_2$(set) $point_1$(basis) $point_2$(basis)
          Define $point_1$(set) and $point_2$(set) as trisection points of the
          line segment from $point_1$(basis) to $point_2$(basis).
(6)   LTTK $point_1$(basis) $point_2$(basis)
          Put the length from $point_1$(basis) to $point_2$(basis) in the
          queue(length, basis).
(7)   GLPA segment(set) point(basis) angle(basis)
          Draw a guide line (environment) segment(set) which has
          angle(basis) and passes point(basis).
(8)   GDEFP point(set) point(basis) segment(basis) exp(basis)
          Define point(set) at a distance of exp(basis) from
          point(basis) along segment(basis).
(9)   SLOOP $point_1$(basis) $point_2$(basis) .. $point_n$(basis)
          Define a seam loop passing through $point_1$(basis),
          $point_2$(basis), .. , $point_n$(basis), in order.  If there are
          points in parenthesis, they are interpolation points.
(10) DEFC constant_name(set) value(basis)
          Define a constant_name(set) as the value(basis).

As described in DESIGN PRINCIPLES, these commands can be also used to develop slopers.  For example, a back waist of Bunka-type basic slopers can be developed as shown in Fig. 1.  These commands are parametric two-dimensional drawing notations, and slopers can be fit to a human body of any size.

**Argument of Command**: When concrete values or names are given as arguments, commands use them directly.

To input argument data flexibly, VIRGO adopts "input request arguments" associated with data queues. An "internal input request argument" is replaced with data taken from the specified data queue. If there is no data in the data queue, the "internal input request argument" is handled as an "external input request argument".  An "external input request argument" means clearing the data queue which has the data type and the data input attribute identical to those of the external input request argument, and requesting users to put in data.  Users can put in not only data themselves but also a sequence of commands which returns the requested data.  This is an extension of usual input request of data.

**Macro Command**: Macro commands can also be defined in VIRGO.  They consist of commands.  Although commands used in editing patterns interactively are executed one by one, commands in macro commands are executed together.  If a sequence of commands in Fig. 1 is made a macro command, a basic sloper is developed automatically.

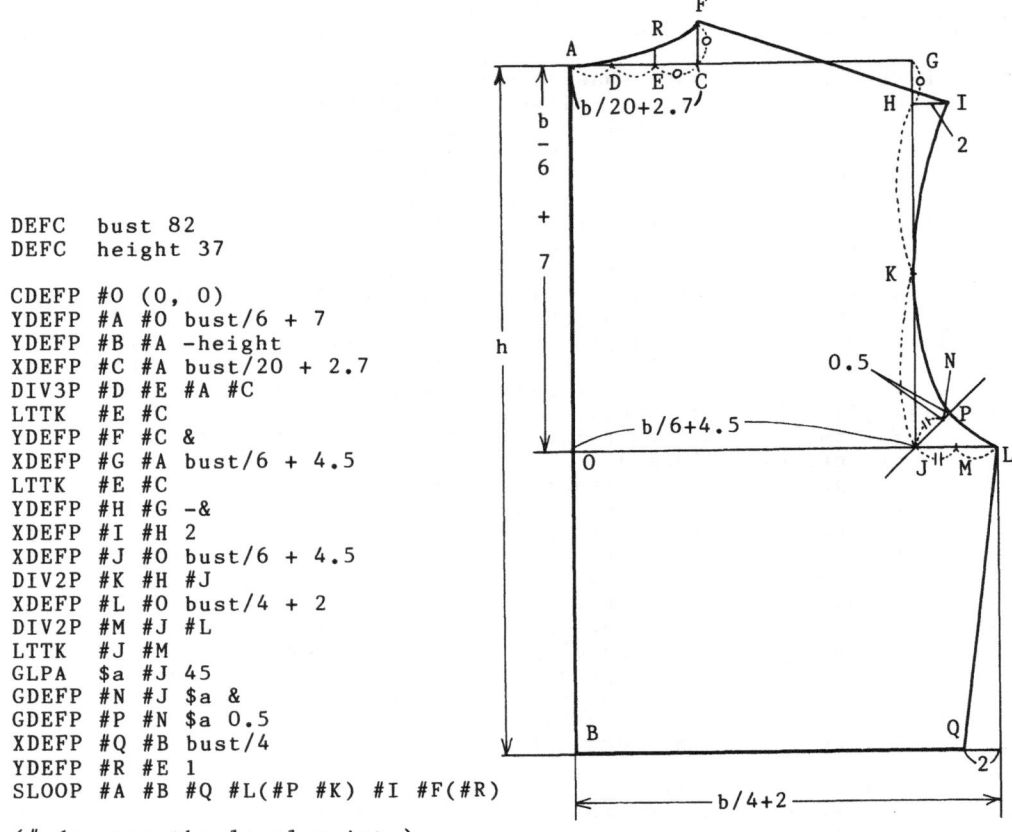

```
DEFC    bust 82
DEFC    height 37

CDEFP #O (0, 0)
YDEFP #A #O bust/6 + 7
YDEFP #B #A -height
XDEFP #C #A bust/20 + 2.7
DIV3P #D #E #A #C
LTTK  #E #C
YDEFP #F #C &
XDEFP #G #A bust/6 + 4.5
LTTK  #E #C
YDEFP #H #G -&
XDEFP #I #H 2
XDEFP #J #O bust/6 + 4.5
DIV2P #K #H #J
XDEFP #L #O bust/4 + 2
DIV2P #M #J #L
LTTK  #J #M
GLPA  $a #J 45
GDEFP #N #J $a &
GDEFP #P #N $a 0.5
XDEFP #Q #B bust/4
YDEFP #R #E 1
SLOOP #A #B #Q #L(#P #K) #I #F(#R)
```

(# denotes the local point.)

Fig. 1. Command sequence generating a sloper

3.3 Design Process Information

With design process information, we can
a) reproduce a pattern constructed in the process of editing, and
   utilize it for other patterns,
b) change a design process into a macro command,
c) store, retrieve, and show a pattern-making process for use through
   a computer assisted instruction system, and
d) execute a reverse operation for interactive use.

Reverse Operation: One of the most important applications of design
process information is the "reverse operation", a kind of undo command
for editors. The reverse operation of VIRGO enables us to return to
any previous stage of editing. Such a function has already been
implemented in a solid modeling system (Chiyokura 1984, 1985; Toriya
1985).

The symmetry of commands is important for reverse operations.

Compression: Design process information often becomes too big to
handle, and involves unnecessary steps. Therefore VIRGO can compress
process information in accordance with certain rules.

# 4. IMPLEMENTATION

## 4.1 Developmental and Target Environment

VIRGO is implemented under the following environment.
(1) Host Computer        Digital Equipment VAX11/750
(2) Operating System     Unix[1] 4.2BSD
(3) Graphic Display      Japan Radio NWX-237
                         (Keyboard and 11" x 11" system tablet)

## 4.2 File Management

VIRGO has two kinds of file formats. One is the drawing file format, and the other is the process file format. The drawing file format is for recording the state of drawing, and the process file format is for recording a design process.

For each part, VIRGO manages three files, that is, an origin file, a process file, and a design file. An origin file and a design file have the drawing file format, and a process file has the process file format. An origin file contains the data for a part and local environment just before editing it. A process file is the record of the design process to transform the state of the origin file to the state of the design file. A design file is the result of editing a part.

We can formalize this as follows: Let D be a set of files having the drawing file format. Let P be a set of files having the process file format, and an element of P is a mapping from D to D. Then for $o, d \in D$, $p \in P$, o, p, and d are an origin file, a process file, and a design file of a part, respectively if and only if $p(o) = d$.

VIRGO also manages macro command files.

## 4.3 Data Manager

Data manager is a subsystem at the data manipulation level. It has a hierarchical structure shown in Fig. 2. Part data manager manages the input and output of parts. Loop data manager treats both seam loops and allowance loops. Vertex data manager deals with both seam vertices and allowance vertices. Point data manager manages nonloop points of parts, local environment points, and global environment points. Segment data manager deals with nonloop segments of parts, local environment segments, and global environment segments. Interpolation data manager treats interpolation data of seam edges, allowance edges, nonloop segments, local environment segments, and global environment segments.

## 4.4 Design Process Information

The difficulty in recording the process information is how to manage the branches of a design process which usually involves multiple trial and error iterations. For example, MODIF by Chiyokura and Kimura (1984) forces users to delete the data representing the process of

---

1 Unix is a trademark of AT&T.

generating B-reps of a given solid. Toriya and others (1985) solved
this difficulty by using tree data structure representation.

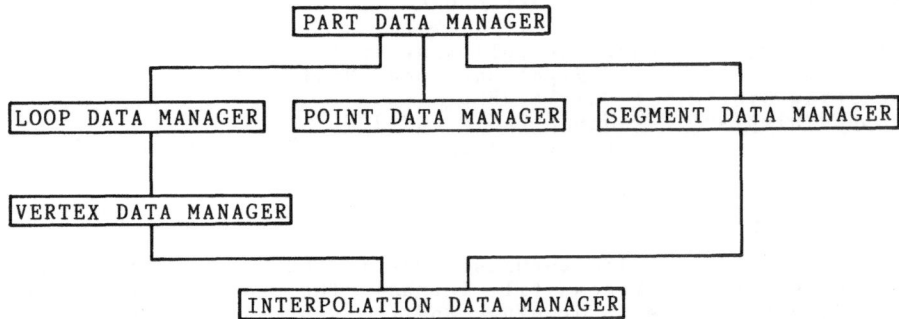

Fig. 2. The structure of data manager

VIRGO adopts simpler method, that is, recording reverse operations
also. An example is shown in Fig. 3. Although this method has a
defect, in the redundancy of information, we can easily cut off the
branches by compression as described below and it is sufficiently
practical.

Compression: The most necessary compression rule in VIRGO is cutting
off the branches of design process. It is easily realized by using
two stacks. The algorithm is described in APPENDIX B.

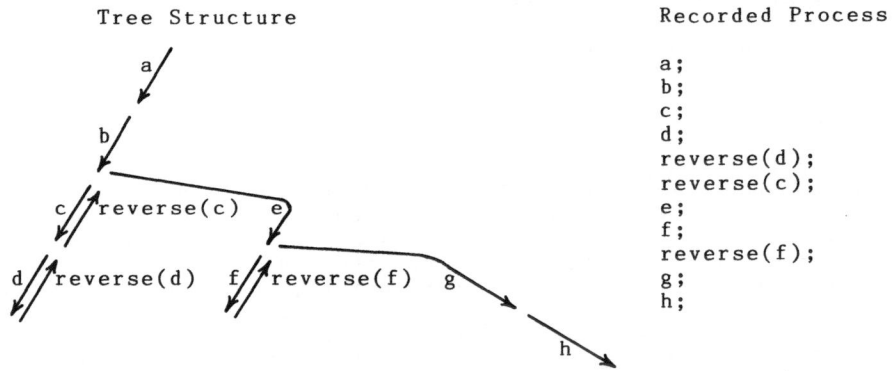

Fig. 3. Branches of a design process made by trial and error
        and recorded reverse operation

5. TOOL

5.1 Graphics Package Generator

To use an intelligent graphic device, a lot of simple subroutines are
necessary. Even if they are supplied with the device as a graphics
package, it is often time-consuming and inflexible.

Therefore a graphics package generator has been developed. All users have to do is to copy the escape sequences of low level graphics instructions out of the manual of the graphic device (Japan 1984) in a file called a source table, to decide subroutine names, and add them to the source table.

For example, low-level commands (instructions), described in the manual, are as follows:

### Extract from the Manual

| name | command |
|------|---------|
| GRAPHIC PLANE ON/OFF | ESC Y D4 |
| SET WINDOW | ESC aF D32 D32 |
| WRITE POLYGON ABSOLUTE | ESC G [ D32 ] . |

ESC means a escape character (033 in octal). the next string is that of the command identifier. D4 and D32 are parameter data formats. A period "." is a command separator. A pair of brackets "[]" denotes repetition.

From the above description, we made the source table shown below.

### An Example of the Source Table

```
graphic     Y D4
setwindow   aF D32 D32
polygonabs  G [ D32 ] .
```

Inputting this source table, the graphics package generator generates three functions written in language C. The generated functions are as follows.

### Generated Functions

void graphic(a1)          set graphic plane to the mode a1.
int a1;

void setwindow(x1,y1,x2,y2)  set window as the rectangle whose bottom-
int x1,y1,x2,y2;             left point is (x1, y1) and top-right
                             point is (x2, y2).

void polygonabs(n1,x1,y1)   write polygon the coordinate values of
int n1,x1[],y1[];           whose vertices are stored in array x1[]
                            and y1[] and the number of vertices is
                            n1.

Write vector absolute command is described as follows:

$$\text{WRITE VECTOR ABSOLUTE} \qquad \text{ESC C} \left\{ \begin{array}{l} [ \ \text{D32C} \ ] \\ [ \ / \ \text{D32C} \ ] \end{array} \right\} .$$

A pair of braces "{}" denotes alternatives, and the function of this command is "to draw a vector from the current point to the point represented by D32C just after no slash is sent", or "to move the current point to the point represented by D32C just after a slash is sent".

From this command, we can generate several functions. An example of the source table and the functions generated from the table are shown below.

<u>An Example of the Source Table</u>

```
lineabs       C D32C .
polylineabs   C [ D32C ] .
polylineabs2  C / [ D32C ] .
linesegabs    C / D32C D32C .
```

<u>Generated Functions</u>

```
void line(x1,y1)            draw a line segment from the current
int x1,y1;                  point to (x1, y1).

void polylineabs(n1,x1,y1)  draw a polyline from the current point.
int n1,x1[],y1[];           The coordinate values of points are
                            stored in array x1[] and y1[], and the
                            number of vertices is n1.

void polylineabs2(n1,x1,y1) draw a polyline from (x[0], y[0]). The
int n1,x1[],y1[];           values of points are stored in array x1[]
                            and y1[], and the number of vertices is
                            n1.

void linesegabs(x1,y1,x2,y2) draw a line segment from (x1, y1) to
int x1,y1,x2,y2;            (x2, y2).
```

This generator is implemented by lex (Lesk 1979) and yacc (Johnson 1979). The syntax of a source table file is described in the Backus-Naur form in <u>APPENDIX C</u>.

Currently, this generator is device-dependent, and only for Japan Radio NWX-237 Graphic Display. However this method can be applied to most of the intelligent raster graphic devices.


6. EXAMPLES


Figure 4 is an example of display on a global sheet. A front and a back waist of Bunka-type basic slopers are drawn on the screen. Figure 5 is an example of display on a local sheet. Only a front waist is shown.


7. DISCUSSIONS


Although VIRGO satisfies the requirements for manufacturing, it is doubtful whether the data structure described in <u>CONCEPTUAL DESIGN</u> can be easily understood by users who are apparel designers and makers. To make the system popular, it is necessary to develop a user's interface accessible to them. Conventional apparel design rules are so complicated and unsystematic that computer scientists have to translate them into systematic rules only with great difficulty.

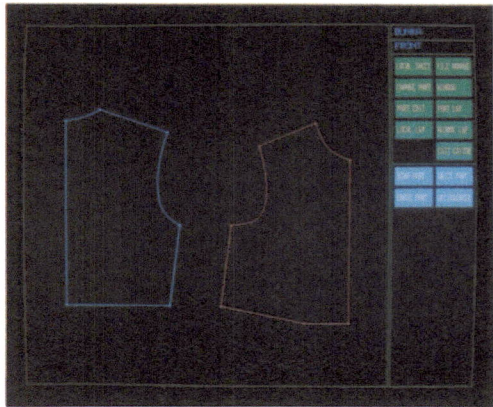 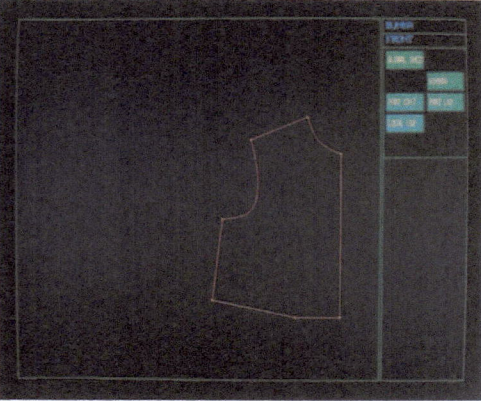

Fig. 4. Display on a global sheet    Fig. 5. Display on a local sheet

ACKNOWLEDGEMENTS

We are grateful to Prof. Geoff Wyvill of University of Otago for his thoughtful comments. Our further gratitude goes to the members of Kunii Laboratory of Computer Science. Mr. Issei Fujishiro offered us a library of interpolation functions he developed. Ms. Emako Aso, Ms. Yoko Nakayama, Ms. Atsuko Sakuraba, and Ms. Nagako Sagayama advised us from the apparel specialists' point of view. Ms. Sachiko Machida made a contribution to the design of commands of VIRGO. Mr. Ying Yuan, Mr. Yasuto Shirai, and Ms. Xiaoyang Mao had valuable discussions with us. This work was partially supported by Ricoh Co., Ltd. Especially, our sincere thanks go to Dr. Hideko S. Kunii of Software Research Center for her continuous encouragement.

REFERENCES

Bunka Woman's University, Bunka Fashion College (eds) (1976) Bunka Apparel Seminar (Bunka Fukusou Kouza), vol 1. Bunka Publishing Bureau, Tokyo :55-60

Chiyokura H, Kimura F (1984) A Representation of Solid Design Process Using Basic Operations. Proc. Computer Graphics Tokyo '84

Chiyokura H, Kimura F (1985) A Method of Representation the Solid Design Process. IEEE CG&A 5(4): 32-41

Japan Radio Co., Ltd. (1984) Japan Radio NWX-237 Graphic Display Operation Manual. Japan Radio Co., Ltd., Tokyo

Johnson SC (1979) Yacc: Yet Another Compiler Compiler. In: Unix Programmer's Manual, 7th edn, vol 2B. Bell Laboratories, Murray Hill

Kato H (1980) Process Design. In: The Textile Machinery Society of Japan (ed) General Remarks of Apparel Science --- Apparel Design (Hifuku Kagaku Souron --- Hifuku Sekkei). The Textile Machinery Society of Japan, Osaka: 95-100

Kopp E, Rolfo V, Zelin B, Gross L (1981) Designing Apparel through the Flat Pattern, 5th edn. Fairchild, New York

Lesk ME, Schmidt E (1979) Lex --- A Lexical Analyzer Generator. In: Unix Programmer's Manual, 7th edn, vol 2B. Bell Laboratories, Murray Hill

Toriya H, Satoh T, Ueda K, Chiyokura H (1985) Invertible Set Operations for Solid Modeling. Proc. Computer Graphics Tokyo '85

APPENDIX A. The Formalization of Data Manipulation Level

Objects, their relations, and actions are formalized as follows:

Objects and Their Relations:

<u>Definition</u> (Patterns and Parts)
   (1) PT  : a set of patterns;
   (2) PA  : a set of parts;
   (3) ptf : part assignment function:
      ptf : $PA \longrightarrow PT$;

<u>Definition</u> (Global Sheet)
   (1)  GS   : a set of global sheets;
   (2)  gsaf : global sheet assignment function:
      gsaf : $PA \times GS \longrightarrow \{ON, OFF\}$;
   (3)  gsrf : global sheet rotation function:
      gsrf : $PA \times GS \longrightarrow R$;
   (4)  gstf : global sheet translation function:
      gstf : $PA \times GS \longrightarrow R^2$;

<u>Definition</u> (Parts)
  A part of a pattern p is given by:
  p = (PSV, PSL, pslf, pscf, so, PAV, PAL, palf, pacf, ao, PNP, PNS,
     pnsf, pncf, PM, pmaf, pmcf, pmdf, PIP, psif, paif, pnif, picf)
  where
    (1)  PSV  : a set of part seam vertices;
    (2)  PSL  : a set of part seam loops;
    (3)  pslf : part seam loop function:
       pslf : $PSL \longrightarrow \bigcup_n PSV^n$;
    (4)  pscf : part seam coordinate function:
       pscf : $PSV \longrightarrow R^2$;
    (5)  so   : a part seam outer loop;
    (6)  PAV  : a set of part allowance vertices;
    (7)  PAL  : a set of part allowance loops;
    (8)  palf : part allowance loop function:
       palf : $PAL \longrightarrow \bigcup_n PAV^n$;
    (9)  pacf : part allowance coordinate function:
       pacf : $PAV \longrightarrow R^2$;
   (10) ao   : a part allowance outer loop;
   (11) PNP  : a set of part nonloop points;
   (12) PNS  : a set of part nonloop segments;
   (13) pnsf : part nonloop segment function:
      pnsf : $PNS \longrightarrow PNP \times PNP$;
   (14) pncf : part nonloop coordinate function:
      pncf : $PNP \longrightarrow R^2$;
   (15) PM   : a set of part marks;
   (16) pmaf : part mark attribute function:
      pmaf : $PM \longrightarrow PMA$;
   (17) pmcf : part mark coordinate function:
      pmcf : $PM \longrightarrow R^2$;
   (18) pmdf : part mark direction function:
      pmdf : $PM \longrightarrow R$;
   (19) PIP  : a set of part interpolation points;
   (20) psif : part seam interpolation function:
      psif : $PSV \longrightarrow \bigcup_n PIP^n$;
   (21) paif : part allowance interpolation function:
      paif : $PAV \longrightarrow \bigcup_n PIP^n$;
   (22) pnif : part nonloop interpolation function:
      pnif : $PNS \longrightarrow \bigcup_n PIP^n$;
   (23) picf : part interpolation coordinate function:
      picf : $PIP \longrightarrow R^2$;

**Definition** (Local Environment)

A local environment, le(p), of a part p is given by:

le(p) = (LEP, LES, lesf, lecf, LIP, leif, licf)

where

    (1)    LEP  : a set of local environment points;

    (2)    LES  : a set of local environment segments;

    (3)    lesf : local environment segment function:

            lesf : LES --> LEP x LEP;

    (4)    lecf : local environment coordinate function:

            lecf : LEP --> $R^2$;

    (5)    LIP  : a set of local environment interpolation points;

    (6)    leif : local environment interpolation function:

            leif : LES --> $\bigcup_{n} LIP^n$;

    (7)    licf : local environment interpolation coordinate function:

            licf : LIP --> $R^2$;

**Definition** (Global Environment)

A global environment, ge(s), of a global sheet s is given by:

ge(s) = (GEP, GES, gesf, gecf, GIP, geif, gicf)

where

    (1)    GEP  : a set of global environment points;

    (2)    GES  : a set of global environment segments;

    (3)    gesf : global environment segment function:

            gesf : GES --> GEP x GEP;

    (4)    gecf : global environment coordinate function:

            gecf : GEP --> $R^2$;

    (5)    GIP  : a set of global environment interpolation points;

    (6)    geif : global environment interpolation function:

            geif : GES --> $\bigcup_{n} GIP^n$;

    (7)    gicf : global environment interpolation coordinate
                  function:

            gicf : GIP --> $R^2$;

## Actions on Objects and Relations:

**Definition** (Actions on Patterns and Parts)

    (1)   create(pt) : create a pattern pt:

```
                {
                        PT <-- PT + {pt};
                }
```

    (2)   delete(pt) : delete a pattern pt:

```
                {
                        for all p ∈ PA
                            ptf(p) = pt
                                ==> PA <-- PA - {p};
                        PT <-- PT - {pt};
                }
```

    (3)   add(p,pt)  : add a part p to a pattern pt:

```
                {
                        PA <-- PA + {p};
                        ptf(p) <-- pt;
                }
```

    (4)   remove(p)  : remove a part p:

```
                {
                        PA <-- PA - {p};
                }
```

<u>Definition</u> (Actions on Global Sheets)
```
(1)   add(p,s)        : add a part p to a global sheet s:
                       {
                               gsaf(p, s) <-- ON;
                               gsrf(p, s) <-- 0;
                               gstf(p, s) <-- (0, 0);
                       }

(2)   remove(p,s)     : remove a part p from a global sheet s:
                       {
                               gsaf(p, s) <-- OFF;
                       }

(3)   rotate(p,s,r)   : rotate a part p on a global sheet s:
                       {
                               gsrf(p, s) <-- r;
                       }

(4)   trans(p,s,x,y)  : translate a part p on a global sheet s:
                       {
                               gstf(p, s) <-- (x, y);
                       }
```

<u>Definition</u> (Actions on Part Seam)
```
(1)   create(l)       : create a part seam loop l:
                       {
                               PSL <-- PSL + {l};
                               pslf(l) <-- ();
                       }

(2)   delete(l)       : delete a part seam loop l:
                       {
                               for all v ∈ PSV
                                   pslf(l) = (.., v,..)
                                   ==> PSV <-- PSV - {v};
                               PSL <-- PSL - {l};
                       }

(3)   divide(l,v,x,y) : divide a part seam edge associated with a
                        part seam vertex v in loop l into two part
                        seam edges and insert a part seam vertex v':
                       {
                               (* suppose pslf(l) is
                               (v1, v2, .. ,v, v", .. ,vn) *)
                               PSV <-- PSV + {v'};
                               pslf(l) <--
                                (v1, v2, .. ,v, v', v", .. ,vn);
                               pscf(v') <-- (x, y);
                               psif(v) <-- ();
                               psif(v') <-- ();
                       }

(4)   connect(l,v)    : connect two part seam edges and delete a
                        part seam vertex v in loop l:
                       {
                               (* suppose pslf(l) is
                               (v1, v2, .. ,v', v, v", .. ,vn)*)
                               pslf(l) <--
                                (v1, v2, .. ,v', v", .. ,vn);
                               PSV <-- PSV - {v};
                               psif(v') <-- ();
                       }
```

```
(5)  move(v,x,y)        : move a part seam vertex v:
                          {
                                  pscf(v) <-- (x, y);
                          }

(6)  add(v,n,p[])        : add the part interpolation points pl,..,pn
                           to a part seam edge associated with a part
                           seam vertex v:
                          {
                                  psif(v) <-- (pl, .., pn);
                          }

(7)  remove(v)           : remove the part interpolation points from a
                           part seam edge associated with a part seam
                           vertex v:
                          {
                                  psif(v) <-- ();
                          }
```

<u>Definition</u> (Actions on Part Allowance)

```
(1)  create(1)           : create a part allowance loop 1:
                          {
                                  PAL <-- PAL + {1};
                                  palf(1) <-- ();
                          }

(2)  delete(1)           : delete a part allowance loop 1:
                          {
                                  for all v ∈ PAV
                                      palf(1) = (.., v,..)
                                      ==> PAV <-- PAV - {v};
                                  PAL <-- PAL - {1};
                          }

(3)  divide(1,v,x,y)     : divide a part allowance edge associated with
                           a part allowance vertex v in loop 1 into two
                           part allowance edges and insert a part
                           allowance vertex v':
                          {
                                  (* suppose pslf(1) is
                                  (v1, v2, .. ,v, v", .. ,vn) *)
                                  PSV <-- PSV + {v'};
                                  pslf(1) <--
                                  (v1, v2, .. ,v, v', v", .. ,vn);
                                  pscf(v') <-- (x, y);
                                  psif(v) <-- ();
                                  psif(v') <-- ();
                          }

(4)  connect(1,v)        : connect two part allowance edges and delete
                           a part allowance vertex v in loop 1:
                          {
                                  (* suppose palf(1) is
                                  (v1, v2, .. ,v', v, v", .. ,vn)*)
                                  palf(1) <--
                                  (v1, v2, .. ,v', v", .. ,vn);
                                  PAV <-- PAV - {v};
                                  paif(v') <-- ();
                          }
```

```
(5)   move(v,x,y)      : move a part allowance vertex v:
                         {
                                 pacf(v) <-- (x, y);
                         }

(6)   add(v,n,p[])     : add the part interpolation points p1,..,pn
                         to a part allowance edge associated with a
                         part allowance vertex v:
                         {
                                 paif(v) <-- (p1, .., pn);
                         }

(7)   remove(v)        : remove the part interpolation points from a
                         part allowance edge associated with a part
                         allowance vertex v:
                         {
                                 paif(v) <-- ();
                         }
```

Definition (Actions on Part Nonloop)

```
(1)   create(s,p1,p2) : create a part nonloop segment s:
                         {
                                 PNS <-- PNS + {s};
                                 pnsf(s) <-- (p1, p2);
                                 pnif(s) <-- ();
                         }

(2)   delete(s)        : delete a part nonloop segment s:
                         {
                                 PNS <-- PNS - {s};
                         }

(3)   set(p,x,y)       : set a part nonloop point p:
                         {
                                 PNP <-- PNP + {p};
                                 pncf(p) <-- (x, y);
                         }

(4)   unset(p)         : unset a part nonloop point p:
                         {
                                 PNP <-- PNP - {p};
                         }

(5)   add(s,n,p[])     : add the part interpolation points p1,..,pn
                         to a part nonloop segment s:
                         {
                                 pnif(s) <-- (p1, .., pn);
                         }

(6)   remove(s)        : remove the part interpolation points from a
                         part nonloop segment s:
                         {
                                 pnif(s) <-- ();
                         }
```

<u>Definition</u> (Actions on Part Mark)
```
   (1)  set(m,a,x,y,d)  : set a part mark m:
                         {
                                 PM <-- PM + {m};
                                 pmaf(m) <-- a;
                                 pmcf(m) <-- (x, y);
                                 pmdf(m) <-- d;
                         }

   (2)  unset(m)         : unset a part mark m:
                         {
                                 PM <-- PM - {m};
                         }
```

<u>Definition</u> (Actions on Part Interpolation)
```
   (1)  set(p,x,y)       : set a part interpolation point p:
                         {
                                 PIP <-- PIP + {p};
                                 picf(p) <-- (x, y);
                         }

   (2)  unset(p)         : unset a part interpolation point p:
                         {
                                 PIP <-- PIP - {p};
                         }
```

<u>Definition</u> (Actions on Local Environment)
```
   (1)  create(s,p1,p2) : create a local environment segment s:
                         {
                                 LES <-- LES + {s};
                                 lesf(s) <-- (p1, p2);
                                 leif(s) <-- ();
                         }

   (2)  delete(s)        : delete a local environment segment s:
                         {
                                 LES <-- LES - {s};
                         }

   (3)  set(p,x,y)       : set a local environment point p:
                         {
                                 LEP <-- LEP + {p};
                                 lecf(p) <-- (x, y);
                         }

   (4)  unset(p)         : unset a local environment point p:
                         {
                                 LEP <-- LEP - {p};
                         }

   (5)  add(s,n,p[])     : add the local environment interpolation
                           points p1,..,pn to a part nonloop segment s:
                         {
                                 leif(s) <-- (p1, .., pn);
                         }

   (6)  remove(s)        : remove the local environment interpolation
                           points from a part nonloop segment s:
                         {
                                 leif(s) <-- ();
                         }
```

```
(7)  set_itpl(p,x,y) : set a local environment interpolation point
                         p:
                       {
                               LIP <-- LIP + {p};
                               licf(p) <-- (x, y);
                       }

(8)  unset_itpl(p)    : unset a local interpolation interpolation
                         point p:
                       {
                               LIP <-- LIP - {p};
                       }
```

Definition (Actions on Global Environment)
```
(1)  create(s,p1,p2) : create a global environment segment s:
                       {
                               GES <-- GES + {s};
                               gesf(s) <-- (p1, p2);
                               geif(s) <-- ();
                       }

(2)  delete(s)        : delete a global environment segment s:
                       {
                               GES <-- GES - {s};
                       }

(3)  set(p,x,y)       : set a global environment point p:
                       {
                               GEP <-- GEP + {p};
                               gecf(p) <-- (x, y);
                       }

(4)  unset(p)         : unset a global environment point p:
                       {
                               GEP <-- GEP - {p};
                       }

(5)  add(s,n,p[])     : add the global environment interpolation
                         points p1,..,pn to a part nonloop segment s:
                       {
                               geif(s) <-- (p1, .., pn);
                       }

(6)  remove(s)        : remove the global environment interpolation
                         points from a part nonloop segment s:
                       {
                               geif(s) <-- ();
                       }

(7)  set_itpl(p,x,y) : set a global environment interpolation point
                         p:
                       {
                               GIP <-- GIP + {p};
                               gicf(p) <-- (x, y);
                       }

(8)  unset_itpl(p)    : unset a global interpolation interpolation
                         point p:
                       {
                               GIP <-- GIP - {p};
                       }
```

APPENDIX B. Compression Algorithm: Cutting the Branches off

In the following algorithm, pop_1() and push_1() are pop and push of stack_1, and pop_2() and push_2() are pop and push of stack_2, respectively.

ALGORITHM CUTTING_THE_BRANCHES_OFF(P)

```
begin
   (* suppose that design process P = (p1, p2, ... , pn) is on the
      stack_1 from top to bottom *)
        p <-- pop_1();
        if(p = empty) then
                return;
        q <-- pop_1();
        while(q != empty) begin
                while(p = reverse(q)) begin
                        p <-- pop_2();
                        if(p = empty) then begin
                                p <-- pop_1();
                                if(p = empty) then
                                        return
                        end;
                        q <-- pop_1();
                        if(q = empty) then begin
                                push_2(p);
                                return
                        end
                end;
                push_2(p);
                p <-- q;
                q <-- pop_1();
        end;
        push_2(p)
   (* compressed design process is on the stack_2 from bottom to top *)
end
```

APPENDIX C. The Syntax of the Source Table File of Graphics Package
           Generator for JRC NWX-237

The syntax of source table file of graphics package generator for
Japan Radio NWX-237 graphic display is given below in Backus-Naur
form.

```
<file> ::= { <line> }

<line> ::=  |
            <name> <list>

<name> ::= <letter> { <letter or digit> }

<letter or digit> ::= <letter> | <digit>

<list> ::= <empty> |
           <string> <list> |
           <parameter> <list> |
           <separator> <list> |
           [ <nested list> ] <list>

<nested list> ::= <empty> |
                  <string> <nested list> |
                  <parameter> <nested list> |
                  <separator> <nested list>

<string> ::= <letter> { <letter> }

<parameter> ::= D4 | D8 | D16 | D16C | D32 | D32C

<separator> ::= / | . | ! | # | $
```

**Tsukasa Noma** is currently a doctor course graduate student of information science at the University of Tokyo. His research interests include computer aided design and computer animation. He received the BSc degree in mathematics in 1984 from Waseda University, and MSc degree in information science in 1986 from the University of Tokyo. He is a member of the Computer Graphics Society.

**Kojun Terai** is currently a master course graduate student of information science at the University of Tokyo. His research interests include computer graphics and its applications. He received the BSc degree in information science in 1985 from the University of Tokyo.

**Tosiyasu L. Kunii** is currently a professor of information and computer science at the University of Tokyo. He started work there in raster graphics in 1968, which led to the Tokyo Raster Technology Project. His research interests include computer graphics, database systems, and software engineering. He has authored and edited 20 computer science books and published 75 refereed academic/technical papers in computer science and applications areas.

Kunii is president of the Computer Graphics Society, chairman of the board of the Handheld Computer Society, and a member of the Editorial Board of CG&A. He is active in IFIP, has organized and is ex-chair of the Technical Committee on Software Engineering of the Information Processing Society of Japan, and has organized and is ex-president of the Japan Computer Graphics Association. He served as general chairman of the Third International Conference on Very Large Data Bases in 1977, program chairman of Intergraphics 83, Computer Graphics Tokyo 84, Computer Graphics Tokyo 85, Computer Graphics Tokyo 86.
Kunii received his BSc, MSc, and DSc in chemistry from the University of Tokyo in 1962, 1964, and 1967.

The authors' address is Department of Information Science, Faculty of Science, the University of Tokyo, 7-3-1 Hongo, Bunkyo-ku, Tokyo 113, Japan.

Chapter 8
# VLSI CAD/CAM

# Efficient Algorithms
# for Validating VLSI Design Database

Yehuda Shiran
SILVAR-LISCO/NCA Corporation, 3250 Jay Street, Santa Clara, CA 95054, USA

ABSTRACT: A generic application-independent validation of VLSI design database is presented. The detected violations are independent of the technology or manufacturing process and the verification is not a substitute for conventional Design Rule Checker (DRC) which is heavily process-dependent. The detection processing is done immediately after completing the VLSI graphic database and is based on a polygon-by-polygon analysis. The various violation types are described and the algorithms are demonstrated. The complexity of the algorithms is linear, compare to N*logN complexity in DRC algorithms. The advantages of using the up-front validation, especially when the database is hierarchical, are discussed.

KEYWORDS: VLSI design database, design verification, scanline algorithms, hierarchical database, database validation.

## INTRODUCTION

The geometry of VLSI artwork is represented by polygons and their non-geometric attributes, such as color and width. For VLSI artwork to be valid and to generate manufacturable chip, it should comply with certain constraints. This paper suggests that the compliance for this constraints can be partially checked immediately after building the database and before subjecting it to pattern generator (PG) interfaces or verification packages. Undetected violations in the graphic database may either cause a fatal error in a later step (e.g. omission of a polygon by the PG interface) or it may be detected by a DRC (Design Rule Checker) package.

Needless to say that a fatal error, in the patter generating step for example, is very expensive in terms or remanufacturing costs and is intolarable. The advantage of validating the data up-front, instead of letting the errors propagate to a DRC step (if at all planned), is the smaller volume of data to be processed. The graphic database is usually structured in a hierarchical fashion. Since DRC checks (among other things) the separation between edges from different polygons, the database needs to be flattened before running DRC and the volume of data checked is much larger then.

The validating described is only for violations that are generic enough to be application- , technology- and process-independent. It does not substitute the function of DRC which is based on application-dependent design rules. The verification is done on a polygon-by-polygon basis and is not designed for detecting violations that involve different polygons.

The paper first presents the various violation types that can be detected up-front, when the hierarchical structure is still intact. Some of these violations are very easy to detect and the corresoponding trivial algorithms are given just for the sake of completeness. Detecting other violations is more complex and involves intersection finding. The second part of this paper presents the corresponding algorithms and estimates their efficiency.


DIGITIZING ERRORS


The following errors will be detected:

1.  <u>Open polygons</u>. The polygons in the mask database must be closed.

2.  <u>Reentrant polygons</u>. These polygons have a mismatch of solid/hole designators and therefore are invalid memebers of the artwork. Figure 1 shows such a reentrant polygon.

    The engineer who digitized the polygon of Fig. 1 intended to draw 2 solid rectangles. Since he didn't break the edge (2-3) at point A, he ended up having one rectangular solid (1-2-A-6-1) and one rectangular hole (A-3-4-5-A). The error is that the hole is not surrounded by solid.

3.  <u>Self-intersected wide lines</u>. Conductive path may be digitized as a polygon with a width attribute. A self-intersection of such wide lines is not allowed.

4.  <u>Invalid angles</u>. Some pattern generators can handle only 45 and 90 degrees polygon angles and different angles are considered errors.

5.  <u>Less-Than-A-Half-Unit features</u>. Two edges may be almost colinear or almost coincident and a simple check determines if a merge operation can take place. Figure 2 shows two

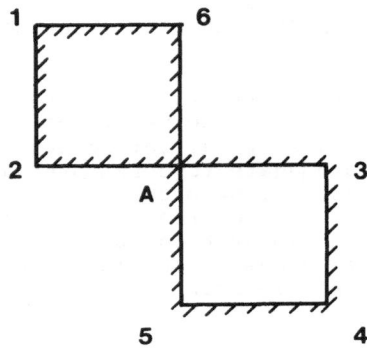

Figure 1. A "reentrant" polygon. The hole A-3-4-5-A is not surrounded by solid.

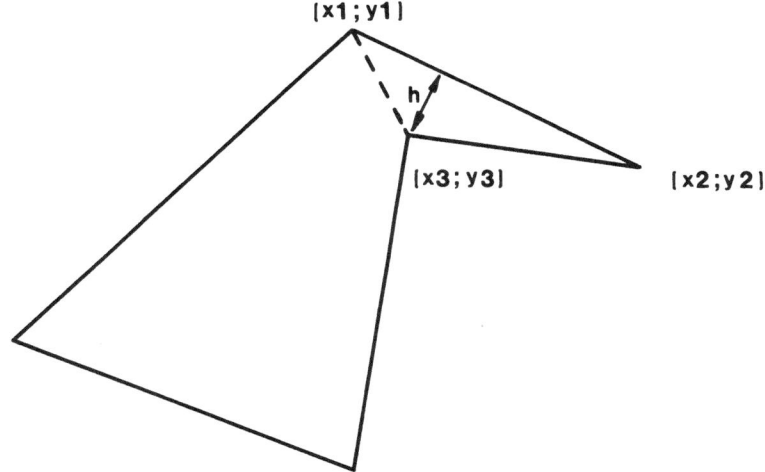

Figure 2. Almost-conicident edges. If h is less than a half
database unit, the vertex (x2;y2) and the edges that are connected to
it are all deleted. A new edge (x1;y1)-(x3;y3) is formed.

almost-coincident edges. Suppose that the edges connecting
(x1;y1) with (x2;y2) and (x2;y2) with (x3;y3) constitute a
triangular section of a polygon. The height of the triangle
is h and is exprssed as:

$$h = \frac{m(x3-x1)-(y3-y1)}{\sqrt{1 + m^2}} \qquad [1]$$

where

$$m = \frac{y2-y1}{x2-x1} \qquad [2]$$

and the condition for deleting the vertex (x2;y2) is

$$h < 0.5 \qquad [3]$$

Figure 3 shows almost-colinear edges for which a similar
test can be applied

ALGORITHMS

The data is analysed in polygon order. Open polygons are detected by
checking the identity of the first and last vertex coordinates.
Invalid angles and Less-Than-A-Half-Unit features are detected by

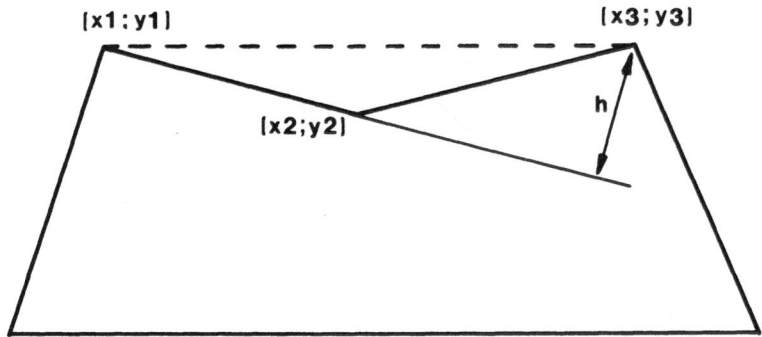

Figure 3. Almost-colinear edges. If h is less than a half database unit, the vertex (x2;y2) and the edges that are connected to it are all deleted. A new edge (x1;y1)-(x3;y3) is formed.

traversing the polygon from head to tail with a 3-vertex-wide detection window. When two edges are found to be too close to each other the candidate vertex for deletion is marked. At the end of the traversal, the deleted vertices are removed and the modified polygon is written out. Figure 4 shows the moving detection window.

The scanline algorithm is used for detecting both self-intersected and reentrant polygons. The main idea in this algorithm is to sweep a horizontal scanline from bottom of the chip to its top, through the plane. The scanline 'combs' the plane, thus defines a horizontal

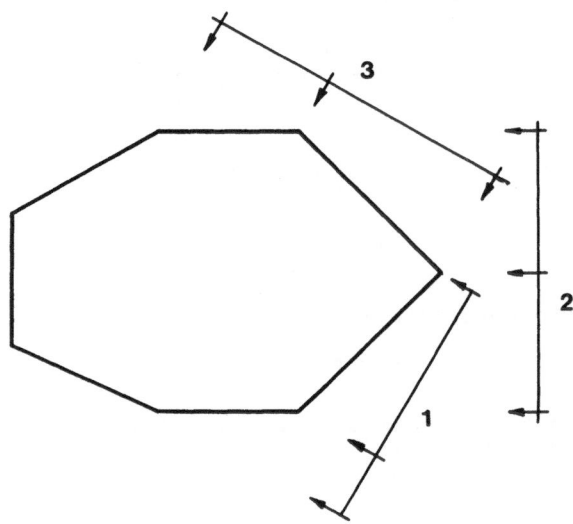

Figure 4. The moving detection window. Three vertices at a time are examined for detection of almost-coincident edges and almost-colinear edges. Deleted vertices are flagged during the traversal of the polygon and all the marked vertices are removed at the end of the polygon scanning.

order on the line segments crossing it. Banltey and Ottman (1979) first used this algorithm to find intersections in a layout database. They used 2 data structures: a list R which contains (in a sorted order) the segments which currently cross the scanline, and a priority queue Q which is used to buffer input edges coming from disk file and new edges resulting from splitting. The complexity of their algorithm is O(N log N), since this is the time associated with both DELETEMIN and INSERT operation defined for the priority queue Q (Aho et al. 1983). DELETEMIN operation deletes the minimal element from a priority queue and INSERT operation inserts an element in a priority queue.

Since the database is processed in polygon order, all of the polygon edges can be kept in main memory without any difficulties. While reading in the polygon data, the edges are entered into a 2-dimensional doubly-linked list. Figure 5 shows the data structure for a simple polygon. The oreder of insertion to the list is the order of the incoming edges of the polygon. The y-header is pointing to the most recently used (MRU) edge on that scanline. The most recently used y-header is also kept in main memory.

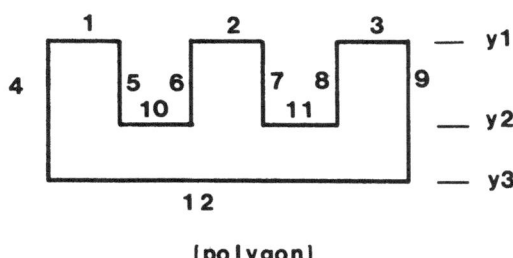

(polygon)

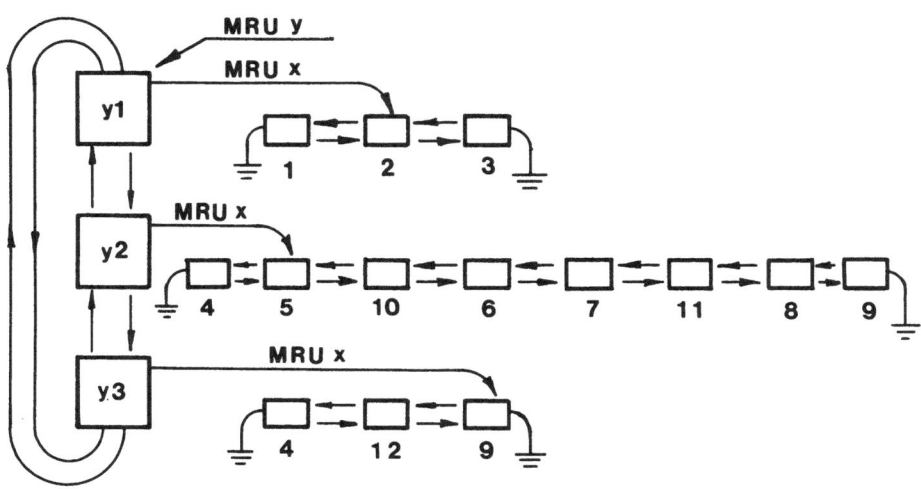

Figure 5. Data structure for the scanline algorithm. The data-structure adjacency of physically adjacent vertices makes the algorithm linear in complexity. MRU stands for Most Recently Used.

The key assumption is that since the edges are read in the order of the polygon traversal, the change in the target scanline for successive insertion (up or down) is O(1). This is due to statistical data that shows that usually an edge will span only a few scanlines, relative to the total number of scanlines. If the database contain N edges, the complexity of the algorithm will be O(N). Figure 6 shows the basic combing algorithm. When traversing a scanline, its edges are linked to the next scanline. If intersection is found a new scanline is created. As always with scanline algorithms, only adjacent edges can intersect each other.

The complexity of combing the layout is linear in H*S, where H is the average number of entries per scanline and S is the number of different scanlines. It was shown by Lauther (1981) and measured by Banteley et al. (1979) that H*S is O(N). In the presented application, there are 2 tasks : reading the edges into the 2-D doubly-linked list with complexity O(N) and scanning the edges with complexity O(N). The complexity of the algorithm is therefore O(N).

When scanning the horizontal lines, the concept of "front" is used. It is constructed from one non-horizontal edge and one horizontal edge (optional). The area to the left of the "front" which bounded by the current scanline and the next scanline is considered checked and irrelevant any more. The process of traversing the scanline is done through repetitive updating of the "front".

When looking for self-intersected wide lines, processing is terminated when the first intersection is found. When checking for reentrant polygons, an accumulator keeps track of the solid/hole designators for all the edges scanned. The accumulator is initialized to zero and then is incremented when a solid is entered and is decremented when the solid is left. A reentrant polygon is detected when this accumulator becomes negative. Figure 7 shows such a polygon. An overlapping polygon is shown on Figure 8. Notice that the accumulator never becomes negative.

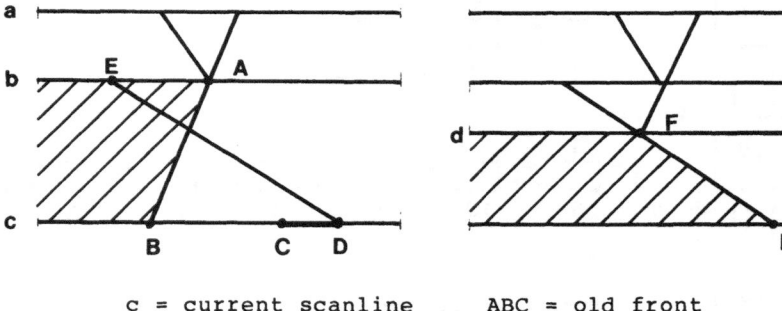

c = current scanline    ABC = old front
b = next scanline       FD  = new front
d = new scanline        ED  = new edge

Figure 6. Intersection finding in the scanline algorithm. The "front" is either one edge (FD) or two edges (ABC) which separates the already-processed zone and the yet-to-be-processed zone between the current scanline and the next scanline.

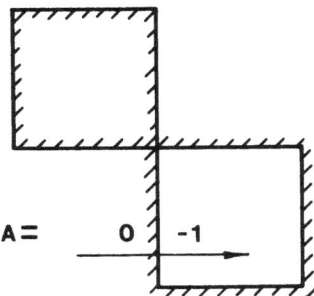

Figure 7. Detecting a "reentrant" polygon. Accumulator A is incremented when a solid is entered and is decremented when a solid is left. A negative accumulator signals a "reentrant" polygon.

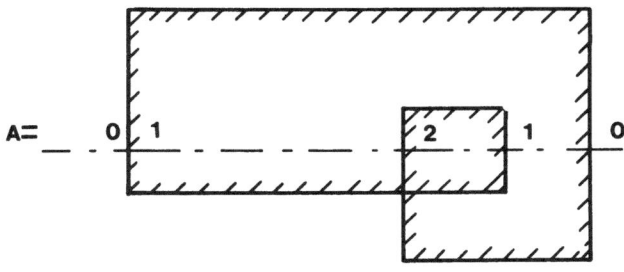

Figure 8. A self-overlapping polygon. Accumulator A never becomes negative.

SUMMARY

The papaer shows a new validating scheme for VLSI graphic database. It outlines the various violation types and describes the algorithms for detecting them. The non-trivial ones are for detecting self-intersecting and reentrant polygons. Since the database is processed in a polygon-by-polygon basis, the complexity of the algorithm is linear. Leaving the violations undetected may cause very expensive errors in the pattern generation process. Validating the hierarchical database saves in CPU time and memory requirements. Only technology- and application-independent violations are detected, so the valid database may be used in several different applications.

# REFERENCES

Aho AV, Hopcroft EJ, Ullman DJ (1983) Data Structures and Algorithms. Addison-Wesley, Reading Menlo Park London Amsterdam Don Syndey.

Bentley JL, Ottman TA (1979) Algorithms for Reporting and Counting Geometric Intersections. IEEE Trans. Comp. 6-28(9): 643-647.

Lauther U (1981) An O (N log N) Algorithm For Boolean Mask Operations. Proc. 18th DA Conf., pp. 555-562.

**Yehuda Shiran** is a Member of Technical Staff at SILVAR-LISCO/NCA Corporation, Santa Clara, California. Before then, he was a research programming consultant at EPRI - Electric Power Research Institute, Palo Alto, California. From 1975 to 1980 he held a technical position with the Israeli Ministry of Defense. His current research areas of interest are IC design verification, silicon compilation, computational geometry, supercomputers in engineering applications and fluid dynamics.

Shiran received his BSc and MSc in Mechanical Engineering from the Technion - Haifa, Israel in 1975 and 1980. He received his MS in Electrical Engineering from Stanford University in 1984 and is currently a Ph.D candidate at Stanford University.

# Format-Independent CAD Software
# for VLSI Mask Data Preparation

Yehuda Shiran

SILVAR-LISCO/NCA Corporation, 3250 Jay Street, Santa Clara, CA 95054, USA

ABSTRACT: IC design database consists of several graphic layers. Manufacturing is based on exposing a glass plate or a silicon wafer to patterns of light, derived from the graphic database. This paper deals with a class of strip-based pattern generators (PG), for which each graphic layer needs fo be partitioned into tiles of machine=dependent dimensions. Format-independent partitioning methodology is shown. It consists of graphic boolean operations between machine-dependent "checkerboard" layer and the design graphic layer. Since these operators are assumed to be off=the=shelf general purpose modules, the new method saves the development of different partitioning modules for different pattern generators.

KEYWORDS: Pattern generators, IC design database, graphic layers, Electron Beam Pattern Generators, Laser Pattern Generators, pattern generator database, trapezoidal representation, vector representation, bit=map representation, magnification, scaling.

INTRODUCTION

The industry trend towards smaller and smaller line width in the layout artwork accelerates the development of those PG (Pattern Generating) machines with smaller wave length beam. The electron beam and the laser beam are the most common now. E=beam is ideal for exposing resist materials with line width in the 0.1 micron range (Fay 1976; Mead and Conway 1980). Laser beam can generate even thinner lines (0.025 micron).

Several companies are involved in the manufacturing of E=beam and laser PG machines. Some of the companies even have several models for the same technology. Usually each model comes with its own data format, into which the system design files (in common intermediate form) must be converted. The generation of PG files is analogous (Mead and Conway 1980) to the loading and executing of machine code to produce output files: All symbol descriptions in the intermediate form must be fully instantiating into a format suitable for a particular machine.

Converting a design database to PG format involves two major steps. The first step is the partitioning of the graphic data in some fashion. Since partitioning of graphic data always involves complex operations like finding intersections and edge breaking, this task is not a trivial one. The experience shows that such a task is in order of 8 man-months of design, programming and testing. Usually, a new partitioning module is developed for every new format coming out of the PG industry. The contribution of the paper is by showing a new way of patitioning the data. The method presented is independent of the target PG format and is based on off-the-shelf software modules such as graphic boolean operators (AND and ANDNOT).

The second step of the conversion depends on the target PG format. The paper shows that this task is usually straight-forward and simpler than the first one.

The paper is structured in a top-down fashion. First, the interface design is outlined. The common format-independent steps are detailed. Secondly, the partitioning algorithm is described and demonstrated. Finally, an overview of the different PG formats is given and the format-dependent part of the conversion is assessed.


INTERFACE DESIGN OUTLINE


Most interfaces may be constructed from the following steps (see Fig. 1):


Magnification; When the foundary uses a mask (as opposite to direct write) there is a vertical gap between the mask and the wafer. The purpose of the gap is to make the etched lines much finer than the lines on the mask. Therefore the features on the mask need to be coarser than those in the original design database. A typical magnification value is 10x.


Scaling; Each PG machine has its own database unit size. It may range from 0.1 micorn to 1.0 micron. The design database unit is different from the PG database unit and scaling should be done. Since the Design Database Unit (Design DBU) is much smaller than the PG-DBU, the scaling operation is a division of every coordinate by the DBUs ratio. Including magnification, each value in the Design Database is converted to PG-DBU by the following formula:

$$PG\text{-}Value = Design\text{-}Value * M * \frac{Design\ DBU}{PG\ DBU} \qquad [1]$$

Where M is the magnification factor.


Partitioning; A PG machine is usually driven by a small microcomputer with a limited amount of main memory. This necessitates the Divide-and-Process method. The design artwork of the chip is divided into rows and columns of small area tiles. Some formats are designed with long stripes to cover the whole chip, so only one-dimensional partitioning is needed. The paper refers here, however, to the general case of 2-D partitioning.


After slicing the chip in both the x-direction and in the y-direction in this checkerboard-like manner, each checker has to surround only self-contained and independent polygons. All polygons within the

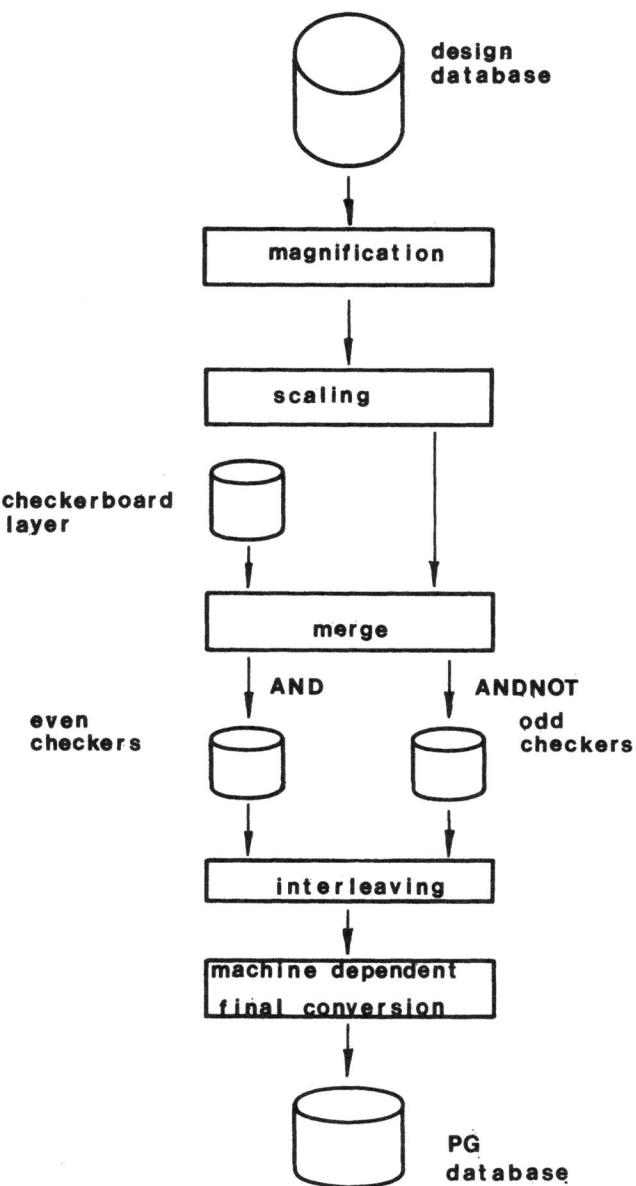

Figure 1.  Data flow in the new PG interface design.

checker  should  be  closed.   Figure  2  shows  a  polygon  in  both
intermediate (design) form and in PG form.  Note that the polygon  is
partitioned  only  when  it  intersects  the  separating line between
adjacent tiles.  PG machines differ from each other in the format  in
which the data within the checker is represented.

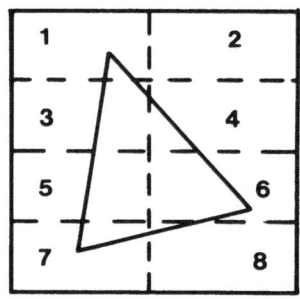    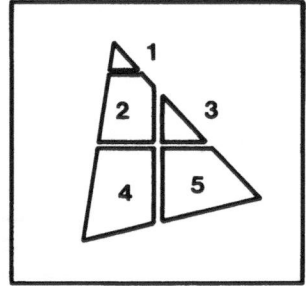

a. design database format       b. PG database format

Figure 2. A triangle in both design format and PG format. The stripes in a and the new polygons in b are both numbered according to the processing order by the PG machine.


Final Conversion; This step is the machine dependent one. The data in the design database needs to be converted to the specific PG format. As described below, we may need to convert it to either triangles and trapezoids, vectors or bit-map representation. Sometimes the coordinates should be reversed. Once the problem is reduced to the checker boundaries, the conversion task is relatively simple: there is no need for intersection search, breaking of edges or boolean operations (except for the trapezoidal format where additional slicing of the polygon is needed).


DATABASE CHECKERBOARD PARTITIONING

The first step in the partitioning uses a ready-and-tested off-the-shelf software module which merge two grphic databases and is capable of generating new database which is the result of a graphic boolean operation between these inputs (Szymanski and Van Wyk 1984). The database is merged with a specially-prepared checkerboard layer. Figure 3 shows such pattern of partitioning layer. The exact size of the checkers is machine dependent. Some of the PG machines require only one vertical column of checkers, some need more than two. There will be 2 boolean operations: AND and ANDNOT. The AND operation will mask the features inside the black checkers (numbered 1-5 in Fig. 3) and the ANDNOT operation will mask the figures inside the white checkers (numbered A-E in Fig. 3). Figure 5 shows the two layers generated by the boolean operations when applied to the shape in Fig. 4.


The partitioning of the design database is completed by interleaving the two outtput databases (coming from the merge operations) into a single database that is later converted to the target PG format. In order to interleave the two databases, all the polygons are labeled with their checker number and then each of the databases is sorted by checker number. Suppose that the polygons in the AND database are

Figure 3. Checkerboard graphic layer. The dimensions of the tiles are machine dependent. Black checkers are labeled with numbers, white checkers are labeled with letters.

Figure 4. An arbitrary polygon to be used in the demonstration of the graphic boolean operations.

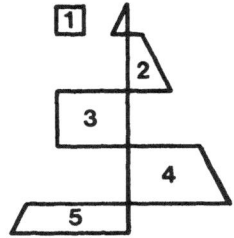
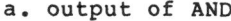

a. output of AND

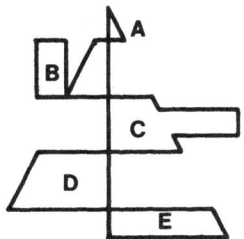

b. output of ANDNOT

Figure 5. The output of AND and ANDNOT operations between the polygon of Fig. 4 and the checkerboard layer of Fig. 3. Polygons labeled with numbers were masked by the white checkers of Fig. 3. Polygons labeled with letters were masked by the black checkers.

labeled with the checker identifiers 1, 2, 3, 4 and 5 and those in the ANDNOT database are labeled with the identifiers A, B, C, D and E.  Both files are then being read and the checkers are interleaved: checker #1 and then checker #A, checker #2 and then checker #B and so on.  Figure 6 shows the reading sequence needed for proper interleaving.  The task of partitioning the database is accomplished now.  Each checker is now containing close polygons which should be converted to the target PG format.  The next section gives an overview of these different formats.

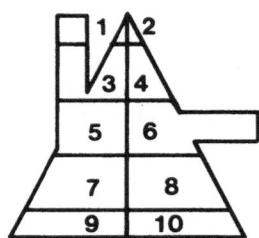

Figure 6.  Interleaving order of AND and ANDNOT databases.  Needs to match the processing order of the PG machine as shown in Fig. 2.


AN OVERVIEW OF PG FORMATS


Since the PG format is used to represent a graphic data, the well-known methods from computer graphics theory are adopted:


Trapezoidal Representation;  Every polygon should be further fractured into triangles and trapezoids.  Figure 7 shows polygon #2 from Fig. 2, represented in this format.  Converting general polygons to trapezoids (triangles included) invovles an additional edge breaking as in the partitioning, but the location of the breaking cannot be determined beforehand and must be tailored to the specific shape.  The mechanism cannot be automated as before – it should have some intelligence.


Vector Representation;  For a machine where the beam scans the stripe from end to end, the vectors on that stripe turn the beam on and off.  Each vector information includes the geometric details and the flag for turning the beam on or off.  As the beam scans the stripe, an accumulator of the on-off bit is kept.  It is initialized to zero before the scan and then is incremented when the beam hits an 'on' vector and is decremented when the vector is an 'off' one.  The beam is actually turned on when the accumulator becomes positive (from zero), stays on as long as it is positive and is turned off when it becomes zero again.  Figure 8 shows how this vector representation drives the beam.  The vectors in the same stripe point to the same direction which may alternate between the odd stripes and the even stripes to shorten the beam idle time.  Since the beam path is always perpendicular to the stripe, the vertical edges are not included in the database, thus reducing the volume of the data to a half (in general).

Converting the design database (after partitioning) to the vector representation is very simple: every non-vertical edge is translated to a vector format in a one-to-one mapping fashion. No fracturing or intersection finding is needed.

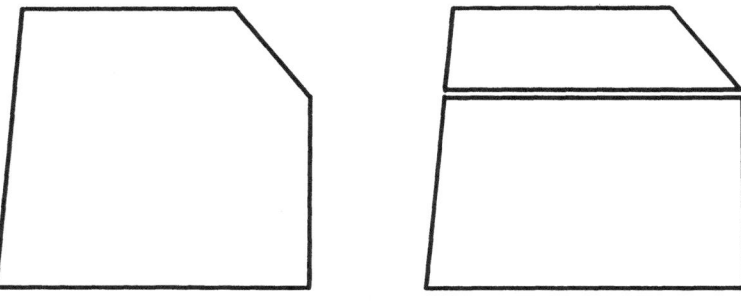

a. design format          b. trapezoidal PG format

Figure 7. Trapezoidal representation of polygon no. 2 of Fig. 2. Slicing of the polygon to trapezoids cannot be automated as the partitioning of the whole chip; It depends on the specific polyon.

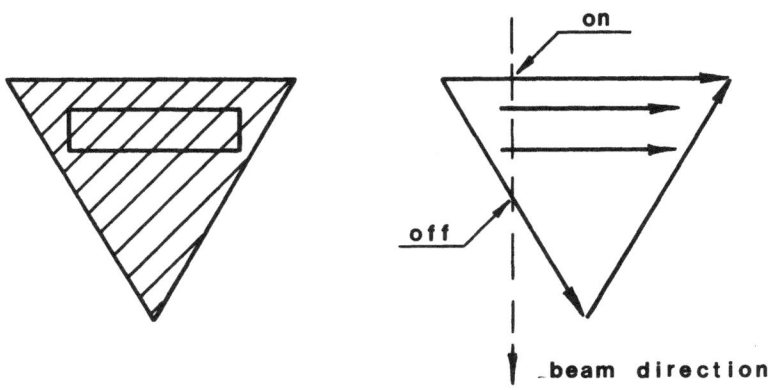

a. design format          b. vector-based PG format

Figure 8. Representation of averlapping polygons in both design database format (a) and vector representation (b). Every vector carries both the geometric details and the on-off bit. Starting from zero, the beam increments the on-off accumulator when it hits an 'on' vector and decrements the accumulator when it hits an 'off' vector. The beam is actually turned on when the accumulator becomes 1 from 0 and it is turned off when the accumulator becomes 0 from 1. The beam does not change its state otherwise.

Bit-map Representation; The database unit in the PG file depends on several factors, among them the beam size and the details of its operation. Each square area of 1 unit is either 'on' (exposed to light) or 'off' (opaque). The partitioning of the chip is designed in such a way, that every line can be represented by a full memory word. For example, if the word length is 32 bits, a row of 32 squares can be accommodated. Figure 9 shows a polygon and its bit-map representation. For a checker of size 20x20 units ≈ 20 memory words are needed, each of 20 bits.

Since the design database is usually in vector-like representation, converting it to a bit-map representation can be done by one of many known vector-to-raster translators. As before, no fracturing or breaking of edges is needed.

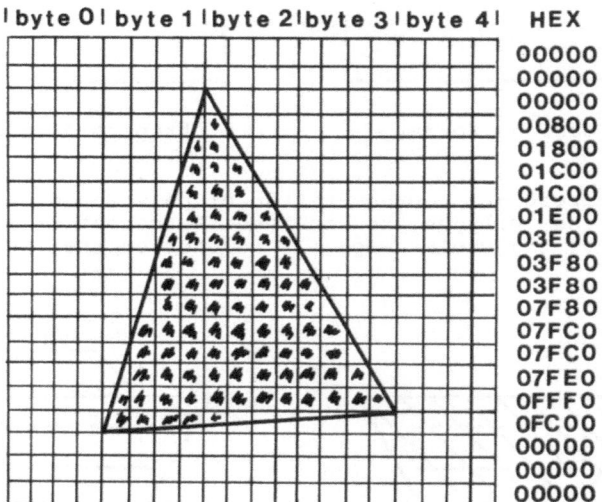

| byte 0 | byte 1 | byte 2 | byte 3 | byte 4 | HEX |

00000
00000
00000
00800
01800
01C00
01C00
01E00
03E00
03F80
03F80
07F80
07FC0
07FC0
07FE0
0FFF0
0FC00
00000
00000
00000

Figure 9. A bit-map representation of a polygon. Assuming that every column is stored in one memory word, the dimension of the tiles are determined by the length of the microcomputer memory word. In this example, the height of the columns is 20 bits. If every bit is representing a micron-by-micron square area, the height of the tile is 20 microns.

SUMMARY

The paper shows how to use general-purpose modules, such as boolean operations, in the design of interfaces for non-optical PG machines. These common programs accomplish most of the complicated tasks associated with the processing of the design database. The PG machine-dependency affects only the checkerboard pattern layer and the final conversion within the checker boundaries. The new method may save about 8 man-months for every interface that uses the proposed sequence of machine-independent modules, instead of a machine-dependent partitioning module. Since all interfaces use the same partitioning modules, savings in maintenance are also significant.

REFERENCES

Fay et al. (1976) X-Ray replication of masks using the synchrotron radiation produced by the ACO storage ring. App. Phys. Lett. 29: 370-372.

Mead CA, Conway LA (1980) Introduction to VLSI systems. Addison-Wesley, Reading Menlo Park London Amsterdam Don Mills Syndey.

Spiller et al. (1976) Application of synchrotron radiation to X-Ray lithography. J. App. Phys. 47: 5450-5459.

Szymanski TG, Van Wyk CJ (1984) GOALIE: A space-efficient system for VLSI artwork analysis. International Conference on Computer Aided Design, pp. 278-280.

Varian/Extrion Division (1979) Ee-BES-40 Electron Beam Lithography System. Varian Corp., Gloucester.

**Yehuda Shiran** is a Member of Technical Staff at SILVAR-LISCO/NCA Corporation, Santa Clara, California. Before then, he was a research programming consultant at EPRI - Electric Power Research Institute, Palo Alto, California. From 1975 to 1980 he held a technical position with the Israeli Ministry of Defense. His current research areas of interest are IC design verification, silicon compilation, computational geometry, supercomputers in engineering applications and fluid dynamics.

Shiran received his BSc and MSc in Mechanical Engineering from the Technion - Haifa, Israel in 1975 and 1980. He received his MS in Electrical Engineering from Stanford University in 1984 and is currently a Ph.D candidate at Stanford University.

# NISC
## Non-Iterative Silicon Compiler

Yehuda Shiran

SILVAR-LISCO/NCA Corporation, 3250 Jay Street, Santa Clara, CA 95054, USA

ABSTRACT: A new silicon compiler system is described. Given a schematic description of the circuit and a physical description of the basic devices or gates, NISC synthesizes the chip layout using a bottom-up hierarchical approach. The main advantage of NISC over other silicon compilers is that it constructs the layout without iterations or feedback loops between the router and the placement module. The other new features of NISC is that it can start its synthesis from device level (FET) instead of gate level and it is driven be a silicon compilation language which is used for design verification as well.

KEYWORDS: Silicon compilers, IC layout synthesis, Design verification, Place and route, IC layout analysis, Hierarchical layout system.

## INTRODUCTION

Silicon Compiler is defined by Goldberg et al. (1985) as "An optimizing transformation program that produces mask-level description of manufacturable VLSI circuits from an intelligent input language description". Janier and Jerraya (1985) pointed out that a lot of software tools can be considered as silicon compilers. One of the reasons why silicon compilers are not widely accepted by the industry (Evanczuk 1985) is their limited spectrum. They produce regular structures of fixed architecture as:

1. Gate arrays.

2. Programmable Logic Arrays (PLAs)(Fung et al. 1982, Powell et al. 1984, Demicheli and Sangiovanni-Vincentelli 1983).

3. Read Only Memories (ROMs), Random Access Memories (RAMs) (Law 1985) and Finite State Machines (FSMs) (Meyer et al. 1984).

4. Arithmetic Logic Units (ALUs) (Law 1985).

5. Parameterized cell generators (Edgington et al. 1984).

6. Weinberger arrays (Southard et al. 1984).

These silicon compilers, sometimes called module generators (Law 1985), may be considered as sophisticated parametrized graphic editors. Each editor is suitable only for a specific predefined graphic structure (PLA, ROM, FSM etc).

Other silicon compilers are broader in spectrum and only the tools belonging to this class can really be called silicon compilers (Janier and Jerraya 1985). Still, several of these compilers are restricted in their target architecture or function as:

1. Signal Processor (Denyer et al. 1982).

2. Data Path (Janier and Jerraya 1985).

3. Path Programmable Logic (PPL) circuits (Peterson and Smith 1984).

4. CMOS Leaf Cells (Nogatch and Hedges 1985).

The third class of silicon compilers includes those that can produce layout for random logic circuits. Since NISC belongs to this group, the paper deals mainly with this type of tools.

Schleider and Rappaport (1985) found that most engineers deemphasized the importance of IC CAD tools and silicon compilers were considered unimportant by the widest margin (64% for early adopters and 80% for mainstream users). Evanczuk (1985) interviewed a couple of CAD managers and tried to pinpoint the reasons for this dissatisfaction. The main finding is that for a silicon compiler to be widely accepted, it needs to be:

1. a general-purpose tool.

2. flexible.

3. intended for engineers without IC design expertise.

The contribution of this paper is in two different levels. First, it shows why NISC is a general-purpose tool, flexible and not intended for experienced IC designers only. As with other silicon compilers, the user needs to provide a library of layout cells. The advantage of NISC is that the cells may be at the device level. In NMOS technology, for example, one may start the compilation from as few as 2 cells: the enhancement-mode and the depletion-mode transistors. Since the primitive-level devices are common to all circuits of the same technology, the capability of NISC to start the compilation from this level makes it a general-purpose tool. NISC is not geared towards a specific target architecture, nor is it intended for a regular predefined structure.

The flexibility of NISC stems from its capability to start the compilation from any level of the layout. Experienced designers may start the process from a high level of cells, while the novice ones will tend to start from a much more primitive level such as the device level (transistors, capacitors, resistors and diodes).

There are two other reasons why NISC is intended for engineers without design proficiency. The first one has to do with the simple input requirements. Besides the layout library, NISC uses the schematic description file which is presumably already used for the design verification of the chip.

The elimination of the user's involvement in the compilation process is the second reason why NISC may appeal to other than IC design engineers. Other systems, such as AIDA (Rose 1985), expect the user to help the compilation in different ways such as partition the chip into functional blocks or placing the diodes individually.

The other area of this paper's contribution is the technical one and is transparent to the user. It shows how methods from Building Block Layout (BBL) systems can be modified and adopted to a hierarchical bottom-up clustering system. Specifically, the integration of a special routing methodology (RRDO) (Dai 1985) makes the whole compiler a non-iterative one.

Different routers are implemented in the current silicon compilers. Most systems use some kind of feedback mechanism between the router and the placement module (Ullman 1984). This feedback initiates the expanding of the layout whenever is needed. Nogatch and Hodges (1985) cut the layout from one end to the other, stretch the two parts and then compact them again. Compaction methods were studied by Schlag et al. (1984), Wolf et al. (1984) and Boyer (1984). Wisniewski and Peters (1984) iteratively expand the routing channels by solving a minimum flow problem. The router of the SILC Silicon Compiler (Ciesielsky 1984) also uses an iterative procedure to release the excessive tracks from routable channels and relocate them to unroutable ones. In the second step of this iterative procedure, each of the remaining unroutable channels is allowed one extra track.

The advantages of non-iterative silicon compiler is obvious. The routing is always guaranteed and the compilation is much faster.

The paper begins with a description of the overall system configuration and the principles of the bottom-up building of the layout library are given. The hierarchical synthesis of the layout is demonstrated via a 4-bit adder chip. The structural compilation language (which is also used in the design verification) is described. The placement/clustering algorithm is then outlined. At last, the routing algorithm is overviewd and demonstrated.

OVERALL SYSTEM CONFIGURATION

The silicon compilation system presented in this paper is a bottom-up implementation of the hierarchical description of the chip. Starting

from a library of manually designed special cells and a schematic
description, NISC generates the PG files for all the layers (see
Fig. 1). During the silicon compilation, new cells are synthesized
at each level of the hierarchical layout from the predefined cells or
from a lower level cells.

In bottom-up layout, the capability of summarizing the current level
designs as library cells for the next higher level of processing is
called ghosting (Rose 1984). Each cell is synthesized using an
automatic placement and routing and then is automatically ghosted and
placed in the library.

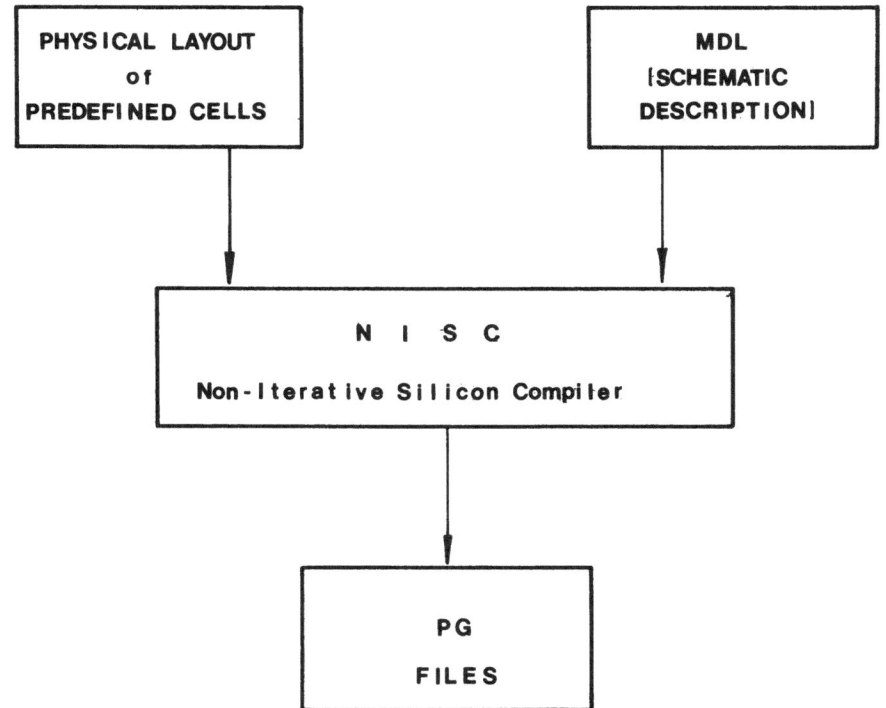

Figure 1. System configuration of NISC.

Figure 2 shows graphically the schematic description of a 4-Bit Adder
chip. The input library of basic cells includes an enhancement-mode
FET (QE), a depletion-mode FET (QD) and a pad cell. Figure 3 shows
the bottom-up layout process and how cells are ghosted to the library
and used again in higher level designs. NISC syntesizes each cell
using its unique router and placement module (described later). Two
predefined cells (QE-enhancement transistor and QD-depletion
transistor) are shown in Fig. 4 and Fig. 5. Figure 6 shows the cell
Al2 that was synthesized from QE, and Fig. 7 shows the cell AN32
which was assembled from the cells QD and Al2. Note that the cells
are not limited to rectangular boundaries.

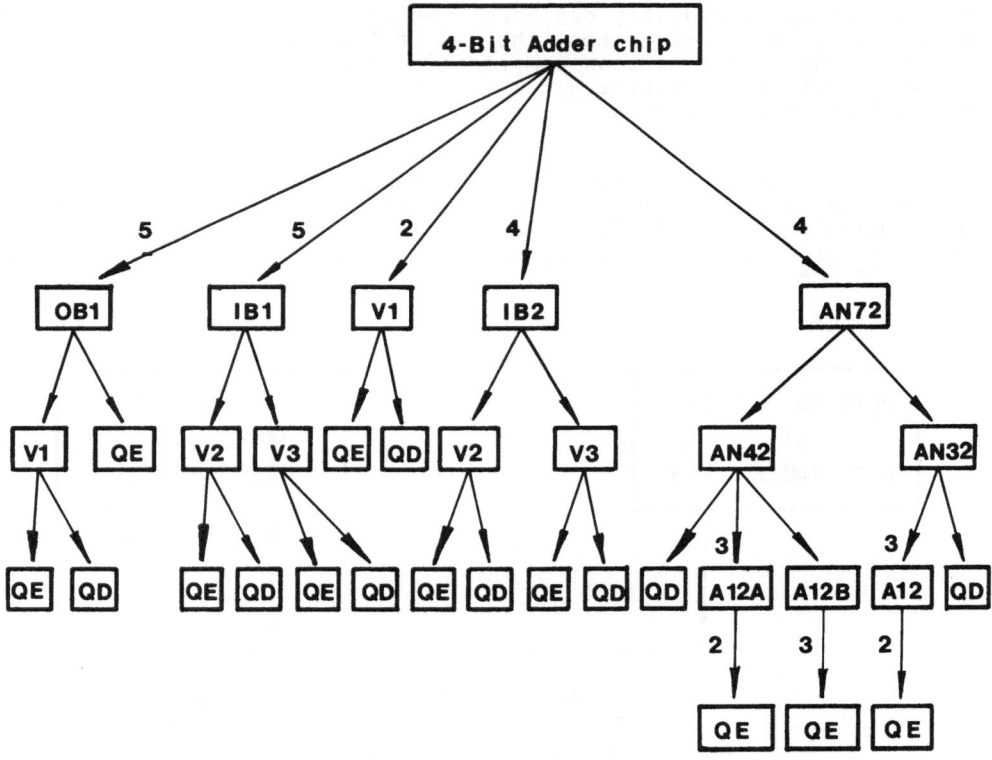

Figure 2. An hierarchical description of the 4-Bit Adder chip.

Once the whole chip is assembled, the pads are placed around it and then automatically routed. The predefined cells are stretchable and their actual dimensions are determined from the layout description file which is written in a Hardware Description Language called MDL - Master Design Language.

MDL – A STRUCTURAL COMPILATION LANGUAGE

MDL is unique in that it serves both the synthesis of the design (NISC) and the analysis of the design (DESIGN VERIFICATION). It has an hierarchical structure of macros similar to the C language preprocessor. Each macro calls other macros or primitive devices. Each predefined or synthesized cell has two views: the schematic view and the layout view. MDL language serves both views by giving the topology of the subcircuit as well as the parameters needed for the final layout view. Figures 4, 5, 6 and 7 show the views of four different cells and the corresponding MDL specifications.

427

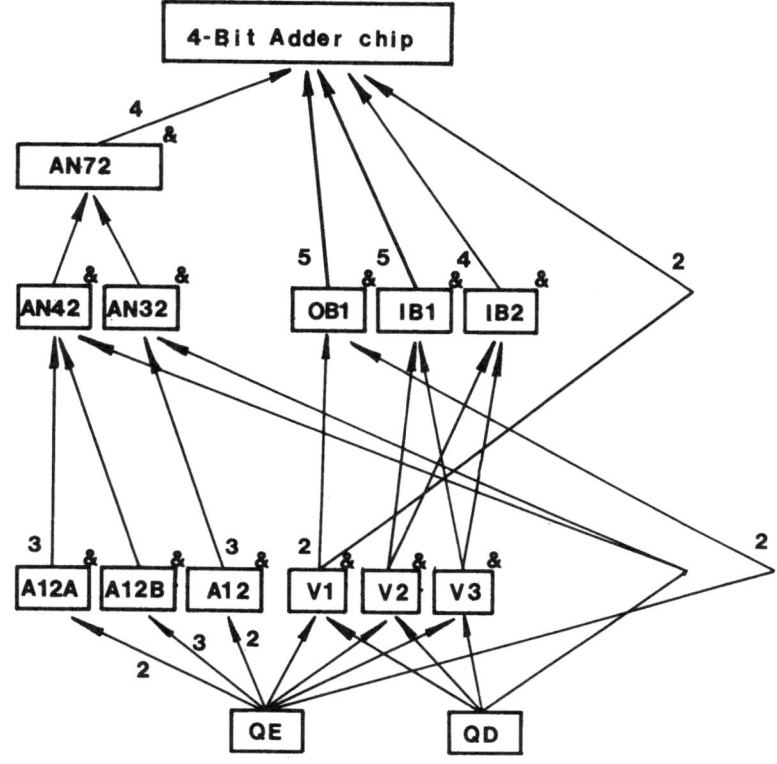

Figure 3. Bottom-up layout synthesis of the 4-Bit Adder chip.

SPECIFICATION

QE   GATE   SOURCE   DRAIN   CW/L   w/l

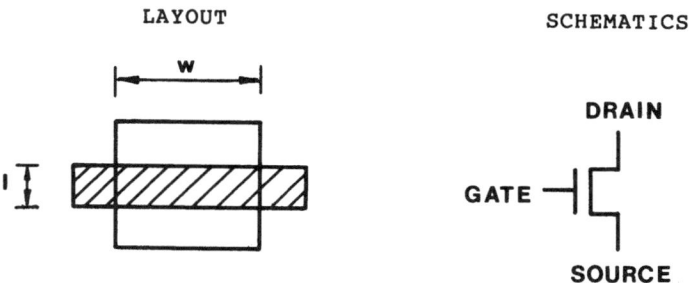

LAYOUT                          SCHEMATICS

Figure 4. Two views of a predefined layout library cell enhancement transistor.

SPECIFICATION

QD    SOURCE    DRAIN    CW/L    w/l

LAYOUT                                                    SCHEMATICS

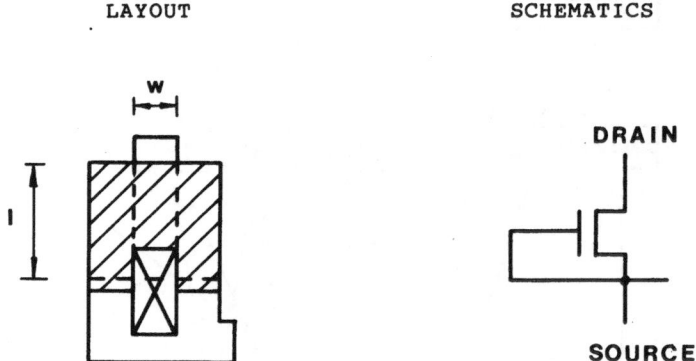

Figure 5.   Two views of a predefined layout library cell -   depletion
transistor.

SPECIFICATION

```
DEFINE   A12   I(G, A, B)   O(OUT)
   QE   B   G   $1     CW/L   10/3
   QE   A   $1   OUT   CW/L    8/3
ENDMACRO
```

LAYOUT                                               SCHEMATICS

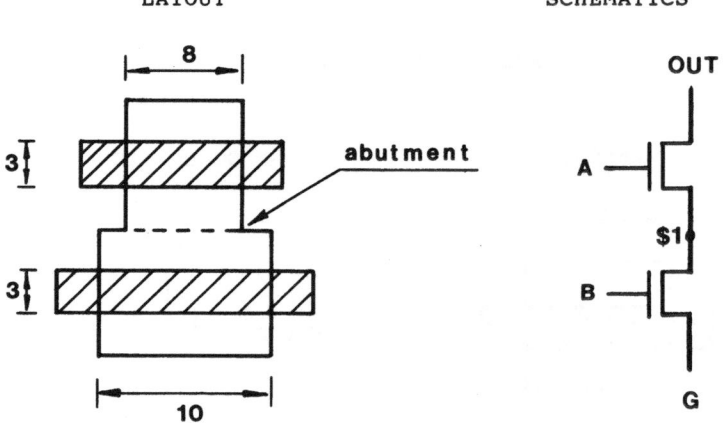

Figure 6.   Two views of a synthesized layout cell -   two   enhancement
transistors in series.   Abutment is used to assemble the cell.

SPECIFICATION

```
DEFINE   AN32  I(D1, E1, D2, E2, D3, E3)   O(OUT)
    A12   I(VSS, D1, E1)   O(OUT)
    A12   I(VSS, D2, E2)   O(OUT)
    A12   I(VSS, D3, E3)   O(OUT)
    QD    OUT   OUT    CW/L   3/8
ENDMACRO
```

SCHEMATICS

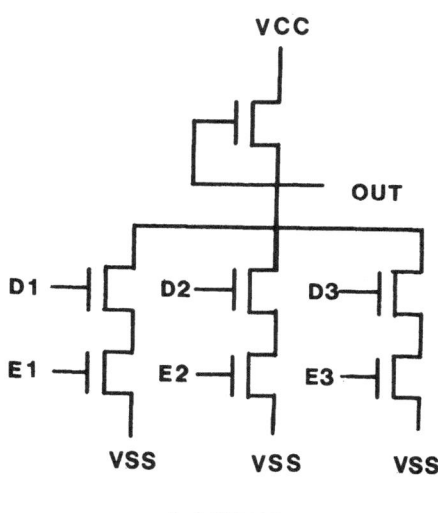

LAYOUT

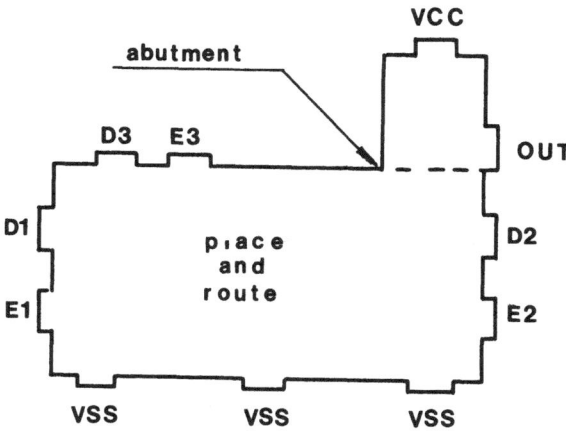

Figure 7.  Two views of a synthesized layout cell ← 2-AND-3-OR  gate.
Both abutment and place-and≠route methods are used.

The MDL language includes several features which are used both in the analysis and in the synthesis of the design. The CW/L check (W/L ratio for FET) is used to stretch the corresponding library cell (QD in Figure 4) to a proper ratio, before placing it. On the gate level, MDL has a CHECK-BETA feature which directs NISC how to stretch the individual devices to arrive at the specified beta ratio. Using a HDL (Hardware Description Language) for both design verification and silicon compilation is very convenient from the point of view of the user: he has to assemble only one description and may use it for both purposes.

PLACEMENT

The placement module of NISC is based on several concepts. The first one is that of abutment. Whenever 2 cells have only 1 interconnect, they will be abutted to each other along that pin, instead of being conventionally routed. Figures 6 and 7 demonstrate this concept. The second concept is a bottom-up pairing, similar to that of BBL (Chen et al. 1983,1984). It is applied after all the singly interconnected cells are abutted. The pairing sequence follows that of the min-cut algorithm and the top-down partitioning of Kim (1984), but in a bottom-up fashion. In this method, the pair with the maximum number of interconnections is placed before all the other pairs. This scheme may be called max-cut algorithm. Once the pair is determined, the actual relative placement of the cells depends on the following prioritized criteria:

1.  Align the modules so that maximum number of common-net pins are facing the routing region between them.

2.  Align the modules along their longer side.

3.  Align the modules to take advantage of the "shoe box" compaction, if at all possible. Since the cell boundaries are not restricted to a rectangular shape, the layout may be significantly compacted by using this method. This built-in compaction is similar to that used by Wolf (1983).

Figure 8 demonstrates the above criteria for the alignment of a pair of cells. In case of a tie in the pairing process, NISC uses the concept of minimum bandwidth of BBL : cells with close dimensions are paired first.

Nisc is designed to arrive at chip aspect ratio close to 1:1. In order to achieve it, it keeps changing the axis of pairing as in the min-cut algorithm. Figure 9 shows this placement concept.

ROUTING

Routing is the key module of NISC. It is based on RRDO algorithm (Dai et al. 1985) which is extended for NISC to handle a cell-based system. It is this algorithm which enables NISC to be non-iterative.

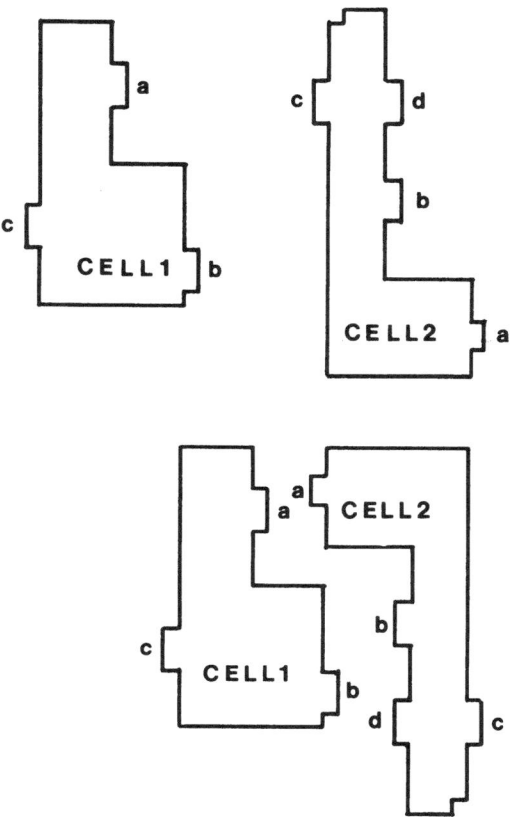

Figure 8. Alignment criteria demonstration. The cells are placed along their longer sides in a "shoe box" position.

The main idea in RRDO is that the placement is "floating" and gradually settles down by the router. First, the routing regions are determined by the placement topology. The order of the routing is assigned in such a way that the placement is adjusted without affecting the placement in the direction of the channel (see Fig. 10), or previously routed regions. Placement is adjusted only perpendicular to the channel direction, so rerouting is not needed. The global routing is done in a similar way to that of SILC (Ciesielski 1984). Since NISC is a hierarchical cell-based system, each cell needs to have its cell-interconnections placed on its boundary. The global routing algorithm is extended to handle the routing of the predefined nets to the closest boundary side. Then the channel routing is taking place. Figure 11 demonstrates the successive steps of routing a demo cell, which is used in RRDO report. Upon completion of routing a region, the two cells bounding the region become a single entity. The routing proceeds in that way until the whole cell becomes a single entity. Each of the cell-interconnection nets (J, K and L) is "floating" until its corresponding channel is routed.

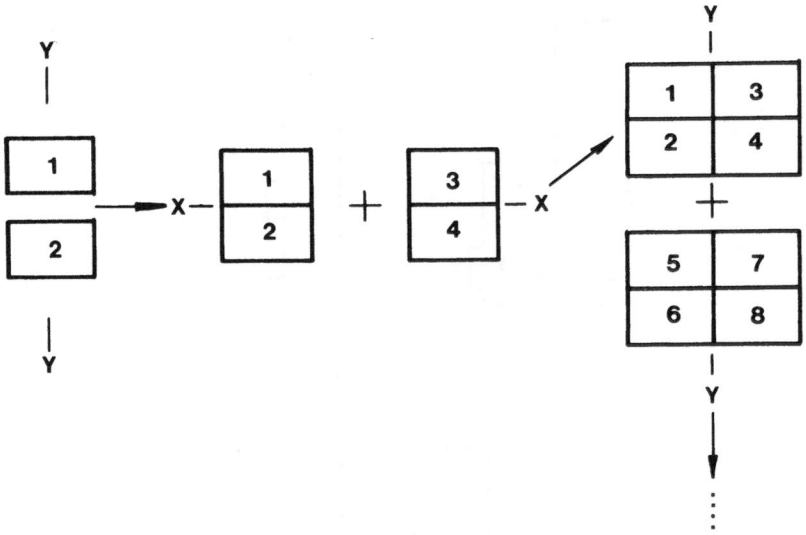

Figure 9. Max-cut algorithm. It is a bottom-up implementation of the min-cut algorithm. The axis of clustering is switching between the x-x and the y-y directions.

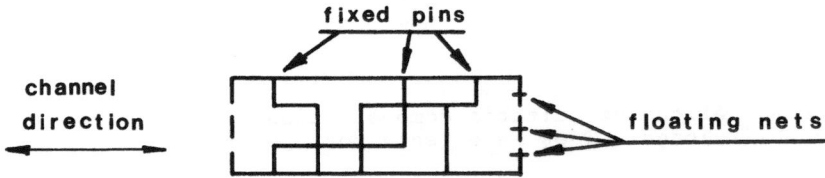

Figure 10. Routing affects placement only perpendicular to channel direction. (Dai et al. 1985). Global routing takes care of cell-interconncections. Nets on entrance and exit (including these cell-interconnections) are "floating" until the channel is routed.

A key feature in RRDO is the ability to route L-shape and non-rectangular regions. Since in a bottom-up clustering layout system the cells are usually not rectangular, and may be compacted as explained above, this capability is extremely helpful in NISC. Figure 12 shows the restrictions of the rectilinear routing channels. The pins must be on the sides that are parallel to the channel direction.

433

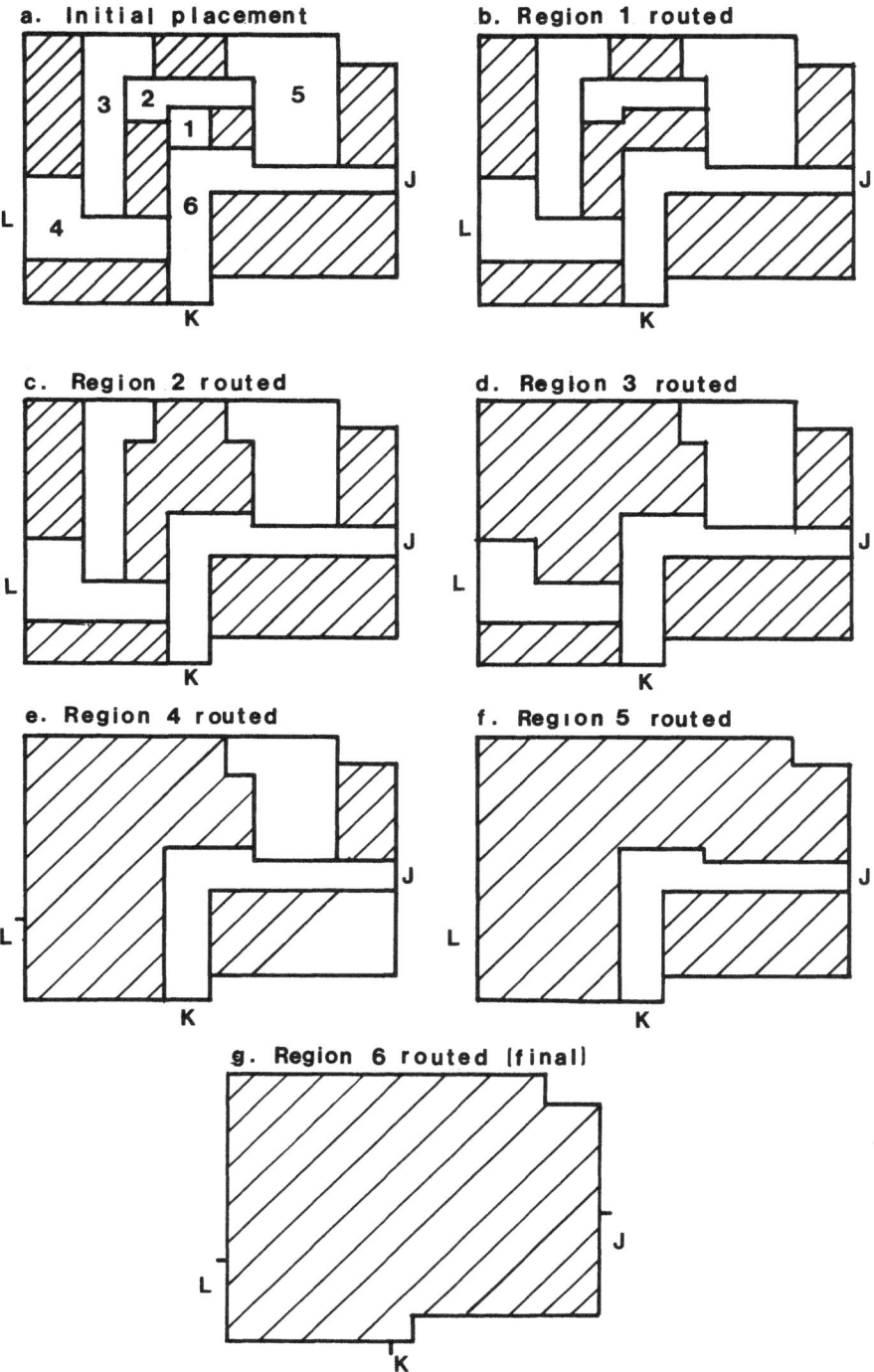

Figure 11. Step-by-step routing of a cell. J, K, L are the external connections of the cell.

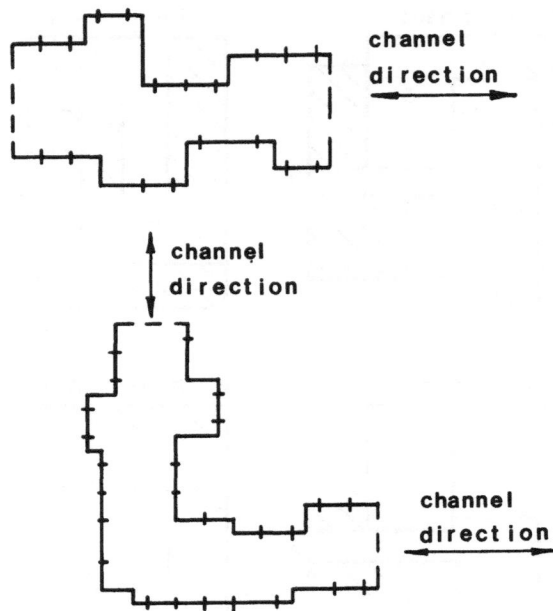

Figure 12.  Horizontal and L-shaped channels.  Pins are restricted to sides parallel to channel direction (Dai et al.  1985).

SUMMARY

We have presented a new silicon compiler, NISC. It has several advantages over other silicon compiler systems. NISC can start the synthesis from the devic level, there are no iterations between the router and the placement module and a high degreee of compaction is achieved by allowing non-rectangular routing region. It also uses a silicon compilation language which may be also used for design verification. These capabilities makes NISC more attractive to non-experienced IC designer as well as to experts.

REFERENCES

Boyer DG (1983) Virtual grid compaction using the Most Recent Layer algorithm. International Conference on Computer-Aided Design (ICCAD), pp.  92-93.
Chen CC, Kuh ES (1984) Automatic placement for Building BLock layout. International Conference on Computer-Aided Design, pp.  90-92.
Chen NP, Hsu CP, Kuh ES, Chen CC, Takahashi M (1983) Building-Block layout system for custom chip IC design. International Conference on Computer-Aided Design, pp.  40-41.
Ciesielski MJ (1984) A new approach to Routing in irregular channels for the SILC silicon compiler. International Conference on Computer-Aided Design (ICCAD), pp.  66-68.

Dai W, Asano T, Kuh ES (1985) Routing Region Definition and Ordering scheme for Building-Block lauout. IEEE Trans. Computer-Aided Design 4: 189-197.

DeMicheli G, Sangiovanni-Vincentelli A (1983) Computer-aided synthesis of PLA based Finite State Machines. International Conference on Computer-Aided Design (ICCAD), pp. 154-156.

Denyer PB, Renshaw D, bergmann N (1982) A silicon compiler for VLSI signal processor. European Solid-State Circuits Conference (ESSCIRC), pp. 215-218.

Edgington D, Walker B, Nance S, Starr C, Dholakia S, Kliment M (1984) CMOS Cell-Layout compilers for custom IC design. Custom Integrated Circuits Conference (CICC), pp. 512-517.

Evanczuk S (1985) Silicon Compilers: No Automatic Route to Acceptence. VLSI DESIGN 6(11): 42-44.

Fung BW, Macnee TJ, Rugila G (1982) A high density PLA macro and its layout generator. International Solid-State Conference (ISSCC), pp. 58-59.

Goldberg AV, Hirschhorn SS, Lieberherr KJ (1985) Approaches towards silicon compilation. IEEE Circuits and Devices Magazine 1(3): 29:39.

Janier R, Jerraya AA (1985) APPOLON, a data-path silicon compiler. IEEE Circuits and Devices Magazine 1(3): 6-14.

Kim CC, Kain RY (1984) A placement algorithm for irregular-sized functional blocks, pp. 93-95.

Law HS (1985) Generating an ALU generator. VLSI DESIGN 6(11): 98-106.

Meyer MJ, Agrawal P, Pfister RG (1984) A VLSI FSM design system. 21st Design Automation Conference, pp. 434-440.

Nogatch JT, Hedges T (1985) Automated Design of CMOS leaf cells. VLSI DESIGN 6(3): 66-78.

Peterson JC, Smith KF (1983) Techniques for automatic layout of constrained PPL circuits. International Conference on Computer-Aided Design (ICCAD), pp. 194-195.

Powell S, Iodice E, Friedman D (1984) An automated, low power, high speed, complementary PLA design system for VLSI application. International Conference on Computer Design (ICCD), pp. 314-319.

Rose F (1984) Application of a hierarchical layout system to VLSI. International Conference on Computer-Aided Design (ICCAD), pp. 125-127.

Sangiovanni-Vincentelly A, Santomauro M, Reed J (1984) A new gridless channel router: Yet Another Channel Router the Second (YACR-II). International Conference on Computer-Aided Design, pp. 72-75.

Schlag M, Liao YZ, Wong CK (1983) An algorithm for optimal two-dimensional compaction of VLSI layout. International Conference on Computer-Aided Design (ICCAD), pp. 88-89.

Schleider PD, Rappaport AS (1985) Users' attitudes about CAE. VLSI DESIGN 6(6): 74-83.

Southard JR, Domic A, Crouch KW (1983) Report on the Linconl Boolean Synthesizer (LBS). International Conference on Computer-Aided Design (ICCAD), pp. 192-193.

Ullman JD (1984) Computational Aspects of VLSI. Computer Science Press, Rockville, Maryland.

Wisniewski JA, Hudson JA (1983) Layout modeling and global routing strategies for rectilinear shaped macrocell assemblies. International Conference on Computer-Aided Design (ICCAD), pp. 134-135.

Wolf W, Mathew R, Newkirk J, Dutton R (1983) Two-dimensional compaction strategies. International Conference on Computer-Aided Design (ICCAD), pp. 90-91.

**Yehuda Shiran** is a Member of Technical Staff at SILVAR-LISCO/NCA Corporation, Santa Clara, California. Before then, he was a research programming consultant at EPRI - Electric Power Research Institute, Palo Alto, California. From 1975 to 1980 he held a technical position with the Israeli Ministry of Defense. His current research areas of interest are IC design verification, silicon compilation, computational geometry, supercomputers in engineering applications and fluid dynamics.

Shiran received his BSc and MSc in Mechanical Engineering from the Technion - Haifa, Israel in 1975 and 1980. He received his MS in Electrical Engineering from Stanford University in 1984 and is currently a Ph.D candidate at Stanford University.

Chapter 9

# Marketing and
# Business/Technical Trends

# Computer Animation around the World
## A Marketing Oriented Overview of Industry Development and Direction

Robi Roncarelli

The Computer Animation News People Inc., 217 George Street, Toronto, Ontario, M5A 2M9, Canada

## Market Definition.

The term "Computer Imaging" is used to cover a wide spectrum of graphics applications, from CAD/CAM to animated cartoons. It is a huge and rapidly growing industry, with CAD/CAM and Business Graphics sales each representing billion dollar markets.

The area we are discussing is the smallest segment of the Computer Imaging industry - the Computer Animation market. We use the term Computer Animation to differentiate our subject from "Computer Graphics", which we use to refer to a single frame or computer generated image, whereas computer animation is used to describe a series of sequential images or frames strung together, resulting in an "animated" picture that moves.

And now when we use the term computer animation we also must include computer simulation - using computer generated images to simulate scenes, events and objects from the real world around us, in our definition. And because the real world never stands still, these simulated images are animated images.

So what we are discussing is computer generated animated images and simulations for use in:

                1) Advertising
                2) TV Broadcast
                3) Entertainment - Films and TV programs
                4) Education
                5) Medicine
                6) Architecture - project representations

Computer Animation also happens to be the most creatively challenging and visually exciting segment of the total industry.


## A Rapidly Growing Market.

This is A Rapidly Growing Market. It is young, verile and brash. These facts tell the story:

                ** Fifteen years ago, the Computer Animation
                   industry didn't exist.

** Eight years ago there were only <u>five</u>
companies actively producing commercial
Computer Animation, for a very limited
market.

** Six years ago, the companies that today
account for almost <u>80%</u> of total Computer
Animation sales volume were not even in
business.

And today, most of the two-dimensional visual effects that ten
years ago were the major output of the few pioneering Computer
Animation producers, with their rooms full of equipment, are
easily produced at the flick of a switch, in 3-D, by a small box
hidden in the middle of a rack of video equipment.

It is <u>A Changing Market.</u>

This growth has been generated by the tremendous public interest
in, and acceptance of, computer generated images, animation,
simulations and effects as used in advertising, entertainment in
films and on television, and in education.

Not so long ago, Computer Animation production was the domain of
the privileged few who had access to large mainframe computers.
Today, it is possible for anyone, using a relatively inexpensive
personal computer, to actually create Computer Animation. This is
opening the flood gates to the increased creative input and fresh
attitudes that the industry sorely needs.

From the viewer's standpoint, the increased use of computer
animation in broadcast and films is generating a familiarity that
manifests itself in an increased appetite for the medium and
<u>heightened expectations</u> for all types of visual effects.

For people involved in the entertainment business — filmmakers
and TV program producers, it means that they must always try to
surpass themselves. It may take over two years to produce a
'high-tech' film loaded with computer animation, but after just 2
hours in a theatre the viewer is ready for the next episode.

The problem is becoming particularly acute for the advertising/TV
commercial producers, especially those working for smaller, local
advertisers. They are trying to attract the attention of those
same viewers who see the latest effects-laden films and then go
home to watch the TV extravaganzas carrying the expensive
commercial productions of the big international advertisers. But
their production budgets are much smaller.

These forces are generating considerable change in the
<u>technical/production</u> areas of the Computer Animation industry.
They also mean that those involved with designing and producing
Computer Animation must pay greater attention to what is
happening in the market on a <u>global</u> scale as well as becoming
much more attuned to regional and nationalistic differences.

## The Global Market.

It was just one year ago that the true size of the Global Computer Animation market was defined and reported upon. These figures became available with the completion of the first Annual Computer Animation Market Report which was published in the March 1985 issue of PIXEL – THE COMPUTER ANIMATION NEWSLETTER.

To produce this report, we started by dividing the computer animation production market into two main catagories:

1) Developmental facilities: those major producers with their own mainframes and who have their own Research and Development departments and software development programs, and

2) Turn-Key facilities, who use either complete packaged hardware/software systems, or software packages to run on computers they already had or purchased separately.

Total annualized dollar volumes for these two segments indicate that the Turn-Key facilities currently account for more than double the production volume of the Developmental facilities. The actual dollar figures for the 12 month period ending September 30, 1985 give an interesting look at how the Computer Animation market is distributed globally.

Developmental Facilities Market Segment:

| Region | Volume US Dollars | % of Total |
|--------|-------------------|------------|
| 1) North/South America – | $ 42,300,000 | 70.1 |
| 2) England – | 4,600,000 | 7.6 |
| 3) Europe – | 4,100,000 | 6.7 |
| 4) Japan – | 9,400,000 | 15.6 |
| TOTAL – | $ 60,400,000 | % 100.0 |

These figures represent a sales volume increase of approximately four million dollars for the six months period from April 1/85 to September 30/85.

While North American Developmental production accounts for over two-thirds of total world production, this commanding position is being steadily eroded by increased production in Europe, England and Japan. This is particularly so in the Turn-Key market segment where North America's share of total world production is significantly lower.

Turn-key Facilities Market Segment:

| Region | Volume US Dollars | % of Total |
|--------|-------------------|------------|
| 1) North/South America – | $ 70,300,000 | 63.1 |
| 2) England – | 11,475,000 | 10.3 |
| 3) Europe – | 7,825,000 | 7.0 |
| 4) Japan – | 21,800,000 | 19.6 |
| TOTAL – | $ 111,400,000 | % 100.0 |

These figures represent a sales volume increase of approximately six million dollars for the six months period from April 1/85 to September 30/85.

The total computer animation market volume, on an annulaized basis, therefore totals (in US dollars):

$ 171,800,000

with the Developmental segment accounting for %35.2 of the total, and the Turn-key segment accounting for 64.8%.

While America has the lead in technology, reflected by the fact that over half of all the Developmental facilities are located there, a larger percentage of major producers in other countries realized that it was quicker to buy existing technology than try to "re-invent the wheel". Therefore a greater percentage of computer animation is produced by Turn-key facilities outside of America than in America.

New Directions in Production Technology.

The technology of the market is also changing. The most expensive of the "Developmental" facilities is Digital Productions of Los Angeles, who use a Cray XMP-2 super-computer. Other than shared-time applications or special projects, we don't believe that you will see any other super-computers dedicated solely to Computer Animation production. Their high initial cost and operating overhead is more than a single facility can support, and although superb number-crunchers, they are not the best or most cost-efficient approach to Computer Animation production.

What we are seeing now is a greatly increased use of "super-mini" computers, often several at one time. These new IMIs, Suns, Ridges, Apollos and Cadmus', among others, are now as widely used as the the 'industry standard' VAX 11/700 series computers. They are very flexible, they allow easy multi-tasking and they are considerably less expensive.

However, the big breakthrough for Computer Animation production is "parallel-processing". These systems that can distribute a production among 50, 70, 100 or even more relatively inexpensive individual processors will deliver the speed and flexibility required for economically feasible high level production. Much development work is now being done in this area in America. Assembling the hardware is relatively easy. Getting the software to make it all work is taking considerably longer.

But the Japanese have already done it! The Links system developed by Dr. Koichi Omura at Osaka University is a parallel processing system, its operating software built upon a ray-tracing algorithym. Besides the two Links 1 systems at Osaka, five systems are being used to produce work by Toyo Links in Tokyo. They range in size from 30 units linked together to more than 100. The soon-to-be-introduced Links 2 system promises to be even faster and more compact.

Yet, impressive as these systems may be, the major portion of the market growth we are experiencing today is being generated by new "Turn-key" facilities. And systems manufacturers and software suppliers are realizing this.

The familiar names of Quantel, Dubner and even the more recent Bosch FGS-4000 are facing stiff competition from new systems entries such as Alias Research, Psyche 3, Symbolics, Liacom, Artronics and the upgraded CubiComp. These systems are usually capable of a variety of media outputs. Entry prices can be as little as US$30,000 but a viable production set-up costs closer to US$250,000 plus, and that doesn't include output recording equipment which can include a variety of media.

Added to this is a recent proliferation of Software Packages. These range from the relatively expensive offerings from experienced developmental producers such as Robert Abel, and NYIT-CGL to the more affordable packages from Wavefront Technologies, Neo-Visuals, Antics and Intelligent Light. These will run on a wide range of computers, so you can, in effect, build your own "turn-key" system.

This approach will cost you closer to US$1,000,000 all-up, and you don't get source-codes, but it is still much less expensive, time consuming and generally less harrowing than developing your own software.

And, if you have the desire and financial resources required to compete at the top end of the market, you can always develop your own software, or try to make licencing arrangements with well established Developmental companies such as Cranston/Csuri, Omnibus and Digital Productions.

But it is the facilities using the Turn-key and packaged software systems that are fulfilling the rapidly growing demands of the lower end of the market — that huge mass of advertisers, program producers, educators and communicators who want the magic of Computer Animation for their projects but want it at a more affordable price. And also some of the "big-budget" users who want to stretch their dollars, or feel they don't need the ultimate visual effect 'this time around'.

American Technology Still Leads.

Most of this technological development originally came from North America. The Americans are working diligently to maintain their early leadership in hardware and software development, but the Japanese are now hard on their heels.

Considerable activity has also been occuring in Canada and France, particularly in software development and systems design. As in many other areas, Canadian ex-patriates are very active in the American Computer Animation industry. And while there are several well established colleges and schools in North America that have computer animation courses, Sheridan College computer animation course graduates are in demand everywhere. In England, graduates of <u>Middlesex Polytechnic</u> are also earning a reputation for excellence that is gaining them top creative and production jobs in the industry.

The North American Computer Animation industry growth activity has been fuelled by the demands of the advertising, commercial television broadcast market and the film business.

Their TV networks were one of the earliest users of the medium — what can you do to make a station's call letters interesting — and their continuing competition for viewers in the 'ratings wars' means they are always changing and updating their on-air graphics. TV program producers must capture the viewer's attention with their show's openings in a matter of seconds. Film producers must constantly offer even more visually exciting fare to keep today's movie fans coming back for more.

Next in Computer Animation industry seniority are the <u>British</u>. While they lacked the financial stimulus of a large commercial television market, they had the technical background of a home-grown computer industry. Some British practitioners have been at it for several years, and have made up in creativity what they lacked in technical resources and large production budgets. Proportionately, there is a large number of Computer Animation production facilities in the UK, including video producers and post-production facilities with "turn-key" systems. The British became more active in this area before the Americans did.

Another area of British expertise, and one where they led the Americans, was in the production of on-line real-time and near-real-time computer animation/graphics production for television news broadcasts. The pioneering work in this area by the <u>BBC</u> and <u>ITN</u> was closely studied by the American TV networks when setting-up for their 1984 Olympics coverage and they are catching-up quickly. The British networks cannot rest on their laurels if they want to maintain their lead.

The <u>Japanese</u>, while strong on hardware production technology, have been hampered by their traditional weakness in software development. Although responsible for the exciting and technically innovative <u>Links</u> system developmental work being done at Osaka University, and the lighting and natural phenomena rendering software developments at Hiroshima University, the Japanese have traditionally imported much of their software from America, but they also now have six British <u>Antics</u> based systems operating. They have an active industry, catering to the large national appetite for 'sci-fi' TV programs and films, and they are not afraid to mix media.

<u>Europe</u>, led by the <u>French</u> and the <u>Italians</u>, is working very hard at catching-up in the computer technology area generally, and particularly Computer Animation. The French are leading the way with recently introduced computers suitable for animation production, and new animation/graphics systems. And the Computer Animation productions of <u>INA</u> and particularly <u>Sogitec</u>, are a match for most of the American facilities. Both write their own software.

In _Italy_, there has been more emphasis on systems based on purchased software packages, although _Eidos_ in Milan is developing their own software and production system as well as operating an EEC backed computer animation, graphics and design school.

Even _Finland_ has its own computer animation facility which has been operating for several years with its own software and hardware configuration. This is a direct result of their commercial television industry and companion television advertising activity.

_Germany_, while using a considerable amount of Computer Animation produced mainly in England and America, has been slow to develop a local production capability. They are rapidly changing this situation with three facilities now being opened based on American software packages. We expect similar developments soon in _Belgium_ and the _Netherlands_.

_South and Central America_, heavy users of Computer Animation right from the start, finally have basis for their own industry, with a _Computer Image System IV_ in _Chile_ and a sophisticated production facility operated by _Brazil's TV Globo_. This digital, 3-D system was developed for them by _Pacific Data Images_ of California, and is being kept very busy filling the Brazilian viewer's heavy appetite for Computer Animation.


A Global Overview.

While the basic production technology is the same, how it is used varies greatly in different parts of the world. It's the _creative direction_ that shows where the big differences are. To a large degree this is a result of different nationalities and backgrounds.

In _America_, many of the people who started the first Computer Animation facilities, and who are still doing a large part of the development work, came from backgrounds in NASA and the aerospace industry. They approached Computer Animation with a technical viewpoint. Their prime interest was for increasing the capabilities of their systems and being at the forefront of technological development.

Their work strives to be technically superior to that of their competitors. Reflectives must be more reflective. Metallics more "glintzy". Resolution ever higher. More perfect 3-D renderings of complicated subjects. Ray-tracing and Fractals for a visual tour-de-force that often does more to amaze and astound viewers than to communicate with them.

This is a great generalization, and there are exceptions.


_Computer Image Corp_ is developing a character animation/cartoon system that they claim is price-competitive with the lowest cost 'cel' animation productions from the Far East.

Bob Abel, who has a background in films and motion control, uses Computer Animation as a tool to solve communications problems, and usually in conjunction with a variety of other techniques. His productions look different from those of his competitors, and he wins many awards.

Outside of America, things are quite different. First, the whole attitude to "animation" is different. In America it means "Walt Disney" and cartoons. In Europe, animation is often used for serious art subjects and 'message' films.

Secondly, most of the British and Europeans involved in Computer Animation design and production come from an art, graphics or film production background. Most of the companies were started by people from the graphics or film industries. They look upon Computer Animation as a tool to be used with other techniques. They are more concerned with content and graphic design than with technical brilliance. Lacking the more powerful computers, research facilities and larger production budgets of their American counterparts, they can't afford the cost of the latest 'highest-tech' or 'cutting-edge' technology.

Therefore they concentrate more on graphic design, the movement and interaction of the various elements in each scene. They tend to use several techniques in one production, and rely less on reflective metallics and complicated transformations. They are more "creative" in the artistic sense, rather than simply displaying "technical brilliance".

Japanese Computer Animation presents yet a third approach. Much of it is for internal consumption in films and television programs, and reflects its lower production budgets in simple design and less complicated movements. In contrast, the developmental work being carried out at the various universities, JCGL and Toyo-Links has a more 'high-tech' look to it and shows a greater interest in replicating natural phenomena.

When you look at a sampling of demo-reels from various countries, these differences become quite apparent. A Ray-traced image may be visually stunning, but the "standout" productions are usually those that combine their Computer Animation with a variety of film, video and motion-control techniques, each contributing what it does best for that particular production.


Future Developments.

There is great diversity in the Computer Animation industry today. This is a healthy sign and helps fuel the market's continuing expansion.

While the "Developmental" segment of the market is where the most interesting high-tech productions will occur, and it should continue to expand at an annual growth rate of 20%, the biggest total market expansion will be recorded by the "Turn-Key" market segment. It already accounts for double the dollar volume of the "Developmental" market, and is the door through which most new users will enter the Computer Animation market.

Many of these initially 'low-end' users will then go on to become prospective clients for the more expensive productions of the "Developmental" companies as their appetite for the medium increases and they try harder to grab the viewer's attention.

The areas where we see increased production activity include Advertising, Education and Training and Medicine. The film industry use of Computer Animation still has to fulfill its potential, and that will take at least two more years. However, using Computer Animation to plan and preview complex action scenes is already being done quite regularly and is a growing film use area.

New uses for Computer Animation will also contribute to market sales volume growth. These include Architectural Presentations, used by builders and developers to show-off their projects to prospective clients instead of using the traditional maquette models, and by research institutions to demonstrate their work.

Fluctuating currency exchange rates, and the visibly different creative/production styles in different areas and countries present interesting opportunities for users of Computer Animation. By having production done in selected countries, an advertiser can reduce his production costs, vary the look of his commercials, or use different approaches and production executions for different products. This particularly applies to advertising uses of Computer Animation, but the advertising industry yet has much to learn about how to best use the medium. Both the film and advertising industries have tended to use Computer Animation as a replacement for more traditional film/optical techniques rather than use the medium creatively as a new tool. This problem will be reduced as they understand the medium better.

Similarly, Computer Animation producers should look beyond their local area or country for prospective clients, and market their product accordingly. The different industry video standards are not a detering factor for those with film output, and new equipment technology is reducing this problem for those restricted to video output.

From a systems standpoint, the suppliers will continue to offer more power for fewer dollars, again expanding the market base by increasing the activity of present users while attracting new users. But developing the new techniques and software for the high-end productions will remain an expensive proposition, affordable by only a relatively small group of "Developmental" facility clients who will be able to afford the standout productions that pave the way for the whole industry.

To maintain its current rapid growth rate, the industry needs continuing top-end development. It also needs to broaden its user base with more affordable, and accessible, low-end production capability. Both these events are already happening. It is becoming more of an international market every day. The most successful companies will be those who understand international marketing and plan for it.

**Robi Roncarelli** is President of PIXEL - THE COMPUTER ANIMATION NEWS PEOPLE, INC, and Editor and Publisher of PIXEL - THE COMPUTER ANIMATION NEWSLETTER, an international publication that reports on the global computer animation market with subscribers in 19 countries. It publishes the only Annual Market Report on the Computer Animation Industry.

He has been involved directly with computer animation since 1978 as a designer, producer and consultant. He has produced work for a wide range of clients including major TV networks, international advertising agencies and film producers and has acted as consultant to several computer animation production, software and systems companies and the Canadian Government Department of Communicaitons. Besides writing extensively about computer animation, he frequently lectures and makes presentations on the subject.

He is Chairman of ASIFA (Association Internationale du Film d'Animation) Commission #1 on New Technologies and Executive Director of The Canadian International Animation Festival.

Roncarelli's address is PIXEL - THE COMPUTER ANIMATION NEWS PEOPLE, INC, 217 George Street, Toronto, Canada M5A 2M9.

# Business Computer Graphics
## Usage and Effectiveness

K. Venkata Rao and S. Sircar

Department of Information Systems and Computer Science, National University of Singapore, Kent Ridge, 0511 Singapore

ABSTRACT

The use of computer graphics in business appear to be extensive. Current developments in the information systems field also indicate the potential of business graphics as a support tool for task scheduling, group decisionmaking, decision and expert systems. It would appear, however, that advances in graphics production and usage is proceeding at a relentless pace but without regard to the large body of relevant research that is available. This paper proposes a taxonomy of business graphics application based on an information systems classification. In addition it reviews the existing inventory of research using a communication psychology and information system orientation with particular reference to memory capacity and preference and the factors contributing to graphics effectiveness. In sum the paper attempts to integrate extant research with recent developments in business graphics technology and to indicate directions for future research.

Keywords: Business Graphics, Computer Graphics, Decision Support, Graphics Taxonomy, Graphics Applications, Graphics Research

## INTRODUCTION

Graphics may be defined as the science and art of presenting data in the form of text, charts, graphs, drawings, paintings or pictures, and computer graphics is the use of computer technology for generating graphics (Jarett 1983). Computer graphics involves "the synthesis of pictures of real or imaginary objects", and "the creation, storage, and manipulation of models of objects and their pictures via computer" (Foley, Van dam 1982).

Computer graphics is now widely used in such diverse areas as cartography, computer-aided drafting and design (CADD), animation, process control, commercial art, office automation and business. The focus of this paper, however, is on business computer graphics(BCG), which is concerned with the use of graphs and other forms of pictorial representations by managers of organisations to present trends and patterns in data in a meaningful and concise fashion in order to increase understanding of complex phenomena and to facilitate decision making (Foley, Van dam 1982). In other words, BCG supports analysis, decision and communication.

This paper examines the purposes for which BCG is currently used in business information systems in the context of previous and current research studies on the effectiveness of graphics-based information support to management. Further, the paper proposes a taxonomy of BCG and recommendations for effective usage. Some suggestions for future research studies are also put forward.


EARLIER STUDIES ON GRAPHICS

Interest in graphics may be traced back to the Joint Committee on Standards for Graphic Presentation which in 1915 suggested a list of guidelines for presenting quantitative data in graphic form. In the 1920s and 1930s, a group of researchers examined the comparative effectiveness of various graph types. A series of studies conducted in the 1940s were concerned with contrasting graphs with tables for their ability to yield quick and accurate interpretation (Fienberg 1979). These studies were simple in design lacked the rigour evident in later research.


Current research in graphics has been undertaken from the perspectives of experimental psychology or of information systems. Experimental psychologists have focussed on manipulating features of visual displays and measuring the effects on readability and comprehension accuracy. The variables examined included brightness, contrast, texture, color and shape (Simcox 1981). While these studies dealt with the use of color in visual displays, there were other studies by cognitive and applied psychologists, on the effects of graphics on memory and visual displays. Studies by cognitive psychologists compared recall and recognition for pictures and words, and the results have implications for understanding memory processing of graphically displayed data. Applied psychologists, in their studies on the effects of visual displays, emphasised interpretation accuracy and comprehension rather than recall or recognition speed. Interpretation of visual phenomena has been found to be influenced by the ability of the individual to perceptually organize information, his current knowledge base and expectations (Witkin et al 1971; Siegler 1983; Bailey 1982). The effects of visual displays were also a subject of research interest to educationists and audio-visual scientists as well as media specialists in advertising.


Researchers in the field of Management Information Systems (MIS) have identified the mode of presenting information as an important variable (Mason, Mitroff 1973; Schroeder 1967). Some previous studies compared the communication effectiveness of computer screen (CRT) and printed copy mediums (Lucas 1980, Senn 1974), and detailed reports with summarised information (Chervany 1974). Schutz (1961) carried out experimental studies on graphics and notes that line-type graphs produced greater accuracy and speed of performance than vertical bar or horizontal graphs. Zmud (1978) compared tabular, bar chart and line-type graphical modes of presentation and found that graphical presentation was preferred over others because they were more relevant, accurate and readable. Benbasat et al (1977) found that the use of graphical displays produced cost-effective decisions. In an earlier study on Decision Support Systems (DSS), researchers observed that graphical displays were more useful in the problem-solving process than tabular reports containing numbers that lack pattern and are difficult to grasp and comprehend (Scott Morton 1978). A recent experimental study by Watson et al (1983) focussed on the effectiveness of presenting three-dimensional graphics on recall abilities but failed to prove their superiority over tabular presentation.

In his comprehensive survey of graphics research for business information systems, Ives (1982) notes that although proponents of graphics promise major improvements in decision maker productivity and decision quality, empirical evidence in justification for this expectation is rather weak. After some initial comments on the methodology used in some of the previous research, Ives offers extensive but tentative guidelines for graphics designers, particularly on the use of color, labels and text, selection of icons, and lines, grids and axes. He also urges continued research to obtain more conclusive evidence.

A more recent analysis of graphics research (Jarvenpaa, Dickson, De Sanctis 1985) is far more critical. It cites several studies which suggest that graphs are no better than tabular presentation of information. On the other hand, many other studies provide evidence that graphics are not only preferred by managers but also have better decision performance in some situations. Javenpaa et al (1985) feel that such conflicting research findings are the result of differential experimental conditions :

(a)   A variety of tasks are being used and it is inappropriate to compare results between task environments.

(b)   The quality of information presentation across different experiments varies greatly.

(c)   There are other differences, such as subject characteristics, and other experimental enviornments.

(d)   Internal validity is questionable, because outcomes being observed may not be truly a function of experimental manipulation of the independent variables.

(e)   External validity is suspect on the grounds that experimentally contrived situations are not representative of the real world scenarios in which managers work and process information.

These problems are, of course, extremely difficult to solve, but the authors provide some guidelines for future researchers in graphics.

BUSINESS GRAPHICS FOR PRESENTATION

Communication is one of the major functions of management, and the graphics support of communication extends to information display, task scheduling and group decision making. Graphics for presentation require greater formatting flexibility to allow management to communicate information more effectively at meetings or seminars. The software for presentation, therefore, should have a wide range of formatting capabilities. Display of information in attractive color combinations for effectiveness is the current preoccupation of BCG.

This represents, to a large extent, the automation of previous manual systems involving graphic form art-work prepared by specialist artists (McLain 1983).

Another area of graphics support for communication is in the organisation of activities, particularly in the management of large complex projects. Gantt charts and Network charts which have been in use for a long time, can now be prepared more easily and accurately with the aid of computer graphics. These charts can now be updated as the project progresses and as new data becomes available. Graphics software in this area is getting more sophisticated and holds promise as a vital support in project management.

Group decision-making also benefits from graphics support. Important decisions are usually made at meetings, which can be transacted via computer conferencing technology. The support of graphics to the computer conferences or 'electronic meetings' has the potential to enhance the quality of discussions and the decisions that follow. Until recently, graphics files could not be exchanged easily between different computers over communication lines. But, with the recent development of NAPLPS (North American Presentation Level Protocol Syntax), graphics files can now be transmitted over phone lines with remarkable economy of data. What NAPLPS essentially does is to allow new interpretations of the ASCII character set, thereby extending the old set to include foreign language and scientific characters, custom characters, font sizes, block graphics, high resolution graphics and color with adequate provision for expansion into three-dimensional drawings. NAPLPS, therefore, is a potential vehicle for electronic conferencing. Managers participating in a sales conference, for example, can generate charts of sales forecasts on their micros and transmit them, without having to worry about the make or type of computer that is sending and receiving the graphics file.

BUSINESS GRAPHICS FOR ANALYSIS AND DECISION MAKING

BCG can contribute to the efficiency of the analyses that precede decision making. Analytical graphics packages are screen-oriented and designed for speed and data management. These packages, unlike those for presentation, do not require wide formatting flexibility. Several analytical software packages, both on mainframes and micros, offer graphics capabilities for analysis purposes. However, they do not match the capabilities of presentation graphics software packages.

Graphics software for decision making depends on what aspect of human information processing system is supported or automated by a decision aid. There are three aspects to human information processing --- short-term memory, long-term memory and processing.

Short-term memory, which is of limited capacity, serves as a temporary storage facility. However, short-term memory can be enhanced in three ways : (a) extension of capacity through the creation of external memory, (b) improved fitting of information into existing capacity, and (c) better organisation and structuring. The computerised version of external memory is represented by multiple screens or windows available with many packages. Improved methods of fitting information into the short-term memory is called 'chunking'. Standard graphs and multi-dimensional displays represent the graphics version of chunking. While most graphics packages have standard graphics (line charts, bar charts, pie charts etc.), multi-dimensional display graphs are offered only by a few. The limited capacity of short-term memory can be overcome by better structuring and utilisation; this can be accomplished by providing status indicators, display alternatives, reserved locations etc. (Lehman 1983).

Long-term memory can be enhanced by extension, structuring and transferring of information. The long-term memory can be extended by having recourse to external sources of knowledge such as on-line reference material. The structuring of long-term memory involves allowing access to the relevant contents of the memory through graphics support in the form of decision trees and prototype trees. Information stored in long-term memory needs to be transferred to other parts of information processing system to enable its utilisation. Although extant graphics packages do not support the integration of information and database retrieval, on-going research and developments of technology will soon remove this constraint.

Processing involves the generation and evaluation of hypotheses. These can be generated by syntactic decomposition which consists of generating novel configurations of possibilities through brainstorming, lateral thinking and the like. Evaluation of the hypotheses can be supported by automating the computational algorithms based on the application of management science/statistical techniques. Graphics support for statistics is available with most statistical packages, while similar support for management science techniques is slowly emerging. Non-conventional aids to idea generation are also not too remote.

A major area of research in human information processing is that of the hemispheric specialization of the brain. Although many of the earlier beliefs about the unique roles of the left and right hemispheres have been disproved, the research has highlighted the fact that traditional information systems have been sequential, structured and "analytic". They have always suited analytical persons, left hemisphere types, operating with structured data reports, doing structured tasks. Less structured tasks are best performed by non-analytic, right hemisphere types of intuitive problem solvers using a flexible, non-linear graphic system (Robey 1982). Because most of the tasks at upper management levels are of a relatively unstructured nature, it is presumed that graphics capabilities will add a substantial dimension to decision support systems.

A TAXONOMY FOR BUSINESS GRAPHICS USAGE

The preceding discussion on applications makes no attempt to classify BCG in a systematic way. We now propose a taxonomy of business graphics usage modelled on the information systems taxonomy formulated by Sprague (1980). Since BCG is intended to provide information support to management at all levels, it should become an integral feature of transaction processing and management information systems, office information systems, and decision support and expert systems. Figure 1 illustrates our taxonomy of graphics-based information systems.

In Transaction Processing Systems (TPS), the graphics component should cover the representation of transactional data in standard graphic forms such as simple line, bar or pie charts. The major use of these graphs is for presentation of information summarising a large volume of data in an easily comprehensible and understandable form.

Management Information Systems (MIS) are designed to assist managers in performance review and control and simple analyses. Therefore, graphics integration with MIS should lead to the generation of appropriate graphs to reveal significant differences, if any, between actual and planned performance. For this, standard but more complex graph forms (grouped or multiple line charts, segmented line charts, grouped bar charts, segmented bar charts, etc.) would be appropriate. In both TPS and MIS, the standard graphs can be produced from what are called graphics primitives (a "dictionary" of basic symbols), and used in supplementing other forms of information presentation at regular/periodical intervals in supporting well defined structured tasks.

Office Information Systems (OIS) are largely characterised by word processing and the exchange of information over local area and wide area networks. Therefore, graphics interfaces in OIS should help facilitate communication, scheduling of individual and organisational activities and computer conferencing. In addition to the standard graph forms, text in varying font sizes, and non-standard pictures may be used with 'windowing' features. Further, the transmission of graphics-based information should relieve the users from such concerns as what type of computer is making, sending, or receiving graphics files.

Unstructured human (user) interaction with the system is typical of both Decision Support Systems (DSS) and Expert Systems (ES); these interactive systems are gradually emerging as systems with 'intelligence'. Further, the current trend is to build sophisticated graphical systems that provide increasing intelligence in the human-system interface. The graphics interfaces, in these systems, should support more complex analyses and decision processes characteristic of unstructured and semistructured tasks. What is essentially required in these systems is to rapidly prepare graphics interfaces for a wide range of management science and expert system models. Current research efforts in this direction, reported in the computer graphics literature, are illustrated by the development of experimental systems. We provide below a brief and broad overview of two such systems to give a flavour of the emerging technology.

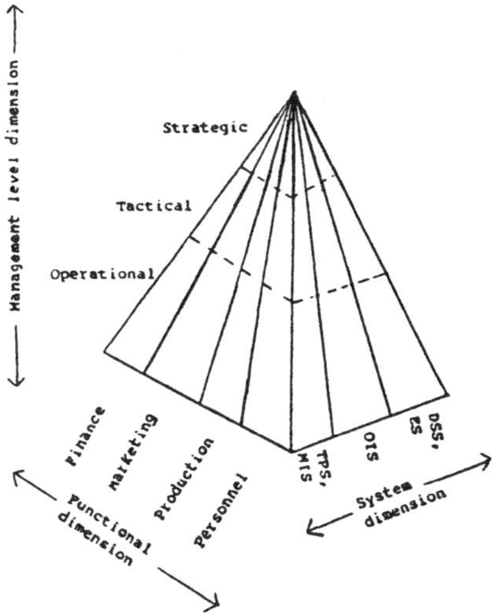

| Systems Classification | Focus | Task Structure | Technology | Graphics Forms | Usage Patterns |
|---|---|---|---|---|---|
| DSS, ES | Decision, Ad hoc reporting | Unstructured, Semi-structured | Data processing, Personal computing, Data communications, Management science, Artificial intelligence | Standard, Non-Standard display forms, including trees, tables, icons, animation, etc, Windowing environment | Interactive, Complex analysis, Problem solving, Automated decision processes |
| OIS | Information, Communication | Semi-structured, Structured | Word processing, Data communication, Office automation | Standard graph forms, Text, Non-standard displays with windowing | Interactive, Communication, Scheduling, Computer conferencing |
| TPS, MIS | Data, Information, Structured reporting | Structured, Well-defined | Data processing | Standard graphs (different forms of line, bar & pie charts) | Non-interactive, Presentation, Simple analyses |

Fig. 1 : Taxonomy of Business Graphics Usage

SAGE (Sensitivity Analysis Graphics interfacE) is an experimental system which permits rapid development of graphics interfaces for sensitivity analysis (Clemons 1985). While the system readily handles such traditional displays as optimisations where variable values are denoted by the icon size, it can also readily handle more sophisticated displays by varying the position, size, shape or color of icons, all of which are based on changes to their values. The SAGE system is indeed very powerful not only for generating a wide range of interesting and effective displays, but also for permitting users to make changes in the model and present the results graphically for quicker evaluation.

APEX (Automated Pictorial EXplanations) is another example of an experimental system which generates pictures showing the performance by a problem solver attending to physical actions in a three-dimensional world (Feiner 1985). The objects in the picture, their level of detail, presentation style and the specification for its viewing are determined by facts about participating objects, proposed actions and user knowledge. Initially, the system is provided with information about the objects in the world, actions to be performed on it and what the user already knows. Thus, APEX generates pictures from the output of an expert system that plans physical actions. Further, APEX itself works like an expert system in the sense that it takes a general description of a set of physical objects, an action to be performed on them and a simple model of the user's knowledge of the problem scene and determines what would be a good graphics description of the planned action for that user.

The above taxonomy provides a framework for analysing not only the variety of commercially available graphics packages, but more importantly, it addresses the issue of BCG usage by an organisation. To which functional area and at what management level in the organisation do graphics users belong? Are graphics being used simply to support reports or are they also being used in decision support and expert systems? Such analyses may result in withdrawal of attention from areas where the cost-benefit balance is adverse and also reveal opportunities for implementation previously ignored.

FACTORS AFFECTING EFFECTIVE GRAPHICS USAGE

In order for BCG to be judged effective, it must make a positive contribution to the value of information used by decision makers. For this, appropriate key factors which contribute to the effectiveness of graphics must be identified. The following three key factors appear to be relevant :

(a) Decision activities or tasks

(b) Features of particular types of graphs and their level of standardisation

(c) Training in graphics usage.

To ensure that BCG resources are effectively employed by the decision makers, there is a need for developing standard guidelines for presentation of graphics on a corporate-wide basis. These guidelines must be directed towards assisting graphics end-users in : (i) identifying the decision activities in which graphics should be used, (ii) deciding what graph formats and features are appropriate in a given situation, and (iii) providing end-users with training on how to create, read and interpret different graph formats efficiently.

## Decision Activities

BCG for decision activities can be classified into perceptual activities and judgmental activities. There is a general feeling that graphics are preferred to tabular reports for the following perceptual tasks : (i) summarizing data, (ii) showing trends and relationships over time, (iii) comparing data points and relationships of variables, and (iv) detecting deviations in data. Previous research studies partially support the claim that graphics are superior to tabular presentations for the above perceptual activities (Carter 1947; Scott Morton 1971; Davis 1981; Ghani 1981; Tullis 1981; Washburne 1927; Lusk 1979; Benbasat 1984). A recent study by Jarvenpaa et al (1985) confirms that graphical forms of presentation lead to better performance in the case of the first two perceptual tasks, whereas tabular form is superior for comparing data points and patterns of variables.

Judgmental or decision making activities include (i) problem finding, (ii) comprehension/interpretation of complex information, (iii) performance review and monitoring, (iv) forecasting, (v) exception reporting, (vi) planning or allocation of resources, and (vii) exploratory data analysis. Previous studies on some of these tasks particularly on planning, did not conclusively establish that graphics will lead to better decision making performance. The studies, however, show that graphics enhance comprehension abilities (Vernon 1952; Wilcox 1964; Power 1982; Firth 1980; Remus 1984). The presentation technique, according to a recent study by Jarvenpaa et al (1985), did not have any impact on problem finding or comprehension; however, graphics turned out to be a superior method in forecasting.

## Standardisation of Graph Forms and Features Used

The standardisation of graph formats and features in organisations will not only improve the human and machine efficiency in graphic generation, but also will reduce the potential for misrepresentation and misinterpretation of data presented graphically. Unless some sort of standardisation for graphic formats, features, and colors is developed, a chaos of incompatible graphics is most likely, particularly as end-user graphics usage becomes more widespread (Widener 1983). The typical formats include line charts, multiple line charts, bar charts and pie charts. The formats have to be reviewed in the light of task or purpose for which graphs are used. For example, a three-dimensional contour chart is likely to be more effective in portraying the relationships among three variables, such as the interactions of the time period, geographical area, and product type in a sales analysis. Bar and line formats seem appropriate for the task of summarizing data. In presenting time series data, line charts are found to be very effective (Schmid

1979). For analysing trends, both line and bar charts seem to have
similar influence on interpretation accuracy. Research supports the
use of multiple-line graphs for segmented or multiple single-line
reports and the use of grouped bars in the place of simple bars
(MacDonald-Ross 1977; Culbertson 1959).

To implement and enforce organisational standards for graphs, a
series of predesigned charts may be developed specifying both
optional and mandatory graphic formats and features. Optional
features might include keys, labels, grids, titles and other
annotations. Mandatory formats should specify the chart types that
should be used as well as the formats that should be avoided. In
addition, shading and color for differentiating organisational sub-
units should also be specified.

## Training of Graphics Users

The users who will produce graphs must be made aware of the graphics
design guidelines and organisational standards through a training
programme. Proper training is also required for decision makers who
will read and interpret computer generated graphs. Since most BCG
users have very little prior experience working with graphs, they
first have to learn how to interpret graphs before any benefits from
their usage can be expected.

The coverage of training programs should include what each graph
symbol represents, how various scales should be interpreted, and how
to interpolate and extrapolate accurately. If the trainees are made
aware of the bias that graphics can generate, they will be more
likely to detect distortions of data. These training sessions are
vital for providing users with heuristics and methods that are
necessary for the effective and efficient viewing of graphical data.

## SUGGESTIONS FOR FUTURE STUDIES IN BUSINESS GRAPHICS

Further studies on the use of computer business graphics as a
decision making tool need to be carried out on the lines of suggested
research frameworks in the MIS/DSS literature. Accordingly,
characteristics of the graph, such as the type of graph (e.g. single
or multiple-line charts, bar charts, pie charts) and its features
(e.g. color, realism, complexity, scale, labelling) should be
considered along with user characteristics and the decision task
context when studying the effectiveness of graphics. With regard to
graph characteristics, the basic issue centers on designing graphs
that can be comprehended quickly and interpreted accurately, for
making informed decisions. Just as one can lie with statistics,
there is also great potential to lie with graphics (Johnson 1980);
therefore, design displays which cause 'poor' information acquisition
or cognitive bias on the part of the reader should be avoided.

Research to date suggests that the user's experience with graphics as
well as the user's decision style are important variables of study.
There are other user characteristics which may be important as well

(e.g. personality variables) and these deserve careful examination. Further work is also needed with regard to the role of the decision context in the effective use of graphics. Information obtained from graphical displays most likely interacts with variables such as task complexity, task content, degree of task structure, or the quality of available decision alternatives, all of which are known to affect decision making (Payne 1982).

The outcome from the use of graphics, following the interactions between graph characteristics, user characteristics and decision context, is the cognitive process that the user experiences when making a decision. The dominance of the right-or-left hemisphere, memory and information processing activities, and the decision strategy adopted by the decision maker who uses BCG are important cognitive aspects in need of study. While many outcome variables deserve consideration, the speed and quality of decision-making are the most important when graphics are used in decision support systems. The ability to properly comprehend the problem at hand affects decision-making; and problem comprehension, in turn, is affected by the user's interpretation of the graph. Postulating premises for further study within the above research framework can lead to clearer understanding of the role of graphics in decision making. Guidelines for further graphics research are given in Jarvenpaa S.L., Dickson G.W., De Sanctis G, (1985).

"The state of the market to-day is not the state of the art" observed Alyce Kaprow (1985) at the National Computer Graphics Association's conference in June 1985. Advanced technology that currently exists include image processors, color separation products and hardware which can take pictures, scan, process and then transmit by satellite to any part of the world. These are likely to have significant impact on the field of BCG. MIS managers do not see BCG as a key management issue. Although BCG is unlikely to be recognised as a key issue or a critical success factor (see Dickson et al, 1984, for survey evidence of this) it is hard at work behind the scenes in contributing (sometimes at a subconscious level) to more informed decision-making. In view of this more vigorous research in BCG is needed in order to provide some direction for a sound and orderly growth of the business graphics market consistent with the needs and effectiveness of graphics-based management information systems.

Unfortunately, published data on the usage of graphics by organizations are scarce, there being only two studies which shed light on current practice. A survey by International Data Corporation conducted in 1984, shows that 15 percent of personal computer users were using graphics, and that in companies with multiple personal computers, more than one-third were using graphics and an additional third planned to use within the next one year. Another study by Davis (1984) describes the heavy use of PCs in his company for converting raw data to a more usable form. Seventy percent of PC time is spent on computational work, 10 percent on "what if" analyses, and 20 percent on graphical presentation of data. He observes that graphical analysis, in particular, "makes the assimilation of large quantities of data very easy, and provides our management team with a common understanding of most issues". He found that decisions were being reached much more quickly than in the past as a result. Many more such studies are required to provide a complete picture of BCG utilization in organizations.

CONCLUSION

Recent advances in computer graphics technology show great potential for the wide use of BCG as an aid to decision making in organisations especially at higher management levels. The various empirical and experimental studies on the use of BCG have established the effectiveness of graphics over other forms of presentation albeit not on all dimensions. Until a few years ago, tabular presentations definitely had a cost advantage. But this situation is fast changing as a result of the declining cost of graphics usage. Not only have the hardware and software costs declined, but graphics software has also become easier to use. Further, the capabilities of packages have also become more versatile. Faced with the bewildering array of graphics technology the user needs considerable guidance in effectively using graphics, through the development of suitable standards taking into account the available graphic formats, decision activities and user characteristics. This requires continuing efforts toward understanding the role of BCG in the decision making process and toward specifying the conditions in which BCG may be effectively employed.

REFERENCES

Bailey W (1982) Human performance engineering : A guide for Systems Designers. Prentice-Hall, Englewood Cliffs N.J.
Benbasat I, Dexter A S (1984) An experimental evaluation of graphical and color-enhanced information presentation. Paper presented at MIS Workshop, University of Minnesota
Benbasat J, Schroeder R (1977) An experimental investigation of some MIS design variables. MIS Quarterly 1-1:37-49
Carter LF (1947) An experiment of the design of tables and graphs used for presenting numerical data. Journal of applied psychology 31:640-650
Chervany NL, Dickson GW (1974) An experimental evaluation of information overload in a production environment. Management Science 20:1335-1344
Clemons EK, Greenfield AJ (1985) The SAGE system architecture : a system for the rapid development of graphics interfaces for decision support. IEEE Computer Graphics and Applications 5-11 : 38-50
Culbertson HM, Powers RD (1959) A study of graph comprehension difficulties. AV Communication Review 7:97-100
Davis D (1984) Computers and top management. Sloan Management Review Spring:63-67
Davis DL (1981) An experimental investigation of the form of information presentation, psychological type of the user, and performance within the context of a management information system. Unpublished Ph.D. thesis, Unversity of Florida
Dickson GW, Leitheiser RL, Wetherbee JC, Nechis M (1984) Key information systems issues for the 1980s, MIS Quarterly 8-3:135-147
Edward J (1983) Graphics punch for low cost computers. Popular Computing 3-1:98-103
Feiner S (1985) APEX : An experiment in the automated creation of pictorial explanations. IEEE Computer Graphics and Applications 5-11:29-37
Fienberg SE (1979) Graphical methods in statistics. American Statistician 33-4:165-178

Firth M (1980) The impact of some MIS design variables on manager's evaluation of subordinates' performance. MIS Quarterly 4-1:45-53

Foley JD, Van dam A (1982) Fundamentals of interactive computer graphics. Addison Wesley, Reading:8-11

Ghani JA (1981) The effects of information representation and modification on decision performance. Unpublished Ph.D. Thesis University of Pennsylvania

Hilt WD (1961) An evaluation of five different abstract coding methods. Human Factors 3-2:120-130

Ives B (1982) Graphical user interfaces for business information systems. MIS Quarterly Special Issue:15-47

Jarett IM (1981) Computer graphics : a reporting revolution. Journal of Accountancy 151-5:49-57

Jarett IM (1983) Computer graphics and reporting financial data. John Wiley, New York, 1983

Jarett IM (1985) Graphics tools for understanding data. National Computer Graphics Association Conference, Los Angeles CA

Jarvenpaa SL, Dickson GW (1985) Managing the use of computer graphics in organisations. MISRC working paper WP-85-11, MIS Research Center, University of Minnesota 1-40

Jarvenpaa SL, Dickson GW, De Sanctis G (1985) Methodological issues in experimented IS Research : experiences and recommendations. MIS Quarterly 9-2:141-156

Johnson JR, Rice RR, Roemmich RA (1980) Pictures that lie: the abuse of graphs in annual reports. Management Accounting 62-4:50-56

Kaprow A (1985) Electronic paint and design systems. National Computer Graphics Association Conference, Los Angeles CA

Lehman JA (1983) Computer graphics for management. MISRC Working Paper WP-83-05, MIS Research Center University of Minnesota 1-11.

Lucas HC, Nielsen NR (1980) The impact of the information presentation on learning and performance. Management Science 26:982-993.

Lusk EJ, Kersnick M (1979) The effect of cognitive style and report format on task performance : the MIS design consequences. Management Science 22:787-798

MacDonald-Ross M (1977) How numbers are shown. AV Communication Review 25:359-409

Mason R, Mitroff I (1973) A program for research on management information systems. Management Science 19:475-487

McLain L (1983) A guided tour of business graphics. Popular Computing 3-1:86-97

Payne JW (1982) Contingent decision behaviour. Psychological Bulletin 92:382-402

Power M, Lashley C, Sanchez P, Shneiderman B (1982) An experimental comparison on tabular and graphic data presentation. Working Paper University of Maryland

Remus W (1984) An empirical investigation of the impact of graphical and tabular data presentation on decision making. Management Science 30:533-542

Robey D, Taggert W (1982) Human information processing in information and decision support systems. MIS Quarterly 6-2:61-73

Schmid CF, Schmid SE (1979) Handbook of Graphic Presentation. John Wiley, New York

Schutz HG (1961) An evaluation of methods for presentation of graphic multiple trends. Human Factors 3-2:108-119

Schroeder H, Driver M, Struefert S (1967) Human information processing. Holt, New York

Scott Morton MS (1971) Management decision systems : Computer-based support for decision making. Division of Research Harvard University Boston

Scott Morton MS, Keen PGW (1978) Decision support systems : an organisational perspective. Addison-Wesley, Reading Massachusetts

Senn JA, Dickson GW (1974) Information system structure and purchasing decision effectiveness. Journal of Purchasing 10:52-64.

Siegler RS (1983) Five generalizations about cognitive development. American Psychologist 38:263-277

Simcox W (1981) Cognitive considerations in display design. National Institute of Education ED 222191 Washington DC

Sprague RH (1980) A framework for the development of decision support systems. MIS Quarterly 4-4:1-26

Takeuchi H, Schmidt AH (1980) New promise of Computer Graphics. Harvard Business Review 58-1:122-131

Tullis TS (1981) An evaluation of alphanumeric, graphic and color information display. Human Factors 23:541-550

Vernon MD (1952) The use and value of graphical material in presenting quantitative data. Occupational Psychology 26:22-34

Washburne JN (1927) An experimental study of various graphic, tabular and textual methods of presenting quantitative material. Journal of Educational Psychology 18:361-376

Watson CJ, Driver RW (1983) The influence of graphics on the recall of information. MIS Quarterly 7-1:45-53

Widener R (1983) The applications of computer graphics to the decision support process at senior management levels. Fifth Annual Conference on Computer Graphics, San Diego California

Wilcox W (1964) Numbers and the news : graph, table or text. Journalism Quarterly 41:38-44

Witkin HA, Oltman PK, Raskin E, Karp SA (1971) A Manual for the embedded figures test. Consulting Psychologists Press Palo Alto, CA

Zmud RW (1978) An empirical investigation of the dimensionality of the concept of information. Decision Sciences 9:187-195

**Sumit Sircar** is currently a Senior Teaching Fellow in the Department of Information Systems and Computer Science at the National University of Singapore. He is on a year's leave of absence from the University of Texas at Arlington, Texas, where he is an Associate Professor in the Systems Analysis Department.

Sircar earned a doctorate degree in 1976 at the Harvard Business School in the field of computer-based systems. Since then his research, teaching and consulting activities have been in the field of information resource management. He has published several articles in various journals on different aspects of information management, including the appropriate management of emerging information technologies. He has also conducted numerous professional seminars on related topics.

**Kharidehal Venkata Rao** is currently a senior lecturer of the National University of Singapore. He has been teaching Information Systems at this University for the past ten years. Before joining this university in 1976, he worked as Management Consultant at the Administrative Staff College of India, and Project Leader with the leading industrial house Tata group of organisations.

His research interest include business computer graphics, decision support and expert systems, and information systems evaluation. He has authored two books on quantitative methods and business information systems, and published over 40 refereed papers on information systems and related areas.

He received BCom (Hons) from Andhra University, India in 1953, ICWA in 1962, and Post-graduate Diploma in Systems Management from University of Bombay in 1971. He is a Fellow of the Institute of Cost & Works Accountants, Member of the British Computer Society, London, Member of ACM, Member of IEEE Computer Society, and Member of the Singapore Computer Society.

# Computer Graphics for Office Automation
## A Case Study

T. Fredrick

Texas Instruments Incorporated, 1001 E. Campbell Road, Richardson, TX 75080, USA

ABSTRACT KEY WORDS: Two major categories of business graphics are
presentation and analytical graphics. Presentation graphics are
the primary focus of personal computers and include charts and
graphs that are presented to others. Analytical graphics, help
individuals understand the meaning of numbers they generate on
their PCs, such as complex spreadsheets, which project numbers in
a sequence. Two major types of graphics programs are either pre-
packaged or customized. ChartMaster, PFs:Graph, and Energraphics,
are good examples of pre-packaged software programs. Customized
programs can be developed externally or internally. Case Study of
Computer Graphics at TI, includes a review of "TI Foils", an
internally developed presentation graphics program to meet the
various needs of a targeted group of users. The corporate
communication culture requires review to determine selection of
either customized or packaged programs. Information Centers speed
up the process of providing quality end user support.
Operational/Functional, Technical, and Software Development Trends
are continually changing and having major impact on Computer
Graphics for Office Automation.

## INTRODUCTION

Business and Management graphics for Office Automation provide visual
output in the form of graphs, charts, and drawings that reflect trends
in business and industry sales, R&D, finance, and manufacturing, which
can be manipulated, stored, and retrieved electronically.

## THE NEED FOR BUSINESS AND MANAGEMENT GRAPHICS

Basic reasons why business and management graphics are important include:

1.  Capability to produce bar, line, organization and text charts,
    which would otherwise have to be done by hand;
2.  End user can produce high quality graphics without special train-
    ing;
3.  Time and money saved in both data input, output and revisions;
4.  High resolution clarity in picture and accurate information dis-
    played on screen;
5.  Professional effect of graphics on presentations for meetings.
    (It was estimated by the Wharton Applied Research Center at the
    University of Pennsylvania that graphics shortened business meet-
    ings by 28%. Roughly 45% of the business graphics market centers
    on presentation graphics that are used for sales promotions, re-
    ports to stockholders, etc.) (Cain 1985)

CORPORATE CULTURE AND COMMUNICATIONS STYLE

Each corporation has its own communication style--one company may favor telephone correspondence while another may prefer letters.

For Business and Management Graphics to be effective, any software or hardware purchased must be evaluated on how the graphics output interacts with the corporate communications style. An example of this would be for a company to purchase a graphics package such as GEM Paint, a free-hand drawing package, when the culture reflects a need for a package that creates charts, such as Chartmaster.

## Selecting a Graphics Program

The key to selecting a graphics program is an understanding of the categories and types available.

The two major categories of business graphics are presentation and analytical graphics. Presentation graphics are the primary focus of personal computers; that include charts and graphs that are presented to others. Analytical graphics, represented by software packages such as Lotus 1-2-3, help individuals understand the meaning of numbers they generate on their PCs. Complex spreadsheets are a good example of analytical graphics because of their ability to project numbers in a sequence, rather than in random columns. (Seymour 1986)

Graphics programs currently available may either be packaged or customized.

Software packages such as Chartmaster, PFs:Graph, SuperCalc, Graphwriter, DR Graph, GEM Chart, Energraphics, etc., are "prepackaged" to meet the general needs of PC users.

However, if no packages can be found to meet the needs of a company, then a decision has to be made to either contract for the development of a software package or design, develop, and distribute one internally.

If a decision is reached to proceed with customizing a graphics program, some potential problems should be considered such as:

> the expense required to develop the program, the long lead-in times involved, the task of finding skilled personnel, and the risk of possible poor documentation because of the constant rush to complete the project. (Krepchin 1985)

Plans must also include the development of correct hardware interfaces, training, and maintenance support for Business and Management Graphics programs to be effective in a corporation.

BUSINESS AND MANAGEMENT GRAPHICS FOR OA:  A CASE STUDY -- TEXAS INSTRUMENTS, INCORPORATED

## The Communications Environment

Texas Instruments has been very active in Electronic Communications, as evidenced by 15,000 PCs and another 18,000 terminals, connected to its worldwide data communications network. "This would average out to be one network-connected terminal for every 2 1/2 people at TI," according to John White, Vice President of Information Systems and Services for TI. "We do have the world's largest single-image, interconnected worldwide communications/data processing network." (White 1986)  (Terminals on the TI network can gain access to multiple computing centers simultaneously.).  Current, Local Area Network strategy is to wire every building at TI by 1987.  In addition, a single-hop satellite link was established in the last quarter of 1985 between the UK and the US, an industry and business first.  It is through this electronic communications environment that Office Automation applications have access to electronic bulletin boards, automated mail/message systems, and on-line document exchange capabilities.

## The TI Culture

TI's culture is to present information during meetings, via "foils" or transparencies on overhead projectors.

The decision to create an inhouse Presentation Graphics Program was arrived at after extensive evaluations of existing packaged programs; the conclusion was that TI needed a package that is easy to learn and use.

A Business and Management presentation graphics package was needed to enable TIers to create transparencies showing charts, graphs, and free-hand drawings, using the TI Professional Computer and the TI Business Pro, with printed output available on TI Omni Series Printers, HP Plotters and HP Laser Printers.  Some departments may also utilize products such as Houston Instruments Plotters, Ricoh and QMS Laser Printers, and Thermal Printers such as the Seiko D-Scan.

## Graphics Survey

In a survey conducted in October, 1985, by Takeshi Ogawa, Chairman of the PC Graphics Users Group at TI, analysis revealed that there are four major groups of graphics users at TI.  The first group is composed of engineers.  The second is made up of programmers, accountants, and consultants.  Another small segment includes the managers and executives at TI, and the last group consists of secretaries and clerks.

For the first group, Auto-Cad was the primary source of software support.

The programmers, accountants and consultants relied heavily on Focus, Lotus 1-2-3, and Tell-A-Graf.  The managers and executives also used these resources, but on a more limited basis.

The final group was composed of those responsible for the creation of presentation graphics, mainly the secretaries and clerks.

## Custom Packages -- TI Foils

To meet the needs of the secretaries and clerks and others, a software package, called "TI Foils," allows text and graphics to be created and edited, was developed by the DRAM Systems Engineering Group.

Bill Egr, a member of this Systems Engineering Group describes the technical process, "TI Foils is written in Microsoft Basic, which supports a Graphics Macro Language (GML) through the draw statement.

"Graphic" type text used in TI Foils was developed as follows:

1.  Each character in the standard character font was
    transposed into a corresponding GML string.

2. Each GML string is loaded into a string array at runtime.

3. A character is generated by using its ASCII value to address a particular GML string with the string array. The X,Y position and color of the character are also specified by using the draw statement."

After completion of TI Foils, the TI Office Automation Strategy Committee reviewed a number of graphics packages, and TI Foils was chosen to be the OA presentation package, in addition to Lotus 1-2-3 Graphics, because of its ease of use over any other packaged program.

## Interfaces

The Office Automation Development Group in the Information Systems and Services Division of Texas Instruments took steps to integrate selected software packages used with various pieces of equipment.

Custom programs were designed to interface Lotus 1-2-3 with the Ricoh Laser Printer, and the QMS LaserGrafix 800, as well as with the Seiko D-Scan.

## Graphics Support Tools

To enable users to understand which Graphics Programs would best meet their needs, a software comparison chart (Table 1), as well as a graphics hardcopy device comparison chart (Table 2), were prepared by the Office Automation Technical Support Staff (Table 2). A tutorial is also being developed to assist first-time users of TI Foils. Additionally, a configuration chart (Example 1), was assembled that shows the correct software "command" for configuring the HP plotter, to the Texas Instruments Professional Computer (TIPC).

## End-User Support - Information Centers

One of the best methods of end-user support is the establishment of "Information Centers". In a newsletter article titled, "Growth News for Better Training," Information Center Study Report, it was noted that Information Centers exist in an estimated 80% of billion-dollar companies. The primary goal of the Information Center is to help employees use computers to solve business problems. Training is the key. (GRWTH Computer Coursewares 1985)

With over 29 Information Centers world-wide at Texas Instruments, continued support is made available to graphics users. One specific area was the development of a graphics symbols library for users of TI Foils, for common applications of TI-related products, symbols, and logos.

If computer graphics will continue to increase productivity, it will come as a result of not just better software or hardware, but also increased support for users.

Table 1.  Graphics software comparison table

| FEATURE: | TI FOILS | BPS | LOTUS | DR. HALO | ENERGRAPHICS |
|---|---|---|---|---|---|
| Pie | Yes | Yes | Yes | No | Yes |
| Exploding Pie | No | Yes | No | No | Yes |
| Horiz. Bar | No | Yes | No | No | Yes |
| Stacked Bar | Yes | Yes | Yes | No | Yes |
| Vertical Bar | Yes | Yes | Yes | No | Yes |
| Hidden Bar | No | No | No | No | Yes |
| 3D Bar | No | No | No | No | Yes |
| Curve Fitting | No | Yes | No | Yes | Yes |
| Mult. Scales | No | No | No | No | Yes |
| Gantt Charts | No | No | No | No | No |
| Area Charts | No | Yes | No | No | Yes |
| Linear Regress | No | Yes | No | No | Yes |
| Color Choice | Yes | Yes | Yes | Yes | Yes |
| Fill Pattern | Yes | Yes | Yes | Yes | Yes |
| Line Styles | No | Yes | No | Yes | No |
| Imports Data | No | Yes | Yes | Yes | Yes |
| Graph Switching | No | Yes | Yes | No | Yes |
| Batch Graphing | No | Yes | No | No | No |
| Interactive | Yes | No | Yes | Yes | Yes |
| Organ. Charts | Yes | No | No | Yes | Yes |
| Curved Line Dr. | No | No | No | Yes | Yes |
| Mouse Interface | No | No | No | Yes | No |
| FreeHand Draw | Yes | No | No | Yes | Yes |
| Text Anywhere | Yes | Yes | No | Yes | Yes |
| Circle | Yes | No | No | Yes | Yes |
| Ellipse | No | No | No | Yes | No |
| Rectangle | Yes | No | No | Yes | Yes |
| Paint | No | No | No | Yes | No |
| Rotate | No | No | No | Yes | Yes |
| Fat Bit Edit | No | No | No | Yes | No |
| Ease of Use | Yes | No | Yes | Yes | Yes |
| Cut & Paste | Yes | No | No | Yes | Yes |
| Copy | Yes | No | No | Yes | Yes |
| Line Thickness | No | No | No | Yes | No |

Table 2.  Graphics device comparison table

| CHARACTERISTICS | HP 7550 | DIABLO C-150 | DATA PRODUCTS 8070 | QMS LG 800 |
|---|---|---|---|---|
| Type | plotter | inkjet | dot matrix | laser |
| Resolution | 1000dpi | 120dpi | 84-168dpi | 300dpi |
| Text Line Printer Capability | no | yes | yes | yes |
| Color | yes | yes | yes | no |
| Prints on Foils | yes | yes | yes | yes |
| Raster Graphics | no | yes | yes | yes |
| Vector Graphics | yes | no | no | yes |
| Price | 2.7K | 1K | 1.7K | 8K |
| Speed | 13min | 2.5min | 15min | 30sec |

NOTE:  The same data was used for all output tested.

EXAMPLE 1.  Plotter Configurations for a TIPC AND AN HP Plotter

---

Hewlett Packard for TI Foils:
      Config LPT1=P?,SP=?,DA=8,ST=1,PA=N,B=X

Hewlett Packard for Lotus 1-2-3:
      Config LPT3=P?,SP=?,DA=8,ST=1,PA=N,B=X

Hewlett Packard for Energraphics:
      Config COM?=P?,SP=?,DA=8,ST=2,PA=N,B=X

---

NOTE:  Substitute your serial port number where there is a question
       mark.  The serial port number can be determined by using the
       MS-DOS diagnostics diskette.  For other HP Plotters, correlate
       the Speed (SP) of the configuration for the software package with
       the manual setting on the HP Plotter.

## TRENDS

There are three main trends emerging in the use of Graphics for Office
Automation.  The first is an operational or functional trend.  The
second involves technical trends that can be expected to continue and
include advances in graphics hardware.  The third involves software
development trends.

### Operational/Functional Trends

Managers are now creating their own charts via mini/micro-computers and
integrating graphics into the daily decisionmaking process, instead of
having system development staffs generate them.  In addition, through
Local Area Networks, more users will be involved in the utilization of
graphics because of the ability to share the cost of the equipment.

### Technical Trends

Future graphics output devices for Business and Management Graphics
include high-resolution, dot-matrix printers, with the ability to do
both text and full-page graphics, and thermal-transfer units that produce color.  Laser printers are now capable of printing both text and
graphics.

Scanners are gaining in popularity.  Using optical-character-recognition (OCR) technology, scanners can recognize popular type styles.
(Aschner 1984)

An optical-character-recognition device performs functions such as
digitizing characters, encoding the characters, matching these encoded
characters with known character sets and then transmitting these characters to a computer.

Image scanning permits users to scan graphics from partial to full-page
size; store and display the scanned image; through the use of a commercial graphics package manipulate and then annotate the image; and
finally produce integrated text and graphic documents.  Many scanners
support 200 dots per inch resolution.  Since there are few low-cost
image scanners available yet, this is an area requiring additional
research and development.

Software Development Trends

Increased end-user productivity is the major theme emerging from graphics software development. Technical developments include interactive design capabilities that allow for on screen editing of charts, and micro-mainframe links that turn the PC into a graphic terminal. Additional developments include full screen menus enabling selection of chart types, and chart books that provide formats that, in the past, were available only to the expert graphics user. (Wright, Bertrand 1985)

SUMMARY

In summary, Business and Management Graphics for Office Automation will play an important role in communicating ideas, especially the microcomputer-graphics software segment of business graphics. It is estimated by industry experts that the business application of computer graphics should exceed 40% of the total graphics market through the rest of this decade, outdistancing even CAD/CAM and CAE segments of the industry. (Cain 1985)

Several considerations necessary to implement effective Business and Management Graphics, based on observations and implementation efforts at Texas Instruments, include understanding the:

1. Corporate communications culture.
2. Types of user needs.
3. Available software packages.
4. Development process for integrating hardware with software to achieve the desired output.
5. Steps for providing end-user training/support.

Most of these areas can be resolved through OA development departments, usually present in large companies. Information Centers, and Education and Training Departments provide a wide variety of services to aid in implementing graphics applications. Familiarization with these products will become commonplace at all levels of management because of future affordability and the accessibility of local area networks. Meeting the needs of users by ensuring proper device configurations, providing corporate information centers for hands-on demonstrations, and offering short courses, will reduce the required learning curve and make more graphics applications available to a wider range of people.

TRADEMARKS

Software:

AutoCad is a product of AutoDesk, Inc.
BPS is a product of Business and Professional Software, Inc.
Chartmaster is a product of the Decision Resources Co.
DR Graph is a product of Digital Research, Inc.
Energraphics is a product of NBI, Inc.
Focus is a product of Information Builders, Inc.
GEM Chart is a product of Digital Research, Inc.
Graphwriter is a product of Graphic Communications
Lotus 1-2-3 is a product of the Lotus Development Corporation
Microsoft BASIC is a product of the Microsoft Corp.
PFS: Graph is a product of Software Publishing Corp.

Supercalc is a product of SORCIM/IUS Micro Software.
Tell-A-Graf is a product of the Integrated Software Systems Corp.
TI Foils is a product of Texas Instruments, Inc.


Hardware:

Data Products 8070 is a product of the Data General Corp.
Diablo C-150 is a product of Diablo Systems, Inc.
HP LaserJet, HP 7550 Plotter, and HP 7220 Plotter are products of the
    Hewlett-Packard Company
QMS LaserGraphix 800, is a product of QMS, Inc.
Seiko D-Scan is a product of Seiko Instruments, Inc.
TI Business Pro, TI Omni Series Printers, and the TI Professional
    Computer are products of Texas Instruments, Inc.


CREDITS


The following individuals provided information used in the preparation
of this report:

C. Davenport, B. Egr, S. Gentry, C. Harker, D. McCammish, T. Ogawa,
J. Weyand, Texas Instruments, Dallas, Texas.



REFERENCES


Auberach Publishers, Inc., (1984) Optical Character Recognition,
    Electronic Office Management and Technology, 6560 North Park Drive,
    Pennsauken, NJ 08109 USA.  810.0000.200.
Cain T (1985) "Business Graphics - Coming of Age for PC Use In
    Smaller Firms," Office Systems, October 1985.
GRWTH News for Better Training, Vol. III, No. 1, Information Center
    Survey Issue:  Special Report, GRWTH Computer Coursewares,
    613 Wilshire Boulevard, Santa Monica, CA 90401.
Krepchin, IP  (Dec. 1985)  "Is Custom or Packaged Right For You?"
    Modern Materials Handling.  The Cahners Magazine Division of Reed
    Publishing USA, 275 Washington Street, Newton, MA 02158.  Pages
    62-65.
Seymour J  (Jan. 1986)  "Do It Yourself PC Graphics:  An Executive Art,"
    Today's Office, Hearst Business Communications, Inc., 645 Stewart
    Ave., Garden City, NY 11530.  Page 27.
White, J  (Oct. 1985)  Dallas Site Newspaper, Texas Instruments, TI
    Internal Communications, P.O. Box 225474. MS 426, Dallas, TX,
    Vol. 16, No. 10.
Wright T, Bertrand R  (1985) "Interactivity, Menus, Chartbooks, -
    Productivity Improvement Mark '85 Development,"  Insight.

**Tom Fredrick** is Market Manager for the Office Automation Department, the Mini-Micro Computing Group, Information Systems and Services Division, for Texas Instruments, Dallas, Texas. Specific areas of research include Business and Management Graphics for Office Automation. Tom has a Master's degree in Business Management from National University, San Diego, California, and a B.S. in Business Administration from Central Michigan University, Mt. Pleasant, Michigan. He has been selected as a guest lecturer for the TI-MIX Convention, (an external association for distributors and added value resellers of TI Equipment), in Dallas, Texas, March 1986, to discuss Business Graphics Application. Additional speaking engagements include "Reshaping the Role of the Office Automation Consultant," for the Association of Information Systems Professionals Convention, in June 1986, San Fransisco, California. Tom is a member of the Association of Information Systems Professionals, the American Management Association, and the TI Graphics Users Group.

# The Influence of CADD on Teaching Traditional Descriptive Geometry and Orthographic Projection

Louis Gary Lamit and Vernon Paige
(with illustrations by Brad Waldron and John Shull)
CADD Facility, De Anza College, 21250 Stevens Creek Boulevard, Cupertino, CA 95014, USA

## INTRODUCTION

With the advent of CADD, especially 3-D CADD, in industry and in educational institutions it has become imperative that educators take a close look at the subject of descriptive geometry, the method of orthographic projection, and their accompanying instructional methodology. This paper investigates the history and uses of descriptive geometry and orthographic projection in industry and in traditional engineering school curriculum. How these topics are being influenced and altered by the addition of CADD systems to engineering graphics classes is the main theme of this paper.

A comparison of the purpose and solution solving capabilites of descriptive geoemtry in a traditional setting is made with CADD systems. This analysis compares 2-D and 3-D design methods.

The primary questions addressed are:

* What types of solutions were derived by descriptive geometry and orthographic projection because the graphical method required a solution based on 2-D projection techniques drawn on paper?

* What data can now be extracted automatically and with a greater degree of accuracy and speed with CADD?

* When traditional engineering graphics education changes to CADD-based graphics how will it influence the student?

* How can educators integrate descriptive geometry into a modern graphic curriculum founded in the use of CADD?

## DRAFTING AND DESIGN

There are two distinct tasks associated with the use of graphical construction in engineering: design and drafting. Design being the process by which an object is conceptualized and then represented pictorially. Drafting being the process of representing the geometry for a part in two dimensions in accordance with standard procedures. 2-D representation is done on paper in manual drafting and on a display device when using 2-D CADD.

The engineer can "design" in two dimensions by drawing a part representation with orthographic projection on paper or on a CRT with a 2-D CADD system. The designer can also create the part using a 3-D

CADD system. 3-D systems are used for design or drafting, but the drafting capability only exists as an add-on feature. Thus, it is correct to say that drafting is always 2-D. Note that both manually prepared drawings and drawings generated on a 2-D CADD system are created using the theory and practices of orthographic projection and descriptive geometry techniques.

Typically, a model of a mechanical design is created in 3-D on the computer. After the design is input into the computer an interactive 2-D drafting and dimensioning module is used to document the model using standard orthographic views and dimensioning. Views, sections, dimensions, tolerances, labels, notes, balloons and crosshatching are easily generated on the system. In addition to these "drafting" capabilities, the system can accurately measure, verify, and calculate specific graphical or mathamatical data. When done manually, this data is subject to a high degree of error or inaccuracy. Projections of specific standard or auxiliary views are generated without the need for specific construction techniques.

Many 3-D systems allow the designer to create the part in user defined views. Later, after the model has been completed, the drafter or the designer may specify standard views (top, front, right side) by simply defining them. Any number of views can be defined for each of an unlimited number of drawing. Only the part model database need be established on one drawing before other drawings of the same model are defined. The designer may wish to work in one of the six standard views or may rotate the part and insert entities while the part is shown isometrically.

Many drafting and design requirements and techniques founded in the theory and practice of descriptive geometry can be eliminated with a 3-D system and automated with a 2-D system. Descriptive geometry techniques are used in industry to answer specific design questions that either require a graphical solution or where a precise mathematical solution is not necessary or too costly in terms of time.


DESCRIPTIVE GEOMETRY

Descriptive geometry is the use of orthographic porjection and auxiliary views to solve three dimensional problems by a two dimensional graphics procedure. The designer is allowed to delete from a specific design everything but the essential points, lines, or planes and therfore, to more easily find a solution by a graphics method. Most solutions to descriptive geometry problems involve establishing such information as the true length of a line, angle between lines or planes, true shape of a surface or clearances. The process remains 2-D and is merely a representation of the actual 3-D part. The designer is still forced to "imagine" what the part looks like from this representation.

Descriptive geometry is used to establish the proper representation and relationships of entities and shapes on a drawing. It provides a relatively accurate method to establish information such as the determination of true shape, true size, and true length. The relationship of elements to one another such as the distance between a line and a point or the angle between two planes is also a typical descriptive geometry problem.

Since both ares share many of the same techniques, egineering graphics/drawing and descriptive geometry are not distinctly different fields since each includes and encompasses much of the other. 2-D drawing is actually elementary descriptive geometry. Constructions in descriptive geometry are done using orthographic projection techniques. Thus, we can start to see that, with the introduction of 3-D CADD in the classroom, the need for both traditional descriptive geometry and orthographic projection become questionable. If the prospective engineer/designer is taught how to "model", then the need for these subjects may diminish or be eliminated.

A developed sense of visualization is essential for the mastering of descriptive geometry. This skill was cultivated by a step by step presentation of the theory and practice of projection. With the introduction of 3-D CADD the ability to visualize a 3-D design in two dimensions is much less important, especially if the system has automatic view generation capabilities.

The designer encounters many situations where traditional visualization techniques and a mastery of the principles of projection are used in the solution of complex engineering and technical problems. The ability to analyze a specific problem, visualize its spatial considerations, and translate the problem into a viable graphical projection is essential for the designer. But, when a 3-D CADD system is available in the classroom and on the job, the type and level of visualization training is different.

Descriptive geometry has been a part of a mechanical, structural or civil engineer's education for a great many years. Point view, true length, true angle, true shape, shortest distance, dihedral angle, bearing, slope, strike, and dip solutions are required in most engineering descriptive geometry classes for engineers.

Descriptive geometry techniques used to determine intersections and development of flat patterns are normally in the domain of the drafter not the engineer/designer. Since these techniques have traditionally been "drafters" work most engineering descriptive geometry classes cover these types of solutions very lightly. With CADD, the designer can automatically extract information from the model database created during the design phase, therefore, the need for this separation of functions (drafter-designer) may be eliminated or greatly reduced. Therefore, the need to develop certain skills in engineering school may at the same time be altered, redefined, and deepened.

Since the prospective engineer currently receives a minimum of training in intersections and developments, it may be necessary to increase coverage in these two areas. Since visualization skills and projection techniques differ considerably between 2-D and 3-D CADD, the concepts and practices associated with each play an important role in the evaluation of the development of new teaching methods for descriptive geometry and engineering graphics.


2-DIMENSIONAL VERSUS 3-DIMENSIONAL

Traditionally, designers and engineers have conceptualized a design in three dimensions and then presented the concept by constructing 2-dimensional views on paper. Designing with a 3-dimensional system is a much more realistic way to produce the model of a part. The 3-D model is the starting point for engineering analysis, drafting, and manufacturing. When using the manual method of projection and solving problems with descriptive geometry, the designer must rely on his or her linework accuracy and projection profiency instead of the quality of the 3-D model database.

Descriptive geometry was devised to provide a method of creating, analyzing, and representing 3-D designs on a 2-D paper surface. That need has changed. If you give a person (engineering student or not) a piece of clay and ask them to create a part/object they would use their hands to mold or model the part as a real object in space. They would not break the clay into three pieces and construct representations of the top, front and side views of the project. This may seem obvious but, when we teach orthographic projection and descriptive geometry, that is just what we do. The process involved in teaching these concepts and techniques actually forces the person to think and create in an unatural way. When teaching design starts with the natural modeling of a conceptualized part, 3-D CADD will provide for a creative breakthrough at the design level. 3-D modeling is just that, though clay or another physical medium is not used, the designer, through computer commands, molds or models the part as if it were clay. The part exists in 3-D space and is defined mathematically within the computer by 3-D coordinates.

For an example, a 3-dimensional CADD system makes it easier to check the spatial relationship between parts in an assembly. The assembly can be rotated to view it from any angle to easily examine the spatial relationships or report can be generated to show any interferences. Complex projections based on the theory and practice of orthographic projection and techniques developed in descriptive geometry are required to achieve the same results with a 2-D system. Since the 3-dimensional system can be used to view an object from any angle, isometric and perspective views can be created with little extra effort. The designer has the freedom and ability to view and observe the assembly from any angle or viewing plane.

Since the model in the 3-dimensional system has an interior as well as an exterior, volumes and mass properties of objects are easily calculated. Hidden lines are easily removed automatically and blending contours between intersecting surfaces can be created.

Even though 2-D systems are limited when compared to 3-D systems, the use of 2-D CADD in descriptive geometry and in projects requiring orthographic projection is still advantagous. A 2-D CADD system is more accurate than manual methods and can extract data automatically. Verifying, measuring, and calculating are very accurate with a CADD system whereas the manual methods of scaling and calculating are prone to errors and inaccuracies.

With a 2-D CADD system the solution to an intersection problem will be more accurate and in the case of flat pattern developments the CADD generated flat pattern will show high levels of accuracy when compared to manually drafted projects.

Because of cost restrictions most colleges are currently installing 2-D systems. But, by the end of this decade, if not sooner, all systems will have 3-D modeling capabilities- including micro-based systems. This technology makes 2-D construction and projection only marginally useful. Views, areas, sizes, and distances are automatically extractable from the 3-D model database. This capability seriously questions whether descriptive geometry and orthographic projection as traditionally taught, belong in "engineering graphics" at the college level. Engineering graphics may eventually be a CADD class that includes design modeling and how to extract 2-D "drawing mode" data such as views, dimensions, labels, and notes.

# THE MODEL

The graphic representation of the part in a CADD system is called the model. This model is mathematically defined and stored in the computer's memory. Since the part is really a mathematical model, all lengths, shapes and relationships to other parts are exact and verifiable. There are three mathematical methods that are used to define this model: wireframe, surfaces, and solids. In addition to the geometry, the design also includes attributes such as material, weight, volume, function, and color. The model may be used to functionally "test" the design before it is built.

A wireframe model uses lines or splines to represent the edges of the part being modeled. Wireframes are relatively easy to create and provide a convenient geometric definition for many engineering applications. Since wireframe modeling closely emulates the process of making drawings, it will suffice for many 2-D design tasks.

Three-dimensional surface models are constructed by stretching a transparent membrane over the wireframe model. These membranes then become the faces of the model. These faces may be simple surfaces such as planes, cylinders, and spheres or they may be more complex surfaces such as ruled surfaces, extrusions, rotations of spline curves, and scuplted surfaces.

Three-dimensional surface models can be used to represent shapes that are difficult to construct with wireframes. Examples of these shapes are styled and warped surfaces, such as the outer skins of automobiles and airplanes, and function surfaces, such as turbine blades and gears. Many of these surfaces were traditionally drawn using techniques from descriptive geometry such as those for warped surfaces, double-curved surfaces, and transition pieces.

Solid models are an unambiguous representation of individual parts or an assembly. In the near future, a solid model will form the master representation of a part in contrast to the current practice of using the engineering drawing as the master representation. The main output of a design/drafting office will be a solid model of the part together with all the associated information that is contained on the engineering drawing and the engineering drawings will be a secondary function. In particular, the drawings, if required, will be automatically generated from the model. The combination of a solid model and the necessary tolerance and associated technical data will be called the "product model". Functions downstream of the design office will take the product model as their primary input. They will extract data from the model using query functions and may also produce secondary models for their own purposes.

# DRAFTING AND DESIGN USING CADD

CADD systems with 3-D capabilities have been designed to be used in as natural a way as possible by recognizing the different thought processes used and associated with design and drafting. In most systems, two modes of operation are used: the model mode (design mode), for designing a part and generating NC data and the drawing mode (drafting mode), for creating detail drawings of the part.

Model geometry is constructed in a 3-D coordinate system. Therefore all spatial relationships of the design can be determined acurately from the model itself, not a 2-D representation of the part. Since true length of each element, size and area of each face plane,

intersection of surfaces, or shapes can be determined directly from
the model, descriptive geometry and orthographic projection have
limited use. Views of the object are generated automatically by the
system from the model. Sections can also be constructed automatically
by the system.

## DESCRIPTIVE GEOMETRY VERSUS 2-D AND 3-D CAD CAPABILITIES

As can be seen from the above description of modeling, there will be a
range of capabilities available for each type of model. Depending on
the type of modeling available, the use of orthographic projection and
descriptive geometry may be similar, lessened or eliminated. Two
important aspects of CADD are discussed below; data retrival and
visualization. Both capabilities will effect the need for descriptive
geometry and orthographic projection.

Data retrival: Based on the type of computer model that was built,
both 2-D and 3-D systems allow the designer to automatically extract a
certain amount of information. A 2-D system will extract accurate
measurements for each view of the part. Therefore, measurements, like
the length of a line can be verified. The area of a surface can be
calculated automatically. The distance between two points or a point
and a line can be extracted. Parallelism, the angle between two lines,
and perpendicularity can be determined. All of the measurements are
possible as long as the elements being measured lie in the plane of
the 2-D coordinate system used by the system.

A 3-D system can also perform any of the above mentioned 2-D
measurements. But the 3-D system offers much more capability. A 3-D
system can calculate volume. It can measure the distance between two
points, lines, or planes regardless of their placement in space.

Visualization: In a 2-D system, visualization is not much better than
manually drawn projects. The benefits over traditional descriptive
geometry techniques are primarily in the quality of the drawing, the
accuracy, and the ability of the system to calculate lengths, areas
and other 2-D data.

Other visualization capabilities include automatic hidden line removal
for the model, and dynamic rotation of the part in three axes. The
projection of designer specified views without constructing each view
individually is a primary feature of a 3-D system.

Intersections of surfaces can be determined by using a number of
different techniques such as Boolean operations where the system
combines simple objects like a cone and a prism or a cone and a
cylinder. The basic objects or primitives are combined automatically
by the system, without the need to do complex descriptive geometry
drawings with edge views or mulitiple cutting planes.

## TRADITIONAL DESCRIPTIVE GEOMETRY PROBLEMS

Traditional descriptive geometry problems involve the relationship of
points, lines, planes, intersections, and developments.

 Since a 3-D system builds a model in 3-D space, a majority of
traditional geometry techniques could be eliminated . The true length
of a line, the distance between a point and a line, the shortest
distance between two lines, and problems in parallelism,
perpendicularity, and revolution could be extracted automatically. The
true angle between lines and the dihedral angle between planes could

be determined by the system; the designer need not know descriptive
geometry. Revolution of lines, planes, or solids would be completed in
3-D space instead of simulated on paper. Values of lengths, angles,
sizes, areas, and volumes could be extracted from the 3-D model
database.

As an example, the angle between intersecting lines solved for
manually using descriptive geometry in Figure 1 required two auxiliary
projections. The CADD generated solution simply required a command to
measure the angle!

Both surface and solid modeling would provide complete capabilities
for intersection problems. Piercing points and intersections of lines,
planes, and solid shapes would be generated automatically with 3-D
CADD.

The manually derived solution for the intersection of the cone and the
plane in Figure 2 required the use of multiple cutting planes. This
intersection can be generated automatically with a 3-D CADD system as
in Figure 2 where a wireframe model of the cone and plane are shown.
The cone and plane were input using 3-D coordinates, a command to
solve for their intersection was then entered. The system determined
the intersection points and constructed the line of intersection
automatically. An engineering student, using traditional descriptive
geometry, needs a substantial amount of time and knowledge to complete
the manually generated solution.

3-D CADD systems are limited to parallel line, radial line, and
transition pieces requiring triangulation for development of flat
patterns. Certain types of warped and double curved surfeces cannot be
developed by the system. But, as it has been previously stated,
engineers are normally not taught in great depth about pattern
developments.  Since this subject is formally in the domain of the
drafter, it is covered lightly.

Because the state of the art in development programs allows the
engineer to create a 3-D model and to request the system to
automatically develop the piece, it may be time for an engineering
student to learn more of the basics of developments. A 3-D CADD system
is able to generate spheres, ellipsiods, and hyperbolic paraboloids
accurately and quickly but it cannot develop warped and double curved
surfaces. Only shapes that can be developed by a CADD system need be
taught.

A 3-D system can develop patterns from parallel lines, radial lines,
and shapes requiring triangulation. At present, the engineer's design
can be unfolded by one of two methods. One method allows the designer
to unbend the 3-D model, adding dimensions, title block and border
automatically. The other method requires each surface to be specified
and unfolded. The designer must then detail the pattern by adding
dimensions. The first method eliminates the need for a drafter.
Therefore, 3-D systems with this capability will require only an
engineer/designer.

A typical parallel line development of a truncated prism is shown in
Figure 3. The manual descriptive geometry method is shown along with a
CADD generated 3-D model and its unfolded flat pattern. The designer
unfolded the model by merely digitizing the surfaces to be developed.

2-D development programs are also available but they either require
the construction techniques found in manual drafting or the pattern is
assembled from polygon elements.  Both 2-D and 3-D CADD flat pattern
programs can calculate bend allowances and compensate for setback.

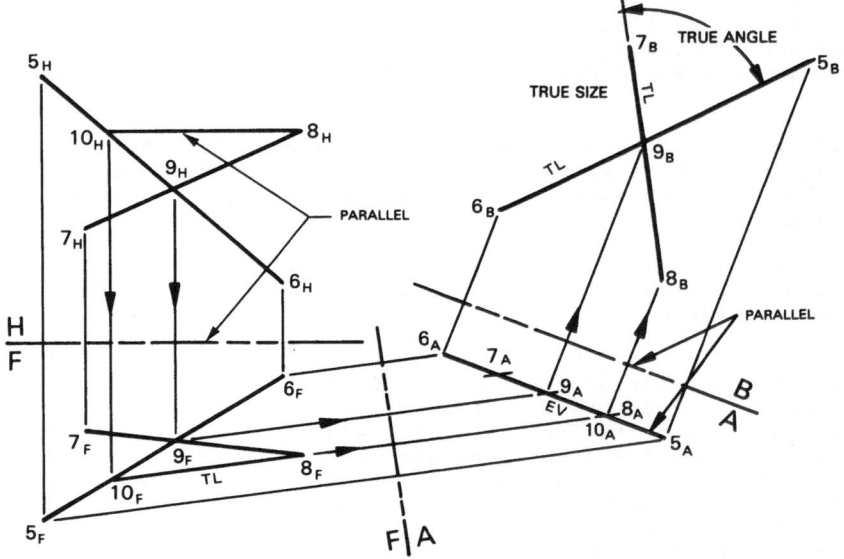

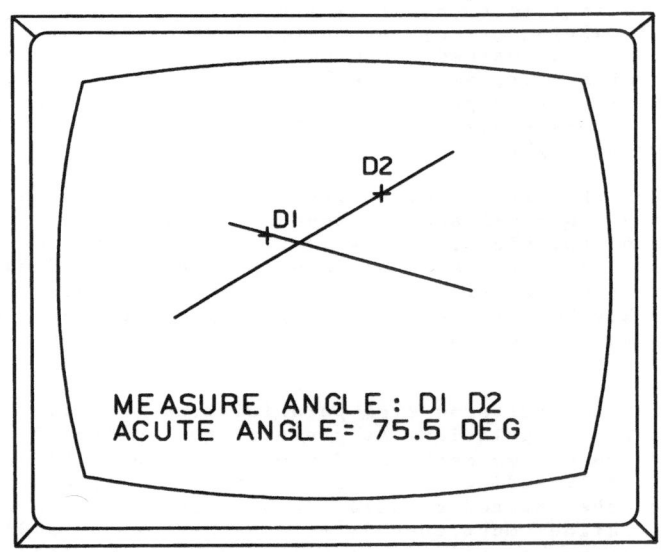

FIGURE 1

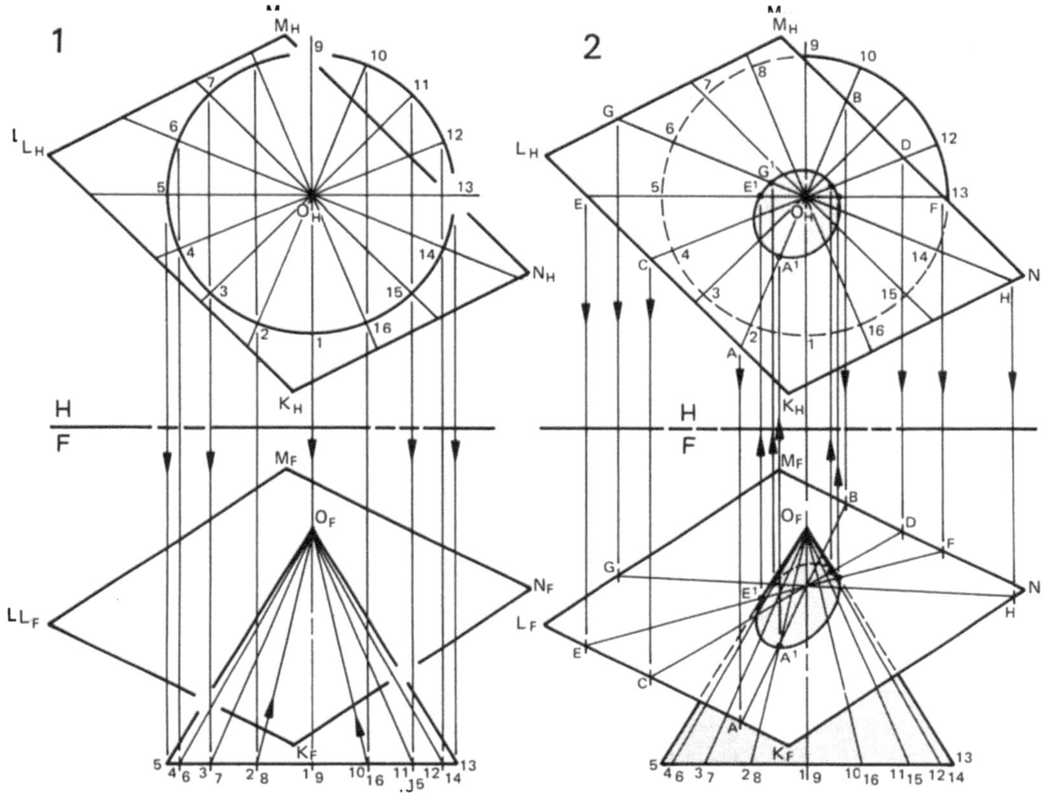

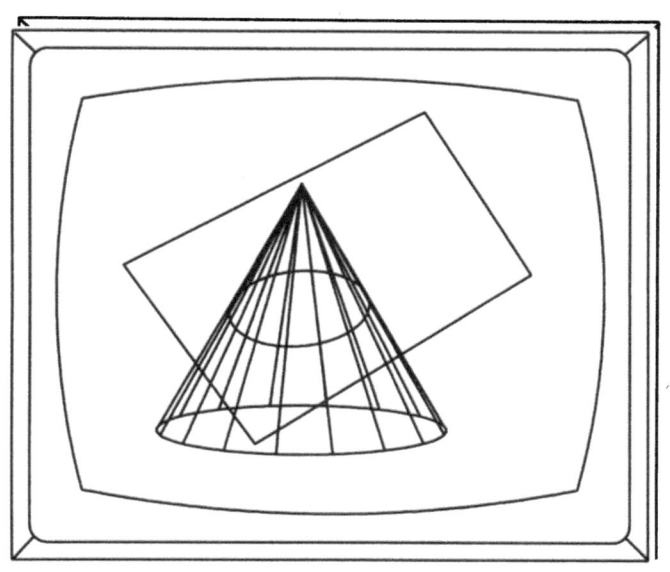

FIGURE 2

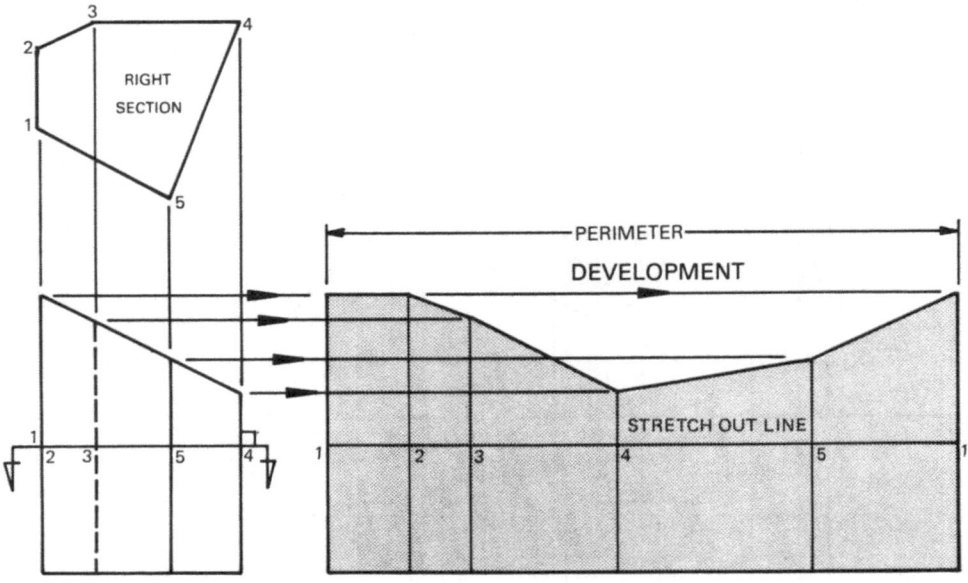

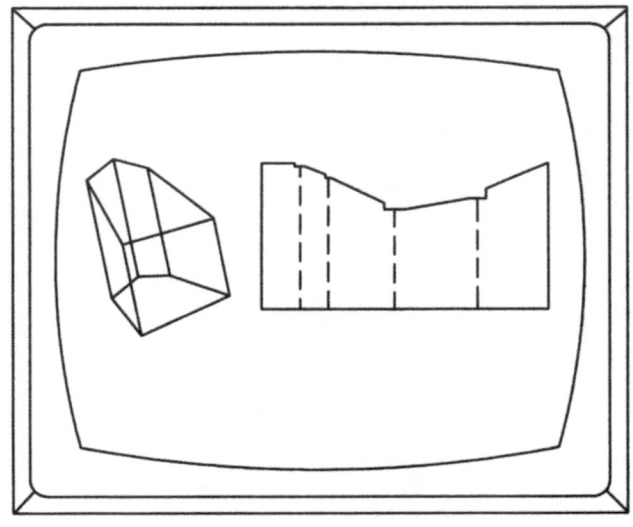

FIGURE 3

CONCLUSIONS

Since perfect lettering and linework are automated with 2-D CADD, it is questionable whether a drafting student need develop these skills. If 3-D modeling is available on a CADD system, the engineering student's education may not need descriptive geometry and orthographic projection as has been presented traditionally.

If this new perspective on descriptive geometry and orthographic projection is to be introduced, a specific capability in a CADD system is essential. 2-D systems, while excellent drafting tools, are not capable of modeling and, therefore, will not eliminate the need for the descriptive geometry or projection skills developed in engineering graphics classes.

Introducing 3-D modeling at an early stage in the engineering graphics curriculum will alter the need to teach a variety of traditional techniques. Point view, true length, true shape, true angle, rotation, view projection, parallelism, and perpendicularity will need be approached from a 3-D model perspective in lieu of construction techniques traditionally used to extract data from a 2-D drawing. 2-D sketching is still necessary but the emphasis must remain on a 3-D model. Once the student learns to generate solid and surface models, the techniques required to generate intersections need need not be taught.

If a 3-D system is available, flat pattern developments should be covered in more depth. But, coverage should be limitted to parallel line, radial line, and triangulation solutions generated by the system, not those solutions generated manually.

2-D CADD systems will not significantly alter the way descriptive geometry is taught, but, the system will offer automated verification and measurements. Problem solving will be enhanced because of the greater accuracy and calculating power of the computer.

As we can see, what is now presented as descriptive geometry and engineering graphics has been profoundly altered by the introduction of the computer into the classroom. As 3-D CADD systems become more commonplace, it will be important to develop curriculum and textbooks that reflect the increased capability of CADD to eliminate the need for 2-D thought processes and projection techniques. This new technology presents engineering instructors with creative possibilities never before available with traditional manual drafting methods.

REFERENCES AND BIBLIOGRAPHY

A. Requicha, "Representation for Rigid Solids:
   Theory, Methods and Systems"
   Computing Surveys , Volume 12, Number 4, December 1980
B.G. Baumgart, "A Polyhedron Representation for Computer Vision",
   AFIPS Conference Procedures, Volume 44, May 1975
Computervision Corporation. CAD Concepts . Bedford, Mass:
   Computervision, 1980
Gardan, Yvon and Lucus, Michel. Interactive Graphics In CAD
   New York, N.Y.: UNIPUB, 1983
Lamit, Louis Gary. Descriptive Geometry . Englewood Cliffs, N.J.:
   Prentice-Hall, 1983
Lamit, Louis Gary and Paige, Vernon. CADD .
   Columbus, Ohio, Charles Merrill Publishers, 1987

**Louis Gary Lamit** is currently an instructor and CADD facility manager at De Anza College in Cupertino, CA, where he teaches computer aided drafting and design.

Between 1966 and 1974 he worked as a drafter, designer, NC programmer, and engineer in the automotive, aircraft and piping industries. A majority of his work experience is in the area of mechanical and piping design.

Since leaving industry Lamit has taught at the community college and university levels and has written a number of textbooks in the areas of Industrial Model Building, Piping Drafting and Design,Pipefitting, Descriptive Geometry and Electronic Drafting and Design.  At present he is under contract to write a general engineering technical drawing text and a text on CADD. Lamit has also written a number of articles, booklets and workbooks in technical areas associated with physical modeling, piping and descriptive geometry.

Lamit received a B.S. degree from Western Michigan University in 1970 and did his masters work at Michigan State University. He has done graduate work at Wayne State University (MI) and University of California at Berkley and holds an NC Programming certificate from Boeing Aircraft Co.

# Trends in Microcomputer-Based CAD in the USA

Terry T. Wohlers and Erich von Stroheim

Department of Industrial Sciences, Colorado State University, Fort Collins, CO 80523, USA

ABSTRACT

Microcomputer-based CAD (microCAD) is gaining tremendous popularity in the U.S., to the point of surpassing conventional CAD systems. The reason for microCAD's success is simple: high performance at a low price.

This paper examines microCAD's development in the USA. By looking at recent software, hardware and systems integration advances, it anticipates the major trends of microCAD in the near future.

MicroCAD software is available for many traditional two-dimensional (2-D) drafting functions, and is beginning to include 3-D capabilities as well. Surface modeling can be achieved in a wire-frame format, with hidden-line removal. Layered drawing storage allows multiple overlapping systems to be developed and viewed separately or together. Translator packages provide communication of drawings and data among different systems.

Standardization is the key to microCAD's modularity and flexibility. A wide variety of hardware and software combinations are available, but compatibility remains a primary area of development. Integration of special purpose hardware and software components into computer-integrated manufacturing systems is a worthy goal, but has not yet been achieved.

The basic trend categories identified in the paper are: 1) Open Architecture Software, 2) Standardization, 3) Translation Packages, 4) Higher Capacity Hardware, 5) Modular Hardware, and 6) Special Purpose Boards and Processors.

KEYWORDS

| | |
|---|---|
| Computer-aided Drafting and Design | CADD |
| Computer-aided Manufacturing | CAM |
| Computer-aided Engineering | CAE |
| Computer-aided Design | CAD |
| Design | Drafting |
| Microcomputer | Micro |
| Personal Computer | PC |
| Microcomputer-based CAD | MicroCAD |
| PC-based CAD | PC-CAD |
| Personal CAD | Low-cost CAD |

INTRODUCTION

Microcomputer-based CAD (microCAD) is taking U.S. industry by storm. Over 90,000 microCAD systems have been installed in the last three years, more than the total number of conventional CAD systems placed in use during the last 10 years. The reason for microCAD's success is simple: high performance at a low price. By contrast, conventional CAD systems, although generally more powerful than microCAD, have been so expensive that only large-scale operations could justify their use.

The purpose of this paper is to examine microCAD's development in the USA. By looking at recent software, hardware and systems integration advances, one can anticipate the major trends of microCAD in the near future. These advances are occurring in many areas. Standardization is beginning to allow interfacing of an ever wider range of components, both in hardware and software.

MicroCAD is defined simply as any CAD system utilizing a low cost microcomputer or personal computer (PC) for its central processing unit. Non-PC multi-user micros exist but are not considered to be low cost ($3,000 to $6000), and consequently are not included among the microCAD systems considered in this paper.

Although microCAD is not as glamorous or powerful as some conventional CAD systems, it provides a tremendous return on investment and is within the price range of nearly any sized business. This fact, along with its flexibility, is the source of microCAD's strength in the marketplace, where a vast array of applications awaits development.

The benefit/cost ratio of a microCAD system may be three to four times that of a mainframe-based system. Since most microcomputers can be used for other applications in addition to CAD, the cost allocatable to the use of CAD may be as little as half the cost of the PC, effectively doubling the benefit/cost ratio.

MicroCAD systems are currently selling at over 6,000 workstations per month, and experts predict this figure will grow ten times by the year 1990. Also by 1990, the power of personal computers will have increased so much that nine of every ten CAD/CAM and CAE workstations will use a personal or desktop computer.


REALIZING MICROCAD'S POTENTIAL

Design professionals are finally beginning to consider microCAD systems as viable drafting and design tools. This was not the case just two or three years ago. At that time, the power and capability of even the best microCAD workstation did not meet the minimum standards for most design professionals.

This change, over the last two years, is due primarily to the developments of powerful and low-cost personal computers such as the IBM PC/AT. This and other comparable PC's such as the Texas Instrument Business Pro and the Hewlett-Packard Vectra, are approximately four times as powerful as the ordinary IBM PC in terms of computational speed and memory capacity.

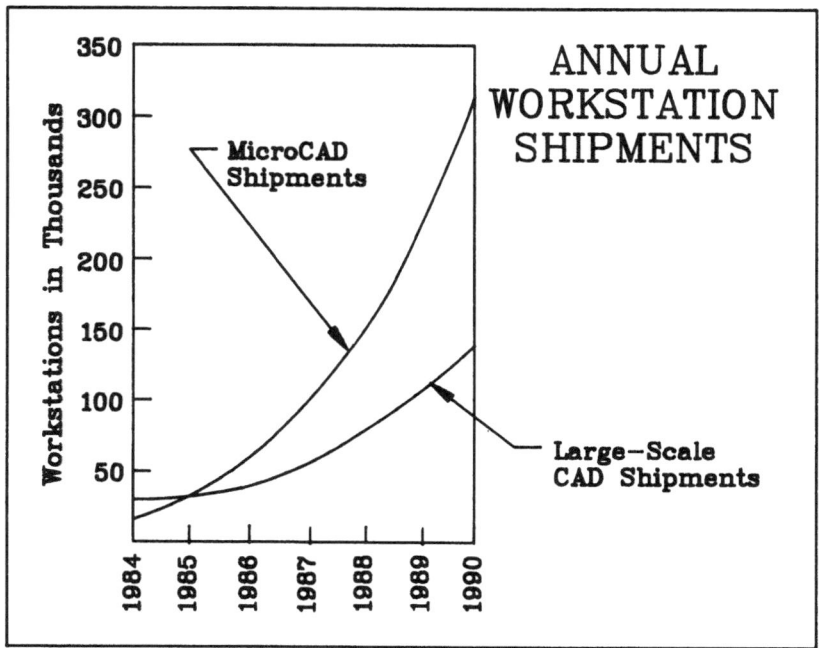

Fig. 1. Expected Growth Rates of MicroCAD vs. Large-Scale
CAD Shipments. (Courtesy of Krouse Associates)

The applications for microCAD are phenomenal. Until microCAD arrived,
most small companies and educational institutions could not justify or
even consider CAD as a tool, because of its high cost. Now, even the
smallest organizations can afford the benefits of CAD. Organizations
are using microCAD for applications as varied as architecture,
mechanical and electrical design, electronics, chemistry, mapping,
facilities management, interior design, and education/training.
MicroCAD is also expanding into non-traditional areas such as theatre
set and lighting design, museum display design, and clothing design.

Internationally recognized CAD-authority Carl Machover estimates that
only a small percentage of the potential applications for microCAD
have emerged. He anticipates microCAD implementations with CNC,
robotics, tool fixture design and simulation.

MicroCAD systems are far easier to learn to use than conventional CAD.
New learners can typically become productive in using a microCAD
system with 40-60 hours of hands-on learning. Conventional CAD
sytems, on the other hand, take up to six months or more to master.
Once a person has learned to use a microCAD system, a large percentage
of the skills learned are transferable to most large CAD systems.
Therefore, microCAD is an excellent means for CAD education and
training.

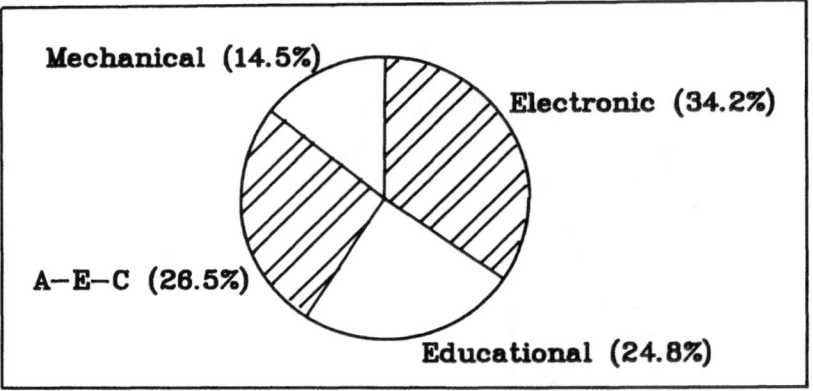

Fig. 2. Types of MicroCAD Users (Courtesy of Daratech, Inc.)

MICROCAD SOFTWARE

MicroCAD software is mostly 2-D drafting oriented, although 3-D
modeling packages are becoming available.  Most microCAD software can
be customized to the users' needs with screen and tablet menus,
macros and easy-to-access symbol libraries.

Relatively small software modules and subroutines can be easily pieced
together into custom-tailored systems.  Users are not locked into one
program's limitations but can use the software tools as building
blocks to create integrated solutions.  For example, one system uses
PROLOG for its user interface, and the C language for its graphics
routines and subroutines.  The flexibility to interface different
languages and subroutines in this way is a direct result of standards
development and acceptance.

Currently, there are about 10 leading general-purpose IBM PC-based CAD
software products available in the USA.  Their capabilities vary
widely, but the most used package called AutoCAD, is extremely
versatile.  AutoCAD is usable on more than 30 different personal
computers, and supports the greatest number of input and output
devices.  In addition, AutoCAD has a large body of third party
software based on it, about 150 programs in all.  Although AutoCAD
allows data-transfer in and out, the lack of clear standards is a big
problem today for computer graphics in general.

The leading U.S. microCAD software packages are AutoCAD by Autodesk,
CADVANCE by Calcomp, VersaCAD Advanced by T & W Systems, CADKEY by
Micro Control Systems, Personal Designer by Computervision, and
Anvil-1000 MD by MCS.  All of the products have their strengths and
weaknesses, but AutoCAD has outsold all others combined.  One reason
is that AutoCAD runs on the widest selection of hardware,
approximately 70 components total. Prices of these microCAD packages
range from $1000 to $6000.

Some microCAD systems include limited 3-D capabilities oriented mainly
toward 3-D wire-frame modeling.  Typically 3-D, and especially surface
and solid modeling, require large amounts of processing power and
storage. For this reason, they have been much easier to implement on

larger systems, and are very limited on micros. But hardware improvements such as faster CPU's, coprocessors and special dedicated accelerator boards are bringing 3-D and solid modeling into the scope of the PC. Software advances in the form of more efficient programming algorithms have also contributed to this progress.

Autodesk has recently introduced its 3-D extension for AutoCAD called 3D Level 1, which allows wire-frame visualization with hidden-line removal. In wire-frame mode, all surfaces are represented by splines, while the hidden-line view shows only visible surfaces and lines. Also, AutoCAD can exchange drawings with about six other big-CAD systems including Computervision, CADAM and Intergraph, through translation packages.

Other software packages available for microCAD include static and dynamic finite element analysis programs (available for both 2-D and 3-D), IGES translator packages for transporting of data into and out of other programs, and a wealth of custom menus and symbol libraries for specific applications.

Like conventional CAD systems, microCAD provides use of different layers which can be turned on or off for representing different aspects of a drawing, such as dimensions, border and title block, and notes and specifications. Layering can also be used for different physical systems within the same drawing space (such as electrical, plumbing and ventilation systems in a plant design drawing). Zooming, panning, dynamic block moving and copying, array creation, windowing, and semi-automatic dimensioning are normal features of microCAD as well. Some microCAD systems provide for storage of attributes within a block for transfer of this information to other software such as dBase III, R:Base 5000 and Lotus 1-2-3.

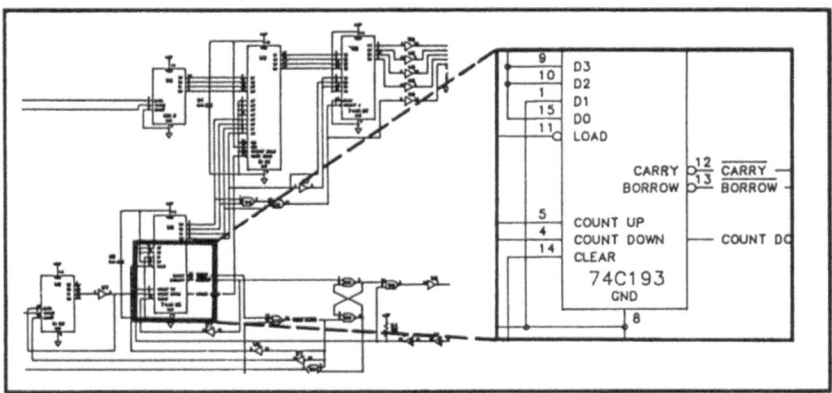

Fig. 3. Electronic Schematic Illustrating Windowing and Zoom Features of MicroCAD

# HARDWARE USED FOR MICROCAD

The IBM Personal Computer series has set the de facto standard for personal computers, including PC's for the microCAD industry. Comparable and even better personal computers have been developed, especially for graphics applications, but the fact remains that the IBM PC series has been the most often used for microCAD workstations.

In addition to the IBM PC series, other popular choices include the Texas Instruments Business Pro, the NEC APC series, the Compaq Deskpro 286, and the Zenith series. Over 35 models of personal computers in the $3000 to $6000 price range can run microCAD software, although many do not hold a significant portion of the market.

The combination of hardware components used for a microCAD system depends directly upon the software chosen. Therefore, it is important for purchasers to consider the software before selecting the hardware. Each microCAD package supports a varying number of personal computers, monitor and graphics board combinations, digitizers, mice, lightpens, printers and plotters.

Even though many dealers package and offer their products as complete turnkey systems, purchasers often select individual components based on their needs, budgets and personal preferences. In some cases, companies already have personal computers for wordprocessing and database management, and choose simply to upgrade their systems to accommodate microCAD software. This is a very practical approach because the personal computer is usually the most expensive part of the system. In this case, only a few thousand dollars are needed to purchase the remaining hardware and software needed to complete the microCAD system.

Over 100 low-cost input and output devices are available for microCAD. One can expect to pay as little as $100 for a simple mouse, or as much as $7000 for a large, sophisticated digitizer. Small digitizing tablets are available in the $600 to $1500 price range. Low-cost pen plotters are manufactured specifically for the low-end CAD market, and are priced as low as $600 for a single-pen A size (8.5" x 11") plotter. Larger, multi-pen plotters are available for $3000 to $14,000.

The microCAD industry has developed an abundance of hardware component choices and their possible combinations. Since the components are modularized but were developed with few standards in mind, seldom are two microCAD workstation installations identical. Fortunately, the typical problems of compatibility will be resolved when better standards are developed. But at present the microCAD industry faces a difficult and challenging problem as purchasers struggle through the various incompatibilities and interfaces currently offered.

Some software producers claim that the low power of the personal computer has been the single biggest limitation of the system. Over the last year, however, there have been developments in personal computers which have resolved some of this problem. But until the new generation of 32-bit personal computers becomes available at a $5000 to $10,000 price range, processing power of the personal computer will continue to be a limitation for microCAD technology.

## INTEGRATION OF MICROCAD

Standardization is a key issue in computer graphics technology. Some packages do, however, have data transfer capabilities (e.g. AutoCAD) by which data can be exchanged with other programs such as spreadsheets, databases and word processors. Additionally, drawings can be converted to other CAD vendors' formats through IGES, even though the process is somewhat expensive and time consuming.

The industry is seeing several enhancements to existing microCAD packages such as templates, customized programs, and symbol libraries. A good example of a program that falls into all of these categories is a product called AE/CADD, which works in conjunction with AutoCAD. AE/CADD was written with the architect/engineer in mind, and offers specialized features such as a complete library of architectural symbols and details, including doors and windows. In addition, AE/CADD allows for automatic double-line wall generation with proper intersection of those double-lines, a feature not provided in the standard AutoCAD package. Like many other specialized programs, AE/CADD builds on an already powerful program, and customizes the program to one specific application.

Since AutoCAD has gained a large percentage of the market, and is considered the leader in the microCAD industry, several companies are developing software to operate with it. MegaCADD was developed as a stand-alone 3-D program a little over a year ago. At that time, AutoCAD did not offer a 3-D option to their program, and MegaCADD therefore was made compatible with AutoCAD. MegaCADD used this as a major selling point of their program, with hopes of reaching the AutoCAD user base. This tactic by MegaCADD is representative of the way many companies are offering what they consider integrated solutions.

Manufacturers are realizing the potential of micro-based CAD/CAM and are developing post-processors to operate with already developed microCAD packages, as well as complete turnkey micro-based CAD/CAM systems. This technology is still in its infancy, but promises huge dividends. One example of a post-processing program is NC Programmer. Designed to operate with AutoCAD, NC Programmer is priced at $1200. In contrast, a similar product by Infinite Graphics Inc. is packaged as a turnkey system for approximately $40,000. Like most microCAD products, both systems are based on the IBM PC series.

Generally speaking, the micro-based CAD/CAM industry is progressing dramatically, but is years away from the total computer-integrated manufacturing (CIM) solution. Until standards are established and communications among products are common, there will be a lag in micro-based CIM, even as the industry sees amazing developments in microCAD for drafting- and design-intensive application areas.

## TRENDS IN MICROCAD

In discussing the current state of microCAD in the marketplace, the authors have identified the following trends as ones which will affect the direction of microCAD. Several of these points have been expanded upon in earlier parts of this paper, while others reflect trends of microcomputer development in general.

-   Open Architecture Software - Modular programming techniques are allowing easy customization through the use of core programs which access subroutines, custom-designed menus and symbol libraries.

Standardization - Much of the modularity described above is
becoming possible through the acceptance of the ASCII character
sets, and through various graphics and telecommunications
standards which allow transfer of drawings and data among
different types of systems.

Translation Packages - As an outgrowth of the standardization
principles mentioned above, translators allow for drawings to be
passed between micros and mainframe CAD systems.

Higher Capacity Hardware - 32-bit microprocessors, high-capacity
RAM, and mass-storage hard-disk and floppy-disk drives are making
microCAD as powerful as earlier mainframe CAD systems.
Eventually, processing and I/O speeds on micros will become
sufficient to support real-time image movement as well as modeling
of solids and surfaces.

Modular Hardware - Interface standards are becoming a reality for
microCAD hardware. Systems will increasingly be assembled from a
variety of components, much as component audio systems are
assembled today.

Special Purpose Boards and Processors - Coprocessors are becoming
available to improve the functionality and performance of microCAD
systems. Floating-point accelerators, array processors, and
special display handlers are other examples. Special purpose
processors will provide specific functions such as a particular
algorithm for anti-aliasing or for representation of shaded
surfaces.

## SUMMARY/CONCLUSION

Whereas mainframe-based CAD has developed beyond the basic needs of
U.S. industry, microCAD has developed and become capable of supporting
industry's needs at an affordable price. Organizations of all sizes
in the USA are recognizing that microCAD is a viable option, and many
therefore, are in the process of replacing their drafting tables with
microCAD workstations.

MicroCAD's potential grows daily as the hardware becomes more
powerful, new software is developed and packages become integrated.

As the array of microCAD system components becomes more sophisticated
and varied, ease of use emerges as a primary issue. The market
winners in the near future will not necessarily be those systems which
are the most powerful, but rather those which combine power with
versatility, flexibility, ease of use and affordability.

## REFERENCES

Orr, Joel N. "Why Not Micros?," Computer Graphics World, September
1985.

Teichoiz, Eric. "The Current State of PC CADD," Computer Graphics
World, August 1985.

Wohlers, Terry T. "Micro-based CAD: Powerful Features at Low
   Cost," Computer Graphics Today, Vol. 2, No. 6, June 1985.

Wohlers, Terry T. "Personal Computer CAD Systems: The Untapped Potential," _Conference Proceedings, Electronic Production Efficiency Exposition_, Birmingham, England, May 1985.

"CAD/CAM, CAE Industry Growth Slows to 30 Percent in 1985," News Release, Daratech Inc., Cambridge, Massachusetts, USA, June 1985.

"The 1990 Graphics Personal Computer Will Have 16 Megabytes," Graphics Newsfront, _Computer Graphics World_, October 1985.

"Forrest: CAD Reactions Reflect Confusion", Interview, _Computer Graphics Today_, Vol. 2, No. 8, August 1985.

**Terry Wohlers** is currently employed by Colorado State University as a Research Associate and Instructor in the Department of Industrial Science's Office of Research, Development and Training. Wohlers received a Master of Sceience degree in Industrial Sciences at Colorado State University, and a Bachelor of Arts degree in Industrial Technology Education at Kearney State College.

At Colorado State University, Wohlers designed and taught the first series of semester courses and industry workshops on microcomputer-based computer-aided design (CAD), and continues to conduct them. His other university responsibilities involve a variety of research and development activities such as analysis of micro-based CAD software and hardware configurations, and curriculum development.

Wohlers has published a dozen articles on micro-based CAD, most recently in Computer Graphics World and Computer Graphics Today. In addition, he has given numerous presentations at regional, national and international meetings and conferences including conferences sponsored by the American Institute of Architects, the National Computer Graphics Association, the Computer & Automated Systems Association, the Society of Manufacturing Engineers, the Urban & Regional Information Systems Association, and the United Kingdom Automatic Test Equipment Group.

In July 1984, Wohlers served as the conference director for the "First Annual International Forum on Micro-based CAD," and currently serves as Director for the 3rd Annual International Forum on Micro-based CAD. Wohlers also serves as the Educational Chairman for the Society of Manufacturing Engineers, Chapter 193.

**Erich von Stroheim** is currently a systems analyst at Creative Consultants Corporation International in Fort Collins, Colorado. He received his Master of Science degree in Computer Information Systems from Colorado State University. He has been a coordinator for the First and Second Annual Micro CAD Forums at Colorado State University, and is currently involved in planning for the Third Annual Forum. His research interests include computer graphics, database systems and telecommunications. He has written articles on computer graphics, and taught courses in computer programming.

Before entering the computer field, Stroheim worked for ten years in filmmaking, photography and video production. He is a member of Beta Gamma Sigma, the business colleges honor society. He received his B.A. from Pomona College in 1972 and his M.S. from Colorado State University in 1985.

Stroheim's address is 1116 W. Mountain Avenue., Fort Collins, Colorado 80521, USA.

# Author Index

The page numbers refer to the list of references povided by each contributor.

# Keywords Index

The page numbers refer to the page on which term is defined.